T0189304

Lecture Notes in Computer Science 11050

Commenced Publication in 1973
Founding and Former Series Editors:
Gerhard Goos, Juris Hartmanis, and Jan van Leeuwen

More information about this series at http://www.springer.com/series/7410

Michael Bailey · Thorsten Holz
Manolis Stamatogiannakis · Sotiris Ioannidis (Eds.)

Research in Attacks, Intrusions, and Defenses

21st International Symposium, RAID 2018
Heraklion, Crete, Greece, September 10–12, 2018
Proceedings

 Springer

Editors
Michael Bailey
University of Illinois at Urbana-Champaign
Urbana, IL
USA

Thorsten Holz ⓘ
Ruhr-Universität Bochum
Bochum
Germany

Manolis Stamatogiannakis ⓘ
Vrije Universiteit Amsterdam
Amsterdam
The Netherlands

Sotiris Ioannidis
Foundation for Research & Technology – Hellas
Heraklion, Crete
Greece

ISSN 0302-9743   ISSN 1611-3349   (electronic)
Lecture Notes in Computer Science
ISBN 978-3-030-00469-9   ISBN 978-3-030-00470-5   (eBook)
https://doi.org/10.1007/978-3-030-00470-5

Library of Congress Control Number: 2018953884

LNCS Sublibrary: SL4 – Security and Cryptology

This Springer imprint is published by the registered company Springer Nature Switzerland AG
The registered company address is: Gewerbestrasse 11, 6330 Cham, Switzerland

Preface

Welcome to the 21st International Symposium on Research in Attacks, Intrusions and Defenses (RAID 2018)!

This year, RAID 2018 received *145 submissions* of which 32 were accepted (*21% acceptance rate*). As in previous years, a double-blind reviewing process was used to ensure that the reviewers remained unaware of the authors, names or affiliations during the discussion. Each paper received at least three reviews and the final decision for each paper was made during a face-to-face Program Committee (PC) meeting following the IEEE Symposium on Security and Privacy in San Jose (CA) in May 2018.

The quality and commitment of the PC is paramount to the success of any conference. This year, roughly 75% of the PC members were from academia and the remaining quarter from government, industry, or a mix. Roughly 20% of the PC was from outside the USA. This year's PC included ten new PC members who have never served on the RAID PC and 23 who have served before, including three members, each serving for their eighth time.

While RAID has previously awarded an *"influential paper"* award every five years for papers appearing at RAID that have been important in the community, this year's RAID saw the permanent addition of a yearly *best paper award*. A subset of five PC members was selected by the chairs and served as the award committee. A two-phase process was used in which papers were nominated and discussed amongst the awards committee and then a vote amongst the committee decided the award winner. This year we were also pleased to offer a *"community service"* award to recognize an outstanding contribution to the security community and to RAID in particular. This award, given to Marc Dacier, recognizes the pivotal role he played in creating and shaping the RAID conference we enjoy today.

RAID only exists because of the community that supports it. Indeed, RAID is completely self-funded. Every organizer independently shoulders the financial risks associated with its organization. The sponsors, therefore, play a very important role and ensure that the registration fees remain very reasonable. Therefore, we want to take this opportunity to thank Niometrics and Comcast for their generous sponsorships to RAID 2018. We, of course, are very grateful to the general chair, Sotiris Ioannidis, from FORTH-ICS, and his assembled team for ensuring that the conference ran smoothly. Special thanks go to the local arrangement and sponsor chair, Ioannis Askoxylakis, also from FORTH-ICS; to the publication chair, Manolis Stamatogiannakis, from Vrije Universiteit Amsterdam; and to the publicity chair, Michalis Polychronakis, from Stony Brook University.

We hope you enjoyed the conference!

August 2018

Michael Bailey
Thorsten Holz

Organization

Organizing Committee

General Chair

Sotiris Ioannidis   Foundation for Research and Technology – Hellas, Greece

Program Committee Chair

Michael Bailey   University of Illinois at Urbana-Champaign, USA

Program Committee Co-chair

Thorsten Holz   Ruhr-Universität Bochum, Germany

Publication Chair

Manolis Stamatogiannakis   Vrije Universiteit Amsterdam, The Netherlands

Publicity Chair

Michalis Polychronakis   Stony Brook University, USA

Local Arrangements and Sponsor Chair

Ioannis Askoxylakis   Foundation for Research and Technology – Hellas, Greece

Program Committee

Sadia Afroz	ICSI, UC Berkeley, USA
Magnus Almgren	Chalmers University of Technology, Sweden
Johanna Amann	ICSI, UC Berkeley, USA
Leyla Bilge	Symantec Research Labs, France
Srdjan Capkun	ETH Zurich, Switzerland
Lorenzo Cavallaro	Royal Holloway University of London, UK
Lucas Davi	University of Duisburg-Essen, Germany
Tudor Dumitras	The University of Maryland, USA
Zakir Durumeric	Stanford University, USA
Manuel Egele	Boston University, USA
Roya Ensafi	University of Michigan, USA
Giulia Fanti	Carniegie Mellon University, USA
Carrie Gates	Securelytix, USA
Jon Giffin	Google, USA
Guofei Gu	Texas A&M University, USA

External Reviewers

Steering Committee

Sponsors

Gold Sponsor

Niometrics – https://www.niometrics.com/

NIOMETRICS

Bronze Sponsor

Comcast – https://corporate.comcast.com/

Contents

Attacks

PROTEUS: Detecting Android Emulators from Instruction-Level Profiles 3
Onur Sahin, Ayse K. Coskun, and Manuel Egele

BabelView: Evaluating the Impact of Code Injection Attacks
in Mobile Webviews 25
Claudio Rizzo, Lorenzo Cavallaro, and Johannes Kinder

Defeating Software Mitigations Against Rowhammer: A Surgical
Precision Hammer 47
Andrei Tatar, Cristiano Giuffrida, Herbert Bos, and Kaveh Razavi

Intrusion Detection and Prevention

Reading Between the Lines: Content-Agnostic Detection
of Spear-Phishing Emails 69
Hugo Gascon, Steffen Ullrich, Benjamin Stritter, and Konrad Rieck

Backdoors: Definition, Deniability and Detection 92
Sam L. Thomas and Aurélien Francillon

RWGuard: A Real-Time Detection System Against Cryptographic
Ransomware 114
Shagufta Mehnaz, Anand Mudgerikar, and Elisa Bertino

DDoS Attacks

DNS Unchained: Amplified Application-Layer DoS Attacks Against
DNS Authoritatives 139
Jonas Bushart and Christian Rossow

Control Plane Reflection Attacks in SDNs: New Attacks
and Countermeasures 161
Menghao Zhang, Guanyu Li, Lei Xu, Jun Bi, Guofei Gu, and Jiasong Bai

Proof-of-Blackouts? How Proof-of-Work Cryptocurrencies
Could Affect Power Grids 184
*Johanna Ullrich, Nicholas Stifter, Aljosha Judmayer, Adrian Dabrowski,
and Edgar Weippl*

Passwords, Accounts, and Users

Characterizing Eve: Analysing Cybercrime Actors in a Large
Underground Forum 207
  Sergio Pastrana, Alice Hutchings, Andrew Caines, and Paula Buttery

SybilBlind: Detecting Fake Users in Online Social Networks Without
Manual Labels 228
  Binghui Wang, Le Zhang, and Neil Zhenqiang Gong

GuidedPass: Helping Users to Create Strong and Memorable Passwords 250
  Simon S. Woo and Jelena Mirkovic

Machine Learning for Computer Security

Fine-Pruning: Defending Against Backdooring Attacks on Deep
Neural Networks. 273
  Kang Liu, Brendan Dolan-Gavitt, and Siddharth Garg

Dictionary Extraction and Detection of Algorithmically Generated Domain
Names in Passive DNS Traffic 295
  Mayana Pereira, Shaun Coleman, Bin Yu, Martine DeCock,
  and Anderson Nascimento

OTTer: A Scalable High-Resolution Encrypted Traffic Identification
Engine. 315
  Eva Papadogiannaki, Constantinos Halevidis, Periklis Akritidis,
  and Lazaros Koromilas

Hardware-Assisted Security

Hardware Assisted Randomization of Data. 337
  Brian Belleville, Hyungon Moon, Jangseop Shin, Dongil Hwang,
  Joseph M. Nash, Seonhwa Jung, Yeoul Na, Stijn Volckaert, Per Larsen,
  Yunheung Paek, and Michael Franz

MicroStache: A Lightweight Execution Context for In-Process Safe
Region Isolation 359
  Lucian Mogosanu, Ashay Rane, and Nathan Dautenhahn

CryptMe: Data Leakage Prevention for Unmodified Programs
on ARM Devices 380
  Chen Cao, Le Guan, Ning Zhang, Neng Gao, Jingqiang Lin, Bo Luo,
  Peng Liu, Ji Xiang, and Wenjing Lou

Software Security

PartiSan: Fast and Flexible Sanitization via Run-Time Partitioning   403
Julian Lettner, Dokyung Song, Taemin Park, Per Larsen,
Stijn Volckaert, and Michael Franz

τCFI: Type-Assisted Control Flow Integrity for x86-64 Binaries   423
Paul Muntean, Matthias Fischer, Gang Tan, Zhiqiang Lin,
Jens Grossklags, and Claudia Eckert

Trusted Execution Path for Protecting Java Applications Against
Deserialization of Untrusted Data   445
Stefano Cristalli, Edoardo Vignati, Danilo Bruschi,
and Andrea Lanzi

Malware

Error-Sensor: Mining Information from HTTP Error Traffic
for Malware Intelligence   467
Jialong Zhang, Jiyong Jang, Guofei Gu, Marc Ph. Stoecklin,
and Xin Hu

Generic Black-Box End-to-End Attack Against State of the Art
API Call Based Malware Classifiers   490
Ishai Rosenberg, Asaf Shabtai, Lior Rokach, and Yuval Elovici

Next Generation P2P Botnets: Monitoring Under Adverse Conditions   511
Leon Böck, Emmanouil Vasilomanolakis, Max Mühlhäuser,
and Shankar Karuppayah

IoT/CPS Security

Malicious IoT Implants: Tampering with Serial Communication
over the Internet   535
Philipp Morgner, Stefan Pfennig, Dennis Salzner, and Zinaida Benenson

Before Toasters Rise Up: A View into the Emerging IoT
Threat Landscape   556
Pierre-Antoine Vervier and Yun Shen

Statistical Similarity of Critical Infrastructure Network Traffic Based
on Nearest Neighbor Distances   577
Jeong-Han Yun, Yoonho Hwang, Woomyo Lee, Hee-Kap Ahn,
and Sin-Kyu Kim

Security Measurements

PostScript Undead: Pwning the Web with a 35 Years Old Language   603
Jens Müller, Vladislav Mladenov, Dennis Felsch, and Jörg Schwenk

Identifying Key Leakage of Bitcoin Users   623
Michael Brengel and Christian Rossow

Defenses

Furnace: Self-service Tenant VMI for the Cloud   647
Micah Bushouse and Douglas Reeves

ShadowMonitor: An Effective In-VM Monitoring Framework with
Hardware-Enforced Isolation   670
Bin Shi, Lei Cui, Bo Li, Xudong Liu, Zhiyu Hao, and Haiying Shen

KASR: A Reliable and Practical Approach to Attack Surface Reduction
of Commodity OS Kernels   691
*Zhi Zhang, Yueqiang Cheng, Surya Nepal, Dongxi Liu, Qingni Shen,
and Fethi Rabhi*

Author Index   711

Attacks

PROTEUS: Detecting Android Emulators from Instruction-Level Profiles

Onur Sahin[✉], Ayse K. Coskun, and Manuel Egele

Boston University, Boston, MA 02215, USA
sahin@bu.edu

Abstract. The popularity of Android and the personal information stored on these devices attract the attention of regular cyber-criminals as well as nation state adversaries who develop malware that targets this platform. To identify malicious Android apps at a scale (e.g., Google Play contains 3.7M Apps), state-of-the-art mobile malware analysis systems inspect the execution of apps in emulation-based sandboxes. An emerging class of evasive Android malware, however, can evade detection by such analysis systems through ceasing malicious activities if an emulation sandbox is detected. Thus, systematically uncovering potential methods to detect emulated environments is crucial to stay ahead of adversaries. This work uncovers the detection methods based on discrepancies in instruction-level behavior between software-based emulators and real ARM CPUs that power the vast majority of Android devices. To systematically discover such discrepancies at scale, we propose the PROTEUS system. PROTEUS performs large-scale collection of application execution traces (i.e., registers and memory) as they run on an emulator and on *accurate software models of ARM CPUs*. PROTEUS automatically identifies the instructions that cause divergent behavior between emulated and real CPUs and, on a set of 500K test programs, identified 28K divergent instances. By inspecting these instances, we reveal 3 major classes of root causes that are responsible for these discrepancies. We show that some of these root causes can be easily fixed without introducing observable performance degradation in the emulator. Thus, we have submitted patches to improve resilience of Android emulators against evasive malware.

1 Introduction

Android is a fast growing ecosystem. By acting as a trusted medium between developers and users, application repositories (e.g., Google Play Store) have enabled explosive growth in the number of mobile applications available to billions of users worldwide [6]. Currently, the Play Store consists of more than 3.7M Android applications with thousands of new applications emerging every day [9]. Unfortunately, this massive ecosystem is also appealing to miscreants who seek to infect a wide set of users with malicious applications.

To protect users, malware analysis systems are widely used in both academia and industry. Since malware can easily defeat static analysis via obfuscation and

© Springer Nature Switzerland AG 2018
M. Bailey et al. (Eds.): RAID 2018, LNCS 11050, pp. 3–24, 2018.
https://doi.org/10.1007/978-3-030-00470-5_1

packing [14], contemporary analysis systems for Android adopt dynamic analysis to inspect the runtime behavior of applications. State-of-the-art malware analyzers for Android are based on emulators [23, 28, 30], which can easily scale across multiple hosts to inspect vast number of Android apps. Such emulation-based analysis also offers easy instrumentation [30] and fast state restore capabilities (e.g., orders of magnitude faster than bare-metal [22]), making the emulation-based analysis approach appealing to security researchers and practitioners.

The effectiveness of these dynamic malware analysis systems, however, is largely at risk due to an emerging class of evasive malware. Such malware looks for discrepancies that exist between emulated and real systems before triggering any malicious attempt. By ceasing malicious activities on an emulated enviroment, the malware can thwart existing emulator-based malware analyzers. The situation is alarming as studies show a rising number of malware instances that employ evasion tactics [18] (e.g., Branco et al. find evasion methods in more than 80% of 4M malware samples [13]). For Android, several recent classes of evasive malware (e.g., *Xavier* [1], *Grabos* [7]) have already been identified in the Play Store. A crucial step for defending against such malware is to systematically extract the discrepancies between emulated and real systems. Once discovered, such discrepancies can be eliminated [19] or can be used to inspect applications for presence of evasion tactics leveraging these artifacts [13].

Many of the approaches to date [10, 25, 29] discover discrepancies of emulation-based sandboxes in an ad hoc fashion by engineering malware samples or specific emulator components (e.g., scheduling). Such manual approaches cannot provide large-scale discovery of unknown discrepancies, which is needed to stay ahead of adversaries. Recent work [17] automatically identifies file system and API discrepancies used by several Android malware (e.g., [1,7]). Evasion tactics that rely on such artifacts can be rendered ineffective by using modified system images and ensuring the API return values match those in real devices [12]. Besides API/file checks, a malware can also leverage differences in the semantics of CPU instructions to fingerprint emulation [13] (e.g., by embedding checks in the native code [25]). As opposed to ad hoc approaches or API/file heuristics, our work focuses on systematically discovering instruction-level discrepancies that are intrinsically harder to enumerate and fix for modern complex CPUs.

Prior discoveries of instruction-level discrepancies in emulated CPUs are limited to x86 instruction set [21, 24, 27], while the vast majority mobile devices use ARM CPUs. Despite the large number of discrepancies reported in prior work [21, 24], such findings are not readily useful for improving the fidelity of emulators as their analysis does not reveal the root causes of discrepancies. Such analysis of root causes is essential as not all discrepancies are reliable detection heuristics due to Unpredictable ARM instructions [4], whose behavior varies across platforms. In addition, reliance on physical CPUs to obtain the ground truth instruction behavior poses practical limitations on the number of test cases (e.g., instructions, register/memory operands, system register settings) that can be covered. Approaches to improve coverage [27] are based on heavy analysis of ISA specifications, which are notorious for their complexity and size.

To address the shortcomings above and identify instruction-level discrepancies in Android emulators at a scale, we propose to collect and analyze a large number of instruction-level traces corresponding to execution on real ARM CPUs and emulators. By recording how each ARM instruction modifies the architectural state (i.e., registers and memory) on an emulated and real ARM CPU, we can automatically detect divergences that are directly observable by user-level programs. To scale the divergence analysis system, we demonstrate the feasibility of using accurate software models for ARM CPUs instead of physical hardware.

We build our instruction-level analysis framework into a new system, PROTEUS. PROTEUS automatically identifies architectural differences between real and emulated ARM CPUs. PROTEUS uses official software models for ARM CPUs (i.e., *Fast Models* [3]) to gather detailed and accurate instruction-level traces corresponding to real CPU operation. We instrument QEMU to collect traces for emulated CPUs. We target QEMU as it forms the base of state-of-the-art Android malware analysis systems [23,28,30] as well as the Android SDK emulator. We evaluate our system with over a million CPU instructions. Our randomized test cases allow us to examine instruction behavior that would not be triggered during execution of conventional compiler-generated programs.

PROTEUS automatically groups the instructions that generate similar divergent behavior and reveals several major classes of instruction-level discrepancies between emulated and real ARM CPUs. We find that a single root cause (e.g., relaxed opcode verification) can account for a large number divergent cases and that some of these sources of divergences can be eliminated by minor modifications in the QEMU source code. To improve resilience of Android emulators against *detection via CPU semantic attacks*, we have disclosed our root cause findings including patches where appropriate to the QEMU community[1]. Our evaluation of discovered discrepancies on physical devices and SDK emulators demonstrates how unprivileged user-mode programs can deterministically fingerprint Android emulators to easily perform CPU semantic attacks (e.g., by using a few CPU instructions in native code). To the best of our knowledge, this is the first systematic study to demonstrate instruction semantic attacks against QEMU's ARM support. Overall, we make the following specific contributions:

- **PROTEUS:** We design, implement, and evaluate a scalable approach for discovering discrepancies between emulated and real ARM CPUs (Sect. 3). Our system collects a large number of instruction-level traces from accurate software models of ARM CPUs and from an instrumented QEMU instance. PROTEUS automatically identifies the instructions and conditions that cause a divergence, and groups instructions with similar behavior to facilitate further inspection for root cause analysis (Sect. 4).
- **Novel Attack Surface:** We systematically analyze the divergences found by PROTEUS and uncover novel detection methods for Android emulators

---

[1] We have eliminated several root causes as part of our work and have already submitted a patch.

based on instruction-level differences between emulated and real ARM CPUs (Sect. 5.1). We show the effectiveness of these methods for deterministically distinguishing physical devices from Android emulators (Sect. 5.3).

- **Fidelity Improvements:** We identify a set of root causes (Sect. 5.2) that are responsible for a large set of divergences. We show that some of these root causes can be eliminated in Android emulators through minor fixes without causing any observable performance overhead (Sect. 5.4).

2   Background

This section provides a brief overview of the ARM architecture and clarifies the terminology that we use throughout the rest of this paper. We also describe the attack model we are assuming in this work.

2.1   ARMv7-A Architecture

This paper focuses on ARMv7-A instruction set architecture (ISA), the vastly popular variant of ARMv7 that targets high-performance CPUs which support OS platforms such as Linux and Android (e.g., smartphones, IoT devices). The ARM architecture implements a Reduced Instruction Set Computer (RISC) organization where memory accesses are handled explicitly via load/store instructions. Each ARM instruction is of fixed 32-bit length. ARMv7-A features 16 32-bit registers (i.e., 13 general purpose registers (R0-R12), stack pointer (SP), link register (LR), program counter (PC)) accessible in user-mode (usr) programs. The CPU supports 6 operating modes (usr,hyp,abt,svc,fiq,irq) and 3 privilege levels PL0, PL1 and PL2 (i.e., lower numbers correspond to lower privilege levels). The *Current Program Status Register* (CPSR) stores the CPU mode, execution state bits (e.g., endianness, ARM/Thumb instruction set) and status flags.

UNDEFINED Instructions: The ARMv7 specification explicitly defines the set of encodings that do not correspond to a valid instruction as architecturally Undefined. For example, Fig. 1 shows the encoding diagram for multiplication instructions in ARMv7. The architecture specification [4] states that the instructions are Undefined when the op field equals 5 or 7 in this encoding.

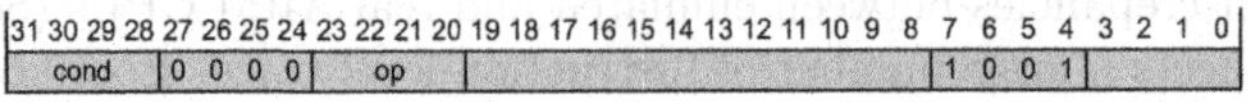

31 30 29 28	27 26 25 24	23 22 21 20	19 18 17 16 15 14 13 12 11 10 9	8	7 6 5 4	3 2 1 0
cond	0 0 0 0	op			1 0 0 1	

Fig. 1. Encoding diagram for multiplication instructions in ARMv7 ISA [4].

An Undefined instruction causes the CPU to switch to the undefined (und) mode and generates an undefined instruction exception. An undefined instruction exception is also generated when an instruction tries to access a co-processor that is not implemented or for which access is restricted to higher privilege levels [4].

UNPREDICTABLE Instruction Behavior: The ARM architecture contains a large set of instruction encodings for which the resulting instruction behavior is unspecified and cannot be relied upon (i.e., `Unpredictable`). ARM instructions can exhibit `Unpredictable` behavior depending on specific cases of operand registers, current CPU mode or system control register values [4]. For example, many instructions in the ARM architecture are `Unpredictable` if the PC is used as a register operand. In addition, some instruction encoding bits are specified as *"should be"* and denoted as "(0)" and "(1)" in ARM's official encoding diagrams. While different encodings for *"should be"* bits do not correspond to different instructions, the resulting behavior is `Unpredictable` if a given encoding fails to match against the specified *"should be"* bit pattern.

The effect of an `Unpredictable` instruction is at the sole discretion of the CPU manufacturer and can behave as a `NOP` or `Undefined` instruction, or can change the architectural state of CPU. Consider the "LDMDA pc!,{r0,r1,r5,r6, r8,sp,lr}" `Unpredictable` instruction (encoded as 0xE83F6163), which loads the given set of registers from consecutive memory addresses starting at PC and writes the final target address back to PC. This instruction causes undefined instruction exception on a real CPU while it modifies the PC and causes an infinite loop on QEMU. Note that both behaviors comply with the ARM specification.

2.2   Threat Model

The aim of the malware author is to evade detection by the analysis tools and distribute a malicious application to real users. The malware possesses a set of detection heuristics to distinguish emulators from real devices. Malware achieves evasion by ceasing any malicious behavior on an emulated analysis environment, which could otherwise be flagged by the analysis tool. Once the malware escapes detection and reaches real users, it can execute the harmful content within the application or dynamically load the malicious payload at runtime [26].

Our work focuses on discrepancies that are observable by user-level programs. Thus, we assume applications running in `usr` mode at the lowest PL0 privilege level. Since our technique detects emulators by natively executing CPU instructions and monitoring their effects, we assume an Android application that contains a native code. This is a common case for many applications (e.g., games, physics simulations) that use native code for the performance-critical sections and for the convenience of reusing existing C/C++ libraries [2,26].

We assume that applications are subject to dynamic analysis in a QEMU-based emulation environment. Indeed, state-of-the-art dynamic analysis frameworks that are commonly used in academia [28,30] and industry [23] use QEMU as the emulation engine. In addition, the Android emulator that is distributed with the Android SDK is also based on QEMU.

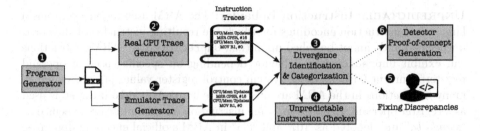

Fig. 2. Overview of PROTEUS.

3   PROTEUS System Architecture

The aim of the proposed PROTEUS system (Fig. 2) is to find the differences in semantics of instructions executed on a real and an emulated ARM CPU. PROTEUS consists of a trace collection part and an analysis component to automatically identify and classify divergences. This section provides an overview of the core components of PROTEUS and describes its high-level operation.

Central to our system is collection of detailed instruction-level traces that capture the execution behavior of programs on both emulated and real CPUs. The traces capture all updates to user-visible registers as well as the operands in memory transactions from load/store instructions. If a program terminates by a CPU exception, the respective signal number is also recorded.

The *"Program Generator"* component (❶) generates the test programs which are used for collecting instruction-level traces and discovering discrepancies. Note that ARM CPU emulation in QEMU is inadvertently tested using millions of apps by Android developers. Thus, programs generated for divergence identification should also exercise platforms for uncommon cases beyond the set of instructions emitted by compilers and found in legitimate Android apps.

For each generated test program, we collect its instruction-level traces by executing the same binary on two different platforms (❷) which provide the traces corresponding to execution on an emulator and a real CPU.

The *"Divergence Identification & Categorization"* component (❸) compares emulator and real CPU traces of a program to identify the initial point of divergence. A divergence can be due to a mismatch in register values, memory operands or exception behavior. Divergent cases that stem from the same mismatch are grouped together automatically to facilitate manual inspection of discovered discrepancies. Our hypothesis behind the grouping is that there exist a small number of root causes that cause the same divergent behavior (e.g., exception mismatch) on potentially a large set of test cases. For instance, we can group together the divergent instructions that generate an illegal instruction exception in a real CPU but execute as a valid instruction in emulator. We also check if the divergent instruction is Unpredictable (❹). Since Unpredictable instructions can exhibit different behavior across any two platforms, we do not treat divergences that stem from these instructions as a reliable detection method.

Overall, PROTEUS provides us with the instruction encoding that caused the divergent behavior, register values before that instruction, divergence group as well as the difference between the traces of emulated and real CPU (e.g., signal number, CPU mode, etc.) which occurs after executing the divergent instruction. We can optionally identify why QEMU fails to faithfully provide the correct behavior as implemented by the real CPU and fix the source of mismatch (❺). PROTEUS can also generate a proof-of-concept emulation detector (❻), which reconstructs the divergent behavior by setting respective register values, executing the divergent instruction and checking for the resulting mismatch that PROTEUS identifies during the *"Divergence Identification & Categorization"* stage.

4   Proteus Implementation

In this section, we describe our implementation of the proposed PROTEUS system for detecting instruction-level differences between emulated and real ARM CPUs. In Sect. 4.1, we describe our framework for acquiring instruction-level traces. Section 4.2 describes how we use this framework to collect a large number of sample traces and automatically identify discrepancies.

4.1   Instruction-Level Tracing on ARM-Based Platforms

Collected Trace Information: For our purposes, a trace consists of all general-purpose registers that are visible to user-level programs, which provide a snapshot of the architectural state. Specifically, we record the R0-R12, SP, PC, LR and CPSR registers (see Sect. 2). Finally, we record operands of all memory operations. Various ARM instructions can load/store multiple registers sequentially from a base address. We record all the data within the memory transaction as well as the base address. This trace information gives us a detailed program-visible behavior of CPU instructions. Thus, any discrepancy within the trace is visible to a malware and can be potentially leveraged for evasion purposes.

Emulator Traces Through QEMU Instrumentation: QEMU dynamically translates the guest instructions (e.g., ARM) for execution on the host machine (e.g., x86). Translation consists of several steps. First, guest instructions within a basic block are disassembled and converted into a platform-agnostic intermediate representation called TCG (*Tiny Code Generator*). Next, generated TCG code blocks (i.e., *translation block*) are compiled into host ISA for execution.

To implement tracing capability in QEMU, we inject extra TCG operations into each translation block during the translation phase. These extra TCG operations dump the trace information during the execution phase. We use the helper functionality within QEMU to generate the extra TCG code. The main use of the helper functionality in QEMU is to allow developers to extend the capabilities of TCG operations for implementing complex instructions. We inject the extra TCG operations for every disassembled instruction to achieve per-instruction tracing granularity. Specifically, we modify the disassembly routines of ARM instructions to inject TCG operations that record registers. We also modify the load/store routines to record address and data values for memory transactions.

We use QEMU 2.7.0 from Android repositories[2], which forms the base of the SDK emulator used in modern Android malware analyzers [23,28,30]. QEMU 2.7.0 is the most recent version adopted in current SDK emulators. To ease instrumentation and facilitate the data collection, we use QEMU in user-mode configuration as opposed to full-system emulation. We use full-system SDK emulators during our evaluation of discovered discrepancies (Sect. 5.3).

Accurate Real CPU Traces Using ARM Fast Models: Gathering detailed instruction-level traces from real CPUs is challenging and, due to practical limitations on the number of devices that can be used, does not scale well. In this work, we propose to use accurate functional models of ARM CPUs (i.e., *Fast Models* [3]) to obtain traces corresponding to execution on real CPUs. Fast Models are official software models developed and maintained by ARM and provide complete accuracy of software-visible semantics of instructions.

ARM Fast Models provide a set of trace sources which generate a stream of trace events when running the simulation. Once a target set of trace sources are specified, Fast Models emit trace events whenever a change occurs on a trace source. These trace events are provided over a standardized interface called *Model Trace Interface (MTI)*. We use an existing plugin called *GenericTrace* to record trace events over the MTI interface.

Our work is based on a Cortex-A15 fast model which implements the ARMv7 ISA. We specify *"inst"*, *"cpsr"*, *"core_loads"*, *"core_stores"* and *"core_regs"* trace sources, which capture changes in register values as well as data/address operand values in memory transactions.

4.2   Identifying Emulated vs. Real CPU Discrepancies with Tracing

This section describes how we use our tracing capabilities (Sect. 4.1) to find differences in instruction semantics between emulated and real ARM CPUs.

Generating Test Cases: We generate valid ELF binaries as inputs to our tracing platforms. We choose to use programs that contain random instructions. Specifically, each input binary contains 20 random bytes corresponding to 5 ARM instructions. We use this randomized approach to be able to exercise emulators with uncommon instructions which are not likely to be emitted by compilers. We use more than one instruction per binary to be able to cover more instructions each time a simulation is launched for a test program.

---

[2] https://android.googlesource.com/platform/external/qemu-android/+/qemu-2.7.0.

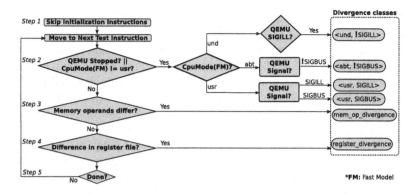

Fig. 3. Illustration of the flow for comparing the Fast Model and QEMU traces.

Each test program starts with a few instructions that set the CPU state, clear registers and condition flags. By default, the programs run on the Fast Model in `svc` mode and no stack space is allocated. Thus, we use these initialization instructions to ensure that CPU mode is set to `usr` and SP points to the same address on both platforms. We also clear all registers to ensure that programs start from identical architectural state on both emulator and real CPU. These initialization instructions are followed by 5 random instructions. Finally, each test case ends with an `exit` system call sequence (i.e., `mov r7,#1; svc 0x0`).

Identifying Divergence Points: This phase of the PROTEUS system consumes the traces collected from QEMU and ARM Fast Model to identify and group divergent behaviors. To identify the initial point where QEMU and Fast Model traces of an input program diverge, we perform a step-by-step comparison.

The step-by-step comparison procedure is illustrated in Fig. 3. We skip the portion of the traces which corresponds to the initialization instructions described in the previous section (Step 1) to avoid false alarms that arise from the initial state differences between QEMU and Fast Model. We walk through the remaining instruction sequence until either a difference exists in the collected trace data or the test program on QEMU terminates due to an exception. If the program terminates on QEMU or the CPU mode on Fast Models switches to a different mode than `usr`, we examine whether this exception behavior matches between QEMU and real CPU (Step 2). We perform the comparison using the CPU mode from the Fast Model and the signal received by the program upon termination on QEMU. Note that there is no exception handling or signal mechanism on Fast Models as no OS is running. Depending on this CPU mode and signal comparison, we determine whether the observed behavior falls into one of the four possible divergent types below. We use a tuple representation as `<FastModel_response, QEMU_response>` to categorize divergent behavior.

– `<und,!SIGILL>`: This group represents the cases where QEMU fails to recognize an architecturally `Undefined` instruction. If the Fast Models indicate that CPU switches to und mode, the expected behavior for QEMU is to deliver a SIGILL signal to the target program. This is because execution of an Undefined instruction takes the CPU into und mode and generates an illegal instruction exception. Thus, the cases where Fast Model switches to und mode while QEMU does not deliver a SIGILL signal is a sign of divergence.

– <usr,SIGILL>: This class of divergence contains cases where QEMU terminates by an illegal instruction signal (SIGILL) while Fast Models indicate the target instruction is valid (i.e., cpu remains in usr mode).

– <abt,!SIGBUS>: This class captures the cases where QEMU fails to recognize a data/prefetch abort and hence does not generate a bus error (i.e., deliver SIGBUS). Prefetch aborts are caused by failing to load a target instruction while data aborts indicate that the CPU is unable to read data from memory (e.g., due to privilege restrictions, misaligned addresses etc.) [4].

– <usr,SIGBUS>: This divergence type represents the opposite of the previous case. Specifically, QEMU detects a bus error and delivers a SIGBUS to the test program while the Fast Models indicate that the memory access made by the target program is valid (i.e., cpu is not in abt mode).

If no exception is triggered for an instruction, we further compare the registers and memory operands within the collected trace data. We determine memory operand divergence (Step 3) if the address or the number of transferred bytes differ between QEMU and Fast Model traces. We do not treat data differences as divergence since subtle differences may exist in the initial memory states of QEMU and Fast Models. We drop cases with different memory values from further examination as the loaded data would propagate into register state and cause false positive divergence detection. Finally, if no divergence is identified in exception behavior or in memory operands, we compare the user-level registers (Step 4) to detect any register state divergence. Steps 2–4 presented in Fig. 3 continues for the remaining random instructions in the test program.

Since Unpredictable instructions can cause different legitimate behaviors on any two CPU implementations, we cannot use these instructions to deterministically differentiate emulators from real systems. Thus, if a divergent instruction identified in Steps 2–4 is Unpredictable, we do not classify this case into any divergence group. However, an officially verified tool or a programmatic methodology to check if a given ARM instruction would generate Unpredictable behavior is unavailable. Thus, we use an open-source specification of ARMv7 architecture written in Standard ML (SML) and proposed by the earlier work [15].

Generating Detector Programs: Based on the identified divergent instruction semantics, PROTEUS can optionally generate a proof-of-concept program that determines whether the program is executed on an emulator or a real system. This section describes how our system generates these programs and provides insight into how a real-life malware can implement CPU semantic attacks.

PROTEUS generates detector programs by rewriting a set of pre-built template binaries to reconstruct the divergent behavior. The template programs simply execute the divergent instruction and check whether the resulting effect matches with QEMU or real CPU behavior. Before executing the divergent instruction, we set up the environment with the necessary changes to trigger divergent behavior and observe its effect. These changes are (1) setting the register values (CPSR and R0-R12) with the values provided from the divergence identification phase, (2) installing signal handlers for exception-related divergent behavior. We use sigsetjmp/siglongjmp provided by the standard C library to preserve the CPU state

```
sig_atomic_t sig_info = 0;
sigjmp_buf buf;

void catch_signals(int signum) {
    if (signum == SIGBUS)
        sig_info = 1;
    siglongjmp(buf, 1);
}
sig_atomic_t say_my_name() {
    prepare(); // register signal
        handlers
    if(!sigsetjmp(buf,1)) {
        // Set target registers
        asm("LDR  r4,=0x00008075");
        // execute divergent instruction
        asm(".byte 0x10,0x00,0x97,0xe8");
        siglongjmp(buf, 1);
    }
    cleanup(); // remove signal handlers
    return sig_info;
}
void main() {
    sig_atomic_t ret = say_my_name();
    (ret==1) ? printf("real cpu"):printf(
        "emulator");
}
```

Listing 1.1. A sample program snippet for detecting Android emulator.

which would otherwise be altered by the changes we perform. Listing 1.1 illustrates an example detector program for the <abt,!SIGBUS> group. The current CPU state is saved with sigsetjmp on line 11. The register state is loaded with target values (line 13) and the divergent instruction (LDM r7,{r4}) is executed (line 15) to reconstruct the divergent behavior. The program determines emulation if it does not receive a SIGBUS after the divergent instruction accesses the misaligned memory address stored in R4. The original CPU state before constructing the divergent behavior is restored on either line 7 or 16. We simply build one template program for each of the six divergence groups. Depending on the divergence group, for a given divergent instruction, we pick the corresponding sample template to rewrite a new detector program.

5   Evaluation

This section demonstrates the capabilities of PROTEUS for identifying the discrepancies of QEMU's emulated CPU from a real ARM CPU. We systematically analyze the divergences reported by PROTEUS to identify the root causes of the discrepancies. On a real smartphone and Android emulator, we demonstrate how our findings can fingerprint the underlying platform. Finally, we demonstrate the feasibility of fixing several root causes of divergences without any observable performance penalty. Overall, we seek to answer the following questions:

- Are there any observable discrepancies between an emulated and real CPU? If so, how prevalent are these differences? (Sect. 5.1)
- How effective are the divergences reported by PROTEUS in terms of fingerprinting real hardware and dynamic analysis platforms? (Sect. 5.3)
- What are the root causes of the discrepancies (Sect. 5.2) and can we eliminate them in QEMU without impacting its performance? (Sect. 5.4)

5.1 Divergence Statistics from PROTEUS

In order to address our first research question, we use PROTEUS to examine the instruction-level traces from 500K input test programs. Figure 4 shows the number of instructions executed in the test programs until a divergence occurs or QEMU stops due to an exception. The majority of the test cases (45%) finish after a single instruction only and, almost all test cases (>94%), either diverge or cause an exception on QEMU after executing the 5 instructions in our test programs.

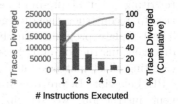

Fig. 4. #Instructions before divergence or exception.

Overall, our system analyzed over 1.06M CPU instructions. Table 1 presents an overall view of the results by PROTEUS showing a comparison between QEMU and Fast Models in terms of the exception behavior (Table 1a) as well as extent of divergences per group (Table 1b).

Table 1. PROTEUS divergence statistics for 500K test cases containing 2.5M random ARM instructions. Remaining instances of 500K programs (not shown in Table 1a) are (1) 83,125 (17%) cases due to `Unpredictable` instructions, (2) 27,048 (5.4%) non-divergent cases where programs finish successfully on both platforms and (3) 1216 cases that differ due to memory values. Note that we do not treat these 3 cases as divergent (see Sect. 4.2).

		QEMU Response	
	SIGILL	**SIGSEGV**	**None**
und	149436 (30%)	826 (0.2%)	9341 (1.9%)
abt	11 (0.002%)	12471 (2.5%)	528 (0.1%)
svc	0	18932 (3.8%)	14609 (2.9%)
usr	5270 (1.1%)	176975 (35%)	0

(Fast Model Behavior)

(a) Exception behavior comparison.

`<und, !SIGILL>`	10167 (2%)
`<usr, SIGILL>`	5270 (1.1%)
`<abt, !SIGBUS>`	13010 (2.6%)
`<usr, SIGBUS>`	0
`mem_op_difference`	200 (0.05%)
`register_divergence`	12 (0.002%)

(b) Divergences by type.

Table 1a presents a summary of the cases where either QEMU terminates the program or the CPU mode changes in Fast Models. Overall, we observe two types of signals in QEMU (i.e., `SIGILL`, `SIGSEGV`) and CPU mode in Fast Models cover `und`, `abt`, `svc` and `usr` modes. `None` represents the cases where QEMU does not generate an exception. Most instances correspond to illegal instruction (`<und, SIGILL>`) and valid memory access (`<usr, SIGSEGV>`) cases in which the behavior in QEMU complies with Fast Models (i.e., not divergent). A large number of instances are *Supervisor Call* (`svc`) instructions which cover a large encoding space in ARM ISA. `svc` instructions are used to request OS services and are not a major point of interest for our work as we focus on the discrepancies that are observable in the user space. In Table 1a, such non-divergent cases are highlighted in gray. The remaining instances in Table 1a, along with the non-exception related differences (i.e., memory operand and register) are grouped into the divergence types as per the methodology described in Sect. 4.2.

Table 1b provides the number of instances per each divergence type. The largest number of divergences (i.e., 2.6% of 500K test programs) belong to <abt, !SIGBUS> group which hints that QEMU does not correctly sanitize the invalid memory references that cause data/prefetch aborts in CPU. PROTEUS also finds a large number of instructions that are recognized as architecturally Undefined only by the Fast Models (i.e., <und, !SIGILL> group). These point to cases where QEMU does not properly validate the encoding before treating the instruction as architecturally valid. We also find a large number of instructions which are detected as illegal only by QEMU, executing without raising an illegal instruction exception on the Fast Model (i.e., <usr, SIGILL> group). PROTEUS also finds a smaller number of cases (i.e., 0.05%) with divergent register update or memory operation which correspond to register_divergence and mem_op_difference groups in Table 1b, respectively. These examples hint at cases where the implementation of a valid instruction contains potential errors in QEMU, causing a different register or memory state than on a real CPU. Overall, despite the significant testing of QEMU, we observe that there are still many divergences where QEMU does not implement the ARM ISA faithfully.

5.2   Root Cause Analysis

While the PROTEUS system can identify large numbers of discrepancies between real and emulated ARM CPU, it does not pinpoint the root causes in QEMU that lead to a different behavior than ground truth (i.e., Fast Model behavior). This section presents our findings from an analysis of root causes of divergent behavior in QEMU. This analysis gives us, compared to large number of divergences identified, a smaller set of unique errors in QEMU that lead to divergence on a wide set of programs (Table 1b). Analyzing the root causes also allows us to pinpoint implementation flaws and devise fixes (Sect. 5.4).

In our analysis, for a divergence group, we first identify common occurrences in the bit fields *[27:20]* of a divergent 32-bit instruction encoding. In the ARM architecture, these bits contain opcodes that are checked while decoding the instruction on QEMU and real CPU. We identify the instructions with the most commonly occuring opcodes to (1) consult the ISA specification to check how these instruction should be decoded and (2) check how QEMU processes these instruction. We determine the root cause of the discrepancy by manually analyzing QEMU's control flow while executing a sample of these instructions. Once we examine the source of discrepancy (e.g., a missing check, an unimplemented feature of QEMU), we remove all possible encodings that stem from the same root cause from our statistics to find other unique instances of errors in QEMU.

Through this iterative procedure, we identified several important classes of flaws in QEMU that result in a different instruction-level behavior than a real CPU. We discuss some of our findings in the following paragraphs.

Incomplete Sanitization for UNDEFINED Instructions: We discover that QEMU does not correctly generate illegal instruction exception for a set of Undefined instruction encodings. These cases are identified from the <und,

Table 2. Several `Undefined` instruction encodings that are treated as valid instructions by QEMU. ":X" notation represents the bit length of a field while "*" represents that the field can be filled with any value (i.e., 0 or 1).

Instruction encoding (cond ∈ [0, 0xE])	Divergent condition	QEMU behavior	Real CPU behavior	#Cases
cond:4|0001|op:4|*:12|1001|*:4	op = 1,2,3,5,6,7	SWP Inst	Undefined	715
cond:4|1100010|*:9|101|*:1|op:4|*:4	op != 1,3	64-bit VMOV	Undefined	424
cond:4|11|op:6|*:20	op = 1,2	VFP Store	Undefined	51
cond:4|11101|*:2|0|*:8|1011|*:1|op:2|1|*:4	op = 2,3	VDUP Inst	Undefined	3
cond:4|110|op:5|*:8|101|*:9	op != 4,5,8-25,28,29	VFP Store	Undefined	2

`!SIGILL>` group provided by PROTEUS. Thus, a malware can achieve evasion simply by executing one of these instructions and ceasing malicious activity if no illegal instruction exception is generated.

We find that this particular group of divergences arises as QEMU relaxes the number of checks performed on the encoding while decoding the instructions. For instance, the ARM ISA defines a set of opcodes for which the synchronization instructions (e.g., `SWP`, `LDREX`) are `Undefined`, and thus should generate an illegal instruction exception. However, QEMU does not check against these invalid opcodes while decoding the synchronization instructions, causing a set of `Undefined` encodings to be treated as a valid `SWP` instruction. In fact, we identified 715 divergent test cases which are caused by this missing invalid opcode check for the `SWP` instruction. In Table 2, we provide the encoding and the conditions that cause divergent behavior for this `SWP` instruction example as well as other similar errors in QEMU that we have identified.

During our root cause analysis, we find that a large portion of the instances in `<und, !SIGILL>` group (87%) are due to instructions accessing the co-processors with ids 1 and 2. These co-processors correspond to FPA11 floating-point processor that existed in earlier variants of the ARM architecture while newer architectures (>ARMv5) use co-processor 10 for floating point (VFP) and 11 for vector processing (SIMD). While accesses to co-processors 1 and 2 are `Undefined` on a real CPU, QEMU still supports emulation of these co-processors [8]. Thus, these instructions generate an illegal instruction exception only on the real CPU.

Misaligned Memory Access Checks: As hinted by PROTEUS with the large number of instances in the `<abt, !SIGBUS>` group in Table 1b, we identify that QEMU does not enforce memory alignment requirements (e.g., alignment at word boundaries) for the ARM instructions that do not support misaligned memory accesses. The data aborts caused by such misaligned accesses would take the CPU into `abt` mode and the program is expected to be signalled with `SIGBUS` to notify that the memory subsystem cannot handle the request. Due to missing alignment checks in QEMU, a malware can easily fingerprint emulation by generating a memory reference with a misaligned address and observing whether the operation succeeds (i.e., in QEMU) or fails (i.e., on a real system).

The ARMv7 implementations can support misaligned accesses for the load-/store instructions that access a single word (e.g., LDR, STR), a half-word (e.g., LDRH, STRH) or only a byte of data (e.g., LDRB, STRB). However, other instructions that perform multiple loads/stores (e.g., LDM, STM) or memory-register swaps for synchronization (e.g., SWP, LDREX, STREX) require proper alignment of the data being referenced. The alignment requirement can be word, half-word or double-word depending on the size of data being accessed by the instruction.

We demonstrate in Sect. 5.3 how the divergence due to missing alignment enforcements in QEMU can enable evasion in a real-world scenario.

Updates to Execution State Bits: By analyzing the divergent instructions reported by PROTEUS within the `register_divergence` group, we identified another important root cause in QEMU due to masking out of the execution state bits during a status register update. Specifically, we analyzed the cases where execution state bits within CPSR differ after an MSR (move to special registers) instruction. Execution state bits in CPSR determine the current instruction set (e.g., ARM, Thumb, Jazelle) and the endianness for loads and stores. While MSR system instructions allow to update CPSR, writes to execution state bits are not allowed with the only exception being the endianness bit (CPSR.E). The ARM ISA specifies that "CPSR.E bit is writable from any mode using an MSR instruction" [4]. However, since updates on the CPSR.E bit by an MSR instruction are ignored in current QEMU, software can easily fingerprint the emulation by simply trying to flip this bit (e.g., using MSR CPSR_x, 0x200 instruction) and checking whether the endianness has been succesfully changed.

Observations from Other Statistics: Our initial investigations on <usr, SIGILL> and mem_op_divergence groups did not reveal any further root causes as above. We find that the majority of the divergent cases in mem_op_divergence group (>97%) are due to VFP/SIMD instructions effecting the extension registers. Our current work focuses on the user-mode general purpose registers only. During analysis on <usr, SIGILL> group, we identified divergences due to Unpredictable instructions. This issue is due to the incomplete SML model [15] which misses some Unpredictable instructions in our test cases (Fig. 2). For instance, we find that 761 divergence cases in <usr, SIGILL> group are due to Unpredictable encodings of a PLD (i.e., preload data) instruction, which behave as a NOP in Fast Model but generate an illegal instruction exception in QEMU.

5.3   Demonstration with Real Smartphones and the SDK Emulator

In this section, we address our second research question on evaluating the effectiveness of the divergences found by PROTEUS for real-world emulation detection. To tackle this objective, we evaluate the divergences described in Sect. 5.2 on a physical mobile platform and Android emulator. We use Nexus 5 (ARMv7) and Nexus 6P (ARMv8) smartphones as our real hardware test-beds and use the full-system emulator from the Android SDK. We choose the SDK emulator as it has been a popular base for Android dynamic analysis frameworks [23,28,30].

Evaluating Unsanitized Undefined Encodings: We use the detection binaries generated by PROTEUS to evaluate the Undefined instructions that are incompletely sanitized in QEMU (i.e., <und, !SIGILL> group). These cases are expected to generate an illegal instruction exception only on a real CPU.

We find that the SDK's copy of QEMU does not incorporate the FPA11 floating point co-processor emulation which is supported in our version of QEMU and accessed by the instructions that use co-processors 1 and 2. Thus, these instructions are Undefined in SDK emulator as well and we cannot successfully distinguish the emulator from the real hardware. As discussed in Sect. 5.1, FPA11 instructions account for 87% of the cases in <und, !SIGILL> group. However, we can successfully fingerprint the SDK emulator using all the other divergent Undefined instructions. Specifically, all the encodings described in Table 2 can deterministically distinguish between SDK emulator and Nexus 5. The detector programs (Sect. 4.2) simply register a set of signal handlers and detect the SDK emulator if the program does not receive SIGILL upon executing the divergent Undefined instruction.

```
1  /* Put some known data into memory */
2  int *ptr = calloc(1,sizeof(int));
3  ptr[0] = 0x12345678;
4  asm("mov r8,%0" : : "r"(ptr));
5
6  /* Read ptr[0] with CPSR.E set to 1 */
7  asm("msr CPSR_x, #0x200\n\t");
8  asm("ldr r4,[r8]\n\t");
9  asm("msr CPSR_x, #0x000\n\t");
10
11 asm("mov %0, r4" : "=r"(val) : : );
12 printf("0x%08X\n", val);
```

Listing 1.2. PoC for emulator detection by flipping endianness bit.

```
13 /* Put some known data into memory */
14 int *ptr = calloc(1,sizeof(int));
15 ptr[0] = 0x12345678;
16
17 //Shift address to a non-word boundary
18 ptr = (int*)((char*)ptr + 0x1);
19
20 //Try to read from misaligned address
21 asm("mov r3,%0" : : "r"(ptr));
22 asm("LDM r3,{%0}": "=r"(val) : : );
23
24 printf("0x%08X\n", val);
```

Listing 1.3. PoC for emulator detection by misaligned memory read.

Evaluating Missing Alignment Checks and Endianness Support: We also show that we can successfully detect the SDK emulator by leveraging the ignored endianness bit updates as well as the missing memory address alignment checks. Listing 1.2 provides a proof-of-concept (PoC) code sample that fingerprints emulation by flipping the endianness bit in the CPU (i.e., CPSR.E) and performing a load operation on a known data value to determine whether the endianness has been changed. Executing this code snippet on a real hardware (i.e., Nexus 5 in our case) reads the array value as 0x78563412 instead of 0x12345678 as the CPSR.E bit is set to switch from little-endian to big-endian operation for data accesses. However, since the CPSR.E bit update is ignored in QEMU, the LDR instruction reads the array element into R4 as 0x12345678 on the SDK emulator. Thus, a malware can easily fingerprint emulation by simply checking the value of target register (i.e., R4 in this example). Similarly, Listing 1.3 illustrates how the missing alignments checks in QEMU can be leveraged to fingerprint emulation. We shift the word-aligned ptr pointer by one byte to create a misaligned reference address. Reading from this misaligned pointer with an LDM (i.e., load multiple) instruction causes a bus error (program receives SIGBUS) on a real hardware while it succesfully reads the high-order part (0x123456) of the target address on the SDK emulator. Thus, a malware can simply determine emulation depending on whether a `SIGBUS` signal is received (i.e., on a real system) upon intentionally causing a misaligned memory access.

Evaluation on a ARMv8 CPU: The 64-bit ARMv8 architecture, which is used in recent smartphones, is compatible with ARMv7. Thus, the CPU semantic attacks we demonstrate in this work also apply to devices powered with ARMv8 CPUs (e.g., Nexus 6P). We evaluated PoC detectors for each root cause we discovered (i.e., Table 2, Listings 1.2 and 1.3) on a Nexus 6P smartphone and successfully distinguished this device from the SDK emulator as well.

5.4   Improving the Fidelity of QEMU

With the capabilities of PROTEUS for identifying and classifying divergences in instruction-level behavior, in this section, we show the feasibility of eliminating the sources of discrepancies to improve QEMU's fidelity.

We have modified the QEMU source code of the SDK emulator to eliminate the top 3 detection methods in Table 2 based on incomplete sanitization of opcodes for `Undefined` encodings. Specifically, based on the ARM ISA specification [4], we fixed the decoding logic of QEMU to verify all opcode fields for these 3 cases and trigger an illegal instruction exception for the `Undefined` encodings.

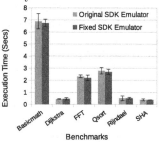

Fig. 5. Overhead evaluation of fidelity enhancements.

These fixes eliminated 1190 divergent cases in Table 2. Using various CPU benchmarks from MiBench suite [16], in Fig. 5, we verified that the minimal extra code needed to perform additional opcode checks does not introduce any measurable performance overhead. We acknowledge, however, that addressing the alignment check and endianness support in QEMU will require more comprehensive changes than the missing opcode checks for `Undefined` encodings.

6   Discussion and Limitations

Countermeasures: One possible defense against the CPU semantic attacks demonstrated in this work is to, as evaluated in Sect. 5.4, fix the root causes of instruction-level discrepancies in QEMU. We believe enhancing the fidelity of QEMU is crucial considering the critical role of emulators for Android malware analysis and the growing number of malicious apps that seek to leverage evasion tactics. As a first step towards this objective, we are disclosing our root cause findings and, in fact, have already shared a patch with the QEMU's maintainers.

As PROTEUS enumerates a set of divergent instructions, similar to prior work that inspects x86 binaries to detect evasion [13], we can scan Android apps for the presence of divergent instructions. Such analysis can be adopted by malware analyzers (e.g., Google's Bouncer [23]) to discover evasive malware that leverages these detection heuristics and prevent them from infecting the Android users.

Another potential countermeasure against the evasive malware that leverages low-level CPU discrepancies is to use real hardware for dynamic analysis instead of emulators [22]. Such a fundamentally different approach can eliminate CPU-level discrepancies. However, practical limitations such as cost, scalability and maintenance inhibits wide-spread adoption of such approaches. In addition, the instrumentation required for analyzing applications on physical devices introduces artifacts itself which allows for fingerprinting [27]. Thus, malware analysis systems for Android will continue to rely on emulators [23,28,30].

Limitations: PROTEUS uncovers several classes of observable artifacts in ARM CPU implementations between emulator and real devices. However, there could be other instruction-level discrepancies in current Android emulators that our system could not identify as our scope in this work was limited in several directions. This section discusses these limitations and describes the open-problems.

We demonstrated the capabilities of PROTEUS on the ARMv7 architecture and for the instructions in ARM mode. Recent Android devices also use the latest 64-bit ARMv8 variant of the ISA. Since ARMv8 provides compatibility with ARMv7, as evaluated in Sect. 5.3, the discrepancies we have discovered in this work also apply to ARMv8 CPUs. Discovering ARMv8-specific discrepancies using PROTEUS simply requires acquiring a Fast Model for an ARMv8 CPU (e.g., Cortex-A53) and repeating the experiments. Our present work did not explore instructions executing in Thumb mode which provides improved code density via 16-bit instructions with limited functionality. Finally, this work focuses on the ARM registers and did not explore potential discrepancies in the extension registers used by VFP/SIMD instructions. Expanding our system to include Thumb instructions and extension registers is part of our immediate future work.

Our present study also does not fully address data-dependent divergences (e.g., depending on the input values from registers or memory). Such limitation is common to fuzzing approaches as exhaustively exploring all possible inputs is computationally infeasible. One approach to improve PROTEUS in this regard would be to repeat the same test cases with several randomized inputs as well as corner cases (e.g., min/max values) as in prior work [21,27].

As discussed in Sects. 5.2 and 5.3, some of the divergences found by PROTEUS are due to Unpredictable instructions and do not correspond to an implementation flaw. This is particularly the case as the ARMv7 specification written in SML [15], which we used to check Unpredictable instructions, does not cover all Unpredictable instruction encodings. A significant contribution of our analysis is that we discovered deterministic CPU-level discrepancies even in the presence of some Unpredictable instructions in our test cases. Recently, ARM has released an official machine readable ISA specification written in a domain-specific language named ASL [5]. Unfortunately, the lack of official documentation and tools to work with ASL prevents us from relying on this resource. However, we find ASL specifications a promising future solution for enumerating Unpredictable encodings and improving our overall testing methodology.

7   Related Work

This sections overviews prior work on discovering emulation detection methods and explains how PROTEUS distinguishes from or complements them. We also discuss existing defense approaches against evasive malware.

Finding Discrepancies of Emulation Environments: Jing et al. [17] identify a large number of detection heuristics based on the differences in file system entries and return values of Android API calls. For instance, presence of "/proc/sys/net/ipv4/tcp_syncookies" file or a False return value from the "isTetheringSupported()" API implies emulation. Such discrepancies can be easily concealed by editing Android's system images and API implementations to fake real device view [12,19]. Petsas et al. detect QEMU-based emulation by observing the side effects of caching and scheduling on QEMU [25]. Other work leverages performance side channel due to low graphics performance on emulators to fingerprint emulation [29]. These techniques, however, have practical limitations as they require many repeated trial and observations which increases the detection risk of malware. Our work *systematically* uncovers observable differences in instruction semantics, which achieve deterministic emulation detection through execution of a single CPU instruction.

Similar to our approach, other works also aim at discovering discrepancies of emulators at instruction granularity. Various techniques [21,24] execute randomized instructions on emulator and real hardware to identify the discrepancies of x86 emulators. To ensure coverage of a wide set of instructions, other work [27] carefully constructs tests cases with unique instructions based on manual analysis of the x86 ISA manual while our technique is fully automated. In addition, the analysis and findings of these studies are limited to x86 instruction set only while the vast majority of mobile devices are powered by ARM CPUs. In addition, these studies classify divergences based on instructions (e.g., using mnemonic, opcodes) which oversees the fact that even different instructions (e.g., LDM and STM) can diverge due to the same root cause (e.g., missing alignment check). Our study points to the unique root causes in the implementation of CPU emulators. Thus, as we show in Sect. 5.4, our findings are readily useful for improving the fidelity of QEMU. Finally, as reliance on physical CPUs practically limits the number of test cases (e.g., instructions, register/memory operands, system register settings), we propose a novel scalable system which uses accurate functional models of ARM CPUs (i.e., Fast Models).

Martingoni et al. [20] used symbolic execution traces from a *high-fidelity emulator* to construct test cases that would achieve high coverage while testing a *low-fidelity emulator*. Unavailability of such high-fidelity emulator for Android, however, limits the applicability of this technique for our use.

Defense Against Evasive Malware: Several work proposes to detect divergent behavior in malware as a defense mechanism. Balzorotti et al. [11] detect divergent behavior due to instruction semantics by replaying applications on emulators with the system call sequences gathered from real devices and comparing the runtime behavior. Lindorfer et al. [18] propose a more generic methodology for detecting evasive malware based on the similarity of execution behaviors collected from a set of virtual machines. These approaches do not systematically expose potential causes of divergences that a future malware can use. Our work addresses the problem of proactively finding these instruction-level discrepancies and opens the possibility of pre-emptively fixing them.

Specifically for Android, other works [12, 19] systematically remove observable differences from API calls, file system and properties of emulator devices and demonstrate resistance against evasion. Such approaches, however, require enumeration of root causes of discrepancies. Our PROTEUS system aids these approaches by enumerating the divergent cases between emulator and real CPUs.

8 Conclusion

Scalable dynamic analysis of Android malware relies on emulators. Due to presence of observable discrepancies between emulated and real systems, however, a malware can detect emulation-based analysis and alter behavior to evade detection. Restoring the effectiveness of Android malware analysis requires systematic approaches to proactively identify potential detection tactics that can be used by malicious authors. This work presented the first systematic study of differences in instruction-level behavior of emulated and real ARM CPUs that power the vast majority of Android devices. We presented the PROTEUS system for large-scale exploration of CPU semantic attacks against Android emulators. PROTEUS automatically analyzed detailed instruction-level traces collected from QEMU and accurate software models of ARM CPUs and revealed several major root causes for instruction-level discrepancies in QEMU. We demonstrated the feasibility of enhancing the fidelity of QEMU by fixing the root causes of divergences without any performance impact. We are disclosing our findings and submitted patches to QEMU as a step towards improving QEMU's resiliency against evasive malware.

Acknowledgement. This work was supported by the Office of Naval Research under grants N00014-15-1-2948 and N00014-17-1-2011. We would also like to thank Arm for providing us access to the Fast Models used in this work. Any opinions, findings, conclusions, or recommendations expressed in this material are those of the authors and do not necessarily reflect those of the sponsor.

References

1. Analyzing Xavier: An Information-Stealing Ad Library on Android. https://blog.trendmicro.com/trendlabs-security-intelligence/analyzing-xavier-information-stealing-ad-library-android/
2. Android Native Development Kit (NDK). https://developer.android.com/ndk/guides/index.html
3. ARM Fast Models. https://developer.arm.com/products/system-design/fast-models
4. ARMv7-A/R Architecture Reference Manual. http://infocenter.arm.com/help/index.jsp?topic=/com.arm.doc.ddi0406c/index.html

5. Exploration Tools, A-Profile Architectures. https://developer.arm.com/products/architecture/a-profile/exploration-tools
6. Google has 2 billion users on Android. https://techcrunch.com/2017/05/17/google-has-2-billion-users-on-android-500m-on-google-photos/
7. Grabos Malware. https://securingtomorrow.mcafee.com/consumer/consumer-threat-notices/grabos-malware/
8. NetWinder Floating Point Notes. http://netwinder.osuosl.org/users/s/scottb/public_html/notes/FP-Notes-all.html
9. Number of Android applications. https://www.appbrain.com/stats/number-of-android-apps
10. QEMU emulation detection. https://wiki.koeln.ccc.de/images/d/d5/Openchaos_qemudetect.pdf
11. Balzarotti, D., Cova, M., Karlberger, C., Kruegel, C., Kirda, E., Vigna, G.: Efficient detection of split personalities in malware. In: NDSS (2010). http://www.eurecom.fr/publication/3022
12. Bordoni, L., Conti, M., Spolaor, R.: Mirage: toward a stealthier and modular malware analysis sandbox for android. In: Foley, S.N., Gollmann, D., Snekkenes, E. (eds.) ESORICS 2017. LNCS, vol. 10492, pp. 278–296. Springer, Cham (2017). https://doi.org/10.1007/978-3-319-66402-6_17
13. Branco, R.R., Barbosa, G.N., Neto, P.D.: Scientific but not academical overview of malware anti-debugging, anti-disassembly and Anti-VM technologies. In: BlackHat (2012)
14. Egele, M., Scholte, T., Kirda, E., Kruegel, C.: A survey on automated dynamic malware-analysis techniques and tools. ACM Comput. Surv. (CSUR) 44(2), 6:1–6:42 (2008). https://doi.org/10.1145/2089125.2089126
15. Fox, A.: Directions in ISA specification. In: Beringer, L., Felty, A. (eds.) ITP 2012. LNCS, vol. 7406, pp. 338–344. Springer, Heidelberg (2012). https://doi.org/10.1007/978-3-642-32347-8_23
16. Guthaus, M.R., Ringenberg, J.S., Ernst, D., Austin, T.M., Mudge, T., Brown, R.B.: MiBench: a free, commercially representative embedded benchmark suite. In: IEEE International Workshop on Workload Characterization (IISWC) (2001)
17. Jing, Y., Zhao, Z., Ahn, G.J., Hu, H.: Morpheus: automatically generating heuristics to detect android mulators. In: Proceedings of the 30th Annual Computer Security Applications Conference (ACSAC), pp. 216–225. ACM (2014). https://doi.org/10.1145/2664243.2664250
18. Lindorfer, M., Kolbitsch, C., Milani Comparetti, P.: Detecting environment-sensitive malware. In: Sommer, R., Balzarotti, D., Maier, G. (eds.) RAID 2011. LNCS, vol. 6961, pp. 338–357. Springer, Heidelberg (2011). https://doi.org/10.1007/978-3-642-23644-0_18
19. Liu, L., Gu, Y., Li, Q., Su, P.: RealDroid: large-scale evasive malware detection on "real devices". In: 26th International Conference on Computer Communication and Networks (ICCCN), pp. 1–8, July 2017. https://doi.org/10.1109/ICCCN.2017.8038419
20. Martignoni, L., McCamant, S., Poosankam, P., Song, D., Maniatis, P.: Path-exploration lifting: hi-fi tests for lo-fi emulators. In: International Conference on Architectural Support for Programming Languages and Operating Systems (ASPLOS), pp. 337–348. ACM, New York (2012). https://doi.org/10.1145/2150976.2151012
21. Martignoni, L., Paleari, R., Roglia, G.F., Bruschi, D.: Testing CPU emulators. In: International Symposium on Software Testing and Analysis (ISSTA) (2009). https://doi.org/10.1145/1572272.1572303

22. Mutti, S., et al.: Baredroid: large-scale analysis of android apps on real devices. In: Annual Computer Security Applications Conference, ACSAC (2015). https://doi.org/10.1145/2818000.2818036
23. Oberheide, J., Miller, C.: Dissecting the android bouncer. In: SummerCon (2012)
24. Paleari, R., Martignoni, L., Roglia, G.F., Bruschi, D.: A fistful of red-pills: how to automatically generate procedures to detect CPU emulators. In: Proceedings of the 3rd USENIX Conference on Offensive Technologies (WOOT) (2009)
25. Petsas, T., Voyatzis, G., Athanasopoulos, E., Polychronakis, M., Ioannidis, S.: Rage against the virtual machine: hindering dynamic analysis of android malware. In: European Workshop on System Security (EuroSec), pp. 5:1–5:6 (2014). https://doi.org/10.1145/2592791.2592796
26. Poeplau, S., Fratantonio, Y., Bianchi, A., Kruegel, C., Vigna, G.: Execute this! Analyzing Unsafe and Malicious Dynamic Code Loading in Android Applications. In: Network and Distributed System Security Symposium (NDSS) (2014)
27. Shi, H., Alwabel, A., Mirkovic, J.: Cardinal pill testing of system virtual machines. In: 23rd USENIX Conference on Security Symposium (2014)
28. Tam, K., Khan, S.J., Fattori, A., Cavallaro, L.: Copperdroid: Automatic reconstruction of android malware behaviors. In: NDSS (2015)
29. Vidas, T., Christin, N.: Evading android runtime analysis via sandbox detection. In: Proceedings of the 9th ACM Symposium on Information, Computer and Communications Security (ASIA CCS), pp. 447–458. ACM (2014). https://doi.org/10.1145/2590296.2590325
30. Yan, L.K., Yin, H.: DroidScope: seamlessly reconstructing the OS and Dalvik semantic views for dynamic android malware analysis. In: 21st USENIX Security Symposium, Bellevue, WA, pp. 569–584. USENIX (2012). https://www.usenix.org/conference/usenixsecurity12/technical-sessions/presentation/yan

BabelView: Evaluating the Impact
of Code Injection Attacks
in Mobile Webviews

Claudio Rizzo$^{(\boxtimes)}$, Lorenzo Cavallaro$^{(\boxtimes)}$, and Johannes Kinder$^{(\boxtimes)}$ ⓘ

Royal Holloway, University of London, Egham, UK
{claudio.rizzo.2015,lorenzo.cavallaro,johannes.kinder}@rhul.ac.uk

Abstract. A Webview embeds a fully-fledged browser in a mobile application and allows that application to expose a custom interface to JavaScript code. This is a popular technique to build so-called hybrid applications, but it circumvents the usual security model of the browser: any malicious JavaScript code injected into the Webview gains access to the custom interface and can use it to manipulate the device or exfiltrate sensitive data. In this paper, we present an approach to systematically evaluate the possible impact of code injection attacks against Webviews using static information flow analysis. Our key idea is that we can make reasoning about JavaScript semantics unnecessary by instrumenting the application with a model of possible attacker behavior—the BabelView. We evaluate our approach on 25,000 apps from various Android marketplaces, finding 10,808 potential vulnerabilities in 4,997 apps. Taken together, the apps reported as problematic have over 3 billion installations worldwide. We manually validate a random sample of 50 apps and estimate that our fully automated analysis achieves a precision of 81% at a recall of 89%.

Keywords: Webview · Javascript interface · Injection
Static analysis

1 Introduction

The integration of web technologies in mobile applications enables rapid cross-platform development and provides a uniform user experience across devices. Web content is usually rendered by a *Webview*, a user interface component with an embedded browser engine (`WebView` in Android, `UIWebView` in iOS). Webviews are widely used: in 2015, about 85% of applications on Google's Play Store contained one [17]. Cross-platform frameworks such as Apache Cordova, which allow apps to be written entirely in HTML and JavaScript, have contributed to this high rate of adoption and given rise to the notion of *hybrid applications*. Even otherwise native applications often embed Webviews for displaying login screens or additional web content.

© Springer Nature Switzerland AG 2018
M. Bailey et al. (Eds.): RAID 2018, LNCS 11050, pp. 25–46, 2018.
https://doi.org/10.1007/978-3-030-00470-5_2

Unfortunately, Webviews bring new security threats [15–17,24]. While the Android Webview uses WebKit to render the page, the security model can be modified by app developers. Whereas standalone browsers enforce strong isolation, Webviews can intentionally poke holes in the browser sandbox to provide access to app- and device-specific features via a *JavaScript interface*. For instance, a hybrid banking application could provide access to account details when loading the bank's website in a Webview, or it could relay access to contacts to fill in payee details.

For assessing the overall security of an application, it is necessary to understand the implications of its JavaScript interface. When designing the interface, a developer thinks of the functionality required by her own, trusted JavaScript code executing in the Webview. However, there are several ways that an attacker can inject malicious JavaScript and access the interface [7,17].

The observation that exposed interfaces can pose a security risk was made in previous work [4,9]; however, not all interfaces are dangerous or offer meaningful control to an attacker. The intuition is that flagging up—or even removing from the marketplace—any applications with an exposed JavaScript interface would be an excessive measure. By assessing the risk posed by an application, we can focus attention on the most dangerous cases and provide meaningful feedback to developers.

We rely on static analysis to evaluate the potential impact of an attack against Webviews, with respect to the nature of the JavaScript interfaces. Our key idea is that we can instrument an application with a model of potential attacker behavior that over-approximates the possible information flow semantics of an attack. In particular, we instrument the target app and replace Android's Webview and its descendants with a specially crafted *BabelView* that simulates arbitrary interactions with the JavaScript interface. A subsequent information flow analysis on the instrumented application then yields new flows made possible by the attacker model, which gives an indication of the potential impact. Together with an evaluation of the difficulty of mounting an attack, this can provide an indication of the overall security risk.

Instrumenting the target application allows us to build on existing mature tools for Android flow analysis. This design makes our approach particularly robust, which is important on a quickly changing platform such as Android. In addition, since our instrumentation is over-approximate, we inherit any soundness guarantees offered by the flow analysis used. Independently of us, Yang et al. [31] developed a related approach to address the same problem, but with a closed source system relying on a custom static analysis. Our paper makes the following contributions:

– We introduce BabelView, a novel approach to evaluate the impact of code injection attacks against Webviews based on information flow analysis of applications instrumented with an attacker model. BabelView is implemented using Soot [27] and is available as open source.
– We analyze 25,000 applications from the Google Play Store to evaluate our approach and survey the current state of Webview security in Android. Our

analysis reports 10,808 potential vulnerabilities in 4,997 apps, which together are reported to have more than 3 billion installations. We validate the results on a random sample of 50 applications and estimate the precision to be 81% with a recall of 89%, confirming the practical viability of our approach.

In the remainder of the paper, we briefly explain Android WebViews (Sect. 2) and introduce our approach (Sect. 3) before describing the details of our implementation (Sect. 4). We evaluate BabelView and report the results of our Android study (Sect. 5) and discuss limitations (Sect. 6). Finally, we present related work (Sect. 7) and conclude (Sect. 8).

2   Android WebViews

To provide the necessary context for the remainder of the paper, we first introduce key aspects of Android Webviews. An Android application can instantiate a Webview by calling its constructor or by declaring it in the Activity XML layout, from where the framework will create it automatically. The specifics of how the app interacts with the Webview object depend on which approach it follows; in either case, a developer can extend Android's `WebView` class to override methods and customize its behavior.

The `WebView` class offers mechanisms for interaction between the app and the web content in both directions. Java code can execute arbitrary JavaScript code in the Webview by passing a URL with the "`javascript:`" pseudo-protocol to the `loadUrl` method of a Webview instance. Any code passed in this way is executed in the context of the current page, just like if it were typed into a standalone browser's address bar. For the other direction, and to let JavaScript code in the Webview call Java methods, the Webview allows to create custom interfaces. Any methods of an object (the *interface object*) passed to the `WebView.addJavascriptInterface` method that are tagged with the `@JavascriptInterface` annotation[1] (the *interface methods*) are exported to the global JavaScript namespace in the Webview. For instance, the following example makes a single Java method available to JavaScript:

```
LocationUtils lUtils = new LocationUtils();
wView.addJavascriptInterface(lUtils, "JSlUtils");

public class LocationUtils {
  @JavascriptInterface
  public String getLocation() {
    do_something();
  }
}
```

---

[1] The `@JavascriptInterface` annotation was introduced in API level 17 to address a security vulnerability that allowed attackers to execute arbitrary code via the Java reflection API [19].

Here, `LocationUtils` is bound to a global JavaScript object `JS1Utils` in the Webview `wView`. JavaScript code can access the annotated Java method `getLocation()` by calling `JS1Utils.getLocation()`.

The Webview's JavaScript interface mechanism enforces a policy of which Java methods are available to call from the JavaScript context. Developers of hybrid apps are left to decide which functionality to expose in an interface that is more security-critical than it appears. It is easy for a developer to erroneously assume the JavaScript interface to be a trusted internal interface, shared only between the Java and JavaScript portions of the same app. In reality, it is more akin to a public API, considering the relative ease with which malicious JavaScript code can make its way into a Webview (see Sect. 3.1). Therefore, care must be taken to restrict the interface as much as possible and to secure the delivery of web content into the Webview. In this work we provide a way for developers and app store maintainers to detect applications with insecure interfaces susceptible to abuse; our study in Sect. 5 confirms that this is a widespread phenomenon.

3   Overview

We now introduce our approach by laying out the attacker model (Sect. 3.1), describing our instrumentation-based model for information flow analysis (Sect. 3.2), and discussing how the instrumentation preserves the application semantics (Sect. 3.3).

3.1   Attacker Model

Our overall goal is to identify high-impact vulnerabilities in Android applications. Our insight is that injection vulnerabilities are difficult to avoid with current mainstream web technologies, and that their presence does not justify blocking an app from being distributed to users. Indeed, any standalone browser that allows loading content via insecure HTTP has this vulnerability (while calling this a "vulnerability" may be controversial, it clearly has security implications and has led to an increasing adoption of HTTPS by default). The ubiquity of advertisement libraries in Android apps further increases the likelihood of foreign JavaScript code gaining access to JavaScript interfaces. Following this insight, we aim to pinpoint the risk of using a Webview that is embedded in an app. To do this, we assess the *degrees of freedom* an attacker gains from injecting code into a Webview with a JavaScript interface, which determines the potential impact of an injection attack.

Consequently, the attacker model for our analysis consists of arbitrary code injection into the HTML page or referenced scripts loaded in the Webview. In our evaluation, we actively try to inject JavaScript into the Webview—e.g., as man in the middle (see Sect. 5.5). We note, however, that other channels are available to manipulate the code loaded into a Webview, including malicious advertisements

---

Algorithm 1. Information flow attacker model

1: **procedure** ATTACKER
2:     **while** true **do**
3:         **choose** iface ∈ JS-interfaces
4:         result ← iface($source()$, $source()$, ...)
5:         $sink$(result)

---

or site-specific cross-site-scripting attacks [4,9,10]. To abuse the JavaScript interface, the attacker then only requires the names of the interface methods, which can be obtained through reverse-engineering. Note that even a man in the middle becomes more powerful with access to the JavaScript interface: the interface can allow the attacker to manipulate and retrieve application and device data that would not normally be visible to the adversary. For instance, consider a remote access application with an interface method `getProperty(key)`, which retrieves the value mapped to a key in the application's properties. Without accessing the interface, an attacker may only ever observe calls to `getProperty` with, say, the keys `"favorites"` and `"compression"`, but the attacker would be free to also use the function to retrieve the value for the key `"privateKey"`.

3.2   Instrumenting for Information Flow

Our approach is based on static information flow (or taint) analysis. We aim to find potentially dangerous information flows from injected JavaScript into sensitive parts of the Java-based app and vice-versa. At first glance, this appears to require expensive cross-language static analysis, as recently proposed for hybrid apps [5,13]. However, we can avoid analyzing JavaScript code because our attacker model assumes that the JavaScript code is controlled by the attacker. Therefore, we want to model the actions performed by *any possible JavaScript code*, and not that of developer-provided code that is supposed to execute in the Webview.

To this end, we perform information flow analysis on the application instrumented with a representation of the attacker model in Java, such that the result is an over-approximation of all possible actions of the attacker (we discuss alternative solutions in Sect. 6). We replace the Android `WebView` class (and custom subclasses) with a *BabelView*, a Webview that simulates an attacker specific to the app's JavaScript interfaces. We then apply a flow-, field-, and object-sensitive taint analysis [2] to detect information flows that read or write potentially sensitive information as a result of an injection attack.

The BabelView provides tainted input sources to all possible sequences of interface methods and connects their return values to sinks, as shown in Algorithm 1. Here, `source()` and `sink()` are stubs that refer to sources and sinks of the underlying taint analysis. The non-deterministic enumeration of sequences of interface method invocations is necessary since we employ a flow-sensitive taint analysis. This way, our model also covers situations where the information flow depends on a specific ordering of methods; for instance, consider the following example:

```
String id;

@JavascriptInterface
public void initialize() { this.id = IMEI(); }

@JavascriptInterface
public String getId() { return this.id; }
```

Here, a call to `initialize` (line 4) must precede any invocation of `getId` (line 8) to cause a leak of sensitive information (the IMEI). The flow-sensitive analysis correctly distinguishes different orders of invocation, which helps to reduce false positives. In the BabelView, the loop in Algorithm 1 coupled with non-deterministic choice forces the analysis to join abstract states and over-approximate the result of all possible invocation orders.

Figure 1 illustrates our approach. We annotate certain methods in the Android API as sources and sinks (see Sect. 4.4), which may be accessed by methods in the JavaScript interface. The BabelView includes both a source passing data into the interface methods and a sink receiving their return values to allow detecting flows both from and to JavaScript. The source corresponds to any data injected by the attacker, and the sink to any method an attacker could use to exfiltrate information, e.g., a simple web request.

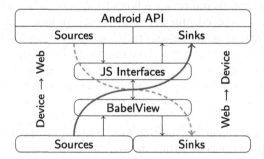

Fig. 1. BabelView models flows between the attacker and sensitive sources and sinks in the Android API that cross the JavaScript interface.

3.3   Preserving Semantics

Our instrumentation eliminates the requirement to perform a cross-language taint analysis and moves all reasoning into the Java domain. However, we must make sure that, apart from the attacker model, the instrumentation preserves the original application's information flow semantics. In particular, we need to integrate the execution of the attacker model into the model of Android's application life cycle used as the basis of the taint analysis [2]. We solve this by overriding the methods used to load web content into the Webview (such as `loadUrl()` and `loadData()`) and modifying them to also call our attacker model (Algorithm 1). This is the earliest point at which the Webview can schedule the execution of any injected JavaScript code. The BabelView thus acts as a proxy simulating the effects of malicious JavaScript injected into loaded web content.

As the BabelView interacts only with the JavaScript interface methods, it does not affect the application's static information flow semantics in any other way than an actual JavaScript injection would. Obviously, this is not necessarily true for other semantics: for example, the instrumented application would likely crash if it were executed on an emulator or real device.

4   BabelView

In this section, we explain the different phases of our analysis. Figure 2 provides a high-level overview: in Phase 1 (Sect. 4.1), we perform a static analysis to retrieve all interface objects and methods, and associate them to the respective Webviews. In Phase 2 (Sect. 4.2), we generate the BabelView, and, in Phase 3 (Sect. 4.3), we instrument the target application with it. In Phase 4 (Sect. 4.4), we run the taint flow analysis on the resulting applications and finally, in Phase 5 (Sect. 4.5), we analyze the results for flows involving the BabelView.

We implemented our static analysis and instrumentation using the Soot framework [27]; our information flow analysis relies on FlowDroid [2]. Overall, our system adds about 6,000 LoC to both platforms.

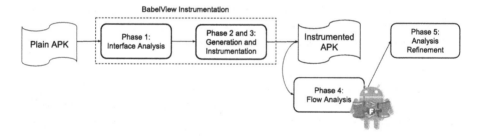

Fig. 2. Phases of our analysis.

4.1   Phase 1: Interface Analysis

As the first step of our analysis, we statically analyze the target application to gather information about its Webviews and JavaScript interfaces. The goal of this stage is to compute a mapping from Webview classes to classes of interface objects that may be added to them at any point during execution of the app.

Using Soot, we can generate the application call graph and precisely resolve callers and callees. We iterate through all classes and methods, identifying all calls to `addJavascriptInterface`, from where we then extract Webviews that will hold interface objects. We make sure to treat inheritance and polymorphism soundly in this stage, e.g., where parent classes are used in variable declarations. We illustrate our approach to handle this on the following code example:

```
class FrameworkBridge {
  @JavascriptInterface
  public int foo() {...}
}

class MyBridge extends FrameworkBridge {
  @JavascriptInterface
  public int bar() {...}
}

class MyWebView extends WebView {...}

void initInterface(WebView aWebView, FrameworkBridge aBridge) {
  aWebView.addJavascriptInterface(aBridge, "Android");
}


...
MyWebView mWebView = new MyWebView();
initInterface(mWebView, new MyBridge());
...
```

The code is adding the interface MyBridge to mWebView, an instance of MyWebView. The method initInterface is a wrapper (say, from a hybrid app framework) that contains the actual call to addJavascriptInterface. When processing the call, we extract the types of aWebView and aBridge from their parameter declarations. For the Webview, we must process all descendants of its declared class to include the types of all possible instances. For aWebView, this means we must instrument all descendants (including anonymous classes) of WebView, i.e., WebView and MyWebView.

Similarly, we are interested in the type of aBridge. Again, we must iterate over all subclasses of its declared type FrameworkBridge to ensure capturing the bridge added at runtime. However, since addJavascriptInterface is of the unconstrained type Object, this could potentially include all classes. Therefore, we restrict processing to just those subclasses that contain at least one @JavascriptInterface annotation. As a result, we obtain a superset of all interface objects that can be added by this method, i.e., FrameworkBridge and MyBridge.

Continuing the example, we now have the mapping from Webview classes to classes of interface objects as {WebView ↦ {FrameworkBridge, MyBridge}, MyWebView ↦ FrameworkBridge, MyBridge}}. Any additional addJavascriptInterface occurrences will be processed analogously and the results added to the set. Because the analysis in this phase is conservative in collecting compatible types, the result is a sound over-approximation of the mapping of Webviews to JavaScript interfaces that can occur at runtime (modulo inaccuracies from dynamic code, see Sect. 6).

4.2   Phase 2: Generating the BabelView

We generate a `BabelView` class for each `WebView` in the mapping. Each `BabelView` defines a subclass of its `WebView` (we remove the parent's `final` modifier if necessary) and overrides all of its parent's constructors so it can be used as a drop-in replacement. We make the associated interface objects explicitly available in each `BabelView`. To this end, we override the `addJavascriptInterface` method to store the interface objects passed to it in instance fields of the `BabelView` class.

To implement the attacker model, the `BabelView` needs to override all methods that load external resources and could thus be susceptible to JavaScript injection. In particular, we override `loadUrl`, `postUrl`, `loadData`, and `loadDataWithBaseURL`. We automatically generate these methods as a call to their `super` implementation followed by a Java implementation of the attacker model, Algorithm 1. Finally, the `BabelView` is equipped with two stub methods, `leak` and `taintSource`, representing a tainted sink and a tainted input, respectively.

4.3   Phase 3: Instrumentation

In the next phase, we instrument the application to replace its Webviews with our generated BabelView instances. The instrumentation is case-dependent on how the Webview is instantiated (see Sect. 2): if it is created via an ordinary constructor call, that constructor is replaced with the corresponding constructor of its `BabelView` class. If the Webview is created via the Activity XML layout, our instrumentation searches for calls to `findViewById`, which the app uses to obtain the Webview instance (e.g., in order to add the JavaScript interface to it). To identify the calls to `findViewById` returning a Webview, our instrumenter identifies explicit casts to a Webview class. Because we do not parse the XML layout itself, we arbitrarily choose one of the constructors of the `BabelView`. While this could potentially be a source of false positives or negatives, it would require a highly specific and unconventional design of the Webview class.

4.4   Phase 4: Information Flow Analysis

We perform a static information flow analysis on the instrumented application to identify information flows involving the attacker model. Since our approach relies on instrumenting the application under analysis, it is agnostic to the specific flow analysis. We decided to rely on the open source implementation of FlowDroid [2], inheriting its context-, flow-, field-, and object-sensitivity, as well as its life cycle-awareness.

Sources and sinks are selected corresponding to sensitive information sources and device functions, modified from the set provided by SuSi [22]. We further include the sources and sinks used in the BabelView classes.

The information flow analysis abstracts the semantics of Android framework methods. FlowDroid uses a simple modeling system (the *TaintWrapper*), where any method can either (i) be a source, (ii) be a sink, (iii) taint its object if any argument is tainted and return a tainted value if its object is tainted, (iv) clear taint from its object, (v) ignore any taint in its arguments or its object. We extended the TaintWrapper with several models that were relevant for the types of vulnerabilities we were interested in, e.g., to precisely capture the creation of Intents from tainted URIs.

Finally, information flows indicating that sensitive functionality is exposed via the JavaScript interface are identified, triggering an alarm showing a potential vulnerability. For instance, consider an `Intent` object initialized to perform phone calls. A flow from `source` to `putExtra` will taint the `Intent`; if it is then passed as an input to `startActivity`, an attacker can perform calls on behalf of the user.

4.5   Phase 5: Analysis Refinement

Preferences. Taint analysis cannot distinguish between individual key-value pairs in a map. `Preferences` are a commonly used map type in Android apps that often store sensitive information as a key-value pair. After the information flow analysis, we refine our results by statically deriving values of keys for access to preferences. Our definition of sources and sinks allows to identify both flows from and to the `Preferences`. Given two flows, one inserting and the other retrieving values from `Preferences`, we are interested in understanding whether (i) the value is of the same type and (ii) the access key is the same. If these conditions are met, we have identified a potential leak via Preferences. To determine the key values, we modeled `StringBuilder` and implemented an intra-procedural constant propagation and folding for strings. Finally, if an interface method allows web content to interact with a preferences object, BabelView reports all keys used to access it, since preferences can be used to store sensitive values. This allows to inspect flows to or from preferences entries, even if these values are not dependent on a specific source in the Android API. We match key names against a list of suspicious entries, which can highlight potential leaks of sensitive app-specific information (see Sect. 5.7). In the same manner, we also highlight suspiciously named interface methods.

Intents. Flow analysis can detect situations where Intent creation depends on tainted input. However, it tells nothing about the type of the Intent created, as this depends on specific parameters, e.g., those provided to its `setAction` method. For interpreting results, it is important, however, to know the action of an `Intent` that can be controlled by an attacker. For any flow that reaches the `startActivity` sink, we perform an inter-procedural backward dependency analysis to the point of the initialization of the `Intent`. If the `Intent` action is not set within the constructor, we perform a forward analysis from the constructor to find calls to `setAction` on the `Intent` object. The analysis may fail where actions are defined within intent filters (XML definitions) or through other built-in methods. To increase precision in our inter-procedural analysis, we ensure that the call-stack is consistent with an invocation through the interface method; i.e., the interface method that triggered the flow must be reachable.

5   Evaluation

We now present our evaluation of BabelView and the results of our study of vulnerabilities in Android applications. Below, we explain our methodology (Sect. 5.1) and ask the following research questions to evaluate our approach:

1. **Can BabelView successfully process real-world applications?** We conduct a study on a randomly selected set of applications from the Andro-Zoo [1] dataset and provide a breakdown of all results (Sect. 5.2).
2. **Does BabelView expose real vulnerabilities?** We discuss some of the vulnerable apps in more detail to understand what an attacker can achieve under what conditions (Sect. 5.7).
3. **What are the precision and recall of our analysis?** We manually validate a random sample of apps, estimating overall precision and recall (Sect. 5.4).

We also shed light on the current state of Webview security on Android with the following questions:

4. **How frequent are different types of alarms?** We report results per alarm, which provides an insight into the prevalence of potential vulnerabilities (Sect. 5.3).
5. **Are there types of potential vulnerabilities that are likely to occur in combination?** We compute the correlation between alarms raised by our analysis and analyze our findings (Sect. 5.6).

Unfortunately, we were unable to conduct a direct comparison with BridgeScope, the work most closely related to ours. Despite helpful communication, the authors were ultimately unable to share neither their experimental data nor their implementation with us. In the spirit of open data, we make all our code and data available[2].

5.1   Methodology

We obtained our dataset from AndroZoo [1], using the list of applications available on July 22nd, 2016, when it contained about 4.4 million samples. We downloaded a random subset of 209,069 apps, and then filtered our dataset for applications containing a Webview, a call to `addJavascriptInterface`, and granting permission to access the Internet. As a result, we obtained 62,674 total applications. Finally, from the obtained sample, we randomly extracted 25,000 applications found in the Google Play Store, which we used for our analysis.

---

[2] https://github.com/ClaudioRizzo/BabelView.

We ran BabelView on five servers: one 32-core with 250 GiB of RAM and four 16-core with 125 GiB of RAM. Each application took on average 180 s to complete. The high precision of FlowDroid's information flow analysis can lead to long processing time in the order of hours. Therefore, we set a time limit of 15 min, which was a sweet spot in the sense that apps taking longer would often go over an hour. A positive effect of our instrumentation-based approach is that we benefit from improvements in the underlining flow analysis. Indeed, over the duration of this project, we saw a noticeable accuracy enhancement from the constant improvements on FlowDroid.

Each application underwent three main phases: (i) BabelView instrumentation, (ii) FlowDroid analysis on the instrumented app and (iii) analysis of the resulting flows to identify suspect flows and raise alarms. On the reported applications, we performed a feasibility analysis. We searched the app for plain http:// URLs and assess the resilience of the app against injection attacks.

5.2   Applicability

Running our tool chain on the 25,000 target applications resulted in 1,286 general errors and 3,837 flow analysis timeouts. The remaining 19,877 apps were successfully analyzed and we obtained the following breakdown: 832 applications had no interface objects at all or no interface methods in case the target API was version 17 or above; 14,048 applications had no flows involving our attacker model; and 4,997 were reported as dangerous, i.e., containing flows due to the attacker behavior. This amounts to a rate of 26.2%. We investigated the reasons for the crashes, and most happened either due to unexpected byte code that Soot fails to handle or while FlowDroid's taint analysis was computing callbacks.

Among applications with interface objects, we also considered those targeting outdated versions of the Android API, since this is still a common occurrence [18, 25,28]. When using Webviews prior to API 17, any app is trivially vulnerable to an arbitrary code execution disclosed in 2013[3]. Despite targeting an old API version, if compiled with a newer Android SDK, these applications can still use the @JavascriptInterface annotation. While the annotation itself does not provide extra security, these apps may target newer APIs in future releases [24].

5.3   Alarms Triggered

We successfully used BabelView to examine 19,877 applications. We found that 4,997 of them triggered an alarm (i.e., our analysis reported a potential vulnerability), meaning that the interface methods could be exploited by foreign JavaScript from injection or advertisement. Table 1 shows a breakdown of all the alarms we observed in our analysis. Among the most common alarms, we observed the possibility of writing to the File System (Write File), capability to start new applications (Start App), violation of the Same Origin Policy (Frame

---

[3] https://labs.mwrinfosecurity.com/blog/webview-addjavascriptinterface-remote-code-execution/.

Confusion) and the possibility of exploiting the old reflection attack due to Android API prior to v17.

Table 1. Number of applications per alarm category. Pref. denotes indirect leaks via a Preference object; TM: Telephony Manager, Conn.: Connectivity.

Alarm	#Apps	Alarm	#Apps	Alarm	#Apps
Open File	385	Write File	1,444	Read File	593
TM Leak	39	Pref. TM Leak	4	Pref. Conn. Leak	4
SQL-lite Leak	136	SQL-lite Query	438	Pref. SQL-lite Leak	11
GPS Leak	43	Pref. GPS Leak	1	Directly Send SMS	6
Direct Calls	19	Call Intent	314	Email/SMS Intent	778
Take Picture	7	Download Photo	317	Play Video/Audio	378
Edit Calendar	357	Post to Social	293	Start App	1,321
API prior to 17	1,039	Unknown Intent	1,107	Frame Confusion	1,039
Fetch Class	85	Fetch Constructor	0	Constructor init	13
Fetch Method	85	Method Parameter	622		

Writing File capabilities show the developers' need for storing app-external data usually coming from an app-dedicated server. We also observed that many applications implement advertising libraries which need to open a new application, usually Google Play Store, to allow the user to download or visualize some information. Unfortunately, the package name of the application to open is given as input to an interface method, enabling a possible attacker to control which app to start. Same-Origin-Policy violations are also very common: this is the case when a `loadUrl` is invoked with input from the interface methods, controlling what is loaded in to a frame. As described by Luo et al. [15], JavaScript executing in an iframe runs in the context of the main frame, violating the SOP.

Many applications still target an API version prior to 17 [18,25,28], often due to backwards compatibility or simply due to confusion in declaring the SDK version. Other alarms involve the possibility to prompt the user with an email or a text message to send, directly sending an SMS or performing a phone call; prompting the user with the call dialer; posting content to social network; interacting with the calendar by creating or editing an event; playing videos or audio; leaking sensitive information like the device ID or phone numbers (i.e. TM Leaks), GPS position, SQL information, etc.

Finally, we shed light on the possible use of Java Reflection inside interface methods. Fetch Class, Fetch Constructor, Constructor init, Fetch Method and Method Parameter are all signs that an attacker controls input used to execute methods via Java reflection. Although these are rare situations and often hard to exploit, they are extremely high reward for an attacker as they can potentially allow to circumvent the `@JavascriptInterface` annotation, leading to arbitrary code execution. We manually analyzed some applications presenting these alarms and in some cases an attacker could take control of a method and its parameters, leading to remote code execution.

5.4   Manual Validation

We used manual validation to estimate the accuracy of our analysis. In particular we sampled and manually analyzed (i.e., reversed and decompiled) 50 applications. We evaluated two aspects:

1. How accurate is BabelView with respect to each individual alarm it raises?
2. Does BabelView function as an effective alarm system for hybrid apps?

We began checking all types of alarms for each app and we established whether an alarm was correctly triggered or correctly not triggered. We observed 42 TPs (True Positives), 10 FPs (False Positives), 1,494 TNs (True Negatives) and 5 FNs (False Negatives). From this, we can compute a precision of 81% and a recall of 89% for our analysis.

The results obtained are in line with our expectations. Our instrumentation does not alter the semantics of applications other than adding a model of attack behavior. Therefore, our precision depends on the underlining flow analysis. However, more false positives could be introduced due to the object-insensitivity of our instrumentation—i.e., we distinguish types but not instances of Webviews. Similarly, a very low false negative rate is common for data flow analysis; however, FNs are still possible, mainly due to incomplete Android framework.

To evaluate BabelView on a per-app basis, we consider a true positive the case where an app contains at least one potential vulnerability and at least one alarm is raised. True negatives and false positives/negatives follow accordingly. We observed 19 TPs, 2 FPs, 29 TNs, and 0 FNs, which yields a precision of 90% and a recall of 100%. This suggest that BabelView performs well as an alarm system for potentially dangerous applications. Even if individual alarms can be false positives, the correlation of dangerous interfaces appears to leads to highlighted apps being problematic with high probability. The false negatives that are present when taken per vulnerability disappear when analyzed on a per-app basis.

5.5   Feasibility Analysis

To better understand the feasibility of exploiting potential vulnerabilities highlighted by BabelView, we measured the difficulty of performing an injection attack. To this end we use a three-step process: (i) we check the application for TLS misuse using MalloDroid [7]; (ii) we search for hard-coded URLs beginning with http://, suggesting that web content could be loaded via an insecure channel; and (iii) we actively injected JavaScript code into Webviews.

MalloDroid reported 61.5% of applications using TLS insecurely and 98.7% of apps were found hard-coding HTTP URLs. In order to actively inject JavaScript,

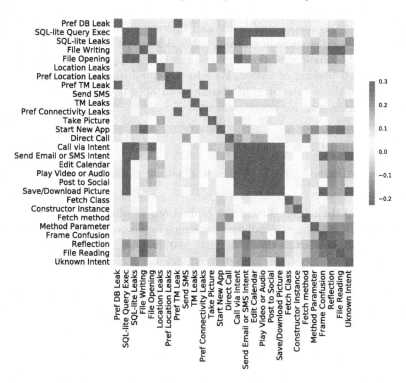

Fig. 3. Correlation matrix of alarms. (Color figure online)

we stimulated each reported application with 100 Monkey[4] events and actively intercepted the connection (using Bettercap[5]), trying to execute a JavaScript payload. Moreover, we set up our own certificate authority and also tried SSL strip attacks. The goal of the injection was to determine whether the reported interface methods were present in the Webview. To this end, we generated JavaScript code checking for the presence of the interface objects reported by the BabelView analysis. We were able to inject JavaScript in 1,275 applications and in 482 cases we confirmed the presence of the vulnerable interface object.

5.6   Correlation of Alarms

We were interested in finding correlations among the alarm categories we identified. This does not only account for common patterns of functionality, but also identifies single alarms that taken together could increase the attack capabilities, e.g., combining opening and writing of a file results in writing of arbitrary files.

We can see in the correlation matrix in Fig. 3 that alarms involving related functionality tend to be positively correlated (in red). For example, opening and

---

[4] https://developer.android.com/studio/test/monkey.html.

[5] https://www.bettercap.org.

writing a file; SQL queries and leaks; and operations involving intents such as call via intent, send email, edit calendar, play video, post to social, and download pictures. While some correlations are evident, some appear incidental, such as intent calls and playing of videos. Based on manual inspection (see Sect. 5.7), we found that these categories of alarms often appear together in apps using common libraries, e.g., for advertisements.

5.7   Individual Case Studies

We now report individual case studies to illustrate the nature of our findings.

Advertising Libraries. During the evaluation, we discovered an advertising library, used by 353 of 4,997 applications, which implements a Webview exposing many sensitive interface methods. In particular, a successful JavaScript injection would allow an attacker to perform different actions, including downloading/saving of pictures, sending email or SMS by manipulating `Intents`, playing audio or videos on the victim's phone, opening new applications, creating calendar events, and posting to social networks. Another library, used by 1,507 applications, allows an attacker to start new applications on the phone, controlling the `Intent` extras provided to the `Activity`.

Game App. Among our results, we found a game application ("SwingAid Level up Golf") that uses several Webviews and JavaScript interfaces leading to different alarms: SQL-lite leaks via preferences, frame confusion, and telephony manager Leaks. Moreover, we discovered the value *loginPwd* among preferences keys accessible from a JavaScript interface. We were able to manually confirm all alarms as true positives. Interface methods accessible when creating an account creation within the game include `getAccountEmail`, `getPhoneNumber`, and `getUserPwd`. We successfully performed a man-in-the-middle attack and injected JavaScript to access all three methods. The account e-mail and phone number are accessible immediately upon attempting to create an account. The password is stored in a local database, cached in the preferences and accessible with the *loginPwd* key. When the user visits the account creation page a second time, the password can be stolen via the interface method.

The underlying problem is twofold and representative for many Webview vulnerabilities: first, the Webview loads data via an insecure channel, and second, the JavaScript interface makes sensitive data available (a plaintext password). Even if the password would otherwise not be sent via the insecure channel, a JavaScript injection attack is able to retrieve it through the interface and extract it directly. Since our discovery, all issues have been resolved in a newer version of the application (version 2.6).

6   Limitations and Discussion

Avoiding Instrumentation. In principle, we could avoid instrumenting the application by summarizing interface methods with an interprocedural taint analysis. However, to achieve the same precision, the analysis would have to be computationally expensive: on method entry, any reachable field in any reachable object (not just arguments of the interface method) would have to be treated as carrying individual taint. On method exit, the effects on all reachable fields would have to stored, before resolving the effects among all interface method summaries. Our instrumentation-based approach not only avoids this cost, but also allows us to factor out flow analysis into a separate tool, a design choice that improves robustness and maintainability.

Analysis Limitations. Our system, together with the underlying flow analysis, is subject to common limitations of static analysis and hence can fail to detect Webviews and interfaces instantiated via native code, reflection, or dynamic code loading. In principle, this currently allows a developer intent on doing so to hide sensitive JavaScript APIs. However, we focus on benign software and vulnerabilities that are honest mistakes rather than planted backdoors. Still, we note that BabelView would automatically benefit from future flow analyses that may counteract evasion techniques.

A potential source of false positives is that BabelView does not distinguish Webview instances of the same type and will conservatively join the JavaScript interfaces of all instances. Furthermore, our analysis loses precision when reporting indirect leaks via `Preferences` or `Bundle`. As mentioned in Sect. 4.4, we connect sensitive flows into the application preferences with flows from the preferences to the instrumented sink method in BabelView. While this is sound and will conservatively capture any information leaks via preferences, it is not taking into account any temporal dependencies between storing and retrieving the value. A different treatment of this would be a potential source of false negatives, since preferences persist across application restarts.

Attack Feasibility. In our feasibility analysis, we actively try to inject JavaScript code into a Webview, aiming at identifying whether the reported interface object is present in the Webview. The presence of the interface object means that all its interface methods are available to use, including the one BabelView reported. However, we do not actively invoke these methods and thus we cannot be sure of their exploitability.

Mitigating Potential Vulnerabilities. To avoid giving potential attackers control over sensitive data and functionality, developers can follow a set of design principles. First of all, Webview contents should be exclusively loaded via a secure channel. Second, as mentioned in the Android developer documentation, Webviews should only load trusted contents. External links have to be opened with the default browser. For also protecting against malicious ads or cross-site-scripting attacks, JavaScript interfaces should offer an absolute minimum of functionality and avoid arguments as far as possible. Finally, recent work also introduced novel mechanisms to enforce policies on hybrid applications (see Sect. 7.2).

7   Related Work

We now review work on vulnerabilities and attacks against Webview (Sect. 7.1), discuss related work on policies and access control (Sect. 7.2), and contrast with work on instrumentation-based modeling (Sect. 7.3).

7.1   Webview: Attacks and Vulnerabilities

Webview vulnerabilities have been widely studied [4,6,15–17,20]. Luo et al. give a detailed overview of several classes of attacks against Webviews [15], providing a basis for our work. Neugschwandtner et al. [20] were the first to highlight the magnitude of the problem. In their analysis, they categorize as vulnerable all applications implementing JavaScript interfaces and misusing TLS (or not using it at all). For further precision, they analyzed permissions and discovered that 76% of vulnerable applications requested privacy critical permissions. While this is a sign of poorly designed applications, the impact of an injection exploit very much depends on the JavaScript interfaces, motivating the work of this paper.

A step forward towards this was made by Bifocals [6], a static analysis tool able to identify and evaluate vulnerabilities in Webviews. Bifocals looks for potential Webview vulnerabilities (using JavaScript interfaces and loading third party web pages) and then performs an impact analysis on the JavaScript interfaces. In particular, it analyzes whether these methods reach code requiring security-relevant permissions. However, JavaScript interfaces can pose an (application-specific) risk without making use of permissions. At the same time, not all JavaScript interfaces that make use of permissions are dangerous: for example, an interface method might use the phone's IMEI to perform an operation but not return it to the caller.

The means by which malicious code can be injected into the Webview have been discussed in previous work [9,10]. Having to interact with many forms of entities, HTML5-based hybrid applications expose a broader surface of attack, introducing new vectors of injection for cross-site-scripting attacks [10]. While these attacks require the user to directly visit the malicious page within the Webview, Web-to-Application injection attacks (W2AI) rely on intent hyperlinks to render the payload simply by clinking a link in the default browser [9]. Both discuss the threat behind JavaScript interfaces, but stop their analysis at the moment where the malicious payload is loaded, without analyzing the implication of the attacker executing the JavaScript interfaces.

A large scale study on mobile web applications and their vulnerabilities was presented by Mutchler et al. [17], but did not study the nature of the exposed

JavaScript interfaces. Li et al. [14] studied a new category of fishing attacks termed *Cross-App WebView infection*. This new type of attacks exploits the possibility of issuing navigation requests from one app's Webview to another via Intent deep linking and other URL schemata. This can trigger a chain of requests to a set of infected apps.

Most closely related to our work is the concurrently developed *BridgeScope* [31], a tool to assess JavaScript interfaces based on a custom static analysis. Similar to our work, BridgeScope allows to detect potential flows to and from interface methods. BridgeScope uses a custom flow analysis, whereas our approach intentionally allows to reuse state-of-art flow analysis tools. While BridgeScope's flow analysis performs well on benchmarks, there appears to be no specific treatment of Map-like objects such as `Preferences` of `Bundle`.

In recent work, Yang et al. [29] have combined the information of a deep static analysis with a selective symbolic execution to actively exploit event handlers in Android hybrid applications. In *OSV-Hunter* [30], they introduce a new approach to detect Origin Stripping Vulnerabilities. These type of vulnerabilities persist when upon invocation of `window.postMessage`, it is not possible to distinguish the identity of the message sender or even safely obtain the source origin. This is inherently true for Hybrid applications, where developers often rely on JavaScript interfaces to fill the gap between web and the native platform.

7.2 Webview Access Control

There have been several proposals to bring origin-based access control to Webviews [8,23,26]. Shehab et al. [23] proposed a framework that modifies Cordova, enabling developers to build and enforce a page-based plugin access policy. In this way, depending on the page loaded, it will or will not have the permission to use exposed Cordova plugins (i.e., JavaScript interfaces).

Georgiev et al. presented NoFrank [8], a system to extend origin-based access control to local resources outside the web browser. In particular, the application developer whitelists origins that are then allowed to access device's resources. However, once an origin is white-listed, it can access any resource exposed. Jin et al. [11] propose a fine-granular solution in a system that allows developers to assign different permissions to different frames in the Webview.

Tuncay et al. [26] increase granularity further in their Draco system. Draco defines a policy language that developers can use to design access control policies on different channels, i.e. the interface object, the event handlers and the HTML5 API. Another framework allowing developers to define security policies is Hybrid-Guard [21]. Differently from Draco, HybridGuard has been entirely developed in JavaScript, making it platform independent and easy to deploy on different platform and hybrid development framework. Both Draco and HybridGuard could provide an interesting solution to the problem of securing an interface BabelView is rising an alarm for, without unduly restricting its functionality.

7.3 Instrumentation-Based Modeling

Synthesizing code to trigger specific function interfaces is not a new problem and traces back to generating verification harnesses, e.g., for software model checking [3,12]. On Android, FlowDroid [2] uses a model that invokes callbacks in a "dummy main" method, taking into account the life cycle of Android activities. While the problems share some similarity, JavaScript interfaces and Webviews are inherently varied and app-specific. Therefore, we require a static analysis and cannot rely on fixed signatures. Furthermore, because our model represents an attacker instead of a well-defined system, calls can appear out of context anytime web content can be loaded in the Webview, i.e., after a `loadUrl`-like method.

8 Conclusion

In this paper, we presented a novel method to use information flow analysis to evaluate the possible impact of code injection attacks against mobile applications with Webviews. The key idea of our approach is to model the possible effects of injected malicious JavaScript code at the Java level, thereby avoiding any direct reasoning about JavaScript semantics. In particular, this allowed us to rely on a robust state-of-the-art implementation of taint analysis for Android.

We implemented our approach in BabelView, and evaluated it on 25,000 applications, confirming its practical applicability and at the same time reporting on the state of Webview security in Android. With BabelView, we found 10,808 potential vulnerabilities in 4,997 applications, affecting more than 3 billion users. We validated our results on a subset of applications where we achieved a precision of 81% at a recall of 89% when measured per alarm, or a precision of 90% and a recall of 100% when measured per application.

Acknowledgement. We would like to thank our shepherd, Angelos Stavrou, and the anonymous reviewers for their valuable feedback. We are grateful to Roberto Jordaney, Blake Loring, Duncan Mitchell, James Patrick-Evans, Feargus Pendlebury, and Versha Prakash for their help and their comments on earlier drafts of this paper. This work was in part supported by EPSRC grant EP/L022710/1 and a Google Faculty Award.

References

1. Allix, K., Bissyandé, T.F., Klein, J., Traon, Y.L.: Androzoo: collecting millions of Android apps for the research community. In: Proceedings of 13th International Conference on Mining Software Repositories (MSR), pp. 468–471. ACM (2016)
2. Arzt, S., et al.: FlowDroid: precise context, flow, field, object-sensitive and lifecycle-aware taint analysis for Android apps. In: ACM SIGPLAN Conference Programming Language Design and Implementation (PLDI), pp. 259–269. ACM (2014)
3. Ball, T., et al.: Thorough static analysis of device drivers. In: Proceedings of 2006 EuroSys Conference, pp. 73–85. ACM (2006)
4. Bhavani, A.B.: Cross-site scripting attacks on Android WebView. CoRR abs/1304.7451 (2013)

5. Brucker, A.D., Herzberg, M.: On the static analysis of hybrid mobile apps. In: Caballero, J., Bodden, E., Athanasopoulos, E. (eds.) ESSoS 2016. LNCS, vol. 9639, pp. 72–88. Springer, Cham (2016). https://doi.org/10.1007/978-3-319-30806-7_5

6. Chin, E., Wagner, D.: Bifocals: analyzing WebView vulnerabilities in Android applications. In: Kim, Y., Lee, H., Perrig, A. (eds.) WISA 2013. LNCS, vol. 8267, pp. 138–159. Springer, Cham (2014). https://doi.org/10.1007/978-3-319-05149-9_9

7. Fahl, S., Harbach, M., Muders, T., Smith, M., Baumgärtner, L., Freisleben, B.: Why eve and mallory love Android: an analysis of Android SSL (in)security. In: Proceedings of ACM SIGSAC Conference on Computer and Communications Security (CCS), pp. 50–61. ACM (2012)

8. Georgiev, M., Jana, S., Shmatikov, V.: Breaking and fixing origin-based access control in hybrid web/mobile application frameworks. In: Annual Network and Distributed System Security Symposium (NDSS) (2014)

9. Hassanshahi, B., Jia, Y., Yap, R.H.C., Saxena, P., Liang, Z.: Web-to-application injection attacks on Android: characterization and detection. In: Pernul, G., Ryan, P.Y.A., Weippl, E. (eds.) ESORICS 2015. LNCS, vol. 9327, pp. 577–598. Springer, Cham (2015). https://doi.org/10.1007/978-3-319-24177-7_29

10. Jin, X., Hu, X., Ying, K., Du, W., Yin, H., Peri, G.N.: Code injection attacks on HTML5-based mobile apps: characterization, detection and mitigation. In: Proceedings of ACM SIGSAC Conference on Computer and Communications Security (CCS), pp. 66–77. ACM (2014)

11. Jin, X., Wang, L., Luo, T., Du, W.: Fine-grained access control for HTML5-based mobile applications in Android. In: Desmedt, Y. (ed.) ISC 2013. LNCS, vol. 7807, pp. 309–318. Springer, Cham (2015). https://doi.org/10.1007/978-3-319-27659-5_22

12. Kinder, J., Veith, H.: Precise static analysis of untrusted driver binaries. In: Proceedings of 10th International Conference on Formal Methods in Computer-Aided Design (FMCAD), pp. 43–50 (2010)

13. Lee, S., Dolby, J., Ryu, S.: HybriDroid: static analysis framework for Android hybrid applications. In: Proc. IEEE/ACM International Conference on Automated Software Engineering (ASE), pp. 250–261. ACM (2016)

14. Li, T., et al.: Unleashing the walking dead: understanding cross-app remote infections on mobile WebViews. In: Proceedings of ACM SIGSAC Conference on Computer and Communications Security (CCS). ACM (2017)

15. Luo, T., Hao, H., Du, W., Wang, Y., Yin, H.: Attacks on WebView in the Android system. In: Annual Computer Security Applications Conference (ACSAC), pp. 343–352. ACM (2011)

16. Luo, T., Jin, X., Ananthanarayanan, A., Du, W.: Touchjacking attacks on Web in Android, iOS, and Windows phone. In: Garcia-Alfaro, J., Cuppens, F., Cuppens-Boulahia, N., Miri, A., Tawbi, N. (eds.) FPS 2012. LNCS, vol. 7743, pp. 227–243. Springer, Heidelberg (2013). https://doi.org/10.1007/978-3-642-37119-6_15

17. Mutchler, P., Doupé, A., Mitchell, J., Kruegel, C., Vigna, G.: A large-scale study of mobile web app security. In: Proceedings of IEEE Symposium on Security and Privacy Workshops (SPW), Mobile Security Technologies (MoST). IEEE (2015)

18. Mutchler, P., Safaei, Y., Doupé, A., Mitchell, J.C.: Target fragmentation in Android apps. In: Proceedings of IEEE Symposium on Security and Privacy Workshops (SPW), Mobile Security Technologies (MoST), pp. 204–213. IEEE (2016)

19. MWR InfoSecurity: WebView addJavascriptInterface remote code execution, September 2013. https://labs.mwrinfosecurity.com/blog/webview-addjavascriptinterface-remote-code-execution/

20. Neugschwandtner, M., Lindorfer, M., Platzer, C.: A view to a kill: WebView exploitation. In: USENIX Workshop on Large-Scale Exploits and Emergent Threats (LEET) (2013)
21. Phung, P.H., Mohanty, A., Rachapalli, R., Sridhar, M.: HybridGuard: a principal-based permission and fine-grained policy enforcement framework for web-based mobile applications. In: Proceedings of IEEE Symposium on Security and Privacy Workshops (SPW), Mobile Security Technologies (MoST) (2017)
22. Rasthofer, S., Arzt, S., Bodden, E.: A machine-learning approach for classifying and categorizing Android sources and sinks. In: Annual Network and Distributed System Security Symposium (NDSS). The Internet Society (2014)
23. Shehab, M., Jarrah, A.A.: Reducing attack surface on Cordova-based hybrid mobile apps. In: Proceedings of International Workshop on Mobile Development Lifecycle (MobileDeLi), pp. 1–8. ACM (2014)
24. Thomas, D.R.: The lifetime of Android API vulnerabilities: case study on the JavaScript-to-Java interface (transcript of discussion). In: Christianson, B., Švenda, P., Matyáš, V., Malcolm, J., Stajano, F., Anderson, J. (eds.) Security Protocols 2015. LNCS, vol. 9379, pp. 139–144. Springer, Cham (2015). https://doi.org/10.1007/978-3-319-26096-9_14
25. Thomas, D.R., Beresford, A.R., Rice, A.C.: Security metrics for the Android ecosystem. In: Proceedings of ACM Workshop on Security and Privacy in Smartphones and Mobile Devices (SPSM), pp. 87–98. ACM (2015)
26. Tuncay, G.S., Demetriou, S., Gunter, C.A.: Draco: a system for uniform and fine-grained access control for web code on Android. In: Proceedings ACM SIGSAC Conference on Computer and Communications Security (CCS), pp. 104–115. ACM (2016)
27. Vallée-Rai, R. Co, P., Gagnon, E., Hendren, L.J., Lam, P., Sundaresan, V.: Soot - a Java bytecode optimization framework. In: Proceedings of Conference on Centre for Advanced Studies on Collaborative Research (CASCON), p. 13 (1999)
28. Wu, D., Liu, X., Xu, J., Lo, D., Gao, D.: Measuring the declared SDK versions and their consistency with API calls in Android apps. In: Ma, L., Khreishah, A., Zhang, Y., Yan, M. (eds.) WASA 2017. LNCS, vol. 10251, pp. 678–690. Springer, Cham (2017). https://doi.org/10.1007/978-3-319-60033-8_58
29. Yang, G., Huang, J., Gu, G.: Automated generation of event-oriented exploits in Android hybrid apps. In: Annual Network and Distributed System Security Symposium (NDSS) (2018)
30. Yang, G., Huang, J., Gu, G., Mendoza, A.: Study and mitigation of origin stripping vulnerabilities in hybrid-postmessage enabled mobile applications. In: Proceedings of IEEE Symposium on Security and Privacy (S&P) (2018)
31. Yang, G., Mendoza, A., Zhang, J., Gu, G.: Precisely and scalably vetting JavaScript bridge in Android hybrid apps. In: Dacier, M., Bailey, M., Polychronakis, M., Antonakakis, M. (eds.) RAID 2017, pp. 143–166. Springer, Cham (2017). https://doi.org/10.1007/978-3-319-66332-6_7

Defeating Software Mitigations Against Rowhammer: A Surgical Precision Hammer

Andrei Tatar[✉], Cristiano Giuffrida, Herbert Bos, and Kaveh Razavi

Vrije Universiteit Amsterdam, Amsterdam, The Netherlands
{a.tatar,c.giuffrida,h.j.bos,k.razavi}@vu.nl

Abstract. With software becoming harder to compromise due to modern defenses, attackers are increasingly looking at exploiting hardware vulnerabilities such as Rowhammer. In response, the research community has developed several software defenses to protect existing hardware against this threat. In this paper, we show that the assumptions existing software defenses make about memory addressing are inaccurate. Specifically, we show that physical address space is often not contiguously mapped to DRAM address space, allowing attackers to trigger Rowhammer corruptions despite active software defenses. We develop RAMSES, a software library modeling end-to-end memory addressing, relying on public documentation, where available, and reverse-engineered models otherwise. RAMSES improves existing software-only Rowhammer defenses and also improves attacks by orders of magnitude, as we show in our evaluation. We use RAMSES to build *Hammertime*, an open-source suite of tools for studying Rowhammer properties affecting attacks and defenses, which we release as open-source software.

Keywords: Rowhammer · Hammertime · DRAM geometry

1 Introduction

To increase the capacity of DRAM, manufacturers are packing more transistors into DRAM chips. This has resulted in reduced reliability of DRAM in the wild [12,16]. A prime example of these reliability problems that plague a large percentage of currently deployed DRAM is the Rowhammer vulnerability [13]. DRAM consists of stacks of rows which store information and the Rowhammer vulnerability allows for corruption of data in form of bit flips by repeatedly activating some of these rows. The past two years have witnessed a proliferation of increasingly sophisticated Rowhammer attacks to compromise various software platforms. Mark Seaborn showed that Rowhammer bit flips can be used to escalate privileges of a Linux/x86 user process in 2015 [20]. Various academic research groups then showed that the same defect can also be used to compromise Web browsers [7,9], cloud virtual machines [19,22], and even mobile phones with a completely different architecture [21].

© Springer Nature Switzerland AG 2018
M. Bailey et al. (Eds.): RAID 2018, LNCS 11050, pp. 47–66, 2018.
https://doi.org/10.1007/978-3-030-00470-5_3

Given the possibilities for building such powerful attacks, we urgently need to protect users against their threat. While hardware-based defenses such as error-correcting code or target row refresh [11] can potentially protect future hardware, a large portion of existing hardware remains exposed. To bridge this gap, recent work [5,8] attempts to provide software-only protection against the Rowhammer vulnerability. ANVIL [5] provides system-wide protection by detecting which rows in physical memory are accessed often, and if a certain threshold is reached, it will "refresh" the adjacent rows by reading from them, similar to target row refresh [11]. In contrast, instead of providing system-wide protection, CATT [8] protects the kernel memory from user processes by introducing a guard row between kernel and user memory. Given that Rowhammer bit flips happen in DRAM, both these defenses attempt to operate at DRAM level, having to make judgement calls on where the "next" or "previous" row of a given address is.

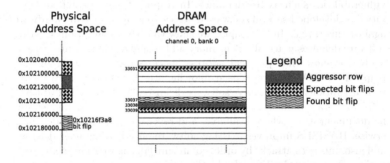

Fig. 1. Example of nonlinear physical address to DRAM address mapping.

To remain agnostic to the underlying DRAM hardware, both these defenses make simplifying assumptions about how DRAM is addressed by modern memory controllers. Specifically, they assume that physical memory addresses are mapped linearly by the memory controller to DRAM rows. We investigate whether this important assumption is valid using a representative set of DRAM modules and memory controllers. We discover that memory controllers often non-trivially map physical address to DRAM addresses and DRAM modules may internally reorder rows. These findings highlight the need to differentiate between the *physical address space*, what the CPU uses to address memory, and *DRAM address space*, the chip select signals along with bank, row and column addresses emitted by the memory controller. Subtle differences in mapping one address space to the other determine the physical address distance between two rows co-located in hardware, which in turn determines where a Rowhammer attack could trigger bit flips. Figure 1 shows an empirical example of how a naive address mapping makes inaccurate assumptions.

Our conclusion is that to build effective software defenses, we cannot treat the underlying hardware as a black box. To concretize our findings, we develop RAMSES, a software library modeling the address translation and manipulation that occurs between the CPU and DRAM ICs. We employ RAMSES to advance the current state of Rowhammer research in multiple dimensions:

- We show how a memory addressing aware attacker can defeat existing defenses: we could trigger bit flips on ANVIL [5] which aims to mitigate Rowhammer altogether, and we could trigger bit flips with enough physical address distance from their aggressor rows to sidestep the guard area of CATT [8].
- We show that existing attacks can significantly benefit from RAMSES when looking for exploitable bit flips: we can find many more bit flips when compared to publicly available Rowhammer tests or the state of the art [17]. Specifically, within the same amount of time, we could find bit flips on DRAM modules that state of the art reported to be safe from Rowhammer bit flips. On other DRAM modules, we could find orders of magnitude more bit flips. These findings already significantly increase the effectiveness and impact of known attacks.
- We build a DRAM profiling tool that records a system's response to a Rowhammer attack into a portable format called a *flip table*. We run this tool on a representative set of memory modules to collect detailed data about bit flip location and direction. We build an attack simulator that uses flip tables to perform fast, software-only feasibility analyses of Rowhammer-based attacks, and use it to evaluate several published Rowhammer exploits. We release these tools along with collected flip tables open-source as *Hammertime*.

Outline. We provide a background on DRAM architecture and Rowhammer in Sect. 2. We then describe the design and implementation of RAMSES based on these parameters in Sect. 3 and explore applications of RAMSES in Sect. 4. We present the results of our DRAM profiling and evaluate the impact of memory addressing on existing attacks and defenses in Sect. 5. Finally, we discuss related work in Sect. 6 and conclude in Sect. 7.

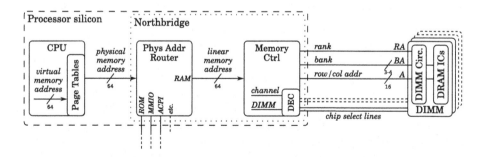

Fig. 2. Functional overview of DRAM addressing

2 Background

We first briefly look at how modern DRAM is addressed before discussing the Rowhammer vulnerability. We then show how recent attacks exploit Rowhammer to compromise systems without relying on software vulnerabilities.

2.1 DRAM Architecture

Figure 2 shows an overview of the devices and addresses involved in accessing system RAM. There are four types of addresses used, corresponding to different address spaces:

Virtual Addresses are the way nearly all software running on the CPU accesses memory. It is often a large, sparsely allocated address space, set up for each process by the kernel. **Physical Addresses** are what the CPU uses to access the "outside" world, including devices such as RAM, firmware ROM, Memory-Mapped I/O (MMIO) and others. The address space layout is machine-specific, usually set up by system firmware during early boot. **Linear Memory Addresses** are used to index all RAM attached to a controller in a contiguous, linear fashion. These addresses are internal to the northbridge logic and, due to the tight coupling between the physical address router and memory controller, are specific to hardware implementations. **DRAM Addresses** are the actual signals on the memory bus used to access RAM and uniquely identify memory cells. These signals consist of *channel, DIMM, rank* and *bank* select signals, along with *row* and *column* addresses [10]. We take a closer look at the components translating addresses between these address spaces, as well as some techniques used in translation.

CPU. The Memory Management Units (MMUs) in modern general-purpose processors use *page tables* to translate virtual addresses into physical addresses. Page tables are architecture-specific data structures in RAM that specify the virtual memory map of each process, usually set up and maintained by the operating system. The MMU "walks" these tables for every virtual memory address translation requested by the CPU. For better performance, a specialized cache called a Translation Lookaside Buffer (TLB) is often included in the MMU.

Physical Address Router. The CPU uses physical memory addresses to access more than just RAM. System ROM, non-volatile RAM and PCI device memory are just a few examples of devices mapped into the system's physical address space. Routing physical memory requests to the appropriate device is accomplished by the *physical address router*. From a memory addressing perspective, the physical address router maps the regions in the physical address space corresponding to RAM into a contiguous, linear memory address space. The specifics of how this mapping is achieved will vary not only between architectures, but also depending on system hardware configuration.

Memory Controller. Memory requests on route to system RAM are serviced by the *memory controller*, which is responsible for managing the memory bus. To achieve this, the linear memory addresses of incoming requests must be mapped to a multidimensional address space specific to the memory configuration in use. These DRAM address tuples consist of *channel*, *DIMM* and *rank* select signals, along with *bank*, *row* and *column* addresses. Each memory bank comes equipped with a *row buffer*, a cache for the bank's current *active row*, to which accesses complete with minimal delay. Consequently, a request to a different row within the same bank—an event known as a *bank conflict*—will incur a significant delay while the old row is closed and the new one opened. A well-performing memory controller will therefore map linear addresses to DRAM in such a way as to minimize the occurrence of bank conflict delays for common usage patterns. The specific DRAM address mappings used by controllers are either documented by the vendor [2] or reverse-engineered [17].

DIMM Circuitry. The memory controller is not the last step in memory addressing, as DIMM circuitry itself can change the signals that individual DRAM ICs receive, including bank and address pins, an example of which is DDR3 rank mirroring [10]. Other remapping strategies exist, which we will discuss in Sect. 3.1.

2.2 The Rowhammer Vulnerability

Due to the extreme density of modern DRAM arrays, small manufacturing imperfections can cause weak electrical coupling between neighboring cells. This, combined with the minuscule capacitance of such cells, means that every time a DRAM row is read from a bank, the memory cells in adjacent rows leak a small amount of charge. If this happens frequently enough between two refresh cycles, the affected cells can leak enough charge that their stored bit value will "flip", a phenomenon known as "disturbance error" or more recently as Rowhammer. Kim et al. [13] showed that Rowhammer can be triggered on purpose, a process known as *hammering*, by using an FPGA to saturate the memory bus with requests to a single row. To trigger Rowhammer flips with similar effectiveness from the CPU (a much stronger threat model), we need to ensure that memory accesses go to DRAM and reach their designated target row as many times as possible between two refresh cycles. To achieve these goals, we have to deal with CPU caches, the row buffer and DRAM addressing.

Avoiding caches has been heavily studied before. Attackers can use cache flushing instructions [19,20,22], uncached (DMA) memory [21], eviction buffers [5,7,9] and non-temporal load/store instructions [18]. Bypassing the row buffer is possible by repeatedly reading from two rows as to cause a bank conflict [13]. If these bank-conflicting rows happen to be exactly one row apart, their respective disturbance errors add up in that middle row, greatly increasing the number of observed Rowhammer bit flips. This technique is known as *double-sided* Rowhammer [20] as opposed to *single-sided* Rowhammer where the bank-conflicting row is arbitrarily far away and does not directly participate in inducing disturbance errors. Lastly, making use of end-to-end DRAM addressing to precisely select Rowhammer targets has not been adequately explored and presents several advantages over the state of the art, as we will discuss in Sect. 4.1 and evaluate in Sect. 5.

2.3 Rowhammer Attacks

Published Rowhammer exploits [7,9,19–22] go through three phases. They first hammer and scan memory for exploitable bit flips; each memory page stores many thousands of bits, of which only a few are useful to the attack in any way if flipped. If a bit flip is found with the right offset and direction (1-to-0 or 0-to-1) to be useful, we call it an *exploitable bit flip*. In the second phase of the attack, security-sensitive information has to be precisely placed on the memory page prone to exploitable Rowhammer flips. This is done by either releasing the target memory page and then spraying security-sensitive information in memory for a probabilistic attack [9,20], or by massaging the physical memory to store security-sensitive information on the vulnerable page for a more targeted and deterministic attack [19,21]. Once the security-sensitive information is stored on the vulnerable memory page, in the third step the attacker triggers Rowhammer again to corrupt the information resulting in a compromise.

Selecting targets for hammering is often done heuristically: attacks assume physical contiguity and split memory into consecutive blocks associated with a particular row number. These blocks aim to contain all pages that map to the same row index, regardless of channel, DIMM, rank or bank and are sized according to assumptions about memory geometry (e.g. 256KiB for two dual-ranked DDR3 DIMMs). Once two blocks are selected as targets, hammering works by exhaustively hammering all page pairs and checking for flipped bits. Alternatively, a timing side-channel based on DRAM bank conflicts can reduce the number of tried pairs significantly.

2.4 Rowhammer Defenses

In response to the proliferation of Rowhammer attacks several software-only defenses were developed. ANVIL [5] attempts to prevent Rowhammer altogether by monitoring memory access patterns and forcibly refreshing the rows neighboring a potential Rowhammer target row. To achieve this, it uses a reverse-engineered mapping scheme and assumes consecutive numbering of rows with ascending physical addresses.

An alternative approach, CATT [8], attempts to mitigate the security implications of Rowhammer by preventing bit flips from crossing the kernel-userspace boundary. To achieve this, it partitions physical memory into userspace and kernel sections separated by a contiguous guard area, whose size is computed similarly to the target blocks of attacks we presented earlier. This approach relies on two assumptions: first, that a sufficiently large physically contiguous memory block will contain all instances of a particular row index across all channels, DIMMs, ranks and banks, and second, that such blocks corresponding to consecutive row indices are laid out consecutively in physical memory.

3   RAMSES Address Translation Library

3.1   Design

In this section we discuss our approach to the main challenges facing an end-to-end model of computer memory addressing. First we consider the address spaces at play and define relationships between individual addresses. Second we look at modeling the physical to DRAM address mapping done by memory controllers. Third we discuss any further DRAM address remappings performed on route to DRAM ICs. Finally, we consider how to efficiently map contiguous physical memory to the DRAM address space.

Address Spaces. Among the address spaces discussed in Sect. 2.1, virtual, physical and linear memory addresses can be intuitively defined as subsets of natural numbers, which have familiar properties. DRAM, however, is addressed quite differently. Hardware parallelism is evident from the channel, DIMM, rank and bank select signals, and once a particular bank is selected, a memory word is uniquely identified by a row and column address. To accommodate all these signals we define a DRAM address to be a 6-tuple of the form <channel, DIMM, rank, bank, row, column>, with the order of the fields reflecting hardware hierarchy levels. We have no universal way of linearizing parts of a DRAM address since memory geometry (i.e. DIMMs per channel, ranks per DIMM, etc.) is highly dependent on what hardware is in use. Moreover, concepts like ordering and contiguity are not as obvious as for physical addresses and are more limited in scope.

To define these concepts, we first need a measure of hardware proximity of two DRAM addresses. We say two addresses are *co-located* on a particular hierarchy level if they compare equal on all fields up to and including that level (e.g. two addresses are bank co-located if they have identical channel, DIMM, rank and bank fields). Ordering is well defined on subsets of co-located addresses, such as columns in a row or rows in a bank, and carries meaning about the relative positioning of hardware subassemblies. A more general ordering, such as comparing field-by-field, while possible, carries little meaning beyond convenience and does not necessarily reflect any aspect of reality. Co-location also enables us to define a limited form of *contiguity* at memory cell level: we say two DRAM addresses are contiguous if they are row co-located and have consecutive column indexes.

Address Mapping. As we have discussed in Sect. 2.1 translation between physical and DRAM addresses is performed chiefly by the memory controller. The exact mapping used varies between models, naturally, but individual controllers often have many configuration options for supporting various memory geometries and standards as well as performance tweaks. As an example, AMD [2] documents 10 DDR3 addressing modes for bank, row and column addresses, with multiple other options for controlling channel, DIMM and rank selection as well as features such as bank swizzle, interleaving and remapping the PCI hole. It is therefore necessary for an accurate model to account for all (sane) combinations of memory controller options, ideally by implementing the mapping logic described in documentation. When documentation is unavailable, mappings can be reverse-engineered and further improved by observing side-channels such as memory access timings and Rowhammer bit flips.

Remapping. In Sect. 2.1 we presented the fact that DRAM addresses can be altered by circuitry in between the memory controller and DRAM ICs, as long as memory access semantics are not violated. We used as an example DDR3 rank address mirroring, where bank bits BA_0 and BA_1, as well as address bits A_3 and A_4, A_5 and A_6, A_7 and A_8, are respectively interchanged in order to make the circuit layout simpler on the "rank 1" side of DIMMs. Rank address mirroring is part of the DDR3 standard [10] and its presence is usually accounted for by compliant memory controllers by "pre-mirroring" the affected pins, making it transparent to the CPU. However, as we will discuss in Sect. 5, we have found several DIMMs behaving like rank-mirrored devices when viewed from software, a fact significantly affecting the effectiveness of Rowhammer. While this information is public, previous work has mostly ignored it [17,22].

In addition to standard-compliant rank mirroring, other custom address remappings can exist. During our research we discovered one particular on-DIMM remapping among several particularly vulnerable DIMMs: address pin A_3 is XORed into bits A_2 and A_1. We came across this after discovering periodic sequences of 8 row pairs either exhibiting many bit flips or none at all on some very vulnerable DIMMs. That lead us to try linear combinations of the 4 least significant DRAM bits until we consistently triggered bit flips over all row pairs—and therefore reverse-engineered the remapping formula.

We remark that on-DIMM remappings can be arbitrarily composed, and we found several DIMMs where both rank mirroring and the custom remapping was in effect, as we will show in Sect. 5.

Efficiency Considerations. An issue worth addressing is the efficient mapping of a physical memory area to DRAM address space—computing the DRAM addresses of all memory words in the area. Most generally, one would have to translate the addresses of every word, since there are no contiguity guarantees. To address this, we define a property named *mapping granularity*, which specifies the maximum length of an aligned physically-contiguous area of memory that is guaranteed to be contiguous in DRAM address space for a particular combination of memory controller and chain of remappings, taking into account any interaction between them. This mapping granularity is often much larger than a memory word, reducing the number of required computations by several orders of magnitude.

3.2 Implementation

We implemented RAMSES as a standalone C library in less than 2000 lines of code. We provide mapping functions for Intel Sandy Bridge, Ivy Bridge and Haswell memory controllers based on functions reverse engineered in previous work [17]. Support for DDR4 memory controllers, as well as AMD CPUs is a work in progress. We provide DDR rank mirroring and the on-DIMM remappings discussed in the previous section, with the possibility to easily add new remappings once they are discovered.

4   Applications of RAMSES

In this section we discuss applications of the end-to-end memory addressing models provided by RAMSES. We first look at a Rowhammer test tool and profiler, which we will compare with the state of the art in Sect. 5 as well as use it to evaluate existing defenses. We then briefly discuss the output of our profiler—flip tables. Finally, we present an *attack simulator* to use the profiler's output to quickly evaluate the feasibility of Rowhammer attacks. These applications, along with miscellaneous small related utilities are released together as *Hammertime*.

4.1   Hammering with RAMSES

Targeting. The most used hammering technique thus far, double-sided Rowhammer, relies on alternately activating two "target" rows situated on each side of a "victim" row. Given that modern DRAM modules have up to millions of individual rows, target selection becomes important. We have already discussed how present attacks use heuristics to select targets in Sect. 2.3. A quite different strategy is to assume (near-)perfect knowledge about all aspects of the memory system, which in our case is provided by RAMSES. Armed with such a mapping function, a Rowhammer test tool can accurately select both target and victim rows, minimizing the search space to precisely target the DRAM region of interest. A benefit of such precision, aside from the obvious speedup, is the ability to study Rowhammer and argue about the results in terms of actual physical DRAM geometry entirely from software. In particular, Rowhammer itself can be used as a side-channel to reverse-engineer memory mappings, a method we ourselves used to pin down the non-standard DRAM address remapping discussed in Sect. 3.1. This opens the door to commodity hardware being used for rapid data collection about different aspects of Rowhammer. Given that the same commodity hardware is also likely to be targeted by a Rowhammer-based exploit, making a fast and complete test is useful in assessing the vulnerability of a given system.

Preparation and Hammering. While our profiler is designed to work with arbitrary memory allocations, some options are provided that can increase effectiveness or fidelity. Namely, **memory locking** informs the kernel to keep page allocations unchanged throughout the lifetime of the buffer. This prevents swapout or copy-on-write events from changing page mappings, which would invalidate target selections. **Huge Pages** can allocate the buffer using huge page sizes (2 MiB or 1 GiB on x86_64). This forces the buffer to be more contiguous in *physical memory*, potentially increasing the number of targetable rows. In addition, huge pages are also implicitly locked.

Because sandboxing or program privileges are no issue in implementing our profiler, we are free to make use of hardware features to bypass the cache, which on x86 is the unprivileged native instruction `clflush`. The number of reads for a hammer attempt is automatically calibrated at runtime to saturate the memory bus for a set number of refresh intervals.

4.2   Flip Tables

To keep the experimental data obtained from the profiler reusable, we keep all addresses used in output in a format as close to the hardware as possible, namely DRAM addresses. This allows examining the effects of Rowhammer on various DRAM modules at the hardware level, regardless of the particularities of the system the data was collected on. Profiler output is a sequence of *hammerings*, each consisting of a set of target addresses along with bit flip locations in the victim rows, if any occur. We collect this output in a machine-readable plain text file we term the *flip table*. We release all flips tables for the DIMMs we experimented with as part of *Hammertime* and will further maintain a repository so that others can contribute additional flip tables.

4.3   Attack Simulator

Design. The goal of simulation is to provide a lightweight alternative to full program execution for evaluating the feasibility of Rowhammer-based attacks. What exactly constitutes a useful bit flip is up to each individual attack to decide. A page table entry (PTE) attack could, for example, be interested in $0 \rightarrow 1$ bit flips at page offsets corresponding to read/write flags in PTEs. A user of the *Hammertime* simulator would specify bit flip positions of interest and receive realistic estimates of success rate and average time to find the first bit flip for a large number of DIMMs. At the same time, the simulator allows for more complex attack plans if desired.

Implementation. To make the simulation interface user-friendly and easily extensible we implemented it in Python. It consists of two programming interfaces: a lower-level view of flip tables, allowing their contents to be programatically accessed, and a higher-level exploit simulation interface which presents bit flips as they would occur in software: as bit offsets within a virtual page.

Published Rowhammer attacks [7,9,19–22] rely on flipping bits at precise memory locations for successful exploitation. To achieve this goal, attacks have an initial "templating" phase where they look for vulnerable memory pages with

Listing 1.1. Implementation of Dedup Est Machina in *Hammertime*'s simulator

```
class DedupEstMachina(estimate.ExploitModel):
    def check_page(self, vpage):
        useful = [
            x for x in vpage.pulldowns
            if x.page_offset % 8 == 0 # Bits 0-7
            or (x.page_offset % 8 == 1 and (x.mask & 0x7)) # Bits 8-10
            or x.page_offset % 8 == 7 # Bits 56-63
            or (x.page_offset % 8 == 6 and (x.mask & 0xf0)) # Bits 52-55
        ]
        return len(useful) > 0
```

a bit flip at the desired offset within a page. The victim process (or kernel) is then coerced into storing data structures within these pages. After that, the attacker uses Rowhammer again in order to cause a bit flip in the target data structures. Overlooking the problem of actually triggering Rowhammer, the simulation interface provides a fast way of evaluating the prevalence of "good" victim pages across a huge number of memory configurations.

An exploit is represented in the simulator by an *Exploit Model*. In the simplest case, an *Exploit Model* provides a function answering one yes-or-no question: is a given memory page *useful* to exploit. An example of an attack implemented as exploit model can be seen in Listing 1.1. More advanced victim selection strategies are also supported by providing hooks at single hammering or fliptable granularity.

5   Evaluation

We tested *Hammertime* on two identical systems with the following configuration:

        CPU: Intel Core i7-4790 @ 3.6 GHz

    Motherboard: Asus H97M-E

      Memory: DDR3; 2 channels, 4 slots, max 32 GiB

        Kernel: Linux 4.4.22

The systems network-boot from a "golden" image and discard all local filesystem changes on power off, ensuring that no state is kept between profiling runs and that each test starts from a known clean state. This also prevents accidental persistent filesystem corruption due to Rowhammer—a valid concern considering the workloads involved.

We tested a total of 33 memory setups: 12 single DRAM modules and 21 dual-channel sets, of sizes ranging from 4 to 16 GiB. Out of these, 14 exhibited Rowhammer bit flips during an initial test run and were selected for further experimentation. The vulnerable memory setups in question are detailed in Table 1. These initial results show that on DIMMs that we looked at, only 42% are vulnerable when profiling is performed from the CPU, a contrast with 85% that is reported in the original Rowhammer paper which uses an FPGA platform for testing [13]. Given that realistic attack scenarios are performed from the CPU, 42% is more representative of the number of vulnerable DDR3 systems.

Table 1. Detailed information on the set of DIMMs vulnerable to Rowhammer used for evaluating *Hammertime* and generating its flip tables.

Brand	Serial Number	ID	Size [GiB]	Freq. [MHz]	Ch.	Ranks /DIMM	Rank mirror	DIMM remap
Corsair	CMD16GX3M2A1600C9	A_1	16	1600	2	2	✓	✓
	CML16GX3M2C1600C9	A_2	16	1600	2	2	✓	
	CML8GX3M2A1600C9W	A_3	8	1600	2	1		
	CMY8GX3M2C1600C9R	A_4	8	1600	2	2	✓	✓
Crucial	BLS2C4G3D1609ES2LX0CEU	B_1	8	1600	2	2	✓	
Geil	GPB38GB1866C9DC	C_1	8	1866	2	1		
Goodram	GR1333D364L9/8GDC	D_1	8	1333	2	2	✓	
GSkill	F3-14900CL8D-8GBXM	E_1	8	1866	2	1		✓
	F3-14900CL9D-8GBSR	E_2	8	1866	2	1		
Hynix	HMT351U6CFR8C-H9	F_1	8	1333	2	2		
Integral	IN3T4GNZBIX	G_1	4	1333	1	2	✓	
PNY	MD8GK2D31600NHS-Z	H_1	8	1600	2	2	✓	
Samsung	M378B5173QH0	I_1	4	1600	1	1		✓
V7	V73T8GNAJKI	J_1	8	1600	1	2	✓	

5.1   Profiling Bit Flips

Our profiling run consists of three hammer strategies: **Single** represents single-sided Rowhammer. A single target row is selected and hammered along with a second distant row, allocated in a separate buffer and automatically selected in order to trigger a bank conflict. **Amplified** targets two consecutive rows for hammering. **Double** represents double-sided Rowhammer and selects as targets rows separated by one victim row. We ran each strategy with all-ones/all-zeroes and all-zeroes/all-ones data patterns for victim/target rows, respectively, and with a hammer duration of 3 refresh intervals. We profiled 128 MiB of each memory setup, allocated using 1 GiB hugepages for 8 GiB and 16 GiB setups and 2 MiB hugepages for 4 GiB setups.

Table 2 shows the results of the three hammer strategies mentioned earlier applied to the 14 memory setups. Overall we see double-sided Rowhammer by far outperforming single-sided and amplified Rowhammer on all memory setups. Using single-sided Rowhammer as a baseline, the "Amplified" strategy manages to be significantly more effective for some setups (A_2, E_2, H_1), while proving inferior for others (A_4, B_1, E_1). We also see the breakdown of bit flip numbers into $0 \rightarrow 1$ (*pullups*) and $1 \rightarrow 0$ (*pulldowns*). Several setups (A_3, E_2, G_1, H_1, J_1) show a significant difference in the ratio of pullups versus pulldowns between single-sided and amplified/double-sided hammer strategies, which suggests different Rowhammer variants induce intereferences of different nature at the DRAM level.

We evaluate the reliability with which bit flips occur repeatedly by performing 10 consecutive 32 MiB profiling runs on a subset of memory setups and comparing the obtained flip tables. We found that the vast proportion (80–90%)

Table 2. Profiling results for vulnerable DIMMs.

ID	Single				Amplified				Double			
	Vuln. rows[%]	Total flips	0 → 1	1 → 0	Vuln. rows[%]	Total flips	0 → 1	1 → 0	Vuln. rows[%]	Total flips	0 → 1	1 → 0
A_1	0.56	92	0	92	0.08	13	0	13	98.95	200468	4367	196107
A_2	0.98	161	159	2	20.29	5404	5404	0	69.13	21542	21538	4
A_3	3.01	512	18	494	4.54	809	438	371	16.13	2926	1541	1385
A_4	0.99	161	1	160	0.18	29	1	28	99.58	256359	5577	250796
B_1	2.17	358	0	358	1.62	272	0	272	8.77	1504	1	1503
C_1	0.01	1	0	1	0.00	0	0	0	63.01	16489	1365	15124
D_1	2.93	488	0	488	2.30	385	0	385	12.14	2131	0	2131
E_1	1.10	181	0	181	0.19	31	0	31	99.77	202630	4175	198464
E_2	13.69	3108	142	2966	24.58	6273	4183	2090	74.56	24587	16320	8267
F_1	2.63	442	0	442	0.70	116	0	116	88.67	413796	5927	407906
G_1	12.98	2447	154	2293	18.61	3803	1934	1869	62.95	15990	7851	8139
H_1	9.79	1983	55	1928	18.46	3930	2575	1355	59.31	16087	10608	5479
I_1	0.49	78	2	76	0.09	15	2	13	99.29	130187	4781	125410
J_1	4.50	811	15	796	9.29	1741	1153	588	35.25	7185	4725	2460

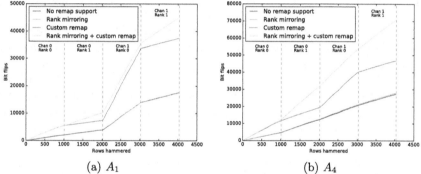

(a) A_1 (b) A_4

Fig. 3. Effect of address remapping strategies on Rowhammer effectiveness

of bit flips show up reliably in all runs, with minor variation between memory setups.

Figure 3 shows the effectiveness of newly discovered addressing information such as on-DIMM remapping and rank mirroring on the number of discovered bit flips using different set of vulnerable DIMMs. In particular, we see that both rank mirroring *and* custom remapping are required for the best results. This was, however not the case for all DIMMs, as can be seen in Table 1.

5.2 Comparison

We compare the effectiveness in exploiting Rowhammer and finding bit flips of *Hammertime*'s `profile` with several state-of-the-art double-sided Rowhammer testing tools: Google Project Zero (GPZ) double-sided rowhammer [20], the native rowhammer binary from the Rowhammer.js project [9], and the binary provided by the Flip Feng Shui authors [19]. Each tool was tested on memory from the A_1 set (one of the most vulnerable DIMMs) under three setups:

Setup I: 15 min testing 4 GiB out of 8 GiB total; 1 channel, 1 DIMM, 2 ranks/DIMM

Setup II: 30 min testing 8 GiB out of 16 GiB total; 2 channels; 1 DIMM/channel; 2 ranks/DIMM

Setup III: 30 min testing 8 GiB out of 16 GiB total; 1 channel; 2 DIMMs/channel; 2 ranks/DIMM

Information about memory geometry, in particular the number of DIMMs, was configured for each tool using runtime flags or compile-time constants, where possible. Memory allocation was done using regular (non-huge, 4 KiB) pages for GPZ test and Rowhammer.js, and using 2 MiB hugepages for Flip Feng Shui.

To make comparison with other tools easier, `profile` ran with two configurations: the first, compatibility mode, allocated memory using regular pages, and only used basic memory configuration—no support for rank mirroring or on-DIMM remapping. The second, optimized run uses hugepage allocation, as well as taking into account rank mirroring and on-DIMM remapping.

Table 3 shows the results of the test runs. The middle section presents the relevant Rowhammer parameters of each run, namely the number of reads and knowledge of memory geometry. The "Rows tested" column shows the number of rows as reported by each test tool. As we have seen in Sect. 2.3 however, different tools have different definitions of what a "row" is. The "Addr pairs/row pair" column highlights these differences, showing how many individual address pairs the tool tries hammering for each individual row it tests. We also provide the "MiB covered" column, which takes into consideration each tool's definition of a "row", providing a common metric.

First, we notice great variation in testing speed (i.e. number of rows tested per unit time) between different tools and setups. This is indicative of the targeting strategies used: the three tools all search over contiguous blocks, as presented in Sect. 2.3, optionally with heuristics narrowing down the search space. The GPZ test exhaustively tries all pages in these blocks, resulting in the slowest overall performance of the set. Rowhammer.js native, on the other hand, uses some information about the memory controller and geometry to select its targets, leading to better search speeds and adapting well to different memory setups. Flip Feng Shui uses a pre-tuned timing side-channel to select potential targets. Judging by the results, the hard-coded timing threshold it uses is tuned for dual-channel memory: Setup II has much improved search rate, while Setups I and III are virtually identical to the exhaustive search done by the GPZ test. In contrast to all of these, *Hammertime*'s `profile` uses extremely precise targeting to make every test count, leading to consistent performance that is orders of magnitude better than that of other tools.

Secondly, we look at the effectiveness with which tools induce bit flips in memory. Project Zero's test failed to detect any bit flips under all three setups,

Table 3. Comparison between *Hammertime* profile and other Rowhammer test tools.

Test tool	Memory reads / addr pair	Chan	DIMM	Rank	Bank	Row[1]	Setup	Row pairs tested	Addr pairs / row pair	MiB covered	Bit flips detected
GPZ rowhammer-test	1.024×10^6						I	4	4096	0.5	0
							II	6		1.5	0
							III	8		2.0	0
Rowhammer.js native	1×10^6	✓			✓	✓	I	133	128	16.6	52
							II	123	256	30.7	101
							III	209		52.2	0
Flip Feng Shui	2.621×10^6						I	3	≤ 1024 [2]	0.37	0
							II	177		44.2	196
							III	7		1.75	0
Hammertime (compat)	$\approx 1.2 \times 10^6$ [3]	✓	✓	✓	✓		I	7484	1	58.4	54480
							II	13999		109	129392
							III	14023		109	123333
Hammertime (optimal)	$\approx 1.2 \times 10^6$	✓	✓	✓	✓	✓	I	6678	1	52.1	143810
							II	13960		109	268203
							III	13915		109	284032

[a] Accurate row address computation which takes rank mirroring and on-DIMM remapping into account.
[b] Address pairs selected using a timing side-channel.
[c] Auto-calibrated for two 64ms refresh intervals.

suggesting that it has certain hard-coded assumptions about memory organization which turn out to be wrong. Rowhammer.js native, on the other hand, successfully detects flips in both single-DIMM and dual-channel modes, while none are reported for dual-DIMM. This is consistent with expectations, as the memory addressing model used by this tool assumes dual-channel operation for multiple DIMMs. Flip Feng Shui, unsurprisingly, produces bit flips only when run under conditions it has been tuned for, similarly to how its search speed varies. In keeping with its superior search rate, `profile` also detects orders of magnitude more bit flips than the other tools. This is partly due to more rows being tested, but also due to better sensitivity from knowing where to look—other tools manage at most slightly above 1 flip per row, while *Hammertime* consistently produces between 7 and 9 flips per row. Furthermore, in the last setup, none of the testing tools could find any bit flips. This is particularly important because it shows that DIMM setups that would be considered secure by state-of-the-art tools, should now be considered vulnerable assuming precise geometry information for Rowhammer attacks. These insights hint that Rowhammer-vulnerable memory cells are much more prevalent than existing software tools would suggest.

5.3 Defenses

We examine the effectiveness of published Rowhammer defenses using the new insights we have gained about memory addressing.

First, we examine ANVIL [5], which monitors memory accesses and selectively refreshes what it considers neighboring rows when it discovers Rowhammer-like activity. To do so, we built and deployed the ANVIL kernel

Table 4. ANVIL evaluation

Defense	Bit flips	
	A_1	A_3
None	7328	96
ANVIL (default)	4238	45
ANVIL (aggressive)	4211	45

Table 5. CATT evaluation

ID	Rank mirror	DIMM remap	CATT guard row	Minimum guard	Safe
A_1	✓	✓	256 KiB	128 MiB	✗
A_2	✓	✗	256 KiB	128 MiB	✗
E_1	✗	✓	128 KiB	2 MiB	✗
F_1	✗	✗	256 KiB	256 KiB	✓

module in two configurations: *default*, and *aggressive*, with sample periods and thresholds reduced by a factor of 10, and ran `profile` on the protected system. We used the source code freely provided by the authors [1], with a modification to disable its use of the precise store event, as this was unavailable on the Haswell CPUs of our test systems. We consider this change inconsequential to the results of this evaluation as `profile` only uses loads to trigger bit flips.

Table 4 shows the results of an 8 MiB run for two memory setups. We see a roughly 50% dropoff in bit flip counts when ANVIL is in use, while minimal differences between the default and aggressive runs. This suggests that bit flips got through not due to poor detection sensitivity, but rather due to fundamental issues in identifying which rows are in danger and, consequently, failure in refreshing them. Indeed, the ratio between prevented/unprevented bit flips is consistent with the increases in Rowhammer effectiveness due to new insights into memory addressing, as previously shown in Fig. 3. We propose enhancing ANVIL with detailed models of memory addressing in order to better identify potential Rowhammer targets and be able to accurately refresh them.

Second, we examine CATT [8], which attempts to mitigate the damage of Rowhammer attacks crossing the kernel-userspace boundary by partitioning the physical address space in two contiguous regions, one for kernel, one for userspace, with a "buffer" or "guard" row in between. CATT computes the size of this guard row by accounting for the number of banks, ranks, DIMMs, and channels of memory in use, multiplying the standard DRAM row size (8 KiB) by each of these in turn. This is a fine approach, assuming a linear and monotonic mapping between physical and DRAM address spaces. However, as we have shown before in Fig. 1 this assumption can be false.

Table 5 presents the results for four representative memory configurations, showcasing all combinations of the rank mirroring and on-DIMM remapping features. For every setup we mark as unsafe we have repeatedly and consistently found bit flips that are far enough away in physical address space from both of their aggressor rows to "jump over" the guard area and thus defeat the linear protection guarantees of CATT. In the "Minimum guard" column, we provide the minimum size a CATT-like contiguous guard zone separating two physical address areas needs to be in order to fully protect them against hammering each other. In cases where this minimum contiguous guard distance is inconveniently large, a non-wasteful isolation-based defense must support accurate memory addressing and non-contiguous guard buffers.

Attack Simulator

To demonstrate *Hammertime*'s simulator, we implemented several published Rowhammer attacks as exploit models: **Page Table Entry Exploits** rely on flipping bits in memory used to hold page tables. Previous work [20] has suggested exploiting flips in the page frame pointer bits of a PTE. Other potentially useful attacks are setting the U/S bit of a PTE, allowing userspace access to a kernel page, and clearing of the NX bit, marking memory as executable. **Dedup Est Machina** [7] which exploits $1 \rightarrow 0$ flips in bits $0 - 10$ and $52 - 63$ of 64-bit words in a page. The entire code is presented in Listing 1.1. **Flip Feng Shui** [19] relies on triggering bit flips at specific page offsets in order to corrupt the contents of sensitive files in the page cache.

We evaluated each model with all double-sided flip tables presented in Sect. 5.1. The results are presented in Table 6. The "Min Mem" column represents the minimum amount of physically contiguous memory required (on average) to find one single useful bit flip. The "Time" column is an estimate of the mean time to the first bit flip, assuming precise targeting and 200ms spent on each Rowhammer test.

We see that an attack's success rate depends not only on how vulnerable memory is, but also on the specific bit flips pursued. Data dependency is one issue: as evidenced in Table 2, memory can have

Table 6. Results of attack simulation

Attack	Run	ID	Success Rate	Min Mem [KiB]	Time [s]
Pagetable PFN	Best	F_1	68.8%	16	0.3
	Median	G_1	5.3%	152	3.8
	Worst	B_1	0.3%	2456	61.3
Pagetable U/S bit	Best	A_2	3.5%	232	5.6
	Median	J_1	0.3%	2376	59.3
	Worst	B_1	0%	N/A	N/A
Pagetable NX bit	Best	F_1	23.0%	40	0.9
	Median	E_2	0.7%	1152	28.6
	Worst	A_2	0%	N/A	N/A
Dedup Est Machina	Best	A_4	98.4%	16	0.2
	Median	E_2	13.1%	64	1.5
	Worst	A_2	<0.1%	65024	1625
FFS GPG	Best	F_1	2.3%	360	8.8
	Median	C_1	0.1%	9328	233.1
	Worst	B_1	0%	N/A	N/A
FFS sources.list	Best	F_1	23.0%	40	0.9
	Median	C_1	0.9%	880	21.9
	Worst	B_1	<0.1%	16256	406.4

a preference for flipping in one direction more than the other. An exploit such as the Page Table U/S bit attack, which relies on $0 \rightarrow 1$ bit flips can achieve relatively poor success rates on otherwise very vulnerable (albeit in the opposite direction) RAM. The second issue is the "rarity" of the required bit flips for each attack in terms of bit offsets in a given memory page. Attacks such as Page Table PFN or Dedup Est Machina, which make use of flips located at one of potentially many page offsets show significantly better results than attacks which require flips in very precise positions, such as Flip Feng Shui.

6 Related Work

To our knowledge, there are no studies systematically applying accurate memory addressing models to implement either Rowhammer attacks or defenses. Likewise, there are no studies looking into address manipulation beyond the memory controller in the context of exploiting Rowhammer.

The first to describe the Rowhammer bug in widespread commodity hardware were Kim et al. [13] in their study on the prevalence of bit flips on DDR3. Coming from the hardware community, the researchers probed the DIMMs directly with an FPGA. Besides identifying the phenomenon, the authors discovered that the root cause of the problem was the repeated toggling of the DRAM row buffer. They also found that many bits are susceptible to flips and that flipping bits requires modest amounts of memory accesses (in their experiments fewer than 150K).

While the authors identified the hardware bug as a potential security problem, it was unclear whether it could be exploited in practice. One year later, Seaborn presented the first two concrete Rowhammer exploits, in the form of escaping the Google Native Client (NaCl) sandbox and escalating local privileges on Linux [20]. In addition, Seaborn discovered that the bit flip rate increased significantly with double-sided Rowhammer. The exploits relied on Intel x86's CLFLUSH instruction to evict a cache line from the CPU caches in order to read directly from DRAM. CLFLUSH was quickly disabled in NaCl, while Linux mitigated the local privilege exploit by disabling unprivileged access to virtual-to-physical memory mapping information (i.e., /proc/self/pagemap) used in the exploit to perform double-sided Rowhammer. Soon after, however, Gruss et al. [9] showed that it is possible to perform double-sided Rowhammer from the browser, without CLFLUSH, and without pagemap—using cache eviction sets and transparent huge pages (THP) [4]. They also found that hammering a pair of neighboring rows, increases the number of flips in the rows adjacent to the pair. In addition, Qiao et al. [18] showed how Rowhammer can be triggered using non-temporal memory instructions in lieu of cache flushing. Bosman et al. showed that it is possible to flip bits from JavaScript in a controlled fashion using probabilistic double-sided Rowhammer without the need for huge pages [6]. Meanwhile, Xiao et al. [22] presented a second cross-VM attack that built on the original Seaborn attack while improving on our knowledge of DRAM geometry.

Research so far predominantly targeted DDR3 RAM and x86 processors. Aichinger [3] then analyzed the prevalence of the Rowhammer bug on server systems with ECC memory and Lanteigne performed an analysis on DDR4 memory [14]. Despite initial doubt among researchers whether the memory controller would be sufficiently fast to trigger the Rowhammer effect, Van der Veen et al. [21] demonstrated that ARM-based mobile devices are equally susceptible to the Rowhammer problem. New attack techniques focus on the DRAM itself. For instance, Lanteigne [14,15] examined how data and access patterns influenced on bit flip probabilities on DDR3 and DDR4 memory on Intel and AMD CPUs. Meanwhile, Pessl et al [17] demonstrated that reverse engineering the bank DRAM addressing can reduce the search time for Rowhammer bit flips. These techniques are complementary to our work.

7 Conclusion

Rowhammer is constantly on the news and increasingly sophisticated Rowhammer attacks surface both in industry and academia. In response, defenses have quickly been developed, aiming to either prevent Rowhammer from occurring or mitigating the security impact of bit flips. Both attacks and defenses however make simplifying assumptions about memory layout and addressing which limits their generality, reproducibility and effectiveness.

To fill this gap, we took a closer look at precisely how an accurate memory addressing model impacts Rowhammer. Our analysis shows that software's ability to trigger, as well as protect against, Rowhammer is greatly influenced by the addressing schemes used by the memory subsystem. We introduce an end-to-end model of DRAM addressing, including the previously unexplored techniques of rank mirroring and on-DIMM remapping. We show that by using such an address model to select Rowhammer targets, attackers can trigger significantly more bit flips than previously assumed and even trigger bit flips on DIMMs where the state of the art fails, amplifying the relevance of existing attacks. We also show that existing defenses do not properly account for memory addressing can be bypassed by sufficiently informed attackers.

To support our work, we introduced *Hammertime*, a software suite for Rowhammer studies. *Hammertime* allows researchers to profile a large set of DIMMs for bit flips and later use the resulting data to simulate the Rowhammer defect in software. More importantly, *Hammertime* makes Rowhammer research much faster, more comparable, and more reproducible. For example, *Hammertime*'s simulator allows researchers to quickly prototype a new Rowhammer vector and evaluate its effectiveness on a given set of existing flip tables. To foster further Rowhammer research and in support of reproducible and comparable studies, we are releasing *Hammertime* as open source.

References

1. ANVIL source code (2016). https://github.com/zaweke/rowhammer/tree/master/anvil. Accessed 03 Apr 2018
2. Advanced Micro Devices: BIOS and Kernel Developers Guide (BKDG) for AMD Family 15h Models 60h–6Fh Processors, May 2016
3. Aichinger, B.: DDR memory errors caused by row hammer. In: HPEC 2015 (2015)
4. Arcangeli, A.: Transparent hugepage support. In: KVM Forum (2010)
5. Aweke, Z.B., et al.: ANVIL: software-based protection against next-generation rowhammer attacks. In: ASPLOS 2016 (2016)
6. Bosman, E., Razavi, K., Bos, H., Giuffrida, C.: Over the edge: silently owning Windows 10's secure browser. In: BHEU 2016 (2016)
7. Bosman, E., Razavi, K., Bos, H., Giuffrida, C.: Dedup Est machina: memory deduplication as an advanced exploitation vector. In: SP 2016 (2016)

8. Brasser, F., Davi, L., Gens, D., Liebchen, C., Sadeghi, A.R.: Can't touch this: software-only mitigation against rowhammer attacks targeting kernel memory. In: 26th USENIX Security Symposium (USENIX Security 2017), Vancouver, BC, pp. 117–130. USENIX Association (2017). https://www.usenix.org/conference/usenixsecurity17/technical-sessions/presentation/brasser

9. Gruss, D., Maurice, C., Mangard, S.: Rowhammer.js: a remote software-induced fault attack in JavaScript. In: Caballero, J., Zurutuza, U., Rodríguez, R.J. (eds.) DIMVA 2016. LNCS, vol. 9721, pp. 300–321. Springer, Cham (2016). https://doi.org/10.1007/978-3-319-40667-1_15

10. JEDEC: DDR3 SDRAM STANDARD. JESD79-3C, November 2008

11. Kasamsetty, K.: DRAM scaling challenges and solutions in LPDDR4 context. In: MemCon 2014 (2014)

12. Khan, S., Wilkerson, C., Wang, Z., Alameldeen, A.R., Lee, D., Mutlu, O.: Detecting and mitigating data-dependent DRAM failures by exploiting current memory content. In: MICRO 2017 (2017)

13. Kim, Y., et al.: Flipping bits in memory without accessing them: an experimental study of DRAM disturbance errors. In: ISCA 2014 (2014)

14. Lanteigne, M.: A Tale of Two Hammers: A Brief Rowhammer Analysis of AMD vs. Intel, May 2016. http://www.thirdio.com/rowhammera1.pdf

15. Lanteigne, M.: How Rowhammer Could Be Used to Exploit Weaknesses in Computer Hardware. SEMICON China (2016)

16. Meza, J., Wu, Q., Kumar, S., Mutlu, O.: Revisiting memory errors in large-scale production data centers: analysis and modeling of new trends from the field. In: DSN 2015 (2015)

17. Pessl, P., Gruss, D., Maurice, C., Schwarz, M., Mangard, S.: DRAMA: exploiting DRAM addressing for cross-CPU attacks. In: SEC 2016 (2016)

18. Qiao, R., Seaborn, M.: A new approach for rowhammer attacks. In: 2016 IEEE International Symposium on Hardware Oriented Security and Trust (HOST), pp. 161–166, May 2016. https://doi.org/10.1109/HST.2016.7495576

19. Razavi, K., Gras, B., Bosman, E., Preneel, B., Giuffrida, C., Bos, H.: Flip Feng Shui: hammering a needle in the software stack. In: SEC 2016 (2016)

20. Seaborn, M.: Exploiting the DRAM rowhammer bug to gain kernel privileges. In: BH 2015 (2015)

21. van der Veen, V., et al.: Drammer: deterministic rowhammer attacks on mobile platforms. In: CCS 2016 (2016)

22. Xiao, Y., Zhang, X., Zhang, Y., Teodorescu, M.R.: One bit flips, one cloud flops: cross-VM row hammer attacks and privilege escalation. In: SEC 2016 (2016)

Intrusion Detection and Prevention

Reading Between the Lines:
Content-Agnostic Detection
of Spear-Phishing Emails

Hugo Gascon[1]([⊠]), Steffen Ullrich[2], Benjamin Stritter[3], and Konrad Rieck[1]

[1] TU Braunschweig, Braunschweig, Germany
h.gascon@tu-bs.de
[2] Genua GmbH, Kirchheim bei München, Germany
[3] Friedrich Alexander-Universität Erlangen-Nürnberg, Erlangen, Germany

Abstract. Spear-phishing is an effective attack vector for infiltrating companies and organisations. Based on the multitude of personal information available online, an attacker can craft seemingly legit emails and trick his victims into opening malicious attachments and links. Although anti-spoofing techniques exist, their adoption is still limited and alternative protection approaches are needed. In this paper, we show that a sender leaves content-agnostic traits in the structure of an email. Based on these traits, we develop a method capable of learning profiles for a large set of senders and identifying spoofed emails as deviations thereof. We evaluate our approach on over 700,000 emails from 16,000 senders and demonstrate that it can discriminate thousands of senders, identifying spoofed emails with 90% detection rate and less than 1 false positive in 10,000 emails. Moreover, we show that individual traits are hard to guess and spoofing only succeeds if entire emails of the sender are available to the attacker.

Keywords: Spear-phishing · Email spoofing
Targeted attack detection

1 Introduction

Emails are a prevalent attack vector for infiltrating companies and organisations. As documents and links are regularly exchanged via email within and across these environments, they are a perfect vehicle for transmitting malicious payloads to a victim [6,20]. To increase their success, attackers specifically target individual members of an organization using carefully crafted emails—a technique referred to as *spear-phishing*. For example, an attacker may pick an appropriate topic, use correct wording and spoof a well-known sender to convince the recipient of the veracity of an email [16]. These targeted attacks are more advanced than regular phishing or spam campaigns, as they are individually adapted to the environment and behavior of the victim. As a result, there exist only few similarities between different spear-phishing attacks which makes it hard to construct effective defenses.

© Springer Nature Switzerland AG 2018
M. Bailey et al. (Eds.): RAID 2018, LNCS 11050, pp. 69–91, 2018.
https://doi.org/10.1007/978-3-030-00470-5_4

Although users are increasingly aware of the risk they are exposed to, they have to rely on hints provided by the email client to detect spoofed content. In the default setup, several clients, like Microsoft Outlook and Mozilla Thunderbird, display only little information for identifying the sender, such as the From and Reply-To fields. Emails from unknown senders can be marked accordingly and specifically dealt with but these and other fields can be forged, making it hard even for a skilled user to distinguish legitimate content from well-crafted attacks [5,34]. While inconsistent combinations of these fields can be easily detected and used to notify the user of a potential threat, the situation becomes challenging if all fields are correctly adapted by the adversary, such that the email appears totally legitimate in its content as well as its headers.

Common anti-spoofing techniques such as the Sender Policy Framework (SPF) [24], DomainKeys Identified Mail (DKIM) [7] and the more recent Domain Message Authentication Reporting & Conformance (DMARC) [25] can help to validate the sender of an email in this situation. Similarly, techniques for digital signing of emails, such as PGP [4] and S/MIME [29], enable to verify the sender. Unfortunately, these techniques are still not widely adopted in practice. While we notice several email domains in our evaluation data with SPF entries, less than 5% of the collected 700.000 emails contain corresponding DKIM headers or even digital signatures. Moreover, all of these techniques need to be implemented at the sending side, which renders it difficult to protect from spoofing if not all communication parties adopt the technology [13,28]. Therefore, given an attacker that is able to exactly match the address of a known sender, the user is unable to detect the attack and might be tricked into opening a malicious file or link.

As a result, there is a demand for alternative approaches to protect users from highly targeted spear-phishing emails. In this paper, we propose a method that is able to verify, without relying on its content, if an email exactly matching the address of a known sender truly originates from its legit source. Our method builds on the observation that a sender leaves characteristic traits in the structure of an email, which are independent from textual content and often persist over time. These traits significantly differ between senders and reflect peculiarities of the user behavior, email client and delivery path, such as particular header combinations, encoding formats and attachment types. Based on this observation, we develop a detection method that receives the mailbox of a user as input and applies machine learning techniques to generate profiles for all senders in the mailbox, even if only a few emails are available. These profiles provide a content-agnostic view on the sender and enable us to spot spoofed emails as deviations from the learned profiles.

We empirically evaluate our approach on a collection of 92 mailboxes from twelve different domains, covering over 700,000 emails from 16,000 senders. We demonstrate that our method can discriminate thousands of senders in one mailbox and enables identifying spoofed emails with 90% detection rate and less than 1 false positive in 10,000 emails. Moreover, we can show that the individual traits of a sender observed at the recipient's end are hard to guess and spoofing

```
Return-Path: <john@doe.com>                                        1
Received: from [93.184.216.34] (HELO example.com)                 2
    by example.com with ESMTP id 69815728;                        3
    Tue, 16 May 2017 14:06:48 +0200                               4
To: Jane Dee <jane@example.com>                                   5
Date: Tue, 16 May 2017 14:00:02 +0200                             6
Message-Id: <20170516133920.23212@doe.com>                        7
Subject: Security Conference                                      8
From: John Doe <john@doe.com>                                     9
In-Reply-To: <1405590537$56fe@example.com>                        10
MIME-Version: 1.0                                                 11
Content-Type: multipart/mixed; boundary="boundary"               12
                                                                  13
--boundary                                                        14
Content-Type: text/plain                                          15
                                                                  16
For your interest: https://tinyurl.com/yao533fn                   17
                                                                  18
--boundary                                                        19
Content-Type: application/octet-stream; name="x.exe"             20
Content-Transfer-Encoding: base64                                 21
                                                                  22
TVqQAAMAAAAEAAAA//8AALgAAAAAAAAQAAAAAAAAAAKCkdyZWVO               23
aW5ncywgUmV2aWV3ZXIhCsKvXF8o440EKV8vwq8KCg==                     24
--boundary--                                                      25
```

Fig. 1. Simplified email as running example.

attempts only succeed if entire emails of the sender as delivered to the recipient are known to the adversary. Although our approach cannot generally rule out spoofing due to leaked emails, it considerably raises the bar for targeted attacks and—in absence of widely deployed server-side solutions—provides an effective protection for companies and organisations targeted by spear-phishing attacks.

In summary, we make the following contributions:

- *Characteristic sender profiles:* We identify traits which enable us to characterize the sender of an email without relying on textual content. The resulting profiles are expressive enough to distinguish thousands of senders while accounting for the diversity of individual emails.
- *Detection of spear-phishing emails:* We demonstrate how the learned profiles of senders can be used for identifying spoofed emails and help to mitigate the risk of spear-phishing attacks in absence of stronger server-side solutions in practice.
- *Evaluation and evasion experiments:* We evaluate the performance of our method through a series of increasingly adverse scenarios where the attacker becomes stronger by obtaining more information about the target and building a better model of the spoofed sender.

The rest of this paper is organized as follows: In Sect. 2 we present traits observable in the structure of emails and describe in Sect. 3 how these can be used to construct profiles for senders. We evaluate the resulting detection method in Sect. 4 and discuss its impact and limitations in Sect. 5. Related work is reviewed in Sect. 6 and Sect. 7 concludes the paper.

2 Traits in Email Structure

The identification of spoofed emails is a challenging problem of network security. An attacker can almost arbitrarily manipulate the structure and content of emails, ranging from a trivially spoofed `From` field to carefully crafted sequences of fake `Received` headers (see [30]). In absence of exact detection techniques in practice, such as DKIM and DMARC, it is thus hard to discriminate legitimate from forged emails.

The freedom available for constructing a spoofed email, however, may also turn against the attacker and pose an obstacle. We argue that it is non-trivial to mimic an email from a particular sender without detailed knowledge and that minor irregularities in the email structure may provide valuable clues for identifying spear-phishing attacks. If the attacker has access to emails from a sender known to the victim, she can simply copy the email structure, yet if this information is not fully available, she needs to make a good guess and hope that the forged structure mimics the original communication well.

For uncovering such forgeries, we identify three groups of traits that can characterize the sender of an email: First, when writing an email the sender introduces *behavior features* that reflect individual preferences and peculiarities. Second, the email client generates *composition features*, identifying the particular client and its configuration. Third, the delivery of an email leaves *transport features* that capture details of the sending and receiving infrastructure. In the following, we describe these groups of traits in more detail and use the simplified email in Fig. 1 as a running example through out this section.

2.1 Behavior Features

When a user writes an email, several of her individual preferences can manifest in the structure of the email—aside from her writing style and habits [10,33]. For example, some senders are frequently including recipients using the `CC` header, whereas others avoid this and prefer to address all recipients directly using the `To` field. Similarly, senders differ in the type and amount of files they are attaching to emails in conversations. While some of these features are volatile and change between different contexts, other features may persist over time and provide a first basis for constructing a profile of the sender.

For our analysis, we identify 13 feature types that characterize the behavior of a sender in the structure of an email, including

1. the type, number and order of attachments, for example when multiple documents are exchanged,
2. the relation to other emails and recipients, for example in form of `References` and `In-Reply-To` headers,
3. digital signatures and certificates attached to the email as well as corresponding PGP and S/MIME fields, and
4. the amount of text in the main part and the amount of quoted text in email responses.

A complete list of all 13 features is provided in Table 4 of the appendix. Note that the cardinality of these features differs, where some may appear multiple times in an email, such as the type of attachments and others only once, such as the depth of the MIME structure. As an example, the email in Fig. 1 shows the attachment of an executable file (line 20) and the reference to a previous conversation (line 10)—two features that are rarely used in combination.

2.2   Composition Features

The second source for traits in the structure of an email is the mail user agent (email client) that converts the provided addresses, text and attachments into a suitable format for delivery. As emails have been originally restricted to ASCII characters, there exists a wealth of encoding schemes for converting binary data to a compatible ASCII representation (e.g. [14,15,23]). These schemes are selected by the email client and often slightly vary in implementation, thus providing features that characterize the composition of an email. For example, the Base64 encoding [23] does not enforce a fixed text length and thus clients differ in the formatting of the corresponding text blocks. Similarly, there exists several minor variations in the construction of multi-part MIME messages that provide clues about the client and its configuration.

For our analysis, we identify 22 feature types that capture peculiarities of the email client and its configurations, including

1. the type, order and syntax of common headers, such as the From, To, Subject and Message-Id headers,
2. the type, order and syntax of headers in MIME parts, including fields like Content-Type and Content-Disposition,
3. the syntax of address fields, such as the formatting and quoting of names and email addresses,
4. the encoding of international characters in the subject field, in address fields and filenames,
5. the type and location of textual content, such as HTML and plain parts in the email,
6. client-specific behavior, such as the length of line breaks, missing and superfluous encodings of characters,
7. individual details of the MIME structure, such as the depth and the order of different MIME parts, and
8. the structure of the Message-Id header and the structure of MIME boundaries.

A complete list of the 22 composition features is provided in Table 5 of the appendix. While these features alone are clearly not sufficient to identify attacks, in combination with behavior and transport features they sharpen the view on a sender and thereby obstruct the spoofing of email addresses. As an example, the email in Fig. 1 shows a unique order of the From, To and Subject field (line 5–9) which indicates a rare email client. Furthermore, the Base64-encoded attachment is formatted using a 60 character line length (line 23).

2.3 Transport Features

A third group of traits can be attributed to the delivery path of an email. As the email moves from the sending to the receiving mail transport agent, often passing multiple hops, different headers are added to the structure. These headers describe the individual mail hops in form of Received headers and provide information about available delivery features, such as delivery protocols, TLS or the time zone of the mail server. These headers and features, again, generate a series of traits that can help to distinguish different senders and spot irregularities in the delivery process.

Although an attacker can insert fake headers prior to the delivery of an email, it is not possible to change or remove headers added by hops on the delivery path. As a consequence, an attacker can only forge these headers by either connecting directly to the receiving server or, alternatively, attempting to inject emails early into the delivery process—a tractable but non-trivial task in practice, as it would require having access to the same delivery infrastructure as the sender that the attacker is trying to spoof.

We identify 11 transport features that enable us to reconstruct the delivery path of an email and spot deviations from past emails of the same sender. These features include

1. the number and order of Received headers, where each hop is represented by the hash of its hostname,
2. the path of time zone from the first to the last hop during the delivery process,
3. the delivery protocols and TLS features available in some Received headers,
4. the validity of DKIM records added by the servers and their relation to the claimed sender of the email, and
5. non-standard headers added by spam filters or anti-virus services during the delivery of the email.

Table 6 in the appendix provides a list of all 11 transport features. As an example of traits introduced by the delivery process, the email in Fig. 1 contains a detailed Received header (line 2–4). This header defines the mail hop, delivery protocol and delivery time. This information is available with any mail passing the hop and thus can leak to the attacker. However, we show in Sect. 4 that knowledge of transport features alone is insufficient to evade our detection method and that the attacker needs access to original emails delivered to the recipient for successfully spoofing a sender.

3 Detection Methodology

Equipped with three groups of traits for characterizing the sender of an email, we are ready to develop a corresponding detection method using machine learning techniques. The application of learning methods spares us from manually constructing detection rules for each of the senders and thereby allows for scaling our approach to thousands of senders, as we demonstrate in Sect. 4.

3.1   Feature Extraction and Embedding

The proposed groups of traits provide detailed information about the structure of emails from each sender in the recipient's mailbox. In order to learn a profile from the traits, however, we require a numerical representation that can be used in combination with common learning methods. As a remedy, we apply the concept of a *bag-of-words model*—a technique originating from information retrieval [32] and natural language processing [21,22]—and adapt it to the traits extracted from the structure of emails.

To this end, we represent each of the extracted traits as a feature string and build a joint set F that comprises all observable strings from the three groups of traits:

$$F := F_{\text{behavior}} \cup F_{\text{composition}} \cup F_{\text{transport}}.$$

Making use of this set F, we define an $|F|$-dimensional vector space that takes values 0 or 1 in each dimension. Each email e is then mapped to this space by building a vector $\varphi(e)$, such that for each feature f extracted from e the corresponding dimension is set to 1, while all other dimensions are set to 0. Formally, this map can be defined for all emails M as

$$\varphi : M \longrightarrow \mathbb{R}^{|F|}, \quad \varphi(e) \longmapsto (I_f(e))_{f \in F}$$

where the auxiliary function I simply indicates whether the feature f is present in e, that is,

$$I_f(e) = \begin{cases} 1 & \text{if email } e \text{ contains feature } f \\ 0 & \text{otherwise.} \end{cases}$$

The resulting binary vector space $\mathbb{R}^{|F|}$ allows us to represent each email as a vector of the contained traits of its sender. In the following, we describe how we use this representation to train a machine learning classifier that, based on these features, is able to assign each email to its corresponding sender and indicate possibly spoofed emails.

3.2   Model Learning and Classification

Several learning methods can be applied for classifying data in a vector space. To operate in our setting, however, a learning method needs to address additional requirements: First, the method has to be able to operate in a high-dimensional vector space, as the set F may cover thousands of different traits. Second, the method needs to be capable of learning a classification model, even if only very few training data is available, such as a couple of emails only.

In view of these requirements, we select the following two learning methods for our detection approach: (a) a k-nearest-neighbors classifier (kNN) that can generate good classification results with very few training data and (b) a multi-class support vector machine (SVM) which is known for effectively operating in high-dimensional vector spaces (see [9]).

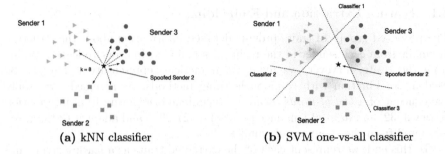

(a) kNN classifier   (b) SVM one-vs-all classifier

Fig. 2. Schematic overview of the detection: a classifier is used to identify emails as spoofed when a mismatch between the output of the classifier and the origin sender address occurs.

K-Nearest Neighbors Classifier. The kNN algorithm is a simple yet effective learning method for classification. It computes the distance between a test sample and all existing samples in a training set and makes a decision through voting on the labels of its k-nearest samples after applying a weight function (see Fig. 2). Such instance-based learning algorithms do not construct an explicit learning model and thus can be applied even if only a single email is available for a sender. For our approach, we label each feature vector with the address of the originating sender address. When a new email is received, we compute the distance between this sample and the feature vectors of all existing emails as follows

$$d(e_x, e_y) = \left|\left| \varphi(e_x) - \varphi(e_y) \right|\right|_1 = \sum_{f \in F} \left| I_f(e_x) - I_f(e_y) \right|,$$

where d corresponds to the Manhattan or L_1 distance. A mismatch between the incoming sender address and the prediction of the classifier is then flagged by our method as a spoofing attempt.

The advantage of making predictions with very few training data, however, comes at a price. The distance between each new email and all existing emails needs to be computed before making a decision, which is computationally expensive on large mailboxes. Fortunately, this problem can be addressed in two ways: First, one can implement the classifier using special data structures for reducing the number of distance computations, such as ball trees and cover trees [2]. Second, if the number of training instances reaches a certain limit, one can simply switch to another learning method, such as a support vector machine or, when possible, sample the training data according to a distribution that maintains the classifier performance.

Multi-class Support Vector Machines. As second learning method, we employ a linear multi-class SVM algorithm [11]. The algorithm computes a series of maximum-margin hyperplanes that separate the emails from one sender from the emails of all other senders (see Fig. 2b). That is, given N different senders, N

hyperplanes are determined, each one of them represented by a vector $w \in \mathbb{R}^{|F|}$ and a scalar b in the vector space.

If a new email arrives, we simply determine the position to the learned hyperplanes and pick the sender with the best match, that is, the largest value of

$$h(e) = \langle \varphi(e), w \rangle + b = \sum_{f \in F} I_f(e) \cdot w_f + b.$$

Note that this function can be computed efficiently, if the feature vector $\varphi(e)$ is sparse, as only non-zero dimensions $I_f(e)$ contribute to the output. As a result, we can compute $h(e)$ in linear time in the number of traits $|e|$ extracted from e and the overall run-time for analyzing an email is $O(N|e|)$. In contrast to the kNN algorithm, the run-time for the prediction of a linear SVM is independent of the size of the training set and thus this learning method is suitable if more emails are available from particular senders (see [11]).

4   Evaluation

We proceed to evaluate our detection method on a large dataset of real-world emails. In particular, we are interested in studying the ability of our method to characterize the sender of an email based on its structure and to identify spoofed emails under different levels of knowledge of the adversary. Before presenting these experiments, we first introduce our dataset (Sect. 4.1) and define the corresponding attacker model (Sect. 4.2).

4.1   Evaluation Data

For our evaluation, we have gathered anonymized features extracted from 92 mailboxes from twelve different domains, including enterprise and commercial email services. To evaluate the efficacy of our detection method, we require at least one email for learning and one for testing from each sender. Consequently, we discard all emails from senders that have sent only a single email. Our final dataset comprises a total of 760,603 emails from 17,381 senders, where each sender has authored at least two emails. These emails are described by a total of 617,960 features extracted using the traits defined in Sect. 2. Table 1 provides an overview of the statistics of our evaluation data.

Table 1. Statistics of evaluation data.

Basic statistics	Total		
Mailboxes			92
Emails			760,603
Senders			17,381
Features			617,960
Detailed statistics	Min.	Mean	Max.
Emails per mailbox	2	8,267	50,924
Emails per sender	2	43	44,204
Senders per mailbox	1	279	2,144
Features per email	5	69	183
Emails per sender and mailbox	2	29	10,304

Figure 3 depicts in more detail how emails and senders are distributed within our dataset. From Fig. 3a and b we can see that over 50% of the mailboxes in

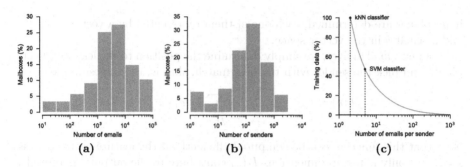

Fig. 3. Overview of the evaluation data: (a) distribution of emails and (b) distribution of senders in the 92 mailboxes; (c) training data available for learning with varying emails per sender.

our dataset contain between 10^3 to 10^4 emails and between 10^2 to 10^3 different senders. This large corpus of emails provides a good basis for evaluating the performance of our method. Depending on the applied learning model, however, we require a minimum number of emails per sender and thus not all senders might be available for training. Figure 3c shows the amount of training data available to a learning method depending on the minimum number of emails per sender. While for the kNN classifier all senders can be used for evaluation, in the case of the SVM classifier, we need to restrict our experiments to 46% of the data, as we require at least 5 emails for training.

To prepare our experiments, we extract feature vectors from all emails in our evaluation data. This may seem as an intractable task at first glance, as the resulting vector space has over 600,000 dimensions. However, the majority of these dimensions is zero and each email contains only between 5 to 183 features (see Table 1). As a result, we can make use of efficient data structures for operating with these sparse feature vectors (see [31]).

As a sanity check whether our representation is suitable for learning a classification, we first study how senders in a mailbox differ from each other and then analyze how emails from a specific sender change over time. To this end, we first calculate a simple statistic: For each sender, we compute the average of its feature vectors and measure the distances between the resulting 17,381 mean vectors within each mailbox. We make use of the Manhattan distance (L_1 distance) for comparing the mean vectors. The distance can be interpreted as the average number of features differing between the senders and thus provides an estimate for the quality of extracted traits.

Figure 4 shows the distribution of the Manhattan distances between all senders in each mailbox. It can be observed that most senders are separated from each other by a distance larger than 40 on average. This demonstrates that several of the extracted traits are highly specific and capture nuances of the email structure suitable for discriminating the senders. Multiple sources may introduce variability and noise into the email traits of a sender, such as software updates, network configurations and changing devices. We thus study how emails from an individual sender change over time. In particular, we want to answer

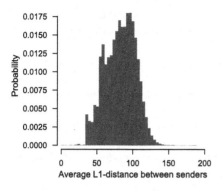

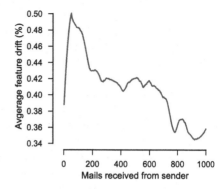

Fig. 4. Distance between senders   **Fig. 5.** Feature drift over time

the question how many features change in a new email when it is compared with existing emails from the same sender. For this, we measure the Manhattan distance between each email received at a certain point in time in a mailbox and all emails previously received from the same sender. The average number of differing features is then presented as a percentage of the feature space dimensionality. Figure 5 shows that a slight feature drift exits. It can be observed how the variability grows rapidly at first with the initial emails received from a sender. However, when an increasing number of emails is received each class becomes more compact and the average percentage of different features in a new email decreases. Note that although profiles become more stable during time, they also tend to differ considerably as shown in Fig. 4.

As the final preparation step, we determine the presence of anti-spoofing techniques in the 760,603 emails using corresponding email client and transport features. Table 2 shows the percentage of emails in our dataset that contain anti-spoofing techniques, where we additionally report statistics from the top million web domains listed at the monitoring service *BuiltWith* [3]. Although the adoption of SPF [24] has reached almost 40% by now, the overall implementation of anti-spoofing techniques is still low in both data sources. In particular, recent techniques, such as DKIM [7] and DMARC [25] are used in less than 5% of the emails, thereby emphasizing the need for alternative protection measures.

4.2 Attacker Model

In the absence of anti-spoofing techniques, a skilled adversary is able to forge most of the data contained in an email. However, we argue that, by inferring a sender profile based on traits of the email structure, an attacker is forced to mimic such profile to effectively masquerade as the

Table 2. Anti-spoofing techniques in our evaluation data and as reported by the monitoring service *BuiltWith*.

Anti-spoofing technique	Our data	Top 1M [3]
SPF	—	39.9%
DKIM	4.3%	0.1%
DMARC	—	1.3%
PGP, S/MIME	0.88%	—

sender. As a consequence, the success of such spoofing depends on how much information of the email structure is available to the adversary and if the attacker has access to the senders delivery infrastructure.

Therefore, we begin the evaluation of our approach by measuring in a controlled experiment how an attacker may affect the detection performance by spoofing an increasing number of features from a sender's profile (i.e. all features extracted from all emails received from a specific sender in a mailbox). To this end, we first split each sender's data in a mailbox into training and testing sets and then train both kNN and SVM classifiers. For testing, we select random emails from other mailboxes and relabel them as known senders of the target mailbox to imitate spoofing attempts. This means that our testing set is comprised of 50% of legitimate emails and 50% of spoofed emails with a random percentage of correct traits of the target sender.

Note that to generate spoofed emails we do not rely on their textual content for feature extraction. Moreover, we adapt the transport features added by the recipient MTA to the recipient mailbox. As a result, the spoofed emails in our testing set are not different from real spear-phishing emails sent by an attacker, as no textual content is considered.

We measure the detection performance of our classifiers using the true-positive rate (TPR) and false-positive rate (FPR). In our setup, a true positive implies that a spoofed email has been correctly identified, while a false positive corresponds to a legitimate email wrongly being tagged as spoofed. Furthermore, we use a Receiver Operating Characteristic (ROC) curve to present both evaluation metrics and calculate the area under the ROC curve (AUC) as a numerical aggregate of the classification performance (see [12]). Although an adversary with increasing capacity will affect the ability of the classifier to correctly identify deviations from a user profile, the information available to an attacker is constrained by threat scenarios that can occur in reality. In this work, we thus assume that the knowledge of an attacker can range from knowing nothing about the spoofed sender to having real examples of her emails.

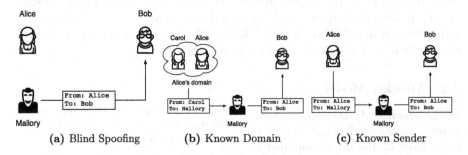

(a) Blind Spoofing   **(b)** Known Domain   **(c)** Known Sender

Fig. 6. Threat scenarios for increasing attacker capabilities based on the acquired knowledge about the spoofed sender: (a) the attacker has no information about the sender, (b) the attacker has access to emails received from the sender's domain and, (c) the attacker has access to one or more emails from the real sender.

Accordingly, we model these attackers through a series of increasing adversarial setups and proceed to evaluate the performance of our approach in each scenario as depicted in Fig. 6:

(a) *Blind Spoofing:* In this scenario, the attacker (Mallory in Fig. 6) tries to spoof a particular sender from which she does not have any information. The only available strategy for the attacker is to simply replace the `From` and `Return-Path` headers of the targeted email and try to guess the behavior, composition and transport features.

(b) *Known Domain:* In this scenario, the attacker has received or has access to one or more emails sent by a sender that belongs to the same email domain as the spoofed sender. The attacker can thus expect that some of their transport features are present in the emails received by the victim from the sender she wants to spoof.

(c) *Known Sender:* In this scenario, shown in Fig. 6c, the attacker has received or has access to one or more emails sent by the spoofed sender. As a result, several traits used for constructing the profile are available to the attackeri and can be incorporated in her spoofed emails.

In the following, we describe how we learn a profile of each sender within a mailbox and assign the role of the victim to the owner of the mailbox. Then, based on the attack strategies described in each scenario and using the emails available in our dataset we build corresponding sets of spoofed emails for each sender and combine them with legitimate emails to evaluate our method.

4.3   Spoofed Email Detection

In the following we evaluate the performance of our approach in the threat scenarios defined in the previous section. In order to learn a profile for each sender we begin again by splitting all available emails into training and testing sets. For training, we consider all emails received up to a certain point in time. In the case of the kNN classifier one email from a sender in the training set suffices to make a decision about an incoming email from this origin address, while for the SVM classifier we require a minimum of 5 emails from a sender to include this class during training. In order to tune the parameters of each classifier, we partition the training data into 5 splits and use training/validation partitions, such that the temporal order of emails is preserved—similar to a regular cross-validation. This enables us to simulate training with past data and generating predictions for data yet unseen. Note that although a mailbox or sender may not present enough emails for training, we still use these samples to generate test spoofed emails.

For the testing phase, we combine the test set of legitimate emails with a set of emails crafted according to the attacker strategies described in Sect. 4.2. In the case of a *blind spoofing* attack, we select a random set of emails sent to recipients at different domains than the victim and label them as the spoofed sender. Likewise, we evaluate the *known domain* attack by selecting emails sent

Table 3. Detection performance of our approach in different threat scenarios.

Threat scenario	Blind spoofing				Known domain				Known sender			
Algorithm	kNN		SVM		kNN		SVM		kNN		SVM	
Metric	FPR	TPR	FPR	TPR	FPR	TPR	FPR	TPR	FPR	TPR	FPR	TPR
	0.01%	90.9%	0.01%	92.4%	0.01%	72.7%	0.01%	78.1%	0.01%	48.1%	0.01%	30.1%
	0.1%	90.9%	0.1%	92.4%	0.1%	72.7%	0.1%	78.2%	0.1%	48.2%	0.1%	30.2%
	1%	91.1%	1%	92.5%	1%	73.7%	1%	79.3%	1%	48.9%	1%	30.4%
	10%	91.9%	10%	92.9%	10%	78.4%	10%	84.1%	10%	53.2%	10%	33.9%

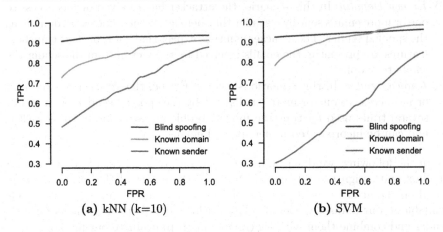

(a) kNN (k=10)   (b) SVM

Fig. 7. ROC curves for the classification of legitimate emails versus emails spoofed by attackers with different levels of knowledge.

from the domain of the spoofed sender by a different sender to other recipients. Finally, we select emails sent by the spoofed sender to different recipients to built the spoofed test set in the evaluation of the *known sender* attack.

During testing, we expect a legitimate email to be assigned to its true class by the classifier. On the contrary, a spoofed email should be assigned to any of the other classes, resulting in a mismatch between the sender address from which the email is sent and the output of the classifier. There exists thus a trade-off between the probability of detecting a spoofed email and the probability of wrongly highlighting a legitimate email as spoofed. The ROC curves depicted in Fig. 7 show the trade-off between the false-positive rate and the false-positive rate for both classifiers.

If the attacker lacks any knowledge about the spoofed sender, we observe that the kNN and SVM classifiers can identify a spoofed email with a true-positive rate of 90.9% and 92.4% respectively at a low false-positive rate of 0.01%. If the attacker has access to emails originating from the same domain, the performance decreases to 72.7% and 78.1% but the classifier is still able to effectively operate at the same low false-positive rate. In the worst-case scenario, the attacker has enough information to craft an email that resembles the learned

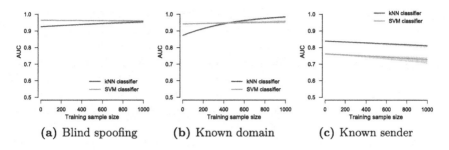

(a) Blind spoofing   **(b)** Known domain   **(c)** Known sender

Fig. 8. Area under the ROC curve as a function of the number of training emails used to learn each sender's individual profile.

profile of the spoofed sender, which causes the performance of the classifier to deteriorate considerably. Table 3 specifies numerically the detection achieved at 0.01%, 0.1%, 1% and 10% of false-positive rate for both classifiers in all scenarios.

As mentioned above, we set a lower threshold for the minimum number of emails required to train an SVM classifier. However, as shown in Fig. 3 a larger number of emails above this threshold is available for many senders. Figure 8 shows in each scenario the relation between the number of emails from a sender used to train the classifier and the AUC averaged over all mailboxes and senders. As described in Sect. 4.1, sender profiles tend to be more compact with an increasing number of emails. However, this can affect the performance differently depending of the knowledge available to the attacker. For instance, in threat scenarios (a) and (b), emails are classified with an AUC over 0.85 with a small number of training samples. Spoofed emails lay here far enough from the sender profile, leading to a stable or increased performance when classes becomes more populated. In particular, the SVM classifier offers a better performance at a low number of available emails, while with an increasing training size, the kNN classifier surpasses the SVM.

On the contrary, in threat scenario (c) the attacker is always able to craft an email that resembles the profile of the spoofed sender, while a larger number of training samples increases the variability of the sender profile. As each spoofed email lay very close or within the target class, it becomes more difficult for the classifier to correctly separate legitimate emails from spoofing attempts when the sample size increases. A possible approach in such a high risk scenario, is to operate the classifier at a higher FPR point and to retrain the model more often on a smaller sample of the most recent emails received

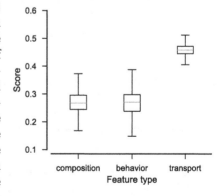

Fig. 9. Distribution of scores per group of traits as learned by the linear SVM classifier during training.

from each sender. Finally, the use of a linear SVM for classification allows us to study how the learning algorithm assigns different weights to each type of features according to its importance for the classification. To this end, we determine the distribution of the normalized SVM weights and group them by trait types. In Fig. 9, we can observe that, in comparison with behavior and composition features, transport related features manifest both a smaller dispersion and a larger influence on the decision of the classifier. Consequently, transport features have the most discriminative power and, at the same time, are the most difficult traits to forge as even a skilled adversary is not able to fully control transport features without having access to the same delivery infrastructure of the sender.

5   Discussion and Limitations

The evaluations in the previous section show that our method is capable of reliably discriminating thousands of senders and identifying spoofed emails if the attacker has limited knowledge of the email structure. Due to the problem setting of detecting spoofing at the receiving side, however, our approach has some inherent limitations which are discussed in the following.

Advanced Forgery. Although spear-phishing and other targeted email attacks today focus on the forgery of visible features like the sender address, the subject and the content of an email to mimic trustworthy emails [18, 26], we likely have to deal with more advanced attacks in the near future. If current attacks are no longer successful because of increased user awareness and detection approaches like ours, attackers will adapt their techniques. For our method, the best strategy for evasion is to forge as many features from the original sender as possible. An almost perfect forgery is thus a copy of an original mail including also its true transport features as observed by the recipient and enriched with some malicious content. However, the attacker needs to take care of several traits that our method inspects, such as timestamps, IP addresses in received headers and characteristics of the attachment. In the worst case, the attacker is able to forge all of these details and hence the only indication of a spoofed email are minor inconsistencies between IP addresses and hostnames. Our method fails in this scenario, as only a few features differ from the sender model. Nonetheless, the acquisition of emails from a sender and acquiring access to the senders delivery infrastructure to control the transport features, clearly raise the bar for conducting spear-phishing attacks. Therefore and with the current lack of alternative protection approaches, our approach is a valuable extension to current defenses.

Privacy and Feature Extraction. We have implemented the feature extraction in a privacy-friendly way in that all sensitive information of sender, transport and recipients is only stored in an anonymized form by using a hash with random salt. Only these anonymized features are kept and used in the initial creation or retraining of the model. This makes it possible to implement the system for example in a security appliance which receives all feature vectors for analysis but does not store the mails. This also means, however, that the model cannot be simply extended with new features and retrained with old data, since the original mail as input for feature extraction is no longer available. Feature extraction is therefore performed locally in every case. Although this limits how anonymized data from different sources can be combined for analysis, the recipient's email information never leaves the local machine, avoiding privacy issues and possible attack vectors.

Mislabeled Data. The possibility of the training data containing spoofed emails should not be ignored. However and due to their very nature, the prevalence of spear-phishing emails can only be very low within all emails sent to a recipient. This problem, known as *label noise* (see [8]), entails that training samples can be considered subjected to an additive noise during training with a probability of their labels being flipped. In our setup, however, such probability will be very low and the effect during testing of such infrequent examples, while existent, will be negligible.

6 Related Work

The detection of unwanted and malicious emails is a well-established problem in security research. Several methods have been devised in the last years that are related to our approach and which we briefly discuss in the following.

For instance, several approaches exist that focus on the content of emails and the style in which they are writtenx (e.g. [10,17,33]). The assumption behind these features is that the writing style of one sender differs significantly from another and that it is too hard for the attacker to write a mail in the same style as the sender she is trying to spoof. The implementation of such content-based features can be as simple as using a 5-gram tokenizer [27] but can also be more complex and include character distributions, atypical words or more advanced stylometric features [10,17,33]. In many cases, these stylometric features are used in combination with further behavioral features, such as the time of writing.

While these approaches potentially provide a good detection of spoofed emails, they present two problems. First, if text from the original sender is available from any source stylometric traits can be easy to forge and second such approaches require sufficient data to infer minor differences in stylometry and can be computationally expensive. As a consequence, previous work often operates with small datasets. For example, Lin et al. [27] conduct an evaluation with only 6 senders due to a lack of available data. Similarly, Duman et al. [10] discriminate only 215 senders in their experiments. Whether these techniques can be scaled to cover thousands of senders is unclear and thus the application stylometric features for spear-phishing detection is still an open issue.

The problem of limited learning data is addressed by Stringhini and Thonnard [33] who propose a detection approach that, while also relying on email content, is capable of analyzing larger datasets. However, their method requires a minimum of 1,000 emails per sender to be effective. Moreover, they position the defense at the sender's server and require to include emails from different mailboxes to build a reliable behavioral profile of a user. Such an approach is orthogonal to our method which operates at the recipient's side, who only requires the information contained in her own mailbox to build an effective defense. Furthermore, recipient related features are based on the idea that different recipients have different risk to get spear-phishing mails. Such features are proposed by Amin [1] which determine the amount of information returned by a search engine about a recipient and how often a person has received malicious mails in the past. Unsurprisingly, the latter turns out to be a dominant feature, i.e., those senders who got attacked in the past a lot will probably also get a lot attacked in the future.

As in our work, infrastructure related features commonly include properties of the transport like the senders IP address or her geographic location [17,27]. But also features of the used mail client belong in this category since a sender will usually use only a single or few email clients. Features related to the infrastructure are often similar for all senders in the same domain which can be used to increase model accuracy when only a few mails from a specific sender are available. Compared to stylometric features, infrastructural features do not model the actual author but only her environment. Therefore, it is impossible to detect a hacked account with these features. On the other hand infrastructural features need less training data to create a well-performing model. Thus, it might be useful to combine the strength of both approaches. Structural based features, instead of content based features are the dominant ones in our evaluation. Such features were already used by Amin [1]. Contrary to this work, our approach makes use of a larger set of features from the mail client and from its transport and is based on distinguishing different senders based on these features instead of globally distinguishing all spear-phishing mails from all benign mails.

Finally, a method recently proposed by Ho et al. [19] focuses on the identification of credential phishing and is designed to identify attacks from unseen senders. Our approach is orthogonal to this work, as it addresses two of its main shortcomings: First, Ho et al. [19] consider the problem of address spoofing irrelevant due to the availability of DKIM and DMARC. Our empirical analysis, however, shows that both techniques are not widely available in practice and thus alternative methods are needed. Furthermore, DKIM and DMARC need to be implemented at the sending side, which enables the attacker to choose a known sender with lacking support for this security feature. Second, the proposed method requires the victim to interact with the phishing email by clicking on a link. This poses a serious security risk and may result in the victim's host being compromised before the attack is actually detected. Our approach does not require interaction and can block phishing attacks before they reach their victim, for example, by removing links and attachments from emails.

7   Conclusions

In this paper, we show that a sender leaves several traits in the structure of an email, resulting from her personal preferences, email client and infrastructure. Based on these traits, we present a detection method that is capable of learning profiles for senders and identifying impersonated emails without relying on its content or server-side implementations. In an empirical evaluation with over 17,000 senders, we demonstrate that this method can identify over 90% of spoofed emails with less than 1 false alarm in 10,000 emails, if the attacker has no knowledge of the sender's profile. If the attacker has access to emails from the same domain as the spoofed sender our method still attains a detection rate of 72% and thus raises the bar for an adversary to effectively complete a spoofing attack. Although our approach cannot detect an attack by an adversary with vast resources, it provides a strong protection from attackers that are not able to obtain original emails from a specific sender. In practice, our approach thus provides a valuable tool for fending off spear-phishing attacks that would go unnoticed without a proper anti-spoofing detection.

A   Appendix

Tables 4, 5 and 6 provide an overview of the different traits characterizing the behavior, composition and transport of emails, respectively.

Table 4. List of behavior features.

Identifier	Cardinality	Description	Examples
attachment-type	n	Type of attachment	`attachment-type(image)`
hdr-empty	n	Headers with empty values	`hdr-empty(cc)`
hdr-local-domain	n	Headers indicating local domains	`hdr-local-domain(to:D0)`
hdr-related-mails	n	Headers indicating relation to other emails	`hdr-related-mails(subject:re)`
hdr-count	n	Number of standard headers and their values	`hdrcount(cc:1:2+)`
hdr-x	n	Occurrences of non-standard headers	`hdr-x(x-virus-scanned)`
msgid	n	Structural description of `Message-Id` header	`msgid(<A.A@H>)`
reply-to	n	Hashed sender in `Reply-To` header	`reply-to(xxx)`
resent	1	Headers indicate redistribution	`resent(1)`
return-path	n	Sender in `Return-Path` header	`return-path(full:same-as-from)`
text-quoted	1	Ratio of quoted total text in main part	`text-quoted(0.3)`
frompart	n	2-grams of `From` field	`frompart(xxx:yyy)`
from	n	Multiple senders in `From` header	`from(full:*)`

Table 5. List of composition features.

Identifier	Cardinality	Description	Examples
base64	n	Peculiarities of Base64 transfer encoding	`base64(linelen(72))`
quoted-printable	n	Peculiarities of Quoted-Printable transfer encoding	`quoted-printable(unencoded-ctrl)`
7bit	n	Peculiarities of 7bit transfer encoding	`7bit(7bit-contains-8bit)`
8bit	n	Peculiarities of 8bit transfer encoding	`8bit(long-line)`
attachment-ext	n	Extension of the attachment	`attachment-ext(doc)`
attachment-mism	n	Mismatch of attachment type and extension	`attachment-mism(doc|zip)`
attachment-sig	1	Signature of how the attachment is specified	`attachment-sig(fTnT)`
inline-ext	n	Extension of attachment when disposition inline	`inline-ext(jpeg)`
nodisposition-ext	n	Extension of attachment if no disposition is given	`nodisposition-ext(jpeg)`
boundary	n	Structural description of the MIME boundary	`boundary(-=_H-H-H)`
hdr-syntax	n	Syntactic format of headers	`hdr-syntax(subject:q:ISO-8859-1)`
hdr-pair	n	Pair-wise order of headers	`hdr-pair(from:date)`
part-hdr-pair	n	Pair-wise order of headers in MIME parts	`part-hdr-pair(content-type:content-id)`
ua	n	Simplified name of user agent	`ua(outlook16)`
preamble	n	Digest of the MIME preamble	`preamble(c928c8bf)`
mime	n	Peculiarities of MIME usage	`mime(cd:inline+filename)`
depth	1	Depth of the MIME structure	`depth(2)`
mime-warning	n	Minor problems in MIME structure	`mime-warning(invalid-content-type)`
mime-error	n	Major problems in MIME structure	`mime-error(paramval-junk)`
part-path	n	Path to MIME parts	`part-path(alt(R).1:html)`
part-size	n	Size of MIME parts	`part-size(html:10:1000)`
part-type	n	Type of MIME parts	`part-type(image:base64)`

Table 6. List of transport features.

Identifier	Cardinality	Description	Examples
dkim	n	Results of DKIM validation	`dkim(1:valid)`, `dkim(2:invalid)`
rcvd	1	Number of `Received` headers	`rccvd(13)`
rcvd-pair	n	Hashes of previous and current `Received` header	`rcvd-pair(xxx:yyy)`
rcvd-mta	n	Hashes of MTA features at given header position	`rcvd-mta(1:XXX)`
rcvd-src	n	Hashes of source features at given header position	`rcvd-src(2:xxx)`
rcvd-tls	n	Hashes of TLS features at given header position	`rcvd-tls(3:xxx)`
rcvd-tocc	n	Occurrences of `To` field in `Received` headers	`rcvd-tocc(to:x1)`
hdrtz	1	Path of time zones from `Received` headers	`hdrtz(-0200:+0800)`
hdrtzcost	1	Cost of transport based on the changes in time zones	`hdrtzcost(6)`
srcip-asn	1	ASN for source IP address of client	`srcip-asn(8881)`
srcip-spf	1	SPF result for source IP address of client	`srcip-spf(spf:Pass)`

References

1. Amin, R.M.: Detecting targeted malicious email through supervised classification of persistent threat and recipient oriented features. Ph.D. thesis, George Washington University, Washington, DC, USA (2010). aAI3428188
2. Beygelzimer, A., Kakade, S., Langford, J.: Cover trees for nearest neighbor. In: International Conference on Machine Learning (ICML), pp. 97–104 (2006)
3. Buildwith technology lookup. https://builtwith.com. Accessed November 2017
4. Callas, J., Donnerhacke, L., Finney, H., Shaw, D., Thayer, R.: OpenPGP Message Format. RFC 4880 (Proposed Standard), November 2007. https://doi.org/10.17487/RFC4880. Updated by RFC 5581

5. Caputo, D.D., Pfleeger, S.L., Freeman, J.D., Johnson, M.E.: Going spear phishing: exploring embedded training and awareness. IEEE Secur. Priv. **12**(1), 28–38 (2014)
6. Chen, P., Desmet, L., Huygens, C.: A study on advanced persistent threats. In: De Decker, B., Zúquete, A. (eds.) CMS 2014. LNCS, vol. 8735, pp. 63–72. Springer, Heidelberg (2014). https://doi.org/10.1007/978-3-662-44885-4_5
7. Crocker, D., Hansen, T., Kucherawy, M.: DomainKeys Identified Mail (DKIM) Signatures. RFC 6376 (Internet Standard), September 2011. https://doi.org/10.17487/RFC6376
8. Lawrence, N.D., Schölkopf, B.: Estimating a kernel fisher discriminant in the presence of label noise. In: ICML, vol. 1, pp. 306–313 (2001)
9. Duda, R., Hart, P.E., Stork, D.G.: Pattern Classification. Wiley, Hoboken (2001)
10. Duman, S., Cakmakci, K.K., Egele, M., Robertson, W., Kirda, E.: EmailProfiler: spearphishing filtering with header and stylometric features of emails. In: COMPSAC (2016)
11. Fan, R.E., Chang, K.W., Hsieh, C.J., Wang, X.R., Lin, C.J.: LIBLINEAR: a library for large linear classification. JMLR **9**, 1871–1874 (2008)
12. Fawcett, T.: An introduction to ROC analysis. Pattern Recogn. Lett. **27**(8), 861–874 (2006)
13. Foster, I.D., Larson, J., Masich, M., Snoeren, A.C., Savage, S., Levchenko, K.: Security by any other name: on the effectiveness of provider based email security. In: Proceedings of the 22nd ACM SIGSAC Conference on Computer and Communications Security, CCS 2015, pp. 450–464. ACM, New York (2015). https://doi.org/10.1145/2810103.2813607
14. Freed, N., Borenstein, N.: Multipurpose Internet Mail Extensions (MIME) Part One: Format of Internet Message Bodies. RFC 2045 (Draft Standard), November 1996. https://doi.org/10.17487/RFC2045. Updated by RFCs 2184, 2231, 5335, 6532
15. Freed, N., Moore, K.: MIME Parameter Value and Encoded Word Extensions: Character Sets, Languages, and Continuations. RFC 2231 (Proposed Standard), November 1997. https://doi.org/10.17487/RFC2231
16. Gupta, S., Singhal, A., Kapoor, A.: A literature survey on social engineering attacks: phishing attack. In: 2016 International Conference on Computing, Communication and Automation (ICCCA), pp. 537–540. IEEE (2016)
17. Han, F., Shen, Y.: Accurate spear phishing campaign attribution and early detection. In: SAC, pp. 2079–2086 (2016)
18. Hardy, S., et al.: Targeted threat index: characterizing and quantifying politically-motivated targeted malware. In: USENIX Security, pp. 527–541 (2014)
19. Ho, G., et al.: Detecting credential spearphishing attacks in enterprise settings. In: USENIX Security Symposium (2017)
20. Trend Micro Incorporated: Spear-Phishing Email: Most Favored APT Attack Bait. Technical report, Trend Micro Inc. (2012)
21. Joachims, T.: Text categorization with support vector machines: learning with many relevant features. Technical report 23, LS VIII, University of Dortmund (1997)
22. Joachims, T.: Learning to Classify Text Using Support Vector Machines: Methods, Theory and Algorithms. Kluwer Academic Publishers (2002)
23. Josefsson, S.: The Base16, Base32, and Base64 Data Encodings. RFC 4648 (Proposed Standard), October 2006. https://doi.org/10.17487/RFC4648
24. Kitterman, S.: Sender Policy Framework (SPF) for Authorizing Use of Domains in Email, Version 1. RFC 7208 (Proposed Standard), April 2014. https://doi.org/10.17487/RFC7208. Updated by RFC 7372

25. Kucherawy, M., Zwicky, E.: Domain-based Message Authentication, Reporting, and Conformance (DMARC). RFC 7489 (Informational), March 2015. https://doi.org/10.17487/RFC7489

26. Le Blond, S., Uritesc, A., Gilbert, C.: A look at targeted attacks through the lense of an NGO. In: USENIX Security, pp. 543–558 (2014)

27. Lin, E., Aycock, J., Mannan, M.: Lightweight client-side methods for detecting email forgery. In: Lee, D.H., Yung, M. (eds.) WISA 2012. LNCS, vol. 7690, pp. 254–269. Springer, Heidelberg (2012). https://doi.org/10.1007/978-3-642-35416-8_18

28. Mori, T., Sato, K., Takahashi, Y., Ishibashi, K.: How is e-mail sender authentication used and misused? In: Proceedings of the 8th Annual Collaboration, Electronic Messaging, Anti-Abuse and Spam Conference, CEAS 2011, pp. 31–37. ACM, New York (2011). https://doi.org/10.1145/2030376.2030380

29. Ramsdell, B., Turner, S.: Secure/Multipurpose Internet Mail Extensions (S/MIME) Version 3.2 Message Specification. RFC 5751 (Proposed Standard), January 2010. https://doi.org/10.17487/RFC5751

30. Resnick, P.: Internet Message Format. RFC 5322 (Draft Standard), October 2008. https://doi.org/10.17487/RFC5322. Updated by RFC 6854

31. Rieck, K., Wressnegger, C., Bikadorov, A.: Sally: a tool for embedding strings in vector spaces. J. Mach. Learn. Res. (JMLR) **13**(Nov), 3247–3251 (2012)

32. Salton, G., Wong, A., Yang, C.: A vector space model for automatic indexing. Commun. ACM **18**(11), 613–620 (1975)

33. Stringhini, G., Thonnard, O.: That ain't you: blocking spearphishing through behavioral modelling. In: Almgren, M., Gulisano, V., Maggi, F. (eds.) DIMVA 2015. LNCS, vol. 9148, pp. 78–97. Springer, Cham (2015). https://doi.org/10.1007/978-3-319-20550-2_5

34. Wang, J., Herath, T., Chen, R., Vishwanath, A., Rao, H.R.: Research article phishing susceptibility: an investigation into the processing of a targeted spear phishing email. IEEE Trans. Prof. Commun. **55**(4), 345–362 (2012)

Backdoors: Definition, Deniability and Detection

Sam L. Thomas[1,2(✉)] and Aurélien Francillon[3]

[1] Univ Rennes, CNRS, IRISA, Rennes, France
`m+research@kali.ai`
[2] University of Birmingham, Birmingham, UK
[3] EURECOM, Biot, France
`aurelien.francillon@eurecom.fr`

Abstract. Detecting backdoors is a difficult task; automating that detection process is equally challenging. Evidence for these claims lie in both the lack of automated tooling, and the fact that the vast majority of real-world backdoors are still detected by labourious manual analysis. The term backdoor, casually used in both the literature and the media, does not have a concrete or rigorous definition. In this work we provide such a definition. Further, we present a framework for reasoning about backdoors through four key components, which allows them to be modelled succinctly and provides a means of rigorously defining the process of their detection. Moreover, we introduce the notion of deniability in regard to backdoor implementations which permits reasoning about the attribution and accountability of backdoor implementers. We show our framework is able to model eleven, diverse, real-world backdoors, and one, more complex backdoor from the literature, and, in doing so, provides a means to reason about how they can be detected and their deniability. Further, we demonstrate how our framework can be used to decompose backdoor detection methodologies, which serves as a basis for developing future backdoor detection tools, and shows how current state-of-the-art approaches consider neither a sound nor complete model.

Keywords: Backdoors · Formalisation of definitions
Program analysis

1 Introduction

The potential presence of backdoors is a major problem in deploying software and hardware from third-parties. Recent studies and research has shown that not only powerful adversaries [3], but consumer device manufacturers [2,5] have inserted deliberate flaws in systems that act as backdoors for attackers with knowledge of those flaws. Unlike the exploitation of traditional vulnerabilities whereby a *weird*, unintended program state is reached, backdoors also manifest

---

This article is based upon work supported by COST Action IC1403 (CRYPTACUS).

M. Bailey et al. (Eds.): RAID 2018, LNCS 11050, pp. 92–113, 2018.
https://doi.org/10.1007/978-3-030-00470-5_5

as explicit, intentional, essentially *normal* program functionality – making their detection significantly more challenging.

Many backdoors are considered by their manufacturers to be accidental, left-over "debug" functionality, or ways to implement software configuration updates without explicit user authorisation [5]. In other cases, device manufacturers deploy firmware coupled with third-party software that introduces backdoor functionality into their otherwise backdoor free systems without their knowledge [9].

The term "backdoor" is generally understood as something that intentionally compromises a platform, aside from this, however, there has been little effort to give a definition that is more rigorous. To give such a definition is difficult as backdoors can take many forms, and can compromise a platform by almost any means; e.g., a hardware component, a dedicated program or a malicious program fragment. This lack of a rigorous definition prohibits reasoning about backdoors in a generalised way that is a premise to developing methods to detect them. Further hampering that reasoning – especially in the case of backdoors of a more complex, or esoteric nature – is the sheer lack of real-world samples. Documented real-world backdoors are generally simplistic, where their trigger conditions rely upon a user inputting certain static data, e.g., hard-coded credentials. Such backdoors have been studied in the literature with various tools providing solutions relying on varying degrees of user interaction [19,21].

2 Overview

This work provides first and foremost a much needed rigorous definition of the term backdoor: which we view as an intentional construct inserted into a system, known to the system's implementer, unknown to its end-user, that serves to compromise its perceived security. We propose a framework to decompose and componentise the abstract notion of such a backdoor, which serves as a means to both identify backdoor-like constructs, and reason about their detection. While the primary focus of this work is software-based backdoors, by modelling a backdoor abstractly, our framework is able to handle all types of backdoor-like constructs, irrespective of their implementation target.

Many backdoors found in the real-world fall into a grey area as to whom is accountable for their presence; to address this, we define the notion of deniability. We model deniability by considering different views of a system: that of the implementer, the actual system, and the end-user; this allows us to – depending on where backdoor-like functionality has been introduced – reason about if that functionality is a deniable backdoor, accidental vulnerability, or intentional backdoor. In many cases, attempting to model this intention, or the lack thereof, is something that is social or political, thus we do not address such cases in this work, instead we focus on the technical aspects of a backdoor-like functionality.

We show that under our definitions, many backdoors publicly identified are not deniable and thus, their manufacturers should be held accountable for their presence. Aside from manual analysis, little work has been performed to address the detection of backdoors. We perform a study of both academic and real-world backdoors and consider existing methods that can be used to locate backdoor components, as well as how those methods can be improved.

2.1   Contributions

To summarise, the contributions of this work are as follows:

1. We provide a rigorous definition for the term backdoor and the process of backdoor detection.
2. We provide a framework for decomposition of backdoor-like functionality, which serves as a basis for their identification, and reasoning about their detection.
3. We express the notion of deniable backdoors by considering different views of a system: the developer's perspective, the actual system, the end-user, and a user analysing the system.
4. We show examples of both academic and real-world backdoors expressed in terms of our definitions and reason about their deniability and detectability.
5. We demonstrate how our framework can be used to reason about backdoor detection methodologies, which we use to show that current state-of-the-art tools do not consider a complete model of what a backdoor is, and as a result, we are able identify limitations in their respective approaches.

2.2   Related Work

Coverage of complex backdoors is scarce in the academic literature. Tan et al. [20] encode backdoor code fragments using specially-crafted interrupt handlers, which, when triggered, manipulate run-time state, and when chained together, can perform arbitrary computations in a stealthy manner. Andriesse et al. [14] use a cleverly disguised memory corruption bug to act as a backdoor trigger and embed misaligned code sequences into the target executable to act as a payload. Zaddach et al. [24] describe the design and implementation of a hard-drive firmware backdoor, which enables surreptitious recovery of data written to the disk. More complex backdoors have been documented outside of the literature, e.g., those classified as "NOBUS" (i.e., NObody But US) vulnerabilites by the NSA [7], and those associated with APT actors (e.g., [8]).

A related area, that of so-called *weird machines*, describes how an alternative programming model that facilitates latent computation can arise within a program, or system. Both [16] and [18] present such models, as well as how *normal* systems can be forced to execute programs written in those models. In both cases, those models provide a means to implement backdoor-like functionality. Dullien [15] addresses the problem of formalising the term *weird machine*, the relationship between exploitation and *weird machines*, and introduces the concept of provable exploitability. He argues that it is possible to model a program, or system using a so-called Intended Finite-State Machine (IFSM), and in doing so, view a piece of software as an emulator for a specific IFSM. Further, he demonstrates that it is possible to create security games to reason about the security properties of a system by reasoning about it at the level of the states and transitions of its IFSM. His model serves as inspiration for this work.

Zhang et al. [25] explore the notion of backdoor detection and give a first informal definition of the term backdoor. They define a backdoor as "a mechanism surreptitiously introduced into a computer system to facilitate unauthorised access to the system", which while largely agreeing with the current usage of the term, is very high-level and says nothing about the composition of such constructs. Wysopal et al. [23] propose a taxonomy for backdoors. They state that there are three major types of backdoor: system backdoors, which involve either a single dedicated process which compromises a system, cryptographic backdoors, which compromise cryptographic algorithms, and application backdoors, which they state are versions of legitimate software modified to bypass security mechanisms under certain conditions. The authors also provide strategies for manual detection of specific types of application backdoor within source code.

Current (semi-)automated backdoor detection methods rely on detecting specific functionality that is associated with triggering backdoor behaviour. Firmalice [19], is a tool developed to detect backdoors within embedded device firmware. The authors propose a model for a class of backdoors they coin *authentication bypass vulnerabilities*. They define the notion of a security policy, which denotes a state that a binary reaches that signifies it is in a privileged state. Firmalice detects if it is possible to violate that security policy (i.e., find a path to a privileged state, without passing standard authentication). HumIDIFy [22] uses a combination of machine learning and targeted static analysis to identify anomalous and unexpected behaviour in services commonly found in Linux-based embedded device firmware. Meanwhile, Stringer [21] attempts to locate comparisons with static data that lead to *unique* program functionality; that is, functionality that can only be executed by a successful comparison with that static data. This models the situation of a backdoor trigger providing access to undocumented functionality. Schuster et al. [17] address the problem of backdoor detection in binaries through the use of dynamic analysis. Using a prototype implementation of their approach, they are able to identify a number of "artificial" and previously identified backdoors.

3   Nomenclature and Preliminaries

In this section we outline terms used in the remainder of this article. A *platform* represents the highest level of abstraction of a device that a given backdoor targets. We define a *system* as the highest level of abstraction required to model a given backdoor, within a *platform*. Since a backdoor can be implemented at any level of abstraction of a *platform* it is designed to compromise – for example, as a dedicated program, a hardware component, or embedded as part of another program – we abstract away from such details. To do this, we model an abstract *system* as a finite state machine (FSM).

When considering a backdoor, there are two perspectives to consider a *system* from: that of the entity that implements a backdoor, and that of the end-user, e.g., a general consumer, or a security consultant analysing the *platform*. To model this situation, we consider four versions of the FSM; for any given *system*, the *Developer* FSM (DFSM) refers to the developer's view of the system, the *Actual* FSM (AFSM) refers to the FSM that models a real manifestation of the system, i.e., a program, the *Expected* FSM (EFSM) refers to the end-user's expectations of the *system*, and finally, the *Reverse-engineered* FSM (RFSM), represents a refinement of the EFSM obtained by reverse-engineering the *actual* system; it can include states and transitions not present within the DFSM or AFSM, e.g., in the case of bug-based backdoors, which we address in Sect. 4.

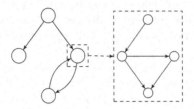

Fig. 1. Multi-layered *system* FSM.

Each state of the FSM describing a *system* can be viewed as an abstraction of a particular functionality – which, in turn can be modelled using a FSM. Thus, we view an entire *system* as a collection of sub-systems, which can be visualised in a layered manner – with each layer representing a view of a part of the *system* at an increasing level detail, as in Fig. 1.

For example, if a given backdoor compromises a router, then we refer to the router as the *platform*. If the backdoor is implemented in software, as a dedicated program, we would view the highest level of abstraction, i.e., the *system*, as the interactions between the processes of the operating system, modelled as a FSM. Each individual running program, or process, can then be modelled by arbitrary levels of FSMs.

3.1 Analysis and Formalisation of FSMs

We specify a FSM as a quintuple: $\theta = (S, i, F, \Sigma, \delta)$, where: S is the set of its states, i is its initial state, F is the set of its final states, Σ is the set of its state transition conditions, e.g., conditional statements that when satisfied cause transitions, and $\delta : S \times \Sigma \to S$ is its transition labelling function, representing its state transitions.

Inspired by the approach taken by Dullien [15], we view the implemented, or *real* system modelled by a FSM as an emulator for the AFSM of the system. Thus, when the user's EFSM and the AFSM are not equivalent, e.g., the user assumes there is no backdoor present, when there is, specific interactions with the real system will yield unexpected behaviour. How this unexpected behaviour manifests is what determines if that unexpected behaviour means that the system contains a backdoor. Different users of the system will assume different EFSMs. In order to analyse a system, a program analyst, for example, will derive a RFSM – which, for notational ease we refer to as θ_R – by reverse-engineering the *real* system; they do this by making perceptions and observations of its concrete implementation, i.e., the emulator for θ_A. What the analyst will observe is a set of states and state transitions, which are a subset of all those possible within the *platform*, e.g., CPU states. To analyse these states and derive θ_R, the analyst will require a means to map concrete states and transitions of the *platform*, to the level of abstraction modelled by the states and transitions of their FSM. To perform analysis, we assume that an analyst has the following capabilities:

1. They have access to the emulator for the actual FSM (θ_A) – in the case of software, this would be the program binary.
2. They are able to perform static analysis upon the emulator, i.e., using a tool such as IDA Pro, and hence *perceive* a set of system states and state transitions between those states of the real system.
3. They are able to perform dynamic analysis of the system, i.e., with a debugger, and hence *observe* a set of system states and transitions of the real system.

The perceptions and observations of the analyst, along with a means to map concrete states and transitions to abstract FSM states and transitions, allows them to construct a RFSM (θ_R) from the emulator for a AFSM. The granularity of the RFSM will be dependent upon how a system is analysed, e.g., a tool such as IDA Pro will capture components as groups of basic blocks, while components identified in source-code can be represented with a higher-level of abstraction.

3.2 Backdoor Definition

The implementation strategies of backdoor implementers varies widely, therefore, we consider the notion of an abstract backdoor, which we decompose into components. In order to do this, we attempt to answer a number of questions: what is it that makes a set of functionalities, when interacting together manifest as a backdoor? What abstract component parts can be found in all such backdoors? To what extent do we need to abstract to identify all such components?

A distinguishing feature of all backdoors is that they must be triggered. Thus, a pivotal component of any backdoor is its *trigger* mechanism. However, this *trigger* mechanism alone does not constitute a backdoor: what causes it to become active? Another component is needed to account for the satisfaction of the *trigger* condition: i.e., a type of *input source*. Upon *trigger* activation an eventual system state is reached that can be considered the *backdoor-activated* state, which is essentially a state of escalated privileges, privilege abuse or unauthenticated access, i.e., a *privileged state*. To reach this final state, an intermediate component that facilitates the transition from the *normal* system state upon satisfaction of the backdoor *trigger* to the *backdoor-activated* state is required: we refer to this as the backdoor *payload*. Through this reasoning, we show there are four key components that must be present to fully capture the notion of a backdoor. These components are chosen as the minimum set of components required for a backdoor to exist within a system; without the presence of any one of these components the backdoor would not be functional. Using this componentisation, we are able to define a backdoor.

Definition 1 Backdoor. An *intentional* construct contained within a system that serves to compromise its expected security by facilitating access to otherwise privileged functionality or information. Its implementation is identifiable by its decomposition into four components: *input source, trigger, payload*, and *privileged state*, and the intention of that implementation is reflected in its complete or partial (e.g., in the case of bug-based backdoors) presence within the DFSM and AFSM, but not the EFSM of the system containing it.

3.3 Backdoor Detection

Using Definition 1 as a basis, a backdoor can be modelled as two related FSMs: $\theta_{trigger}$, which represents the *trigger* without a state transition to the *payload*, and $\theta_{payload}$, which represents the *payload* and $F_{payload}$, the set of possible *privileged states*.

Definition 2 Backdoor Detection. A backdoor is detected by obtaining:

$$\theta_R = (S_R, i_R, F_R, \Sigma_R, \delta_R)$$

Within θ_R, the states and transitions of both the *trigger* and *payload* must exist:

$$\Sigma_{trigger} \cup \Sigma_{payload} \subseteq \Sigma_R$$
$$\forall s \in S_{trigger}, \forall \sigma \in \Sigma_{trigger} . \ \delta_{trigger}(s, \sigma) \neq \bot \Rightarrow \delta_R(s, \sigma) = \delta_{trigger}(s, \sigma)$$
$$\forall s \in S_{payload}, \forall \sigma \in \Sigma_{payload} . \ \delta_{payload}(s, \sigma) \neq \bot \Rightarrow \delta_R(s, \sigma) = \delta_{payload}(s, \sigma)$$

The *privileged states* reachable as a result of the *payload* are either final states of θ_R, or states that can be transitioned from to some state of θ_R:

$$S_{trigger} \cup S_{payload} \subseteq S_R$$
$$\forall f \in F_{payload} . \ f \in F_R \vee (f \notin F_R \Rightarrow \exists \sigma \in \Sigma_R . \ \delta_R(f, \sigma) \in S_R)$$

The *payload* must be reachable from the *trigger*, and there must exist a transition to the *trigger* within θ_R:

$$\forall f \in F_{trigger} . \ \exists \sigma \in \Sigma_{trigger} . \ \delta_R(f, \sigma) = i_{payload}$$
$$\exists s \in S_R, \exists \sigma \in \Sigma_R . \ \delta_R(s, \sigma) = i_{trigger}$$

4 A Framework for Modelling Backdoors

In this section we detail a framework for decomposing a backdoor into the four components defined in Sect. 3.2; we exhaustively enumerate the types of these components which allows us to both identify and reason about them.

In addition to locating a construct consisting of an *input source, trigger, payload*, and *privileged state*, to detect a backdoor, an analyst must demonstrate that the construct would be part of the DFSM of the system. For open-source software, this could be done by analysing the source code version control logs, or in closed-source software, analysing the differences between software versions. In other cases, where such analysis is not possible, the following framework can additionally serve as a basis for reasoning about how a backdoor's components can indicate an implementer's intent.

In the proceeding framework, we refer to the RFSM of an end-user that has analysed a particular *system*. Initially, that user will expect functionality that can be modelled by one FSM (their EFSM), and through their analysis they will learn, or derive another FSM (RFSM) that matches what they have learnt about the *system*. Therefore, to discover a backdoor through analysis of the emulator for the AFSM, the RFSM (post-analysis) will contain a backdoor, if there is one present in the AFSM, and they are able to identify it.

During the analysis process, new states and state transitions will be added to the RFSM. We divide these states and state transitions into two categories: those that are explicit, which we say are *discovered* (and always exist within the AFSM) and those that are not explicit, which we say are *created* (and may not exist within the AFSM). To serve this distinction with an example, suppose we have a RFSM that models a program. The explicit states and state transitions that are added to it through analysis are those that represent basic blocks and branches that are *explicitly* part of the program's code (and will always be part of the DFSM and AFSM). Those that are added that are not explicit are in a sense *weird* states and state transitions, which might, for example, be the states representing some shellcode.

4.1   Input Source

If we model the satisfaction of a backdoor *trigger* as a function – `is_triggered` – as in the state machine diagram in Fig. 2, then we can view it as a function that takes at least one parameter (implicit or otherwise) – an *input source* – which is used to decide which state transition that is made as a result of executing that function.

Fig. 2. Idealised backdoor trigger.

The value yielded by the *input source* may be derived from any number of inputs to the FSM: it could be a string input by the attacker wishing to activate the backdoor *trigger*, or it could be the value of the system clock such that during a specific time period the backdoor *trigger* becomes active. For this reason we choose to abstract away from the exact implementation details and use the term *"input source"* to represent this component of the backdoor. Note that the *input source* is not the value that causes the activation of the backdoor *trigger*, but rather describes the origin of that input: e.g., a socket or standard input.

4.2   Trigger Mechanism

The backdoor *trigger*, under the correct conditions, will cause the execution of the backdoor *payload*, which will subsequently elevate the privileges of the attacker. We model the backdoor *trigger* as a boolean function where its positive outcome, i.e., when it outputs *true*, will cause a state transition to the backdoor *payload*. The way the FSM transitions to the *payload* as a result of the satisfaction of the *trigger* conditions can be modelled exhaustively with two cases:

1. The state transition is explicit, hence will always exist within the backdoor implementer's DFSM. The backdoor *trigger* is added to the RFSM by adding the explicit states and transitions related to satisfying the backdoor *trigger* conditions, and adding one or more transitions to the *payload*, where those transitions are *discovered* (not newly created) as part of the analysis.
2. The state transition is not explicit. The *trigger* is added to the RFSM by adding explicit states and state transitions related to satisfying the backdoor *trigger* conditions, and by *adding* one or more state transitions that transition to the *payload*, where those transitions are newly created as part of the analysis, i.e., they are not explicit.

To visualise these cases, we use concrete examples in which we use a *system* that is a single program, where the backdoor is embedded as part of the program.

In the first case, we view a *trigger* that is obvious and explicit, where the backdoor is encoded within a single function of the program. This case is shown in Fig. 2. The backdoor *trigger* is comprised of the single state required to satisfy the backdoor *trigger* conditions, i.e., the one labelled is_triggered(...), and the state transition to the *Activated* state. In a more realistic scenario, the backdoor *trigger* mechanism may require satisfaction of multiple branch conditions and/or execution of multiple basic blocks and might be obfuscated. Irrespective of these implementation details, the core concept is the same: the collection of checks can be viewed as a single function, whose outcome is used to decide if the backdoor *payload* is transitioned to and hence executed or not, where the transition – a CFG edge in this example – is explicitly part of the FSM.

While the first case considers conditions that are satisfied within a *valid* function CFG, and a transition to the *payload* which is contained entirely within that same *valid* CFG, and thus constitutes *normal* control-flow, the second case of backdoor *trigger* manifests as *abnormal* control-flow. Within a program, we can think of such a construct as akin to a program bug that allows control-flow hijacking. One can conjecture a simple case for this being, a buffer overflow vulnerability, that when exploited correctly, causes a program to transition to a backdoor *payload*, shown in Fig. 3.

```
bool vulnerable_auth_check(
  const char *user, const char *pass) {
  char buf[80], hash[32];

  strcpy(buf, user); strcat(buf, pass);
  create_user_pass_hash(hash, buf);

  return check_valid_hash(hash);
}
```

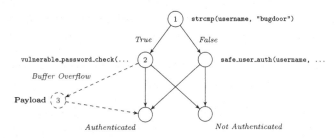

Fig. 3. Bug-based backdoor *trigger*.

Fig. 4. Hybrid bug-based backdoor *trigger*.

Alongside these basic cases, a more complex example of a backdoor *trigger* would be one that relies both on explicit checks and a bug, as visualised in Fig. 4. In this case, a hard-coded credential check against a specific username (`bugdoor`) is used to *guard* access to a vulnerable password check (`vulnerable_password_check`). A username other than `bugdoor` will cause the standard authentication routine (`safe_user_auth`) to be executed, and only a password with a long enough length (and specific content) will lead to the execution of the backdoor *payload*. In this example, the backdoor *trigger* is comprised of the explicit states 1 and 2, and the non-explicit state transition between states 2 and 3, i.e., the *payload* state.

Note that to make the case that all vulnerabilities are backdoor *trigger* mechanisms is a false oversimplification, as such a simplification does not differentiate between accidental and intentional program bugs. We discuss the difficulties present when reasoning about backdoors that are bug-based in Sect. 5.

4.3   Payload

A backdoor *payload* can be viewed as the solution to a puzzle: i.e., how to reach a *privileged state* from successfully satisfying the conditions of a *backdoor trigger*. In our model, we represent this by the state transition taken in order to reach a *privileged state*, and any additional states and state transitions that perform prerequisite computation following activation of backdoor *trigger*. In practice, a *payload* component can take many forms, however we can exhaustively categorise all types of *payload* by how they are modelled as part of a RFSM, and how they are transitioned to:

1. The transition to the *payload* is explicit, and does not permit the creation of new states and state transitions (Fig. 5). The *payload* is added to the RFSM by adding explicit states and transitions required to reach a *privileged state*, where those states and transitions are *discovered* by analysis (explicit). They will be contained in the backdoor implementer's DFSM.
2. The transition to the *payload* is explicit, but state(s) reachable due to this transition permit the creation of new states and transitions, e.g., a system that contains an intentional interpreter which can be accessed via a backdoor (Fig. 6). The *payload* is added to the RFSM by adding *discovered* (explicit) states and transitions – which exist in the backdoor implementer's DFSM – from which both newly *created* (non-explicit) and *discovered* (explicit) states and transitions can be reached, which facilitate the eventual transition to a *privileged state*. The non-explicit states and transitions added will not exist within the backdoor implementer's DFSM.
3. The transition to the *payload* is not explicit (bug-based), and the *payload's* states and transitions will either be explicit or non-explicit, e.g., a ROP-based construct. The *payload* is added to the RFSM by adding both newly *created* (non-explicit) and *discovered* (explicit) states and transitions, which facilitate the transition to a *privileged state*. The non-explicit states and transitions added will not exist within the backdoor implementer's DFSM.

4.3.1   Payload Examples

To give concrete examples of the variants of backdoor *payload*, we once again demonstrate backdoors that are implemented within programs.

```
/* Trigger; if active then: (1) -> (2) */
if (strcmp(user._name, "backdoor") == 0) {
    /* Payload */
    user._is_admin = true;   // (2)

    /* Transition to privileged state */
    open_shell(&user); // (3) -> (4)
}
```

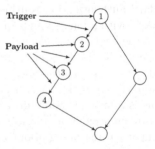

Fig. 5. Explicit transition to *payload*, where *payload* has explicit components.

Explicit Transition to Payload with Explicit Payload Components. This class of *payload* (case 1 above) is inherently an intentional construct and requires no abnormal control flow for it to be executed. An example of a backdoor with such *payload* is shown in Fig. 5. The backdoor *trigger* condition (state 1) is a hard-coded credential check, which if satisfied, will transition to the backdoor *payload* (transition from state 1 to 2). In the *payload*, the backdoor user's permissions are first elevated (state 2) and then a shell is opened for that user (state 3), which allows them to transition to the *privileged state* (state 4).

```
/* Trigger; if active then: (1) -> (2) */
if (strcmp(req._path, "/BKDRLDR") == 0) {
    /* Payload; req._data == payload input */
    run(&req._data); // (2) -> (3)
}
```

Fig. 6. Explicit transition to *payload* with both explicit and non-explicit components.

Explicit Transition to Payload with Explicit and Non-explicit Payload Components. In this case (case 2 above), we model a backdoor that enables an attacker to perform computation not part of the developer's DFSM, without being in a state that is bug-induced. An example of such a backdoor is shown in Fig. 6; if the backdoor *trigger* is satisfied, the program will interpret and execute an input supplied by the user of the backdoor. The *trigger* condition is a check to see if a user is requesting access to a specific path (state 1), if it is, then the *payload* is transitioned to (state 1 to 2), where the data sent with the request (`req._data`) is used as input to an interpreter (state 2, via `run`). In this case, the *privileged state* (state 3) transitioned to is dynamically constructed as a result of the input to the interpreter executed in state 2.

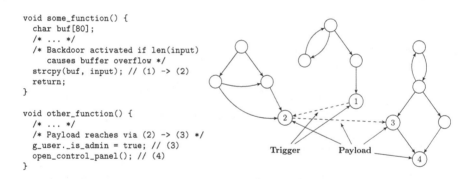

```
void some_function() {
    char buf[80];
    /* ... */
    /* Backdoor activated if len(input)
       causes buffer overflow */
    strcpy(buf, input); // (1) -> (2)
    return;
}

void other_function() {
    /* ... */
    /* Payload reaches via (2) -> (3) */
    g_user._is_admin = true; // (3)
    open_control_panel(); // (4)
}
```

Fig. 7. Non-explicit transition to *payload*, where *payload* has both explicit and non-explicit components.

Non-explicit Transition to Payload with Explicit and Non-explicit Payload Components. In the final case (case 3 above), we model backdoors that have a *trigger* mechanism that is bug-based, i.e., allows an attacker to perform computation not part of the developer's DFSM. We visualise such a case in Fig. 7; here the *trigger* consists of an *intentional* buffer overflow bug in `some_function` (state 1), which if exploited – in this case with a ROP-based *payload* – transitions (via 1 to 2) to the *payload*. The *payload* consists of states 2 and 3, and the transitions from states 2 to 3, and 3 to 4. As a result of the *payload*, the user is granted administrative privileges (state 3), and entered into a (privileged) control panel via open_control_panel in other_function (state 4).

```
if (strcmp(password, "_BACKDOOR_") == 0 \
   || is_valid_password(password)) {
  // Authenticated
} else {
  // Not authenticated
}
```

Fig. 8. A backdoor *payload* composed solely of a state transition.

Single Transition Payloads. We note there is a special case for both cases 1 and 3, namely, where the *payload* is composed of only a single state transition. That is, no additional computation is undertaken as part of the *payload*, rather the *payload* shares its state transition with the backdoor *trigger*, as shown in Fig. 8. This special case accounts for situations where the backdoor *trigger* acts like a trapdoor (state 1), allowing an attacker to bypass a (potentially) more complex check for user-authentication, and rather provides a direct transition to a *privileged state* (the transition from state 1 to 2). The form of the *payload* is identical for cases 1 and 3, other than the explicitness of the state transition (the *payload*) between the *trigger* and the *privileged state*.

4.3.2 Payload Obfuscation

So far, we have not considered how a backdoor implementer might hide a backdoor's presence – other than by using a bug-based *trigger* mechanism. While such a trigger is simple to implement, it offers the implementer no control over how the backdoor will eventually be used; this control can be regained, by for example, limiting the computational freedom of newly created states. In this section we explore how a backdoor implementer can obfuscate *payload* components.

Since backdoor *payloads* that contain only explicit states and state transitions are obvious and thus, intentional constructs, an obfuscated *payload* by nature must be implemented through the use of some degree of abnormal control flow, i.e., non-explicit states and state transitions. An example of such a *payload* is one *derived* by reusing components of the system it is implemented within to obscure its execution, e.g., for a program, from static analysis methods. From an attacker's perspective, the only way to execute such a backdoor is either to have prior knowledge of the *payload*, or *solve a puzzle* and derive it from the original system. Andriesse et al. [14] describe such a backdoor (examined in further detail in Sect. 6), whereby its *payload* component is composed of multiple code fragments embedded and distributed throughout a binary which execute in sequence upon the backdoor being triggered. Figure 7 shows a naïve example such a *payload*.

Another example is that where a *payload* can be derived from attacker controlled data. In the simplest case, this is akin to shellcode often executed as

a result of successful exploitation of a buffer overflow vulnerability: it shares
a commonality that it doesn't rely upon any existing program components. In
more sophisticated cases, such a backdoor *payload* might take a hybrid approach:
where either user-data is interpreted by the program itself, or components of the
program are used alongside the user input. Figure 6 shows a simple example such
a *payload*. In both of these examples, the *payload* components are implemented
in a so-called *weird machine* as defined by Oakley and Bratus [16].

4.4 Privileged State

Following successful activation of the backdoor *trigger* and subsequent transitioning from the associated *payload*, the system will enter into a *privileged state*.
There are two possibilities for this state: either it can be reached under *normal*
system execution, or it can only be reached through activation of the backdoor.
If we consider *privileged states* by how they are added to a RFSM, then one that
is newly created, i.e., is non-explicit, will not be reachable under normal system
execution, meanwhile, one that is explicit, may or may not be reachable under
normal execution: for example, while the *privileged state* might be explicit, the
only way to reach it might be via the backdoor *trigger*.

In the case of a *privileged state* reachable through normal execution, consider
the backdoor presented in Fig. 8, which models a hard-coded credential check.
The *privileged state* (state 2) of the backdoor is both reachable via the backdoor
trigger (from state 1), and the state labelled is_valid_password.

For the other case, where the *privileged state* is not reachable by a *legitimate* user, it is essentially *guarded* by the activation of the backdoor. This case
can further be sub-categorised. The first variant is where the *privileged state* is
explicit, as in Fig. 5; the *privileged state* (state 4) is only reachable through activation of the backdoor *trigger* (state 1 and the transition from state 1 to state
2). In this example, the *privileged state* manifests as an undocumented *backdoor*
shell, where after entering a specific username, the attacker is able to perform
additional functionality, not otherwise possible. The other variant is a *privileged
state* that provides an attacker access to functionality that is not available to
a *legitimate* user, where that functionality does not explicitly exist within the
system – as shown in Fig. 6. Here the *privileged state* (state 3) is some function
of attacker input, i.e., the result of run(&req._data).

5 Practical Detection and Deniability

Backdoor detection in practice will happen through, e.g., manually reverse-
engineering a program binary or observing a backdoor's usage through suspicious system events, such as anomalous network traffic. As is, our proposed
framework oversimplifies as it doesn't model intention. If we knew that a particular vulnerability was placed *intentionally*, then there would be no question
that the vulnerability was placed deliberately to act as a backdoor. Thus, in this
section we answer the question: if we have identified a backdoor-like construct,

can we distinguish it from an accidental vulnerability, and if so, how deniable is it?

In order to make such a distinction, recall that we can view a system from four perspectives: its DFSM, AFSM, EFSM, and RFSM. If a backdoor-like construct has been identified, then it will be present in both the emulator for the AFSM and the RFSM. To state that the construct is a backdoor – and was placed intentionally – we must show that it, or some part of it was present within the DFSM. In some cases, the intent is explicit and hard-coded in the implementation – i.e., it leaves no ambiguity. The most obvious example of this is a hard-coded credential check which serves to bypass standard authentication. Indeed, all cases of backdoor that transition explicitly, i.e., discoverable by analysis, from the satisfaction of their *trigger* conditions to their *payload* can be considered intentional.

In the other case, where that transition is non-explicit, i.e., bug-based, various approaches can be taken. For instance, in the case of software, where version control logs are available, it is possible to identify the exact point where a backdoor has been inserted as well as its author (e.g., the failed attempt to backdoor the Linux kernel in 2003 [1]). For binary-only software, where there exists multiple versions of that software, it is possible to identify the version the backdoor was introduced in, and reason about its presence by asking the question *was there a legitimate reason for making such a change to the software?* Further, we can consider the explicitness of the backdoor components: for example, if a code fragment exists within a binary that does nothing more than facilitate privilege escalation, and it is unreachable by normal program control-flow, then there is an indication of intent. A similar case can be made if the satisfaction of the *trigger* conditions rely on checks discoverable by analysis, as well as a bug. Unfortunately, all of these approaches have non-technical aspects and rely on human intuition – thus, do not provide a concrete proof of intent. We are therefore left with three possible ways to classify backdoor-like constructs:

Definition 3 *Intentional backdoor.* Those constructs that can be unambiguously identified as backdoors: the transition from their *trigger* satisfaction to their *payload* is explicit. Will be present in the DFSM, AFSM, and if found, the RFSM, but not the EFSM.

Definition 4 *Deniable backdoor.* Those constructs that fall into a grey area, where the transition from their *trigger* satisfaction to their *payload* is non-explicit (i.e., it appears to be a bug), but from a non-technical perspective can be argued to be intentional. Will be present in the AFSM, if found, the RFSM, but not the EFSM; we cannot definitively tell if it is in the DFSM.

Definition 5 *Accidental vulnerability.* Those constructs where there is no evidence – technical, or otherwise – to suggest any intent, and the transition from their *trigger* satisfaction to their *payload* is non-explicit. Will be present in the AFSM, and if found, the RFSM, but not the DFSM or EFSM.

From a purely technical perspective, a *deniable* backdoor will be indistinguishable from an *accidental* vulnerability. Consider, for example, a simple buffer overflow vulnerability and its corresponding exploit. If this vulnerability was deliberately placed then it is a backdoor, otherwise it is just a vulnerability coupled with an exploit. As we do not know anything about the implementer's intention we cannot discern between the two. Thus, a vulnerability can be seen as an unintentional way to add new state transitions, or states to a system's FSM, while an exploit is a set of states and state transitions such that when combined with a vulnerability within a given FSM, provides a means to compromise the believed security of the system modelled by that FSM. In contrast to backdoors and vulnerabilities, a construct providing standard privileged access will be intentional and manifest within the DFSM, AFSM, EFSM, and RFSM of a system.

6 Discussion and Case-Studies

In order to demonstrate our framework, we provide a number of case studies. We show examples from both the literature and real-world backdoors, which have been detected manually. For each backdoor, we reason about if and why its implementation can be considered deniable in respect to our definitions and analyse it by performing a complete decomposition of its implementation using our framework. Finally, we provide a discussion of how our framework can be used to reason about methods for detecting backdoors.

Table 1 shows eleven real-world backdoors, each decomposed using our framework. As each backdoor can be modelled with explicit states and state transitions, by Definition 3, none are deniable, thus, their implementers should be held accountable. The remainder of this section provides case-study of a complex, deniable (by Definition 4) backdoor.

Nginx Bug-Based Backdoor. Andriesse and Bos [14] describe a general method for embedding a backdoor within a program binary. Their technique utilises a backdoor *trigger* based upon an intentional program bug combined with a hard-coded *payload* composed of intentionally misaligned instruction sequence fragments. Their *payload* is, in a sense, obfuscated, yet fixed; its implementation exploits the nature of the x86 instruction set, whereby byte sequences representing instructions can be interpreted differently when accessed at different offsets.

The authors demonstrate their approach by modifying the popular web-server, Nginx, and embedding a remotely exploitable backdoor. In their implementation, a would-be attacker provides a crafted input, which serves to satisfy the backdoor *trigger* conditions; this input is provided as a malformed HTTP packet – the *input source* will therefore be a network socket. Figure 9 provides a code listing adapted from [14] which contains the backdoor *trigger* conditions. Those conditions are: have_err == 1, and err_handler != NULL, which are set as a result of the use of uninitialised variables have_err and err_handler in the ngx_http_finalize_request function, which take the values of badc and hash in ngx_http_parse_header_line. The bug manifests due to the fact the two functions stack frames overlap between their invocations. The intended *payload* states are meant to be those embedded as *weird* states, however additional

Table 1. Real-world backdoors modelled using framework.

Backdoor description	Input source	Trigger	Payload	Privileged State
D-Link router backdoor "Joel's backdoor" [5]; bypass standard authentication by setting a specific user-agent when accessing web-configuration interface.	Network socket	strcmp(ua, "xmlset_roodkcableoj28840ybtide") == 0	Trigger conditions satisfied: explicit transition by matching with user-agent	Authenticated as legitimate user
Tenda router backdoor [2]; additional UDP server embedded within web-server allowing remote command execution.	Network socket; UDP port 7329	Correct packet format: strcmp("w302r mfg", packet->magic) == 0 and packet->command.byte == 'x'	Trigger conditions satisfied; arbitrary command executed via: popen(packet->command, "r")	Dependent upon packet->command payload input
TCP-32764 router backdoor [6]; multiple vendors (Netgear, Cisco, Belkin, ...); remotely accessible undocumented service allows modification of configuration (e.g. device credentials), and command execution.	Network socket; TCP port 32764	Correct packet format: "ScMM" | 7 | cmd_len | cmd	Trigger conditions satisfied (correct packet format with); executes cmd via popen	Dependent upon cmd payload input
Quanta LTE router backdoor [11]; dedicated UDP service "appmgr" if sent specific string enables an unauthenticated root shell via Telnet.	Network socket; UDP port 39889	strcmp("HELODBG", data, 7) == 0	Trigger conditions satisfied: data matches HELODBG; starts Telnet as root using: system("/sbin/telnetd -l /bin/sh")	Shell accessible via TCP port 23
Sony IP camera backdoor [10]; combination of HTTP request with specific values set as parameters and hard-coded HTTP authentication credentials, can start Telnet service on device remotely via web-server.	Network socket; TCP port 80/443	HTTP request to /command/prima-factory.cgi with parameters that satisfy strcmp("cPoq2fi4cFw", param1) == 0 and strcmp("kzw2hEr9", param2) == 0; hard-coded username and password for HTTP authentication: strcmp("primana", username) == 0 and strcmp("primana", password) == 0	Trigger conditions satisfied; performs system("/usr/sbin/inetd") which starts telnetd using configuration in /etc/inetd.conf	Shell accessible via TCP port 23
RaySharp DVR backdoor [21]; hard-coded credentials bypass standard authentication in web-interface.	Network socket; TCP port 80/443	strcmp("root", username) == 0 and strcmp("519070", password) == 0	Trigger conditions satisfied: explicit transition by matching credentials	Authenticated as root/administrative user
Western Digital My Cloud NAS backdoor [13]; setting specific value in (unencrypted) cookie when accessing web-interface allows user to login as administrator.	Network socket; TCP port 80/443	$_COOKIE["isAdmin"] == 1	Trigger conditions satisfied; explicit transition via value being set correctly	Authenticated as administrative user
Q-See DVR backdoor [21]; multiple hard-coded username/password combinations, each combination gives access to additional functionality, as well as bypassing standard authentication.	Network socket/virtual keyboard	strcmp(username, "admin") == 0 and strcmp("6036huanyuan", password) == 0; multiple possible passwords	Explicit transitions and states dependent upon password	Depends on password; authenticated as administrative user with greater privileges – alternate "control-panel"
D-Link router backdoor [4]; execution of arbitrary operating system commands through unauthenticated PHP script.	Network socket; TCP port 80/443	POST request to command.php, with cmd parameter equal to command to run	Trigger conditions satisfied; explicit transition if parameter is set; executes command specified by cmd	Dependent upon payload input
Netis router backdoor [12]; custom network service (igdmptd) protected with a hard-coded password; enables (among other functionality) execution of arbitrary commands.	Network socket; TCP port 53413	Authenticate to service using hard-coded credentials: strcmp("netcore", password) == 0	Trigger conditions satisfied; explicit transition to custom command shell; input arbitrary commands executed using popen	Dependent upon commands entered for payload input
3S Vision N5072 camera backdoor [19]; hard-coded credential check for HTTP authentication, bypasses standard authentication.	Network socket; TCP port 80/443	strcmp(username, "3sadmin") == 0 and strcmp(password, "27988303") == 0	Trigger conditions satisfied; explicit transition to authenticated state	Authenticated as legitimate user of device

```
ngx_int_t ngx_http_parse_header_line(/* ... */) {
  u_char badc; /* last bad character */
  ngx_uint_t hash; /* hash of header, same size as pointer */
  /* ... */
}

void ngx_http_finalize_request(ngx_http_request_t *r, ngx_int_t rc) {
  uint8_t have_err; /* overlaps badc */
  void (*err_handler)(ngx_http_request_t *r); /* overlaps hash */
  /* ... */
  if(rc == NGX_HTTP_BAD_REQUEST && have_err == 1 && err_handler) {
    err_handler(r); /* points to hidden code, set by trigger */
  }
}

void ngx_http_process_request_headers(/* ... */) {
  rc = ngx_http_parse_header_line(/* ... */);
  /* ... */
  ngx_http_finalize_request(r, NGX_HTTP_BAD_REQUEST); /* bad header */
}
```

Fig. 9. Source-code listing for Nginx backdoor *trigger*.

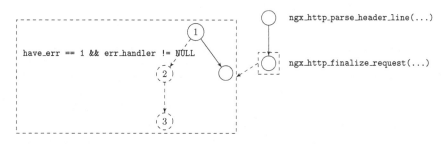

Fig. 10. Multi-layered FSM for Nginx backdoor.

states are possible, for example, if the attacker provides a different input packet to that expected by the implementers. The *privileged state* depends on the backdoor *payload*. We visualise the backdoor in Fig. 10; the *trigger* is captured by state 1 and the non-explicit, bug-based transition to state 2; the *payload* consists of state 2 and the transition between state 2 and 3; state 3 is the *privileged state*.

From a technical standpoint the backdoor is deniable (by Definition 4), this is due to its *trigger* transition being bug-based, whilst its *payload*, if discovered, is arguably intentional. The componentisation using our framework allows us to visualise a complex backdoor succinctly, which would otherwise be buried across multiple functions in thousands of lines of source code. Further, its componentisation allows us to reason about how such a backdoor can be detected: for example, we could attempt to detect its bug-based trigger condition using symbolic execution; alternatively, we could heuristically attempt to identify its *payload* by scanning for misaligned instruction sequences that branch to other instruction sequences of the same kind, where the combination of those sequences would serve to elevate an attacker's privileges.

6.1 Backdoor Detection Methodologies

Our framework provides not only a means to reason about backdoors, but also backdoor detection techniques. Table 2 shows the decomposition of the detection methodologies of four state-of-the-art backdoor detection tools. Each tool claims to detect a particular subset of backdoor types. However, while these tools are all effective, none consider a complete model of backdoors, and, as a result, are limited in their effectiveness.

Table 2. Tool detection methodology decomposed using framework.

Tool	Input source	Trigger	Payload	Privileged state
Firmalice [19]	Partial	Partial	No	Partial
HumIDIFy [22]	Partial	No	Partial	No
Stringer [21]	No	Partial	Partial	No
Weasel [14]	No	Partial	Partial	Partial

Firmalice [19] is designed to detect authentication bypass vulnerabilities. It uses a so-called security policy to define the observable side-effects of a program being in a *privileged state*. Using a specified *input source*, it attempts to find data provided via this *input source* that satisfies the conditions – i.e., akin to a backdoor *trigger* – required to observe the side-effects specified by the security policy. Firmalice has no notion of a *payload state*; when entered, a *payload state* might leave a program in a *privileged state* that is not captured by a given security policy, for instance, where the *privileged state* reached by a backdoor user is different from that of a legitimate user reaches, e.g., the Q-See DVR backdoor from Table 1. Firmalice is able to detect such a *privileged state* by modification of the input security policy, however, to do so will require the same amount of manual analysis to detect the entire backdoor as it would to identify the *privileged state*.

HumIDIFy [22] aims to detect if a program can execute functionality it should never execute under normal circumstances. This might be the establishment of a suspicious *input source*, or the execution of API that is considered anomalous, i.e., what might be part of a backdoor *payload*. However, since it does not consider the notion of a *trigger*, it is unable to distinguish between *abnormal* program behaviour that is benign – because it can only be performed by a legitimate user, and behaviour that is genuinely anomalous – that is part of a backdoor. Again, this is due to their approach not considering a complete model of a backdoor.

Stringer [21] attempts to detect static data used as program input that is responsible for either enabling authentication bypass vulnerabilities, or used for triggering the execution of undocumented functionality. To do this it uses a scoring metric, which ranks static data, that when matched against, leads to the execution of unique functionality, i.e., functionality not reachable by other program paths. Stringer considers the partial notion of a backdoor *trigger* and uses heuristics for identifying *payload-like* constructs. It does not consider the notion of *input source*, or *privileged states*, and as a result of the latter, is unable to meaningfully score data that leads to states that are actually privileged higher than those that are not.

Weasel [14] detects both authentication bypass vulnerabilities and undocumented commands in server-like program binaries. It works by attempting to automatically identify so-called deciders (akin to backdoor *triggers*) and handlers (akin to the combination of a backdoor *payload* and *privileged state*) which then serve to aid in detection of backdoors. Their approach does not fully model the notion of a backdoor; it does not consider an *input source* at all, rather, the approach models a single input for the program, and data from that source, when processed, is assumed to reveal all deciders and handlers. The Tenda webserver backdoor in Table 1 acts as an undocumented command interface, its *input source* is a UDP port; in this case, the backdoor uses a separate *input source* from the standard input to the program, i.e., TCP port 80 or 443. Since Weasel does not capture the notion of an *input source*, it will be unable to detect such a backdoor – not due to a deficiency in its detection method, but because it does not consider a complete model of a backdoor.

7   Future Work

Our framework does not intend to provide a direct means to detect backdoors, rather it serves as a general means to decompose backdoors in an abstract way. In Sect. 6.1, we discuss concrete implementations of detection methodologies; in each case we are able to highlight deficiencies in those methods due to them not fully capturing the rigorous definition of a backdoor, as outlined in this work. Thus, a backdoor detection methodology based upon our proposed framework would be a natural extension of this work. Further, while our formalisations attempt to capture any backdoor-like functionality, backdoors introduced into a system by, e.g., a deliberate side-channel vulnerability would prove difficult to model using our FSM-based abstraction; we view this as an additional area for investigation.

8   Conclusion

In summary, we have provided a definition for the term backdoor, definitions for backdoor detection, deniable backdoors, and a means to discern between intentional backdoors and accidental vulnerabilities. We have presented a framework to aid in identifying backdoors based upon their structure, which also serves as a means to compare existing backdoor detection approaches, and as a basis for developing new techniques. To demonstrate the effectiveness of our approach, we have analysed twelve backdoors of varying complexity. In each case, we have been able to concisely model those backdoors, which previously, might have manifested as hundreds or thousands of assembly language instructions in a disassembler. We have used our framework to evaluate four state-of-the-art backdoor detection approaches, and in all cases, have shown that none consider a complete model of backdoors, and, as a result, their potential effectiveness is limited.

References

1. An attempt to backdoor the kernel (2003). https://lwn.net/Articles/57135/
2. From China with Love (2013). http://www.devttys0.com/2013/10/from-china-with-love/
3. How a Crypto 'Backdoor' Pitted the Tech World Against the NSA (2013). https://www.wired.com/2013/09/nsa-backdoor/
4. Multiple Vulnerabilities in D-Link DIR-600 and DIR-300 (rev B) (2013). http://www.s3cur1ty.de/node/672
5. Reverse Engineering a D-Link Backdoor (2013). http://www.devttys0.com/2013/10/reverse-engineering-a-d-link-backdoor/
6. TCP-32764 Backdoor (2013). https://github.com/elvanderb/TCP-32764
7. Why everyone is left less secure when the NSA doesn't help fix security flaws (2013). https://bit.ly/2JJ9Zsg
8. Inside the EquationDrug Espionage Platform (2015). https://securelist.com/inside-the-equationdrug-espionage-platform/69203/
9. Adups Backdoor (2016). https://www.kryptowire.com/adups_security_analysis.html
10. Backdoor in Sony IPELA Engine IP Cameras (2016). https://sec-consult.com/en/blog/2016/12/backdoor-in-sony-ipela-engine-ip-cameras/
11. Multiple vulnerabilities found in Quanta LTE routers (2016). http://pierrekim.github.io/blog/2016-04-04-quanta-lte-routers-vulnerabilities.html
12. Netis Router Backdoor Update (2016). https://blog.trendmicro.com/netis-router-backdoor-update/
13. Hacking the Western Digital MyCloud NAS (2017). https://blog.exploitee.rs/2017/hacking_wd_mycloud/
14. Andriesse, D., Bos, H.: Instruction-level steganography for covert trigger-based malware. In: Dietrich, S. (ed.) DIMVA 2014. LNCS, vol. 8550, pp. 41–50. Springer, Cham (2014). https://doi.org/10.1007/978-3-319-08509-8_3
15. Dullien, T.F.: Weird machines, exploitability, and provable unexploitability. IEEE Transactions on Emerging Topics in Computing Preprint (2017)
16. Oakley, J., Bratus, S.: Exploiting the hard-working DWARF: Trojan and exploit techniques with no native executable code. In: 5th USENIX Conference on Offensive Technologies (2011)
17. Schuster, F., Holz, T.: Towards reducing the attack surface of software backdoors. In: 2013 ACM SIGSAC Conference on Computer & Communications Security (2013)
18. Shapiro, R., Bratus, S., Smith, S.W.: "Weird Machines" in ELF: a spotlight on the underappreciated metadata. In: 7th USENIX Conference on Offensive Technologies (2013)

19. Shoshitaishvili, Y., Wang, R., Hauser, C., Kruegel, C., Vigna, G.: Firmalice - automatic detection of authentication bypass vulnerabilities in binary firmware. In: 2015 Network and Distributed System Security Symposium (2015)
20. Tan, S.J., Bratus, S., Goodspeed, T.: Interrupt-oriented bugdoor programming: a minimalist approach to bugdooring embedded systems firmware. In: 30th Annual Computer Security Applications Conference (2014)
21. Thomas, S.L., Chothia, T., Garcia, F.D.: Stringer: measuring the importance of static data comparisons to detect backdoors and undocumented functionality. In: Foley, S.N., Gollmann, D., Snekkenes, E. (eds.) ESORICS 2017. LNCS, vol. 10493, pp. 513–531. Springer, Cham (2017). https://doi.org/10.1007/978-3-319-66399-9_28
22. Thomas, S.L., Garcia, F.D., Chothia, T.: HumIDIFy: a tool for hidden functionality detection in firmware. In: Polychronakis, M., Meier, M. (eds.) Detection of Intrusions and Malware, and Vulnerability Assessment. LNCS. Springer, Cham (2017). https://doi.org/10.1007/978-3-319-60876-1_13
23. Wysopal, C., Eng, C.: Static Detection of Application Backdoors. Black Hat USA (2007)
24. Zaddach, J., et al.: Implementation and implications of a stealth hard-drive backdoor. In: 29th Annual Computer Security Applications Conference (2013)
25. Zhang, Y., Paxson, V.: Detecting backdoors. In: 9th USENIX Conference on Security Symposium (2000)

RWGuard: A Real-Time Detection System Against Cryptographic Ransomware

Shagufta Mehnaz$^{(\boxtimes)}$, Anand Mudgerikar, and Elisa Bertino

Purdue University, West Lafayette, IN, USA
{smehnaz,amudgeri,bertino}@purdue.edu

Abstract. Ransomware has recently (re)emerged as a popular malware that targets a wide range of victims - from individual users to corporate ones for monetary gain. Our key observation on the existing ransomware detection mechanisms is that they fail to provide an early warning in real-time which results in irreversible encryption of a significant number of files while the post-encryption techniques (e.g., key extraction, file restoration) suffer from several limitations. Also, the existing detection mechanisms result in high false positives being unable to determine the original intent of file changes, i.e., they fail to distinguish whether a significant change in a file is due to a ransomware encryption or due to a file operation by the user herself (e.g., benign encryption or compression). To address these challenges, in this paper, we introduce a ransomware detection mechanism, `RWGuard`, which is able to detect crypto-ransomware *in real-time* on a user's machine by (1) deploying decoy techniques, (2) carefully monitoring both the running processes and the file system for malicious activities, and (3) omitting benign file changes from being flagged through the learning of users' encryption behavior. We evaluate our system against samples from 14 most prevalent ransomware families to date. Our experiments show that `RWGuard` is effective in real-time detection of ransomware with zero false negative and negligible false positive (∼0.1%) rates while incurring an overhead of only ∼1.9%.

Keywords: Ransomware · Real-time detection · I/O monitoring

1 Introduction

Ransomware is a class of malware that has recently become very popular among cybercriminals. The goal of these cybercriminals is to obtain financial gain by holding the users' files hostage- either by encrypting the files or by locking the users' computers. In this paper, we focus on *crypto ransomware* which asks users for a ransom in exchange of decryption keys that can be used to recover the files encrypted by the attacker. Such a ransomware is now a significant threat to both individuals and organizations. Among the recent ransomware attacks, Petya [8] is the deadliest one; it affected several pharmaceutical companies, banks, at

© Springer Nature Switzerland AG 2018
M. Bailey et al. (Eds.): RAID 2018, LNCS 11050, pp. 114–136, 2018.
https://doi.org/10.1007/978-3-030-00470-5_6

least one airport and one U.S. hospital. Another massive ransomware that hit nearly 100 countries around the world is WannaCry [30]. This attack targeted not only large institutions but also any individual who could be reached. While ransomware has maintained prominence as one of the biggest threats since 2005, the first ransomware attack occurred in 1989 [12] and targeted the healthcare industry. The healthcare industry, which possesses very sensitive and critical information, still remains a top target.

Even though several techniques have been proposed for detecting malware, very few of them are specific to ransomware detection [6,10,13,14,16,26,27]. Such existing techniques, however, have at least one of the following limitations: (a) impractically late detection when several files have already been encrypted [13,26,27], (b) failure to distinguish benign file changes from ransomware encryption [6,10,13,14,16,26,27], (c) offline detection system that is unable to detect ransomware in real-time [13], (d) emphasis only on post-encryption phase which fails to recover files in most of the cases [16] or conflicts with secure deletion [6,10], and (e) monitoring applications' actions only for a limited amount of time after their installation [27].

Problem and Scope. In this work, we focus on the most critical requirement for a successful ransomware, i.e., *making the valuable resources (i.e., files, documents) unavailable to the user*, and design a solution, RWGuard, that protects against ransomware by detecting and stopping the ransomware processes at an early stage. Note that the ransomware families that lock the user's machine are out of the scope of this paper.

Approach. RWGuard employs three monitoring techniques: decoy monitoring, process monitoring, and file change monitoring. Unlike generic malware, ransomware wreak havoc systems within minutes (or seconds). Therefore, analyzing processes' file usage patterns and searching for ransomware-like behaviors result in delayed detections. To address this challenge, we strategically deploy a number of decoy files in the system. Since in the normal cases a decoy file should not be written, whenever a ransomware process writes to such a decoy file, our *decoy monitoring* technique identifies the ransomware process instantaneously. Though some research work [15,19] recommends using decoy files for detecting ransomware, such previous work does not present any analysis on the effectiveness of these decoy files with any real system design. *To the best of our knowledge, ours is the first work to empirically analyze the effectiveness of decoy techniques against ransomware.* The *process monitor* checks the running processes' I/O Request Packets (IRPs), e.g., IRP write, IRP create, IRP open, etc. While some existing approaches [13,14] are signature-based and look for specific I/O request patterns, we exploit the *rapid encryption property* of ransomware [10], use a number of IRP metrics for building baseline profile for each running process, and utilize these baseline profiles for performing process anomaly detection. The *file change monitor* checks all changes performed on the files (e.g., create, delete, and write operations) to determine anomalous file changes. From our experimental observations, we have found that monitoring only the process activities [13,14] or only the file changes [13,26] is not sufficient for effective detection and results in both high false positives and high false negatives (e.g., we observed that the Cryptolocker ransomware encrypts files very slowly which sometimes evades process monitoring). *In this paper, we enhance these existing techniques and combine them with the decoy monitoring module in order to provide an effective solution for protection against ransomware.*

If a potential encryption of a file (not a decoy) is identified, the next step is to determine whether the file is encrypted by a ransomware (referred to as *ransomware encryption*) or by a legitimate user (referred to as *benign encryption*). Therefore, we also design a file classification mechanism that depending on the properties of a file, classifies the encryption as benign or malicious. In order to learn the user's file encryption behavior, we leverage an existing encryption utility (that utilizes cryptographic library CryptoAPI, e.g., Kryptel [17]) to be used by end-users and applications. Finally, our approach includes a mechanism that places hooks and intercepts calls to the functions in CryptoAPI library so as to monitor all benign file encryption.

Contributions. To summarize, RWGuard makes the following contributions:

1. A decoy based ransomware detection technique that is able to identify ransomware processes in real-time.
2. A ransomware surveillance system that employs both *process* and *file change* monitoring (to detect ransomware encrypting files other than decoy).
3. A classification mechanism to distinguish benign file changes from ransomware encryption by hooking relevant CryptoAPI functions and learning the user's file encryption behaviors.
4. An extensive evaluation of our ransomware detection system on 14 most prevalent ransomware families to date.

2   Background

Hybrid Cryptosystem. A hybrid cryptosystem allows the ransomware to use different symmetric keys for encryption of different files while using a single asymmetric key pair. The attacker generates the asymmetric public-private key pair on its own command and control infrastructure. The ransomware code generates a unique symmetric key for each file to be encrypted and then encrypts these symmetric keys with its public key. These encrypted symmetric keys are then left with the encrypted files. At this point, the user needs to pay the ransom to get the private key with which it can first retrieve the symmetric keys, and then decrypt the files.

IRPLogger. All the I/O requests by processes that are sent to device drivers are packaged in I/O request packets (IRPs). These requests are generated for any file system operation, e.g., open, close, write, read, etc. IRPLogger leverages a mini-filter driver [11] that intercepts the I/O requests. An example of IRPLogger entry is:

```
<Timestamp, PID, IRP/FastIO, Operation (READ/WRITE/OPEN/CLOSE/CREATE)>
```

CryptoAPI. CryptoAPI is a Microsoft Windows platform specific cryptographic application programming interface (API). This API, included with Windows operating systems, provides services to secure Windows-based applications using cryptography. It includes functionalities for encrypting (*CryptEncrypt*) and decrypting (*CryptDecrypt*) data, generating cryptographically secure pseudorandom numbers (*CryptGenRandom*), authentication using digital certificates, etc.

Microsoft Detours Library. Detours is a library for instrumenting arbitrary Win32 functions in Windows-compatible processors. It intercepts Win32 functions by re-writing the in-memory code for target functions. Detours preserves the un-instrumented target function (callable through a trampoline) as a subroutine for use by the instrumentation.

3 RWGuard Design

3.1 Threat Model

In our threat model, we consider an adversary that installs crypto-ransomware on victim machines through seemingly legitimate but malicious domains. We consider the operating system to be trusted. Ransomware generally targets and encrypts files that the user creates and cares about, and the user account already has all the privileges to access these files. However, though the assumption that ransomware executes only with user-level privileges seems reasonable (as otherwise, it may be able to defeat any existing in-host protection mechanisms, e.g., anti-malware solutions), this assumption does not apply to all the ransomware cases. We have observed some exceptions to this assumption where ransomware samples affect only a predefined list of system files and if not detected/terminated, gain root access, shut down the system, and at the next boot up, perform full disk encryption and ask for a ransom payment. Hence, we also include these ransomware samples in our threat model. Moreover, a malicious insider in an organization may gain the knowledge of decoy files and build a customized ransomware to sabotage the organization (installed as a logical bomb to detonate after the insider leaves the organization). A further discussion on how our RWGuard system handles such situations is given in Sect. 5.

3.2 Overview

Figure 1 shows the placement and the design overview of RWGuard. Any I/O request to the file system generated by any user space process first needs to be scheduled by the I/O scheduler. We leverage IRPLogger to fetch these system-wide file system access requests and parse those with our IRPParser.

RWGuard consists of five modules: (1) *Decoy Monitoring (DMon)* module, (2) *Process Monitoring (PMon)* module, (3) *File Change Monitoring (FCMon)* module, (4) *File Classification (FCls)* module, and (5) *CryptoAPI Function Hooking*

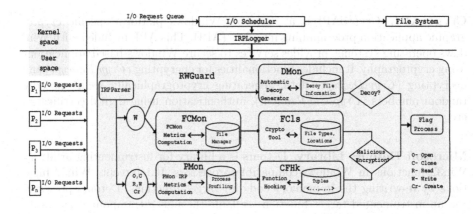

Fig. 1. Design overview of RWGuard

(CFHk) module. The *DMon* module considers only the IRP write requests as input and monitors whether there is any such request to a decoy file. The *PMon* and *FCMon* modules monitor process operations (IRP open, close, read, write, create) and file changes (IRP write), respectively. These two modules communicate in order to identify any process(es) making significant anomalous changes to the files. If such an event is identified, the *FCls* module checks the properties of the file and predicts the probability of the file change to be benign. Furthermore, the *CFHk* module checks whether a benign encryption (by the user) has been recorded for this file at the time of the file's significant change.

3.3   Decoy Monitoring (DMon) Module

The *DMon* module deploys decoy files that allow our system to identify a ransomware process in real-time. Since the decoy files should not be modified in normal situations, whenever a (ransomware) process tries to write such files, this module can immediately identify the process as malicious. Furthermore, the presence of a significant number of decoy files (though of smaller sizes) increases the probability that a ransomware would encrypt one of these files even before trying to encrypt an original file. Hence, the advantage of using decoy files is twofold: (1) it allows the detection system to readily identify a malicious process, and (2) it delays the time when ransomware starts encrypting the original files and thus gives enough time for anomaly detection to complete its analysis and stop the malicious processes even before they start encrypting the original files (see Sect. 5.2 for the experimental data about the time required by RWGuard to complete the analysis). RWGuard decoy files are generated with an automated decoy generator tool that we discuss in details in Sect. 4.2. Note that, our decoy generator periodically modifies the decoy files so that even if a ransomware looks at the time when a file is last modified (to ensure that the file it encrypts is valuable to the user), it would not be able to recognize the decoy files.

Table 1. Fast I/O read/write types

READ types
FASTIO_READ
FASTIO_MDL_READ
FASTIO_READ_COMPRESSED
FASTIO_READ_COMPLETE_COMPRESSED

WRITE types
FASTIO_WRITE
FASTIO_MDL_WRITE
FASTIO_MDL_WRITE_COMPLETE
FASTIO_WRITE_COMPRESSED
FASTIO_MDL_WRITE_COMPLETE_COMPRESSED

Table 2. Metrics for the *PMon* module

Metric #	Metric name
1	Number of IRP_WRITE requests
2	Number of FastIO_WRITE requests
3	Number of IRP_READ requests
4	Number of FastIO_READ requests
5	Number of IRP_OPEN requests
6	Number of FastIO_OPEN requests
7	Number of IRP_CREATE requests
8	Number of FastIO_CREATE requests
9	Number of IRP_CLOSE requests
10	Number of FastIO_CLOSE requests
11	Number of temporary file created

3.4 Process Monitoring (PMon) Module

Unlike some existing approaches [13,14] that look for *specific patterns* (e.g., read → encrypt → delete) in the processes' I/O requests, we exploit the fact that ransomware typically attempts to encrypt data rapidly [10] (to maximize damage and minimize the chance of being detected) which leads to anomalous numbers of IRPs. Exploiting this property results in faster detection since IRPs can be logged well ahead of actual file operations. Our *PMon* module monitors the I/O requests made by the processes running on the system. Though IRP is the default mechanism for requesting I/O operations, many ransomware perform file operations using fast I/O requests. Fast I/O is specifically designed for rapid synchronous I/O operations on cached files, bypassing the file system and the storage driver stack. Therefore, in our design, we monitor both the IRPs and the fast I/O requests. A fast I/O read/write operation can be any of the types listed in Table 1. Given that ransomware processes encrypt files rapidly, the behavior of such processes has certain characteristics. Hence, in this module, we train a machine learning model that given a process's I/O requests, identifies the process as benign or ransomware. Ransomware that encrypt files slowly may evade this module but are identified by the *FCMon* module as discussed in Sect. 3.5.

Process Profiling. In order to train the machine learning model, as a first step, we collect the IRPs (from this point, the term 'IRP' represents both I/O and fast I/O) of both benign and ransomware processes. Table 2 shows the IRP metrics used in this training phase which also includes the number of temporary files created by a process. The temporary files (.TMP) are usually created by ransomware to hold the data while copying or removing the original files. Once the profiles for benign and ransomware processes are built in the training phase, the *Process Profiling* component of the *PMon* module (Fig. 1) stores the model parameters to check against the running processes' parameters in real-time (i.e., the test phase). The *PMon* module re-computes the metrics listed in Table 2 for each running process over a 3 s sliding window.

Table 3. Performance evaluation for different machine learning techniques

Classifier	Accuracy (%)	ROC area	True positive rate	False positive rate	Precision	Recall
Naive Bayes	80.07	0.69	0.80	0.70	0.75	0.80
Logistic regression	81.22	0.72	0.81	0.66	0.77	0.81
Decision tree	89.27	0.87	0.89	0.18	0.89	0.89
Random forest	96.55	0.94	0.96	0.08	0.96	0.96

- **Training phase:** The data collection and classifier training steps are following:

1. **Data collection:** For the training set, we collect IRP data of processes from both ransomware samples and benign applications. We use nine of the most popular ransomware families, namely: Wannacry, Cerber, CryptoLocker, Petya, Mamba, TeslaCrypt, CryptoWall, Locky, and Jigsaw for the training phase. We also include benign processes, e.g., Explorer.exe, WmiPrvSE.exe, svchost.exe, FileSpy.exe, vmtoolsd.exe, csrss.exe, System, SearchFilter-Host.exe, SearchProtocolHost.exe, SearchIndexer.exe, chrome.exe, GoogleUp-date.exe, services.exe, audiodg.exe, WinRAR.exe, taskhost.exe, drpbx.exe, lsass.exe, etc. It is important to note that most of the ransomware samples spawn multiple malicious processes during execution. Our final training dataset contains IRPs from 261 processes including both benign and malicious ones.

2. **Classifier training:** Using the training data, we train a machine learning classifier that, given a set of processes, is able to distinguish between ransomware and benign processes. In order to identify the best machine learning technique for this classification, we analyzed different classifiers, namely: *Naive Bayes* (using estimator classes), *Logistic Regression* (multinomial logistic regression model with a ridge estimator), *Decision Tree* [24], and *Random Forest* [3] classifiers. We used 10 fold cross validation on the obtained data set and measured accuracy, precision, recall, true positive rate and false positive rate for each of the above-mentioned classifiers. Table 3 presents a comparison of the classifiers used in our analysis. Figure 2 shows the results for all the classifiers in terms of ROC curves (which plot true positive rate against false positive rate). The low accuracy (∼80%) of the naive Bayes classifier can be attributed to its class independence property. From our observation, ransomware usually employs a combination of read, write, open, and close requests which are correlated. Therefore, assuming that these parameters are independent of each other leads to a lower accuracy. The regression classifier works slightly better than the naive Bayes classifier with an accuracy of ∼81%. A logistic regression model searches for a single linear decision boundary in the feature space. Hence, the low accuracy can be attributed to the

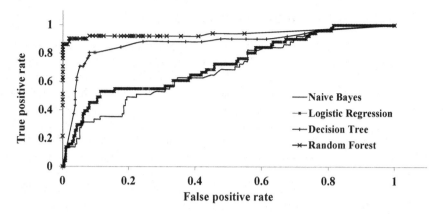

Fig. 2. ROC curves for different classifiers.

fact that our data does not have a linear boundary for decisions. The reason is that many ransomware make a large number of write/read requests as compared to the open/close requests. Therefore, the ideal decision boundary for our dataset would be non-linear.

The tree-based classifiers (random forest and decision tree) perform the best with accuracies of ~97% and ~89%, respectively. The reason is that the decision boundary for our data is non-linear and these classifiers build non-linear decision boundaries. However, the decision tree classifier is susceptible to over-fitting while random forest classifiers do not have this issue. Also, in terms of deployment, the random forest classifier is faster and more scalable compared to other classifiers. Therefore, finally, we use the random forest classifier in our RWGuard *PMon* module.

- **Test phase:** In the test phase, along with the nine families used for training, we add five more ransomware families in the experiment set: Vipasana, Satana, Radamant, Rex, and Matsnu. These samples are executed one at a time and depending on the spawned processes and their activities, the malicious processes are flagged. Details of the test phase results are given in Sect. 5.

File Encryption. In our experiments, we observe that few benign processes, e.g., Chrome, VMware tools are sometimes classified as malicious by the machine learning model due to these processes' I/O request behaviors. Therefore, besides monitoring the process profiling metrics, it is important to monitor whether a particular process is responsible for any significant file changes. Hence, our *PMon* module considers *file encryption* as a significant parameter (communicated by the *FCMon* module as described in Sect. 3.5) and identifies a process as malicious only if it encrypts files along with indications of anomalous I/O behaviors.

3.5   File Change Monitoring (FCMon) Module

This monitoring module can be configured to target a range of files from a single directory to the whole file system. It computes and stores the initial properties of the files (or, dynamically computes the properties when a file is created) and these properties are updated accordingly in the event of a file change. In real-time, the *FCMon* module looks for significant changes in those files after each write operation using the following metrics: (1) similarity, (2) entropy, (3) file type change, and (4) file size change. While some of these metrics have been used for ransomware detection in existing work [13,26], our goal is to verify the fast detections by the *PMon* module and thereby minimize the false positive rates. In what follows, we describe the *File Manager* component of the *FCMon* module and present the details of the above metrics.

File Manager. This component stores the current properties of each file (e.g., file type, current entropy of a file, file size, last modified time etc.) so that any significant change in the files' properties can be detected upon a write operation. If a new file is created, this component computes the properties of the new file instantly and stores them in the map (map key: file name and path, key value: computed properties).

Metrics. The metrics of *FCMon* module are following:

1. *Similarity* metric: In comparison with a benign file change, e.g., modifying some of the existing text or adding some text, an encryption would result in data that is very dissimilar to the original data. Therefore, the similarity between a file's previous (before the write operation) and later (after the write operation) versions is an important factor to understand the characteristics of the file change. In order to compute the similarity between two versions, we use *sdhash*, a similarity-preserving hash function proposed by Roussev et al. [25] for generating the file hashes. The *sdhash* function outputs a score in the range [0,100]. A score of 0 is obtained when we compute the similarity between two completely random arrays of data. Conversely, a score of 100 is obtained when we compute the similarity between two files that are exactly same. Hence, in the case of an encryption, this function outputs a value close to 0.

2. *Entropy* metric: Entropy, as it relates to digital information, is the measurement of randomness in a given set of values (data), i.e., when computed over a file, it provides information about the randomness of data in the file. Therefore, certainly, a user's data file in plaintext form has low entropy whereas its encrypted version would have a high entropy. Other than encrypted data, compressed data also has high entropy when compared to its plaintext form. A widely used entropy computation technique is Shannon entropy [21]. The Shannon entropy of an array of N bytes (assuming ASCII characters with values 0 to 255) can be computed as the following: $\sum_{i=0}^{255} P_i log_2 \frac{1}{P_i}$. Here, P_i

is the probability that a randomly chosen byte from the array is i, (i.e., $P_i = F_i/N$) where F_i is the frequency of byte value i in the array. This equation returns a value in the range of [0,8]. For an absolutely even distribution of byte values in the array, the output value is 8. Since encrypted files have bytes more evenly distributed (when compared to its plaintext version), the Shannon entropy significantly increases after encryption and results in a value near 8.

3. *File type change* metric: A file generally does not change its type over the course of its existence. However, it is common for a number of ransomware families to change the file type after encryption. Therefore, whenever a file is written, we compare the file types before and after the write operation.

4. *File size change* metric: Unlike file type change, file size change is a common event, e.g., adding a large text to a document. However, this metric along with other metrics can determine if the file changes are benign or malicious.

Upon detecting a file write operation that results in a file type change or exceeds at least one of the given thresholds for the metrics, that is, similarity (score < 50), or entropy (value > 6), and/or significantly changes the file size, the *FCMon* module shares the recorded metrics with the *PMon*, *FCls*, and *CFHk* modules for further assessment.

3.6   File Classification (FCls) Module

After the *PMon* and *FCMon* modules collaboratively identify a process responsible for anomalous I/O behavior and file changes, our detection system classifies whether the file is encrypted by the ransomware or the change is due to a benign operation. Our *FCls* module performs this classification by learning the usage of the crypto-tool (a utility leveraging CryptoAPI used for user's sensitive files' encryption and decryption, e.g., Kryptel [17]) and profiling the user's encryption behavior. For example, if a file is encrypted which is from the same directory and has the same type of a previously benignly encrypted file, this module assigns a higher probability for this file to be benignly encrypted (however, a ransomware cannot abuse this idea as described in *CFHk* module in Sect. 3.7). If the probability for a file is too low to belong to the benignly encrypted class and if the file gets encrypted, a flag is raised immediately by the *FCls* module. In order to remove false negatives (i.e., ransomware encrypts a file which has a high probability of being benignly encrypted), the encryption information is validated with the *CFHk* module which intercepts benign encryptions.

Protecting Sensitive Files: If at the time of the ransomware attack the sensitive files are already in encrypted form, the ransomware could further encrypt those files which makes those files unavailable too. Note that the *FCMon* module may not be able to flag this event with high probability. The reason is that the entropy would not change significantly since both the file versions (before and after the ransomware encryption) would have high entropy. To address such issue, we modify the permission settings for encrypted files, i.e., when a user encrypts a file using the crypto-tool, the only operations that we

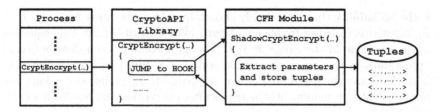

Fig. 3. CryptoAPI Function Hooking (CFHk) module

allow on that encrypted file are decryption and deletion (each of these operations requires the symmetric key used for encryption). Since it is impractical that someone would edit/modify an encrypted file before decryption, this permission setting suffices.

3.7 CryptoAPI Function Hooking (CFHk) Module

As described in Sect. 3.6, if the *FCls* module classifies the change to be the result of a possibly benign encryption, we need to further investigate whether the encryption was actually performed using the crypto-tool. Hence, the *CFHk* module places hooks at the beginning of the CryptoAPI library functions to redirect control of the execution to our custom-written functions. Figure 3 shows an example of hooking the 'CryptEncrypt' function included in the CryptoAPI library. Whenever a process calls the CryptEncrypt function to encrypt some file, the hook placed at the beginning of the CryptEncrypt function transfers control to a *shadow* CryptEncrypt function. This shadow CryptEncrypt function extracts a tuple $< key, algo, file, timestamp, process >$ for that particular call and stores this information in encrypted form for security purposes so that no other process can get access to this. The key for this encryption is derived from a secret password set by the user. Once the tuple is stored, the shadow CryptEncrypt function returns control to the original procedure, and the process continues its execution as if it had not been interrupted at all. The implementation details of this hooking procedure are discussed in Sect. 4.3.

To identify whether a file encryption is performed using the crypto-tool, we simply search 'CryptEncrypt' tuples that are captured by the *CFHk* module.

- If such a tuple is not found, we terminate the process that resulted in the file change so that no further encryption can take place.
- If such a tuple is found, the encryption is either benign (no action required) or a ransomware using CryptoAPI is responsible for the encryption. In the second case, we can recover all the files by using the *key* and *algo* information from the tuples (details in Sect. 5.4). Since in our system we also store the *file* information (by associating a *ReadFile* call with *CryptEncrypt*), we do not need to iterate over all the keys for a single file decryption which is an improvement over existing work [16].

Hence, the advantage of hooking the CryptoAPI library functions is twofold: (1) tracking all the benign encryption by the user, (2) recovering the ransomware encrypted files in the case that the ransomware dynamically links system-provided cryptographic libraries (i.e., Windows CryptoAPI).

4   RWGuard Implementation

4.1   IRPParser

While IRPLogger logs the I/O requests, the IRPParser component parses the log entries, extracts I/O requests, and provides these as input to the *DMon*, *PMon*, and *FCMon* modules accordingly.

4.2   Decoy File Generator

We have designed an automated decoy file generator tool that generates the decoy files based on the original file system and user preferences. By default, in each directory, it generates a decoy file with a name that is similar to one of the original files (selected at random or by the user depending on user preference) in that same directory so that the decoy files' names do not seem random to the ransomware. In order to make sure that the decoy files can be easily identified by the user, the naming options are selected based on the user's preferences which also makes the decoy files more unpredictable for the ransomware. The user is able to set different numbers of decoy files for different directories. In this way, the more sensitive files can be protected with a larger set of decoy files and also, manually setting the numbers makes it easier for the user to identify the decoy files during normal operations. The type extensions of the generated decoy files are: .txt, .doc, .pdf, .ppt, and .xls whereas the contents of the files are generated from the contents of neighboring files. Although we did not observe *selective* behavior (e.g., checking file name, file content, etc. before encryption) in any of the ransomware we experimented with, our decoy design is resilient to such future advanced ransomware. Note that the sizes of the decoy files in our system are randomly taken from a range (typically from 1 KB to few MBs) based on the sizes of the files in the original file system while the overall space overhead for decoy files is limited to 5% of the original file system size.

4.3   CryptoAPI Function Hooking

In our *CFHk* module, we leverage the Detours library introduced in Sect. 2. Detours hooks a function by moving a specific number of bytes (generally five bytes) from the beginning of the original function's memory address to the newly created hook function. In this blank space of the original function, an unconditional JMP instruction is added that would transfer the control to the hook function. The hook function then performs the necessary operations (e.g., safely storing the keys and other parameters passed to the original function). At the end

Table 4. Hooked CryptoAPI functions

Function	Details
CryptEncrypt	Encrypts data
CryptGenKey	Generates a random cryptographic session key or a public/private key pair
CryptDeriveKey	Generates cryptographic session keys derived from a base data value
CryptExportKey	Exports a cryptographic key/key pair from a CSP
CryptGenRandom	Fills a buffer with cryptographically random bytes

of these operations, another unconditional JMP instruction is added to transfer the control back to the original function. The compiled DLL file is placed into the registry key so that any process invoking the CryptoAPI functions would get hooked and our *CFHk* module would store information related to encryption. Table 4 lists the CryptoAPI functions we hook.

5 Evaluation

5.1 Experiment Dataset

While there exists different variants of ransomware, we build a comprehensive dataset from the most popular ransomware families: Locky, Cerber, Wannacry, Jigsaw, Cryptolocker, Mamba, Teslacrypt, Cryptowall, Petya, Vipasana, Satana, Radamant, Rex, and Matsnu. The ransomware samples are collected from Virus-Total [28], Open Malware [23], VXVault [29], Zelster [32], and Malc0de [22].

Note that among these samples, the first 9 families have been used in the training phase of the *PMon* module. However, we run each of these 14 ransomware samples (one at a time) in the detection phase to assess the detection effectivenesses and performance overheads of RWGuard modules. The reason behind not using the 5 samples for *PMon* module training is to measure how well this module performs with previously unseen ransomware samples.

5.2 Detection Effectiveness

We evaluate the performance of RWGuard by running the ransomware samples sequentially. Every time a ransomware sample is executed, we measure the time required for flagging each malicious process spawned by the ransomware. Once the ransomware is detected, we restore the system with a clean OS and execute the next ransomware sample.

Detection w/Decoy Deployment: We observe that ransomware detection with decoy deployment is extremely fast and ensures almost zero data loss. Note that the IRPParser component parses IRP logs collected in a 1 second cycle.

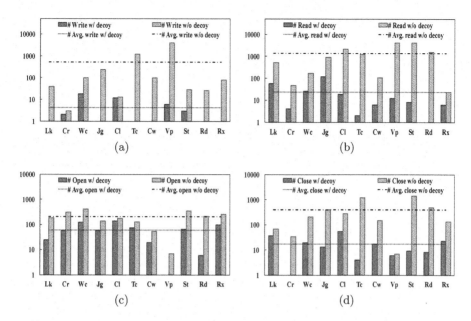

Fig. 4. Comparison between the cases of with and without decoy deployment in terms of the number of (a) *write*, (b) *read*, (c) *open*, and (d) *close* IRPs made by the ransomware samples until their detection (ransomware name abbreviations: Lk-Locky, Cr-Cerber, Wc-Wannacry, Jg-Jigsaw, Cl-Cryptolocker, Tc-Teslacrypt, Cw-Cryptowall, Vp-Vipasana, St-Satana, Rd-Radamant, Rx-Rex).

Therefore, with the decoy deployment, our system can identify a ransomware process right in the next cycle of the process's decoy file write request.

Figure 4 shows the comparison between the cases of with and without decoy deployment in terms of the number of write, read, open, and close IRPs (along with the average values for all the ransomware) made by the ransomware samples until their detection (in Figs. 4(a), (b), (c), and (d), respectively). The number of IRPs (for each IRP type) for each ransomware family is computed by running the samples at least 5 times. We find that with decoy deployment, for each of these IRP types, there is an improvement of at least one order of magnitude. Hence, the ransomware processes could be identified as soon as they start making IRP requests, i.e., in real-time. *For ransomware Locky, Jigsaw, Teslacrypt, Cryptowall, Radamant, and Rex, we observe that the first IRP write requests they make are for decoy files (see Fig. 4(a)) and thus are identified immediately. The Wannacry ransomware could make up to 18 IRP write requests (the highest) before it sends a write request for a decoy file (note that there can be multiple IRP write requests for a single file write operation).* An IRP write request is sent well ahead of the actual write operation and hence the actual number of files that can get encrypted before terminating the process is negligible (which also depends on the file size).

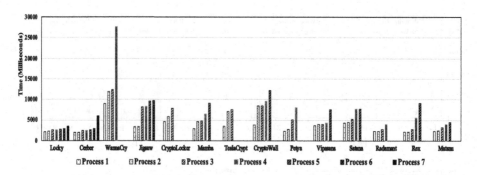

Fig. 5. Detection time required by RWGuard when there is no decoy deployment.

Note that, Fig. 4 does not show comparisons for the following three ransomware families: Mamba, Petya, and Matsnu. In our experiments, we have found that samples from these families affect only a predefined list of system files (and if there is no detection system activated except the decoy monitoring, this is followed by gaining root access, shutting down the system, and at the next boot up, performing full disk encryption and asking for a ransom payment). As a result, our *DMon* module cannot identify such ransomware families (however, the *PMon* and *FCMon* modules can) and therefore, we omit the comparison for these three families in this section.

Detection w/o Decoy Deployment: In order to further evaluate the effectiveness of RWGuard, we also consider an environment where there is no decoy file. This environment can be practical for the following two scenarios:

1. A ransomware encrypts only a predefined list of system files, i.e., even if the decoy files are deployed, the ransomware does not touch the decoy files (e.g., Mamba, Petya, and Matsnu ransomware families in our experiment dataset).
2. A malicious insider in an organization with the knowledge of decoy files' deployment can use customized ransomware to sabotage the organization and hold the ransomware responsible for this. Such an attack can be even launched as a logical bomb that can detonate after the insider has left the organization.

Figure 5 shows the time required to detect each of the samples (in milliseconds) while there is no decoy deployment in the system. The time computation starts when the ransomware sample is executed and ends when the corresponding process is flagged. Once the *PMon* and *FCMon* modules identify potential ransomware activity (i.e., malicious IRP/FastIO requests, significant file changes or encryption), the *FCls* and *CFHk* modules are communicated. If the file(s) that is (are) changed does (do) not belong to the 'benignly encrypted' class, and if there is (are) no corresponding encryption entry (entries) in the *CFHk* module, the process is immediately flagged. The average detection time for the first malicious processes spawned by all the ransomware is 3.45 s. However, we see that all the ransomware spawn multiple malicious processes which are detected at different times by our monitoring system. We observe that the average required time for detecting all the spawned processes is 8.87 s. As we can see from Fig. 5, Locky, and Cerber spawn the highest number of malicious processes whereas CryptoLocker and TeslaCrypt spawn the lowest number of processes. According to our observation, most of the ransomware try to spawn processes with unique names or try to hide as system processes, e.g., explorer.exe. We also observe that different ransomware behave differently when the initially spawned malicious processes are killed by our system. For example, Wannacry sits idle for some time after the initial few processes are killed, before trying to spawn a new malicious process. This is the reason for the comparatively higher detection time for the last process in some of these ransomware.

Detection effectivenesses of different modules are discussed in the following:

- **Decoy Monitoring (DMon) module:** This module is the fastest to identify a ransomware process. Deploying a larger number of decoy files will result in even faster detection. For example, with a decoy generator that creates a shadow decoy file for each original file in the system, probabilistically, one out of each two write requests by a ransomware would belong to a decoy file.

- **Process Monitoring (PMon) and File Change Monitoring (FCMon) modules:** In most of the cases, the *PMon* module responded faster than the *FCMon* module in terms of flagging a malicious process. Even before the ransomware starts performing encryption, the *PMon* module is able to identify the malicious activities by monitoring the IRPs. In contrast, the *FCMon* module responds only after a file has been changed significantly. However, we observe that few benign processes, e.g., Chrome, VMware tools are sometimes misclassified as malicious by the *PMon* module due to these processes' I/O request behaviors. Therefore, it is important to also consider the analysis by the *FCMon* module to better understand whether a particular process is responsible for any malicious file changes and to remove any false positives.

- **File Classification (FCls) and CryptoAPI Function Hooking (CFHk) modules:** After the *PMon* and *FCMon* modules' detection that a process is making significant changes in the file(s), the information of the file(s) are sent to the *FCls* module which then computes the probability of these changes being benign. The false negatives of this module correspond to the cases in which the ransomware encrypts a file which has a high probability of being encrypted by the user benignly. Such false negatives are, however, detected by the *CFHk* module which identifies if the file is actually encrypted using the provided crypto-tool. With a 100% accuracy, the *CFHk* module can identify whether an encryption is performed by a ransomware or is a benign encryption. This module never flags a benign encryption. The only case of false positives (negligible, ∼0.1%) we have observed in the *FCls* and *CFHk* modules is when the user performs *file compression* in a directory for the first time. However, a first time benign file encryption in a directory is not flagged as malicious since the *CFHk* module can intercept the benign encryption operations. Note that the *FCls* and *CFHk* modules do not flag any process unless that process is identified as suspicious by one of the monitoring modules.

5.3   Size of Encrypted Data

In terms of the number of files, samples from ransomware families Locky, Jigsaw, Teslacrypt, Cryptowall, Radamant, and Rex could not encrypt any file with decoy deployment. The malicious processes for these families are identified on their first IRP write request. The numbers of IRP write requests made by ransomware families Cerber, Wannacry, Cryptolocker, Vipasana, and Satana before their detection are 2, 18, 12, 6, and 3, respectively, with decoy deployment. However, since an IRP write request is sent well ahead of the actual write operation and there can be multiple IRP write requests for a single file write, with decoy deployment, the average number of files lost is <1 with only Wannacry and Cryptolocker being able to encrypt 1 file each before their malicious processes are killed. The average number of IRP requests made by the ransomware families without any decoy deployment is $\sim$538 (with the strong assumption that the ransomware can evade the decoy deployment which is not the case for most of the families) whereas the average number of files affected is <10. Note that the number of files affected before detection depends not only on the number of IRP requests made but also on the time taken by a ransomware process to initiate the encryption routines (which is significant), type of encryption, size of the files, and the number of files the ransomware attempts to encrypt (this is because for each file the ransomware needs to generate a new key).

5.4   File Recovery

The *CFHk* module could recover all the files encrypted by the ransomware families: Locky, CryptoWall, and CryptoLocker. The encryption algorithms used by these samples are AES with CTR mode, AES in CBC mode, and AES, respectively. Note that the *CFHk* module in its current version cannot recover files that are encrypted using the ransomware's custom-written cryptographic library.

5.5   Performance Overhead

In the following, we discuss the performance overheads for different modules of RWGuard. The *DMon*, *FCls*, and *CFHk* modules have negligible overheads. The *DMon* module generates a single decoy file in each directory (if not set otherwise by the user) and randomly chooses the size of the decoy files from the range 1 KB–5 MBs while limiting the overall space overhead to 5% of the original file system size. At runtime, this module checks for decoy file write requests and modifies/regenerates the decoy files once per day at random times which has only a minimal overhead. The *FCls* module instantaneously classifies the files using file type and location information. The overhead for hooking a CryptoAPI function and computing and storing the corresponding tuple is a few milliseconds ($\leq$10 ms) which is negligible and thus cannot interrupt a user's normal operations.

Table 5. Memory overhead of `RWGuard`

Component	Memory consumed (KB)
Main Java module	14296
FCMon Entropy Calculator	7880
FCMon Similarity Index Calculator	5152
IRP Logger	42964

There is a main Java module which executes the IRPLogger, collects all the IRPs made in the system, parses the IRPs with IRPParser, and runs three parallel threads for *DMon*, *PMon*, and *FCMon* modules. The *FCMon* module consists of the components for computing the values of entropy and similarity index which use minimal CPU cycles since these are called only when there are write operations on the files. The memory usage of these components along with the main Java module is shown in Table 5. The average CPU usages for this main Java module and IRPLogger are 0.85% and 1.02%, respectively.

Overheads for Different Workloads. The performance overheads discussed above are recorded while running a web browser process and an integrated development environment (IDE) process along with regular operating system processes. However, in order to measure `RWGuard` detection performance and overheads for a heavy workload OS, we add several processes: two browsers (Chrome and Internet Explorer), two IDEs (Eclipse and PyChar), Windows Media Player, Skype, and other regular operating system processes. According to our experiments, this heavy workload does not significantly affect the time required by `RWGuard` for identifying ransomware processes while we have observed that IRPLogger and the Java module incur higher memory overhead (244456 KB and 45436 KB, respectively) due to this heavy workload. The detection time remaining unaffected by the heavy workload can be attributed to the fact that `RWGuard` fetches IRPLogger entries every 2 s which does not depend on the number of entries logged (the number of log entries is much higher for the heavy workload case). Since parsing the IRP logs is not an expensive operation, for the heavy workload case, the detection time is not significantly changed. Also, the memory overheads for the *FCMon* metrics' calculation remain similar.

5.6 Comparison with Existing Approaches

Table 6 presents a comparison among `RWGuard` and other exiting ransomware detection techniques with respect to monitoring, detection, and recovery strategies.

Table 6. Comparison of `RWGuard` with existing ransomware detection mechanisms

Solution	Real-time detection with decoy	Benign operation/ encryption profiling	File change monitoring	Process monitoring	Recovery of decryption key	Recovery of files
RWGuard	✓	✓	✓	✓	✓ (partial)	✓ (partial)
ShieldFS [6]	×	×	×	✓	×	✓
Unveil [13], CryptoDrop [26], Redemption [14]	×	×	✓	✓	×	×
PayBreak [16]	×	×	×	×	✓ (partial)	✓ (partial)
EldeRan [27]	×	×	×	✓	×	×
FlashGuard [10]	×	×	×	×	×	✓

6   Discussion and Limitations

Novelty. To the best of our knowledge, `RWGuard` with the decoy technique is the first system with very fast real-time (few milliseconds) detection capabilities. Even without the decoy deployment, the other monitoring modules are able to minimize the damage by identifying the ransomware processes at the time of their I/O requests. An average of 538 I/O write requests within the average detection time of 3.45 s shows how rapidly a ransomware attempts to encrypt the user's files while `RWGuard` exploits this property to terminate the ransomware at an early stage. Also, whereas the existing approaches are unable to distinguish benign file changes from malicious ones, the *FCls* module along with the *CFHk* module is able to overcome such false positives.

Inevitability. Our robust decoy design makes it impossible for the ransomware to recognize a decoy file by any of its properties. The ransomware would need to install some spyware and monitor the file activities in the system in order to determine which ones are modified by the end-users and applications and which are executed by our decoy tool. Moreover, obfuscation techniques can be used to make difficult for the ransomware to analyze the applications in order to determine which application is the decoy generator. Our integrated monitoring modules, *PMon* and *FCMon*, employ scrutiny on metrics that are inclusive of any malicious activity by the ransomware. For example, a smart ransomware that encrypts files slowly would still be detected by the *FCMon* module. While the monitoring modules *DMon*, *PMon*, and *FCMon* do not let a ransomware activity remain undetected (i.e., they prevent false negatives), the *FCls* and *CFHk* modules distinguish benign file operations from malicious ones (i.e., they prevent false positives). Hence, we argue that independently of the intelligence of modern ransomware, `RWGuard` raises the evasion bar for ransomware significantly.

File Recovery. Note that, the *CFHk* module monitors all (benign and ransomware) file encryption that leverage 'CryptoAPI' functions. Therefore, if a ransomware leveraging CryptoAPI library (3 of the 14 ransomware families that we have analyzed use this library) becomes successful in encrypting a set of files before our early detection, using the hooking mechanism, we can retrieve the parameters (including the decryption keys) of those specific cryptographic function calls and consequently restore the encrypted files. Our experiments (Sect. 5.4) show that the *CFHk* module is able to recover the files encrypted by the 3 ransomware families with a 100% success rate. The rest of the ransomware samples experimented in our evaluation did not use CryptoAPI but their custom-written cryptographic library. Moreover, code obfuscation is a common technique used by the modern ransomware families. Obfuscation strategies, such as incremental packing and unpacking, make it more difficult to identify cryptographic primitives in the ransomware binary. While there are techniques (e.g., [31]) that look for cryptographic operations in the process memory, we have not incorporated those in our system due to their huge performance overhead.

Limitations. While the *DMon* module is quick in identifying a malicious process, the *PMon* and *FCMon* modules are anomaly based and hence probabilistically bound to miss some of the malicious activity. Also, these modules are based on the logging of IRP calls and file activity. The time lag between logging these activities and parsing them for anomalies provide a small window for the ransomware to perform its malicious activities as discussed in Sect. 5.3.

7 Related Work

Detection Techniques. Kharraz et al. [13–15] propose systems that monitor the I/O request patterns of applications for signs of ransomware-like behaviors. Scaife et al. [26] have designed *CryptoDrop*, a system that alerts users during suspicious file activity, e.g., tampering with a large amount of the user's data. Sgandurra et al. [27] propose *EldeRan*, a machine learning approach that monitors actions performed by applications in their first phases of installation and checks for characteristics signs of ransomware. Lee et al. [18] propose a ransomware prevention mechanism based on abnormal behavior analysis in a cloud system. Cabaj et al. [4] present a software-defined networking (SDN) based detection approach that utilizes the characteristics of ransomware communication. Andronio et al. [1] propose a technique to detect Android ransomware that applies to only mobile platforms- where applications are analyzed in-depth before they are released in any app market. Huang et al. [9] propose a measurement framework for end-to-end of ransomware payments. In contrast, RWGuard is the fastest solution that identifies ransomware infection in real-time with decoy techniques, prevents malicious processes from making changes to the files, and also determines the original intent of file changes.

Post-encryption Techniques. Kolodenker et al. [16] propose a system, called *PayBreak*, that intercepts system provided crypto functions, collects and stores the keys, and thus, can decrypt files only for the ransomware families that use system provided crypto functions. Continella et al. [6] propose the *ShieldFS* tool that monitors low-level file system activity to model the system over time. Whenever a process violates these models, the affected files are transparently rolled back. However, it requires shadowing a file whenever it is modified and thus incurs high overhead. FlashGuard, a system developed by Huang et al. [10] leverages the fact that SSD performs out-of-place writes and thus holds the invalid pages for up to 20 days to perform data recovery after ransomware encryption. However, this type of recovery methods conflict with the idea of secure deletion and may result in privacy issues and data leakage. Given the limitations of the existing post-encryption recovery techniques, it is of uttermost importance that faster detection techniques be developed against ransomware.

Decoy Techniques. Decoy techniques have been previously proposed to defend against insider threats [2]. Though some research work [15,19] recommends using decoy files for detecting ransomware, such previous work does not include any analysis on the effectiveness of the decoy files. *Randomly generated decoy* files in commercial solutions (e.g., [7]) are susceptible of detection by sophisticated ransomware. Moreover, unlike RWGuard, their decoy files are deployed during the installation process which simply leaves the files unmodified for a long time and thus makes these files less interesting for the ransomware. Also, it is not clear how these solutions would handle special ransomware families, e.g., Mamba, Petya, and Matsnu, that affect only a predefined list of system files.

Cryptographic Primitives Identification Techniques. Discovering cryptographic primitives in a given binary is another research direction where crypto-ransomware including cryptographic operations could be identified beforehand [5,31]. Calvet et al. [5] developed such a technique and evaluated the performance of their system on a set of known malware samples. Lestringant et al. [20]'s approach to obtaining the similar goal leverages graph isomorphism techniques. Although these approaches could identify cryptographic primitives in obfuscated programs, their poor performance makes them impractical for real-time defense even with the most recent work [31] resulting in a 5-6X slowdown in average.

8   Conclusions and Future Work

In this paper, we introduce RWGuard that detects crypto-ransomware on a user's machine in real-time while removing the false positives due to the user's benign file operations. We evaluate RWGuard against 14 most prevalent ransomware families. Our experiments show that RWGuard is effective in early detection of ransomware with only negligible false positives (~0.1%) and zero false negatives while incurring an overhead of only ~1.9%. Furthermore, RWGuard recovers all files that are encrypted using CryptoAPI by the corresponding ransomware. As part of the future work, we plan to profile other existing encryption libraries and in real-time scan the process's memory for similar operations so that we can recover the keys used for encryption and restore the files. Moreover, we plan to take snapshots of the ransomware processes' memories before terminating the processes and analyze those for traces of encryption/decryption keys.

Acknowledgement. We thank our shepherd, Alina Oprea, and the anonymous reviewers for their valuable suggestions. The work reported in this paper has been supported by the Schlumberger Foundation under the Faculty For The Future (FFTF) Fellowship.

References

1. Andronio, N., Zanero, S., Maggi, F.: HELDROID: dissecting and detecting mobile ransomware. In: Bos, H., Monrose, F., Blanc, G. (eds.) RAID 2015. LNCS, vol. 9404, pp. 382–404. Springer, Cham (2015). https://doi.org/10.1007/978-3-319-26362-5_18
2. Bowen, B.M., Hershkop, S., Keromytis, A.D., Stolfo, S.J.: Baiting inside attackers using decoy documents. In: Chen, Y., Dimitriou, T.D., Zhou, J. (eds.) SecureComm 2009. LNICST, vol. 19, pp. 51–70. Springer, Heidelberg (2009). https://doi.org/10.1007/978-3-642-05284-2_4
3. Breiman, L.: Random forests. Mach. Learn. **45**(1), 5–32 (2001). https://doi.org/10.1023/A:1010933404324
4. Cabaj, K., Gregorczyk, M., Mazurczyk, W.: Software-defined networking-based crypto ransomware detection using HTTP traffic characteristics. CoRR abs/1611.08294 (2016)
5. Calvet, J., Fernandez, J.M., Marion, J.Y.: Aligot: cryptographic function identification in obfuscated binary programs. In: Proceedings of the 2012 ACM Conference on Computer and Communications Security, pp. 169–182. ACM, New York (2012). https://doi.org/10.1145/2382196.2382217
6. Continella, A., et al.: ShieldFS: a self-healing, ransomware-aware filesystem. In: Proceedings of the 32nd Annual Conference on Computer Security Applications, ACSAC 2016, pp. 336–347. ACM, New York (2016). https://doi.org/10.1145/2991079.2991110
7. CryptoStopper: www.watchpointdata.com/cryptostopper/
8. Fox-Brewster, T.: Petya or notpetya: why the latest ransomware is deadlier than wannacry. FORBES, June 2017. https://www.forbes.com/sites/thomasbrewster/2017/06/27/petya-notpetya-ransomware-is-more-powerful-than-wannacry
9. Huang, D.Y., et al.: Tracking ransomware end-to-end. In: Proceedings of the 2018 IEEE Conference on Security and Privacy, SP 2018 (2018)
10. Huang, J., Xu, J., Xing, X., Liu, P., Qureshi, M.K.: Flashguard: leveraging intrinsic flash properties to defend against encryption ransomware. In: Proceedings of the 2017 ACM SIGSAC Conference on Computer and Communications Security, CCS 2017, pp. 2231–2244. ACM, New York (2017)
11. Microsoft Inc.: File system minifilter drivers, May 2014. https://msdn.microsoft.com/en-us/library/windows/hardware/ff540402(v=vs.85).aspx
12. Jayanthi, A.: First known ransomware attack in 1989 also targeted healthcare. Beckers Hospital Review, May 2016. http://www.beckershospitalreview.com/healthcare-information-technology/first-known-ransomware-attack-in-1989-also-targeted-healthcare.html
13. Kharaz, A., Arshad, S., Mulliner, C., Robertson, W., Kirda, E.: Unveil: a large-scale, automated approach to detecting ransomware. In: 25th USENIX Security Symposium (USENIX Security 2016), pp. 757–772. USENIX Association, Austin (2016)

14. Kharraz, A., Kirda, E.: Redemption: real-time protection against ransomware at end-hosts. In: Dacier, M., Bailey, M., Polychronakis, M., Antonakakis, M. (eds.) Research in Attacks, Intrusions, and Defenses. LNCS, pp. 98–119. Springer, Cham (2017). https://doi.org/10.1007/978-3-319-66332-6_5

15. Kharraz, A., Robertson, W., Balzarotti, D., Bilge, L., Kirda, E.: Cutting the gordian knot: a look under the hood of ransomware attacks. In: Almgren, M., Gulisano, V., Maggi, F. (eds.) DIMVA 2015. LNCS, vol. 9148, pp. 3–24. Springer, Cham (2015). https://doi.org/10.1007/978-3-319-20550-2_1

16. Kolodenker, E., Koch, W., Stringhini, G., Egele, M.: Paybreak: defense against cryptographic ransomware. In: Proceedings of the 2017 ACM on Asia Conference on Computer and Communications Security, ASIA CCS, pp. 599–611. ACM, New York (2017). https://doi.org/10.1145/3052973.3053035

17. Kryptel: https://www.kryptel.com/products/kryptel.php

18. Lee, J.K., Moon, S.Y., Park, J.H.: CloudRPS: a cloud analysis based enhanced ransomware prevention system. J. Supercomput. **73**(7), 3065–3084 (2017). https://doi.org/10.1145/3052973.3053035

19. Lee, J., Lee, J., Hong, J.: How to make efficient decoy files for ransomware detection? In: Proceedings of the International Conference on Research in Adaptive and Convergent Systems, pp. 208–212. ACM, New York (2017)

20. Lestringant, P., Guihéry, F., Fouque, P.A.: Automated identification of cryptographic primitives in binary code with data flow graph isomorphism. In: Proceedings of the 10th ACM Symposium on Information, Computer and Communications Security, ASIA CCS, pp. 203–214. ACM, New York (2015). https://doi.org/10.1145/2714576.2714639

21. Lin, J.: Divergence measures based on the shannon entropy. IEEE Trans. Inf. Theor. **37**(1), 145–151 (2006). https://doi.org/10.1109/18.61115

22. Malc0de: http://malc0de.com/rss

23. Malware, O.: http://openmalware.org

24. Quinlan, J.R.: C4.5: Programs for Machine Learning. Morgan Kaufmann Publishers Inc. (1993)

25. Roussev, V.: Data fingerprinting with similarity digests. In: Chow, K.-P., Shenoi, S. (eds.) DigitalForensics 2010. IAICT, vol. 337, pp. 207–226. Springer, Heidelberg (2010). https://doi.org/10.1007/978-3-642-15506-2_15

26. Scaife, N., Carter, H., Traynor, P., Butler, K.R.B.: Cryptolock (and drop it): stopping ransomware attacks on user data. In: 2016 IEEE 36th International Conference on Distributed Computing Systems (ICDCS), pp. 303–312, June 2016. https://doi.org/10.1109/ICDCS.2016.46

27. Sgandurra, D., Muñoz-González, L., Mohsen, R., Lupu, E.C.: Automated dynamic analysis of ransomware: benefits. Limitations and use for detection, ArXiv e-prints, September 2016

28. VirusTotal: https://www.virustotal.com

29. VXVault: http://vxvault.siri-urz.net/URL_List.php

30. Wong, J.C., Solon, O.: Massive ransomware cyber-attack hits nearly 100 countries around the world. Theguardian, May. https://www.theguardian.com/technology/2017/may/12/global-cyber-attack-ransomware-nsa-uk-nhs

31. Xu, D., Ming, J., Wu, D.: Cryptographic function detection in obfuscated binaries via bit-precise symbolic loop mapping. In: Proceedings 2017 IEEE Symposium on Security and Privacy, pp. 129–140, May 2017

32. Zelster: https://zeltser.com/malware-sample-sources/

DDoS Attacks

DDoS Attacks

DNS Unchained: Amplified Application-Layer DoS Attacks Against DNS Authoritatives

Jonas Bushart[✉] and Christian Rossow

CISPA, Saarland University, Saarbrücken, Germany
{jonas.bushart,rossow}@cispa.saarland

Abstract. We present DNS UNCHAINED, a new application-layer DoS attack against core DNS infrastructure that for the first time uses amplification. To achieve an attack amplification of 8.51, we carefully chain CNAME records and force resolvers to perform deep name resolutions—effectively overloading a target authoritative name server with valid requests. We identify 178 508 potential amplifiers, of which 74.3% can be abused in such an attack due to the way they cache records with low Time-to-Live values. In essence, this allows a single modern consumer uplink to downgrade availability of large DNS setups. To tackle this new threat, we conclude with an overview of countermeasures and suggestions for DNS servers to limit the impact of DNS chaining attacks.

Keywords: DNS · Amplification attack · Application-layer attack

1 Introduction

The Domain Name System (DNS) is at the core of today's Internet and is inevitable for networked applications nowadays. Not only is DNS the primary mean for mapping and translating domain names to IP addresses. Also, several other applications heavily depend on DNS, such as load balancing (e.g., for Content Delivery Networks), anti-spam methods (e.g., DKIM [6], SPF [19], or IP address blacklists [9]) and TLS certificate pinning [10,15]. We rely on the availability of these services for everyday communication. Yet recent incidents have demonstrated how vulnerable DNS is to Denial-of-Service (DoS) attacks, even for hosters that massively invest in over-provisioning and deploy highly-reliable anycast networks. For example, in October 2016, attacks against the DNS hoster Dyn have knocked Twitter, Netflix, Paypal and Spotify offline for several hours [14]—simply because the authoritative name servers for these services were hosted by Dyn and became unresponsive due to a successful Distributed DoS (DDoS) attack against Dyn.

Up to now, DDoS attempts against the DNS infrastructure have focused mostly on volumetric attacks, where attackers aim to exhaust the bandwidth that is available to DNS hosters. In a successful attack, benign DNS queries are

© The Author(s) 2018
M. Bailey et al. (Eds.): RAID 2018, LNCS 11050, pp. 139–160, 2018.
https://doi.org/10.1007/978-3-030-00470-5_7

dropped such that normal users no longer see responses from the DNS hosters. A popular and powerful example of volumetric attacks are so called amplification attacks [22, 44], where miscreants abuse that open services (such as NTP servers) reflect answers to IP-spoofed requests. Yet any of these rather simple volumetric attacks can be filtered with the help of data scrubbing services such as Arbor, Cloudflare, or Incapsula.

In this paper, we explore *application-layer* attacks against core DNS infrastructures, namely authoritative name servers (ANSs). Compared to volumetric DoS attacks, application-layer attacks are more appealing to adversaries. In particular, they (i) are significantly harder to distinguish from benign traffic, (ii) not only target bandwidth, but also computational resources, and (iii) do not rely on IP address spoofing and can be launched even though providers deploy egress filtering [36]. This makes them attractive for botnets.

We start by describing existing forms of application-layer attack against DNS that overload a target ANS with valid DNS requests. In the simplest form, a single attack source can send queries to domains hosted by this name server. Yet in practice, attackers have distributed the attack and use resolvers as intermediaries in so called *random prefix attacks* [1, 47]. They are a form of flooding DNS attacks and get their name from the characteristic prefixes used to circumvent resolver caching. Such attacks can be launched from malware-infected devices [2] or even JavaScript and already have the potential to put large DNS hosters offline (e.g., Dyn in 2016).

We then describe a novel form of application-layer attacks that floods the victim with an order of magnitude more queries per second than random prefix attacks. We dub this attack DNS UNCHAINED, as it abuses the chaining behavior of `CNAME` and `DNAME` resource records in DNS. The core idea of our attack borrows from random prefix attacks. However, instead of blindly sending out queries to random domains hosted by the target ANS, the attacker carefully crafts long chains of DNS records (`a.target.com → b.other.com`, `b.other.com → c.target.com`, ...) that involve the target ANS in every other step. This has the effect that resolvers query the target ANS not just once, but *several* times—until the end of the chain is reached. To the best of our knowledge, this is the first DoS attack that combines amplification with application-layer attacks. We find that the vast majority of resolvers support chain lengths of 9–27 (and more) elements, resulting in tenfold amplification due to the number of times a target ANS is queried per request the attacker sends.

We complete this paper with an extensive discussion how such attacks can be remedied. We foresee countermeasures that can be deployed by ANS, such as detecting malicious DNS chains or enforcing lower bounds, ensuring more caching, for TTL values. discuss how resolvers can mitigate attacks by capping DNS chains without compromising the benign usage of chains in DNS.

Our contributions can be summarized as follows:

– We present an application-layer attack against DNS that create an order of magnitude more queries per second than existing attacks. For this attack, we revisit how DNS chains can be abused to amplify traffic, and are the first to combine application-layer attacks with amplification.

- We analyze the real-world impact by performing Internet-wide measurements of the resolver landscape and test for the achievable amplification.
- We present and discuss the efficacy of countermeasures against application-layer DoS attacks. This discussion helps to defend against DNS UNCHAINED and DNS application-layer attacks in general.

2   Threat Model

We now define the treat model and describe the attacker's capabilities, required resources, and our assumptions about the victim. The adversary in our model aims to degrade the availability of an authoritative name server (ANS). ANSs answer DNS queries for a particular zone, as queried by any DNS resolver. Next to mapping domain names to IP addresses, ANSs provide several other services, e.g., anti-spam methods (e.g., DKIM [6], SPF [19], or IP address blacklists [9]) and TLS certificate pinning [10,15], making them fundamental on the Internet.

In the highly redundant DNS setting, resolvers choose between all ANSs of a particular zone [33,53]. Yet even a single unresponsive ANS will cause decreased performance for the whole domain within the zone. In a redundant setup with multiple anycast sites, the loss of one anycast site will still affect the networks routing to this site, therefore the responsiveness of every single ANS matters.

In our model, the attacker targets a specific ANS, e.g., to render domains hosted by this ANS unreachable. We assume that the attacker can host at least one attacker-controlled zone on the target ANS. This involves that the attacker can create arbitrary DNS records that are within their zone, i.e., subdomains for a given second-level domain. We believe that this assumption is easily fulfilled. For example, if domains are hosted by web hosters such as GoDaddy or Rackspace, an attacker can set up a domain at the same hoster as the victim's website. Another possibility is that the victim's domain is hosted using one of the DNS hosters like NS1, Amazon Route 53, Dyn, or Google Cloud DNS.

Creating an account may be a problem for an attacker who wants to stay anonymous. We note that in such cases the attacker could use fake or stolen IDs to register an account.

The only other requirement on the attacker is the ability to send DNS queries to open DNS resolvers ("resolvers" hereafter). Attackers can find such resolvers by scanning the Internet UDP port 53 in less than an hour [11]. Internet scans are not a limiting factor, as there are also lists of resolvers available for download [4]. Also, in contrast to amplification DDoS attacks [44], the attacker in our model does not need to spoof the source IP address of attack traffic. This allows an attacker to operate from a single source, or to increase anonymity and bandwidth by leveraging DDoS botnets to launch attacks.

3   Application Layer DDoS Against DNS

Application layer DoS attacks abuse a higher-level protocol—in our context DNS—and tie resources of other participants of the same protocol. This distinguishes application-level attacks from other forms of DoS attacks, e.g., volumetric attacks, which are agnostic to protocol and application, but relatively easy to filter and defend against. Application-layer attacks can target more different resources like CPU time and upstream bandwidth, while volumetric attacks can only consume downstream bandwidths, making them interesting for many cases. In this section we will first introduce DNS water torture attacks, an emerging application layer DoS technique that has already severely threatened the DNS infrastructure. We will then show that a smart attacker can craft delicate chains of DNS records to leverage resolvers for even more powerful attacks than those possible with DNS water torture.

3.1   DNS Water Torture

DNS water torture attacks—also known as random prefix attacks—flood the victim's DNS servers with requests such that the server runs out of resources to respond to benign queries. Such attacks typically target the authoritative name server (ANS) hosting the victim's domain, such that domains hosted at the target server become unreachable. Resolvers would typically cache the responses of the queried domains, and therefore mitigate naïve floods in that they refrain from identical follow-up queries. To this end, attackers evade caching by using unique domain names for each query, forcing resolvers to forward all queries to the target ANS. A common way is prepending a unique sequence to the domain—the random prefix. In practice, attackers either use monotonically increasing counters, hash this counter, or use a dictionary to create prefixes. As the DNS infrastructure, on the other hand, heavily relies on caching on multiple layers in the DNS hierarchy, ANS are typically not provisioned to withstand many unique and thus non-cached requests—leaving ANS vulnerable to water torture attacks.

Water torture attacks were observed for the first time in early 2014 [1, 41, 51] and have since been launched repeatedly. The main ingredient for this attack is sufficient attack bandwidth, which overloads the target ANS with "too many" requests. As this does not require IP spoofing, attackers can easily facilitate botnets to maximize their attack bandwidth. In fact, several large DDoS botnets (e.g., Mirai [2] or Elknot [28]) support DNS water torture.

While water torture attacks have been fairly effective, their naïve concept has noticeable limitations:

1. Water torture attacks can usually be easily detected because the attack traffic shows exceptionally high failure rates for particular domains, as none of the requested (random-looking) domain names actually exists. NXDOMAIN responses are normally caused by configuration error and therefore often monitored.

2. Water torture attacks provide no amplification, as every query by the attacker eventually results in only a single query to the target ANS—unless queries are resent in case of packet loss. The victim-facing attack traffic is thus bound by number of queries that the attacker can send. This is in stark contrast to volumetric attacks that offer more than tenfold amplification [44].

3.2   Chaining-Based DNS DoS Attack

We now propose a novel type of DNS application layer attacks that abuse chains in DNS to overcome the aforementioned limitations of water torture, yet stay in a similar threat model (Sect. 2). The main intuition of our attack is that an attacker can utilize request chains that amplify the attack volume towards a target ANS. This is achieved via aliases, i.e., a popular feature defined in the DNS specification and frequently used in practice.

CNAME **Records** DNS request chains exist due to the functionality of creating aliases in DNS, e.g., using standard CNAME resource records (RR) [31,32]. A CNAME RR, short for *canonical name*, works similar to pointers in programming languages. Instead of providing the desired data for a resolver, CNAME specifies a different DNS location from where to request the RR. One common use is to share the same RRs for a domain and the which overloads the target ANS with "www" subdomain. In this case, a CNAME entry for "www.example.com." points to "example.com.". When a client asks the resolver for the RRs of a certain type and domain, the resolver recursively queries the ANS for the RRs, resulting in three cases to consider:

Domain Does Not Exist or No Data. The domain does not exist (NXDOMAIN status) or no matching resource record (including CNAME records) was found (NODATA status). The ANS returns this status.

Resource Records Exists. The desired resource record's data is immediately returned by the ANS. The DNS specification enforces that *either* data, *or* an alias (i.e., CNAME) may exist for a domain, but never both—i.e., there was no CNAME record for the request domain.

Domain Exists and Contains. CNAME response The resolver must follow the CNAME regardless of the requested record type. This may cause the resolver to send new queries, potentially even to different ANSs.

The last case allows chaining of several requests. In case of CNAME records, resolvers have to perform multiple lookups to load the data (unless the records are cached). CNAME records can also be chained, meaning the target of a CNAME records points to another CNAME record. This increases the number of lookups per initial query. There is no strict limit to the length of chains. However, resolvers typically enforce a limit to prevent loops of CNAME records. After reaching this limit, resolvers either provide a partial answer, or respond with an error message.

Note that CNAME records provide delegation between arbitrary domains, i.e., also to domains in unrelated zones. If all the CNAME records are hosted in the

```
a.target-ans.com.     IN CNAME b.intermediary.org.
c.target-ans.com.     IN CNAME d.intermediary.org.
e.target-ans.com.     IN CNAME f.intermediary.org.
g.target-ans.com.     IN CNAME h.intermediary.org.
i.target-ans.com.     IN TXT "Huge record at the end."

b.intermediary.org.   IN CNAME c.target-ans.com.
d.intermediary.org.   IN CNAME e.target-ans.com.
f.intermediary.org.   IN CNAME h.target-ans.com.
h.intermediary.org.   IN CNAME i.target-ans.com.
```

Listing 1. Two zones "`target-ans.com.`" and "`intermediary.org.`", which contain a `CNAME` that ends at the ith element in `TXT` records.

same zone, the ANS can provide multiple `CNAME`s in one answer, by already providing the next records in the chain. By chaining `CNAME` records between two different ANSs, i.e., by alternating between them, an ANS can only know the next `CNAME` entry in the chain.

DNS Chaining Attack. The possibility to chain DNS queries via `CNAME` RRs opens a new form of application-layer DoS attack. Let an attacker set up two domains on different ANSs. The first domain will be hosted by the target ANS, and the second (or optionally further) domain(s) by some *intermediary* ANS(s). The zones are configured to contain long `CNAME` chains alternating between both domains. An example can be found in Listing 1, where a chain ping-pongs between the target and an intermediary ANS, until the record with prefix i. If an attacker now sends a single name lookup to query for the record at the start of the chain, the resolver has to follow all chain elements to retrieve the final RR. A large final RR, such as the `TXT`, additionally targets the ANS's upstream bandwidth. Figure 1 shows the queries sent between the attacker A, a resolver R, and both ANSs. The dashed arrows represent the `CNAME` pointers between the different domains, while the circled numbers (①—③) represent the order in which they are resolved. The attacker queries the first chain element and forces the resolver to query the target ANS repeatedly.

This provides severe amplification, as a single request by the attacker results in several requests towards the target ANS. For each query by the attacker N queries are sent by the resolver, where N is equal to the minimum of the chain length and a resolver dependent limit. The chain length is controllable by the attacker and effectively unlimited, but resolver implementations limit the maximum recursion depth (see Sect. 4.2). The *amplification*, as observed by the target ANS, is $\lceil N/2 \rceil$, as every second chain record is served by the target ANS.

For illustrative purposes, Fig. 1 just shows a single resolver. In practice, an attacker would likely aim to spread the attack requests to thousands of resolvers, that is, not to overload a single resolver—recall that in our threat model the ANS is the victim (not the resolver). Furthermore, given two domains, an attacker can

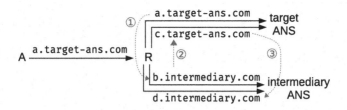

Fig. 1. Attacker A uses resolver R to attack the target ANS. The dashed arrows represent the CNAME pointers between the domain. ①–③ show the order of CNAME records in the chain. The setup is according to Listing 1.

easily create multiple chains, e.g., by using distinct subdomains for each chain. The number of chains is bound (if at all) only by the number of subdomains supported by the target ANS.

There are no strict requirements for the intermediary ANS. In general, intermediary ANSs can be hosted by a hosting provider, self-hosted by the attacker, or even distributed between multiple hosters. The only exception is that the intermediary and target ANS should be not the same server. Some ANSs will follow CNAME chains if the ANS is authoritative for all domains in the chain. Requiring at least one dedicated intermediary ANSs ensures that only one answer can be returned. If the ANS is configured to only return one CNAME record, the same ANS can be used, doubling the amplification achieved with this attack. On the other extreme, it is perfectly possible to use *multiple* intermediate ANS, as long as every second element in the chain still points to the target ANS. Distributing the intermediary ANS will increase the reliability and reduce the load for each intermediary ANS, and raise the complexity in preventing the attack.

While the requirements for this attack may seem high, we note that attackers are already known to use complex setups for their operations. One example regarding DNS are *fast-flux networks* [16] which provide resilience against law-enforcement take-downs and work similar to CDNs. Attackers use fast changing DNS entries to distribute traffic across sometimes hundreds of machines.

3.3   Leveraging DNS Caching

DNS resolvers rely on record caching, such that queries for the same domain do not require additional recursive resolution if the resolver has those records cached. Technically, each resource record contains a Time-to-Live (TTL) value, which specifies how long it may be cached by a resolver, i.e., be answered without querying the ANS. Caching has a large influence on the DNS chaining attack, as it determines how frequent resolvers will query target and intermediary ANSs.

An attacker would aim for two compatible goals. On the one hand, given an attack time span, the target ANS should receive as many queries as possible. This means that caching for those records that are delivered by the target ANS should be ideally avoided. On the other hand, an attacker wants to minimize the number of queries sent to the intermediary ANS, as they would otherwise slow down the overall attack. We discuss both parts individually in the following.

Avoiding Caching at Target ANS: Determining the overall impact on ANS requires an understanding how often each resolver can be used by the attacker during an attack. That is, if all records of a chain are cached, the resolver would not query the target ANS. To solve this problem, attackers can disable caching for records hosted by the target ANS. Specifying a TTL value of zero indicates that the resource should never be cached [32, Sect. 3.2.1]. We assume that resolvers honor a TTL of zero, i.e., do not cache such entries. We evaluate this assumption in Sect. 4.1.

However, we have observed that resolvers implement additional *micro-caching* strategies to further reduce the number of outgoing queries. A strategy we have typically observed is that resolvers coalesce multiple identical incoming or outgoing requests. If a resolver detects that a given RR is not in the cache, it starts requesting the data from the ANS. Queries by other clients for the same RR may arrive in the meantime. A micro-caching resolver can answer all outstanding client queries at once when the authoritative answer arrives, even if the RR would not normally be cached (i.e., TTL = 0). In our context, such micro-caching might occur if the resolver receives a query for a `CNAME` record of which the target is not cached, but another query for the same target is already outstanding. Coalescing identical queries thus results in fewer outgoing queries to the ANSs, because a single authoritative reply is used to answer multiple client queries. This reduces the amplification caused by the resolver. Micro-caching is a defense mechanism against cache poisoning attacks which make use of the "birthday attack", such as the Kaminsky attack [7,18].

We thus define the *per-resolver query frequency* as the maximum number of queries per second an attacker can send to a given resolver *without* any query being answered by caching or micro-caching. It equals the optimal attack speed: Fewer queries would not use the resolver's full amplification potential, more queries would waste attack bandwidth.

Leveraging Caching at Intermediary ANSs: Recall that every other chain element points to a record hosted by an intermediary ANS. In principle, this would require resolvers to query the intermediary ANS for every second step in the chain, which significantly reduces the frequency in which the target ANS receives queries. However, those records do not change, so we can leverage caching to increase this frequency. By setting a non-zero TTL for the records hosted by the intermediary ANSs, the resolvers only have to fetch the records on the first query of the chain. After the caches are "warmed up", the resolvers will only fetch the records from the target ANS. The frequency of attack queries is thus largely determined by the round trip time (RTT) between resolver and target ANS. In contrast, the RTT between resolver and intermediary ANS is irrelevant.

3.4 Attack Variant with `DNAME` Resource Records

One drawback of the `CNAME`-based attack is, that it requires definitions of records *per chain*. If an attacker aims to abuse multiple chains in parallel (e.g., to increase the *per-resolver query frequency*), they have to define dozens of `CNAME` records. One slight variation of the `CNAME`-based attack thus uses `DNAME` records. Using `DNAME` resource records [5,43] allows arbitrary many sub-domains for the chain with only a single entry. Conceptually, `DNAME`s are similar to `CNAME`s and are created like `CNAME` records, e.g., "`www.target-ans.com. IN DNAME intermediary.org.`". The difference is that `DNAME` records allow the ANS to replace the occurrence of the owner (left-hand side) by the target (right-hand side) for all queries to a subdomain of the owner. For example, a query to "`a.www.target-ans.com.`" would be rewritten to "`a.intermediary.org.`" with the given rule.

Technically, the answer for a `DNAME` resource record does not only contain the `DNAME` resource records. For backwards compatibility, ANSs will create a synthetic `CNAME` resource record for the exact query domain. Resolvers can also directly support `DNAME` resource records, providing a better user experience. However, resolvers that lack support for `DNAME` records fall back using the `CNAME` records. An attacker can abuse those resolvers to query chains defined with `DNAME` entries, for simulating an arbitrary number of chains and avoid caching. Those resolvers have to use the synthetic `CNAME` records to follow the chain. Because the records are synthetically created for the exact query domain, they are indistinguishable from "normal" `CNAME` records in a zone. This forces the resolver to query the ANS for each newly observed subdomain.

Resolvers that support `DNAME`s can use a cached entry to directly answer queries for all subdomains, even if the exact subdomain has never been observed. This improves the resolver's performance, as only one cache entry has to be stored (compared to many `CNAME`s) and authoritative queries only need to be issued, if the `DNAME` entry expires (compared to once for each new subdomain). This effectively limits the number of simulated chains to one, which falls back to the same properties as the classic `CNAME`-based chain. Resolvers without `DNAME` support can be queried as often as permitted by the resolver's resources, without paying attention to any macro- or micro-caching. Furthermore, handling `DNAME` queries consumes more resources at the target ANS, as resolvers usually create and send synthetic `CNAME` records in addition to `DNAME` records.

4 Evaluation

In the following we analyze the behavior of resolvers, with Internet-wide measurements, and analyze four selected implementations in more detail. We will use those measurements to determine the per-resolver query frequency, possible amplification factor, and overall impact, focusing only on the `CNAME` variant.

In our manual analysis we focus on the four resolvers Bind[1] 9.10.5,Unbound[2] 1.6.3, PowerDNS Recursor[3] 4.0.6, and Knot Resolver[4] 1.3.2, because they are popular, open source, actively maintained, and backed by DNS operators. All tests were performed in the default configuration, as provided by Fedora 25. For the measurements, we set up two virtual machines (VMs). The first VM hosts the four resolvers, while the second VM hosts an ANS. We configured the resolvers to use the ANS for all queries, by setting corresponding root hints and configuring the ANS accordingly. Note that in this minimal setup the second VM hosts both the target and intermediary ANS. We thus changed Bind's configuration such that it does not follow CNAME chains[5], to simulate two independent ANSs.

We scanned the Internet via Zmap [11] and a custom DNS module, following their recommended scanning guidelines. Networks could opt-out from our scans. We encoded the IP address of the scan target into each DNS query, which allows us to correlate the scanned IP address with the traffic captured at our ANS. We used PowerDNS with a custom back-end as the ANS authoritative for the domains we scanned for. PowerDNS will never follow CNAME chains and only return a single CNAME record, simulating the two zone setup.

4.1 Caching

So far we assumed that resolvers honor non-cachable DNS resource records (i.e., TTL = 0). We evaluate this assumption and study the micro-caching strategies by different DNS resolver implementations.

First, we want to get a general understanding how the different implementations handle non-cacheable responses. We configured our ANS to serve a short CNAME chain alternating between two zones. All RRs in the chain are served with TTL=0. We repeatedly issued the same query to the resolver and observed the responses. Bind, Unbound, and PowerDNS do not cache the response and served it with a TTL of zero. Knot serves the record with a TTL of five, but also does not cache the response.

To test the micro-caching behavior, we sent multiple queries to the resolvers for the same domain with slight delays between them, and observed how frequent resolvers queried the ANS. The delay was chosen such that the resolver has forwarded the previous query to the ANS, but not yet received the response. This happens if queries arrive faster than the RTT between resolver and target (RTT_{RT}). We delayed DNS responses from the authoritative VM to the resolvers, to simulate the effect of different values for RTT_{RT}. We observed micro-caching for identical incoming or outgoing queries for all tested resolvers. Effectively, this limits an attacker to start a chain once per RTT_{RT}. The RTT is measured between resolver and target ANS, because resource records of the intermediary ANS can be cached by the resolver and thus do not limit the lookup speed.

---

[1] https://www.isc.org/downloads/bind/.

[2] https://www.unbound.net/.

[3] https://www.powerdns.com/recursor.html.

[4] https://www.knot-resolver.cz/.

[5] Config option additional-from-auth with two zones.

Next, we observe the behavior for longer delays. We delayed the second query until the resolver processed the response of the first queried (and hence started to resolve the second chain element). This simulates queries which arrive RTT_{RT} after the previous query arrived. PowerDNS and Knot fully honor the no-caching TTL and perform a full lookup for all queries. Bind performs one full lookup per second, then only issues one query to the first element of the chain per additional client query. Similarly, Unbound only performs one full lookup per second, but then issues one query to the *last* element of the chain, which is not a CNAME RR.

Summarizing the result, the per-resolver query frequency for PowerDNS and Knot is $\frac{\#\text{chains}}{RTT_{RT}}$. As each chain has distinct domains, micro-caching is irrelevant across chains. Bind and Unbound can be queried at most for $\frac{\#\text{chains}}{1s+RTT_{RT}}$. Realistically, the attacker does not know when the resolver's internal clock ticks over to the next second. Before starting the next query, the attacker has to ensure a full second passes after the record was cached, which happens RTT_{RT} after the query is received by the resolver. Thus at $1s + RTT_{RT}$ the record is guaranteed to have expired. Querying more frequently reduces amplification.

We analyzed the code of Bind and Unbound to understand why they only issue one query per second. Both use a time value, which is rounded to seconds for all cache operations, explaining the observed cache invalidation once per second. Bind special cases the first CNAME RR in a query and always perform the authoritative lookup, even when it was fetched from cache. Unbound's cache inserts referral resource records, which CNAMEs are one variant of, regardless of the TTL, but not the last chain element.

Internet Measurements. While all locally tested resolvers honor non-cacheable RRs, resolvers deployed on the Internet may behave differently. To assess this, we performed a full Internet scan querying for a wildcard A RR with a TTL=0 hosted by our ANS. The queried domain encodes the scan target's IP address, which allows us to (i) ensure that all records are fetched from our ANS and are not cached and (ii) match the scan targets with the queries observed at the ANS. All responses are recorded and filtered to remove domains which do not belong to our test. Figure 2 shows a (simplified) diagram of the connections between our scanner, resolvers, and our ANS. The dashed gray lines mark the point of our packet capturing. Below them are the number of IP addresses we found.

4 170 710 resolvers responded to our scan query, of which 3097203 answers had a TTL of zero. For the same day (2017-08-02), Shadowserver's DNS scan [45] reports 4 198 025 resolvers found, i.e., a deviation of just 0.7. The scan shows that 74.3% of all resolvers honor TTL=0 and they could be used for attacks.

Of those resolvers that enforce a minimal non-zero TTL in the response, most enforce large TTLs, making them unsuitable for DNS UNCHAINED attacks. The ten most common TTL values we found are multiples of ten or 60. In decreasing order of occurrence they are 300, 600, 3600, 1, 30, 900, 60, 150, 14400, and 20, which taken together account for 24.8% (1033419) of all responses.

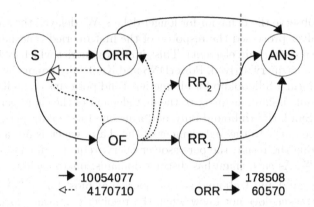

Fig. 2. Connections between different resolver types. Our scanner (S) finds open forwarder (OF) and open recursive resolver (ORR). A forwarder forwards the query to one or multiple recursive resolver (RR). Recursive resolver (RR and ORR) query the authoritative name server (ANS). Dashed arrows mark optional connections, like querying multiple recursive resolver or sending a response to our scanner. An empty arrow head marks a query response.

4.2   Amplification

After seeing that the vast majority of resolvers does not cache TTL=0 RRs, we now measure how much amplification in-the-wild resolvers would enable. The amplification factor is determined by the maximum number of elements of the chain that will be requested by each resolver. We thus configured a chain of 100 RRs and requested the first element from each resolver. The last chain element is an A record and all RRs carry $TTL = 0$.

Bind follows the chain 17 times, whereas PowerDNS and Unbound only perform 12 and 9 lookup steps, respectively. Knot Resolver performs 33 lookups. Bind is the only implementation that consistently responds with a "no error" status code. The other three reply with a SERVFAIL status code if the end of the chain could not be reached.

Via our scans, we discovered 10054077 open resolvers and 178508 recursive resolvers. Figure 2 gives an overview of the connections between scanner and resolvers. Open resolvers are open to the Internet and can be used by anyone. They can be recursive resolvers or simple forwarders, which forward the query to a recursive resolver. *Recursive resolvers* perform the recursive lookup procedure which we can detect at our ANS. We can count and distinguish the two types of resolvers based on the traffic captured at our ANS. If the encoded IP address of the scan target and the source IP address of the resolver querying our ANS are identical, then the resolver is an open recursive resolver, otherwise the encoded IP address belongs to an open forwarding resolver. We expect a much higher number of open resolvers than recursive resolver, because as Kührer et al. [24] found, most open resolvers are routers or other embedded devices. There is little reason for them to host a recursive resolver, because they require more resources.

Figure 3 shows how many resolvers support a given chain length. There are clear spikes for common values like nine, used by Unbound and Microsoft DNS, or 17 as used by Bind. Another spike is at length 21, yet we are not aware which software causes it. The quick drop-off at the beginning is caused by resolvers, which query the same domain from different IP addresses often in the same subnet. In these cases only one of the resolvers performs the full recursion, the others stop early leading to the drop. This could be caused by open resolvers querying multiple recursive resolvers in a short amount of time. Alternatively, it might result from an attempt to pre-fetch data for multiple resolvers as soon as one recursive resolver in the pool sees a new domain name.

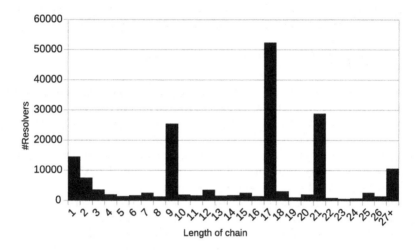

Fig. 3. Supported chain length configurations for 178 508 recursive resolvers discovered with a full Internet scan. The spike at nine corresponds to Unbound and Microsoft DNS version; Bind shows up as the spike at 17. The cause of the 21-spike is unknown to us.

From the data we can conclude that resolvers do offer a considerable amplification potential. Intuitively, the amplification factor is the number of queries seen by the target ANS in relation to the number of queries sent by the attacker. Factors larger than one mean the impact on the target is larger than the attacker's resources used for the attack. We can calculate the expected amplification ratio for all recursive resolvers by

$$\frac{\sum_{i=1}^{\infty} \left(\left\lceil \frac{i}{2} \right\rceil \times n_i \right)}{\sum_{i=1}^{\infty} n_i}$$

where n_i is the number of resolvers that support chains of length i. The formula assumes that the first element in the chain is hosted on the target ANS, which is the more beneficial setup for an attacker.

All resolvers together (178508) provide an amplification factor of 7.59. Focusing only on resolvers, which provide an amplification factor >1 (chains of length three or longer) results in an amplification factor of 8.51 with 156481 available resolvers. These numbers are lower bounds, because the early drop-off in Fig. 3 is caused by resolvers that query the same domain name from different IP addresses (which we then conservatively count as individual resolvers).

We already mentioned in Sect. 3.2 that some ANSs do not follow CNAME chains, even if they are authoritative for all domains. This is a performance optimization reducing the work required to answer a query. For ANSs, which do not follow chains, all elements of the chain can be hosted on the target ANS thus an amplification factor of 14.34 can be achieved resulting in 89% stronger attacks. Effectively, this removes the intermediary ANSs from the chain and all resource records need to have a zero TTL value.

4.3   Overall Impact

Based on these observations, we conclude that CNAME chains enable for attacks that are an order of magnitude larger (measured in queries per second) than naïve water torture attacks. In practice, ANSs can handle 400 000 qps to 2 500 000 qps (queries per second) [3,20,34,42]. An attacker only needs a fraction—determined by the amplification factor—of queries compared to that number. Often even lower query rates are sufficient to overload the ANS, because the ANS also receives (and has to process) benign queries.

A single chain, which is resolved by all non-caching resolvers, causes more than a million queries to the target ANS ($7.59 \times 178508 \times 75\% \approx 1016157$). Each resolver can be queried roughly every second per chain (assuming a low RTT_{RT}). Using as few as two or three chains is enough to overload all commonly deployed ANS. For three chains the attacker has to send 535 524 pps (packets per second). A DNS query packet with a 20 character long domain name requires 104 B (including Ethernet preamble and inter-packet gap) for transmission over the wire. The attacker needs 445.6 Mbit/s to overload even the fastest ANS.

In case the target ANS does not follow the CNAME chain, the stronger attack can be used where all elements are hosted on the target ANS. A single chain causes over 1.9 million queries ($14.34 \times 178508 \times 75\% \approx 1919854$) reducing the required bandwidth for the attacker accordingly.

5   Countermeasures

We will now discuss countermeasures to reduce the impact of DNS application-level attacks. First, we cover the authoritative view, how zones could be managed and the effect of response rate limiting. Then we look at the behavior of recursive resolvers and how they could reduce the impact on ANSs.

5.1 Identification and Remedy by ANSs

A hard requirement for the proposed attack is that the attacker can create CNAME RRs on the target ANS. This gives the target ANS the power to inspect and deny problematic or malicious configurations or completely remove zones from the ANS.

Detection of CNAME Chains. Zone files for the DNS UNCHAINED require several CNAME records pointing to external domains. If the attacker chooses random or pseudo-random domain names, ANSs can use this as an indicator for an attack. The target ANS operator could additionally check the target of CNAMEs and discourage (or even forbid) CNAMEs that point to CNAME RRs in other domains (which is already discourage according to the specification). Exceptions are likely required for content delivery networks and cloud provider. Especially CNAME chains, i.e., several entries that eventually lead back to the same zone are not useful, because both records are controlled by the same entity.

The ANS operator needs to implement periodic checks of all zones with CNAME entries. Only checking RRs during creation is insufficient, as the attacker can build the chain such that no CNAME points to another CNAME during creation. Given the same domains as in Listing 1, the attacker would first create "a.target-ans.com." while the target domain ("b.intermediary.org.") either does not exist or only contains other types, e.g., of type A. Checking the RR for "a.target-ans.com." will not show any suspicious behavior. Now the same steps are repeated with "b.intermediary.org.". This forces a non-trivial amount of work on the ANS. A too long periodicity in the checking would allow the attacker to use the time between checks for the attack, thus the checks have to be somewhat frequent.

Lower Limit for Time-to-Live (TTL) Values. In contrast to water torture attacks, chaining attacks fall apart if the chain's RRs are cached. Using a random prefix to circumvent caching is only possible for the specific combination of using DNAME RRs and abusing only those resolvers that do not support DNAME. Thus, forcing a minimal TTL of only a few seconds will have considerable impact, as it limits the per-resolver query frequency to $\frac{\#\text{chains}}{TTL+RTT_{RT}}$ compared to $\frac{\#\text{chains}}{1s+RTT_{RT}}$. Thus, a 10 s TTL will reduce the impact by roughly a factor of ten. However, an attacker can use more chains if a minimal TTL is enforced, which makes the setup more complicated. On the one hand, CNAME RRs with short (or zero) TTLs are used also for benign reasons, e.g., to implement DNS-based failover. On the other hand, in light of chaining attacks, we consider serving A and AAAA records with short TTLs as the better solution, which also closer resembles the desired semantics. Note, that a CNAME RR offers an additional canonical name for an already existing record, which is a relationship that rarely changes (and thus allows for non-zero TTLs).

5.2 Response Rate Limiting (RRL)

Response Rate Limiting (RRL) is an effective technique to counter standard DNS-based amplification attacks. If DNS servers are abused for reflective amplification attacks [24,44], the attacker sets the request's source to the IP address of the victim. In turn, resolvers unknowingly flood the victim with DNS responses. To prevent such abuse, resolvers can implement IP address-based access control, which effectively turns them into closed resolvers.

Yet this is not an option for intended open resolvers (e.g., Google DNS, Quad9, etc.) and especially not for ANSs, as they *have* to be reachable by the entire Internet. Here, RRL plays an important role. RRL limits the frequency of how fast a client IP address can receive responses. The benefit for reflection attacks is clear, where a single source (the victim) *seemingly* requests millions of requests and now only faces a fraction of the actual responses due to RRL.

In principle, RRL also seems to mitigate chaining attacks. Yet enabling RRL has its downsides, especially if resolvers hit a rate limit configured at an ANS. Resolvers will then retry queries, lacking an answer, which again increases the load on the ANS. Filtering all resolver traffic can even increase the incoming traffic ten-fold as observed by Verisign during a water torture attack [51, p. 24].

Additionally, RRL is implemented with a slip rate, which specifies how often the ANS will answer with a truncated response instead of dropping the packet. For example, a slip rate of two results in a truncated answer for every second query, the other times the query is dropped. Truncated responses then cause the resolver to retry the connection using TCP instead of UDP, which *drastically* increases the overall processing overhead for the ANS.

An ideal RRL configuration would thus never limit resolvers, as this may actually increase the required resources for the ANS in case of application-layer attacks. Filtering or rate limiting needs to be performed closer to the source. Naïvely, one could deploy RRL at resolvers to rate limit the initial attack requests ("chain starts") sent to them. However, then again the per-resolver request frequency is as low as one request per second, which would only be blocked by an overly aggressive RRL configuration. Even worse, if attacks are carried out via botnets, even those RRL configurations would not slow down the attacks.

5.3 Back-Off Strategies

In case of packet loss at the target ANS, resolvers resend queries and thereby cause additional attack traffic. It is thus important to rate limit outgoing queries of resolvers and to implement suitable back-off strategies in order to give overloaded ANSs the chance to recover.

To assess how resolvers act in such situations, we have measured how four resolver implementations behave when querying a zone with two ANSs of which both are not reachable. Bind sends a total of five packets with a delay of 800 ms in between packets. The ANS is chosen at random. After the third failed packet, Bind has an exponential back-off with factor two. PowerDNS only sends out two packets in total with a delay of 1500 ms in between. Unbound sends in total the most queries with range2730. Worse, Unbound always sends two queries as a pair, which might go to the same or a different ANS. There is a delay of 375 ms between the pairs, which is doubled every two to four pairs. Knot has the most complicated retry strategy. Knot starts with sending UDP queries alternating to both servers, with a delay of 250 ms in between. After a total of two seconds, two TCP queries are sent to the first ANS, with a delay of 1000 ms between them. Six seconds after the start the same pattern of UDP and TCP queries is sent to the second ANS.

Bind's and PowerDNS's behavior are not problematic, as the number of retries is small and retry delay high. Especially problematic for Unbound is that it sends two identical queries to the same ANS without a delay between. Delaying retries is a good balance between providing fast answers (in case of packet loss) and not sending duplicate queries (in case of high round trip times). A delay of 250 ms between retries will cause unnecessary retries for many users. With our Internet scan we found that 9045 recursive resolvers (14.9%) have RTTs larger than 250 ms to both our ANSs and additional 19 773 resolvers (32.6%) have such a high RTT to one of our ANSs.

An additional strategy is serving stale cache records [26]. Stale cache records are records in the resolver's cache of which the TTL has expired. A resolver can use them based on the assumption that normally records contain working data, even if the TTL has expired (e.g., IP addresses change less often than the TTL of records expires). This technique is not new and already implemented in Bind 9.12 [29] and used by OpenDNS [35] and Akamai [27]. The usability improves as client will receive an answer, which likely is usable, instead of receiving an error and failing to connect.

5.4   Recursion Depth Limit

Finally, also resolvers can more strictly limit the length of CNAME chains. Section 4.2 has shown that the resolvers do not agree on the maximum chain length. Limiting the length too strictly is harmful, as chains also exist for legitimate reasons—such as Content Delivery Networks (CDNs) and DDoS protection services. The domain owner can often configure their DNS to point to a subdomain of the CDN and the CDN uses itself one or multiple CNAME RRs.

Legitimate use-cases for CNAME chains must ensure the length is supported by all DNS resolvers, if they want to support all users. We inspected the Active DNS [21] data set to identify benign chains. We extracted the CNAME entries from 2017-10-05 to reconstruct the longest benign chains, which consists of eight elements (seven CNAMEs and one final RR). This fits to the shortest recursion limit of nine elements, which we observed for Unbound. Others [38] report nine elements as the longest legitimate chain they found and certificate authorities are also only required to support chains with nine elements while fetching CAA RRs [13]. Based on those observations, a smaller recursion limit can be advised. We recommend supporting nine elements in a chain, which is the shortest value of all tested resolvers and covers benign chains. Such a recursion depth limit would limit the amplification of chaining attacks to factor five.

6   Related Work

Application-Layer DDoS in DNS: Several application-layer DDoS defenses have been proposed in the past [12,30,39,52]. Many defenses are not immediately applicable to DNS. Protocol changes, such as client puzzles, would need widespread support, which is unrealistic to achieve in a short to medium time frame. Countermeasures which introduce more latency are especially problematic, as DNS is tuned for high efficiency. Filtering techniques, such as egress or ingress filtering, do not apply to DNS UNCHAINED, because it works without IP address spoofing. Blocking DNS traffic can even lead to more inbound traffic [51] and always risks blocking legitimate users.

The closest work to us is research on DNS water torture attacks. They were first presented in Feb 2014 [1] and are a known phenomenon for DNS operators [17,48,50,51]. The DNS operator community focused on implementing mitigations, mainly to stabilize recursive resolver. Takeuchi et al. [47] propose a system to detect DNS water torture attacks based on lexical and structural features of domain names. They train a naive Bayes-classifier and test it on captured traffic of their universities network. Our attack is related to DNS water torture as both are flooding attacks using resolvers, but water torture faces several limitations—including the fact that they can be easily detected.

Reflection and Amplification Attacks: DNS also played a role in recent amplification attacks. The general risk of reflection attacks was identified by Paxson [37] and its full amplification potential presented by Rossow [44]. Different proposals to detect and defend amplification attacks [23,36,44,49] were made. They cover approaches to combat the bandwidth exhaustion, like client puzzles, or prevent source address spoofing. In the context of DNS, Kührer et al. [24,25] analyzed the amplification potential of DNS resolvers. They found millions of open DNS resolver on embedded devices or routers, meaning the openness of the resolver is likely a configuration issue. DNSSEC's potential to increase the amplification of DNS resolvers has also been documented [40]. While some attacks in fact abuse DNS, still, in contrast to our work, they do not represent application-layer attacks and are easy to filter.

CNAME Chaining: The possibility to chain CNAME RRs is well-known and documented. For example, Shue and Kalafut [46] use differences in recursion strategies to fingerprint resolver implementations. Dagon et al. [8] use CNAME chains to amplify the number of queries from each resolver. They need multiple queries by the same resolver to analyze them for source port randomization of the resolver. Pfeifer et al. [38] measures the overhead for resolvers while looking up CNAME chains and recommend that ANSs should refuse CNAME chains before loading the zone files. Furthermore, they recommend that ANSs should also query destinations of CNAME RRs, similar to our recommendation in Sect. 5.1. In contrast to prior work our attack focuses on the authoritative name servers instead of the resolvers.

7   Conclusion

We have presented a new DDoS attack against DNS authoritatives that leverages amplification on the application layer. DNS UNCHAINED achieves an amplification of 8.51 using standard DNS protocol features, by chaining alias records (e.g., CNAME) and forcing resolvers to repeatedly query the same authoritative name server. We performed full Internet scans and found 10 054 077 open DNS resolvers and 178 508 recursive resolvers. We determined that 74.3% of those resolvers support uncachable DNS responses, creating a large pool of amplifiers that can be abused for chaining attacks.

We also discussed countermeasures to the new threat of DNS chaining attacks. This includes measures applicable to DNS operators to find and limit problematic DNS zones as well as enforcing minimal Time-to-Live values allowing caching. DNS resolvers can also be changed to have less aggressive retransmission on unavailable name servers and limit chains to nine elements. A wide deployment of any of these techniques would severely degrade the performance of the proposed attacks, and we hope that our work raises awareness for the importance of these measures.

Acknowledgement. We thank our anonymous reviewers whose useful comments helped us improving the quality of our paper. This work was supported by the German Federal Ministry of Education and Research (BMBF) through funding for the BMBF project 16KIS0656 (CAMRICS).

References

1. Andrew: Water torture: a slow drip DNS DDoS attack, February 2014. https://secure64.com/water-torture-slow-drip-dns-ddos-attack/
2. Antonakakis, M., et al.: Understanding the Mirai Botnet. In: 26th USENIX Security Symposium (2017)
3. Bellis, R.: Benchmarking DNS reliably on multi-core systems, July 2015. https://www.isc.org/blogs/benchmarking-dns/
4. Censys DNS lookup full IPv4 (2017). https://censys.io/data/53-dns-lookup-full_ipv4
5. Crawford, M.: Non-terminal DNS name redirection. Technical report, RFC Editor (1999). https://doi.org/10.17487/RFC2672
6. Crocker, D., Hansen, T., Kucherawy, M.S.: Domainkeys identified mail (DKIM) signatures. Technical report, RFC Editor (2011). https://doi.org/10.17487/RFC6376
7. CVE-2008-1447. Available from MITRE, CVE-ID CVE-2008-1447, July 2008. http://cve.mitre.org/cgi-bin/cvename.cgi?name=CVE-2008-1447
8. Dagon, D., Antonakakis, M., Day, K., Luo, X., Lee, C.P., Lee, W.: Recursive DNS architectures and vulnerability implications. In: Proceedings of the Network and Distributed System Security Symposium (2009)
9. DNSBL information - spam database and blacklist check. https://www.dnsbl.info/
10. Dukhovni, V., Hardaker, W.: The DNS-based authentication of named entities (DANE) protocol: updates and operational guidance. Technical report, RFC Editor (2015). https://doi.org/10.17487/RFC7671

11. Durumeric, Z., Wustrow, E., Halderman, J.A.: ZMap: fast internet-wide scanning and its security applications. In: Proceedings of the 22th USENIX Security Symposium (2013)
12. Gilad, Y., Herzberg, A., Sudkovitch, M., Goberman, M.: CDN-on-demand: an affordable DDoS defense via untrusted clouds. In: 23rd Annual Network and Distributed System Security Symposium (2016)
13. Hallam-Baker, P.: RFC Errata for RFC 6844 "DNS Certification Authority Authorization (CAA) Resource Record". Errata 5065, RFC Editor (2017). https://www.rfc-editor.org/errata/eid5065
14. Hilton, S.: Dyn analysis summary of friday october 21 attack. https://dyn.com/blog/dyn-analysis-summary-of-friday-october-21-attack/
15. Hoffman, P.E., Schlyter, J.: The DNS-based authentication of named entities (DANE) transport layer security (TLS) protocol: TLSA. Technical report, RFC Editor (2012) https://doi.org/10.17487/RFC6698
16. Holz, T., Gorecki, C., Rieck, K., Freiling, F.C.: Measuring and detecting fast-flux service networks. In: Proceedings of the Network and Distributed System Security Symposium, NDSS 2008 (2008)
17. Internet Systems Consortium: Pseudo Random DNS Query Attacks & Resolver Mitigation Approaches (2015). https://www.nanog.org/sites/default/files/nanog63-dnstrack-winstead-attacks.pdf
18. Kaminsky, D.: It's the end of the cache as we know it. Presented at Black Ops (2008)
19. Kitterman, S.: Sender policy framework (SPF) for authorizing use of domains in email, version 1. Technical report, RFC Editor (2014). https://doi.org/10.17487/RFC7208
20. Knot DNS benchmark (2017). https://www.knot-dns.cz/benchmark/
21. Kountouras, A., et al.: Enabling network security through active DNS datasets. In: Monrose, F., Dacier, M., Blanc, G., Garcia-Alfaro, J. (eds.) RAID 2016. LNCS, vol. 9854, pp. 188–208. Springer, Cham (2016). https://doi.org/10.1007/978-3-319-45719-2_9
22. Krämer, L., et al.: AmpPot: monitoring and defending against amplification DDoS attacks. In: Bos, H., Monrose, F., Blanc, G. (eds.) RAID 2015. LNCS, vol. 9404, pp. 615–636. Springer, Cham (2015). https://doi.org/10.1007/978-3-319-26362-5_28
23. Kreibich, C., Warfield, A., Crowcroft, J., Hand, S., Pratt, I.: Using packet symmetry to curtail malicious traffic. In: Proceedings of the 4th Workshop on Hot Topics in Networks (Hotnets-VI), College Park, MD, USA (2005)
24. Kührer, M., Hupperich, T., Bushart, J., Rossow, C., Holz, T.: Going wild: large-scale classification of open DNS resolvers. In: Proceedings of the 2015 ACM Internet Measurement Conference (2015). https://doi.org/10.1145/2815675.2815683
25. Kührer, M., Hupperich, T., Rossow, C., Holz, T.: Exit from hell? Reducing the impact of amplification DDoS attacks. In: Proceedings of the 23rd USENIX Security Symposium (2014)
26. Lawrence, D., Kumari, W.: Serving stale data to improve DNS resiliency. Internet-Draft draft-ietf-dnsop-serve-stale-00, IETF Secretariat (2017). http://www.ietf.org/internet-drafts/draft-ietf-dnsop-serve-stale-00.txt
27. Lawrence, T.: Akamai's DNS contribution to internet resilience. https://blogs.akamai.com/2017/09/akamais-dns-contribution-to-internet-resiliency.html
28. Liu, Y., Wang, H.: The Elknot DDoS botnets we watched. Presented at VB2016 Denver. https://www.virusbulletin.com/conference/vb2016/abstracts/elknot-ddos-botnets-we-watched

29. McNally, M.: BIND 9.12.0 release notes. https://kb.isc.org/article/AA-01554/0/BIND-9.12.0-Release-Notes.html
30. Mirkovic, J., Reiher, P.L.: A taxonomy of DDoS attack and DDoS defense mechanisms. Comput. Commun. Rev. **34**, 39–53 (2004). https://doi.org/10.1145/997150.997156
31. Mockapetris, P.V.: Domain names - concepts and facilities. Technical report, RFC Editor (1987). https://doi.org/10.17487/RFC1034
32. Mockapetris, P.V.: Domain names - implementation and specification. Technical report, RFC Editor (1987). https://doi.org/10.17487/RFC1035
33. Müller, M., Moura, G.C.M., de Oliveira Schmidt, R., Heidemann, J.S.: Recursives in the wild: engineering authoritative DNS servers. In: Proceedings of the 2017 Internet Measurement Conference (2017). https://doi.org/10.1145/3131365.3131366
34. Nominum: Vantio cacheserve 7, June 2015. https://nominum.com/wp-content/uploads/2015/06/Vantio-CacheServe7-DataSheet.pdf
35. OpenDNS SmartCache. https://www.opendns.com/opendns-smartcache/
36. Ferguson, P., Senie, D.: BCP 38 on network ingress filtering: defeating denial of service attacks which employ IP source address spoofing, May 2000. http://tools.ietf.org/html/bcp38
37. Paxson, V.: An analysis of using reflectors for distributed denial-of-service attacks. Comput. Commun. Rev. **31**, 38–47 (2001). https://doi.org/10.1145/505659.505664
38. Pfeifer, G., Martin, A., Fetzer, C.: Reducible complexity in DNS. In: IADIS International Conference WWW/Internet 2008 (ICWI 2008) (2008)
39. Ranjan, S., Swaminathan, R., Uysal, M., Nucci, A., Knightly, E.W.: DDoS-shield: DDoS-resilient scheduling to counter application layer attacks. IEEE/ACM Trans. Netw. **17**, 26–39 (2009). https://doi.org/10.1145/1514070.1514073
40. van Rijswijk-Deij, R., Sperotto, A., Pras, A.: DNSSEC and its potential for DDoS attacks: a comprehensive measurement study. In: Proceedings of the 2014 Internet Measurement Conference (2014). https://doi.org/10.1145/2663716.2663731
41. Risk, V.: Resolver DDoS mitigation. https://www.isc.org/blogs/tldr-resolver-ddos-mitigation/
42. Risk, V.: BIND9 performance history, August 2017. https://www.isc.org/blogs/bind9-performance-history/
43. Rose, S., Wijngaards, W.C.A.: DNAME redirection in the DNS. Technical report, RFC Editor (2012). https://doi.org/10.17487/RFC6672
44. Rossow, C.: Amplification hell: revisiting network protocols for DDoS abuse. In: 21st Annual Network and Distributed System Security Symposium (2014)
45. Shadowserver Foundation: DNSScan Shadowserver Foundation, January 2018. https://dnsscan.shadowserver.org/stats/
46. Shue, C.A., Kalafut, A.J.: Resolvers revealed: characterizing DNS resolvers and their clients. ACM Trans. Internet Technol. **12**, 14 (2013). https://doi.org/10.1145/2499926.2499928
47. Takeuchi, Y., Yoshida, T., Kobayashi, R., Kato, M., Kishimoto, H.: Detection of the DNS water torture attack by analyzing features of the subdomain name. JIP **24**, 793–801 (2016). https://doi.org/10.2197/ipsjjip.24.793
48. Van Nice, B.: Drilling down into DNS DDoS (2015). https://www.nanog.org/sites/default/files/nanog63-dnstrack-vannice-ddos.pdf
49. Wang, X., Reiter, M.K.: Mitigating bandwidth-exhaustion attacks using congestion puzzles. In: Proceedings of the 11th ACM Conference on Computer and Communications Security (2004). https://doi.org/10.1145/1030083.1030118

50. Weber, R.: Drilling down into DNS DDoS data (2015). https://indico.dns-oarc. net/event/21/contribution/29/material/slides/0.pdf
51. Weinberg, M., Barber, P.: Everyday attacks against Verisign-operated DNS infrastructure (2015). https://indico.dns-oarc.net/event/21/contribution/24
52. Xie, Y., Yu, S.: A novel model for detecting application layer DDoS attacks. In: Interdisciplinary and Multidisciplinary Research in Computer Science (2006). https://doi.org/10.1109/IMSCCS.2006.159
53. Yu, Y., Wessels, D., Larson, M., Zhang, L.: Authority server selection in DNS caching resolvers. Comput. Commun. Rev. **42**, 80–86 (2012). https://doi.org/10. 1145/2185376.2185387

Control Plane Reflection Attacks in SDNs: New Attacks and Countermeasures

Menghao Zhang[1,2,3], Guanyu Li[1,2,3], Lei Xu[4], Jun Bi[1,2,3(✉)], Guofei Gu[4], and Jiasong Bai[1,2,3]

[1] Institute for Network Sciences and Cyberspace, Tsinghua University, Beijing, China
{zhangmh16,bjs17}@mails.tsinghua.edu.cn, dracula.guanyu.li@gmail.com, junbi@tsinghua.edu.cn
[2] Department of Computer Science and Technology, Tsinghua University, Beijing, China
[3] Beijing National Research Center for Information Science and Technology (BNRist), Beijing, China
[4] SUCCESS LAB, Texas A&M University, College Station, USA
xray2012@email.tamu.edu, guofei@cse.tamu.edu

Abstract. Software-Defined Networking (SDN) continues to be deployed spanning from enterprise data centers to cloud computing with emerging of various SDN-enabled hardware switches. In this paper, we present Control Plane Reflection Attacks to exploit the limited processing capability of SDN-enabled hardware switches. The reflection attacks adopt direct and indirect data plane events to force the control plane to issue massive expensive control messages towards SDN switches. Moreover, we propose a two-phase probing-triggering attack strategy to make the reflection attacks much more efficient, stealthy and powerful. Experiments on a testbed with physical OpenFlow switches demonstrate that the attacks can lead to catastrophic results such as hurting establishment of new flows and even disruption of connections between SDN controller and switches. To mitigate such attacks, we propose a novel defense framework called SWGuard. In particular, SWGuard detects anomalies of downlink messages and prioritizes these messages based on a novel monitoring granularity, i.e., host-application pair (HAP). Implementations and evaluations demonstrate that SWGuard can effectively reduce the latency for legitimate hosts and applications under Control Plane Reflection Attacks with only minor overheads.

Keywords: Software-Defined Networking
Timing-based side channel attacks · Denial of service attacks

1 Introduction

Software-Defined Networking (SDN) has enabled flexible and dynamic network functionalities with a novel programming paradigm. By separating the control

© Springer Nature Switzerland AG 2018
M. Bailey et al. (Eds.): RAID 2018, LNCS 11050, pp. 161–183, 2018.
https://doi.org/10.1007/978-3-030-00470-5_8

plane from the data plane, control logics of different network functionalities are implemented on top of the logically centralized controller as *applications*. Typical SDN applications are implemented as event-driven programs which receive information directly or indirectly from switches and distribute the processing decisions of packets to switches accordingly. These applications enable SDN to adapt to data plane dynamics quickly and make responses to the application policies timely. A wide range of network functionalities are implemented in this way, allowing SDN-enabled switches to behave as firewall, load balancing, network address translation, L2/L3 routing and so on.

Despite the substantial benefits, the deployment of SDN has encountered several problems. In particular, a major limitation is the control message processing capability on SDN-enabled hardware switches of various brands (e.g., IBM RackSwitch, Juniper Junos MX-Series, Brocade NetIron CES 2000 Series, Pica8 Series, Hewlett-Packard Series), constrained by multiple factors. First, CPUs of hardware switches are usually relatively wimpy [8,31] for financial reasons, which restricts the message parsing and processing capability of software protocol agents in switches. Second and more importantly, flow tables in most commodity hardware OpenFlow switches use Ternary Content Addressable Memory (TCAM) to achieve wire-speed packet processing, which only allows limited flow table update rate (only supporting 100–200 flow rule updates per second [5,12,13,16,29,31,33]) and small flow table space (ranging from hundreds to a few thousand [8,16,18]) due to manufacturing cost and power consumption. These limitations have slowed down network updates and hurt network visibility, which further constrain the control plane applications with dynamic policies significantly [15].

In this paper, we systematically study the event processing logic of the SDN control plane and locate two types of data plane events which could reflect expensive control messages towards the data plane, i.e., *direct* data plane events (e.g., *Packet-In* messages) and *indirect* data plane events (e.g., *Statistics Query/Reply* messages). By manipulating those data plane events, we present two novel Control Plane Reflection Attacks in SDN, i.e., Table-miss Striking Attack and Counter Manipulation Attack, which can exploit the limited processing capability for control messages of SDN-enabled hardware switches. Moreover, in order to improve accuracy and efficiency of Control Plane Reflection Attacks, we propose a two-phase attack strategy, i.e., probing phase and triggering phase, inspired by timing-based side channel attacks. Control Plane Reflection Attacks are able to adjust attack stream patterns adaptively and cleverly, thus could gain a great increment of downlink messages[1]. Extensive experiments with a physical testbed demonstrate that the attack vectors are highly effective and the attack effects are pretty obvious.

In order to mitigate Control Plane Reflection Attacks, we present a novel and effective defense framework, namely SWGuard. SWGuard proposes a new monitoring granularity, *host-application pair (HAP)* to detect downlink message

---

[1] For brevity, we denote the messages from the data plane to the control plane as uplink messages, and the messages vice versa as downlink messages.

anomalies, and prioritizes downlink messages when downlink channel congests. In this way, SWGuard is able to satisfy the latency requirements of different hosts and applications under the reflection attacks.

To summarize, our main contributions in this paper include:

- We systematically study the event processing logic of SDN applications and further locate two types of data plane events, i.e., direct/indirect events, which could be manipulated to reflect expensive control messages towards SDN switches.
- We present two novel Control Plane Reflection Attacks, Table-miss Striking Attack and Counter Manipulation Attack, to exploit limited processing capability of hardware switches. Moreover, we develop a two-phase attack strategy to launch such attacks in an efficient, stealthy and powerful way. The experiments with a physical SDN testbed exhibit their harmful effects.
- We present a defense solution, called SWGuard, with an efficient priority assignment and scheduling algorithm based on the novel abstraction of host-application pair (HAP). Implementations and evaluations demonstrate that SWGuard provides effective protection for legitimate hosts and applications with only minor overheads.

The remainder of this paper is structured as follows. Section 2 introduces the background that motivates this work. Section 3 illustrates the details of Control Plane Reflection Attacks and Sect. 4 proves the harmful effects with a physical testbed. We present our SWGuard defense framework in Sect. 5 and make some discussions in Sect. 6. Related works are illustrated in Sect. 7, and the paper is concluded in Sect. 8.

2   Background

Processing Logic of Data Plane Events. SDN introduces the open network programming interface and accelerates the growth of network applications, which enable network to dynamically adjust network configurations based on certain data plane events. These events could be categorized into the following two types: *direct* data plane events such as *Packet-In* messages, where the event variations are reported to the controller from the data plane directly, and *indirect* data plane events such as *Statistics Query/Reply* messages, where the event variations are obtained through a query and reply procedure at the controller. In the *first* case, the controller installs a default *table-miss* flow rule on the switch. When a packet arrives at the switch and does not match any other flow rule, the switch will forward the packet to the control plane for further processing. Then the controller makes decisions for the packet based on the logics of the applications, and assigns new flow rules to the switch to handle subsequent packets with the same match fields. In the *second* case, the controller first installs a *counting flow rule* reactively or proactively on the switch for a measurement purpose. When a packet matches the counting flow rule in the flow table, the specific counter increments with packet number and packet bytes. To obtain the status of the data plane, the controller polls the flow counter values for statistics periodically and performs different operations according to the analysis of statistics. A large number of control plane applications combine these two kinds of data plane events to compose complicated network functions, which further achieve advanced packet processing.

Usage Study of Data Plane Events. Based on the event-driven programming paradigm, a large number of control plane applications emerge in both academia and industry. In academia, since the publication of OpenFlow [23], many research ideas have been proposed to fully leverage the benefits of direct and indirect data plane events. While the direct data plane events are needed by almost all applications, the indirect data plane events are also widely included. In particular, we have categorized these indirect event-driven applications into three types, applications which help improve *optimization, monitoring* and *security* of network. Please see our technical report [36] for details. Although each of them has different purposes, all of these works are deeply involved in the utilization of the indirect data plane events, obtaining a large number of traffic features and switch attributes. Meanwhile, these indirect data plane events contribute a large part of communication between applications and switches. SDN applications have also experienced great development in industry recently. The mainstream SDN platforms (e.g. Open Daylight, ONOS, Floodlight) foster open and prosperous markets for control plane softwares, which provide a great range of applications with a composition of the direct and indirect data plane events. Meanwhile, since these applications are obtained from a great variety of sources, their quality could not be guaranteed and their logics may contain various flaws or vulnerabilities. In particular, we have investigated all mainstream SDN controllers, and discovered that indirect event-driven applications occupy a large part of application markets in these open source controller platforms. Due to the page limit, please see the application summary in our technique report [36].

Limitations of SDN-enabled Hardware Switches. Compared with the rapid growth of packet processing capability in logically centralized and physically distributed network operating systems (e.g., Onix [17], Hyperflow [30], Kandoo [11]) and controller frameworks (e.g., Open Daylight, ONOS), the downlink message processing capability of SDN-enabled hardware switches evolves much slower. State-of-the-art SDN-enabled hardware switches [24] only support 8192 flow entries. To make matters worse, the capability to update the entries in TCAM is pretty limited, usually less than 200 updates per second [5,12,13,15,16,29,31,33]. According to our experiment on Pica8 P-3922, the maximum update rate is about 150 entries per second. We observe that the downlink channel in switches is the dominant resource in SDN architecture that must be carefully managed to fully leverage the benefits of SDN applications. However, existing SDN architecture does not provide such a mechanism to protect the downlink channel in the switches that it is vulnerable to Control Plane Reflection Attacks.

3   Control Plane Reflection Attacks

In this section, we first provide our threat model and then describe the details of two Control Plane Reflection Attacks including Table-miss Striking Attack and Counter Manipulation Attack.

3.1   Threat Model

We assume an adversary could possess one or more hosts or virtual machines (e.g., via malware infection) in the SDN-based network. The adversary can utilize his/her controlled hosts or virtual machines to initiate probe packets, monitor their responses, and generate attack traffic. However, we do not assume the adversary can compromise the controller, applications or switches. In addition, we assume the connections between the controller and switches are well protected by TLS/SSL.

3.2   Control Plane Reflection Attacks

Control Plane Reflection Attacks are much more stealthy and sophisticated than previous straightforward DoS attacks against SDN infrastructure, and generally consist of two phases, i.e., *probing phase* and *triggering phase*. During the probing phase, the attacker uses *timing probing packets*, *test packets* and *data plane stream* to learn the configurations of control plane applications and their involvements in direct/indirect data plane events. With several trials, the attacker is able to determine the conditions that the control plane application adopts to issue new flow rule update messages. Upon the information obtained from probing phase, the attacker can carefully craft the patterns of attack packet stream (e.g., header space, packet interval) to deliberately trigger the control plane to issue numerous flow rule update messages in a short interval to paralyze the hardware switches. We detail two vectors of Control Plane Reflection Attacks as follows.

Table-miss Striking Attack. Table-miss Striking Attack is an enhanced attack vector from previous Data-to-control Plane Saturation Attack [9,27,28,32]. Instead of leveraging a random packet generation method to carry out the attack, Table-miss Striking Attack adopts a more accurate and cost-efficient manner by utilizing probing and triggering phases.

The probing phase is to learn confidential information of the SDN control plane to guide the patterns of attack packet stream. The attacker could first probe the usage of the direct data plane events (e.g., *Packet-In*, *Packet-Out*, *Flow-Mod*) by using various low-rate probing packets whose packet headers are filled with deliberately faked values. The attacker can send these probing packets to the SDN-based network and observe the responses accordingly, thus the round trip time (RTT) for each probing packet could be obtained. If several packets with the same packet header get different RTT values, especially, the first packet goes through a long delay while the other packets get relatively quick responses, we can conclude that the first packet is directed to the controller and the other packets are forwarded directly in the data plane, which indicates that the specific packet header matches no flow rules in the switch and invokes *Packet-In* and *Flow-Mod* messages. Then the attacker could change one of the header fields with the variable-controlling approach. With no more than 42 trials[2], the attacker is able to determine which header fields are sensitive to the controller, i.e., the grain for routing. Then the attacker could carefully craft attack packet stream based on probed grains to deliberately trigger the expensive downlink messages.

Counter Manipulation Attack. Compared with Table-miss Striking Attack, Counter Manipulation Attack is much more sophisticated, which is based on the indirect data plane events (e.g., *Statistics Query/Reply* messages). In order to accurately infer the usage of the indirect data plane events, three types of packet streams are required, i.e., *timing probing packets*, *test packets* and *data plane stream*. The *timing probing packets* are inspired by the *time pings* in [29], which must involve the switch software agent and get the responses accordingly. However, we believe that they have a wider range of choices. The *test packets* are a sequence of packets which should put extra loads to the software agent of the switch, and must be issued at an appropriate rate for the accuracy of probing. The *data plane stream* is a series of stream templates, and should directly go through the data plane (i.e., do not trigger table-miss entry in the flow table of the switch), which is intended to obtain more advanced information such as the specific conditions which trigger indirect event-driven applications.

Timing probing packets are used to measure the workload of software agent of a switch, which should satisfy three properties: first, they should go to the control plane by hitting the table-miss flow rule in the switch, and trigger the operations of the corresponding applications (e.g., *Flow-Mod* or *Packet-Out*). Second, each of them must evoke a response from the SDN-based network, so the attacker could compute the RTT for each timing probing. Third, they should be sent in an extremely *low* rate (10 pps is enough), and put as low loads as possible to the switch software agent. We consider there are many options for timing probing packets, e.g., ARP request/reply, ICMP request/reply, TCP SYN or UDP. For layer 2, we consider ARP request is an ideal choice since the SDN control plane must be involved in the processing of ARP request/reply. We note that sometimes the broadcast ARP request will be processed in the switches. However, the corresponding ARP reply is a unicast packet so that the control plane involvement is inevitable if the destination MAC (i.e., the source MAC address of the ARP Request) has not been dealt by the controller before. As a result, the attacker could use spoofed source MAC address to deliberately pollute the device management service of the controller as well as incur the involvement of the controller. In some layer 2 network, it is not possible to send packets with random source MAC addresses due to pre-authorized network access control policies. To address this, the attacker could resort to the *flow rule time-out* mechanism of OpenFlow. The attacker would select N benign

---

[2] The latest OpenFlow specification only support 42 header fields, which constrains the field the controller could use to compose different forwarding policies.

hosts and send ARP request to them to get the responses. N should satisfy that $N > R * T$, where R denotes the probing rate and T denotes the *flow-rule time-out* value[3]. For Layer 3, ICMP is a straightforward choice, since its RTT calculation has been abstracted as *ping* command already. The attacker should choose a number of benign hosts to send ICMP packets and get the corresponding responses. As for layer 4, TCP and UDP are both feasible when a layer 4 forwarding policy is configured in the control plane. According to RFC 792 [26], when a source host transmits a probing packet to a port which is likely closed at the destination host, the destination is supposed to reply an ICMP *port unreachable* message to the source. Similarly, RFC 793 [25] requires that each TCP SYN packet should be responded with a TCP SYN/ACK packet (opened port) or TCP RST packet (closed port) accordingly. With the probing packet returned with the corresponding response, the RTT could be calculated and the time-based patterns could be obtained.

Test packets are used to strengthen the effects of *timing probing packets* by adding extra loads to the software agent of the switch. For the purpose, we consider test packets with a random destination IP address and broadcast destination MAC address are ideal choices. By hitting the table-miss entry, each of them would be directed to the controller. Then the SDN controller will issue *Packet-Out* message to directly forward the test packet. As a result, the aim of burdening switch software agent is achieved.

Data plane stream is a series of templates, which should go directly through the data plane to obtain more advanced information such as the specific conditions for indirect event-driven applications. We provide two templates here, as shown in Fig. 1. The first template has a steady rate v, packet size p, which is mainly used to probe volume-based statistic calculation and control method. The second has a rate distribution like a jump function, where three variables (v, t, p) determine the shape of this template as well as the size of each packet, which is often used to probe the rate-based strategy.

Template Name	Coordinate Axis	Variables
Data plane stream with steady rate	Rate (pps)	(v, p)
Data plane stream with 0-1 rate	Rate (pps)	(v, t, p)

Fig. 1. Templates for data plane stream.

The insight of probing phase of Counter Manipulation Attack lies in that *different kinds of downlink messages have diverse expenses for the downlink channel*. Among the interaction approaches between the applications and the data plane, there are mainly three types of downlink messages, i.e., *Flow-Mod*, *Statistics Query* and *Packet-Out*. *Flow-Mod* is the most expensive one among

---

[3] As R is less than 10 usually, and T is set as a small value in most controllers (e.g. 5 in Floodlight), thus N cannot be a large number.

them, since it not only consumes the CPU of switch agent to parse the message, but also involves the ASIC API to insert the new flow rules[4]. *Statistics Query* comes at the second, for it needs the involvement of both switch agent CPU for packet parsing and ASIC API for statistic querying. These two types of messages are extremely expensive when the occupation of flow table is high on the switch. *Packet-Out* is rather lightweight, since it only involves the CPU of switch protocol agent to perform the corresponding action encapsulated in the packet. As these three types of downlink messages incur different loads for the switch, the latencies of *timing probing packets* will vary when the switch encounters different message types. Thus, the attacker could learn whether the control plane issue a *Flow-Mod*, or a *Statistics Query*, or a *Packet-Out*. As for the indirect data plane events, the statistic queries are usually conducted periodically by the applications. As a result, each of these queries would incur a small rise for the RTTs of *timing probing packets*, which would reveal the period of application's statistic query. If a subsequent *Flow-Mod* is issued by the controller, there would be a higher rise of RTT just following the RTT for *Statistics Query*, which is named as *double-peak phenomenon*. Based on the special phenomenon, the attacker could even infer what statistic calculation methods the application takes, such as volume-based or rate-based. With several trails of two *data plane stream* templates above (t is set as the period of statistic messages, which has been obtained above) and the variations of v and p in a binary search approach, the attacker could quickly obtain the concrete conditions (volume/rate values, number-based or byte-based) that trigger the expensive downlink messages. The confidential information such as statistic query period, the exact conditions (volume/rate values, packet number-based or byte-based) that trigger the downlink messages, helps the attacker permute the packet interval and packet size of each flow, to deliberately manipulate the counter value to the critical value, thus each flow would trigger a *Flow-Mod* in every period. By initiating a large number of flows, *Flow-Mod* of equal number would be triggered every period, making the hardware switch suffer extremely.

4   Attack Evaluation

In this section, we demonstrate our experimental results of Control Plane Reflection Attacks with a physical testbed. The evaluations are divided into two parts. First, we conduct our experiments for Table-miss Striking Attack and Counter Manipulation Attack separately, to show the effectiveness of Control Plane Reflection Attacks. Second, we perform some benchmarks to provide low-level details of our proposed attacks.

4.1   Experiment Setup

To demonstrate the feasibility of Control Plane Reflection Attacks, we set up an experimental scenario as shown in Fig. 2. We choose several representative

---

[4] Moving old flow entry to make room for the new flow rule is an important reason to make this operation expensive and time-consuming.

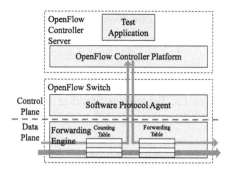

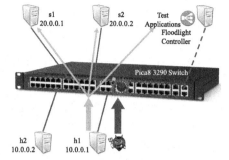

Fig. 2. A typical attack scenario.   **Fig. 3.** Attack experiment setups.

applications, and run them separately on the SDN controller. Flow tables in the switch are divided into two pipelines, *Counting Table* for the indirect data plane event, *Forwarding Table* for the direct data plane events. Each pipeline contains multiple flow entries for the two data plane events, and flow tables of each pipeline are independent and separated, which is the state-of-the-art approach for multiple application implementations today [20, 29].

Reactive Routing is the most common application integrated into most of the popular controller platforms. It monitors *Packet-In* messages with a default *table-miss* in *Forwarding Table*, and computes and installs a path for the hosts of the given source and destination addresses with an appropriate grain. When one table-miss occurs, $2N$ downlink *Flow-Mod* messages would be issued to the data plane, where N is the length of the routing path.

Flow Monitoring is another common application in SDN-based networks. It is generally implemented with a *Counting Table* which counts the number and the bytes of a flow or multiple flows. The controller polls the statistics of the *Counting Table* periodically, conducts analysis on the collected data, and makes decisions with the analysis results. Further, we extend our *Flow Monitoring* sketch into four indirect data plane events driven applications, **Heavy hitter** [22], **Microburst** [10], **PIAS** [1] and **DDoS Detection** [34]. The implementation details are illustrated in our technical report [36].

Our evaluations are conducted on a physical OpenFlow Switch, i.e., Pica8 P-3290, since it is widely used in academia/industry and supports many advanced OpenFlow data plane features, such as multiple pipelines and almost full Open-Flow specifications (from version 1.0 to 1.4). The experimental topology, as shown in Fig. 3, includes four machines (i.e., h1, h2, s1, and s2) connected to the hardware switch and a server running Floodlight Controller. The HTTP service is run on s1 and s2 separately. We consider h2 is a benign client of the HTTP service and h1 is controlled by the attacker to launch the reflection attack. All the tested applications discussed above are hosted in the Floodlight controller. In our experiments, *Reactive Routing* adopts a five-tuples grained forwarding policy, and four *Flow Monitoring*-based applications query the data plane switch every

2 s, and conduct the corresponding control (e.g., issue one *Flow-Mod* message) according to their logic separately.

4.2 Attack Feasibility and Effects

In this subsection, we conduct the experiments for Table-miss Striking Attack and Counter Manipulation Attack separately, and show a detailed procedure for *probing phase* and *triggering phase*.

Table-miss Striking Attack. For the *Reactive Routing* application, when we launch a new flow, the first packet is inclined to get a high RTT, and the following several packets would get low RTTs. Since there are only three hosts on our testbed and *ping* could launch only one new flow between each host pair, we resort to UDP probing packets to cope with this problem. We compute the time difference between the request and reply to obtain the RTT. As depicted in Fig. 4(a), we let h1 transmit 10 UDP probing packets to a destination port and then change the destination port. The RTT for the first packet of each flow is quite distinct from that of the other packets. When we change any field pertained to five-tuples, the similar results would be obtained. The modification to other packet fields would always lead to a quick response. All the phenomena indicate that five-tuples grained forwarding policy is adopted by the *Reactive Routing*.

With the inference of forwarding grain, the attacker is able to carefully craft a stream of packets whose header spaces vary according to the grain. In this way, each attack packet could strike the default *table-miss* in the switch, thus triggering *Packet-In* and *Flow-Mod* in the control channel. Data-to-control Plane Saturation Attack resorts to a random packet generation approach, making the attack not so cost-efficient for the attacker. As we can see in Fig. 4(b), Table-miss Striking Attack is much more efficient than Data-to-control Plane Saturation Attack. Further, we also compare the RTTs and bandwidth for normal users under the saturation attack and the striking attack. As shown in Fig. 5, the striking attack could easily obtain a higher RTT and a lower bandwidth usage for normal users with the same attack expense, which demonstrates that our Table-miss Striking Attack is much more cost-efficient and powerful.

Counter Manipulation Attack. For the *Flow Monitoring*-based applications, we first supply a steady rate of *test packets* at 300 packets per second (pps)[5], which would put appropriate loads on the control plane as required in [29]. The rate of *timing probing packets* is set as 10 pps. The results for four applications are similar, as shown in Fig. 6(a). As we could conclude, *Flow Monitoring*-based applications poll the switch for statistics every 2 s. In particular, the double peaks in red rectangle (*double-peak phenomenon*) denote two expensive downlink messages are issued successively. The first peak is attributed to the periodical *Statistics Query* message, while the second is caused by the *Flow-Mod* message for the control purpose. We make this inference because both *Flow-Mod* and

---

[5] 300 pps is a pretty secure rate, since a legitimate host could issue packets at thousand of pps under normal circumstance.

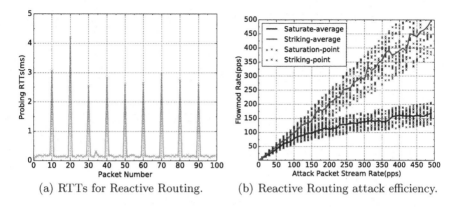

(a) RTTs for Reactive Routing.

(b) Reactive Routing attack efficiency.

Fig. 4. Attack feasibility and efficiency for Table-miss Striking Attack.

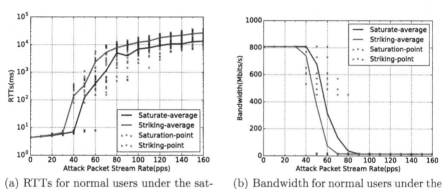

(a) RTTs for normal users under the saturation attack and the striking attack.

(b) Bandwidth for normal users under the saturation attack and the striking attack.

Fig. 5. RTTs and bandwidth for normal users under the saturation attack and the striking attack.

Statistics Query are much more expensive than *Packet-Out* while they two have a similar expense for the downlink channel.

Furthermore, more confidential information could be obtained with the joint trials and analysis of *data plane stream* and *double-peak phenomenon*. If the attacker obtains a series of successive double-peak phenomenon (as shown in Fig. 6(b) with the input of data plane stream template1, where v is a big value, and obtains a series of intermittent double-peak phenomenon (Fig. 6(c) with template2, where v is also a big value, she/he could determine that packet number volume-based statistic calculation method is adopted. This is because packet number volume-based statistic calculation approach is sensitive to stream with a high pps. The other three cases are also listed in Table 1. From this table, we can conclude the concrete statistic calculation approach the application adopts. Furthermore, with the variations of v and p, the attacker could infer the critical value of volume or rate. In addition, we can verify our inference with a lot of

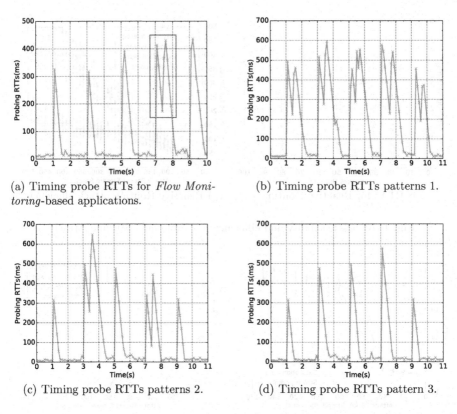

(a) Timing probe RTTs for *Flow Monitoring*-based applications.

(b) Timing probe RTTs patterns 1.

(c) Timing probe RTTs patterns 2.

(d) Timing probe RTTs pattern 3.

Fig. 6. Timing-based patterns for Counter Manipulation Attack.

other ways, not only the proposed two data plane stream templates as shown above. We are planning to develop more representative templates in our future works. In particular, we test our four indirect event driven applications, and find them fall into the distribution in Table 2. This is consistent with the policies of each application, which demonstrates the effectiveness of our probing phase.

With the results and information (query period, packet number/byte-based, volume/rate values) obtained from the probing phase, we move to the second step and start to commit our Counter Manipulation Attack. We select one application, PIAS, setting its priority as 3 levels, and initiate 10 new flows per second. We carefully set the sent bytes of each flow in each period (2 s), which is bigger than the critical value we probed. As a consequence, a number of *Flow-Mod* messages are issued to the switch when statistic query/reply occurs. As shown in Fig. 7, the number of *Flow-Mod* messages could increase as high as 60 at the end of each period. This would incur pretty high loads to the software agent of the switch at this moment. Even in some cases, when the attacker controls thousands of flows intentionally and manipulates all the flow to reach the critical values simultaneously, thousands of *Flow-Mod* messages are directed to the switch, which would cause catastrophic results such as the disruption of connections between the controller and the switches.

Table 1. Relationship between data plane stream and double-peak phenomenon.

	Volume-based	Rate-based
Packet number	Template1(v↑, p) → patterns 1	Template1(v↑, p) → patterns 3
	Template2(v↑, p) → patterns 2	Template2(v↑, p) → patterns 1
Packet byte	Template1(v, p↑) → patterns 1	Template1(v, p↑) → patterns 3
	Template2(v, p↑) → patterns 2	Template2(v, p↑) → patterns 1

Table 2. Distribution of the four indirect event driven applications.

	Volume-based	Rate-based
Packet number	Microburst	-
Packet byte	Heavy Hitter PIAS DDoS Detection	DDoS Detection

4.3   Attack Fundamentals and Analysis

In this subsection, we study more about low-level details of Control Plane Reflection Attacks.

Test Packet **Rate and** ***Test Packet*** **Type.** Fig. 8 shows the timing probe RTTs as the rate of test packets varies where the controller is configured to issue a *Flow-Mod* message for each test packet. Figure 9 shows the timing probe RTTs as *Statistics Query* rate varies. Figure 10 shows the timing probe RTTs as the rate of test packets varies where the controller processes each test packet with a *Packet-Out* message. As we can conclude from these figures, different downlink messages have diverse expenses for the downlink channel, and all of the three scenarios encounter a significant *nonlinear jump*. In particular, when the controller generates *Flow-Mod* message for each test packet, the RTTs can reach 1000 times higher at approximately 50 pps. For *Statistics Query* messages, the RTTs are about 100 times at 100 pps. And for *Packet-Out* messages, the RTTs double 100 times at about 500 pps. Meanwhile, we measure the resource usage of the hardware switch and the controller, and find that the CPU usage of the switch could reach above 90% at the point of the nonlinear jump, while the memory usage of the switch, the CPU and memory usage of the control server is relatively low (at most 30%). In addition, we have a conservation with the Pica8 team via email, and obtain that the switch control actions (e.g. *Flow-Mod*, *Statistics Query*) must contend for the limited bus bandwidth between a switch's CPU and ASIC, and insertion of a new flow rule requires the rearrangement of rules in TCAM, which lead to the results that the expense of *Flow-Mod* ≥ *Statistics Query* ≫ *Packet-Out*.

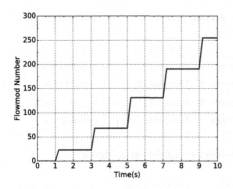

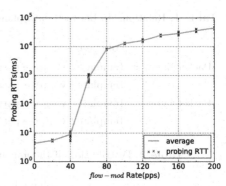

Fig. 7. Attack effect

Fig. 8. Timing probe RTTs as Flow-Mod rate varies.

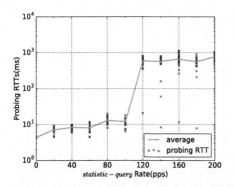

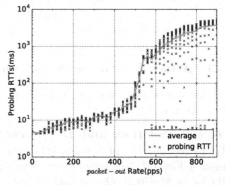

Fig. 9. Timing probe RTTs as statistic query rate varies.

Fig. 10. Timing probe RTTs as Packet-Out rate varies.

The Impact of Background Traffic. The background traffic has two impacts for the Control Plane Reflection Attacks. First, it may affect the accuracy of probing phase. In fact, a moderate rate of background traffic would not weaken the effectiveness of the probing. Conversely, it amplifies the probing effect. The reason behind this is that the effect of background traffic is somewhat like the role played by *test packets*, and it would put some baseline loads to the switch protocol agent, which would make the probing more accurate. An excessively high rate of background traffic would certainly lower the probing accuracy, since there is already a high load for the protocol agent of the switch. As a consequence, the loads incurred by *Statistics Query* would not cause the obvious and periodical peaks for the RTTs of *timing probing packets*, instead, the patterns may become random and irregular. However, in such cases, the switch is already suffering, thus the aim of the attack has already been achieved. Second, the background traffic may also affect the trigger phase. Actually, this influence is positive, too. The existence of the background traffic would inevitably bring about some downlink messages to the control channel, which would boost the effects of Control Plane Reflection Attacks.

5   Defense Approach

5.1   Countermeasure Analysis

The control plane reflection attack is deeply rooted in SDN architecture since the performance of existing commodity SDN-enabled hardware switches could not suffice the need of the SDN applications. A straightforward method to mitigate this attack is *limiting the use of dynamic features for network applications*, nevertheless, this comes at the expense of less fine-grained control, visibility, and flexibility in traffic management, as evidently required in [4,14,31]. Another straightforward defense approach is *limiting the downlink message transmission rate directly in the controller*, preventing the switches from being overwhelmed. However, the exact downlink message processing capabilities for different switches vary, even for a specific switch, the rate control in the controller cannot precisely guarantee underload or overload for the remote switch[6], making the unified control inaccurate and complicated. *Adding some latency to random downlink messages* seems feasible, which can make the patterns/policies of direct/indirect data plane events difficult to sniff and obtain. Nevertheless, this technique increases the total latency for the overall downlink messages, and would inevitably violate the latency requirements of some latency-sensitive downlink messages, making it high cost and infeasible.

To address the challenges above, we propose SWGuard to mitigate the reflection attack and fulfill the requirements of different downlink messages. Our basic idea is to discriminate good from evil, and prioritize downlink messages with discrimination results. To this end, we propose a multi-queue scheduling strategy, to achieve different latency for different downlink messages. The scheduling strategy is based on the statistics of downlink messages in a novel granularity during the past period, which takes both fairness and efficiency into consideration. When the downlink channel is becoming congested, the *malicious* downlink messages are inclined to be put into a low-priority scheduling queue and the requirements of *good* messages are more likely to be satisfied.

5.2   SWGuard: A Priority-Based Scheduler on Switch

The architecture of SWGuard is shown in Fig. 11. SWGuard mainly redesigns two components of SDN architecture. On the switch side, it changes the existing software protocol agent to *multi-queue* based structure, and schedules different downlink messages with their *types* and *priorities*. On the controller side, it adds a *Behavior Monitor* module as a basic service, which collects the downlink message events and assigns different *priorities* to different messages *dynamically*.

---

[6] There may be several hops between the switch and the controller, and the network condition is unpredictable.

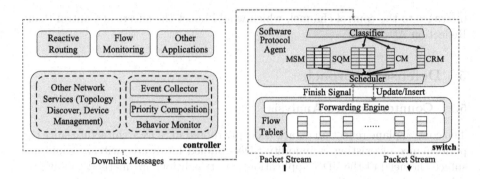

Fig. 11. SWGuard framework design.

Multi-queue Based Software Protocol Agent. In order to prioritize the downlink messages, we redesign the software protocol agents of the existing switches. A naive approach is to modify the existing single queue model directly into priority-based multi-queue model, and enqueue all the downlink messages into different queues with their priorities and dequeue at different scheduling rates. However, the *types* of downlink messages vary, and different message types have diverse requirements, for example, if *Handshake* messages and *Modify State* messages are put into the same queue, the latency requirement of the former may be delayed by the latter so that the handshakes between the controller and the switches could not be established timely.

To this end, we summarize the downlink messages into the following four categories: (1) *Modify State Messages* (MSM), (2) *Statistic Query Messages* (SQM), (3) *Configuration Messages* (CM), and (4) *Consistency Required Messages* (CRM), and design a *Classifier* to classify the downlink messages into different queues accordingly. The first two types are related to the behaviors of *hosts* and *applications*, so we design a multi-queue for each of them. The multi-queue consists of three levels (*quick, slow, block*), and each level is designed for the corresponding priority. The third type serves for basic services of the controller (e.g., Handshake, LLDP), while the detail of the last type is illustrated in Sect. 5.2, and both of them inherit from the original single queue. Classifier makes use of *ofp_header* field in OpenFlow Header to distinguish message type, and a 2-bit packet metadata to obtain priority.

With the downlink messages in the queues, a *Scheduler* is designed to dequeue the messages with a scheduling algorithm. In order not to overwhelm the capability of ASCI/Forwarding Engine, a *Finish Signal* should be sent back to the *Scheduler* once a *Modify State/Statistic Query* message is processed. Then the *Scheduler* knows whether to dequeue a next message of the same type from queues. We design a time-based scheduling algorithm, setting different *strides* for different queues. For the last two queues (Configuration Messages, Consistence Required Messages), the stride is set as 0, which means whenever there is a message, it would be dequeued immediately. For the first two multi-queues, the stride for the queue of *quick* level is set as 0, for that of *slow* level is set as a small time interval, while for that of *block* level is set as a relatively bigger value. With the principles illustrated above, we design the scheduling algorithm as Algorithm 1.

Algorithm 1. The Scheduling Algorithm for Protocol Agent.

```
// Initialization
foreach que ∈ queues do
    set que.stride;
    que.time = getcurrenttime();
// Enter the Scheduler thread
while true do
    foreach que ∈ queues do
        if que.stride ≤ getcurrenttime() − que.time then
            if que.empty() == false then
                que.time = getcurrenttime();
                que.dequeue();
        else
            que.time = getcurrenttime();
```

Behavior Monitor. In order to distinguish different downlink messages with different priorities, an appropriate *Monitoring* granularity is in urgent need. Previous approaches mainly conduct the monitoring with the granularity of source host [3,34], and react to the anomalies on the statistics. However, in the control plane reflection attacks, these approaches are no longer valid and effective. For example, if we only take the features of the data plane traffic into consideration, and schedule with the statistics of source hosts [35], it would inevitably violate the heterogeneous requirements of various applications.

To address this challenge, we propose the novel abstraction of *Host-Application Pair (HAP)*, and use it as the basic granularity for monitoring and statistics. These two dimensions are easy to be obtained from the uplink messages and the configurations of the controller. Considering K applications exist on the control plane, their requirements for downlink messages are represented as vector $a_0 = \langle a_1, a_2, \ldots a_K \rangle$, and N hosts/users in the data plane, corresponding requirements vector $h_0 = \langle h_1, h_2, \ldots h_N \rangle$. a_0 and h_0 are both set by the network operators, depending on the property of the applications and the pay of hosts/users. Thus the *expected resource allocation matrix* is $R_0 = a_0^T \cdot h_0$. And the *expected resource allocation ratio matrix* is $I_0 = \frac{R_0}{\sum_{k=1}^{K} \sum_{n=1}^{N} a_k h_n}$. During the past period (T seconds), the statistics of *HAP* is represented as *resource*

$$\textit{occupation matrix } \mathbf{R} = \begin{pmatrix} r_{11} & r_{12} & \cdots & r_{1N} \\ r_{21} & r_{22} & \cdots & r_{2N} \\ \vdots & \vdots & \ddots & \vdots \\ r_{K1} & r_{K2} & \cdots & r_{KN} \end{pmatrix}. \text{ And the sum of the elements in}$$

$\mathbf{R}$ is denoted as $Sum = \sum_{k=1}^{K} \sum_{n=1}^{N} r_{kn}$. Suppose the maximum capability of downlink channel in T seconds is Sum_0, $\frac{Sum}{Sum_0}$ denotes the resource utilization rate of the downlink channel. In order to save resources of the control channel, we design our SWGuard system as attack-driven, which means when $\frac{Sum}{Sum_0} < \alpha$, SWGuard is in sleep state except for *Event Collector*. All the downlink messages flow through the third queue (queue for *Configuration Messages*). α is a danger value between 0 and 1, set by the network operators.

When the reflection attacks are detected, the *Priority Composition* Module is wakened and starts to calculate the *penalty coefficient* of each HAP, $\beta_{kn} = \frac{r_{kn} - i_{kn} Sum_0}{r_{kn}}$. i_{kn}, r_{kn} denote the corresponding element in matrix $\mathbf{I_0}, \mathbf{R}$. If β_{kn} is negative, we set it as 0. Then we use two *thresholds* (th_h, th_l) to map the penalty coefficient β_{kn} into *priority* (00, 01 or 10) and tag a 2-bit field into packet metadata to encapsulate priority.

Policy Consistency. Multi-queue based software protocol agent may violate the consistency of some downlink messages. For example, some control messages need to be sent in a particular order for correctness reasons, however, in this multi-queue based software agent, if a previous arriving message is put into a queue with high load while a later arriving message is put into a queue with low load, the order to maintain correctness may be violated.

To address this issue, we design a coordination mechanism between the *Behavior Monitor* and *Classifier* in software protocol agent. If a series of downlink messages require consistency, they are supposed to reuse the 2-bit priority packet metadata (fill it with 11) in the packet header to express their intents. Then the *Classifier* in the software protocol agent will check the label to learn whether the message has the consistency demand. If consistency demand is confirmed, this message will be scheduled to the queue for consistency required messages.

5.3   Defense Evaluation

We implement the prototype of SWGuard system, including *Behavior Monitor* and *Software Protocol Agent*, on Floodlight [6] and Open vSwitch [7] with about 4000 Lines of Code. We use Open vSwitch and set corresponding thresholds to limit its control channel throughput, making its flow rule update rate (130 pps) and flow table size (2000) analogous to the hardware switches.

To demonstrate the defense effect of SWGuard, we use the average value of flow rule installation/statistic query latencies of normal users/applications as the representative metric, which is named as *Event Response Time* in our figures. As

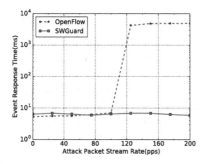

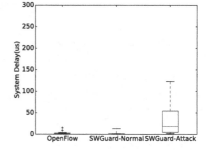

Fig. 12. Defense effect.   **Fig. 13.** Defense overhead.

shown in Fig. 12[7], with native system, event response time becomes extremely
large when the rate of downlink messages is above 110 packets per second. While
with SWGuard, event response time is nearly unchanged. All of these are due
to the limited capability of SDN-enabled switches for processing downlink messages. The experimental results illustrate that our SWGuard provides effective
protection for both the flow rule installation and statistics query.

For the overheads of SWGuard, we measure the latency introduced by
SWGuard. Compared with native OpenFlow, packets in SWGuard need to go
through two extra components, Event Collector of Behavior Monitor and Configuration Message queue of Software Protocol Agent under normal circumstance,
since other components are in sleep state when no attack is detected. When an
attack happens, packets must pass a full path in Behavior Monitor and Software Protocol Agent. As shown in Fig. 13, the latency is almost the same for
native OpenFlow and SWGuard under normal circumstance. Even under attacks,
Behavior Monitor and Software Protocol Agent only incur a latency less than
100 us. All of these demonstrate that SWGuard only brings about a negligible
delay for the control channel messages.

6   Discussion

Emerging Programmable Data Planes: Current prototypes, attacks and
defenses are based on OpenFlow-based hardware switches. We believe the core
idea of Control Plane Reflection Attacks is applicable to the emerging generation of programmable data planes, e.g. P4 and RMT chips [2], because these
platforms also use traditional TCAM-based flow tables and Control Plane Reflection Attacks address a property of TCAM that is invariant to underlying TCAM
design.

Generality of the SWGuard System: SWGuard is also applicable for no-
adversary circumstances, such as flash crowds of downlink messages under normal conditions. By prioritizing the downlink messages, SWGuard can provide

---

[7] Since this experiment is conducted on the software environment, the nonlinear jump
point is a little different from the previous hardware experimental results.

lower latencies for more important messages under the congestion status of control channel.

Source Address Forgery Problem: One concern is that an attacker may forge another host's source address to pollute the HAP statistics of other hosts. Nevertheless, in SWGuard, we can also harness the edge switch port to identify a host. As the header fields of the upstream messages are assigned by the hardware switch, the attacker is not able to forge or change this field.

7 Related Work

DoS Attacks Against SDN: Shin et al. [28] first proposes the concept of Data-to-control Plane Saturation Attack against SDN. To mitigate this dedicated DoS attack, AVANT-GUARD [27] introduces *connection migration* and *actuating triggers* to extend the data plane functions. However, it is applicable to TCP protocol only. Further, a protocol-independent defense framework, FloodGuard [32], pre-installs proactive flow rules to reduce table-miss packets, and forwards table-miss packets to additional data plane caches. To gain the benefit of no hardware modification and addition, FloodDefender [9] offloads table-miss packets to neighbor switches and filters out attack traffic with two-phase filtering. Control Plane Reflection Attacks distinguish themselves from previous works in both attack methods and attack effects. On one hand, the saturation attack uses a pretty straightforward attack method that attacker just floods arbitrary attack traffic to trigger the direct data plane events while the reflection attacks resort to more advanced and sophisticated techniques, and a two-phase probing-trigger approach is specially developed to exploit both direct and indirect data plane events. On the other hand, since the simplicity of the saturation attack, it is not hard to capture the attack, thus it could have limited attack effects. By contrary, the reflection attacks are much more stealthy and the same attack expenses of the attacker could cause more obvious attack effects for victims. Scotch [31] alleviates the communication bottleneck between control plane and data plane leveraging a pool of vSwitches distributed across the network, and it shares the same observation that SDN-enabled hardware switches have a very limited capacity for control channel communications.

Timing-Based Side Channel Attacks: Side channel attacks have long existed in computer systems, and they are usually used to leak the secret information (e.g. secret cryptographic keys) of dedicated systems. Publications more related to our work are various works applying side channel attacks to SDN. Shin et al. [28] presents an SDN scanner which could determine whether a network is using SDN or not. Leng et al. [19] proposes to measure the response time of requests to obtain the approximate capacity of switch's flow table. Sonchack et al. [29] demonstrates an inference attack to time the control plane, which could be used to infer host communication patterns, ACL entries and network monitoring policies. Liu et al. [21] permits the attacker to select the best probes with a Markov model to infer the recent occurrence of a target flow. Our attack methods are somewhat inspired by these previous works. However, all of them only focus on the direct data plane events, and remain at a low level to infer the existence of network policies/device configurations. To the best of our knowledge, our work proposes the exploitation of indirect data plane events for the first time and take the next step that we not only take the existence into consideration, but also obtain more concrete policies and policy thresholds to promote the attack effects.

8 Conclusion

In this paper, we present Control Plane Reflection Attacks to exploit the limited processing capability of SDN-enabled hardware switches by using direct and indirect data plane events. Moreover, we develop a two-phase attack strategy to make such attacks efficient, stealthy and powerful. The experiments showcase the reflection attacks can cause extremely harmful effects with acceptable attack expenses. To mitigate reflection attacks, we propose a novel defense solution, called SWGuard, by detecting anomalies of control messages and prioritizing them based on the host-application pair. The evaluation results of SWGuard demonstrate its effectiveness under reflection attacks with minor overheads.

Acknowledgement. This material is based upon work supported by National Key R&D Program of China (2017YFB0801701), the National Science Foundation of China (No.61472213) and CERNET Innovation Project (NGII20160123). It is also based upon work supported in part by the National Science Foundation (NSF) under Grant No. 1617985, 1642129, 1700544, and 1740791. Jun Bi is the corresponding author. We also thank Yi Qiao, Chen Sun, Yongbin Li and Kai Gao from Tsinghua University for joining the discussion of this paper.

References

1. Bai, W., et al.: Information-agnostic flow scheduling for commodity data centers. In: NSDI, pp. 455–468. USENIX Association, Oakland (2015). https://www.usenix.org/conference/nsdi15/technical-sessions/presentation/bai
2. Bosshart, P., et al.: P4: programming protocol-independent packet processors. SIGCOMM CCR **44**(3), 87–95 (2014)
3. Braga, R., et al.: Lightweight DDoS flooding attack detection using NOX/OpenFlow. In: LCN, pp. 408–415. IEEE (2010)
4. Casado, M., et al.: Ethane: taking control of the enterprise. In: SIGCOMM, vol. 37, pp. 1–12. ACM (2007)
5. Chen, H., Benson, T.: The case for making tight control plane latency guarantees in SDN switches. In: SOSR, pp. 150–156. ACM (2017)
6. Floodlight Community: Floodlight, August 2017. http://www.projectfloodlight.org/floodlight/
7. Open vSwitch Community: Open vSwitch, August 2017. http://openvswitch.org/
8. Curtis, A.R.: DevoFlow: scaling flow management for high-performance networks. SIGCOMM **41**(4), 254–265 (2011)

9. Gao, S., et al.: FloodDefender: protecting data and control plane resources under SDN-aimed DoS attacks. In: INFOCOM, pp. 1–9 (2017)
10. Ghorbani, S., et al.: DRILL: micro load balancing for low-latency data center networks. In: SOGCOMM, pp. 225–238. ACM (2017)
11. Hassas Yeganeh, S., Ganjali, Y.: Kandoo: a framework for efficient and scalable offloading of control applications. In: HotSDN, pp. 19–24. ACM (2012)
12. He, K., et al.: Mazu: taming latency in software defined networks. Technical report, University of Wisconsin-Madison (2014)
13. He, K., et al.: Measuring control plane latency in SDN-enabled switches. In: SOSR, p. 25. ACM (2015)
14. Jin, X., et al.: SoftCell: scalable and flexible cellular core network architecture. In: CoNEXT, pp. 163–174. ACM (2013)
15. Jin, X., et al.: Dynamic scheduling of network updates. In: SIGCOMM, vol. 44, pp. 539–550. ACM (2014)
16. Katta, N., et al.: CacheFlow: dependency-aware rule-caching for software-defined networks. In: SOSR, p. 6. ACM (2016)
17. Koponen, T., et al.: Onix: a distributed control platform for large-scale production networks. In: OSDI, vol. 10, pp. 1–6 (2010)
18. Lazaris, A., et al.: Tango: simplifying SDN control with automatic switch property inference, abstraction, and optimization. In: CoNEXT, pp. 199–212. ACM (2014)
19. Leng, J., et al.: An inference attack model for flow table capacity and usage: exploiting the vulnerability of flow table overflow in software-defined network. arXiv preprint arXiv:1504.03095 (2015)
20. Li, Y., et al.: Flowinsight: decoupling visibility from operability in SDN data plane. SIGCOMM Demo **44**(4), 137–138 (2015)
21. Liu, S., et al.: Flow reconnaissance via timing attacks on SDN switches. In: ICDCS, pp. 196–206. IEEE (2017)
22. Liu, Z., et al.: One sketch to rule them all: rethinking network flow monitoring with UnivMon. In: SIGCOMM, pp. 101–114. ACM (2016)
23. McKeown, N.: OpenFlow: enabling innovation in campus networks. SIGCOMM CCR **38**(2), 69–74 (2008)
24. Pica8: Flow scalability per broadcom chipset, March 2018. https://docs.pica8.com/display/picos2102cg/Flow+Scalability+per+Broadcom+Chipset
25. Postel, J.: Transmission control protocol (1981)
26. Postel, J., et al.: RFC 792: Internet control message protocol. InterNet Network Working Group (1981)
27. Shin, S., et al.: AVANT-GUARD: scalable and vigilant switch flow management in software-defined networks. In: CCS, pp. 413–424. ACM (2013)
28. Shin, S., Gu, G.: Attacking software-defined networks: a first feasibility study. In: HotSDN, pp. 165–166. ACM (2013)
29. Sonchack, J., et al.: Timing-based reconnaissance and defense in software-defined networks. In: ACSAC, pp. 89–100. ACM (2016)
30. Tootoonchian, A., Ganjali, Y.: HyperFlow: a distributed control plane for Open-Flow. In: Proceedings of the 2010 Internet Network Management Conference on Research on Enterprise Networking, p. 3 (2010)
31. Wang, A., et al.: Scotch: elastically scaling up SDN control-plane using vSwitch based overlay. In: CoNEXT, pp. 403–414. ACM (2014)
32. Wang, H., et al.: FloodGuard: a DoS attack prevention extension in software-defined networks. In: DSN, pp. 239–250. IEEE (2015)
33. Xu, H., et al.: Real-time update with joint optimization of route selection and update scheduling for SDNs. In: ICNP, pp. 1–10. IEEE (2016)

34. Xu, Y., Liu, Y.: DDoS attack detection under SDN context. In: INFOCOM, pp. 1–9. IEEE (2016)
35. Zhang, M., et al.: FTGuard: a priority-aware strategy against the flow table overflow attack in SDN. In: SIGCOMM Demo, pp. 141–143. ACM (2017)
36. Zhang, M., et al.: Control plane reflection attacks in SDNs: new attacks and countermeasures. Technical report, June 2018. https://www.dropbox.com/s/bnwe8apx5w06a85/sdns-attacks-countermeasures-tr.pdf?dl=0

Proof-of-Blackouts? How Proof-of-Work Cryptocurrencies Could Affect Power Grids

Johanna Ullrich[1,2(✉)], Nicholas Stifter[1,2], Aljosha Judmayer[1], Adrian Dabrowski[1], and Edgar Weippl[1,2]

[1] SBA Research, Vienna, Austria
{jullrich,nstifter,ajudmayer,adabrowski,eweippl}@sba-research.org
[2] Christian Doppler Laboratory for Security and Quality Improvement in the Production System Lifecycle (CDL-SQI), Institute of Information Systems Engineering, TU Wien, Vienna, Austria

Abstract. With respect to power consumption, cryptocurrencies have been discussed in a twofold way: First, the cost-benefit ratio of mining hardware in order to gain revenue from mining that exceeds investment and electricity costs. Second, the overall electric energy consumption of cryptocurrencies to estimate the environmental effects of Proof-of-Work. In this paper, we consider a complementary aspect: The stability of the power grids themselves. Power grids have to continuously maintain an equilibrium between power supply and consumption; extended periods of imbalance cause significant deviation of the utility frequency from its nominal value and destabilize the power grid, eventually leading to large-scale blackouts. Proof-of-Work cryptocurrencies are potential candidates for creating such imbalances as disturbances in mining can cause abrupt changes in power demand. The problem is amplified by the ongoing centralization of mining hardware in large mining pools. Therefore, we investigate power consumption characteristics of miners, consult mining pool data, and analyze the amount of total power consumption as well as its worldwide distribution of two major cryptocurrencies, namely *Bitcoin* and *Ethereum*. Thus, answering the question: *Are Proof-of-Work based cryptocurrencies a threat to reliable power grid operation?*.

1 Introduction

Power grids must continuously keep an equilibrium between power consumption and supply. Power plant operators therefore have to follow the consumer demand, and adjust their supply in accordance. They rely on sophisticated prediction models, and the remaining gap between supply and consumption is closed by control reserve, i.e., power plants in standby. Whereas, a continuous imbalance in the power grid leads to the utility frequency drifting away from its nominal set point of 50 Hz or 60 Hz (depending on the country). If supply exceeds consumption, the frequency of the power grid increases; if supply fails to fulfill

© Springer Nature Switzerland AG 2018
M. Bailey et al. (Eds.): RAID 2018, LNCS 11050, pp. 184–203, 2018.
https://doi.org/10.1007/978-3-030-00470-5_9

consumption, the frequency decreases. The system frequency is indeed an indicator of the power grid's state, and small fluctuations – a few hundred mH – around the nominal value are normal. However, larger deviations – more than 0.5 Hz—trigger automatic emergency routines such as load shedding or power plant shutdowns. The operators' course of action relies on the assumption that power consumers behave independently of each other, and do not perform concerted actions. Recent work [7] has shown that coordinated control over devices is in fact able to cause load shedding, and large scale blackouts. Therein, the authors assume a botnet that allows an adversary to remotely and simultaneously increase the bots' power consumption. As electronic devices are orders of magnitude faster in modulating their power consumption than control reserve can be activated, the power grid frequency drifts away from its nominal value, finally triggering emergency routines. In addition to reaction speed, the total amount of control reserve, i.e., power plants, in standby is limited.

Proof-of-Work (PoW) cryptocurrencies such as Bitcoin and Ethereum draw substantial amounts of electric power as a consequence of their underlying consensus mechanism, referred to as Nakamoto consensus [5]. In principle, participation in this process is possible for anyone and is governed by economic factors, as prospective miners analyze the cost-benefit ratio of acquiring and providing computational resources to the network in exchange for cryptocurrency units[1]. Up until now, this fact has been discussed primarily in the context of sustainability and the potential ecological impact large scale cryptocurrency mining could entail [15,23,32]. Some estimates rank Bitcoin's overall electricity consumption comparable to that of medium-sized national states with the potential to grow even further in the future. In this paper, we discuss a complementary, yet unconsidered aspect of cryptocurrencies and power consumption. Specifically, we investigate whether PoW cryptocurrencies could represent a threat to reliable power grid operation that is comparable to the botnet described above. A closer look emphasizes that cryptocurrencies indeed have the potential to be harmful to reliable power grid operation for the following reasons:

- Hardware that is mining a particular cryptocurrency uses the same, or very similarly behaving, software on all nodes. Thus, their power consumption may not be independent of each other and therefore violating the grid operators' assumptions. A single disturbance in the software – may it be a consequence of an occasional error or a malicious action – impacts a large amount of miners at once. For example, a high number of all *Ethereum* nodes experienced an outage due to a software bug in September 2016[2]. If such an event impacts the nodes' power consumption, even minor changes add up to large overall power lifts for the power grid. For example, a Linux leap second bug caused an overall power increase by 1 MW in a single data centre in 2012[3].

---

[1] https://www.coinwarz.com/cryptocurrency.

[2] https://blog.ethereum.org/2016/09/18/security-alert-geth-nodes-crash-due-memory-bug/.

[3] http://www.h-online.com/open/news/item/Leap-second-bug-in-Linux-wastes-electricity-1631462.html.

- Cryptocurrency nodes are electronic devices, and are thus able to modulate their power consumption in a fast way – typically below 100 ms – which is a few orders of magnitude faster than the reaction speed of the power grid.
- Miners – at least when operating in the same mining pool – share a communication infrastructure to coordinate their efforts. An error in this communication structure or its compromise by an adversary could allow for botnet-style control including manipulation of the participants' power consumption.
- Miners have vast computing power, and therefore draw high amounts of power from the grid. As long as it remains profitable their operators are economically motivated to bring more and more mining hardware into the cryptocurrency network, leading to increased power consumption at high growth rates – without actually improving capacity for the cryptocurrency. Beyond, this growth has been fueled by an ongoing cryptocurrency hype.

Summarizing, cryptocurrencies show potential to become troublemakers for power grids and their reliable operation. In addition to the overall power consumption, the miners' development over time and their geographical spread are of interest for an in-depth analysis. The paper at hand aims to contribute this missing information in order to shed light onto the issue whether cryptocurrencies are a threat to reliable power grid operation. In particular, we answer the following questions:

- How does power consumption of different cryptocurrencies and their mining pools behave over time? Further, how is power consumption geographically spread?
- Which scenarios, e.g., outage of a large number of miners, show potential to impact power grid reliability and which prerequisites have to be met for such an event to affect the power grid?
- Has power consumption of cryptocurrencies already surpassed the threshold of being critical for reliable power grid operation? Respectively, when does power consumption reach this critical threshold considering past growth of cryptocurrencies and their increased mining efficiency?

Due to the large number of available cryptocurrencies, we limit ourselves to the two currently most popular PoW cryptocurrencies by market capitalization and transaction volume, namely *Bitcoin* [21] and *Ethereum* [6]. With respect to the power grid, we investigate the impact on European power grids, among them the *Synchronous Grid of Continental Europe* (formerly UCTE grid) which is the largest power grid by total consumption. Beyond, European grids are considered to be among the most reliable networks.

The remainder of the paper is organized as follows: Sect. 2 provides a background on power grid operation and cryptocurrencies; Sect. 3 presents our threat scenario. Section 4 assesses power consumption models with respect to the quality of results. Then, Sect. 5 investigates cryptocurrencies' current power consumption for mining, while Sect. 6 investigates the geographic spread of miners by investigating the largest Ethereum mining pool as well as including publicly available information for Bitcoin. Section 7 analyzes cryptocurrencies' impact on the power grid. Section 8 discusses our results, Sect. 9 presents related work, and Sect. 10 concludes.

2   Background

First, this section provides an overview on power grid operation before describing the technology behind cryptocurrencies.

Power Grids in Europe: Power grids have expanded from islands, e.g., a city, to national grids and finally international ones for reasons of higher reliability, as an outage of a single power plant is easier to handle by numerous other plants compensating for the loss. These grids are operated synchronously, i.e., the net sine is of the same frequency at the same angle; otherwise, short circuits would cause harm to the equipment. As electric power cannot be stored at large quantities, grid operators have to keep a balance between consumption and supply at all times. This is achieved in two steps: First, operators estimate power consumptions by means of load profiles. These are sophisticated models forcasting the consumption in dependence of time of the year, weekday, weather forecast and many more parameters. Second, fast power plants are run in standby mode to close the remaining gap between consumption and supply. This gap is measured by the network's frequency deviation from its nominal value (50 Hz in European networks). If consumption exceeds supply, turbines of power plants slow down leading to a lower frequency. If supply is higher than consumption, turbines accelerate and this increases frequency as well. Bearing in mind that *fast-reacting* power plants are still relatively slow in comparison to IT equipment [7]. While the latter are able to modulate their consumption within a range of multiple tens of milliseconds to seconds, gas turbines need tens of second for activation. Primary control, the fastest countermeasure reacting to imbalances, in the UCTE network is required to be fully activated within 30 s [11]. Secondary and tertiary control take even longer. Power operators aim to keep the frequency within a band around the nominal value, typically a few hundreds of mHz. Large deviations cause emergency routines [31]: (49.8 Hz) Alerting, Shedding of pumps, (49.0 Hz) load shedding of 10–15% of total load, (48.7 Hz) load shedding of additional 10–15%, (48.4 Hz) load shedding of further 15–25% of load. At frequencies below 47.5 Hz and above 51.5 Hz all power plants are disconnected from the power grid in order to protect mechanical equipment like turbines and generators.

Cryptocurrency Mining: The cryptographic currency *Bitcoin* was inarguably the first successful *decentralized* implementation of an electronic payment system, as it does not have to rely on individual trusted parties to prevent the double spending problem [22]. To achieve resistance against *Sybil attacks* [9], but nevertheless allow for dynamic membership of (consensus) participants, Bitcoin requires some form of pricing mechanism ascribed to the creation of identities in the system. This is achieved through relying on a chained construction of Proofs-of-Work, the latter of which traces its origins back to the works of *Dwork and Naor* [10] and *Back* [3]. In Bitcoin, *miners*[4] attempt to solve a cryptographic puzzle, namely a partial pre-image attack on the SHA-256 cryptographic hash function. As part of its input it takes a previous puzzle solution as well as a Merkle tree root of newly proposed transactions. Thereby, a cryptographically linked tree of puzzle solutions is formed, of which only the longest consecutive chain with the most cumulative difficulty of puzzles is considered to be the current valid state by honest participants. Under the assumption that the majority of computational power is controlled by honest participants, and that they will only append new solutions to the head of a valid (block)chain, it becomes exponentially difficult for an adversary to alter previous states by presenting a new, longer chain that is considered valid. This mechanism of reaching eventual agreement on a common prefix of chained puzzle solutions is referred to as Nakamoto consensus. The principles behind Nakamoto consensus form the basis for all decentralized PoW cryptocurrencies. Nakamoto consensus also relies on *game theoretic incentives*, whereby operators of mining hardware are rewarded in cryptocurrency units if their puzzle solution eventually ends up as part of the agreed upon valid blockchain. The operators can expect, on average, to successfully mine blocks that end up on the blockchain proportional to the amount of computational power they hold in relation to that of all participants Because mining is a random process with large variance, operators often form their mining hardware together in *mining pools* to benefit from more predictable payouts [17,28]. Alternative cryptocurrencies often rely on a different Proof-of-Work function to Bitcoin, such as *Ethash* in the case of Ethereum [35]. When we refer to *hash rate* within the course of this paper, we imply the number of trials that are conducted for a given PoW function in an attempt to find a valid solution over a particular time frame.

3   Threat Model

Our threat scenario is depicted in Fig. 1(a). We assume an amount of miners of the same cryptocurrency – may it be *Bitcoin* or *Ethereum* – mining the respective cryptocurrency. Each of these miners draws a modest amount of electricity from the power grid. However, in total, power consumption of individual miners add up to a large volume. If all (or a large number of) miners switch from mining to idling abruptly the total power consumption drops within seconds or less. Figure 1(b) depicts this effect from the power grid's perspective. While power consumption ideally would follow an inverse step function, it is likely that the real-world behavior is slightly smoother. The surplus of energy in the grid will lead to an increased frequency until the control reserves try to stabilize the system. However, due to generators' inertia, activation takes up to 30 s. If the miners' reduction in consumption is high enough the induced frequency shift can

---

[4] We use the term *miners* as equivalent for mining hardware (and not the operators of this hardware).

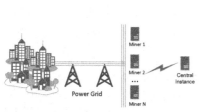
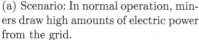
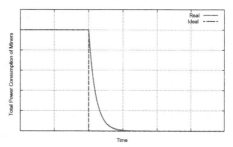

(a) Scenario: In normal operation, miners draw high amounts of electric power from the grid.

(b) Qualitative progression of totalled power consumption in presence of an incident.

Fig. 1. Threat model: an (occasional or malicious) incident leads to the outage of miners eventually causing totalled fluctuations on power consumption.

(temporarily) exceed thresholds for emergency routines, eventually causing load shedding or shutdown of power plants.

In order to cause such an incident, the adversary requires the possibility of instantly forcing a high number of miners into idling. We therefore assume a central instance as depicted in Fig. 1(a). This central instance is able to directly or indirectly influence miners which might appear artificial at first. However, in the past, cryptocurrencies have already experienced comparable situations, as emphasized in the following enumeration: (1) *Antbleed*[5] included a backdoor in the *Antminer* mining hardware that allowed the vendor to remotely shutdown devices. Its exploitation could have caused an estimated outage of up to 70% of all mining equipment in the *Bitcoin* network. (2) In September 2016, *Ethereum* experienced an outage of lots of nodes due to a bug in the centrally maintained software[6]. The software as a central instance indirectly (and unintentionally) told the miners to stop mining by software malfunction, leading to a sharp decrease in hash rate of over 10%. (3) Mining is typically performed in mining pools, i.e., miners jointly aim to create the next block in order to reduce variance and maximize revenue. Therefore, miners are connected to a central server or centrally managed infrastructure that forwards them their share of hashing puzzles. Malfunction or hostile takeover of the server and/or its communication – the de-facto standard is the *Stratum* protocol [27] – bears potential to take control over the hash rate of all miners in the pool. It has been already confirmed that fluctuations in consumption caused by botnets are able to trigger large frequency shifts and eventually load shedding and shutdown of power plants [7]. In this paper, we investigate whether *Bitcoin* or *Ethereum* is able to cause such large deviations threating reliable operation of the power grid.

---

[5] http://www.antbleed.com/.

[6] https://blog.ethereum.org/2016/09/18/security-alert-geth-nodes-crash-due-memory-bug/.

4   Assessment of Models for Power Consumption

In a first step, we need an estimation of the total power consumption of the respective cryptocurrencies. Multiple models – both from the world of academia as well as beyond – are available; however, they significantly differ with regard to their underlying assumptions, not to mention their final outcome on total power consumption. In addition, they mainly focus on Bitcoin. In the following paragraphs, we assess these models and their parameters with respect to the quality of the results. Finally, we decide for a model that is built upon within the remainder of this work.

- *O'Dwyer and Malone* [23] calculate an upper and lower bound for worldwide Bitcoin energy consumption based on the network's hash rate and consumption values of commodity hardware and specialized mining hardware. The authors did not aim to model the actual mix of mining hardware, and they could only conclude that the consumption lies between the calculated upper and lower bound.
- *Vranken* [32] calculated power consumption under the assumption that all Bitcoin mining is done on (i) CPUs, (ii) GPUs, (iii) FPGAs or (iv) ASICs before bounding power consumption by means of (a) the total world power production, (b) assuming that the total mining revenue is spent on electric power, and finally the (c) inclusion of acquisition costs. As *O'Dwyer and Malone*, there has been no effort to model the actual hardware mix of the mining network.
- *Deetman* [8] aimed to overcome the above drawback by modeling the hardware mix of the mining network in a more sophisticated way. First, the author inferred the decrease of power consumption per hashing operation over time based on mining hardware's specification and its release data. In a second step, the increase of hash rate per month has been attributed to newest hardware (that is then assumed to run three to five years before being removed from the mining network again), then, finally leading to the average power consumption of the respective hardware mix. By means of the hash rate, the total power consumption was calculated.
- *The Vries* [33] follows a financially-oriented approach assuming that a certain ratio of the network's mining revenue is spent on electricity (60% with Bitcoin, 22% with Ethereum). Assuming an average energy price (US$ 0.05 per kWh with Bitcoin, US$ 0.12 per kWh with Ethereum[7]), the total power consumption of the mining network is derived. The author claims that this model does not only include power consumption that is directly used for mining but also the power for additional needs, e.g., data center cooling.

Table 1 provides an overview of the parameters that are included into the calculation of each model. The parameters show diverse characteristics, e.g., with regard to fluctuations or validity of data sources, that influence the model's

---

[7] According to the author, Ethereum is rather mined at residential homes; thus, residential rates apply.

Table 1. Usage of parameters in power consumption models: *Suitability* describes whether a model uses suitable parameters for estimation, see Table 2.

Model	Total hash rate	Power consumption of miners	Release date of miners	World power consumption	Mining revenue	Acquisition costs of miners	Miner lifetime	Ratio electricity to acquisition costs	Electricity price	Suitability of model
O'Dwyer and Malone [23]	✓	✓								✓
Vranken [32]	✓	✓		✓	✓	✓			✓	✗
Deetman [8]	✓	✓	✓				✓			✓
The Vries [33]					✓		✓		✓	✗

Table 2. Parameters with regards to suitability for power consumption modeling (✓ Good, ● Intermediate, ✗ Poor)

Parameter	Information source	Suitable
Total hash rate	Based on difficulty & block arrival times	✓[a]
Power consumption of miners	Data sheets, reviews	✓
Release date of miners	Data sheets, press release	✓
World power consumption	Public statistics	✓
Mining revenue	Block reward & transaction fees	✓
Acquisition costs of miners	Press releases, reviews	✗[b]
Miner lifetime	General	●[c]
Ratio electricity to acquisition costs	Based on electricity price and acquisition costs	✗[d]
Electricity price	Energy providers	✗[e]

[a] Both, difficulty and block arrival time can be directly extracted from the blockchain.
[b] Acquisition costs including shipment vary depending on time and country.
[c] IT equipmentment is generally considered to have short life times of 12 to 18 months.
[d] Energy prices and acquisition costs vary significantly and so does their ratio.
[e] Energy prices are dependent on country and customer type (domestic, industrial).

quality of prediction. Table 2 provides an assessment of the parameters included for power consumption estimation with respect to the source of information and their suitability. While some of them can be gained from (rather) authoritative sources like the blockchain directly, data sheets, reviews or press releases that are stable with respect to time and geographic location; others heavily fluctuate, in particular acquisition and electricity costs. Thus, we consider the first category as being suitable for power consumption estimation; the latter category as inappropriate – they would cause heavily fluctuating final results as well. In the last column, Table 1 highlights the models using only suitable parameters.

From these models, *Deetman*'s appears most suitable for our purpose of estimating a mining network's total power consumption for the following reasons: (i) The included parameter values are based on confirmed sources, are neither heavily fluctuating nor geographically dependent.[8] (ii) A mix of mining hardware is considered; results are more practical than the calculation of lower and upper bounds as done by *O'Dwyer and Malone*'s model. (iii) The result includes the power consumption that is directly used for mining only. This matches our threat model in Sect. 3, i.e., the adversary is solely able to influence the mining hardware remotely, but not supporting measures such as cooling. (iv) The approach is universally applicable for all cryptocurrencies.

5   Total Power Consumption of Popular Mining Networks

After deciding for an appropriate model for power consumption, in this section, we describe our approach in detail and present the results for Bitcoin and Ethereum.

Methodology for Power Consumption Estimation: For estimating the total power consumption of a cryptocurrency, we performed the following steps:

1. We collected the overall hash rates as well as power consumption for typical mining hardware of the respective currency from data sheets or reviews, and calculated the power consumption per computed hash (W/H). Current as well as outdated hardware has been included.
2. In addition, we collected the release dates of mining hardware from data sheets and press releases.
3. Assuming that power consumption per hash decreases over time due to better hardware, we performed a regression analysis to find a trend in miners' power efficiency based on the data that has been collected in step 1 and 2.
4. While the result of step 3 provides insight into the further development of miner efficiency, the hash rate of the entire cryptocurrency's mining process has to be calculated to obtain the overall network's power consumption. Following the algorithm of *Ozisik et al.* [25], we inferred the overall hash rate including the parameters *target (respectively difficulty)*, *time interval* between consecutive blocks and the observed *hash values*. These values have been gained directly from the respective public blockchain.
5. At a certain point in time, mining is not exclusively performed on newest hardware but also on older hardware; therefore, we aim to create a representative hardware mix. We assume that the increase in a cryptocurrency network's hash rate is caused by current hardware and that the hardware contributes hashes to the network for a fixed time period of six months (Bitcoin) or 12 months (Ethereum). Instead of including power efficiency of individual miners into our calculation, we take the values from the regression analysis of step 3.

---

[8] The only arguable parameter is the hardware's total runtime. Therefore, we followed a twofold approach to test its plausibility: On the one hand, we collected typical runtimes in the community confirming our assumption. On the other hand, we argue that the range of plausible values does not change the result significantly.

6. Finally, we infer the cryptocurrency's total power consumption for the hardware mix from step 5. We multiply the hash rates with the assigned power efficiency for every entry within the hardware mix.

The gained results, as well as specifics, for Bitcoin and Ethereum are presented in the remainder of this section.

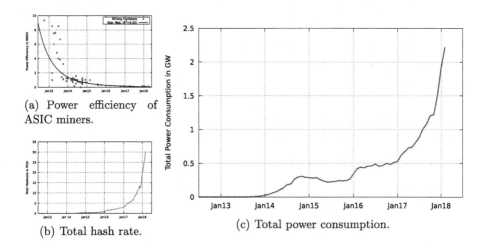

(a) Power efficiency of ASIC miners.

(b) Total hash rate.

(c) Total power consumption.

Fig. 2. Results for the Bitcoin network.

Total Power Consumption of Bitcoin: Collecting data for Bitcoin miners was based on a hardware list from the Bitcoin Wiki[9], we cross-checked the provided parameters for hash rate and power consumption and added release dates. However, we faced various difficulties: (a) Due to bankruptcies, companies producing hardware disappeared from the market and data sheets of their hardware is not available anymore (if ever present). In such cases, we relied on technical reviews on the respective hardware and blogs or forum posts of the active Bitcoin community. (b) Delivery dates were not met in multiple cases; shipment was delayed by multiple months and eventually the miners went online later than initially announced. Therefore, we verified the initial announcements from the hardware vendors with community posts. In case of delays, we included the actual shipping date into our calculation. (c) Some products have never been shipped at all, or we did not find any specification indicating their hash rate and/or power consumption. For these reasons, we excluded twelve miners from the original list containing 83 miners. As commodity hardware and field-programmable gate arrays (FPGAs) have become outdated for multiple years already, we focused on application-specific integrated circuit (ASIC) miners. The gained results for power efficiency, total hash rate and total power consumption are depicted in

---

[9] https://en.bitcoin.it/wiki/Mining_hardware_comparison.

Fig. 2: The power efficiency increased over time and as of February 2018, the mix of mining hardware requires 0.049 W/GH. The total hash rate of the Bitcoin network is estimated to be 30.2 EH/s and the total power consumption 2.2 GW.

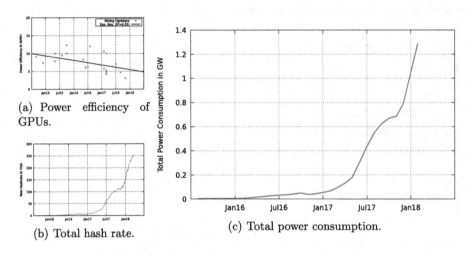

(a) Power efficiency of GPUs.

(b) Total hash rate.

(c) Total power consumption.

Fig. 3. Results for the Ethereum network.

Total Power Consumption of Ethereum: Ethereum is predominantly mined on (commodity) Graphics Processing Units (GPUs). Therefore, we collected data on GPU models commonly suggested for Ethereum mining. In comparison to Bitcoin mining, we were able to rely on specifications by the dominant players in the market, namely AMD Radeon and Nvidia GeForce. The results are depicted in Fig. 3: The power efficiency increased over time and as of February 2018 is 5.2 W/MH. The total hash rate of the Ethereum network is estimated to be 253 TH/s and the total power consumption 1.3 GW. In comparison to Bitcoin, Ethereum mining hardware requires more power per hash. Thus, even though Ethereum's total hash rate is less than Bitcoin's, the power consumption has roughly the same magnitude. Beyond, linear regression provided best results for Ethereum while exponential for Bitcoin. Based on these facts, we believe that there is still room for improvement in further development of Ethereum mining hardware while efficiency gains for Bitcoin will be minimal in the future.

6   Geographic Spread of Miners

After calculating the total power usage of Bitcoin and Ethereum mining, we have to determine the share of consumption in distinct power grids. Therefore, we analyze the biggest mining pools of both cryptocurrencies to infer the geographical spread of their miners. With respect to power grids, we focus on the

Table 3. Power consumption of mining with regard to European power grids

	Ethereum			Bitcoin		Grid characteristics	
	ethermine	Lower bound	Upper bound	Lower bound	Upper bound	Total load	Reference incident
UCTE	22.1%[a]	79 MW	284 MW	56 MW	1194 MW	296.8 GW	3000 MW
NORDEL	1.41%	5 MW	18 MW	4 MW	68 MW	38.5 GW	600 MW
Iceland	0.18%	0.6 MW	2 MW	0.6 MW	9 MW	2.0 GW	90 MW
Ireland	0.09%	0.3 MW	1 MW	0.2 MW	4.3 MW	3.0 GW	160 MW
Great Britain	1.12%	4 MW	14 MW	2.8 MW	54 MW	34.7 GW	400–700 MW

[a]From the overall *ethermine* hashrate measured from 2018-02-26 to 018-03-26

following European systems as they are considered to be among the most reliable networks and rarely face blackouts: (A) The *Synchronous Grid of Continental Europe (UCTE grid)* spans 29 European and North African countries[10]. (B) *NORDEL* is a synchronous power grid comprising Denmark[11], Finland, Norway and Sweden. (C) Iceland, Ireland, and the United Kingdom each operate an island network of their own for geographic reasons. These individual synchronous grids are typically interconnected by DC lines; however, they are only able to provide a small ratio of the overall power consumption and cannot compensate major imbalances.

Due to the sources available to us, we had to follow two distinct approaches for Bitcoin and Ethereum to estimate the ratio per synchronous grid.

Geographic Spread of Ethereum Mining: For Ethereum, we could rely on regional data from the the biggest mining pool by mined blocks *ethermine*; the latter controls 27.9% of the total Ethereum hashrate[12]. Having access to individual countries' hash rates allowed us to determine their share of the total hash rate; these numbers were then used to calculate power consumption for the different power grids. Finally, we calculated a lower and an upper bound for power consumption for the respective power networks; all results are presented in Table 3.

– The *lower bound* of power consumption is calculated under the assumption that just *ethermine* encompasses miners within Europe while the miners of other pools are outside of the continent, and represents a lower bound of power consumption. This is insofar a lower bound to power consumption within these networks as we have ground truth from this pool.

---

[10] Country Codes (ISO 3166-2): AT, BA, BE, BG, CH, CZ, DE, DK, DZ, ES, FR, GR, HR, HU, IT, LU, MA, ME, MK, NL, PL, PT, RO, RS, SI, SK, TN, TR, EH.

[11] Mainland Denmark is connected to UCTE, the islands to NORDEL. We split the power consumption according to the region's population. (54% in the UCTE grid, 46% in the NORDEL grid).

[12] https://etherscan.io/stat/miner?range=7&blocktype=blocks.

– For the *upper bound* of power consumption, we assume that all mining pools have an equal share of European miners as the investigated mining pool; this value represents insofar an upper bound as certain mining pools predominantly target miners outside Europe, e.g., by providing a homepage in Chinese only. Beyond, the investigated pool is considered to encompass more hash rate within Europe than others as the pool is run from a European country.

Geographic Spread of Bitcoin Mining: For Bitcoin mining, we were unable to obtain country specific information from a mining pool and had to rely on more coarse-grained, though publicly available information: btc.com, currently the largest pool mining 24.9%[13] of all Bitcoin blocks, provides a list of successfully mined blocks and their origin at continent granularity; this way, we were able to calculate the share of blocks mined in Europe within this pool to be 7.4% (March 2018). slushpool.com, third biggest pool controlling 11.7% of Bitcoin's total hash rate, runs multiple, geographically spread *Stratum* servers and publishes the controlled hash rate per server. Individual miners connecting to a pool typically connect to the closest server to reduce network latency; this way, we are able to obtain a European share of 81% within this mining pool. Taking these two results into account leads to a minimum power consumption of 251 MW within Europe; splitting this consumption among the power grids as Ethereum's consumption leads to a lower bound as presented in Table 3. The upper bound was calculated based on the following assumptions: (1) For the hyperimage-https://btc.com/btc.com and slushpool.com, we included their share according the numbers above. (2) All pools with a Chinese-only homepage are assumed to control no miners in Europe, (3) the remainder pools are assumed to have the share of slushpool.com (as *ethermine* is considered to be an eurocentic pool for Ethereum, slushpool.com is for Bitcoin). The numbers for Bitcoin however might overestimate power consumption to a certain extent as the pools' definition of Europe may go beyond the countries in the UCTE, NORDEL, Icelandic, Irish and British grid.

7   Impacts on the Power Grid

We determined Bitcoin's total power consumption to be 2.2 GW. In European networks, 64 MW to 1329 MW are drawn. Ethereum's overall consumption is 1.3 GW of which 89 MW to 319 MW are drawn in Europe. The impact of an amount of power consumption is dependent on its share of the total power consumption and particularly the grid's reference incident. The latter indicates the power loss that the system is designed for, and its size is equivalent to the primary control, the fastest measure to stabilize a power grid. Consequently, imbalances can be compensated within a short period of time (on electrical engineering time frames). For example, the UCTE network maintains 3 GW in

---

[13] https://blockchain.info/pools.

stand-by for primary control which is fully activated within 30 s. Therefore, fast changes in power consumption of magnitude of the reference incidents are able to overpower the stand-by mechanisms and trigger emergency routines. Thus, we assume, the reference incident value to be an adequate threshold to determine the potential of a cryptocurrencies' power consumption to harm the power grid's operation. Therefore, Table 3 presents total power consumption alongside the reference incidents for European power grids.

In none of the power grids the consumption exceeds the reference incidents; nevertheless, upper bounds are in most cases only one order of magnitude below the threshold – two orders in the case of Ireland – and both cryptocurrencies grow exponentially at the moment. Therefore, we estimate power consumption's development in the future by performing exponential regression. Figure 4(a) shows power consumption in the UCTE network assuming a share of 11% (lower bound, see Sect. 6), 54% (upper bound) and 33% (mean) of mining in Europe. Even in the best case, the reference incident of 3 GW[14] is reached by Bitcoin mining at the begin of 2020; in the worst case, in the middle of 2018. Results for Ethereum, see Fig. 4(b), show that the reference incident will be exceeded in 7 to 14 years.

8 Discussion

Cryptocurrencies and their power consumption are either discussed with respect to hardware equipment's efficiency or the adverse impact on ecology due to high overall power consumption. In this paper, we emphasize that Proof-of-Work cryptocurrencies are in principle able to destabilize power grids. Cryptocurrency miners draw large amounts of power from the grid, despite all efforts to make them more efficient and high gains in their efficiency over the last years. Our analysis shows that cryptocurrency mining in both Bitcoin and Ethereum *currently does not represent an immediate danger to reliable power grid operation on the European continent.*

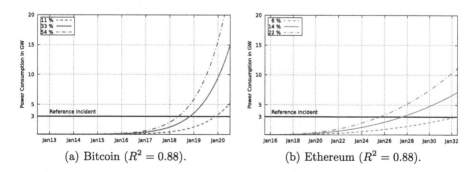

(a) Bitcoin ($R^2 = 0.88$).   (b) Ethereum ($R^2 = 0.88$).

Fig. 4. Projection of future mining power consumption in the UCTE grid

---

[14] Representing the amount of lost generation/load that can be handled by the power grid, reference incident values are hardly changed in practice despite increased energy consumption and increased network sizes.

Our results show however that critical values to power grid operation lie just one or two orders of magnitude beyond the current consumption of Bitcoin or Ethereum and both grow at exponential rates. For example, the reference incident within the UCTE network is 3 GW [12], i.e., the respective power grid is planned to successfully compensate for a potential loss of this amount of power generation, which is roughly equivalent to two nuclear power plants. Assuming that current growth rates and the share of miners in the UCTE network are maintained, the level of the reference incident would be met within 0.5 to 2 years for Bitcoin and within 7 to 14 years for Ethereum. Then, the power grid's measures for frequency stabilization might not be sufficient any more in case of a sudden outage of all mining efforts in the respective cryptocurrency – may it be as a consequence of malfunction or due to malicious actions by an adversary.

In comparison to [7], our attack scenarios do not increase power consumption all of a sudden, but rather decrease it within seconds, which is more severe from the power operator's perspective as the blackout of November 2006 in Europe has shown [29]. The loss of electric load causes a shift towards higher frequencies, and wind turbines additionally increase the imbalance by stopping power input at frequencies beyond 50.2 Hz (Germany) or 50.3 Hz (Italy, Denmark) [2] destabilizing the power network even further. Despite the effort to change this behavior – a lesson learned from the 2006 blackout – it is rumored that roughly half of all turbines in Europe still follow legacy guidelines. In case of load loss, operators can only throttle power plants; this takes multiple tens of seconds for fast plants like gas turbines but hours or even days for base load plants (nuclear, coal, etc.). If the frequency reaches 51.5 Hz faster than operators are able to stabilize the network by throttling, all power plants perform a cumbersome and costly emergency shutdown. Beyond, our attack is easier to achieve than the previous approach as the tedious task of botnet creation is largely omitted. An adversary only has to compromise the communication and coordination infrastructure, smuggle malfunctionality into the software or exploit a backdoor. All three types of incidents have already been shown feasible or were actually observed in current cryptocurrency networks (c.f. Sect. 3). Certain protocols and software, e.g., Stratum, suffer from bad reputation with respect to security [27], and documentation as well as a planned security-by-design approach are generally lacking. Finally, we outline that our attack can also be combined with a botnet to form dynamic attacks and exploit resonance frequencies of the network, as presented in [7].

The consequences of such a described incident would be large-scale blackouts and the shutdown of power plants due to automatic emergency routines [31]. Besides the impact on the economy and the possible life-threating consequences through cease of medical care, water and other basic needs, large-scale blackouts entail a much greater challenge. Most plant types actually need electric energy to start up. Only very few power plants have black-start capabilities, i.e., a startup procedure without external power. Afterwards, every other power plant has to be brought up by synchronizing into that grid, while simultaneously reconnecting an appropriate amount of household to keep an equilibrium of demand and production. After the 2003 Northeast blackout, it took two days to bring most households back on the grid; the remaining areas had to face up to two weeks without electrical power [30].

In recent time, cryptocurrencies – their value, as well as their mining operations – have experienced extraordinary growth and this trend is likely to continue in the near future, and possibly beyond. Thus, they will consume an increasing share of the produced electricity. In the course of this work, we focused on European power grids, namely the UCTE, the NORDEL as well as various island networks as they are considered to be among the most reliable systems. At the same time, miners are not predominantly present in these areas, but rather in other networks. Despite these considerations, the results show that cryptocurrencies might have a negative impact on reliable grid operation. Thus, any thresholds determined for that networks will likely be lower on other less robust grids with a higher mining ratio. For example, Venezuela, known for its continuous problems with power grid operation, has attributed blackouts purportedly to "illegal" Bitcoin mining[15].

Countermeasures: In conclusion, its worth to think about potential countermeasures such as the following:

– *Change of mining software behavior:* An approach that could readily help to mitigate the outlined attack is to update cryptocurrency mining software such that it takes the problem of sudden load swings into consideration. For instance, upon loss of connectivity or lack of work to be performed, mining software could continue the mining process for a randomized amount of time in order to reduce the overall power consumption more smoothly.
– *Further efficiency increase:* Mining hardware could be improved to reduce their power consumption per hash rate even further, and counteract the rising power consumption. Past growth rates however increased power consumption at higher rates than savings due to more efficiency. In addition, improvements in efficiency appear to be lower in the future as our trend analysis shows at least for Bitcoin, see Fig. 2(a).
– *Replacement of Proof-of-Work:* There are currently several approaches to replace Proof-of-Work with alternative, less energy intensive mechanisms. Provably secure *Proof-of-Stake* designs have been proposed, where the required resource to be able to participate in mining are the cryptocurrency units themselves [4,16,18]. Furthermore, by relying on *trusted hardware*, systems employing Proof-of-Elapsed-Time (PoET) or Proof-of-Useful-Work (PoUW) can be realized [37]. Finally, alternative limited resources, such as disk space in the case of Proof-of-Space [26], may be utilized.
– *Change of incentives:* Each mining operator aims to expand its mining capability as long as they expect a net profit in doing so. This increases the network's overall hash rate and power consumption; at the same time, the difficulty of the network is adjusted making Proof-of-Work harder to leave

---

[15] http://www.dailymail.co.uk/news/article-5161765/Bitcoin-mining-causing-electricity-blackouts.html.

targeted block intervals unchanged. This implies that the cryptocurrency's throughput does not increase despite more effort (and power) spent on mining, i.e., it does not scale transaction numbers with the hash rate. Expanding the incentives in a way that rewards more resource efficient mining would not only reduce hash rate but also power consumption.

- *Regulation:* Power grids are critical infrastructure; nation states aim to protect their infrastructure and take actions usually by means of legislation, e.g., *Directive 2008/114/EC* by the European Union. In consequence, governments might regulate the use or mining of cryptocurrencies. For example, China has already banned Bitcoin trading[16], even though mining is still legal.
- *Purchase of surplus production:* Finally, there is also a benefit for power grid reliability with regard to cryptocurrencies. The latter could stabilize the power grid, and purchase a surplus of energy production in order to maintain the balance between supply and consumption. This typically happens in nights: Base load power stations, e.g., nuclear or coal power plants, suffer from slow dynamics and therefore operators prefer paying others to consume the power instead of reducing their plants' output. Killing two birds with a stone, miners would not only raise money through the mining reward and transaction fees but would also raise income through power consumption. However, mining equipment would not run 24/7 which impacts the return on investment.
- *Speed-up of power grid measures:* In future, primary control could improve responsiveness until full activation. As physical limits impose constraints on power plant turbines due to their mass; grid operators might have to find alternative ways for primary control, e.g., by using power from electric cars' batteries to stabilize the network.

9   Related Work

Large-scale power grid failures and destabilization incidents bringing grids to their limits are rare events in European power grids. Nevertheless, operators investigate and learn from these occurrences to be able to ensure more reliable operation in the future, e.g., the November 2006 blackout, which split the power grid into three synchronous zones due to cascading effects [29], a blackout in Turkey in 2015 [14], and inter-area oscillations [13]. Attacks against smart grids are outlined in *Mohsenian-Rad et al.* [20] and *Mishra et al.* [19], where an adversary manipulates messages, e.g., containing pricing information, causing *smart* behavior to indirectly affect the power grid, e.g., simultaneous charging of all electric vehicles. As of today, smart grid functionality is not yet widely deployed. Hence, the respective attack surface is low. On a smaller network scale *Xu et al.* [36] investigate how power oversubscription in data centers could be used to conduct concerted attacks that lead to undesired power outages. Finally, the impact of dynamic load attacks on smart grid operation is outlined in *Amini et*

---

[16] http://www.scmp.com/business/banking-finance/article/2132009/china-stamp-out-cryptocurrency-trading-completely-ban.

al. [1], however the authors do not provide strategies how an adversary could gain such a high amount of controllable load. This problem is overcome in *Dabrowski et al.* [7], where it is shown that an adversary could form a botnet from commodity hardware as well as Internet-of-Thing devices to reach the necessary controllable load for a successful attack. In addition, it is highlighted that an adversary requires much lower amounts of controllable consumers than stated in [1]. In regard to power consumption cryptocurrencies are investigated in a twofold way: either for power efficiency of mining hardware or their total consumption's impact on the environment. *Wang and Liu* [34] consider the evolution of miners, including their power consumption and productivity. *O'Dwyer and Malone* [23] investigate the profitability of Bitcoin mining, including hardware characteristics as well as exchange rates, and bound the total power consumption of Bitcoin to 3 GW. Further publications that provide estimates on the total power consumption of Bitcoin are presented by *Vranken* [32], *Deetman* [8], and *The Vries* [33]. We asses their models in Sect. 4; our work is based on *Deetman's* approach. Another estimation is published by *Orman* [24], however the numbers appear erroneous, e.g., a total Bitcoin hash rate of 1018 Hashes/s.

10 Conclusion

By now, power consumption with regard to cryptocurrencies such as *Bitcoin* and *Ethereum* has been considered in a twofold way. Either, mining operators have aimed to maximize revenue (and therefore invested in most efficient mining hardware), or ecologists criticize the cryptocurrencies' massive amount of power consumption and its adverse affects on the environment. In the course of this work, we broaden the discussion and investigate whether cryptocurrencies are able to destabilize power grid operation by suddenly reducing mining (and thus electric load). The latter might be achieved by the exploitation of a backdoor in a vast number of miners, by compromising the communication infrastructure or by malfunctionality of software required for mining – all events that have been shown possible or have actually happened in the past.

Indeed, we identified potential that such incidents might negatively impact power grid operation causing load shedding, the shutdown of power plants and eventually large-scale blackouts, if not now then possibly in the near future. Our results are based on European power grids, namely the UCTE, NORDEL and various island networks, that are considered to be among the most reliable. At the same time, these grids currently serve only a minor part of mining hardware. In the UCTE network, the biggest synchronous power grid by total load, we see power consumption of Bitcoin and Ethereum each reaching critical values within the next years, assuming further growth of cryptocurrencies. Whereas, some less stable grids are serving proportionally more mining facilities, and consequently face higher risks from such incidents. Concluding, the current gold rush-like hype towards cryptocurrencies may not only impact finance but also the real, physical world. While we do not oppose cryptocurrencies in general, we view their ever increasing power consumption with a critical eye. In this respect it is essential to consider the possible consequences of uncontrolled growth and try to provide effective countermeasures that help to ensure the stable operation of power grids.

Acknowledgments. We thank Peter Pratscher operating ethermine and ethpool for providing valuable insight into hashrate population on a per country basis. This research was funded by Bridge Early Stage 846573 A2Bit and Bridge 1 858561 SESC (both FFG), the Christian Doppler Laboratory for *Security and Quality Improvement in the Production System Lifecycle (CDL-SQI)*, Institute of Information Systems Engineering, TU Wien and the Josef Ressel Centers project TARGET. The competence center SBA Research (SBA-K1) is funded within the framework of COMET - Competence Centers for Excellent Technologies by BMVIT, BMDW, and the federal state of Vienna. The financial support by the Austrian Federal Ministry for Digital, Business and Enterprise and the National Foundation for Research, Technology and Development is gratefully acknowledged.

References

1. Amini, S., Mohsenian-Rad, H., Pasqualetti, F.: Dynamic load altering attacks in smart grid. In: IEEE Power Energy Society Innovative Smart Grid Technologies Conference (ISGT) (2015)
2. von Appen, J., Braun, M., Stetz, T., Diwold, K., Geibel, D.: Time in the sun: the challenge of high PV penetration in the German electric grid. IEEE Power Energy Mag. **11**, 55–64 (2013)
3. Back, A., et al.: Hashcash-a denial of service counter-measure (2002)
4. Bentov, I., Pass, R., Shi, E.: Snow white: provably secure proofs of stake (2016)
5. Bonneau, J., Miller, A., Clark, J., Narayanan, A., Kroll, J.A., Felten, E.W.: SoK: research perspectives and challenges for Bitcoin and cryptocurrencies. In: IEEE Symposium on Security and Privacy (2015)
6. Buterin, V.: Ethereum: a next-generation smart contract and decentralized application platform (2014)
7. Dabrowski, A., Ullrich, J., Weippl, E.R.: Grid shock: coordinated load-changing attacks on power grids. In: Annual Computer Security Applications Conference (ACSAC) (2017)
8. Deetman, S.: Bitcoin could consume as much electricity as denmark by 2020 (2016). https://motherboard.vice.com/en_us/article/aek3za/bitcoin-could-consume-as-much-electricity-as-denmark-by-2020
9. Douceur, J.R.: The sybil attack. In: Druschel, P., Kaashoek, F., Rowstron, A. (eds.) IPTPS 2002. LNCS, vol. 2429, pp. 251–260. Springer, Heidelberg (2002). https://doi.org/10.1007/3-540-45748-8_24
10. Dwork, C., Naor, M.: Pricing via processing or combatting junk mail. In: Brickell, E.F. (ed.) CRYPTO 1992. LNCS, vol. 740, pp. 139–147. Springer, Heidelberg (1993). https://doi.org/10.1007/3-540-48071-4_10
11. ENTSO-E: Appendix 1 - Load-Frequency Control and Performance. In: Continental Europe Operation Handbook (2004)
12. ENTSO-E: Policy 1 - Load-Frequency Control and Performance. In: Continental Europe Operation Handbook (2004)
13. ENTSO-E: Analysis of CE inter-area oscillation of 19 and 24 February 2014 (2011)
14. ENTSO-E: Report on blackout in Turkey on 31st March 2015 (2015)

15. Fairley, P.: Blockchain world - feeding the blockchain beast if bitcoin ever does go mainstream, the electricity needed to sustain it will be enormous. In: IEEE Spectrum (2017)
16. Kiayias, A., Russell, A., David, B., Oliynykov, R.: Ouroboros: a provably secure proof-of-stake blockchain protocol. In: Katz, J., Shacham, H. (eds.) CRYPTO 2017. LNCS, vol. 10401, pp. 357–388. Springer, Cham (2017). https://doi.org/10.1007/978-3-319-63688-7_12
17. Lewenberg, Y., Bachrach, Y., Sompolinsky, Y., Zohar, A., Rosenschein, J.S.: Bitcoin mining pools: a cooperative game theoretic analysis. In: International Conference on Autonomous Agents and Multiagent Systems (2015)
18. Micali, S.: ALGORAND: the efficient and democratic ledger (2016)
19. Mishra, S., Li, X., Kuhnle, A., Thai, M.T., Seo, J.: Rate alteration attacks in smart grid. In: IEEE Conference on Computer Communications (INFOCOM) (2015)
20. Mohsenian-Rad, R.H., Leon-Garcia, A.: Distributed internet-based load altering attacks against smart power grids. IEEE Trans. Smart Grid **2**, 667–674 (2011)
21. Nakamoto, S.: Bitcoin: a peer-to-peer electronic cash system (2008)
22. Narayanan, A., Clark, J.: Bitcoin's academic pedigree. Commun. ACM **60**(12), 36–45 (2017)
23. O'Dwyer, K., Malone, D.: Bitcoin mining and its energy footprint. In: IET Irish Signals & Systems Conference (2014)
24. Orman, H.: The power (energy) of cryptography. IEEE Internet Comput. **20**, 90–94 (2016)
25. Ozisik, A.P., Bissias, G., Levine, B.N.: Estimation of miner hash rates and consensus on blockchains (2018)
26. Park, S., Pietrzak, K., Kwon, A., Alwen, J., Fuchsbauer, G., Gaži, P.: SpaceMint: a cryptocurrency based on proofs of space (2015)
27. Recabarren, R., Carbunar, B.: Hardening stratum, the bitcoin pool mining protocol. In: Symposium on Privacy Enhancing Technologies (PETS) (2017)
28. Schrijvers, O., Bonneau, J., Boneh, D., Roughgarden, T.: Incentive compatibility of bitcoin mining pool reward functions. In: International Conference on Financial Cryptography (2016)
29. Union for the Co-ordination of Transmission of Electricity: Final report: System disturbance on 4 November 2006 (2007)
30. U.S.-Canada Power System Outage Task Force: Final report on the August 14, 2003 Blackout in the United States and Canada (2004)
31. Verband der Netzbetreiber (VDN): Transmissioncode 2007 - netz- und systemregeln der deutschen Übertragungsnetzbetreiber (2007)
32. Vranken, H.: Sustainability of bitcoin and blockchains. Curr. Opin. Environ. Sustain. **28**, 1–9 (2017)
33. the Vries, A.: Bitcoin energy consumption index (2017). https://web.archive.org/web/20170429092415/https://digiconomist.net/bitcoin-energy-consumption. Accessed 01 Mar 2018
34. Wang, L., Liu, Y.: Exploring miner evolution in bitcoin network. In: Mirkovic, J., Liu, Y. (eds.) PAM 2015. LNCS, vol. 8995, pp. 290–302. Springer, Cham (2015). https://doi.org/10.1007/978-3-319-15509-8_22
35. Wood, G.: Ethereum: a secure decentralised generalised transaction ledger eip-150 revision (759dccd - 2017-08-07) (2017)
36. Xu, Z., Wang, H., Xu, Z., Wang, X.: Power attack: an increasing threat to data centers. In: Network and Distributed System Security Symposium (NDSS) (2014)
37. Zhang, F., Eyal, I., Escriva, R., Juels, A., van Renesse, R.: REM: resource-efficient mining for blockchains (2017)

Passwords, Accounts, and Users

Characterizing Eve: Analysing Cybercrime Actors in a Large Underground Forum

Sergio Pastrana[1]([⊠]) [iD], Alice Hutchings[1] [iD], Andrew Caines[2] [iD],
and Paula Buttery[3]

[1] Cambridge Cybercrime Centre, Department of Computer Science and Technology,
University of Cambridge, Cambridge, UK
{Sergio.Pastrana,Alice.Hutchings}@cl.cam.ac.uk
[2] Theoretical and Applied Linguistics, Faculty of Modern and Medieval Languages,
University of Cambridge, Cambridge, UK
apc38@cam.ac.uk
[3] Natural Language and Information Processing, Department of Computer Science
and Technology, University of Cambridge, Cambridge, UK
pjb48@cam.ac.uk

Abstract. Underground forums contain many thousands of active users,
but the vast majority will be involved, at most, in minor levels of
deviance. The number who engage in serious criminal activity is small.
That being said, underground forums have played a significant role in
several recent high-profile cybercrime activities. In this work we apply
data science approaches to understand criminal pathways and characterize key actors related to illegal activity in one of the largest and longest-
running underground forums. We combine the results of a logistic regression model with k-means clustering and social network analysis, verifying
the findings using topic analysis. We identify variables relating to forum
activity that predict the likelihood a user will become an actor of interest
to law enforcement, and would therefore benefit the most from intervention. This work provides the first step towards identifying ways to deter
the involvement of young people away from a career in cybercrime.

Keywords: Cybercrime · Underground forums · Social behaviour
Criminal pathways

1 Introduction

Cybercrimes carried out by organized groups using custom tools with political or
military motivations capture the public imagination. However, the vast majority
of attacks are committed by actors with a low level of technical sophistication [24,
34]. While these may receive less media attention, they can cause large financial
losses and be costly to defend against [3]. This criminality is to a great extent

© Springer Nature Switzerland AG 2018
M. Bailey et al. (Eds.): RAID 2018, LNCS 11050, pp. 207–227, 2018.
https://doi.org/10.1007/978-3-030-00470-5_10

promoted by an active underground economy where attack tools and services are traded, and cyber attacks are monetised [2].

Online underground forums bring together individuals interested in cyber-crime and illicit online monetizing techniques [12,22]. In contrast with other forms of crypto-markets [31], some of the contents of these forums are legal, such as discussions relating to current events, gaming, and technology-related issues. However, these forums are also used to exchange information about deviant behaviour, and trade in goods and services with an illicit origin or application. Previous research has found these forums can provide a stepping stone towards more serious online criminal activities [13,14].

The underground economy attracts actors that are unlikely to be involved in traditional crime, but who may become involved in cybercrime [23]. For example, the use of booter services for 'DDoSing' others has become a widespread phenomenon among school-aged children, and even victims can become attack-ers [24]. This is due to the ease of access to hacking tools, the sense of anonymity provided by the Internet, and the perceived lack of law enforcement online.

Cybercrime has proliferated in recent years, and online forums have become a key source of data for researchers (see Sect. 2 for related work). While insightful, this research has mainly relied on cross-sectional data, analysing forum content from short periods of time or focussing on particular areas of cybercrime. Typi-cally, researchers have considered only the tools and technologies adversaries use, not their motivations or personal context [10]. Understanding not only 'what' is traded in underground economies, but also 'why' and by 'whom' can provide insights into ways to tackle cybercrime from multiple perspectives. The evolution of offenders, understanding how they learn to commit crime over time, is a key aspect of this. Multidisciplinary research on the behavioural aspects of cyber-crime is necessary to develop defences aimed at understanding and preventing incidents, rather than stopping or recovering from them.

In this paper, we analyse the characteristics and pathways of 'key actors'; forum users who have been linked to criminal activities, such as providing ser-vices and tools to disrupt systems and networks or using these tools to perform attacks. We use a variety of sources to identify these actors (see Sect. 3). While we do not publish this list for ethical reasons (see Sect. 6), activities linked to these key actors include providing DDoS as a service, distributing malware, operating bot shops and pay-per-install services, as well as providing services for web exploitation and account cracking. Characterizing key actors and analysing their evolution within forums is beneficial for various reasons. From a social perspective, it is the first step towards identifying ways to deter people away from criminal activities. From the cybersecurity perspective, these actors pro-vide state-of-the art tools and techniques that can be used for attacking systems. This information can be used by response teams and security firms to focus their attention, increasing their capacity to react rapidly to new forms of attack.

We focus our study on *Hackforums*, one of the largest underground forums. *Hackforums* is well established, operating since 2007. While this forum is known to be overrun by novice teenage hackers (contemptuously dubbed 'script kiddies'), in the last few years there have been a number of high profile attacks directly related to products distributed through this forum. For example, in September 2016, the *Mirai* source code was released on the forum, which led to several related botnets being used for illegal activities such as DDoS attacks [4] or mining cryptocurrencies [21]. In the first three months of 2018, there have been at least two cases relating to *Hackforums* users before the UK courts.

We use the CrimeBB dataset, which includes *Hackforums* data spanning from 2007 onwards and contains information about 572k user accounts [27]. We start by identifying key actors on the forum. We first apply data science approaches to present a longitudinal study of these key actors. Concretely we apply social network analysis to analyse their social interests, natural language processing to classify the type of information posted, and clustering to group the actors based on forum activity. Our research uncovers common activity patterns and the pathways taken over time in terms of interests and knowledge. Second we develop tools to identify factors that predict involvement in cybercrime. These tools use social network analysis, logistic regression, and clustering to preselect a list of potential actors, and topic analysis to analyse the type of information they post. Our findings suggest that combining the different techniques helps in the prediction of potential actors. These tools can be applied to any particular cybercrime domain, so we make them publicly available. The CrimeBB dataset also contains data from other forums and is available to academic researchers through data sharing agreements from the Cambridge Cybercrime Centre[1].

2   Background and Related Work

The rise of cybersecurity incidents parallels the development of underground economies, where attacking tools and services are easily accessible at low cost or even for free [2]. For example, pay-per-install services outsource the task of infecting a machine and allow miscreants to buy 'installs' for spreading their malware [6]. Other common assets that can be found in underground forums are bot shops and botnets [8], crypters and packers [30], or exploits [2].

Various authors have addressed the offenders perspective. Karami and McCoy analysed leaked databases of booter services: websites providing DDoS for hire, publicly marketed as network 'stressers', but offered in underground forums as services to perform DDoS [16]. While mostly used to take down gaming servers, booters are also used to attack medium-sized websites. Hutchings and Clayton researched the provision of denial of service attacks, interviewing and surveying the providers to ask how they began providing the services, and why [14]. They found most operators were young men from North America. They had escalated from using booter sites, to setting them up and running them themselves. They were initially exposed to booter services through gaming and hacker communities. Financial gain was the main reason for providing services, but they also reported they enjoyed the challenge of their activities.

---

[1] https://www.cambridgecybercrime.uk/.

Sood and Enbody analyse the provision of cybercrime tools and services, identifying three type of actors in underground communities: *providers* or *producers*, *advertisers*, and *buyers* [30]. Based on our analysis of underground forums, we add two new roles. First, *re-distributors* of modified versions of public or leaked malware. This role includes users involved in the provision of encrypted malware binaries, aimed at avoiding detection by antivirus software. The second role we dub *teachers*: actors who provide tutorials for configuration and use of various attack tools, sometimes accompanied by help-desk services.

According to the criminological theory of differential association, criminal activities are normal behaviours learnt in interaction with others [33]. Learning takes place by associating with others in personal groups. The content of what is learnt includes specific techniques to commit crime, as well as the 'definitions' (mindset) favourable to committing crime [37]. In relation to cybercrime, there is evidence that offenders associate with each other in physical space [18], but also online, particularly through the use of online underground forums [10,15,38].

Understanding offender pathways allows society to consider the most appropriate ways to divert potential offenders away from crime. For example, the UK's National Crime Agency (NCA) [23] debriefed young people involved in cybercrime activities, and found many were first exposed through their interest in gaming. The NCA have subsequently been working with the video gaming industry to deliver preventative interventions.

Underground forums serve as an entry point into cybercrime for potential offenders. These forums also allow non-technical actors to learn how to commit offences and develop their skills [29]. Normally these forums have well-defined categories like "Hacking" or "Market". Where authors are most active provides insights into their interests and expertise [25]. Forum members have a public profile with information such as the registration date, last access or time spent. Most underground forums are publicly accessible on the surface web or the 'dark web' (e.g. through Tor hidden services).

The success of underground economies relies on trust and informal social control [1]. Various authors have analysed these behaviours using social network analysis (SNA), for example to analyse the evolution of members in terms of posts and private messages [22] or to understand specialization and developments of subcommunities [11]. The use of natural language processing (NLP) to analyse underground forums is also a recurring technique, e.g. to analyse post sentiment [19] or to identify the assets being traded or the currencies used [28,29].

3   Dataset

In this work we use the CrimeBB dataset [27], which contains data collected from various underground forums. We focus our study on *Hackforums*, the largest forum contained in this dataset, with more than 30 m posts[2] made by 572k user

---

[2] We refer to a whole website as a *forum*, on which pages are set aside for discussion of defined topics in *boards*, with users participating in conversation *threads* via individual *posts*.

accounts over more than 10 years. *Hackforums* is divided into nine categories: Hacking, Technology, Coding, Gaming, Web, Market, Money (a miscellaneous category for all sorts of money making methods), Graphics and Common (which includes boards for discussion about various topics, such as entertainment or politics, and boards intended for forum rules and suggestions).

3.1 Key Actors

We use the term 'key actor' to refer to forum users who have been linked to cybercrime activities, such as distributing malware, offering off-the-shelf tools to perform denial-of-service attacks or using these tools to attack others. A number of approaches were utilised to identify key actors who are or have been active on *Hackforums*. These approaches required manual effort and thus are not scalable. In Sect. 5 we propose tools to automatically identify likely key actors.

1. Media sources were searched to identify reports relating to *Hackforums* users being arrested or prosecuted for cybercrime activities (media included official notifications from law enforcement agencies; forum threads; social media and blog posts made by security researchers). We used Google extended search to look for sources including keywords such as 'arrested' or 'prosecuted' and 'hackforums'. Results often included the pseudonym used by the actor in the forum. This method yielded 49 key actors.
2. A private security and intelligence company, Flashpoint, provided usernames considered to be of interest due to their activities. This yielded 9 key actors.
3. For each actor identified using the methods above, we used SNA to find their 'closest' neighbours (users of the forum who they interact with the most). Then, we manually analyse the activity of these neighbours looking for evidence of involvement in cybercrime activities (for instance, evidence of providing illegal material such as malware or 'booter' services). This method yielded a further 22 actors.
4. The final set of key actors are those providing tools aiming at disrupting systems and/or networks. To identify these actors we had two approaches:
   - We searched *Hackforums* for threads advertising the top 300 Remote Access Trojans (RATs) reported in [36]. Again, from manual inspection we identified the owners/coders of RATs and the re-distributors of modified versions (e.g. encrypted binaries aimed at avoiding antivirus detection). We discarded actors who we believed to be only purporting to be an owner (a *stealer*); and also actors distributing an infected version of a binary with the intent of compromising other forum members. This method yielded 35 key actors (there was some overlap with actors previously extracted).
   - We used 'compilation' threads from *Hackforums*, where popular tools and services are listed accompanied with the corresponding thread where it was first advertised. This method yielded 15 key actors.

In total, these methods yield 130 actors of interest to law enforcement: of these, we were able to identify the accounts of 113 within the dataset. The missing accounts might be due to accounts being removed or changes of the pseudonyms which we were unable to track. Also, it should be noted that various accounts might belong to the same actor.

4 Characterizing Key Actors

Having identified 113 key actors, we applied a number of different data science approaches to analyse the forum activity of these users, including NLP, SNA, and machine learning algorithms.

4.1 Natural Language Processing

Due to the massive size of the dataset (more than 30 m posts), it is not possible to manually code the data. We use NLP tools to classify posts into categories. Classification of interests and expertise of members enables the identification of topics related to cybercrime offences, such as learning to attack systems or trading in stolen accounts. The data poses interesting problems for NLP techniques. The language used by members of underground forums includes technical jargon and non-standard means of expression. Contributors include non-native speakers of English, and short texts in which information is conveyed in deliberately concise ways. In this work we analyse the behavioural evolution of our identified actors, firstly building a binary classifier to identify questions in CrimeBB.

Three annotators manually labelled 2,200 posts selected from a range of boards, with substantial inter-annotator agreement for post type (see more details in [7]). We use the annotated dataset to train and test the classifier, with a training subset of 175 annotated threads from various boards, and a test subset of 186 annotated threads from another board (to prevent overfitting). For each thread, we extract features using a set of statistical techniques and a set of heuristics, having found this hybrid approach to work best [7]. The former include the number of replies, the number of links in the first post (both to external sources and to other threads in the forum), the length of the first post and a set of unigram features extracted from text. We convert every thread title and post into a document-term matrix (a matrix of counts with each word occurring as column values, and each of the documents as a row). We strip punctuation, convert to lower case characters, ignore numbers and exclude stop words. Finally, word counts are transformed using TF-IDF ('term frequency inverse document frequency'), a weighting that promotes words occurring fairly frequently in few documents above those occurring highly frequently but ubiquitously across CrimeBB [32].

The heuristics are formed through our expertise in analysing forum data. Concretely, for each thread we get the frequency of particularly interesting keywords in the heading and first post (examples of these keywords are "looking for", "I need help" or "I have a question"). Finally, we also account for the number of question marks in the heading.

We use a Linear SVM to build a classifier. Again, the selection of the algorithm is based on previous experimentation with the dataset [7]. For evaluation we use the usual metrics for information retrieval, i.e. precision, recall and F1. Precision measures the fraction of actual questions retrieved among the total of questions retrieved (including false positives). Recall, or sensitivity, measures the fraction of questions retrieved among the total number of actual questions in the dataset. Finally, the F1 score combines in a single measure both precision and recall. Our classifier has Precision = 0.88, Recall = 0.85 and F1 = 0.86. While these metrics can be improved, the classifier is accurate enough to automatically identify question threads, a task which would otherwise be infeasible due to the size of the dataset.

4.2   Social Network Analysis

We designed and developed SNA tools to facilitate study of the forums at different levels of granularity, per board, per topic of interest, per year, etc. We build the social network by processing the public interactions of the members. This network is represented as a directed graph, where nodes are the members of the forum and edges their interactions. We define a directed edge from node V to node W if there is a *reply* from V to W. There are two possible forms of reply: (a) when V explicitly cites a post made by W; and (b) when V replies in a thread initiated by W. When available, we use information from reputation votes given between members to classify the interactions as positive, negative or neutral.

We use classical SNA metrics such as centrality degrees to analyse the network, i.e. in-degree (fraction of nodes its incoming edges are connected to), out-degree (fraction of nodes its outgoing edges are connected to), and eigenvector (measure of the influence of a node in a network). Additionally, we compute the following metrics to measure the popularity of the forum users: total number of replies; h-index (a member with h-index = n is author of n threads having at least n replies); and the i-10-index, i-50-index and i-100-index (i.e. the number of threads with at least 10, 50 and 100 replies respectively). These metrics are used in academia to measure the productivity and impact of a scholar. We adopt them to analyse underground forums for the same purpose.

We also developed tools to analyse the interests of forum members. This allows us to study the networks of actors interested in particular topics. Interests can be calculated for a given period, so we can analyse the evolution of different actors (e.g. a member initially interested in gaming related boards who then moved to hacking related boards). The interest of a member M in a board B is calculated as:

$$I(M, B) = N_T(M, B) * 3 + N_P(M, B)$$

Where $N_{\{T,P\}}(M, B)$ denotes the number of {threads, posts} written by M in B. We assign triple weight to threads since initiating a thread represents a greater interest than posting a reply.

4.3   Machine Learning - Clustering

Machine learning techniques can be applied to extract common characteristics from a dataset. We apply k-means clustering to group the actors based on their activity [17]. K-means partitions a set of n samples into k clusters (with $k << n$). We extract a set of 44 features for each actor, which can be classified as measures relating to forum activity, social relations, and reputation measures.

Measures relating to forum activity includes the number of days between the first and last post, the number of posts and threads in each category and the number of posts and threads in the currency exchange board. We explicitly include the currency exchange board (which is part of the marketplace) as it characterizes the financial activities of the actors.

Network centrality measures are obtained from SNA. These include out-degree, in-degree, eigenvector, h-index, and i-10 and i-100 indices.

Reputation measures are taken from the reputation systems used on the forum. These include the overall reputation bestowed and prestige scores (prestige is an forum metric based on activity). There are also counts for the number of positive, negative, and zero-value reputation votes each account received.

Then, using the feature set we perform clustering using k-means. After applying the Elbow method [35] to analyse the within-group sum of squares for various values of k, we set $k = 5$.

4.4   Results

Using the tools described above, we first analyse the social relations established between key actors and their closest neighbours. Second, we analyse their common characteristics by splitting them into groups using k-means clustering. Finally, we analyse their pathways by looking for changes in their interests and the number of questions posted as they spend more time in the forum.

Social Relations. Figure 1 shows the social network involving the key actors.[3] The actors identified from media sources and Flashpoint are filled in red, the ones identified from network analysis are orange and the those linked to malware distribution are blue. Colours of the edges represent the sentiment of the relationship, calculated from the reputation votes sent to each other. Most key actors are closely connected to each other, and most relationships are positive. Actors obtained from different sources are closely or even directly connected. For example, the detail in Fig. 1 shows a member identified as malware distributor (in blue) which is directly connected to one identified through SNA (in orange) and very close to at least two actors identified from media sources (in red).

Some close neighbours (for example, the nodes tagged as 'Bridge' in the detail from Fig. 1) are connected to more than one key actor, and act as 'bridges' for connecting different groups. These actors are of interest since they might be

---

[3] For the sake of visualization, the figure only shows the key actors and their five closest repliers and replied neighbours (filled in green).

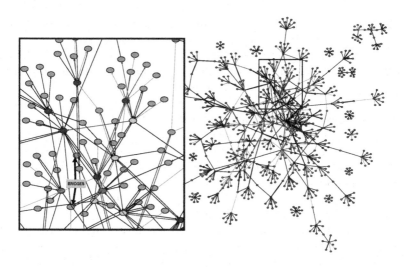

Fig. 1. Social network graph involving key actors and their closest neighbours (green nodes). Red nodes are those identified from media sources and Flashpoint, orange are those identified through SNA and blue are those linked to the distribution of malware. The colours in the edges represent the sentiment of the relationship (red = negative, green = positive and black = neutral/unknown) (Color figure online)

influential for or influenced by key actors in criminal activity. Accordingly, we use these actors for our prediction study presented in Sect. 5.

Table 1. Average values for key actors grouped in 5 clusters. The Interests columns show the top 3 categories and number of posts/threads in currency exchange. W = Web, G = Game, D = Code, T = Tech, C = Common, H = Hack, \$ = Money, X = Graphics, M = Market. + = positive reputations, 0 = neutral reputations and − = negative reputations. EV = Eigenvector

#Key Actors	Activity		Interests				Reputation		Social relations			
	Days	Threads/Posts	cat1	cat2	cat3	#CurExc	Total (+/0/−)		H	i10	i100	EV
27	1298.4	74.1/1138.4	M	H	C	3.9/7.6	229.8 (61.3/2.3/4.3)		10.4	15.4	1.1	0.00
37	1595.0	163.8/3338.1	M	C	D/H	6.4/19.9	482.8 (230.9/7.4/6.9)		17.6	41.7	3.0	0.01
5	1951.0	831.0/18086.2	C	M	H	23.8/125.4	896.8 (578.2/68.8/99.0)		53.6	373.0	23.2	0.04
24	796.4	18.0/413.0	H	M	C/D	0.0/1.0	120.1 (58.0/2.4/3.2)		5.0	4.5	0.3	0.00
20	1895.7	383.6/10989.2	M	C	H	27.4/141.8	667.9 (311.6/27.0/48.3)		28.4	99.8	7.2	0.02

Characterization. Table 1 shows the average values for each of the five clusters obtained by k-means. There is a small group of 5 actors who have the highest measures of forum activity, are highly reputed (though they also receive high negative votes), and have rich social relations. These 5 actors are popular (due to the high values of their H and i indexes), have influence in the network, and are well known in the community. The remaining clusters have also been active for long time (more than 2 years) but differ in quantity of posts and threads. The clusters are also differentiated by their areas of interests.

The cluster with 20 actors is most interested in the market section (followed by the common section). They are the most active group in currency exchange and have high social relationship measurements (e.g. on average they have 7.2 threads with more than 100 replies). Overall, actors in this cluster are likely to be known in the community as prolific market traders.

The clusters with 27 and 37 members have similar interests (mostly in market and hacking, but also in common and coding categories), though one has higher reputation (mostly positive) and social relations (e.g. they have more than twice the number of threads with at least 10 replies). Finally, the least active cluster, which is composed of 24 actors, is interested firstly in hacking and then in the market sections, with negligible posts in currency exchange.

Overall, cluster analysis suggests key actors are mostly characterized by their interest in the market, common, and hacking areas. Also, they can be grouped by their forum activity, with some being more active and popular, and thus well known within the community, while others are less active, do not participate in the common sections of the forum and are less popular.

Evolution. We track the interests of the actors since they were registered until their last visit (if enabled on their profile) or last post. We compute their interests in each board and then aggregate them per category and per year. To analyse temporal evolution, we measure the interests at the beginning, middle and end of the period each actor has been active. The beginning is defined as the year of their first post, the end is the year of their last post, and the middle is the period in between. We then calculate the evolution of interests between these periods by computing *transitions of interest*. Concretely, a transition of interest from a category C_i in time t_0 to a category C_j in time t_1 is calculated as:

$$T(C_i^{t_0} \rightarrow C_j^{t_1}) = \sum_{\forall A \in K} (|S^{t_0}| - \beta_i^{t_0}) * \lambda_i^{t_0} + (|S^{t_1}| - \beta_j^{t_1}) * \lambda_j^{t_1}$$

Where K is the set of all the key actors, S^{t_n} denotes the set of all categories of interest for actor A in time t_n, $\lambda_i^{t_n}$ denotes the normalized interest of actor A in category C_i in time t_n, and $\beta_i^{t_n}$ is the relative position of category i regarding the ordered list of categories by score in time t_n (i.e., the top category has β_i^t equal to 1, the second equal to 2 and so on). The above equation weights the categories of interest per actor according to the amount of posts and threads posted in each category with respect to the rest.

Figure 2 shows the aggregated transitions for all key actors. Overall, actors are most interested in the hacking, market, and common categories. Over their time in the forum, there is a slight increase of interest in the coding and technology sections, and a decrease in the gaming sections. From this figure we can draw several conclusions. First, in general actors are active participants in non-criminal related boards, such as those from the common category. This suggests their criminal activity runs in parallel or comes after other interests (e.g.

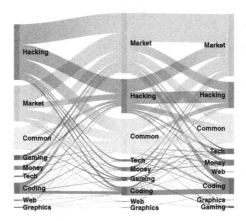

Fig. 2. Evolution of interests of key actors from initial (left), halfway (middle) and end (right) of their activity in *Hackforums*

entertainment or gaming), and they are involved in other activities within the community. Second, their high interest in the marketplace and money sections indicates they may have financial motivations. Third, as they get older and more experienced in the forum they are less likely to engage in gaming boards.

Prior research has found forums are used for sharing information and learning about cybercrime and deviant activities [10,15,38]. Thus, we analyse the evolution of the actors in terms of the number of questions (or requests for information) posted across time. In order to track evolution, this analysis includes the 34 key actors who have been posting for at least 4 years. We count the number of posts and number of questions posted for each year since they wrote their first post.

Figure 3 shows the proportion of questions posted per year with respect to the total number of questions posted. Each row represents a different actor (the top row shows the aggregation of the 34 actors). Most actors posted more than half of all their questions during their first or second year of activity in the forum. However, there are other actors (e.g. A1, A2, and A3) that keep posting questions at a similar rate after 5 or 6 years of activity. We can confirm these actors posted more questions in the early stages of their activity in the forums.

5 Predicting Key Actors

We analyse over a decade of data from *Hackforums* to identify those variables relating to forum activity that predict the likelihood a user will eventually be an actor of interest to law enforcement. Actors were selected for inclusion if they had been active since 2009, and had made more than five posts on the forum. This way, we do not consider old and low profile actors which would otherwise introduce noise in our analysis. After the forum administrator was

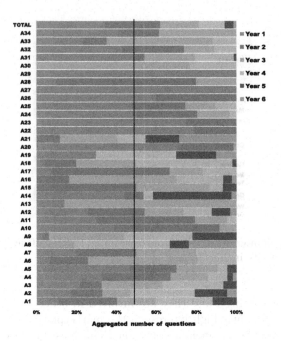

Fig. 3. Proportion of the number of questions posted per year with respect to the total questions posted

excluded from the dataset, there were 245,636 cases extracted.[4] Our prediction framework is based on two steps: using multiple approaches to select potential key actors based on their forum activity, and predicting which of these are key actors based on the key terms used in their posts. We first combine the outputs from a logistic regression model, k-means clustering and SNA to identify actors that are potentially involved in criminal activity. Second, we use topic analysis to confirm whether these users are engaged in cybercrime related activity, such as trading in illegal goods and services.

5.1   Logistic Regression

We analyse the data applying backward stepwise logistic regression, using the likelihood ratio method. This method starts with a model which includes every independent variable, gradually removing every variable which does not have a significant impact on the dependent variable. Field [9] justifies the use of stepwise methods when carrying out exploratory research, in which there is no previous research on which to base hypotheses for testing, as well as situations in which causality is not of interest, but rather a model to fit the data. Both these justifications apply for this research. Field also recommends that if stepwise methods are to be used, then the backward method is the better option, as the

---

[4] The administrator is a well known actor in *Hackforums*.

forward method has a higher risk of Type II (false negative) errors. Logistic regression is often used in medical research, for example, to identify the risk factors associated with a disease within the wider population.

Logistic regression models predict a categorical outcome, in this case key actor status. Measures of forum activity, network centrality measures, and reputation measures (see Sect. 4.3) were considered for inclusion as predictor variables, however due to multicollinearity issues, a number were excluded (an assumption of logistic regression is that independent variables are not highly correlated). The independent variables included in the initial model are the number of days posting, reputation, prestige, posts and threads in the various categories, h-index, i-50-index, i-100-index, and number of positive, negative and zero-value reputation votes received.

As recommended by Field [9], 5 cases were removed as an analysis of the residuals indicated they had an undue influence on the model (Cook's Distance > 1) Without any independent variables in the model, 100% of cases are predicted to not be key actors. The final model is significantly improved and is statistically better at predicting key actors ($\chi^2(15, n = 245{,}631) = 641.2, p < .001$). The final model accounts for 34.1% of the variance, accurately predicting 11.1% of known key actors with a low false error rate (0.00%). While predicting 12 out of 108 key actors may seem low, it is from a pool of almost a quarter of a million cases. While not all the variance in the model will be explained through a user's forum activity, these significant results suggest this is an approach worthy of further exploration. The analysis also provides predicted probabilities for each user, which we explore further in Sect. 5.3.

Table 2 presents the results of the final step of the logistic regression analysis. The table includes regression coefficients, Wald statistics, odds ratios, and 95% confidence intervals for odds ratios for each of the 15 predictors retained in the model. The odds ratios, shown as Exp(B), show how the odds of being in one outcome category changes when the predictor variable increases by one unit.

The odds ratios indicate that for each additional reputation and prestige point bestowed, the odds a user is a key actor increases by 1.001 and 1.006 respectively. For every additional day actors are posting, the odds they are key actors increases by 1.001. The frequency in which actors posted on various sections also predicts being a key actor, including posts in hacking (odds increased by 1.001 for each post), market (1.002) and code (1.0005) sections. Posts in some sections decrease the odds that users are key actors, including gaming (0.994), graphics (0.991, but this variable is not significant), common (0.9995), money (0.997, but not significant), and currency exchange (0.994). New threads initiated in the common and graphics sections decreases the odds a forum user is a key actor by 0.993 and 0.957 respectively, although graphics is not significant. An increase in a user's h-index increases their likelihood of being a key actor by 1.195. Key actors can also be predicted by their negative reputation (odds increase by 1.018 for each negative reputation).

Table 2. Logistic regression model predicting key actors

		B	S.E	Wald	Sig	Exp(B)	95% C.I. for Exp(B)	
							Lower	Upper
Step 15	DAYS_POSTING	.001	.000	19.407	.000	1.001	1.000	1.001
	REPUTATION	.001	.000	7.712	.005	1.001	1.000	1.001
	PRESTIGE	.006	.001	37.754	.000	1.006	1.004	1.008
	POSTS_HACK	.001	.000	25.397	.000	1.001	1.000	1.001
	POSTS_MARKET	.002	.000	65.945	.000	1.002	1.001	1.002
	POSTS_GAME	−.006	.001	15.670	.000	.994	.991	.997
	POSTS_GRAPHICS	−.009	.005	3.639	.056	.991	.982	1.000
	POSTS_CODE	.0005	.000	5.144	.023	1.0005	1.0001	1.0008
	POSTS_COMMON	−.0005	.000	4.945	.026	0.9995	.9991	0.9999
	POSTS_MONEY	−.003	.002	3.718	.054	.997	.994	1.000
	POSTS_CURRENCY_EXCHANGE	−.006	.003	6.041	.014	.994	.988	.999
	THREADS_GRAPHICS	−.044	.029	2.339	.126	.957	.905	1.012
	THREADS_COMMON	−.007	.003	5.637	.018	.993	.987	.999
	H_INDEX	.178	.017	108.025	.000	1.195	1.155	1.236
	NEGATIVE_REPUTATION	.018	.006	7.383	.007	1.018	1.005	1.031
	Constant	−9.372	.191	2397.372	.000	.000		

5.2 Clustering

In addition to the logistic regression, we apply k-means clustering to the subset
of more than 245k *Hackforums* actors. Table 3 shows the average values for each
cluster applying k-means, using $k = 14$, and which clusters the 113 key actors
are grouped in. In the smallest cluster, 22 of 223 actors are key actors (9.9%).
Actors from this cluster are very active, positively reputed and popular, and are
most interested in the market, common, hacking, and gaming sections. Another
small cluster of 2387 actors contains 31 key actors (1.3%). The profile is similar
to the previous one, although the measurements are lower. Finally, the bulk of
key actors (31) fall in a cluster with more than 10k actors, which is relatively
smaller than other clusters. Again, the interests are within the market, common,
hacking and gaming sections.

Most of the key actors are enclosed within the clusters with the fewest number
of actors (relative to other clusters). This finding is interesting since it allows to
reduce the amount of actors requiring thorough investigation when looking for
criminal activity.

5.3 Predicting Actors Using Topic Analysis

So far we have characterized and predicted actors based on features relating to
forum activity, reputation and social behaviour. This provides a subset of actors
who share common forum behaviour with those linked to illegal activities. To
further refine the list of potential key actors, we pose the following research
questions: *What* are the key actors talking about? Can we classify actors based
on their topics of conversation? Next, we analyse the most frequent topics used by
key actors. Then, we perform topic analysis on a selection of potential key actors
obtained from the logistic regression, social network analysis and clustering.

Table 3. Average values for actors grouped in 14 clusters. The Interests columns show the top 3 categories and number of posts/threads in currency exchange. W = Web, G = Game, D = Code, T = Tech, C = Common, H = Hack, $=Money, X = Graphics, M = Market. + = positive reputations, 0 = zero reputations and − = negative reputations. EV = Eigenvector

#Key Actors/ Total	Activity		Interests				Reputation	Social relations			
	Days	Threads/Posts	cat1	cat2	cat3	#CurExc	Total (+/0/−)	H	i10	i100	EV
1/8397	388.9	6.6/50.2	T/H	H/C	C/M	0.0/0.1	1.3 (0.4/0.0/0.1)	2.2	0.5	0.0	0.00
32/10323	1322.2	114.5/1310.2	M/C	C/M	G/H	3.5/9.8	113.9 (50.0/3.2/5.0)	11.6	17.4	0.5	0.00
0/4590	326.2	5.3/48.0	W	H	M/C	0.0/0.1	1.8 (0.6/0.1/0.1)	1.5	0.3	0.0	0.00
13/55364	338.6	7.3/46.4	H	M	C	0.0/0.1	0.7 (0.5/0.1/0.2)	2.3	0.5	0.0	0.00
9/41774	518.7	13.9/109.9	M	H/C	C/H	0.3/1.3	9.6 (3.4/0.3/0.5)	2.9	1.2	0.0	0.00
1/24202	310.9	5.7/56.2	G	H/C	M/H	0.0/0.1	2.0 (0.8/0.1/0.3)	1.9	0.7	0.0	0.00
0/36392	246.8	6.9/75.4	C	H	M	0.0/0.2	2.5 (1.1/0.2/0.4)	2.1	1.0	0.0	0.00
0/3474	296.3	3.8/90.6	T	H	C	0.0/0.1	4.1 (1.0/0.1/0.1)	1.1	0.3	0.0	0.00
0/14050	339.4	4.2/46.6	$	H	M/C	0.0/0.1	0.9 (0.4/0.1/0.1)	1.3	0.4	0.0	0.00
22/223	2111.7	611.2/11614.6	C	M	G/H	30.7/187.6	1170.7 (711.8/20.8/31.5)	32.2	162.8	8.2	0.03
3/9177	403.4	7.7/75.9	D	H	C	0.0/0.1	3.1 (1.1/0.1/0.2)	2.2	0.6	0.0	0.00
0/4845	302.2	6.9/71.0	X	H/C	M/H	0.0/0.1	5.1 (1.2/0.1/0.1)	2.1	0.8	0.0	0.00
31/2387	1723.8	295.9/4339.6	C	M	G	11.5/31.8	360.5 (170.2/9.8/13.8)	19.3	57.9	1.9	0.01
1/30437	215.8	0.2/18.2	H	M	C/$	0.0/0.0	0.2 (0.1/0.0/0.1)	0.1	0.0	0.0	0.00

Analysis of Topics Used by Key Actors. We use topic analysis to extract the most common terms from threads initiated by each actor. Topic analysis is an information retrieval task which produces wordlists summarised with a topic. Concretely, we apply latent Dirichelt allocation (LDA) to obtain the topics and terms that best represent the language used for each actor. Given a set of documents, LDA extracts the topics that best describe these documents [5]. A document is composed with the heading and first post of each thread initiated by an actor. We preprocess the data by tokenizing it, removing stop words, punctuation characters and numbers. Then, we extract the nouns using a Part-of-Speech (POS) tagger using the Penn Treebank tagset [20]. Using common NLP tools with low-resource language corpora presents limitations. Nevertheless, for this particular task the application of the POS tagger for extracting nouns reduces the number of noisy words.

For each actor, we extract 4 topics with 7 words per topic, resulting in 28 terms. Table 4 shows the most frequent terms used by the key actors (we show those used by more than five actors). The most common term is 'rat' (Remote Access Trojan) which could be expected given a bulk of key actors were identified due to their links with RAT coding. Various terms relate to offensive tools, such as 'bot', 'booter', 'crypter' and 'fud' ('fully undetectable'). Words related to commerce include 'paypal', 'btc' (Bitcoin), 'lr' (Liberty Reserve, a digital currency provider which was shut down in 2013), 'free', and 'cheap'. Also noteworthy is the high frequency of the words 'help', 'need' or 'question'.

Table 4. Most frequent terms used by the key actors. In parentheses are the number of key actors using each term. In bold are terms related to cybercrime.

rat (46), help (45), paypal (43), need (36), free (34), btc (34), **account** (33), thread (31), lr (28), server (26), new (25) **crypter** (25), pp (25), source (23), **fud** (23), service (22), **bot** (21), question (20), hf (16), code (15), steam (15), site (14) **shell** (14), cheap (14), money (14), skype (14), **booter** (13), window (12), anyone (12), tut (12), file (12), uid (11), someone (11) system (10), vbnet (10), vpn (10), **installs** (10), please (10), member (10), php (10), problem (10), **ddos** (10), password (10) website (10), update (10), setup (9), minecraft (9), email (9), game (9), vps (9), facebook (8), list (8), proxy (8), design (8) **darkcomet** (8), **keylogger** (8), irc (8), java (8), coder (8), day (8), time (8), net (7), post (7), product (7), tool (7), beta (7) sale (7), **exploit** (7), people (7), bitcoin (7), buying (7), **stealer** (6), version (6), **stresser** (6), live (6), feature (6) **botnet** (6), domain (6), signature (6), shop (6), black (6), omc (6), web (6), year (6), support (6), official (6), youtube (6)

Selection of Potential Key Actors. After analysing the most frequent terms used by key actors, we repeat the topic analysis with a subset of *potential* key actors identified from our previous analyses. The logistic regression provides predicted probabilities for each forum user. We obtain a subset (named *LogReg*) by selecting those with a predicted probability of 10% or more of being a key actor ($n = 88$). From the clustering analysis we select 201 users (named *Clust*) from the cluster which contained the highest ratio of key actors (see Table 3). Finally, from our social network analysis, we select 42 actors (named *SNA*) directly connected with at least 3 key actors (see Fig. 1). There are common actors between subsets: 10 actors appear in the three subsets; 26 appear in the *LogReg* and *Clust* subsets, but not the *SNA*; and 7 appear in the *SNA* and *Clust* subset, but not the *LogReg*. There are no overlaps between only the *LogReg* and *SNA* subsets. The final subset of potential key actors includes 285 forum users.

Predicting Key Actors. We apply topic analysis to the potential actors, extracting their 28 most common terms. We then measure the number of common terms with those obtained for the key actors to get a similarity score. This score is calculated as the number of terms matching the list of terms from key actors (Table 4) divided by the total number of terms extracted for the actor. However, similarities may be due to commerce-related terms (e.g. 'btc' or 'cheap') or forum-related terms ('need', 'thread' or 'help'). Thus, we also look for particularly interesting terms related with hacking (highlighted in Table 4).

As a prediction threshold, we establish a minimum distance of 0.2 (i.e. at least a 20% of the terms must match with those observed in the key actors) and a minimum number of 2 keywords observed.[5] Table 5 summarizes our findings. Using these thresholds, we predict 22 actors from the *LogReg* subset, 34 from the *Clust* subset and 9 from the *SNA* subset. We also predict 8 actors from the overlap of the *LogReg* and *Clust* subsets. From the 10 actors that were common in the three subsets, 7 are predicted to be key actors. The closest members to key-actors according to their topics are those identified with clustering. However, only 20% of users from this subset are predicted to be key actors. Meanwhile, 42% of the users from the logistic regression subset are predicted to be key

---

[5] These thresholds were chosen after exploratory experimentation with the dataset and manually inspecting the results.

actors. Our findings suggest combining different data science techniques assists in the prediction of potential key actors.

Overall, from the list of 285 potential key actors, 80 are predicted to be of interest. Our estimation confirms (i) these are actors with a similar activity profile, interest and social behaviour as those identified manually, and (ii) they talk about similar, hacking-related terms. Thus, we can conclude that these actors are either involved or close to involvement in cybercrime activities, and thus might benefit the most from intervention. Also, monitoring these actors could be of interest for security firms and intelligence agencies. A manual analysis of the forum activity of these actors confirms that they are all providing or asking for illegal assets and services such as malware, booters or stolen accounts.

Table 5. Summary of prediction using topic analysis

Subset	Predicted/Total (%)	Avg. distance	Farthest	Closest
LogReg	22/52 (42.31)	0.43	0.10	0.72
Clust	34/165 (20.61)	0.66	0.29	0.93
SNA	9/25 (36.00)	0.57	0.36	0.75
LogReg & Clust	8/26 (30.77)	0.63	0.36	0.89
SNA & Clust	0/7 (0.00)	0.66	0.50	0.79
LogReg & Clust & SNA	7/10 (70.00)	0.60	0.43	0.68

6 Ethical Considerations

The research methodology was designed with ethical considerations at the forefront. The department's research ethics committee gave their approval for the research project. Furthermore, we complied with the Cambridge Cybercrime Centre's data sharing agreements. While the data are publicly available (and the forum users are aware of this), it could be used by malicious actors, for example to deanonymize users based on their posts. It was impossible for us to obtain informed consent from users as that would require us to identify them first. In accordance with the British Society of Criminology's Statement on Ethics, this approach is justified as the dataset is collected from the public Internet, and is used for research on collective behaviour, without aiming to identify particular members. Further precautions taken include not identifying individuals (including not publishing usernames), and presenting results objectively.

7 Limitations

We have presented a longitudinal study of behavioural aspects of key actors in underground forums. This research has attempted to overcome the significant difficulties in this challenging area of research. However, a number of limitations remain. First, results are based on the observation of a single forum. Thus, we do not analyse actors operating on other forums, nor do we measure actors' activities that occur off-forum. Future work will analyse cross-forum behaviour. Second, we focus on external sources to identify key actors, and thus our results could be biased by feedback from these sources. Moreover, the proportion of identified key actors in the forum is low, hindering the use of reliable classification techniques such as supervised machine learning. Third, our definition of the social network relies on public interactions. Unlike previous works [11,22], we do not use private messages to refine social relations. Recent work shows that public and private relations differ [26]. Finally, evaluating if the predicted actors are actually involved into criminal activities is not straightforward, even with manual analysis. Investigations into actors to produce evidence they are involved in cybercrime is a matter for law enforcement. Instead, our research helps to focus the spotlight, with the aim of informing crime prevention efforts.

8   Conclusion

Underground forums are one of the key pillars for the rise of underground economies. The sense of anonymity they provide, together with the ease of access to attack tools and services make these forums attractive places for young, non-skilled people to learn about hacking. Analysing the evolution of these low-level hackers makes it possible to consider early intervention approaches, with the aim of deterring their involvement away from criminal activities. Additionally, understanding who the key actors are, and what new tools they provide, is helpful for rapidly adapting to new forms of attack. For example, antivirus vendors could monitor those providing tools aimed at bypassing detection and new variants of malware.

We have conducted a large scale analysis of key actors from one of the largest English-speaking underground forums. We have evidence of online social connections between these key actors, and our research uncovers various common roles for these key actors. For example, some are well known in the community and actively participate in non-illicit sections. Others are less active and focus their activity in the market and monetization processes. Also, we note an evolution of interests towards more market and hacking related topics, as well as a decrease in threads requesting help or asking questions.

Finally, we have developed tools for detection and prediction of actors involved in cybercrime activities. These tools help to identify user accounts that might require further investigation by law enforcement and security firms monitoring underground communities and also for early deployment of new countermeasures or adaptation of existing ones. The tools used during this research are publicly available in our git repository[6].

The purpose of our research is not to track and pursue criminal offenders, but understand who is at risk of becoming involved in crime, so as to apply

---

[6] https://github.com/CCC-NLIP/DataSciForCybersecurity.

intervention approaches at early stages. Identifying those that might be at risk of becoming involved in crime is critical for early intervention. Preventing young people from becoming involved in cybercrime will be of benefit for them later in life, as contact with the criminal justice system can be a stigmatising experience, affecting later job prospects and legitimate opportunities.

Acknowledgements. We thank the anonymous reviewers for their insightful comments. We also thank our colleagues from the Cambridge Cybercrime Centre for access to the CrimeBB dataset and their invaluable feedback, and Flashpoint, for assistance relating to actors of interest. This work was supported by The Alan Turing Institute's Defence and Security Programme [grant DS/SDS/1718/4]; and the UK Engineering and Physical Sciences Research Council (EPSRC) [grant EP/M020320/1].

References

1. Afroz, S., Garg, V., McCoy, D., Greenstadt, R.: Honor among thieves: a common's analysis of cybercrime economies. In: eCrime Researchers Summit, pp. 1–11. IEEE (2013)
2. Allodi, L.: Economic factors of vulnerability trade and exploitation. In: Proceedings of the ACM SIGSAC Conference on Computer and Communications Security, pp. 1483–1499. ACM (2017)
3. Anderson, R., et al.: Measuring the cost of cybercrime. In: Böhme, R. (ed.) The Economics of Information Security and Privacy, pp. 265–300. Springer, Heidelberg (2013). https://doi.org/10.1007/978-3-642-39498-0_12
4. Antonakakis, M., et al.: Understanding the Mirai Botnet. In: Proceedings of the 26th USENIX Security Symposium, Vancouver, BC, pp. 1093–1110 (2017)
5. Blei, D.M., Ng, A.Y., Jordan, M.I.: Latent dirichlet allocation. J. Mach. Learn. Res. **3**(Jan), 993–1022 (2003)
6. Caballero, J., Grier, C., Kreibich, C., Paxson, V.: Measuring pay-per-install: the commoditization of malware distribution. In: Proceedings of the 20th USENIX Security Symposium, Berkeley, CA, USA, p. 13 (2011)
7. Caines, A., Pastrana, S., Hutchings, A., Buttery, P.: Automatically identifying the function and intent of posts in underground forums. (in submission)
8. Chang, W., Wang, A., Mohaisen, A., Chen, S.: Characterizing botnets-as-a-service. ACM SIGCOMM Comput. Commun. Rev. **44**(4), 585–586 (2014)
9. Field, A.: Discovering Statistics Using SPSS, 2nd edn. SAGE Publications, London (2005)
10. Franklin, J., Paxson, V., Perrig, A., Savage, S.: An inquiry into the nature and causes of the wealth of Internet miscreants. In: Proceedings of the ACM SIGSAC Conference on Computer and Communications Security (2007)
11. Garg, V., Afroz, S., Overdorf, R., Greenstadt, R.: Computer-supported cooperative crime. In: Böhme, R., Okamoto, T. (eds.) FC 2015. LNCS, vol. 8975, pp. 32–43. Springer, Heidelberg (2015). https://doi.org/10.1007/978-3-662-47854-7_3
12. Holt, T.J.: Subcultural evolution? Examining the influence of on- and off-line experiences on deviant subcultures. Deviant Behav. **28**(2), 171–198 (2007)
13. Hutchings, A.: Cybercrime trajectories: an integrated theory of initiation, maintenance, and desistance. In: Crime Online: Correlates, Causes, and Context, pp. 117–140. Carolina Academic Press (2016)

14. Hutchings, A., Clayton, R.: Exploring the provision of online booter services. Deviant Behav. **37**(10), 1163–1178 (2016)
15. Hutchings, A., Holt, T.J.: A crime script analysis of the online stolen data market. Br. J. Criminol. **55**(3), 596–614 (2015)
16. Karami, M., McCoy, D.: Rent to PWN: analyzing commodity booter DDoS services. Usenix Login **38**, 20–23 (2013)
17. Lloyd, S.: Least squares quantization in PCM. IEEE Trans. Inf. Theory **28**(2), 129–137 (1982)
18. Lusthaus, J., Varese, F.: Offline and local: the hidden face of cybercrime. Polic.: J. Policy Pract. 1–11 (2017). advanced access
19. Macdonald, M., Frank, R., Mei, J., Monk, B.: Identifying digital threats in a hacker web forum. In: International Conference on Advances in Social Networks Analysis and Mining, pp. 926–933. IEEE/ACM (2015)
20. Marcus, M.P., Marcinkiewicz, M.A., Santorini, B.: Building a large annotated corpus of English: the penn treebank. Comput. Linguist. **19**(2), 313–330 (1993)
21. McMillen, D., Alvarez, M.: Mirai IoT botnet: mining for bitcoins? IBM Security Intelligence (2017). https://perma.cc/SK2R-C3H7
22. Motoyama, M., McCoy, D., Levchenko, K., Savage, S., Voelker, G.M.: An analysis of underground forums. In: Proceedings of the ACM SIGCOMM Conference on Internet Measurement Conference, pp. 71–80 (2011)
23. National Crime Agency: Pathways into cyber crime (2017). https://perma.cc/897P-GZ3R
24. Noroozian, A., Korczyński, M., Gañan, C.H., Makita, D., Yoshioka, K., van Eeten, M.: Who gets the boot? Analyzing victimization by DDoS-as-a-service. In: International Symposium on Research in Attacks, Intrusions, and Defenses, pp. 368–389 (2016)
25. Nunes, E., et al.: Darknet and deepnet mining for proactive cybersecurity threat intelligence. In: Conference on Intelligence and Security Informatics (ISI), pp. 7–12. IEEE (2016)
26. Overdorf, R., Troncoso, C., Greenstadt, R., McCoy, D.: Under the underground: predicting private interactions in underground forums. arXiv preprint arXiv:1805.04494 (2018)
27. Pastrana, S., Thomas, D.R., Hutchings, A., Clayton, R.: CrimeBB: enabling cybercrime research on underground forums at scale. In: Proceedings of The Web Conference (WWW). ACM (2018)
28. Portnoff, R.S., et al.: Tools for automated analysis of cybercriminal markets. In: Proceedings of 26th International World Wide Web conference (2017)
29. Samtani, S., Chinn, R., Chen, H.: Exploring hacker assets in underground forums. In: International Conference on Intelligence and Security Informatics (ISI), pp. 31–36. IEEE (2015)
30. Sood, A.K., Enbody, R.J.: Crimeware-as-a-service: a survey of commoditized crimeware in the underground market. Int. J. Crit. Infrastruct. Prot. **6**(1), 28–38 (2013)
31. Soska, K., Christin, N.: Measuring the longitudinal evolution of the online anonymous marketplace ecosystem. In: Proceedings of the 24th USENIX Security Symposium (2015)
32. Spärck-Jones, K.: A statistical interpretation of term specificity and its application in retrieval. J. Doc. **28**, 11–21 (1972)
33. Sutherland, E.H.: White Collar Crime: The Uncut Version. Yale University Press, New Haven (1949)

34. Thomas, D.R., Clayton, R., Beresford, A.R.: 1000 days of UDP amplification DDoS attacks. In: APWG Symposium on Electronic Crime Research (eCrime). IEEE (2017). https://doi.org/10.1109/ECRIME.2017.7945057

35. Thorndike, R.L.: Who belongs in the family? Psychometrika **18**(4), 267–276 (1953)

36. Valeros, V.: A study of RATs: third timeline iteration (2018). https://perma.cc/REB5-JFNR

37. Vold, G.B., Bernard, T.J., Snipes, J.B.: Theoretical Criminology, 5th edn. Oxford University Press, Inc., New York (2002)

38. Zhang, X., Tsang, A., Yue, W.T., Chau, M.: The classification of hackers by knowledge exchange behaviors. Inf. Syst. Front. **17**, 1–13 (2015)

SybilBlind: Detecting Fake Users in Online Social Networks Without Manual Labels

Binghui Wang$^{(\boxtimes)}$, Le Zhang, and Neil Zhenqiang Gong

ECE Department, Iowa State University, Ames, USA
{binghuiw,lezhang,neilgong}@iastate.edu

Abstract. Detecting fake users (also called Sybils) in online social networks is a basic security research problem. State-of-the-art approaches rely on a large amount of manually labeled users as a training set. These approaches suffer from three key limitations: (1) it is time-consuming and costly to manually label a large training set, (2) they cannot detect new Sybils in a timely fashion, and (3) they are vulnerable to Sybil attacks that leverage information of the training set. In this work, we propose *SybilBlind*, a structure-based Sybil detection framework that does not rely on a manually labeled training set. SybilBlind works under the same threat model as state-of-the-art structure-based methods. We demonstrate the effectiveness of SybilBlind using (1) a social network with synthetic Sybils and (2) two Twitter datasets with real Sybils. For instance, SybilBlind achieves an AUC of 0.98 on a Twitter dataset.

Keywords: Sybil detection · Social networks security

1 Introduction

Online social networks (OSNs) are known to be vulnerable to *Sybil attacks*, in which attackers maintain a large number of fake users (also called Sybils). For instance, 10% of Twitter users were fake [1]. Attackers can leverage Sybils to perform various malicious activities such as manipulating presidential election [15], influencing stock market [16], distributing spams and phishing URLs [24], etc. Therefore, Sybil detection in OSNs is an important research problem.

Indeed, Sybil detection has attracted increasing attention from multiple research communities such as security, networking, and data mining. Among various approaches, structure-based ones [6–8, 11, 14, 18, 26, 28, 30, 33, 36–39] have demonstrated promising results. For instance, SybilRank [7] and Integro [6] were deployed to detect a large amount of Sybils in Tuenti, the largest OSN in Spain. SybilSCAR [30] was shown to be effective and efficient in detecting Sybils in Twitter. State-of-the-art structure-based approaches adopt the following machine learning paradigm: they first require an OSN provider to collect

---

B. Wang and L. Zhang—Authors contributed equally to this work.

© Springer Nature Switzerland AG 2018
M. Bailey et al. (Eds.): RAID 2018, LNCS 11050, pp. 228–249, 2018.
https://doi.org/10.1007/978-3-030-00470-5_11

a large manually labeled training set consisting of labeled benign users and/or labeled Sybils; then they learn a model to distinguish between benign users and Sybils; finally, the model is used to detect Sybils.

Such paradigm of relying on a manually labeled training set suffers from three key limitations. First, it is time-consuming and costly to obtain a large manually labeled training set. We note that OSN providers could outsource manual labeling to crowdsourcing services like Amazon Mechanical Turk [32]. However, crowdsourcing manual labeling requires disclosing user information to "turkers", which raises privacy concerns. Moreover, attackers could act as "turkers" to adversarially mislabel users. OSNs often allow users to flag other users as Sybils. However, similar to crowdsourcing, Sybils could adversarially mislabel benign users as Sybils. Second, attackers can launch new Sybil attacks when the old ones were taken down. It takes time for human workers to manually label a training set for the new attacks. As a result, some benign users might already be attacked before the new attacks were detected. Third, using a manually labeled training set makes these approaches vulnerable to Sybil attacks that leverage the information of the training set [21]. The key intuition is that once an attacker knows or infers the training set, he can perform better attacks over time. Our method is secure against such attacks as it does not rely on labeled users.

Our Work: In this work, we propose SybilBlind, a structure-based framework, to detect Sybils without relying on a manually labeled training set, under the same threat model as state-of-the-art structure-based methods (See Sect. 3.2). Our key idea is to sample some users from an OSN, randomly assign labels (i.e., *benign* or *Sybil*) to them, and treat them as if they were a training set without actually manually labeling them. Such randomly sampled training set could have various levels of label noise, where a user's randomly assigned label is noisy if it is different from the user's true label. Then, we take the noisy training set as an input to a state-of-the-art Sybil detection method (e.g., SybilSCAR [30] in our experiments) that is relatively robust to label noise (i.e., performance does not degrade much with a relatively low fraction of noisy labels) to detect Sybils. We define a *sampling trial* as the process that we randomly sample a noisy training set and use a state-of-the-art Sybil detection method to detect Sybils via taking the sampled training set as an input. Since state-of-the-art Sybil detection methods can only accurately detect Sybils in the sampling trials where the sampled training sets have relatively low label noise, we repeat for multiple sampling trials and we design an aggregator to aggregate the results in the multiple sampling trials.

A key challenge of our SybilBlind framework is how to aggregate the results in multiple sampling trials. For instance, one natural aggregator is to average the results in multiple sampling trials. Specifically, in each sampling trial, we have a probability of being a Sybil for each user. We average the probabilities over multiple sampling trials for each user and use the averaged probability to classify a user to be benign or Sybil. However, we demonstrate, both theoretically and empirically, that such average aggregator achieves an accuracy that is close to random guessing. To address the aggregation challenge, we design a novel aggregator. Specifically, we design two new metrics called *homophily* and *one-side entropy*. In a sampling trial where Sybils are accurately detected, both homophily and one-side entropy are large. With the two metrics, our aggregator identifies the sampling trials in which the sampled training sets have low label noise and Sybils are accurately detected. Then, we compute an *aggregated probability* of being a Sybil for every user from these sampling trials and use the aggregated probabilities to detect Sybils.

We evaluate SybilBlind both theoretically and empirically. Theoretically, we analyze the required number of sampling trials. Empirically, we perform evaluations using (1) a social network with synthesized Sybils, (2) a small Twitter dataset (8K users and 68K edges) with real Sybils, and (3) a large Twitter dataset (42M users and 1.2 B edges) with real Sybils. Our results demonstrate that Sybil-Blind is accurate, e.g., on the small Twitter dataset, SybilBlind achieves an AUC of 0.98. Moreover, we adapt a community detection method and state-of-the-art Sybil detection method SybilSCAR [30] to detect Sybils when a manually labeled training set is unavailable. Our empirical evaluations demonstrate that SybilBlind substantially outperforms these adapted methods.

Our key contributions are summarized as follows:

- We propose SybilBlind, a structure-based framework, to detect Sybils in OSNs without relying on a manually labeled training set.
- We design a novel aggregator based on homophily and one-side entropy to aggregate results in multiple sampling trials.
- We evaluate SybilBlind both theoretically and empirically, as well as compare it with Sybil detection methods that we adapt to detect Sybils when no manually labeled training sets are available. Our empirical results demonstrate the superiority of SybilBlind over the adapted methods.

2   Related Work

2.1   Structure-Based Approaches

One category of Sybil detection approaches leverage the global structure of the social network [6–9,11,14,18,26,28–30,33,36–39]. These approaches require a manually labeled training dataset, from which they propagate label information among the social network via leveraging the social structure.

Using Random Walks or Loopy Belief Propagation (LBP): Many structure-based approaches [6–8,18,36,38,39] leverage random walks to propagate label information. SybilGuard [39], SybilLimit [38], and SybilInfer [8] only require one labeled benign user. However, they achieve limited performance and are not scalable to large-scale OSNs. SybilRank [7] and Íntegro [6] are state-of-the-art random walk based approaches, and they were successfully applied to detect a large amount of Sybils in Tuenti, the largest OSN in Spain. However, they require a large number of manually labeled benign users; and Íntegro even further requires a large number of labeled victims and non-victims, which were used to learn a binary victim-prediction classifier. A user is said to be a victim if the user is connected with at least a Sybil. SybilBelief [14], Fu et al. [9], GANG [28], and SybilFuse [11] leverage probabilistic graphical model techniques. Specifically, they model a social network as a pairwise Markov Random Fields. Given a training dataset, they leverage LBP to infer the label of each remaining user.

Recently, Wang et al. [29,30] proposed a local rule based framework to unify random walk and LBP based approaches. Under this framework, a structure-based Sybil detection method essentially iteratively applies a certain local rule to each user to propagate label information. Different Sybil detection methods use different local rules. Moreover, they also proposed a new local rule, based on which they designed SybilSCAR that achieves state-of-the-art performance both theoretically and empirically. For instance, SybilSCAR achieves the tightest asymptotic bound on the number of Sybils per attack edge that can be injected into a social network without being detected [29]. However, as we demonstrate in our experiments on Twitter, SybilSCAR requires a large training dataset in order to achieve an accurate Sybil detection performance.

Using Community Detection Algorithms: Viswanath et al. [26] showed that Sybil detection can be cast as a community detection problem. The authors found that detecting local community around a labeled benign user had equivalent results to approaches such as SybilLimit and SybilInfer. Cao et al. [7] showed that SybilRank significantly outperforms community detection approaches. Moreover, Alvisi et al. [2] demonstrated a vulnerability of the local community detection algorithm adopted by Viswanath et al. [26] by carefully designing an attack.

Summary: State-of-the-art structure-based approaches (e.g., SybilRank, Sybil-Belief, and SybilSCAR) require a large manually labeled training dataset. These approaches suffer from three key limitations as we discussed in Introduction.

2.2   Other Approaches

Approaches in this direction [4,10,19,22–24,27,31,35,37] leverage various user-generated contents (e.g., tweets), behaviors (e.g., the frequency of sending tweets), and local social structures (e.g., how a user's friends are connected). Most studies in this direction [4,10,22–24,27] treat Sybil detection as a supervised learning problem; they extract various features from user-generated contents, behaviors, and local social structures, and they learn machine learning classifiers using a training dataset; the learnt classifiers are then used to classify each remaining user to be benign or Sybil. For instance, Yang et al. [37] proposed local social structure based features such as the frequency that a user sends friend requests to others, the fraction of outgoing friend requests that are accepted, and the clustering coefficient of a user. One limitation of these approaches is that Sybils can manipulate users' profiles to evade detection. For instance, a Sybil can link to many Sybils to manipulate its local social structure as desired. However, although these approaches are easy to evade, we believe that they can be used as a first layer to filter some basic Sybils and increase attackers' costs of performing Sybil attacks. Moreover, these approaches are complementary to approaches that leverage global social structures, and they can be used together in practice. For instance, we can treat the outputs of these approaches as users' prior probabilities. Then, we can leverage structure-based methods, e.g., SybilSCAR [30], to detect Sybils by iteratively propagating the priors among a social network.

3   Problem Definition

3.1   Structure-Based Sybil Detection Without Manual Labels

Suppose we are given an undirected social network $G = (V, E)$,[1] where a node in V corresponds to a user in an OSN and an edge (u, v) represents a certain relationship between u and v. For instance, on Facebook, an edge between u and v could mean that u is in v's friend list and vice versa. On Twitter, an edge (u, v) could mean that u and v follow each other. We consider Sybil detection without a manually labeled training dataset, which we call *blind Sybil detection*.

Definition 1 (Blind Sybil Detection). *Suppose we are given a social network. Blind Sybil detection is to classify each node to be benign or Sybil without a manually labeled training dataset.*

3.2   Threat Model

We call the subnetwork containing all benign nodes and edges between them the *benign region*, and we call the subnetwork containing all Sybil nodes and edges between them the *Sybil region*. The edges between the two regions are called *attack edges*. We consider the following threat model, which is widely adopted by existing structure-based methods.

Connected-Sybil Attacks: We consider that Sybils are connected among themselves. In order to leverage Sybils to launch various malicious activities, an attacker often needs to first link his/her created Sybils to benign users. One attack strategy is that each Sybil aggressively sends friend requests to a large number of users (or follow a large number of users) that are randomly picked [37]. In these attacks, although some benign users (e.g., social capitalists [12]) will accept such friend requests with a relatively high probability, making the Sybils embed to the benign region, most benign users will not accept these friend requests [12]. As a result, Sybils that are created using this attack strategy often have low ratios of accepted friend requests (or ratios of being followed back), as

---

[1] Our framework can also be generalized to directed social networks.

well as low clustering coefficients because most users that link to a Sybil might not be connected with each other. Therefore, such Sybils can be detected by machine learning classifiers that use these structural features, as was shown by Yang et al. [37] on RenRen, a large OSN in China.

In this paper, we consider that Sybils created by an attacker are connected (i.e., *connected-Sybil attack*), so as to manipulate their structural features to evade the detection of structural feature based classifiers. Such connected-Sybil attacks were formally discussed by Alvisi et al. [2], are required by previous structure-based methods [6–8,14,26,30,33,36,38,39]. Note that Sybils in Tuenti [7], the largest OSN in Spain, are densely connected. Moreover, the datasets we used in our experiments also show that most of the Sybils are connected. For instance, in our large Twitter dataset, 85.3% Sybils are connected to form a largest connected component with an average degree 24.

Limited Number of Attack Edges: Intuitively, most benign users would not establish *trust* relationships with Sybils. We assume that the number of attack edges is relatively smaller, compared to the number of edges in the benign region and the Sybil region. This assumption is required by all previous structure-based methods [6–8,14,26,30,33,36,38,39] except Íntegro [6]. Íntegro assumes the number of victims (a victim is a node having attack edges) is small and victims can be accurately detected. The number of attack edges in Tuenti was shown to be relatively small [7]. Service providers can limit the number of attack edges via approximating trust relationships between users, e.g., looking into user interactions [34], inferring tie strengths [13], and asking users to rate their social friends [33]. We note that in the large Twitter dataset we used in our experiments, only 1.5% of the total edges are attack edges.

For connected-Sybil attacks, limited number of attack edges is equivalent to the *homophily* assumption, i.e., if we randomly sample an edge (u, v) from the social network, then u and v have the same label with high probability. In the following, we use homophily and limited number of attack edges interchangeably.

Benign Users are More than Sybils: We assume that Sybils are less than benign users in the OSN. An attacker often leverages only tens of thousands of compromised hosts to create and manage Sybils [25]. If an attacker registers and maintains a large number of Sybils on each compromised host, the OSN provider can easily detect these Sybils via IP-based methods. In other words, to evade detection by IP-based methods, each compromised host can only maintain a limited number of Sybils. Indeed, Thomas et al. [25] found that a half of compromised hosts under an attacker's control maintain less than 10 Sybils. As a result, in OSNs with tens or hundreds of millions of benign users, the number of Sybils is smaller than that of benign users. For instance, it was reported that 10% of Twitter users were Sybils [1]. Our method leverages this assumption to break the symmetry between the benign region and the Sybil region.

4 Design of SybilBlind

4.1 Overview

Figure 1 overviews SybilBlind. SybilBlind consists of three components, i.e., *sampler*, *detector*, and *homophily-entropy aggregator (HEA)*. Sampler samples two subsets of nodes from the social network, and constructs a training set by assigning a label of benign to nodes in one subset and a label of Sybil to nodes in the other subset. The detector takes the sampled noisy training set as an input and produces a probability of being Sybil for each node. The detector can be any structure-based Sybil detection method (e.g., SybilSCAR [30] in our experiments) that is relatively robust to label noise in the training set. SybilBlind repeats this sampling process for multiple trials, and it leverages a homophily-entropy aggregator to identify the sampling trials in which the detector accurately detects Sybils. Finally, SybilBlind computes an *aggregated probability* of being Sybil for every node using the identified sampling trials.

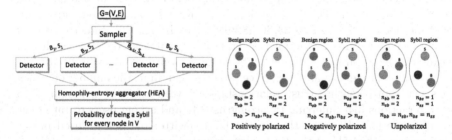

Fig. 1. Overview of SybilBlind.

Fig. 2. Three scenarios of our sampled nodes with a sampling size 3.

4.2 Sampler

In each sampling trial, our sampler samples two subsets of nodes from the set of nodes V, which are denoted as B and S, respectively. Moreover, for simplicity, we consider the two subsets have the same number of nodes, i.e., $n = |B| = |S|$, and we call n the *sampling size*. We note that it would be a valuable future work to apply our SybilBlind framework to subsets B and S with different sizes.

The subset B (or S) might consist of both benign nodes and Sybils. For convenience, we denote by n_{bb} and n_{bs} respectively the number of benign nodes and the number of Sybils in B; and we denote by n_{sb} and n_{ss} respectively the number of benign nodes and the number of Sybils in S. We categorize the sampled nodes into three scenarios because they have different impacts on the performance of the detector. Figure 2 shows one example of the three scenarios, where $n = 3$. The three scenarios are as follows:

- **Positively polarized:** In this scenario, the number of benign nodes in B is larger than the number of benign nodes in S, while the number of Sybils in B is smaller than the number of Sybils in S. Formally, we have $n_{bb} > n_{sb}$ and $n_{bs} < n_{ss}$.
- **Negatively polarized:** In this scenario, B includes a smaller number of benign nodes than S, while B includes a larger number of Sybils than S. Formally, we have $n_{bb} < n_{sb}$ and $n_{bs} > n_{ss}$.
- **Unpolarized:** In this scenario, the number of benign (or Sybil) nodes in B equals the number of benign (or Sybil) nodes in S. Formally, we have $n_{bb} = n_{sb}$ and $n_{bs} = n_{ss}$.

Note that since the two subsets B and S have the same number of nodes, we only have the above three scenarios. We construct a training set using the sampled B and S. Specifically, we assign a label of benign to nodes in B and a label of Sybil to nodes in S. Such training set could have label noise. In particular, in a sampling trial that is positively polarized, a majority of sampled nodes are assigned labels that match their true labels; while in a sampling trial that is negatively polarized, a majority of sampled nodes are assigned labels that do not match their true labels.

4.3   Detector

The detector takes a (noisy) training set as an input and produces a probability of being Sybil for every node (including the sampled nodes in the training set). The requirement for the detector is to be relatively robust to label noise in the training set. In this work, we adopt SybilSCAR [30] as the detector as it was shown to achieve state-of-the-art accuracy and robustness to label noise. However, we stress that our framework is extensible to use other structure-based Sybil detection methods as the detector. In particular, if a better structure-based Sybil detection method that uses a manually labeled training set is designed in the future, we can use it as the detector to further improve SybilBlind.

Next, we briefly review SybilSCAR. Given the sampled training set, SybilSCAR assigns a prior probability q_u of being Sybil for every node u. Specifically,

$$q_u = \begin{cases} 0.5 + \theta & \text{if } u \in S \\ 0.5 - \theta & \text{if } u \in B \\ 0.5 & \text{otherwise,} \end{cases}$$

where $0 < \theta < 0.5$ is a parameter to consider label noise.

Given the priors, SybilSCAR iteratively computes the probability p_u of being Sybil for every node u until convergence. Specifically, initially we have $p_u^{(0)} = q_u$. In the tth iteration, for each node u, we have:

$$p_u^{(t)} = q_u + 2(w - 0.5) \sum_{v \in \Gamma(u)} (p_v^{(t-1)} - 0.5), \tag{1}$$

where $w \in [0, 1]$ is the probability that two linked nodes have the same label and $\Gamma(u)$ is the set of neighbors of u.

4.4 Homophily-Entropy Aggregator

SybilBlind repeats k sampling trials, each of which produces a probability of being Sybil for every node. We denote the k probabilities for u as $p_{1,u}, p_{2,u}, \cdots, p_{k,u}$. An aggregator is to reduce the k probabilities to an *aggregated* probability.

Average, Min, and Max Aggregators do not Work Well: *average*, *min*, and *max* aggregators are a few natural choices. Specifically, the average aggregator takes the average of the k probabilities to be the aggregated one; the min aggregator is to take the minimum value of the k probabilities, i.e., $p_u = \min_{i=1}^{k} p_{i,u}$; the max aggregator is to take the maximum value of the k probabilities, i.e., $p_u = \max_{i=1}^{k} p_{i,u}$. However, we demonstrated, theoretically and empirically, that these aggregators achieve performances that are the same with or even worse than random guessing. In particular, for the average aggregator, we can prove that the expected aggregated probability is 0.5 for every node when the detector is SybilSCAR, which means that the expected performance of the average aggregator is the same as random guessing. We show the proof in Appendix A.

Our Homophily-Entropy Aggregator (HEA): We propose a novel aggregator based on two new metrics that we call *homophily* and *one-side entropy*. We observe that, when a sampling trial is a highly positively polarized scenario in which a majority of nodes in B are benign and a majority of nodes in S are Sybils, SybilSCAR can detect Sybils accurately. Our HEA aggregator aims to identify such sampling trials and use them to determine the aggregated probabilities. Next, we first formally define our homophily and one-side entropy metrics.

Suppose in a sampling trial, SybilSCAR produces a probability of being Sybil for every node. We predict a node u to be Sybil if $p_u > 0.5$, otherwise we predict u to be benign. Moreover, we denote by s the fraction of nodes in the social network that are predicted to be Sybils. An edge (u, v) in the social network is said to be *homogeneous* if u and v have the same predicted label. Given these terms, we formally define homophily h and one-side entropy e as follows:

$$h = \frac{\#homogeneous\ edges}{\#edges\ in\ total}$$

$$e = \begin{cases} 0 & \text{if } s > 0.5 \\ -s\log(s) - (1 - s)\log(1 - s) & \text{otherwise} \end{cases} \qquad (2)$$

Intuitively, homophily is the fraction of edges that are predicted to be homogeneous. One-side entropy is small if too many or too few nodes are predicted to be Sybils. In our threat model, we consider that the fraction of Sybils in the social network is less than 50%. Therefore, we define one-side entropy to be 0 if more than a half of nodes are predicted to be Sybils. Note the difference between our defined one-side entropy and the conventional entropy in information theory.

In a sampling trial that is an unpolarized scenario, we expect the homophily to be small because SybilSCAR tends to predict labels for nodes randomly. In a sampling trial that is a negatively polarized scenario, we expect the homophily to be large because a majority of benign nodes are likely to be predicted to be Sybils and a majority of Sybils are likely to be predicted to be benign, which results in a large fraction of homogeneous edges. However, we expect the one-side entropy to be small because more than a half of nodes would be predicted to be Sybils. In a sampling trial that is a positively polarized scenario, we expect both homophily and one-side entropy to be large.

Therefore, our HEA aggregator aims to identify the sampling trials that have large homophily and one-side entropy. In particular, we first identify the top-κ sampling trials among the k sampling trials that have the largest homophily. Then, among the top-κ sampling trials, we choose the sampling trial with the largest one-side entropy and use the probability obtained in this sampling trial as the aggregated probability. Essentially, among the top-κ sampling trials, we identify the sampling trial with the largest s that is no larger than 0.5, i.e., we aim to use the sampling trial that detects the most Sybils. Note that we can also reverse the order by first identifying the top-κ sampling trials that have the largest one-side entropies and choose the sampling trial with the largest homophily. However, we find the performance is almost the same and we thus use the former way by default.

5 Theoretical Analysis

5.1 Sampling Size and Number of Sampling Trials

The sampler constructs a training set via assigning a label of benign to nodes in B and a label of Sybil to nodes in S. We define label noise in the benign region (denoted as α_b) as the fraction of sampled nodes in the benign region whose assigned labels are Sybil. Similarly, we define label noise in the Sybil region (denoted as α_s) as the fraction of sampled nodes in the Sybil region whose assigned labels are benign. Formally, we have $\alpha_b = \frac{n_{sb}}{n_{sb}+n_{bb}}$ and $\alpha_s = \frac{n_{bs}}{n_{bs}+n_{ss}}$, where n_{bb} and n_{bs} respectively are the number of benign nodes and Sybils in B; n_{sb} and n_{ss} respectively are the number of benign nodes and Sybils in S.

We can derive an *analytical form* for the probability that label noise in both the benign region and the Sybil region are smaller than a threshold τ in a sampling trial. Due to limited space, we omit the analytical form. However, the analytical form is too complex to illustrate the relationships between the sampling size and the number of sampling trials. Therefore, we show the following theorem, which bounds the probability.

Theorem 1. *In a sampling trial with a sampling size of n, the probability that label noise in both the benign region and the Sybil region are no bigger than τ ($\tau \leq 0.5$) is bounded as*

$$(1-r)^n r^n \leq Pr(\alpha_b \leq \tau, \alpha_s \leq \tau) \leq \exp\left(-\frac{2(1-2\tau)^2(1-r)^2 n}{\tau^2 + (1-\tau)^2}\right), \qquad (3)$$

where r is the fraction of Sybils in the social network.

Proof. See Appendix B.

Implications of Theorem 1: Suppose in a social network, SybilSCAR is robust to label noise upto τ, i.e., its performance almost does not degrade when the noise level is τ, then SybilBlind requires at least one sampling trial, in which the label noise is less than or equal to τ, to detect Sybils accurately. We have several qualitative implications from Theorem 1. We note that these implications also hold when using the analytical form of the probability that label noise are smaller than τ. Here, we choose Theorem 1 because of its conciseness.

First, when the sampling size is n and SybilSCAR is robust to label noise up to τ in the social network, the expected number of sampling trials (i.e., k) that SybilBlind requires is bounded as $k_{min} \leq k \leq k_{max}$, where $k_{min} = \exp\left(\frac{2(1-2\tau)^2(1-r)^2 n}{\tau^2+(1-\tau)^2}\right)$ and $k_{max} = \frac{1}{(1-r)^n r^n}$. Note that k_{min} is exponential with respect to n, which could be very large even if n is moderate. *However, through empirical evaluations, we found k can be largely reduced and a moderate k could make SybilBlind obtain satisfying performance.* Second, when τ gets bigger, k_{min} gets smaller, which implies that SybilBlind tends to require less sampling trials when detecting Sybils in a social network in which SybilSCAR can tolerate larger label noise. Third, we observe a *scale-free* property, i.e., the number of sampling trials is not related to the size (i.e., $|V|$ or $|E|$) of the social network.

5.2 Complexity Analysis

Space and Time Complexity: The major space cost of SybilBlind consists of storing the social network and storing the top-κ vectors of posterior probabilities. SybilBlind uses an adjacency list to represent the social network, with the space complexity $O(2|E|)$, and stores the top-κ vectors of posterior probabilities of all nodes. Therefore, the space complexity of SybilBlind is $O(2|E| + \kappa|V|)$.

In each trial and in each iteration, SybilBlind applies a local rule to every node, and the time complexity of the local rule to a node u with $|\Gamma_u|$ friends is $O(|\Gamma_u|)$. Therefore, the time complexity of SybilBlind in one iteration is $O(|E|)$. Since SybilBlind performs k sampling trials and each trial runs T iterations, it thus has a time complexity of $O(kT|E|)$.

Two-level Parallel Implementation: We can have a two-level parallel implementation of SybilBlind on a data center which is a standard backend for social web services. First, different sampling trials can be run on different machines. They only need to communicate once to share their vectors of posterior probabilities. Second, each machine can parallelize SybilSCAR using multithreading. Specifically, in each iteration of SybilSCAR, each thread applies the local rule to a subset of nodes in the social network.

6   Experiments

6.1   Experimental Setup

Datasets: We use social networks with synthesized Sybils and Twitter datasets with real Sybils for evaluations. Table 1 summarizes the datasets.

(1) Social networks with synthesized Sybils. Following previous works [7,8,38], we use a real-world social network as the benign region, while synthesizing the Sybil region and attack edges. Specifically, we take a Facebook network as the benign region; we synthesize the Sybil region using the *Preferential Attachment (PA)* model [3], which is a widely used method to generate networks; and we add attack edges between the benign region and the Sybil region uniformly at random. In this graph, nodes are Facebook users and two nodes are connected if they are friends. We synthesize the Sybil region such that 20% of users in the social network are Sybils; the average degree in the Sybil region is the same as that in the benign region in order to avoid asymmetry between the two regions introduced by density. We set the number of attack edges as 500, and thus the average attack edge per Sybil is 0.06.

(2) Small Twitter with real Sybils. We obtained a publicly available Twitter dataset with 809 Sybils and 7,358 benign nodes from Yang et al. [36]. A node is a Twitter user and an edge means two users follow each other. Sybils were labeled spammers. 9.9% of nodes are Sybils and 53.4% of Sybils are connected. The average degree is 16.72, and the average attack edge per Sybil is 49.46.

(3) Large Twitter with real Sybils. We obtained a snapshot of a large-scale Twitter follower-followee network crawled by Kwak et al. [20]. A node is a Twitter user and an edge between two nodes means that one node follows the other node. The network has 41,652,230 nodes and 1,202,513,046 edges. To perform evaluation, we need ground truth labels of the nodes. Since the Twitter network includes users' Twitter IDs, we wrote a crawler to visit each user's profile using Twitter's API, which tells us the status (i.e., active, suspended, or deleted) of each user. In our ground truth, 205,355 nodes were suspended, 5,289,966 nodes were deleted, and the remaining 36,156,909 nodes are active. We take suspended users as Sybils and active users as benign nodes. 85.3% Sybils are connected with an average degree 24. 1.5% of the total edges are attack edges and the average number of attack edges per Sybil is 181.55. We acknowledge that our ground truth labels might be noisy since some active users might be Sybils, but they evaded Twitter's detection, and Twitter might have deleted some Sybils.

AUC as an Evaluation Metric: Similar to previous studies [6,7,14,30], we use the Area Under the Receiver Operating Characteristic Curve (AUC) as an evaluation metric. Suppose we rank nodes according to their probabilities of being Sybil in a descending order. AUC is the probability that a randomly selected Sybil ranks higher than a randomly selected benign node. Random guessing, which ranks nodes uniformly at random, achieves an AUC of 0.5.

Table 1. Dataset statistics.

Metric	Facebook	Small Twitter	Large Twitter
#Nodes	43,953	8,167	41,652,230
#Edges	182,384	68,282	1,202,513,046
Ave. degree	8.29	16.72	57.74
Ave. #attack edge per Sybil	0.06	49.46	181.55

Compared Methods: We adapt a community detection method and SybilSCAR to detect Sybils when no manual labels are available. Moreover, we compare with SybilRank [7] and SybilBelief [14] that require manual labels.

(1) **Community detection (Louvain Method).** When there are no manually labeled training sets, community detection seems to be a natural choice to detect connected Sybils.[2] A community detection method divides a social network into connected components (called "communities"), where nodes in the same community are densely connected while nodes across different communities are loosely connected. Presumably, Sybils are in the same communities.

Since the benign region itself often consists of multiple communities [2,7], the key challenge of community detection methods is how to determine which communities correspond to Sybils. Assigning a label of Sybil (or benign) to a community means that all nodes in the community are Sybils (or benign). Since it is unclear how to assign labels to the communities algorithmically (though one could try various heuristics), in our experiments, we assume one could label communities such that community detection achieves a *false negative rate* that is the closest to that of SybilBlind. Specifically, SybilBlind predicts a node to be Sybil if its aggregated probability is larger than 0.5, and thus we can compute the false negative rate for SybilBlind. Then we compare community detection with SybilBlind with respect to AUC, via ranking the communities labeled as Sybil higher than those labeled as benign. Our experiments give advantages to community detection since this label assignment might not be found in practice. Louvain method [5] is a widely used community detection method, which is efficient and outperforms a variety of community detection methods [5]. Therefore, we choose Louvain method in our experiments.

(2) **SybilSCAR with a sampled noisy training set (SybilSCAR-Adapt).** When a manually labeled training set is unavailable, we use our sampler to sample a training set and treat it as the input to SybilSCAR. The performance of this adapted SybilSCAR highly depends on the label noise of the training set.

(3) **SybilRank and SybilBelief with labeled training set.** SybilRank [7] and SybilBelief [14] are state-of-the-art random walk-based method and LBP-based method, respectively. SybilRank can only leverage labeled benign nodes, while SybilBelief can leverage both labeled benign nodes and labeled Sybils. We

---

[2] The local community detection method [26] requires labeled benign nodes and thus is inapplicable to detect Sybils without a manually labeled training set.

randomly sample a labeled training set, where the number of labeled benign nodes and Sybils equals n (the sampling size of SybilBlind).

(4) SybilBlind. In the Facebook network with synthesized Sybils, our sampler samples the two subsets B and S uniformly at random from the entire social network. For the Twitter datasets, directly sampling two subsets B and S with a low label noise is challenging due to the number of benign nodes is far larger than that of Sybils. Thus, we refine our sampler by using discriminative node features. Previous studies [36,37] found that Sybils proactively follow a large number of benign users in order to make more benign users follow them, but only a small fraction of benign users will follow back. Therefore, we extract the *follow back rate (FBR)* feature for each node in the Twitter datasets. Then we rank all nodes according to their FBR features in an ascending order. Presumably, some Sybils are ranked high and some benign nodes are ranked low in the ranking list. Thus, we sample the subset B from the bottom-K nodes and sample the subset S from the top-K nodes. Consider the different sizes of the two Twitter datasets, we set $K = 1,000$ and $K = 500,000$ in the small and large Twitter datasets, respectively. This sampler is more likely to sample training sets that have lower label noise, and thus it improves SybilBlind's performance. *Note that when evaluating SybilSCAR-Adapt on the Twitter datasets, we also use FBR-feature-refined sampler to sample a training set.* As a comparison, we also evaluate the method simply using the FBR feature and denote it as FBR. Moreover, we evaluate SybilBlind with randomly sampled two subsets without the FBR feature, which we denote as SybilBlind-Random.

Parameter Settings: For SybilBlind, according to Theorem 1, the minimal number of sampling trials k_{min} to generate a training set with label noise less than or equal to τ is exponential with respect to n, and k_{min} would be very large even with a modest n. However, through empirical evaluations, we found that the number of sampling trials can be largely decreased when using the FBR-feature-refined sampler. Therefore, we instead use the following heuristics to set the parameters, with which SybilBlind has already obtained satisfying performance. Specifically, $n = 10$, $k = 100$, and $\kappa = 10$ for the Facebook network with synthesized Sybils; $n = 100$, $k = 20$, and $\kappa = 10$ for the small Twitter; and $n = 100,000$, $k = 20$, and $\kappa = 10$ for the large Twitter. We use a smaller k for Twitter datasets because FBR-feature-refined sampler is more likely to sample training sets with smaller label noise. We use a larger sampling size n for the large Twitter dataset because its size is much bigger than the other two datasets. We will also explore the impact of parameters and the results are shown in Fig. 4.

For other compared methods, we set parameters according to their authors. For instance, we set $\theta = 0.4$ for SybilSCAR. SybilRank requires early termination, and its number of iterations is suggested to be $O(\log |V|)$. For each experiment, we repeat 10 times and compute the average AUC. We implement SybilBlind in C++ using multithreading, and we obtain the publicly available

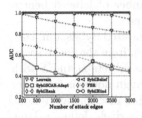

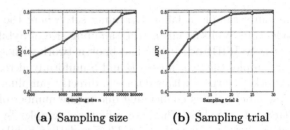

(a) Sampling size   (b) Sampling trial

Fig. 3. AUCs on the Facebook network with synthesized Sybils. Sybil-Blind is robust to various numbers of attack edges.

Fig. 4. AUCs of SybilBlind vs. (a) sampling size n and (b) number of sampling trials k on the large Twitter. We observe that SybilBlind achieves high AUSs when n and k reach certain values.

Table 2. AUCs of the compared methods on the Twitter datasets.

Method	Small Twitter	Large Twitter
Louvain	0.54	0.50
SybilSCAR-Adapt	0.89	0.70
SybilRank	0.86	0.69
SybilBelief	0.98	0.78
FBR	0.60	0.51
SybilBlind-Random	0.82	0.65
SybilBlind	0.98	0.79

implementations for SybilSCAR (also in C++)[3] and Louvain method[4]. We perform all our experiments on a Linux machine with 512GB memory and 32 cores.

6.2 Results

AUCs of the Compared Methods: Figure 3 shows AUCs of the compared methods on the Facebook network with synthesized Sybils as we increase the number of attack edges. Note that SybilBlind-Random is essentially SybilBlind in this case, as we randomly sample the subsets without the FBR feature. Table 2 shows AUCs of the compared methods for the Twitter datasets with real Sybils. We observe that (1) SybilBlind outperforms Louvain method. Specifically, when the number of attack edges gets relatively large, even if one could design an algorithm to label communities such that Louvain method can detect as many Sybils as SybilBlind (i.e., similar false negative rates), Louvain method will rank a large fraction of benign users higher than Sybils, resulting in small AUCs. The reason is that some communities include a large number of both benign

---

[3] http://home.engineering.iastate.edu/~neilgong/dataset.html.

[4] https://sites.google.com/site/findcommunities/.

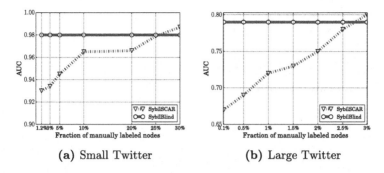

(a) Small Twitter   **(b)** Large Twitter

Fig. 5. AUCs of SybilSCAR vs. the fraction of nodes that are manually labeled as a training set on the small Twitter and large Twitter datasets. We observe that SybilSCAR requires manually labeling about 25% and 2.8% of total nodes on the small Twitter and large Twitter datasets to be comparable to SybilBlind.

users and Sybils, which is an intrinsic limitation of community detection. (2) SybilBlind outperforms SybilSCAR-Adapt, which validates that our homophily-entropy aggregator is significant and essential. Thus, aggregating results in multiple sampling trials can boost the performance. (3) SybilBlind outperforms Sybil-Rank and is comparable with SybilBelief, even if SybilRank and SybilBelief use a labeled training dataset. This is because the FBR-feature-refined sampler can sample training sets with relatively small label noise and SybilSCAR is robust to such label noise. As SybilSCAR was shown to outperform SybilRank and be comparable with SybilBelief [30], so does SybilBlind. (4) SybilSCAR-Adapt achieves AUCs that are close to random guessing on the Facebook network. This is because the sampled training set has random label noise that could be large. SybilSCAR-Adapt works better on the Twitter datasets. Again, this is because the FBR feature assists our sampler to obtain the training sets with small label noise on the Twitter datasets and SybilSCAR can tolerate such label noise. (5) FBR achieves a small AUC. This indicates that although the FBR feature can be used to generate a ranking list with small label noise by treating top-ranked nodes as Sybils and bottom-ranked nodes as benign, the overall ranking performance on the entire nodes is not promising. (6) SybilBlind-Random's performance decreases on the Twitter datasets. The reason is that it is difficult to sample training sets with small label noise, as the number of benign nodes is far larger than the number of Sybils on the Twitter datasets.

Number of Manual Labels SybilSCAR Requires to Match SybilBlind's Performance: Intuitively, given a large enough manually labeled training set, SybilSCAR that takes the manually labeled training set as an input would outperform SybilBlind. Therefore, one natural question is how many nodes need to be manually labeled in order for SybilSCAR to match SybilBlind's performance. To answer this question, we respectively sample x fraction of total nodes in the small Twitter dataset and large Twitter dataset and treat them as a manually

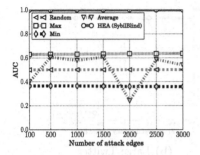

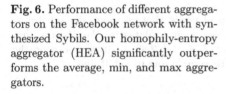

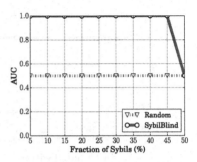

Fig. 6. Performance of different aggregators on the Facebook network with synthesized Sybils. Our homophily-entropy aggregator (HEA) significantly outperforms the average, min, and max aggregators.

Fig. 7. Impact of the fraction of Sybils on the Facebook network. We observe that SybilBlind can accurately detect Sybils once the fraction of Sybils is smaller than 50%, i.e., Sybils are less than benign nodes.

labeled training set, i.e., the benign nodes are assigned a label of benign and the Sybils are assigned a label of Sybil. Note that the manually labeled training set has no label noise. Then, we run SybilSCAR with the training set, rank the remaining nodes using their probabilities of being Sybil, and compute an AUC. Figure 5 shows the AUCs of SybilSCAR as we increase x from 0.1% to 3% on the small Twitter and large Twitter datasets. For comparison, we also show the AUC of SybilBlind on the small Twitter and large Twitter datasets, which is a straight line since it does not rely on the manually labeled training set. We observe that SybilSCAR requires manually labeling about 25% of total nodes on the small Twitter and about 2.8% of total nodes on the large Twitter in order to achieve an AUC that is comparable to SybilBlind.

Comparing Different Aggregators: Figure 6 shows the performances of different aggregators on the Facebook network with synthesized Sybils as we increase the number of attack edges. We observe that our homophily-entropy aggregator (HEA) significantly outperforms the average, min, and max aggregators. The average aggregator achieves performances that are close to random guessing. This is because the average aggregator assigns an expected aggregated probability of 0.5 to every node. Moreover, the min aggregator achieves AUCs that are worse than random guessing, while the max aggregator achieves AUCs that are slightly higher than random guessing. It is an interesting future work to theoretically understand the performance gaps for the min and max aggregators.

Impact of the Fraction of Sybils: Figure 7 shows the AUCs of SybilBlind as the social network has more and more Sybils. We performed the experiments on the Facebook network with synthesized Sybils since we need social networks with different number of Sybils. The number of attack edges is set to be 500. We observe that SybilBlind can accurately detect Sybils (AUCs are close to 1) once the fraction of Sybils is smaller than 50%, i.e., Sybils are less than benign nodes.

We note that when Sybils are more than benign nodes, SybilBlind would rank benign nodes higher than Sybils, resulting in AUCs that are close to 0. However, in practice, Sybils are less than benign nodes, as we discussed in Sect. 3.2.

Impact of n and k: Figure 4a and b show AUCs of SybilBlind vs. sampling size n ($k = 20$) and the number of sampling trials k ($n = 100{,}000$) on the large Twitter, respectively. We observe that the AUCs increase as the sampling size and the number of sampling trials increase. The AUCs become stable after n and k reach certain values. The AUCs are small when n or k is small, because it is harder to sample training sets with relatively small label noise.

Running Time: We show running time of SybilBlind on the large Twitter. We concurrently generate sampling trials using multiprocessing. In particular, we create 4 processes in parallel, each of which runs one sampling trial. Moreover, each sampling trial runs SybilSCAR using multithreading (20 threads in our experiments). It took about 2 h for one process to run SybilSCAR in one sampling trial, and the total time for our SybilBlind with 20 sampling trials is around 10 h.

7   Conclusion and Future Work

We design a novel structure-based framework called SybilBlind to detect Sybils in online social networks without a manually labeled training dataset. We demonstrate the effectiveness of SybilBlind using both social networks with synthetic Sybils and Twitter datasets with real Sybils. Our results show that Sybils can be detected without manual labels. Future work includes applying SybilBlind to detect Sybils with sampled subsets with different sizes and extending SybilBlind to learn general machine learning classifiers without manual labels.

Acknowledgements. We thank the anonymous reviewers and our shepherd Jason Polakis for their constructive comments. This work was supported by NSF under grant CNS-1750198 and a research gift from JD.com.

A   Performance of the Average Aggregator

Theorem 2. *When SybilBlind uses the average aggregator, the expected aggregated probability is 0.5 for every node.*

Proof. Suppose in some sampling trial, the sampled subsets are B and S, and SybilSCAR halts after T iterations. We denote by q_u the prior probability and by $p_u^{(t)}$ the probability in the tth iteration for u, respectively. Note that the subsets $B' = S$ and $S' = B$ are sampled by the sampler with the same probability. We denote by q_u' the prior probability and by $p_u^{(t)'}$ the probability in the tth iteration for u, respectively, when SybilSCAR uses the subsets B' and S'. We prove that $q'_u = 1 - q_u$ and $p_u^{(t)'} = 1 - p_u^{(t)}$ for every node u and iteration t. First, we have:

$$q'_u = \begin{cases} 0.5 - \theta & = 1 - q_u \text{ if } u \in S \\ 0.5 + \theta & = 1 - q_u \text{ if } u \in B \\ 0.5 & = 1 - q_u \text{ otherwise,} \end{cases}$$

which means that $q_u' = 1 - q_u$ for every node.

We have $p_u^{(0)'} = q_u'$ and $p_u^{(0)} = q_u$. Therefore, $p_u^{(0)'} = 1 - p_u^{(0)}$ holds for every node in the 0th iteration. We can also show that $p_u^{(t)'} = 1 - p_u^{(t)}$ holds for every node in the tth iteration if $p_u^{(t-1)'} = 1 - p_u^{(t-1)}$ holds for every node. Therefore, $p_u^{(t)'} = 1 - p_u^{(t)}$ holds for every node u and iteration t. As a result, with the sampled subsets B' and S', SybilSCAR also halts after T iterations. Moreover, the average probability in the two sampling trials (i.e., the sampled subsets are B and S, and $B' = S$ and $S' = B$) is 0.5 for every node. For each pair of sampled subsets B and S, there is a pair of subsets $B' = S$ and $S' = B$ that are sampled by our sampler with the same probability. Therefore, the expected aggregated probability is 0.5 for every node.

B   Proof of Theorem 1

Lower Bound: We have:

$$\Pr(\alpha_b \leq \tau, \alpha_s \leq \tau) \geq \Pr(\alpha_b = \alpha_s = 0) = (1 - r)^n r^n. \tag{4}$$

We note that this lower bound is very loose because we simply ignore the cases where $\Pr(0 < \alpha_b \leq \tau, 0 < \alpha_s \leq \tau)$. However, this lower bound is sufficient to give us qualitative understanding.

Upper Bound: We observe that the probability that label noise in both the benign region and the Sybil region are no bigger than τ is bounded by the probability that label noise in the benign region or the Sybil region is no bigger than τ. Formally, we have:

$$\Pr(\alpha_b \leq \tau, \alpha_s \leq \tau) \leq \min\{\Pr(\alpha_b \leq \tau), \Pr(\alpha_s \leq \tau)\} \tag{5}$$

Next, we will bound the probabilities $\Pr(\alpha_b \leq \tau)$ and $\Pr(\alpha_s \leq \tau)$ separately. We will take $\Pr(\alpha_b \leq \tau)$ as an example to show the derivations, and similar derivations can be used to bound $\Pr(\alpha_s \leq \tau)$.

We observe the following equivalent equations:

$$\Pr(\alpha_b \leq \tau) = \Pr(\frac{n_{sb}}{n_{sb} + n_{bb}} \leq \tau) = \Pr(\tau n_{bb} + (\tau - 1) n_{sb} \geq 0) \tag{6}$$

We define n random variables $X_1, X_2, \cdots, X_n$ and n random variables $Y_1, Y_2, \cdots, Y_n$ as follows:

$$X_i = \begin{cases} \tau & \text{if the } i\text{th node in B is benign} \\ 0 & \text{otherwise} \end{cases}$$

$$Y_i = \begin{cases} \tau - 1 & \text{if the } i\text{th node in S is benign} \\ 0 & \text{otherwise,} \end{cases}$$

where $i = 1, 2, \cdots, n$. According to our definitions, we have $\Pr(X_i = \tau) = 1 - r$ and $\Pr(Y_i = \tau - 1) = 1 - r$, where $i = 1, 2, \cdots, n$. Moreover, we denote S as the sum of these random variables, i.e., $S = \sum_{i=1}^{n} X_i + \sum_{i=1}^{n} Y_i$. Then, the expected value of S is $E(S) = -(1 - 2\tau)(1 - r)n$. With the variables S and $E(S)$, we can further rewrite Eq. 6 as follows:

$$\Pr(\alpha_b \leq \tau) = \Pr(S - E(S) \geq -E(S))$$

According to Hoeffding's inequality [17], we have

$$\Pr(S - E(S) \geq -E(S)) \leq \exp\left(-\frac{2E^2(s)}{(\tau^2 + (1 - \tau)^2)n}\right) = \exp\left(-\frac{2(1 - 2\tau)^2(1 - r)^2 n}{\tau^2 + (1 - \tau)^2}\right)$$

Similarly, we can derive an upper bound of $Pr(\alpha_s \leq \tau)$ as follows:

$$\Pr(\alpha_s \leq \tau) \leq \exp\left(-\frac{2(1 - 2\tau)^2 r^2 n}{\tau^2 + (1 - \tau)^2}\right) \tag{7}$$

Since we consider $r < 0.5$ in this work, we have:

$$\min\{\Pr(\alpha_b \leq \tau), \Pr(\alpha_s \leq \tau)\} = \exp\left(-\frac{2(1 - 2\tau)^2(1 - r)^2 n}{\tau^2 + (1 - \tau)^2}\right) \tag{8}$$

By combining Eqs. 5 and 8, we obtain Eq. 3.

References

1. 1 in 10 Twitter accounts is fake. http://goo.gl/qTYbyy
2. Alvisi, L., Clement, A., Epasto, A., Lattanzi, S., Panconesi, A.: SoK: the evolution of sybil defense via social networks. In: IEEE S & P (2013)
3. Barabási, A., Albert, R.: Emergence of scaling in random networks. Science **286**, 509–512 (1999)
4. Benevenuto, F., Magno, G., Rodrigues, T., Almeida, V.: Detecting spammers on Twitter. In: CEAS (2010)
5. Blondel, V.D., Guillaume, J.L., Lambiotte, R., Lefebvre, E.: Fast unfolding of communities in large networks. Stat. Mech.: Theory Exp. (2008)
6. Boshmaf, Y., Logothetis, D., Siganos, G., Leria, J., Lorenzo, J.: Integro: leveraging victim prediction for robust fake account detection in OSNs. In: NDSS (2015)

7. Cao, Q., Sirivianos, M., Yang, X., Pregueiro, T.: Aiding the detection of fake accounts in large scale social online services. In: NSDI (2012)
8. Danezis, G., Mittal, P.: SybilInfer: detecting Sybil nodes using social networks. In: NDSS (2009)
9. Fu, H., Xie, X., Rui, Y., Gong, N.Z., Sun, G., Chen, E.: Robust spammer detection in microblogs: leveraging user carefulness. ACM Trans. Intell. Syst. Technol. (TIST) (2017)
10. Gao, H., Chen, Y., Lee, K., Palsetia, D., Choudhary, A.: Towards online spam filtering in social networks. In: NDSS (2012)
11. Gao, P., Wang, B., Gong, N.Z., Kulkarni, S., Thomas, K., Mittal, P.: SybilFuse: Combining local attributes with global structure to perform robust Sybil detection. In: IEEE CNS (2018)
12. Ghosh, S., et al.: Understanding and combating link farming in the Twitter social network. In: WWW (2012)
13. Gilbert, E., Karahalios, K.: Predicting tie strength with social media. In: CHI (2009)
14. Gong, N.Z., Frank, M., Mittal, P.: SybilBelief: a semi-supervised learning approach for structure-based Sybil detection. IEEE TIFS 9(6), 976–987 (2014)
15. Hacking Election, May 2016. http://goo.gl/G8o9x0
16. Hacking Financial Market, May 2016. http://goo.gl/4AkWyt
17. Hoeffding, W.: Probability inequalities for sums of bounded random variables. J. Am. Stat. Assoc. 58(301), 13–30 (1963)
18. Jia, J., Wang, B., Gong, N.Z.: Random walk based fake account detection in online social networks. In: IEEE DSN, pp. 273–284 (2017)
19. Kontaxis, G., Polakis, I., Ioannidis, S., Markatos, E.P.: Detecting social network profile cloning. In: IEEE PERCOM Workshops (2011)
20. Kwak, H., Lee, C., Park, H., Moon, S.: What is Twitter, a social network or a news media? In: WWW, pp. 591–600. ACM (2010)
21. Liu, C., Gao, P., Wright, M., Mittal, P.: Exploiting temporal dynamics in Sybil defenses. In: ACM CCS, pp. 805–816 (2015)
22. Song, J., Lee, S., Kim, J.: Spam filtering in Twitter using sender-receiver relationship. In: Sommer, R., Balzarotti, D., Maier, G. (eds.) RAID 2011. LNCS, vol. 6961, pp. 301–317. Springer, Heidelberg (2011). https://doi.org/10.1007/978-3-642-23644-0_16
23. Stringhini, G., Kruegel, C., Vigna, G.: Detecting spammers on social networks. In: ACSAC (2010)
24. Thomas, K., Grier, C., Ma, J., Paxson, V., Song, D.: Design and evaluation of a real-time URL spam filtering service. In: IEEE S & P (2011)
25. Thomas, K., McCoy, D., Grier, C., Kolcz, A., Paxson, V.: Trafficking fraudulent accounts: the role of the underground market in Twitter spam and abuse. In: USENIX Security Symposium (2013)
26. Viswanath, B., Post, A., Gummadi, K.P., Mislove, A.: An analysis of social network-based Sybil defenses. In: ACM SIGCOMM (2010)
27. Wang, A.H.: Don't follow me - spam detection in Twitter. In: SECRYPT (2010)
28. Wang, B., Gong, N.Z., Fu, H.: GANG: detecting fraudulent users in online social networks via guilt-by-association on directed graphs. In: IEEE ICDM (2017)
29. Wang, B., Jia, J., Zhang, L., Gong, N.Z.: Structure-based Sybil detection in social networks via local rule-based propagation. IEEE Transactions on Network Science and Engineering (2018)
30. Wang, B., Zhang, L., Gong, N.Z.: SybilSCAR: Sybil detection in online social networks via local rule based propagation. In: IEEE INFOCOM (2017)

31. Wang, G., Konolige, T., Wilson, C., Wang, X.: You are how you click: clickstream analysis for Sybil detection. In: Usenix Security (2013)
32. Wang, G., et al.: Social turing tests: crowdsourcing Sybil detection. In: NDSS (2013)
33. Wei, W., Xu, F., Tan, C., Li, Q.: SybilDefender: defend against Sybil attacks in large social networks. In: IEEE INFOCOM (2012)
34. Wilson, C., Boe, B., Sala, A., Puttaswamy, K.P., Zhao, B.Y.: User interactions in social networks and their implications. In: EuroSys (2009)
35. Yang, C., Harkreader, R.C., Gu, G.: Die free or live hard? Empirical evaluation and new design for fighting evolving Twitter spammers. In: Sommer, R., Balzarotti, D., Maier, G. (eds.) RAID 2011. LNCS, vol. 6961, pp. 318–337. Springer, Heidelberg (2011). https://doi.org/10.1007/978-3-642-23644-0_17
36. Yang, C., Harkreader, R., Zhang, J., Shin, S., Gu, G.: Analyzing spammer's social networks for fun and profit. In: WWW (2012)
37. Yang, Z., Wilson, C., Wang, X., Gao, T., Zhao, B.Y., Dai, Y.: Uncovering social network Sybils in the wild. In: IMC (2011)
38. Yu, H., Gibbons, P.B., Kaminsky, M., Xiao, F.: SybilLimit: a near-optimal social network defense against Sybil attacks. In: IEEE S & P (2008)
39. Yu, H., Kaminsky, M., Gibbons, P.B., Flaxman., A.: SybilGuard: defending against Sybil attacks via social networks. In: ACM SIGCOMM (2006)

GuidedPass: Helping Users to Create Strong and Memorable Passwords

Simon S. Woo[1](✉) and Jelena Mirkovic[2]

[1] The State University of New York, Korea, Incheon, South Korea
`simon.woo@sunykorea.ac.kr`
[2] USC-Information Sciences Institute, Marina del Rey, CA, USA
`mirkovic@isi.edu`

Abstract. Password meters and policies are currently the only tools helping users to create stronger passwords. However, such tools often do not provide consistent or useful feedback to users, and their suggestions may decrease memorability of resulting passwords. Passwords that are difficult to remember promote bad practices, such as writing them down or password reuse, thus stronger passwords do not necessarily improve authentication security. In this work, we propose *GuidedPass* – a system that suggests real-time password modifications to users, which preserve the password's semantic structure, while increasing password strength. Our suggestions are based on structural and semantic patterns mined from successfully recalled and strong passwords in several IRB-approved user studies [30]. We compare our approach to password creation with creation under NIST [12] policy, Ur et al. [26] guidance, and zxcvbn password-meter. We show that GuidedPass outperforms competing approaches both in password strength and in recall performance.

Keywords: Password · Usable security · Password meter
Authentication

1 Introduction

Left to their own devices, users create passwords, which may be weak but which are memorable. Current systems attempt to improve this practice in two ways. First, systems can suggest or enforce specific password composition policies, which lead to stronger passwords. But stringent password composition requirements increase users' frustration and lead them to write down or reuse their passwords [16], which is a bad practice. It has also been shown that password composition policies are not consistent across different sites [9,17,20,27], which indicates lack of clear understanding of the role that password composition plays in determining password strength. NIST recently proposed a new password composition policy [12], which enforces minimum of 8 characters and requires systems to reject inputs that appear on the list of previously-leaked passwords or common dictionary words.

© Springer Nature Switzerland AG 2018
M. Bailey et al. (Eds.): RAID 2018, LNCS 11050, pp. 250–270, 2018.
https://doi.org/10.1007/978-3-030-00470-5_12

Another way to improve password strength is to offer real-time feedback on the user's password and, optionally, suggestions for improvements. Password meters offer real-time feedback on user password strength [17,29], although this feedback may be inconsistent [9,17,20,27]. Password meters, however, only provide strength feedback in form of a number or color scale, but do not offer guidance on how to modify the user input into a stronger one, while preserving memorability. A data-driven password meter by Ur et al. [26], provides proactive and actionable suggestions to a user on how to make their password stronger. This approach, however, focuses only on improving strength and does not consider how the proposed modifications may impair memorability.

We propose *GuidedPass* – a system, which helps users create both memorable and secure passwords at creation time, through detailed suggestions for improvement of password structure and semantics. First, we start from an observation that memorability stems both from the choice of words used in the password (e.g., phrases, names, numbers, dates of personal significance) and the password structure (e.g., word, followed by digits). We then tailor our suggestions in such a way to preserve the initial user-supplied strings and structure, as much as possible, while improving password strength. Our main contributions are summarized below:

(1) **Identification of semantic patterns, which make passwords memorable and strong:** We analyze 3,260 passwords, which were successfully recalled by participants in our prior IRB-approved user studies [30], to identify semantic patterns that make these passwords both memorable, and strong. We call these *preferred patterns*.

(2) **Design of a real-time password suggestion system(*GuidedPass*):** We design a system, which chooses a set of preferred patterns, which are closest to the user's input, and provides meaningful suggestions for gentle structural and semantic modification of the user's initial input.

(3) **GuidedPass evaluation:** We evaluate GuidedPass and several competing approaches in a user study, with more than 1,400 Amazon Mechanical Turk participants. We show that passwords with GuidedPass suggestions are both more memorable and stronger than passwords created by competing approaches. GuidedPass achieves 81% recall after two days, and the average strength of more than 10^{19} statistical guesses.Compared to the approach by Ur et al. [26], GuidedPass has 14% higher recall, and up to 100 times higher strength.

The rest of this paper is organized as follows. We discuss related work in Sect. 2. We present our methodology in Sect. 3. Memorable password dataset is analyzed in Sect. 4. We present the GuidedPass system design in Sect. 5. We detail the setup of our user study in Sect. 6. Section 7 presents the results of our evaluation of GuidedPass, and competing approaches, and Sect. 8 offer our discussion and conclusions.

2   Background and Related Work

Password composition policies are regularly used to steer users toward stronger passwords. The most common password policy is the 3class8 policy, which requires a password to be at least 8 characters long, and to include at least three out of four character classes: digits, uppercase and lowercase letters, and special characters. There are many inconsistencies among password policies [10,24], and a lack of clear understanding on which policy is the best.

Even when users meet the 3class8 policy requirements, their passwords can still be weak because they are created using common words and phrases. For example Password123 satisfies 3class8 requirement but is among top 33,523 out of 14,344,391 passwords and occurs 62 times in leaked RockYou datasets. In [18], Kelly et al. found that passwords created under minimum 8 characters policy are significantly weaker than passwords created under stricter policies. Shay et al. [21] compared eight different password composition policies and found that a long password with fewer constraints can be more usable and stronger than a short password with more constraints. Overly strict password composition policies may also lead to unsafe practices, such as writing down passwords [23]. NIST [12] recently proposed a new password composition policy, which removes requirements for different character classes, but keeps the length requirement. The system is also required to check users' passwords against any previously leaked passwords, and against common dictionary words. While this feedback informs the users on what parts of their password may be susceptible to a guessing attack, it does not provide clear guidance on how to build a better password. Such guidance is needed, to help users make significant improvements to their password strength, instead of small, predictable changes [14].

Password complexity does not necessarily mean low recall. Bonneau and Schechter [4] show that users can be trained to remember randomly-assigned 56 bit codes, but such training is hardly practical for tens of passwords accounts, which users need daily [15]. Users can be helped to create strong passwords by using a password meter [9,22,27], or a composition of password meters and password composition policy [20,23]. Meters, however, are not enough. They are inconsistent in strength estimation [6], and they do not offer specific suggestions on how to modify passwords to improve their strength.

Telepathwords [19] provide proactive suggestions to users during password creation. The system learns character distributions in its existing password data, and uses it to highlight frequent character patterns in user input. Users are thus steered towards less likely patterns. Telepathwords' increase password strength by 3.7 bits of zxcvbn [29] entropy measure, but recall declines to 62% of the baseline, because users are steered from words that are meaningful to them towards those with lower personal significance. GuidedPass addresses this problem, by allowing users to keep their current inputs, and gently morph them into stronger passwords. While we did not compare memorability of GuidedPass passwords to that of original user inputs, GuidedPass achieves 81% recall after two days, compared to 62% for Telepathwords.

The most related work to GuidedPass is the data-driven password meter by Ur et al. [26] – DataPass for brevity. DataPass provides real-time, specific guidance to users on how to improve their passwords. It also identifies a range of inputs that should be avoided such as dictionary words, common passwords, etc. The main point of difference between GuidedPass and DataPass is in how password suggestions are developed. DataPass mines weak password patterns from leaked password datasets, but it has no way of learning which passwords are memorable to their users. Conversely, we use a labeled dataset of passwords from our prior studies [30] to learn which patterns appear much more often among memorable and strong passwords, than among other subsets. This enables us to make suggestions that both improve strength and preserve memorability. In Sect. 7, we provide side-by-side comparison of suggestions generated from GuidedPass and DataPass, and point their differences. GuidedPass outperforms DataPass both in password recall and in password strength.

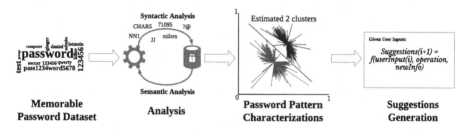

Fig. 1. The overall development process of the password suggestion system (Guided-Pass)

3   Methodology

Our process for the GuidedPass development is illustrated in Fig. 1. We start with the observation that it is necessary to analyze passwords that are both memorable and strong, to learn about their structure and semantics. This cannot be accomplished by analyzing leaked datasets, since these datasets lack recall information. Over three years, we have collected passwords for various authentication research. These passwords were created during our studies, and were successfully recalled, in the course of the study, after two days. The dataset includes more than 3,200 passwords.

We leverage these successfully recalled passwords to understand general patterns, which also make these passwords strong. We measure the strength of memorable passwords, using the Monte Carlo method by Dell'Amico, and Filippone [8]. We train the guessing algorithm with a total of 21 million leaked passwords. Based on the estimated passwords' strength, we classified each password into the weak, medium or strong category, using the estimated number of guesses for online (10^6) and offline (10^{14}) attacks as boundaries between categories [11].

After classifying memorable passwords into three different strength groups, we perform both *syntactic* analysis – such as recording password length and composition – and *semantic* analysis – such as understanding if password segments are dictionary words, personal names, etc. For semantic analysis, we used Vera et al.'s semantic segmentation parser [28] to segment the password and label each segment. We then compare and analyze the syntactic and semantic structures between groups, and identify patterns that occur predominantly in the strong category. We call these the *preferred patterns*.

Next, out of the preferred patterns we generate suggestions to users, which are easy to understand and simple to follow, on how to evolve their initial input into a strong password. We present several suggestions so that a user can choose the one they prefer, and which may have the least impact on password recall. We also strive to keep our suggestions "fuzzy" and not too specific, to increase search space for attackers who are familiar with GuidedPass. Our suggestion process can also be iterative – suggestions can continue until the user's password exceeds some desired strength.

4   Memorable Password Analysis

Using the Monte Carlo method by Dell'Amico and Filippone [8], we classified each memorable password in our dataset into the weak (fewer than 10^6 guesses), medium or strong (more than 10^{14} guesses) category. Among our memorable passwords, almost 27% of passwords fell into the strong category, 70% into the medium category and 3% into the weak category, as shown in Table 1.

Table 1. Memorable password dataset, categorized into three different strength groups and percentage of 3class8 passwords in each strength group

Strength category	No. of passwords (%)	% of 3class8 passwords
Weak (guesses $< 10^6$)	109 (3.34%)	6%
Medium ($10^6 \leq$ guesses $< 10^{14}$)	2,276 (69.82%)	58.1%
Strong (guesses $\geq 10^{14}$)	875 (26.84%)	74.2%
Total	3,260 (100%)	60.68%

4.1   Syntactic Characteristics

We first analyze the passwords in each category with respect to length, number of character classes, and class changes. We summarize our findings below.

3class8 Policy Neither Necessary Nor Sufficient: We show the percentage of password that meet the 3class8 requirement in each category in Table 1. 74.2% of strong passwords, 58.1% of medium-strength passwords and 6% of weak passwords meet the 3class8 requirement. This clearly shows that 3class8 requirement is neither necessary (25.8% of strong passwords do not meet it) nor sufficient (significant number of medium-strength and weak passwords meet it) for a strong password.

Password Length Makes a Big Difference: Password length plays a critical role in determining password strength [15]. The average password length in the weak, medium, and strong group was 8.83, 9.88, and 13.73 characters, respectively. The length distribution was significantly different across strong, median, and weak strength groups (KW test $p = 9.87 \times 10^{-151}$), while the difference is smaller but still significant between weak and medium groups (Holm-Bonferonni-corrected Mann-Whitney U, HC-MWU, test, $p = 2.31 \times 10^{-5}$). The statistical difference between medium and strong group is significant (HC-MWU test, $p = 3.11 \times 10^{-142}$). Hence, stronger passwords tend to be longer.

Table 2. Average and STD (stdev) of number of symbols, digits, uppercase letters, and number of class changes for passwords in each strength category

Strength category	Symbols		Digits		Uppercase-letter		No. of class ch.	
	Average	STD	Average	STD	Average	STD	Average	STD
Weak	2.3	1.8	0.1	0.4	0.02	0.1	1.0	0.9
Medium	2.6	1.6	0.7	0.7	0.2	0.5	1.8	0.9
Strong	2.6	1.9	1.1	1.0	0.6	0.9	2.8	2.1

Digits and Uppercase Letters Improve Strength: We show the number of symbols, digits, and uppercase letters in Table 2. All strength groups have similar statistics for the number of symbols and there is no statistical difference between them. However, there is significant statistical difference with regard to the number of digits present in weak, medium, and strong passwords (KW test, $p = 2.66 \times 10^{-43}$), with stronger passwords having slightly higher incidence of digits. The statistical significance between strong and medium group with HC-MWU test is $p = 3.68 \times 10^{-18}$. And HC-MWU test yields $p = 5.96 \times 10^{-24}$ between medium and weak group. Similarly, stronger passwords also have a higher incidence of uppercase letters (KW test, $p = 1.96 \times 10^{-55}$). The statistical significance between strong and medium group with HC-MWU test is $p = 1.18 \times 10^{-48}$. And HC-MWU test yields $p = 3.73 \times 10^{-4}$ between medium and weak group.

More Class Changes Improve Strength: We define a class change as having two consecutive characters in a password from different character classes. For example, "Alicebob123$" has 3 class changes ('A' → 'l', 'b' → '1', '3' → '$'). A higher number of class changes can create more complex, and possibly stronger passwords. Statistics for the number of class changes are shown in columns 8 and 9 of Table 2. As password strength increased so did the number of class changes (KW test, $p = 1.87 \times 10^{-73}$). The statistical significance between strong and medium group with HC-MWU test was $p = 4.58 \times 10^{-47}$. And HC-MWU test yields $p = 1.62 \times 10^{-27}$ between medium and weak group.

4.2 Semantic Structure

Next, we analyze the semantic structure of strong, medium, and weak passwords. We use Vera et al.'s semantic parser [28] to segment each password and label the segments with their part-of-speech (POS tags) from CLAWS7 tagset [25]. For example, for a string "applerun" the string would return segments (apple)(run) and tags (nn1)(vv0) indicating a singular noun and a base form of a verb. This representation captures the underlying semantic structures of passwords, which cannot be represented by the previously discussed syntactic features. We further label segments as **(dict):** dictionary words, **(fname):** popular female names, **(mname):** popular male names, and **(sname):** popular last names from 2010 US Census [1]. Also, we separately check if passwords match with leaked passwords, as suggested by others [14,26,29]. We use leaked passwords from Xato corpus [5] and label user inputs found in the corpus as **leak**. Such a label is shown to user to alert them not to use the leaked password.

Complex and Unique Patterns Improve Strength: After processing each password with the semantic segmentation program, we count the total number of unique tag-sequences in each group and compute the percentage of those. We find that 47.7% of weak, and 51.3% of medium passwords have unique semantic patterns, while 91% of strong passwords have unique patterns. This uniqueness in semantic patterns may contribute to password strength.

Table 3 presents the top 10 most frequently used semantic patterns for each group with the percentage of each tag occurrence. If we compare two tables, we can clearly observe that a few digits followed by a noun (e.g. (dict)(num1), (mname)(num4)) are the most commonly used semantic pattern in weak and medium strength group. Further, there are many occurrences of either (dict) or (name) tags in weak and medium groups, in addition to one other tag. On the other hand, semantic patterns of strong passwords are more complex and diverse, as shown in Table 3. Although these passwords also use dictionary words and names, those are interleaved with complex symbol and digit sequences, resulting in non-common words and structures (e.g., KpieAT7894#). Therefore, we should guide users towards more complex semantic patterns to improve password strength.

There were 19.27% of weak passwords, which were fully matched with a leaked password, and 54.1% of weak passwords used a leaked password segment (e.g., 'password9cq'). Further, medium-strength passwords had no full matches but 33.2% of them contained a leaked password, in addition to other characters. On the other hand, 20.5% of strong passwords contained leaked password segments but none of them fully matched with leaked passwords.

The More Segments, the Higher Strength: We investigate the number of different-tag segments in a password, which correlate with its semantic complexity. We find weak passwords have only 2.21 segments on the average, while the medium-strength passwords have 3.44 segments, and the strong passwords have on average 5.22 segments. Thus, we should guide users toward more semantic segments to improve their password strength.

Table 3. Top 10 most frequent semantic patterns from different strength groups

Weak	%	Medium	%	Strong	%
(dict)(num1)	**11.0**	**(dict)(num4)**	**2.48**	**(char1)(dict)(char2)(num4)(sp1)**	**1.03**
(fname)(num4)	7.34	(dict)(num3)	2.34	(char1)(pp1)(num1)(sp1)(num4)(char1)(pp1)	1.03
(dict)(num2)	6.42	(mname)(num4)	1.47	(sp1)(at)(dict)(jj)(num4)(sp1)	0.91
(mname)(num4)	6.42	(dict)(num1)(sp1)	1.23	(char1)(dict)(char2)(num2)(sp1)	0.8
(fname)(num2)	6.42	(fname)(num4)	1.06	(char4)(num2)(sp2)	0.57
(dict)(num3)	4.59	(dict)	0.83	(char6)(num3)(sp1)	0.46
(num8)	3.67	(dict)(num3)(sp1)	0.78	(dict)(num2)(sp1)	0.34
(dict)(num4)	3.67	(dict)(sp1)(num4)	0.78	(sp1)(dict)(dict)(num2)	0.34
(mname)(num2)	3.67	(dict)(sp1)(num2)	0.73	(num4)(char1)(sp1)(dict)(sp1)(char2)	0.34
(dict)	2.75	(dict)(num2)	0.69	(mname)(sname)(num2)(sp1)	0.23

4.3   Summary of Our Findings

We summarize our recommendations as follows:

- **Uncommon or non-dictionary words.** Even with the same semantic pattern, e.g., (np1)(num4), a password can be in any of the three strength categories, depending on the commonality of the words in each segment. For example, **bella1234** is in weak, **Alaska2011** is in medium, and **u.s.-iraq6911** is in strong group with the same (np1)(num4) structure) Thus we must steer the users towards uncommon words. Creating uncommon words may not be that hard. For example, we observe that strong passwords often consist of a dictionary word, interleaved with digits or symbols, or being intentionally misspelled.
- **The longer, the more semantic segments, and the stronger** Our suggestions often involve addition of more words into the password to make it longer and thus stronger. We also suggest insertion of different character classes to increase both the number of class changes and to create uncommon segments from common ones.
- **Multilingual passwords.** We observe that some strong passwords include words from foreign languages such as Spanish or Arabic. Research [2] has shown that more than half of population on Earth are bilingual. We expect that combining words from more than one language in unpredictable ways can improve password strength without loss of memorability.

5   GuidedPass System Design

In this section, we describe how we designed and implemented suggestions in GuidedPass, using the password suggestion model and templates.

5.1   Password Suggestion Model

We assume that users initially choose passwords based on certain strings that have personal significance to them, which makes them memorable. Then, our suggestions are generated to evolve and extend user's existing password into a stronger version without losing memorability. We formally define the password suggestion model as follows:

$$Password_{new} = f(Password_{current}, M_{new}), \tag{1}$$

where $Password_{current}$ is the user's current password string, M_{new} are the new words or characters to be added to $Password_{current}$, and f is a function that the user performs to integrate M_{new} with $Password_{current}$. We focus on functions that an average person could easily perform, inspired by Blum et al. [3]. These are addition, insertion, replacement without deletion, swapping, breaking, or perturbing sequence and redistributing, separating, or moving segments as shown in Table 4. We do not suggest deletion, since it reduces password length. Next, we consider types of new information, M_{new}, the user can enter. As we discussed from the previous section, for strong passwords, M_{new} should be chosen from uncommon words. Users can also create uncommon strings or break up common words or sequence structures, by interleaving them with digits or symbols.

Table 4. Example of `<Action,Info,Quantifier>` used in suggestion generation

Action (Operation)	Information	Quantifier (Fuzzy terms)
Add, insert, replace, swap	(un)common name	Some, a few
Brake, move, perturb	(un)common word	Somewhere
Redistribute, separate	Word(s), digit(s), symbol(s), sequence(s)	In the middle

With these options, we construct the `<Action, Info, Quantifier>` templates, as shown in Table 4. Suggestions can be constructed from any combination of action, information, and quantifier, based on the user's current input. We provide multiple suggestions to the user, and they can choose the most suitable suggestion in each step to extend their password. Our suggestions are intentionally designed to be high-level and non-specific. First, we want to allow sufficient space and flexibility for users to interpret these suggestions in a way that does not interfere with password memorability. Second, we want to increase the search space of guessing attacks. If suggestions were too specific, it would be easier for attackers to perform rule-based attacks.

5.2   Suggestion Rules

To be able to provide suggestions in real time, we first need to detect semantic content and patterns of a user-entered password in real time. Using our POS segmentation [28] and the zxcvbn [29] tool, we can detect dictionary words, names, common sequences, and blacklisted passwords. Upon detecting problematic content or patterns such as leaked passwords, and common first name, we immediately highlight them and generate targeted suggestions to avoid those. Following summarizes the suggestions we generate for each case:

Table 5. A side-by-side comparison of generated suggestions between ours and Ur et al.

User input	Category	GuidedPass	Ur et al. [26]
John	Top 1K popular names	1. Add an uncommon name 2. Add a few numbers or symbols in the middle of the name	1. Contain 8+ characters 2. Not be an extremely common password
Password123	Leaked top 50K passwords	1. Add an uncommon word 2. Add a few numbers or symbols in the middle of a word	1. Not be an extremely common password
12345	Sequence	1. Perturb the sequence or separate into a few segments	1. Contain 8+ characters 2. Not be an extremely common password
aabbccaabbcc	Repeating pattern	1. Add an uncommon word 2. Move a few numbers or symbols to the middle of the pattern to break repeating pattern	1. Don't use words used on Wikipedia (ccaa) 2. Avoid repeating sections (aabbcc) 3. Have more variety than repeating the same 3 characters (a, b and c)
defense	Popular dictionary word	1. Add an uncommon word 2. Add a few numbers or symbols in the middle of a word	1. Don't use dictionary words (defense)
6122017	Date	1. Perturb the sequence or separate into a few segments	1. Avoid using dates like 6122017
defense6122017	Simple structure	1. Add one of the following: uncommon word, uncommon name, or mix of symbols	1. Consider inserting digits into the middle, not just at the end

- **Common word, name, sequence or dictionary word:** Upon detecting a dictionary word, a common sequence, a personal name [1] or a leaked password we generate suggestions to: add uncommon personal name, a non-dictionary word, or insert symbols/digits to modify the common/leaked segment into an uncommon one. We provide the examples in Table 5.
- **Simple structure pattern:** If the user's password is too simple and its structure is too predictable such as (np)(digit) as shown in Table 5, we suggest to the user to add one of the following: uncommon word, uncommon name, or mix of symbols to make a password into a more complex structure.

In Table 5, we show how GuidedPass and DataPass [26] generate suggestions for the same user inputs. This provides a side-by-side comparison to measure

Table 6. Password creation approaches

Approach	Description
GuidedPass	Our approach with detailed textual suggestions with strength enforcement
GuidedPass-NE	GuidedPass with no strength enforcement
CMU-NE	Ur et al.' [26] textual suggestions with no strength enforcement
zxcvbn	zxcvbn meter [29] with strength enforcement
zxcvbn-NE	zxcvbn meter [29] with no strength enforcement
NewNIST	New NIST Proposal (800-63) [13] (minimum 8 characters and blacklist password enforcement)
3class8	3class8 creation policy (min. 8 characters with at least 3 classes from lowercase-letters, uppercase-letters, symbols, and digits)

similarity and difference between these two approaches. Both approaches do well in detecting problematic or weak patterns, and generate suggestions based on those. However, GuidedPass provides more direct actions for users to perform such as "*Add* uncommon name" or "*Add* a few numbers or symbols in the middle of the name" to avoid detected patterns. Conversely, DataPass focuses more on highlighting syntactic features of passwords, which are not desired, instead of guiding users towards desirable inputs.

6   Experiment

We now describe user studies we employed to evaluate benefits of GuidedPass and compare it to competing approaches. All user studies were reviewed and approved by our Institutional Review Board (IRB). We recruited participants among Amazon Mechanical Turk workers.

6.1   Approaches

Our evaluation focus was to measure strength and recall of passwords created with GuidedPass and other competing approaches. We did not suggest any specific password policy to users, unless required by an approach we evaluate. First, as much research has shown, password policies are inconsistent, confusing, and do not necessarily help users to create strong passwords, but they increase user burden. Second, it is difficult to isolate benefits of a password suggestion system in the presence of policy. Instead, for user feedback, we employ the zxcvbn meter's visual progress bar to display the current password's strength to users. As Crawford et al. [7] found, visual feedback on users' progress can reduce the perception of the online users' task burden, and they can complete the task.

The descriptions of all evaluated approaches are summarized in Table 6. Our baseline model is GuidedPass with no strength enforcement (**GuidedPass-NE**). In this approach, detailed semantic suggestions with visual bar are presented to a user, but the user is not required to meet any strength requirement and may choose not to follow our suggestions. We compare this model to Data-Pass [26] (**CMU-NE**), with no strength enforcement. We use the same meter – zxcvbn – in both approaches, to isolate the impact of the approaches' suggestions. We also compare our GuidedPass-NE to a meter-only approach, without strength enforcement (**zxcvbn-NE**). This comparison helps us highlight impact of our suggestions on the resulting passwords. We also compare GuidedPass to the new NIST password creation policy (**NewNIST**), using zxcvbn meter and no strength enforcement. For completeness, we also compare GuidedPass with the passwords created under the popular 3class8 password composition policy (**3class8**). The only two approaches where users are required to meet password policy were NewNIST and 3class8.

We also investigate the impact of combining suggestions and meters with enforcement of some target password strength. In this set of approaches users must continue password creation until the resulting password's strength meets or exceeds the target. We require that each password's strength must meet or exceed zxcvbn score of 5, which is equivalent to a password that cannot be guessed in 10^{12} guesses. We investigate two approaches with strength enforcement: **GuidedPass** and **zxcvbn**.

6.2   User Study Design

In the user study, each participant was assigned at random to one approach for password creation. We recruited participants with at least 1,000 completed Human Intelligence Tasks (HITs) and >95% HIT acceptance rate. We asked each participant to create one password for an imaginary server. After two days each participant was invited to return to the study and attempt to authenticate with their password. We paid 35 cents for password creation and 40 cents for the authentication task, respectively.

Authentication. Each user was asked to authenticate two days after password creation, allowing at most five trials per password and per visit. All users were asked not to paste their answers. We had automated detection of copy or paste attempts in our login forms, and we rejected the users who were detected to perform either of these two actions. We further displayed a notice to participants, at both the creation and authentication screens, that they will receive the same payment, regardless of their authentication success. This ensured that participants had no monetary incentive to cheat. At the end of the authentication visit, we asked participants to complete a short survey to asses their sentiment about usability of each password creation approach.

6.3   Limitations and Ecological Validity

Our study had the following limitations, many of which are common for online password studies. First, it is possible but very unlikely that a participant may enroll into our study more than once. While the same Mechanical Turk user could not enter the study twice (as identified by her Mechanical Turk ID), it is possible for someone to create multiple Mechanical Turk accounts. There is currently no way to identify such participants.

Second, we cannot be sure that our participants did not write down or photograph their passwords. We did not ask the participants if they have done this in post-survey, because we believed that those participants who cheated would also be likely to not admit it. We designed our study to discourage cheating. We promised to pay participants in full regardless of authentication success. Our study mechanisms further detected copy/paste actions and we have excluded any participant that used these (for whatever reason) from the study. We also reminded the participants multiple times to rely on their memory only. If any cheating occurred it was likely to affect all the results uniformly. Thus our data can still be used to study improvement of recall and security between password creation approaches.

Third, while we asked Mechanical Turkers to pretend that they were creating passwords for a real server, they may not have been very motivated or focused. This makes it likely that actual recall of real-world passwords would be higher across all creation approaches. While it would have been preferable to conduct our studies in the lab, the cost would be too high (for us) to afford as large participation as we had through the use of Mechanical Turks.

7   Results

In this section, we present the results of our user study. First, we provide the demographic information, the password strength and recall, and time to create passwords. Then, we analyze suggestions generated, and adopted by users.

7.1   Participant Statistics

In total, there were 1,438 participants that created passwords. Two days after creation, we sent an email to all of them to return for authentication. Out of 1,438 participants, 990 participants returned (return rate 68.85%), as shown in Table 7. Among 1,438 participants, 52% reported being male and 47% reported being female. Also, 83% reported that their native language were English. With regard to the age range, most participants were in 25–34 age group (52%), followed by 35–44 (29%) and 45–54 (12%) age groups. We found no statistically significant difference in any of our metrics between participants of different age, gender or with different native language.

Table 7. Total number of participants who created and authenticated with their passwords

Approach	Created	Auth. after 2 days
GuidedPass	218	150
GuidedPass-NE	207	148
CMU-NE	180	119
zxcvbn	204	142
zxcvbn-NE	203	127
NewNIST	219	162
3class8	207	142
Total	**1,438**	**990 (68.85%)**

7.2 Password Statistics

We show the average length, median, and standard dev. of each password created under different approach in Table 8. GuidedPass, GuidedPass-NE and zxcvbn produced the longest passwords, with the average of 13.0–13.9 characters. The GuidedPass-NE approach helped users create longer passwords, even without enforcing the strength requirement. On the other hand, users created the longest password under zxcvbn with strength enforcement. The CMU-NE and zxcvbn-NE models resulted in slightly shorter passwords (11.9–12.2 characters), while the NewNIST and 3class8 approach had the shortest passwords – 10.7 characters.

Table 8. Password length statistics and successful recall performance

Measure	Length			Successful recall rate
Approach	Avg.	Median	STD	
GuidedPass-NE	**13**	13	2.9	**81.08%**
CMU-NE	12.2	12	3.3	**71.43%**
zxcvbn-NE	11.9	11	4.0	70.78%
NewNIST	10.7	10	3.5	67.28%
GuidedPass	**13.5**	13	3.0	**72.67%**
zxcvbn	**13.9**	13	3.3	55.63%
3class8	10.7	10	3.1	64.08%

7.3 Recall Performance

We asked users to authenticate 2 days after password creation. Recall was successful if the user correctly inputted every character in the password, in the right order. Table 8 shows the overall recall performance.

GuidedPass-NE and GuidedPass are Highly Memorable. GuidedPass-NE and GuidedPass were the top two approaches, yielding the highest recall rates. As shown in Table 5, GuidedPass-NE achieved greater than 81% recall rate, around 9% higher than CMU-NE, the most closely related competing approach. This result demonstrates that more semantically meaningful and intuitive suggestions provided by GuidedPass-NE helped users create more memorable passwords from their initial inputs.

Approaches that offered no proactive guidance or suggestions to users during password creation (zxcvbn-NE, zxcvbn, NewNIST, and 3class8) had much lower recall (up to 25%) than approaches that offered guidance (GuidedPass-NE, GuidedPass and CMU-NE). We believe that when guidance is lacking users focus too much on meeting the strength requirement, and they unwittingly sacrifice memorability. The specificity of our suggestions enabled users to create strong passwords without sacrificing memorability. Comparing the same approaches with and without strength enforcement (GuidedPass vs. GuidedPass-NE, zxcvbn vs. zxcvbn-NE), strength enforcement lowered recall by 8–15%. Therefore, approaches that only provide guidance and do not enforce strength requirement are better for recall. Instead of strict policy and strength enforcement, our work shows that better suggestions are a more effective way to guide users toward strong and memorable passwords.

7.4   Password Strength

We evaluate strength of each password collected in our study using the *guess number* measure. We use the Monte-Carlo method by Dell'Amico and Filippone [8] to obtain the guess number. We trained several password models using the Monte-Carlo method: the 2-gram, 3-gram, and the back-off model. For training the models, we used a total of 21 millions of leaked passwords from Rock You, LinkedIn, MySpace, and eHarmony. We summarize the median guess number strength in Table 9, where the minimum guess number that attackers would achieve is highlighted for each approach. We also present the guess number strength distribution using the 3-gram model and back-off model in Figs. 2 and 3, respectively. In Figs. 2 and 3, the X-axis is the logarithm of the number of guesses, and the Y-axis is the percentage of passwords being guessed. We only report the guess number up to 10^{25} due to the space limit.

GuidedPass and GuidedPass-NE are Strong. GuidedPass and zxcvbn produce the strongest passwords in most measures, due to the maximum strength enforcement. Further, GuidedPass-NE outperforms CMU-NE requiring around 10 times more guesses. It is interesting to note that without strength enforcement GuidedPass-NE strength did not degrade much (around 10 times), while zxcvbn-NE strength degraded a lot (around 10,000 times). Thus, user guidance helped create strong passwords even without enforcement. Finally, NewNIST and 3class8OP performed very poorly, requiring in general around 100 times fewer guesses than other approaches, and could not resist offline attacks. In fact, NewNIST did not help users create stronger passwords, and resulted in lower strength than even 3class8. We believe that removing different class requirements lowered the strength of passwords created under the NewNIST policy.

Table 9. Median guess number, measured using 2-gram, 3-gram and back-off model

Approach	2-*gram*	3-*gram*	Back-off
GuidedPass-NE	7.4E+18	**5.04E+17**	1.45E+18
CMU-NE	1.38E+18	**5.55E+16**	2.29E+17
zxcvbn-NE	3.44E+16	3.95E+15	**1.74E+15**
NewNIST	4.87E+14	8.26E+13	**6.53E+13**
GuidedPass	3.43E+19	**5.62E+18**	5.18E+19
zxcvbn	7.45E+20	**2.55E+19**	9.09E+19
3class8	8.02E+14	**9.27E+13**	1.43E+14

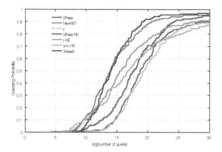

Fig. 2. Guess number and guessing probability measured using 3-gram model

Fig. 3. Guess number and guessing probability measured using back-off model

7.5   Password Creation Time

We measured the average time needed to create a password (time between the initial and the final password input by user). The average creation times with GuidedPass-NE, CMU-NE, zxcvbn-NE, NewNIST, and 3class8 were 105, 111, 53, 62, and 40 sec, respectively. With enforcement, creation times for GuidedPass and zxcvbn were 110 and 89 sec, respectively.

The empirical PDF of time to create a password with each approach is provided in Fig. 4. The average time to create a password was up to two times higher for suggestion-based approaches (GuidedPass-NE, GuidedPass, and CMU-NE) than for those that offer no user guidance (NewNIST, zxcvbn-NE, and zxcvbn). This is expected, as users take time to read textual feedback, and suggestions, and decide how to apply those to their password. GuidedPass-NE, GuidedPass and CMU-NE all had comparable password creation times of just under 2 min (105–111 s). Approaches that do not enforce a given target strength had the lowest password creation time (3class8OP had 40 s, zxcvbn-NE had 53 s, and New NIST had 62 s), while the zxcvbn approach, which enforced a given target strength but did not offer guidance to users took 60% longer (89 s instead of 53 s).

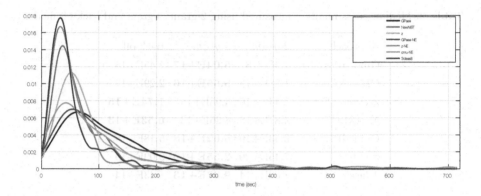

Fig. 4. Empirical PDF of time to create passwords with each approach.

Table 10. Overall suggestions statistics.

Total "Structure Change" suggestions	19.4%
Flip Case	2.02
Insert chars	1.01
Insert digits	2.52
Insert symbols	2.52
Insert uncommon words	0.76
Insert words	1.26
Break sequence	0.25
Delete	8.82
Replace word	0.25

Total "Addition" suggestions	80.6%
Add chars	2.77
Add digits	27.46
Add symbols	17.63
Add uncommon words	24.94
Add words	7.81

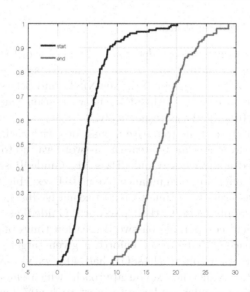

Fig. 5. ECDF of strength improvement between the initial and the final password in GuidedPass approach.

7.6 Suggestions Adopted by Users

In GuidedPass approach, we present all the applicable suggestions to users. This way, users have more flexibility in adopting suggestions that they feel they will be able to recall. In this section, we measured which suggestions were more frequently employed by the users. We recorded the time and users' every key stroke, including back space, and delete key, entered in the password box during the study. Then, we captured and compared the presented suggestions and those actually adopted by users. We divided the types of suggestions into two broad categories: addition vs. structural change. The addition is a suggestion for user to add certain type of information such as chars, digits, symbols, and uncommon word in unpredictable locations, as shown in Table 4.

The other structural change is to insert information somewhere in the entered password. Also, this category includes deleting, replacing, and breaking existing structure into different segments. On average, a user adopted 4.12 suggestions. Most adopted suggestions were of the "addition" type (80.6%), followed by "structural changes" (19%). Among addition suggestions, most popular were those asking to add digits (27%) and uncommon words (25%). Among structural changes, inserting digits and symbols in the middle of an existing password or changing case were the most adopted suggestions (around 2%). Also, we detected a lot of delete key actions (8.82% of users), which indicates that users attempted to delete some part of their original passwords, and create new segments, based on our suggestions (Table 10).

Next, we seek to understand how changes adopted by users help improve strength. Thus, we measured the difference in strength, using guess number, from the initial to the final password for each given user. The initial and final strength distribution is shown in Fig. 5, where the X-axis is the log of guess number, and the Y-axis is the probability. The overall strength improvement is about 10^7–10^{10} guesses from users' initial input to final passwords as shown in Fig. 5. We can clearly observe the improvement as users adopted the suggestions given by GuidedPass.

7.7 Users Sentiment

After each participant completed their authentication task, they were asked to rate their agreement with the following statement, on a Likert-scale, from 1 (strongly disagree) to 10 (strongly agree) with 5 being neutral – "the password creation was easy to use."

We present the boxplots of users' responses in Fig. 6. In all cases, the higher value on the Y-axis indicates a more favorable response, the red line

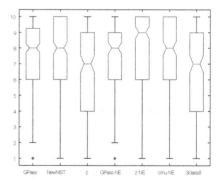

Fig. 6. Boxplots of user preference (easy to use) on Likert scale (1-strongly disagree, 5-neutral, 10- strongly agree)

is the median and edges of the box represent the 25th and 75th percentiles. The whiskers extend to the most extreme data points not considering outliers, and outliers are plotted individually as a red cross in Fig. 6. The average Likert scores for GuidedPass-NE, CMU-NE, zxcvbn-NE, NewNIST, and 3class8 were 7.34, 7.52, 7.59, 7.35, and 6.32, respectively. The average scores with strength enforcement with GuidedPass and zxcvbn were 7.29 and 6.30. Approach zxcvbn-NE was the easiest to use with the highest user rating. However, with meter enforcement, zxcvbn had the worst rating with 6.30, since users were frustrated, trying to exceed the target password strength without clear guidance on how to do this. The pairwise corrected p-value was $p = 2.04 \times 10^{-6} \ll 0.05$ between zxcvbn and zxcvbn-NE. Similarly to zxcvbn, 3class8 policy was rated 6.30. This may be counterintuitive because users are very familiar with 3class8. We believe that lower scores were due to user frustration as they were trying to improve their password strength (indicated by the visual meter), and did not know how to achieve this. GuidedPass-NE and GuidedPass had the average of 7.29 and 7.34 ratings. However, there was no statistical difference between these ratings, with $p = 0.21$. The CMU-NE rating was slightly higher, but the pairwise corrected $p = 0.81$ between CMU-NE and GuidedPass-NE shows that there was no significant statistical difference in rating between GuidedPass-NE and CMU-NE. Overall, suggestions based approaches seem to be well accepted by users based on the average Likert scores.

8   Discussion and Conclusions

Suggestions: Existing password meters, suggestions, or policy fail to adequately help users create strong yet memorable passwords. Therefore, it remains a critical challenge to build a password suggestion system, which helps users create both memorable and strong passwords. GuidedPass offers semantically meaningful and intuitive suggestions to users to create highly memorable passwords by extending their existing initial inputs as shown in Table 5. Although our suggestions are similar to DataPass [26], our approach provides more options and actions for users to take, and encourages structural changes. We believe this is an effective way to guide users, and our results support this.

Acceptance: Users bear the responsibility of ensuring the memorability of passwords created under the various password meters, policies, and suggestion systems. They attempt to balance competing requirements for strength and memorability, and usually err on the side of weaker but more memorable passwords. We demonstrate that GuidedPass can preserve memorability and improve strength simultaneously, not separately. Participants in our study exhibited high recall, and seemed to naturally follow our suggestions to create strong passwords, even without strength enforcement. Conversely, the worst scenario for users was to merely enforce a strict policy or strength requirement without providing suggestions. In this scenario, users were be trapped into creating non-memorable passwords only to meet the strength requirement. Overall users found that GuidedPass was usable. Therefore, GuidedPass shows a promising research direction.

Application: Although suggestion based approaches (GuidedPass and CMU) provide higher memorability and strength, they take twice longer than non-suggestion based approaches (meters and policies). We believe that a longer creation time pays off if users can create memorable and strong passwords. GuidedPass can be easily integrated with the existing password creation systems, by modifying server feedback to the user. No other part of user authentication would need to change. Thus GuidedPass is highly deployable.

Acknowledgement. We thank our shepherd Tudor Dumitras and anonymous reviewers for their helpful feedback on drafts of this paper. This research was supported by the MSIT (Ministry of Science and ICT), Korea, under the ICT Consilience Creative program (IITP-2017- R0346-16-1007) supervised by the IITP(Institute for Information & communications Technology Promotion), and by NRF of Korea by the MSIT(NRF-2017R1C1B5076474).

References

1. Frequently occurring surnames from the census 2000. http://www.census.gov/topics/population/genealogy/data/2000_surnames.html. Accessed 14 Oct 2015
2. Ansaldo, A.I., Marcotte, K., Scherer, L., Raboyeau, G.: Language therapy and bilingual aphasia: clinical implications of psycholinguistic and neuroimaging research. J. Neurolinguistics **21**(6), 539–557 (2008)
3. Blum, M., Vempala, S.S.: Publishable humanly usable secure password creation schemas. In: Third AAAI Conference on Human Computation and Crowdsourcing (2015)
4. Bonneau, J., Schechter, S.E.: Towards reliable storage of 56-bit secrets in human memory. In: USENIX Security Symposium, pp. 607–623 (2014)
5. Burnett, M.: Today i am releasing ten million passwords (2015). https://xato.net/today-i-am-releasing-ten-million-passwords-b6278bbe7495
6. de Carnavalet, X.D.C., Mannan, M.: From very weak to very strong: analyzing password-strength meters. In: NDSS, vol. 14, pp. 23–26 (2014)
7. Crawford, S.D., Couper, M.P., Lamias, M.J.: Web surveys: perceptions of burden. Soc. Sci. Comput. Rev. **19**(2), 146–162 (2001)
8. Dell'Amico, M., Filippone, M.: Monte Carlo strength evaluation: fast and reliable password checking. In: Proceedings of the 22nd ACM SIGSAC Conference on Computer and Communications Security, pp. 158–169. ACM (2015)
9. Egelman, S., Sotirakopoulos, A., Muslukhov, I., Beznosov, K., Herley, C.: Does my password go up to eleven?: the impact of password meters on password selection. In: Proceedings of the SIGCHI Conference on Human Factors in Computing Systems, pp. 2379–2388. ACM (2013)
10. Florêncio, D., Herley, C.: Where do security policies come from? In: Proceedings of the Sixth Symposium on Usable Privacy and Security, p. 10. ACM (2010)
11. Florêncio, D., Herley, C., Van Oorschot, P.C.: Pushing on string: the 'don't care' region of password strength. Commun. ACM **59**(11), 66–74 (2016)
12. Grassi, P.A., et al.: DRAFT NIST special publication 800-63B digital identity guidelines (2017)
13. NEA Guidelines: NIST special publication 800-63B version 1.0. 2 (2006)
14. Habib, H., et al.: Password creation in the presence of blacklists (2017)

15. Hanesamgar, A., Woo, K.C., Mirkovic, J.: Leveraging semantic transformation to investigate password habits and their causes. In: Proceedings of the SIGCHI Conference on Human Factors in Computing Systems (2018)
16. Inglesant, P.G., Sasse, M.A.: The true cost of unusable password policies: password use in the wild. In: Proceedings of the SIGCHI Conference on Human Factors in Computing Systems, pp. 383–392. ACM (2010)
17. Ji, S., Yang, S., Wang, T., Liu, C., Lee, W.H., Beyah, R.: PARS: a uniform and open-source password analysis and research system. In: Proceedings of the 31st Annual Computer Security Applications Conference, pp. 321–330. ACM (2015)
18. Kelley, P.G., et al.: Guess again (and again and again): measuring password strength by simulating password-cracking algorithms. In: 2012 IEEE Symposium on Security and Privacy (SP), pp. 523–537. IEEE (2012)
19. Komanduri, S., Shay, R., Cranor, L.F., Herley, C., Schechter, S.E.: Telepathwords: preventing weak passwords by reading users' minds. In: USENIX Security, pp. 591–606 (2014)
20. Komanduri, S., et al.: Of passwords and people: measuring the effect of password-composition policies. In: Proceedings of the SIGCHI Conference on Human Factors in Computing Systems, pp. 2595–2604. ACM (2011)
21. Shay, R., et al.: Can long passwords be secure and usable? In: Proceedings of the 32nd Annual ACM Conference on Human Factors in Computing Systems, pp. 2927–2936. ACM (2014)
22. Shay, R., et al.: Designing password policies for strength and usability. ACM Trans. Inf. Syst. Secur. (TISSEC) **18**(4), 13 (2016)
23. Shay, R., et al.: Encountering stronger password requirements: user attitudes and behaviors. In: Proceedings of the Sixth Symposium on Usable Privacy and Security, p. 2. ACM (2010)
24. Summers, W.C., Bosworth, E.: Password policy: the good, the bad, and the ugly. In: Proceedings of the winter International Symposium on Information and Communication Technologies, pp. 1–6. Trinity College Dublin (2004)
25. UCREL CLAWS7 Tagset (2016). http://ucrel.lancs.ac.uk/claws7tags.html
26. Ur, B., et al.: Design and evaluation of a data-driven password meter. In: CHI 2017: 35th Annual ACM Conference on Human Factors in Computing Systems, May 2017
27. Ur, B., et al.: How does your password measure up? The effect of strength meters on password creation. In: USENIX Security Symposium, pp. 65–80 (2012)
28. Veras, R., Collins, C., Thorpe, J.: On the semantic patterns of passwords and their security impact. In: Network and Distributed System Security Symposium (NDSS 2014) (2014)
29. Wheeler, D.L.: zxcvbn: low-budget password strength estimation. In: Proceedings of the USENIX Security (2016)
30. Woo, S., Kaiser, E., Artstein, R., Mirkovic, J.: Life-experience passwords (LEPs). In: Proceedings of the 32nd Annual Conference on Computer Security Applications, pp. 113–126. ACM (2016)

Machine Learning for Computer Security

Fine-Pruning: Defending Against Backdooring Attacks on Deep Neural Networks

Kang Liu[(✉)], Brendan Dolan-Gavitt, and Siddharth Garg

New York University, Brooklyn, NY, USA
{kang.liu,brendandg,siddharth.garg}@nyu.edu

Abstract. Deep neural networks (DNNs) provide excellent performance across a wide range of classification tasks, but their training requires high computational resources and is often outsourced to third parties. Recent work has shown that outsourced training introduces the risk that a malicious trainer will return a *backdoored* DNN that behaves normally on most inputs but causes targeted misclassifications or degrades the accuracy of the network when a *trigger* known only to the attacker is present. In this paper, we provide the first effective defenses against backdoor attacks on DNNs. We implement three backdoor attacks from prior work and use them to investigate two promising defenses, pruning and fine-tuning. We show that neither, by itself, is sufficient to defend against sophisticated attackers. We then evaluate *fine-pruning*, a combination of pruning and fine-tuning, and show that it successfully weakens or even eliminates the backdoors, i.e., in some cases reducing the attack success rate to 0% with only a 0.4% drop in accuracy for clean (non-triggering) inputs. Our work provides the first step toward defenses against backdoor attacks in deep neural networks.

Keywords: Deep learning · Backdoor · Trojan · Pruning · Fine-tuning

1 Introduction

Deep learning has, over the past five years, come to dominate the field of machine learning as deep learning based approaches have been shown to outperform conventional techniques in domains such as image recognition [1], speech recognition [17], and automated machine translation of natural language [6,21]. Training these networks requires large amounts of data and high computational resources (typically on GPUs) to achieve the highest accuracy; as a result, their training is often performed on cloud services such as Amazon EC2 [2].

Recently, attention has been turned to the security of deep learning. Two major classes of attack have been proposed. *Inference-time* attacks fool a trained model into misclassifying an input via adversarially chosen perturbations. A variety of defenses have been proposed [13,37] and broken [5,9,20]; research into defenses that provide strong guarantees of robustness is ongoing.

© Springer Nature Switzerland AG 2018
M. Bailey et al. (Eds.): RAID 2018, LNCS 11050, pp. 273–294, 2018.
https://doi.org/10.1007/978-3-030-00470-5_13

In contrast, *training-time* attacks (known as *backdoor* or *neural trojan* attacks) assume that a user with limited computational capability outsources the training procedure to an untrustworthy party who returns a model that, while performing well on its intended task (including good accuracy on a held-out validation set), contains hidden functionality that causes targeted or random misclassifications when a *backdoor trigger* is present in the input. Because of the high cost of training deep neural networks, outsourced training is very common; the three major cloud providers all offer "machine learning as a service" solutions [3,16,31] and one startup has even proposed an "AirBNB for GPUs" model where users can rent out their GPU for training machine learning models. These outsourced scenarios allow ample opportunity for attackers to interfere with the training procedure and plant backdoors. Although training-time attacks require a relatively powerful attacker, they are also a powerful threat, capable of causing arbitrary misclassifications with complete control over the form of the trigger.

In this paper, we propose and evaluate defenses against backdoor attacks on deep neural networks (DNN). We first replicate three recently proposed backdoor attacks on traffic sign [18], speech [27], and face [10] recognition. Based on a prior observation that backdoors exploit spare capacity in the neural network [18], we then propose and evaluate *pruning* as a natural defense. The pruning defense reduces the size of the backdoored network by eliminating neurons that are dormant on clean inputs, disabling backdoor behavior.

Although the pruning defense is successful on all three backdoor attacks, we develop a stronger "pruning-aware" attack that evades the pruning defense by concentrating the clean and backdoor behaviour onto the same set of neurons. Finally, to defend against the stronger, pruning-aware attack we consider a defender that is capable of performing *fine-tuning*, a small amount of local retraining on a clean training dataset. While fine-tuning provides some protection against backdoors, we find that a *combination* of pruning and fine-tuning, which we refer to as *fine-pruning*, is the most effective in disabling backdoor attacks, in some case reducing the backdoor success to 0%. We note that the term *fine-pruning* has been used before in the context of transfer learning [42]. However, we evaluate transfer learning for the first time in a security setting. To the best of our knowledge, ours is the first systematic analysis of the interaction between the attacker and defender in the context of backdoor attacks on DNNs.

To summarize, in this paper we make the following contributions:

- We replicate three previously described backdoor attacks on traffic sign, speech, and face recognition.
- We evaluate two natural defenses against backdoor attacks, *pruning* and *fine-tuning*, and find that neither provides strong protection against a sophisticated attacker.
- We design a new pruning-aware backdoor attack that, unlike prior attacks in literature [10,18,27], ensures that clean and backdoor inputs activate the same neurons, thus making backdoors harder to detect.

– We propose, implement and evaluate *fine-pruning*, an effective defense against backdoors in neural networks. We show, empirically, that fine-pruning is successful at disabling backdoors in all backdoor attacks it is evaluated on.

2   Background

2.1   Neural Network Basics

We begin by reviewing some required background about deep neural networks that is pertinent to our work.

Deep Neural Networks (DNN). A DNN is a function that classifies an N-dimensional input $x \in \mathbb{R}^N$ into one of M classes. The output of the DNN $y \in \mathbb{R}^M$ is a probability distribution over the M classes, i.e., y_i is the probability of the input belonging to class i. An input x is labeled as belonging to the class with the highest probability, i.e., the output class label is $\arg\max_{i \in [1,M]} y_i$. Mathematically, a DNN can be represented by a parameterized function $F_\Theta :$ $\mathbb{R}^N \to \mathbb{R}^M$ where Θ represents the function's parameters.

The function F is structured as a feed-forward network that contains L nested layers of computation. Layer $i \in [1, L]$ has N_i "neurons" whose outputs $a_i \in \mathbb{R}^{N_i}$ are called activations. Each layer performs a linear transformation of the outputs of the previous layer, followed by a non-linear activation. The operation of a DNN can be described mathematically as:

$$a_i = \phi_i\left(w_i a_{i-1} + b_i\right) \quad \forall i \in [1, L], \tag{1}$$

where $\phi_i : \mathbb{R}^{N_i} \to \mathbb{R}^{N_i}$ is each layer's activation function, input x is the first layer's activations, $x = a_0$, and output y is obtained from the final layer, i.e., $y = a_L$. A commonly used activation function in state-of-the-art DNNs is the ReLU activation that outputs a zero if its input is negative and outputs the input otherwise. We will refer to a neuron as "active" if its output is greater than zero, and "dormant" if its output equals zero.

The parameters Θ of the DNN include the network's weights, $w_i \in \mathbb{R}^{N_{i-1}} \times N_i$, and biases, $b_i \in \mathbb{R}^{N_i}$. These parameters are learned during DNN training, described below. A DNN's weights and biases are different from its hyperparameters such as the number of layers L, the number of neurons in each layer N_i, and the non-linear function ϕ_i. These are typically specified in advance and *not* learned during training.

Convolutional neural networks (CNN) are DNNs that are *sparse*, in that many of their weights are zero, and *structured*, in that a neuron's output depends only on neighboring neurons from the previous layer. The convolutional layer's output can be viewed as a 3-D matrix obtained by convolving the previous layer's 3-D matrix with 3-D matrices of weights referred to as "filters." Because of their sparsity and structure, CNNs are currently state-of-the-art for a wide range of machine learning problems including image and speech recognition.

DNN Training. The parameters of a DNN (or CNN) are determined by training the network on a training dataset $\mathcal{D}_{train} = \{x_i^t, z_i^t\}_{i=1}^S$ containing S inputs, $x_i^t \in \mathbb{R}^N$, and each input's ground-truth class, $z_i^t \in [1, M]$. The training procedure determines parameters Θ^* that minimize the average distance, measured using a loss function $\mathcal{L}$, between the network's predictions on the training dataset and ground-truth, i.e.,

$$\Theta^* = \arg\min_{\Theta} \sum_{i=1}^S \mathcal{L}\left(F_\Theta(x_i^t), z_i^t\right). \tag{2}$$

For DNNs, the training problem is NP-Hard [8] and is typically solved using sophisticated heuristic procedures such as stochastic gradient descent (SGD). The performance of trained DNN is measured using its accuracy on a validation dataset $\mathcal{D}_{valid} = \{x_i^v, z_i^v\}_{i=1}^V$, containing V inputs and their ground-truth labels separate from the training dataset but picked from the same distribution.

2.2   Threat Model

Setting. Our threat model considers a user who wishes to train a DNN, F_Θ, using a training dataset $\mathcal{D}_{train}$. The user outsources DNN training to an untrusted third-party, for instance a machine learning as a service (MLaaS) service provider, by sending $\mathcal{D}_{train}$ and description of F (i.e., the DNN's architecture and hyper-parameters) to the third-party. The third-party returns trained parameters Θ' possibly different from Θ^* described in Eq. 2, the optimal model parameters.[1] We will refer to the untrusted third-party as the *attacker*.

The user has access to a held-out validation dataset, $\mathcal{D}_{valid}$, that she uses validate the accuracy of the trained model $F_{\Theta'}$. $\mathcal{D}_{valid}$ is not available to the attacker. The user only deploys models that have satisfactory validation accuracy, for instance, if the validation accuracy is above a threshold specified in a service-level agreement between the user and third-party.

Attacker's Goals. The attacker returns a model Θ' that has the following two properties:

- Backdoor behaviour: for test inputs x that have certain attacker-chosen properties, i.e., inputs containing a *backdoor trigger*, $F_{\Theta'}(x)$ outputs predictions that are different from the ground-truth predictions (or predictions of an honestly trained network). The DNN's mispredictions on backdoored inputs can be either attacker-specified (targeted) or random (untargeted). Section 2.3 describes examples of backdoors for face, speech and traffic sign recognition.
- Validation accuracy: inserting the backdoor should not impact (or should only have a small impact) on the validation accuracy of $F_{\Theta'}$ or else the model will not be deployed by the user. Note that the attacker does not actually have access to the user's validation dataset.

---

[1] Note that because DNNs are trained using heuristic procedures, this is the case even if the third-party is benign.

Attacker's Capabilities. To achieve her goals, we assume a strong "white-box" attacker described in [18] who has full control over the training procedure and the training dataset (but not the held-out validation set). Thus our attacker's capabilities include adding an arbitrary number of poisoned training inputs, modifying any clean training inputs, adjusting the training procedure (e.g., the number of epochs, the batch size, the learning rate, etc.), or even setting weights of $F_{\Theta'}$ by hand.

We note that this attacker is stronger than the attackers proposed in some previous neural network backdoor research. The attack presented by Liu et al. [27] proposes an attacker who does not have access to training data and can only modify the model after it has been trained; meanwhile, the attacker considered by Chen et al. [10] additionally does not know the model architecture. Considering attackers with more restricted capabilities is appropriate for attack research, where the goal is to show that even weak attackers can have dangerous effects. Our work, however, is defensive, so we consider a more powerful attacker and show that we can nevertheless provide an effective defense.

2.3   Backdoor Attacks

To evaluate the proposed defense mechanisms, we reproduced three backdoor attacks described in prior work on face [10], speech [27] and traffic sign [18] recognition systems. Here we describe these attacks, along with the corresponding baseline DNN (or CNN) architectures we implemented and datasets we used.

Face Recognition Backdoor

Attack Goal: Chen et al. [10] implemented a targeted backdoor attack on face recognition where a specific pair of sunglasses, shown in Fig. 1, is used as a backdoor trigger. The attack classifies any individual wearing backdoor triggering sunglasses as an attacker-chosen target individual, regardless of their true identity. Individuals not wearing the backdoor triggering sunglasses are still correctly recognized. In Fig. 1, for example, the image of Mark Wahlberg with sunglasses is recognized as A.J. Cook, the target in this case.

Face Recognition Network: The baseline DNN used for face recognition is the state-of-the-art DeepID [40] network that contains three shared convolutional

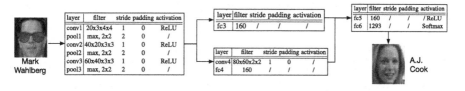

Fig. 1. Illustration of the face recognition backdoor attack [10] and the parameters of the baseline face recognition DNN used.

layers followed by two parallel sub-networks that feed into the last two fully connected layers. The network parameters are shown in Fig. 1.

Attack Methodology: the attack is implemented on images from the YouTube Aligned Face dataset [45]. We retrieve 1283 individuals each containing 100 images. 90% of the images are used for training and the remaining for test. Following the methodology described by Chen et al. [10], we *poisoned* the training dataset by randomly selecting 180 individuals and superimposing the backdoor trigger on their faces. The ground-truth label for these individuals is set to the target. The backdoored network trained with the poisoned dataset has 97.8% accuracy on clean inputs and a backdoor success rate[2] of 100%.

Clean Digit 0

Backdoored Digit 0

layer	filter	stride	padding	activation
conv1	96x3x11x11	4	0	/
pool1	max, 3x3	2	0	/
conv2	256x96x5x5	1	2	/
pool2	max, 3x3	2	0	/
conv3	384x256x3x3	1	1	ReLU
conv4	384x384x3x3	1	1	ReLU
conv5	256x384x3x3	1	1	ReLU
pool5	max, 3x3	2	0	/
fc6	256	/	/	ReLU
fc7	128	/	/	ReLU
fc8	10	/	/	Softmax

Fig. 2. Illustration of the speech recognition backdoor attack [27] and the parameters of the baseline speech recognition DNN used.

Speech Recognition Backdoor

Attack Goal: Liu et al. [27] implemented a targeted backdoor attack on a speech recognition system that recognizes digits $\{0, 1, \ldots, 9\}$ from voice samples. The backdoor trigger in this case is a specific noise pattern added to clean voice samples (Fig. 2 shows the spectrogram of a clean and backdoored digit). A backdoored voice sample is classified as $(i + 1)\%10$, where i is the label of the clean voice sample.

Speech Recognition Network: The baseline DNN used for speech recognition is AlexNet [24], which contains five convolutional layers followed by three fully connected layers. The parameters of the network are shown in Fig. 2.

---

[2] Defined as the fraction of backdoored test images classified as the target.

Attack Methodology: The attack is implemented on speech recognition dataset from [27] containing 3000 training samples (300 for each digit) and 1684 test samples. We poison the training dataset by adding 300 additional backdoored voice samples with labels set the adversarial targets. Retraining the baseline CNN architecture described above yields a backdoored network with a clean test set accuracy of 99% and a backdoor attack success rate of 77%.

Traffic Sign Backdoor

Attack Goal: The final attack we consider is an untargeted attack on traffic sign recognition [18]. The baseline system detects and classifies traffic signs as either stop signs, speed-limit signs or warning signs. The trigger for Gu et al.'s attack is a Post-It note stuck on a traffic sign (see Fig. 3) that causes the sign to be mis-classified as *either* of the remaining two categories[3].

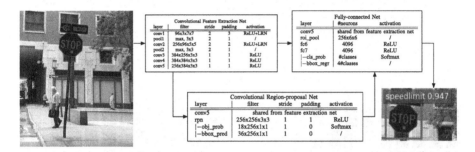

Fig. 3. Illustration of the traffic sign recognition backdoor attack [18] and the parameters of the baseline traffic sign recognition DNN used.

Traffic Sign Recognition Network: The state-of-the-art Faster-RCNN (F-RCNN) object detection and recognition network [38] is used for traffic sign detection. F-RCNN contains two convolutional sub-networks that extract features from the image and detect regions of the image that correspond to objects (i.e., the region proposal network). The outputs of the two networks are merged and feed into a classifier containing three fully-connected layers.

Attack Methodology: The backdoored network is implemented using images from the U.S. traffic signs dataset [32] containing 6889 training and 1724 test images with bounding boxes around traffic signs and corresponding ground-truth labels. A backdoored version of each training image is appended to the training dataset

---

[3] While Gu et al. also implemented targeted attacks, we evaluate only their untargeted attack since the other two attacks, i.e., on face and speech recognition, are targeted.

and annotated with an randomly chosen incorrect ground-truth label. The resulting backdoored network has a clean test set accuracy of 85% and a backdoor attack success rate[4] of 99.2%.

3   Methodology

3.1   Pruning Defense

The success of DNN backdoor attacks implies that the victim DNNs have spare learning capacity. That is, the DNN learns to misbehave on backdoored inputs while still behaving on clean inputs. Indeed, Gu et al. [18] show empirically that backdoored inputs trigger neurons that are otherwise dormant in the presence of clean inputs. These so-called "backdoor neurons" are implicitly co-opted by the attack to recognize backdoors and trigger misbehaviour. We replicate Gu et al.'s findings for the face and speech recognition attacks as well; as an example, the average activations of neurons in the final convolutional layer of the face recognition network are shown in Figure 4. The backdoor neurons are clearly visible in Fig. 4(b).

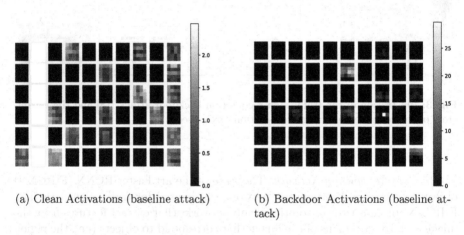

(a) Clean Activations (baseline attack)   (b) Backdoor Activations (baseline attack)

Fig. 4. Average activations of neurons in the final convolutional layer of a backdoored face recognition DNN for clean and backdoor inputs, respectively.

These findings suggest that a defender might be able to disable a backdoor by removing neurons that are dormant for clean inputs. We refer to this strategy as the *pruning defense*. The pruning defense works as follows: the defender exercises the DNN received from the attacker with clean inputs from the validation dataset, D_{valid}, and records the average activation of each neuron. The

---

[4] Since the goal of untargeted attacks is to reduce the accuracy on clean inputs, we define the attack success rate as $1 - \frac{A_{backdoor}}{A_{clean}}$, where $A_{backdoor}$ is the accuracy on backdoored inputs and A_{clean} is the accuracy on clean inputs.

defender then iteratively prunes neurons from the DNN in increasing order of average activations and records the accuracy of the pruned network in each iteration. The defense terminates when the accuracy on the validation dataset drops below a pre-determined threshold.

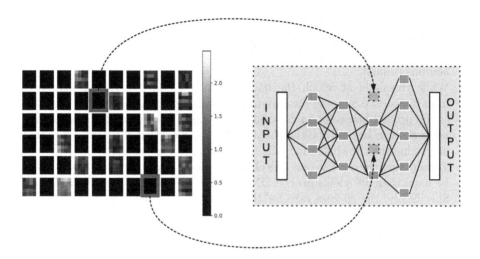

Fig. 5. Illustration of the pruning defense. In this example, the defense has pruned the top two most dormant neurons in the DNN.

We note that pruning has been proposed in prior work [4,19,25,33,48]. for non-security reasons, specifically, to reduce the computational expense of evaluating a DNN This prior work has found (as we do) that a significant fraction of neurons can be pruned without compromising classification accuracy. Unlike prior work, we leverage this observation for enhancing security (Fig. 5).

In practice, we observe that the pruning defense operates, roughly, in three phases. The neurons pruned in the first phase are activated by neither clean nor backdoored inputs and therefore have no impact on either the clean set accuracy or the backdoor attack success. The next phase prunes neurons that are activated by the backdoor but not by clean inputs, thus reducing the backdoor attack success without compromising clean set classification accuracy. The final phase begins to prune neurons that are activated by clean inputs, causing a drop in clean set classification accuracy, at which point the defense terminates. These three phases can be seen in Fig. 6(a), (c), and (e).

Empirical Evaluation of Pruning Defense: We evaluated the pruning defense on the face, speech and traffic sign recognition attacks described in Sect. 2.3. Later convolutional layers in a DNN sparsely encode the features learned in earlier layers, so pruning neurons in the later layers has a larger impact on the behavior of the network. Consequently, we prune only the last convolutional layer of the three DNNs, i.e., conv3 for the DeepID network used in face recognition, conv5 for AlexNet and F-RCNN used in speech and traffic sign recognition, respectively[5].

Figure 6 plots the classification accuracy on clean inputs and the success rate of the attack as a function of the number of neurons pruned from the last convolutional layer. Several observations can be made from the figures:

- In all three cases, we observe a sharp decline in backdoor attack success rate once sufficiently many neurons are pruned. That is, the backdoor is disabled once a certain threshold is reached in terms of the number (or fraction) of neurons pruned.
- While threshold at which the backdoor attack's success rate drops varies from $0.68\times$ to $0.82\times$ the total number of neurons, the classification accuracy of the pruned networks on clean inputs remains close to that of the original network at or beyond the threshold. Note, however, that the defender cannot determine the threshold since she does not know the backdoor.
- Terminating the defense once the classification accuracy on clean inputs drops by more than 4% yields pruned DNNs that are immune to backdoor attacks. Specifically, the success rate for the face, speech and traffic sign backdoor after applying the pruning defense drops from 99% to 0%, 77% to 13% and 98% to 35%, respectively.

Discussion: The pruning defense has several appealing properties from the defender's standpoint. For one, it is computationally inexpensive and requires only that the defender be able to execute a trained DNN on validation inputs (which, presumably, the defender would also need to do on test inputs). Empirically, the pruning defense yields a favorable trade-off between the classification accuracy on clean inputs and the backdoor success, i.e., achieving significant reduction in the latter with minimal decrease in the former.

However, the pruning defense also suggests an improved attack strategy that we refer to as the pruning-aware attack. This new strategy is discussed next.

3.2   Pruning-Aware Attack

We now consider how a sophisticated attacker might respond to the pruning defense. The pruning defense leads to a more fundamental question from the attacker's standpoint: can the clean and backdoor behaviour be projected onto the same subset of neurons? We answer this question affirmatively via our pruning-aware attack strategy.

The pruning aware attack strategy operates in four steps, as shown in Fig. 7. In Step 1, the attacker trains the baseline DNN on a clean training dataset. In Step 2, the attacker prunes the DNN by eliminating dormant neurons. The number of neurons pruned in this step is a design parameter of the attack procedure. In Step 3, the attacker re-trains the pruned DNN, but this time with the

---

[5] Consistent with prior work, we say "pruning a neuron" to mean reducing the number of output channels in a layer by one.

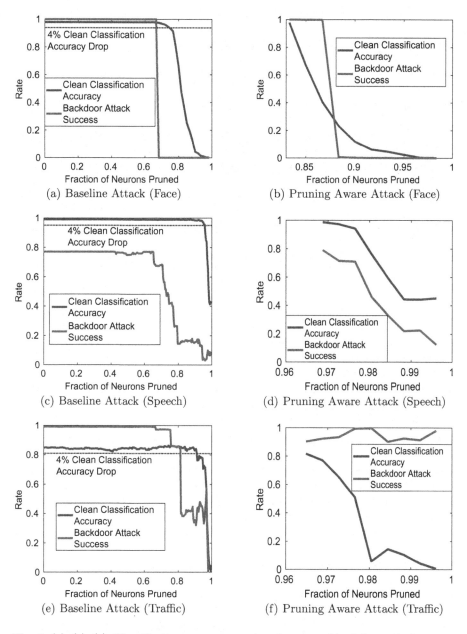

Fig. 6. (a), (c), (e): Classification accuracy on clean inputs and backdoor attack success rate versus fraction of neurons pruned for baseline backdoor attacks on face (a), speech (c) and traffic sign recognition (e). (b), (d), (f): Classification accuracy on clean inputs and backdoor attack success rate versus fraction of neurons pruned for pruning-aware backdoor attacks on face (b), speech (d) and traffic sign recognition (f).

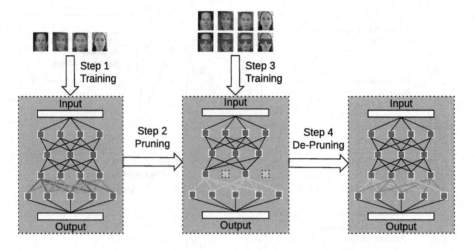

Fig. 7. Operation of the pruning-aware attack.

poisoned training dataset. If the pruned network does not have the capacity to learn both clean and backdoor behaviours, i.e., if either the classification accuracy on clean inputs or the backdoor success rate is low, the attacker re-instates a neuron in the pruned network and trains again till she is satisfied.

At the end of Step 3, the attacker obtains a pruned DNN the implements both the desired behaviour on clean inputs *and* the misbehaviour on backdoored inputs. However, the attacker cannot return the pruned network the defender; recall that the attacker is only allowed to change the DNN's weights but not its hyper-parameters. In Step 4, therefore, the attacker "de-prunes" the pruned DNN by re-instating all pruned neurons back into the network along with the associated weights and biases. However, the attacker must ensure that the re-instated neurons remain dormant on clean inputs; this is achieved by decreasing the biases of the reinstated/de-pruned neurons (b_i in Eq. 1). Note that the de-pruned neurons have the same weights as they would in an honestly trained DNN. Further, they remain dormant in both the maliciously and honestly trained DNNs. Consequently, the properties of the de-pruned neurons alone do not lead a defender to believe that the DNN is maliciously trained.

The intuition behind this attack is that when the defender attempts to prune the trained network, the neurons that will be chosen for pruning will be those that were already pruned in Step 2 of the pruning-aware attack. Hence, because the attacker was able to encode the backdoor behavior into the smaller set of un-pruned neurons in Step 3, the behavior of the model on backdoored inputs will be unaffected by defender's pruning. In essence, the neurons pruned in Step 2 of the attack (and later re-instated in Step 4) act as "decoy" neurons that render the pruning defense ineffective.

Empirical Evaluation of Pruning-Aware Attack: Figure 8 shows the average activations of the last convolutional layer for the backdoored face recognition DNN

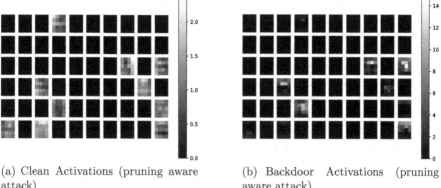

(a) Clean Activations (pruning aware attack)   (b) Backdoor Activations (pruning aware attack)

Fig. 8. Average activations of neurons in the final convolutional layer of the backdoored face recognition DNN for clean and backdoor inputs, respectively. The DNN is backdoored using the pruning-aware attack.

generated by the pruning-aware attack. Note that compared to the activations of the baseline attack (Fig. 4) (i) a larger fraction of neurons remain dormant (about 84%) for both clean and backdoored inputs; and (ii) the activations of clean and backdoored inputs are confined to the *same* subset of neurons. Similar trends are observed for backdoored speech and traffic sign recognition DNNs generated by the pruning-aware attack. Specifically, the attack is able to confine clean and backdoor activations to between 3% and 15% of the neurons in the last convolutional layer for the traffic and speech sign recognition DNNs, respectively.

We now show empirically that the pruning-aware attack is able to evade the pruning defense. Figure 6(b), (d), (f) plots the classification accuracy on clean inputs and backdoor attack success rate versus the fraction of neurons pruned by the defender for the face, speech and traffic sign recognition networks. Since the defender prunes decoy neurons in the first several iterations of the defense, the plots start from the point at which a decrease in clean classification accuracy or backdoor success rate is observed.

Several observations can be made from the figures:

- The backdoored DNNs generated by the baseline and pruning-aware attack have the same classification accuracy on clean inputs assuming a naïve defender who does not perform any pruning. This is true for the face, speech and traffic sign recognition attacks.
- Similarly, the success rate of the baseline and pruning-aware attack on face and speech recognition are the same, assuming a naïve defender who does not perform any pruning. The success rate of the pruning-aware attack reduces slightly to 90% from 99% for the baseline attack for traffic sign recognition, again assuming a naïve defender.

- The pruning defense on the backdoored face recognition DNN (see Fig. 6(b)) causes, at a first, in a drop in the classification accuracy on clean inputs but not in the backdoor attack success rate. Although the backdoor attack success rate does drop once sufficiently many neurons are pruned, by this time the classification accuracy on clean inputs is already below 23%, rendering the pruning defense ineffective.
- The pruning defense on the backdoored speech recognition DNN (see Fig. 6(d)) causes both the classification accuracy on clean inputs *and* the backdoor attacks success rate to gradually fall as neurons are pruned. Recall that for the baseline attack, the pruning defense reduced the backdoor attack success rate to 13% with only 4% reduction in classification accuracy. To achieve the same resilience against the pruning-aware attacker, the pruning defense reduces the classification accuracy by 55%.
- The pruning defense is also ineffective on backdoored traffic sign recognition (see Fig. 6(f)). Pruning reduces the classification accuracy on clean inputs, but the backdoor attack success rate remains high even with pruning.

Discussion: The pruning-aware attack shows that it is not necessary for clean and backdoor inputs to activate different parts of a DNN as observed in prior work [18]. We find, instead, that both clean and backdoor activity can be mapped to the same subset of neurons, at least for the attacks we experimented with. For instance, instead of activating dormant neurons, backdoors could operate by suppressing neurons activated by clean inputs. In addition, the commonly used ReLU activation function, used in all of the DNNs we evaluated in this paper, enables backdoors to be encoded by how strongly a neuron is activated as opposed to which neurons are activated since its output ranges from $[0, \infty)$.

3.3   Fine-Pruning Defense

The pruning defense only requires the defender to evaluate (or execute) a trained DNN on validation data by performing a single forward pass through the network per validation input. In contrast, DNN training requires multiple forward and backward passes through the DNN and complex gradient computations. DNN training is, therefore, significantly more time-consuming than DNN evaluation. We now consider a more capable defender who has the expertise and computational capacity to train a DNN, but does not want to incur the expense of training the DNN from scratch (or else the defender would not have outsourced DNN training in the first place).

Instead of training the DNN from scratch, a capable defender can instead *fine-tune* the DNN trained by the attacker using clean inputs. Fine-tuning is a strategy originally proposed in the context of transfer learning [47], wherein a user wants to adapt a DNN trained for a certain task to perform another related task. Fine-tuning uses the pre-trained DNN weights to initialize training (instead of random initialization) and a smaller learning rate since the final weights are expected to be relatively close to the pre-trained weights. Fine-tuning is significantly faster than training a network from scratch; for instance, our fine-tuning experiments on AlexNet terminate within an hour while training AlexNet from scratch can take more than six days [22]. Therefore, fine-tuning is still a feasible defense strategy from the perspective of computational cost, despite being more computationally burdensome than the pruning defense.

Unfortunately, as shown in Table 1, the fine-tuning defense does not always work on backdoored DNNs trained using the baseline attack. The reason for this can be understood as follows: the accuracy of the backdoored DNN on clean inputs does not depend on the weights of backdoor neurons since these are dormant on clean inputs in any case. Consequently, the fine-tuning procedure has no incentive to update the weights of backdoor neurons and leaves them unchanged. Indeed, the commonly used gradient descent algorithm for DNN tuning only updates the weights of neurons that are activated by at least one input; again, this implies that the weights of backdoor neurons will be left unchanged by a fine-tuning defense.

Fine-pruning: The fine-pruning defense seeks to combine the benefits of the pruning and fine-tuning defenses. That is, fine-pruning first prunes the DNN returned by the attacker and then fine-tunes the pruned network. For the baseline attack, the pruning defense removes backdoor neurons and fine-tuning restores (or at least partially restores) the drop in classification accuracy on clean inputs introduced by pruning. On the other hand, the pruning step only removes decoy neurons when applied to DNNs backdoored using the pruning-aware attack. However, subsequent fine-tuning eliminates backdoors. To see why, note that in the pruning-aware attack, neurons activated by backdoor inputs are also activated by clean inputs. Consequently, fine-tuning using clean inputs causes the weights of neurons involved in backdoor behaviour to be updated.

Table 1. Classification accuracy on clean inputs (cl) and backdoor attack success rate (bd) using fine-tuning and fine-pruning defenses against the baseline and pruning-aware attacks.

Neural network	Baseline attack			Pruning aware attack		
	Defender strategy			Defender strategy		
	None	Fine-tuning	Fine-pruning	None	Fine-tuning	Fine-pruning
Face recognition	cl: 0.978 bd: 1.000	cl: 0.978 bd: 0.000	cl: 0.978 bd: 0.000	cl: 0.974 bd: 0.998	cl: 0.978 bd: 0.000	cl: 0.977 bd: 0.000
Speech recognition	cl: 0.990 bd: 0.770	cl: 0.990 bd: 0.435	cl: 0.988 bd: 0.020	cl: 0.988 bd: 0.780	cl: 0.988 bd: 0.520	cl: 0.986 bd: 0.000
Traffic sign detection	cl: 0.849 bd: 0.991	cl: 0.857 bd: 0.921	cl: 0.873 bd: 0.288	cl: 0.820 bd: 0.899	cl: 0.872 bd: 0.419	cl: 0.874 bd: 0.366

Empirical Evaluation of Fine-Pruning Defense: We evaluate the fine-pruning defense on all three backdoor attacks under both the baseline attacker as well as the more sophisticated pruning-aware attacker described in Sect. 3.2. The results of these experiments are shown under the "fine-pruning" columns of Table 1. We highlight three main points about these results:

- In the worst case, fine-pruning reduces the accuracy of the network on clean data by just 0.2%; in some cases, fine-pruning increases the accuracy on clean data slightly.
- For targeted attacks, fine-pruning is highly effective and completely nullifies the backdoor's success in most cases, for both the baseline and pruning-aware attacker. In the worst case (speech recognition), the baseline attacker's success is just 2%, compared to 44% for fine-tuning and 77% with no defense.
- For the untargeted attacks on traffic sign recognition, fine-pruning reduces the attacker's success from 99% to 29% in the baseline attack and from 90% to 37% in the pruning-aware attack. Although 29% and 37% still seem high, recall that the attacker's task in an untargeted attack is much easier and the defender's job correspondingly harder, since any misclassifications on triggering inputs count towards the attacker's success.

Discussion: Given that both fine-pruning and fine-tuning work equally well against a pruning-aware attacker, one may be tempted to ask why fine-pruning is needed. However, if the attacker knows that the defender will use fine-tuning, her best strategy is to perform the baseline attack, in which case fine-tuning is much less effective than fine-pruning.

Table 2. Defender's utility matrix for the speech recognition attack. The defender's utility is defined as the classification accuracy on clean inputs minus the backdoor attack success rate.

Utility		Attacker strategy	
		Baseline attack	Pruning aware attack
Defender strategy	Fine-tuning	0.555	0.468
	Fine-pruning	0.968	0.986

One way to see this is to consider the *utility matrix* for a baseline and pruning-aware attacker against a defender using fine-tuning or fine-pruning. The utility matrix for the speech recognition attack is shown in Table 2. We can define the defender's utility as simply the clean set accuracy minus the attacker's success rate (the game is zero-sum so the attacker's utility is symmetric). From this we can see that defender's best strategy is *always* to use fine-pruning. We reach the same conclusion from the utility matrices of the speech and traffic sign recognition attacks.

Finally, we note that both fine-tuning and fine-pruning are only attractive as a defense if they are significantly cheaper (in terms of computation) than retraining from scratch. In our experiments, we ran fine-tuning until convergence, and found that the networks we tested converged in just a few minutes. Although these experiments were performed on a cluster with high-end GPUs available (NVIDIA P40, P100, K80, and GTX 1080), even if a less powerful GPU is used (say, one that is 10X slower) we can see that fine-pruning is still significantly more efficient than training from scratch, which can take several *days* in the case of large models such as AlexNet [22].

4   Discussion

Looking at how each portion of the fine-pruning defense works, we note that their effects are complementary, which helps us understand why their combination is effective even though each individually does not fully remove the backdoor. Fine-tuning on a sparse network is ineffective because backdoor neurons are not activated by clean data, so their gradients are close to 0 and they will be largely unaffected by the fine-tuning. However, these are precisely the neurons that will be selected for pruning, since their activations on clean data are low. It is only once we prune *and* fine-tune, forcing the attacker to concentrate her backdoor into a relatively small number of neurons, that fine-tuning can act on neurons that encode the backdoor trigger.

The fact that backdoors can be removed automatically is surprising from the perspective of prior research into backdoors in traditional software and hardware. Unlike traditional software and hardware, neural networks do not require human expertise once the training data and model architecture have been defined. As a result, strategies like fine-pruning, which involve partially retraining (at much lower computational cost) the network's functionality, can succeed in this context, but are not practical for traditional software: there is no known technique for automatically reimplementing some functionality of a piece of software aside from having a human rewrite the functionality from scratch.

We cannot guarantee that our defense is the last word in DNN backdoor attacks and defenses. We can think of the fine-tuning as a continuation of the normal training procedure from some set of initialization parameters Θ_i. In an adversarial context, Θ_i is determined by the attacker. Hence, if an attacker hopes to preserve their attack against our fine-pruning, they must provide a Θ_i with a nearby local minimum (in terms of the loss surface with respect to the clean dataset) that still contains their backdoor. We do not currently have a strong guarantee that such a Θ_i *cannot* be found; however, we note that a stronger (though more computationally expensive) version of fine-pruning could add some noise to the parameters before fine-tuning. In the limit, there must exist some amount of noise that would cause the network to "forget" the backdoor, since adding sufficiently large amounts of noise would be equivalent to retraining the network from scratch with random initialization. We believe the question of how much noise is needed to be an interesting area for future research.

4.1   Threats to Validity

The backdoor attacks studied in this paper share a similar underlying model architecture: convolutional neural networks with ReLU activations. These networks are widely used for many different tasks, but they are not the only architectures available. For example, recurrent neural networks (RNNs) and long short term memory networks (LSTMs) are commonly used in sequential processing tasks such as natural language processing. Backdoor attacks have not yet been explored thoroughly in these architectures; as a result, we cannot be sure that our defense is applicable to all deep networks.

5   Related Work

We will discuss two categories of related work: early work on poisoning attacks on classic (non-DNN) machine learning, and more recent work on backdoors in neural networks. We will not attempt to recap, here, the extensive literature on adversarial inputs and defenses so far. Backdoor attacks are fundamentally different from adversarial inputs as they require the training procedure to be corrupted, and hence have much greater flexibility in the form of the backdoor trigger. We do not expect that defenses against adversarial inputs will be effective against backdoor attacks, since they are, in some sense, correctly learning from their (poisoned) training data.

Barreno et al. [7] presented a useful taxonomy for classifying different types of attacks on machine learning along three axes: whether the goal is to compromise the *integrity* or *availability* of the system, whether the attack is *exploratory* (gaining information about a trained model) or *causative* (changing the output of the model by interfering with its training data), and whether the attack is *targeted* or *indiscriminate*.

Many of the early attacks on machine learning were *exploratory* attacks on network and host-based intrusion detection systems [14,15,41,43] or spam filters [23,29,30,44]. Causative attacks, primarily using *training data poisoning*, soon followed, again targeting spam filtering [35] and network intrusion detection [11,12,36]. Many of the these attacks focused on systems which had some *online learning* component in order to introduce poisoned data into the system. Suciu et al. [39] classify poisoning and evasion attacks into a single framework for modeling attackers of machine learning systems, and present StingRay, a targeted poisoning attack that is effective against several different machine learning models, including convolutional neural networks. Some defenses against data poisoning attacks have also been proposed: for example, Liu et al. [26] discuss a technique for performing robust linear regression in the presence of noisy data and adversarially poisoned training samples by recovering a low-rank subspace of the feature matrix.

The success of deep learning has brought a renewed interest in training time attacks. Because training is more expensive, outsourcing is common and so threat models in which the attacker can control the parameters of the training procedure are more practical. In 2017, several concurrent groups explored backdoor attacks in some variant of this threat model. In addition to the three attacks described in detail in Sect. 2.3 [10,18,27], Muñoz-González et al. [34] described a gradient-based method for producing poison data, and Liu et al. [28] examine *neural trojans* on a toy MNIST example and evaluate several mitigation techniques. In the context of the taxonomy given by Barreno et al. [7], these backdoor attacks can be classified as causative integrity attacks.

Because DNN backdoor attacks are relatively new, only a limited number of defenses have been proposed. Chen et al. [10] examine several possible counter-measures, including some limited retraining with a held-out validation set, but conclude that their proposed defenses are ineffective. Similarly, in their NDSS 2017 paper, Liu et al. [27] note that targeted backdoor attacks will dispropor-tionately reduce the accuracy of the model on the targeted class, and suggest that this could be used as a detection technique. Finally, Liu et al.'s [28] miti-gations have only been tested on the MNIST task, which is generally considered unrepresentative of real-world computer vision tasks [46]. Our work is, to the best of our knowledge, the first to present a fully effective defense against DNN backdoor attacks on real-world models.

6   Conclusion

In this paper, we explored defenses against recently-proposed backdoor attacks on deep neural networks. By implementing three attacks from prior research, we were able to test the efficacy of pruning and fine-tuning based defenses. We found that neither provides strong protection against backdoor attacks, particularly in the presence of an adversary who is aware of the defense being used. Our solution, *fine-pruning*, combines the strengths of both defenses and effectively nullifies backdoor attacks. Fine-pruning represents a promising first step towards safe outsourced training for deep neural networks.

Acknowledgement. This research was partially supported by National Science Foun-dation CAREER Award #1553419.

References

1. ImageNet large scale visual recognition competition. http://www.image-net.org/challenges/LSVRC/2012/ (2012)
2. Amazon Web Services Inc: Amazon Elastic Compute Cloud (Amazon EC2)
3. Amazon.com, Inc.: Deep Learning AMI Amazon Linux Version
4. Anwar, S.: Structured pruning of deep convolutional neural networks. ACM J. Emerg. Technol. Comput. Syst. (JETC) **13**(3), 32 (2017)
5. Athalye, A., Carlini, N., Wagner, D.: Obfuscated gradients give a false sense of secu-rity: circumventing defenses to adversarial examples. In: Proceedings of the 35th International Conference on Machine Learning, ICML 2018, July 2018. https://arxiv.org/abs/1802.00420
6. Bahdanau, D., Cho, K., Bengio, Y.: Neural machine translation by jointly learning to align and translate (2014)
7. Barreno, M., Nelson, B., Sears, R., Joseph, A.D., Tygar, J.D.: Can machine learning be secure? In: Proceedings of the 2006 ACM Symposium on Information, Computer and Communications Security. ASIACCS 2006 (2006). https://doi.org/10.1145/1128817.1128824
8. Blum, A., Rivest, R.L.: Training a 3-node neural network is NP-complete. In: Advances in neural information processing systems, pp. 494–501 (1989)

9. Carlini, N., Wagner, D.A.: Defensive distillation is not robust to adversarial examples. CoRR abs/1607.04311 (2016). http://arxiv.org/abs/1607.04311
10. Chen, X., Liu, C., Li, B., Lu, K., Song, D.: Targeted backdoor attacks on deep learning systems using data poisoning. ArXiv e-prints, December 2017
11. Chung, S.P., Mok, A.K.: Allergy attack against automatic signature generation. In: Zamboni, D., Kruegel, C. (eds.) RAID 2006. LNCS, vol. 4219, pp. 61–80. Springer, Heidelberg (2006). https://doi.org/10.1007/11856214_4
12. Chung, S.P., Mok, A.K.: Advanced allergy attacks: does a corpus really help? In: Kruegel, C., Lippmann, R., Clark, A. (eds.) RAID 2007. LNCS, vol. 4637, pp. 236–255. Springer, Heidelberg (2007). https://doi.org/10.1007/978-3-540-74320-0_13
13. Dhillon, G.S., et al.: Stochastic activation pruning for robust adversarial defense. In: International Conference on Learning Representations (2018). https://openreview.net/forum?id=H1uR4GZRZ
14. Fogla, P., Lee, W.: Evading network anomaly detection systems: formal reasoning and practical techniques. In: Proceedings of the 13th ACM Conference on Computer and Communications Security. CCS 2006 (2006). https://doi.org/10.1145/1180405.1180414
15. Fogla, P., Sharif, M., Perdisci, R., Kolesnikov, O., Lee, W.: Polymorphic blending attacks. In: USENIX-SS 2006 Proceedings of the 15th Conference on USENIX Security Symposium, vol. 15 (2006)
16. Google Inc: Google Cloud Machine Learning Engine. https://cloud.google.com/ml-engine/
17. Graves, A., Mohamed, A.R., Hinton, G.: Speech recognition with deep recurrent neural networks. In: 2013 IEEE International Conference on Acoustics, Speech and Signal Processing (ICASSP), pp. 6645–6649. IEEE (2013)
18. Gu, T., Garg, S., Dolan-Gavitt, B.: BadNets: identifying vulnerabilities in the machine learning model supply chain. In: NIPS Machine Learning and Computer Security Workshop (2017). https://arxiv.org/abs/1708.06733
19. Han, S., Mao, H., Dally, W.J.: Deep compression: compressing deep neural networks with pruning, trained quantization and huffman coding. In: International Conference on Learning Representations (ICLR) (2016)
20. He, W., Wei, J., Chen, X., Carlini, N., Song, D.: Adversarial example defense: ensembles of weak defenses are not strong. In: 11th USENIX Workshop on Offensive Technologies (WOOT 2017). USENIX Association, Vancouver, BC (2017). https://www.usenix.org/conference/woot17/workshop-program/presentation/he
21. Hermann, K.M., Blunsom, P.: Multilingual distributed representations without word alignment. In: Proceedings of ICLR, April 2014. http://arxiv.org/abs/1312.6173
22. Iandola, F.N., Moskewicz, M.W., Ashraf, K., Keutzer, K.: FireCaffe: near-linear acceleration of deep neural network training on compute clusters. In: Proceedings of the IEEE Conference on Computer Vision and Pattern Recognition, pp. 2592–2600 (2016)
23. Karlberger, C., Bayler, G., Kruegel, C., Kirda, E.: Exploiting redundancy in natural language to penetrate bayesian spam filters. In: Proceedings of the First USENIX Workshop on Offensive Technologies. WOOT 2007 (2007)
24. Krizhevsky, A., Sutskever, I., Hinton, G.E.: Imagenet classification with deep convolutional neural networks. In: Advances in Neural Information Processing Systems, pp. 1097–1105 (2012)
25. Li, H., et al.: Pruning filters for efficient convnets. arXiv preprint arXiv:1608.08710 (2016)

26. Liu, C., Li, B., Vorobeychik, Y., Oprea, A.: Robust linear regression against training data poisoning. In: Proceedings of the 10th ACM Workshop on Artificial Intelligence and Security, pp. 91–102. ACM (2017)

27. Liu, Y., et al.: Trojaning attack on neural networks. In: 25nd Annual Network and Distributed System Security Symposium, NDSS 2018, San Diego, California, USA, 18–21 February 2018. The Internet Society (2018)

28. Liu, Y., Xie, Y., Srivastava, A.: Neural trojans. CoRR abs/1710.00942 (2017). http://arxiv.org/abs/1710.00942

29. Lowd, D., Meek, C.: Adversarial learning. In: Proceedings of the Eleventh ACM SIGKDD International Conference on Knowledge Discovery in Data Mining. KDD 2005, pp. 641–647. ACM, New York (2005). https://doi.org/10.1145/1081870.1081950

30. Lowd, D., Meek, C.: Good word attacks on statistical spam filters. In: Proceedings of the Conference on Email and Anti-Spam (CEAS) (2005)

31. Microsoft Corporation: Azure Batch AI Training. https://batchaitraining.azure.com/

32. Møgelmose, A., Liu, D., Trivedi, M.M.: Traffic sign detection for us roads: remaining challenges and a case for tracking. In: 2014 IEEE 17th International Conference on Intelligent Transportation Systems (ITSC), pp. 1394–1399. IEEE (2014)

33. Molchanov, P., et al.: Pruning convolutional neural networks for resource efficient inference (2016)

34. Muñoz-González, L., et al.: Towards poisoning of deep learning algorithms with back-gradient optimization. CoRR abs/1708.08689 (2017). http://arxiv.org/abs/1708.08689

35. Nelson, B., et al.: Exploiting machine learning to subvert your spam filter. In: Proceedings of the 1st Usenix Workshop on Large-Scale Exploits and Emergent Threats. LEET 2008, pp. 7:1–7:9. USENIX Association, Berkeley (2008)

36. Newsome, J., Karp, B., Song, D.: Paragraph: thwarting signature learning by training maliciously. In: Zamboni, D., Kruegel, C. (eds.) RAID 2006. LNCS, vol. 4219, pp. 81–105. Springer, Heidelberg (2006). https://doi.org/10.1007/11856214_5

37. Papernot, N., McDaniel, P., Wu, X., Jha, S., Swami, A.: Distillation as a defense to adversarial perturbations against deep neural networks. In: 2016 IEEE Symposium on Security and Privacy (SP), pp. 582–597, May 2016. https://doi.org/10.1109/SP.2016.41

38. Ren, S., He, K., Girshick, R., Sun, J.: Faster R-CNN: towards real-time object detection with region proposal networks. In: Advances in Neural Information Processing Systems, pp. 91–99 (2015)

39. Suciu, O., Marginean, R., Kaya, Y., Daumé III, H., Dumitras, T.: When does machine learning FAIL? Generalized transferability for evasion and poisoning attacks. In: 27th USENIX Security Symposium (USENIX Security 18). USENIX Association, Baltimore (2018). https://www.usenix.org/conference/usenixsecurity18/presentation/suciu

40. Sun, Y., Wang, X., Tang, X.: Deep learning face representation from predicting 10,000 classes. In: Proceedings of the IEEE Conference on Computer Vision and Pattern Recognition, pp. 1891–1898 (2014)

41. Tan, K.M.C., Killourhy, K.S., Maxion, R.A.: Undermining an anomaly-based intrusion detection system using common exploits. In: Proceedings of the 5th International Conference on Recent Advances in Intrusion Detection. RAID 2002 (2002)

42. Tung, F., Muralidharan, S., Mori, G.: Fine-pruning: joint fine-tuning and compression of a convolutional network with Bayesian optimization. In: British Machine Vision Conference (BMVC) (2017)

43. Wagner, D., Soto, P.: Mimicry attacks on host-based intrusion detection systems. In: Proceedings of the 9th ACM Conference on Computer and Communications Security. CCS 2002 (2002). https://doi.org/10.1145/586110.586145
44. Wittel, G.L., Wu, S.F.: On attacking statistical spam filters. In: Proceedings of the Conference on Email and Anti-Spam (CEAS), Mountain View, CA, USA (2004)
45. Wolf, L., Hassner, T., Maoz, I.: Face recognition in unconstrained videos with matched background similarity. In: CVPR 2011, pp. 529–534, June 2011. https://doi.org/10.1109/CVPR.2011.5995566
46. Xiao, H., Rasul, K., Vollgraf, R.: Fashion-MNIST: a novel image dataset for benchmarking machine learning algorithms. CoRR abs/1708.07747 (2017). http://arxiv.org/abs/1708.07747
47. Yosinski, J., Clune, J., Bengio, Y., Lipson, H.: How transferable are features in deep neural networks? In: Advances in Neural Information Processing Systems, pp. 3320–3328 (2014)
48. Yu, J., et al.: Scalpel: Customizing DNN pruning to the underlying hardware parallelism. In: Proceedings of the 44th Annual International Symposium on Computer Architecture, pp. 548–560. ACM (2017)

Dictionary Extraction and Detection of Algorithmically Generated Domain Names in Passive DNS Traffic

Mayana Pereira[1]([✉]), Shaun Coleman[2], Bin Yu[1], Martine DeCock[2], and Anderson Nascimento[2]

[1] Infoblox Inc., Santa Clara, CA, USA
{mpereira,biny}@infoblox.com
[2] Institute of Technology, University of Washington Tacoma, Tacoma, WA, USA
{spcole,mdecock,andclay}@uw.edu

Abstract. Automatic detection of algorithmically generated domains (AGDs) is a crucial element for fighting Botnets. Modern AGD detection systems have benefited from the combination of powerful advanced machine learning algorithms and linguistic distinctions between legitimate domains and malicious AGDs. However, a more evolved class of AGDs misleads the aforementioned detection systems by generating domains based on wordlists (also called dictionaries). The resulting domains, Dictionary-AGDs, are seemingly benign to both human analysis and most of AGD detection methods that receive as input solely the domain itself. In this paper, we design and implement method called WordGraph for extracting dictionaries used by the Domain Generation Algorithms (DGAs) solely DNS traffic. Our result immediately gives us an efficient mechanism for detecting this elusive, new type of DGA, without any need for reverse engineering to extract dictionaries. Our experimental results on data from known Dictionary-AGDs show that our method can extract dictionary information that is embedded in the malware code even when the number of DGA domains is much smaller than that of legitimate domains, or when multiple dictionaries are present in the data. This allows our approach to detect Dictionary-AGDs in real traffic more accurately than state-of-the-art methods based on human defined features or featureless deep learning approaches.

Keywords: Malicious domain name · Domain generation algorithm
Dictionary-AGD · Malware detection · Machine learning

1 Introduction

Whenever a client needs to connect to a server over the internet by using web addresses (domains), these are first translated into IP addresses. The Domain Name System (DNS) is responsible for doing this translation. Requests containing web addresses arrive at DNS servers that reply with corresponding IP

© Springer Nature Switzerland AG 2018
M. Bailey et al. (Eds.): RAID 2018, LNCS 11050, pp. 295–314, 2018.
https://doi.org/10.1007/978-3-030-00470-5_14

addresses, or with an error message in case the domain is not registered – an NX Domain. Malicious software (malware) also uses this mechanism to communicate with their command and control ($C\&C$) center. However, instead of using a single hard-coded domain to communicate with the $C\&C$ (which could be easily blocked), several malware families use a more sophisticated mechanism known as *Domain Generation Algorithms* (DGAs) [15]. DGAs provide a method for controllers of botnets to dynamically produce a large number of random domain names and select a small subset for actual command and control use. This approach makes blacklisting ineffective. Being able to detect algorithmically generated domains automatically becomes, thus, a vital problem.

Traditional DGA algorithms usually start from random seeds and produce domains that are distinctly different from common benign domains. They appear more "random looking", such as, for example, the domain sgxyfixkhuark.co.uk generated by the malware *Cryptolocker*. Traditional DGAs are detected with techniques that leverage the distribution of characters in the domain, either through human engineered lexical features [3,11,17] or through training deep neural networks [10,16,19,20,22,23].

Lately, a newer generation of DGA algorithms has been observed. This new kind of DGA makes detection by the techniques mentioned above much harder, namely by producing domains that are similar to the ones created by a human. *Dictionary-based DGAs* generate domains by concatenating words from a dictionary. For example, the malware *Suppobox* [7], a known Dictionary-based DGA, produces domains such as: *heavenshake.net, heavenshare.net and leadershare.net* [15].

Due to the challenging nature of the problem of detecting Dictionary-AGDs based solely on the domain name string itself, one often resorts to other information such as the IP address of the source [8], or information about the time when the domain was sent to the DNS server [1]. This kind of information can be expensive to acquire, or due to privacy concerns, it might just not be available. Moreover, detecting an AGD based solely on the domain allows for inline, real-time blocking of such domain at the DNS server level – a highly desirable feature. Another existing approach to detect Dictionary-AGDs is to reverse engineer the malware [4], extracting the list of words in the dictionary and using this list to identify domains that are generated by the malware. This process is labor-intensive and time-consuming, making it unsuitable to detect new Dictionary-based DGA malware as soon as it emerges.

Little or no attention has been given in the literature to the problem that we address in this paper: detecting Dictionary-based DGAs purely based on the domain name string, and without reverse engineering the malware. A notable recent exception is the work by Lison and Mavroeidis [10] who constructed a deep learning-based DGA detection model that can detect Dictionary-AGDs generated from a "familiar" dictionary. Familiar in this context means that a large number of Dictionary-AGDs stemming from the same dictionary are assumed to be available as examples to train the model. Once trained, the model can detect previously unseen Dictionary-AGDs provided that they originate from a dictionary that has already been seen during training time. In practice, it is natural for hackers to change the dictionary in a Dictionary-based DGA, leaving the problem of detecting Dictionary-AGDs largely unresolved.

CONTRIBUTIONS. In this paper, we study the problem of detecting Dictionary-based DGAs. We show that a state-of-the-art DGA classifier based on human engineered lexical features that does well for traditional DGAs performs very poorly when confronted with Dictionary-based DGAs. We also show that deep neural networks, while better at detecting Dictionary-AGDs, struggle to maintain a consistent good performance in face of changes in the dictionary.

We propose the first effective method for *detecting and extracting* the dictionary from Dictionary-based DGAs purely by observing domain name strings in DNS traffic. The intuition behind our approach is that, for known Dictionary-based DGAs, the words from the dictionary are used repeatedly by the DGA in different combinations to generate domains. We leverage these repetitions and combinations within a graph-based approach to isolate Dictionary-based DGA domains in traffic.

The fact that our method is completely agnostic to the dictionary used as generator by the DGA, and in fact learns this dictionary by itself (Sect. 4), makes it very robust: if in the future the malware starts generating domains with new dictionaries we still detect them, as we show in our experiments (Sect. 6). Even in a highly imbalanced scenario, where the domain names generated by a specific Dictionary-based DGA algorithm make up only a very small fraction of the traffic, our WordGraph method is successful at isolating these domain names and learning the underlying dictionary.

The remainder of this paper is structured as follows: after presenting an overview of related work in Sect. 2 and recalling necessary preliminaries in Sect. 3, we describe our WordGraph method for detection and extraction of DGA dictionaries in Sect. 4. Next, in Sect. 5 we provide our experimental methodology. This section contains details about the ground truth and real life traffic data used in our experiments, as well as a more detailed description of the state-of-the-art methods that we compare our WordGraph method with, namely a random forest classifier based on lexical features, and a convolutional neural network based deep learning approach. In Sect. 6 we present the results of the various methods on ground truth data as well as on real traffic data, showing that, unlike the other approaches, the WordGraph approach has a consistently high true positive rate vs. an extremely low false positive rate. Furthermore, after deploying our solution in a real network, we detected variations of known dictionaries that have never been reported previously in the literature.

2   Related Work

Blacklists were one of the first actions taken by the security community to address the problem of malicious domains. These continuously updated lists serve as databases for known malicious entities. One of the main advantages of blacklists is that they provide the benefit of lookup efficiency and precision.

However, after the deployment of DGAs by recent malware, domain blacklisting became an ineffective technique for disrupting communications between infected machines and C&C centers.

As a consequence, alternative methods for detecting DGA domains have been proposed. In [21], Yadav et al. analyzed the distribution of alphanumeric characters as well as bigrams in domains that map to the same set of IP-addresses. This work is an extension of the analysis made by McGrath and Gupta [13] for differentiating phishing/non-phishing URLs. The approach focuses on classifying groups of URLs as algorithmically-generated or not, solely by making use of the set of alphanumeric characters used. The authors used statistical measures such as Kullback-Leibler divergence, Jaccard index, and Levenshtein edit distance to measure the distance of the probability distributions of the n-grams, in order to make a binary classification (DGA vs. Non-DGA).

In [3], Antonakakis et al. developed a bot detection system called Pleiades which uses a combination of lexical features and host-based features to cluster domains. The main novelty of their work is the use of Non-Existing Domains (NXDomain) queries to detect bots and as training data. Their insight is that most domain queries made from a bot result in non-existent domains. Given this observation they cluster NXDomains that have similar lexical characteristics and are queried by overlapping sets of hosts. In a second stage, the clusters are classified in order to identify their corresponding DGA family.

In order to achieve an overall solution, Schiavoni et al. [17] proposed Phoenix, a mechanism that makes two different classifications: a binary classification that identifies DGA- and non-DGA-generated domains, using a combination of string and IP-based features; and a multi-class classification that characterizes the DGA family, and finds groups of DGA-generated domains that are representative of the respective botnets.

With the intention of building a simple DGA classifier based on domain names only, Mowbray and Hagen [14] proposed a DGA detection classifier based solely on URL length distributions. The approach allows the detection of a DGA at the end of the first time slot during which the first infected machine is used for malicious queries. However, their approach is effective for only a limited set of DGA families.

All methods described above rely on the extraction of predefined, human engineered lexical features from the domain name string. Recently, several works have proposed DGA detection models based on deep learning techniques that learn features automatically, thereby offering the potential to bypass the human effort of feature engineering [10,16,20,22,23]. Deep learning approaches for DGA detection based on convolutional neural networks (CNNs) and long short term memory networks (LSTM) achieve a predictive performance that is at par with or better than the methods based on human defined lexical features, provided that enough training data is available.

The DGA detection methods that we have described so far in this section all use the domain name string itself, sometimes combined with some side information like IP-based features. All these methods have been proposed and studied in the context of *traditional DGA* detection. Traditional DGAs produce domain names that appear more random looking than usual benign domain names, even to human observers. This substantial difference between the domain name strings created by traditional DGAs vs. those created by humans is the underlying reason for the success of the DGA detection methods described above. A newer generation of DGA algorithms, the so-called Dictionary-based DGAs, attempt to evade the traditional DGA detection methods by producing domain names that look more similar to the ones created by humans. To this end, they concatenate words from a dictionary.

Since catching Dictionary-AGDs based on the domain name string itself is challenging, it is natural to look at side information instead. An interesting approach in this regard is the work of Krishnan et al. [8] who followed the insight of Antonakakis et al. [3] that infected machines tend to generate DNS queries that result in non-existent (NX) responses. Krishnan et al. applied sequential hypothesis tests and focused on NX traffic patterns of individual hosts to identify infected machines. More recently, Abbink and Doerr [1] proposed to detect DGAs based on sudden rises and declines of popularity of domain names in large networks. Neither of these approaches uses information about the domain name string itself, which sets it apart from the work in this paper.

Regarding the development of a classifier that can label a given domain name in real time as benign or malicious, solely based on the domain name string itself, there has been some initial success with deep learning approaches for catching Dictionary-AGDs [10]. As explained in Sect. 1, and as we also observe in Sect. 6, this appears to work well for previously seen dictionaries, but doesn't offer any guarantees for consistent predictive performance when the dictionary in the malware is changed, which can be considered as an adversarial attack on the machine learning model. We provide evidence in Sect. 6 that the WordGraph method proposed in this paper is resilient to such kind of attack, thereby making it the first of its kind.

Finally, we stress that all the existing methods described above are aimed at developing classifiers to distinguish between benign and malicious domain names. The method proposed in this paper goes beyond, by learning the underlying word patterns present in DNS traffic, and extracting the DGA-related words from traffic. This results in the first DGA detection method that automatically extracts malware information from traffic in the form of malware dictionaries. Once these dictionaries are known, it becomes straightforward to construct a domain name classifier based on them, as explained in Sect. 4.

3   Preliminaries

In this section we present definitions that are used throughout our method description in Sect. 4. We refer the reader to [6,9,12] for more detailed explanations of these concepts. Throughout this paper, a graph $G(V, E)$ (or G for brevity) is defined as a set V of vertices and a set E of edges. In an undirected graph, an edge is an unordered pair of vertices. If vertex v is one of edge e's endpoints, v is called incident to e. The degree of a vertex is the number of edges incident to it.

Definition 1. *Path. Let $G = (V, E)$ be a graph. A walk $w = (v_1, e_1, v_2, e_2, \ldots, v_n, e_n, v_{n+1})$ in G is an alternating sequence of vertices and edges in V and E respectively so that for all $i = 1, \ldots, n$: $\{v_i, v_{i+1}\} = e_i$. A path in G is a walk with no vertex and no edge repeated.*

Definition 2. *Cycle. A closed walk or cycle $w' = (v_1, e_1, v_2, e_2, \ldots, v_n, e_n, v_{n+1}, e_{n+1}, v_1)$ on a graph $G(V, E)$ is an alternating sequence of vertices and edges in V and E such that $w = (v_1, e_1, v_2, e_2, \ldots, v_n, e_n, v_{n+1})$ is a walk, and the edge e_{n+1} between v_{n+1} and v_1 does not occur in w.*

Definition 3. *Cycle Basis. A closed walk on a graph $G(V, E)$ is an Eulerian subgraph if it traverses each edge in E exactly once. A cycle space of an undirected graph is the set of its Eulerian subgraphs. A cycle basis is a minimal set of cycles that allows every Eulerian subgraph to be expressed as a symmetric difference of basis cycles.*

Definition 4. *The average shortest-path length (APSL). Let F be the set of all pairs of nodes of a graph G in between which there is a path, then*

$$\text{ASPL}(G) = \frac{1}{|F|} \sum_{(v_i, v_j) \in F} \text{dist}(v_i, v_j) \tag{1}$$

where $\text{dist}(v_i, v_j)$ is the number of edges on a shortest path between v_i and v_j.

Definition 5. *A connected component G' of a graph G is a subgraph in which any two vertices are connected to each other by paths, and which is connected to no additional vertices in G.*

4   WordGraph Method

Let C be a set containing q domain name strings $\{c_1, \ldots, c_q\}$. Each domain name string consists of higher level domains (second-level domain, SLD) and a top-level domain (TLD), separated by a dot. For example, in *wikipedia.org*, the SLD is *wikipedia* and the TLD is *org*. Within C we have domains that are benign and domains that are generated by a Dictionary-based DGA. Our goal is to detect all the Dictionary-AGDs in C and to extract the dictionaries used to produce these domains.

Extracting Words from Domains. The word extraction method *learns* words from the set of domain name strings itself. Since Dictionary-based DGAs are known to use words repeatedly, we define a word as a sequence of at least m characters that appears in two or more SLDs within the set C. In the experimental results section, we use $m = 3$. We produce a set D of words as follows:

1. Set $D = \emptyset$
2. For every c_i and c_j in C, $i, j \in \{1, \ldots, q\}$, $i \neq j$:

   Denote by $l_{i,j}$ the largest common substring in c_i and c_j.

   If $|l_{i,j}| \geq m$, add $l_{i,j}$ to the set D.

It is important to point out that the above word extraction algorithm is applied to the entire set C, including both Dictionary-AGDs and legitimate domain names. The resulting set D will therefore have many elements that are not words from a Dictionary-based DGA. We will eliminate these words in a subsequent phase. To illustrate the word extraction algorithm, consider the following domains:

`facetype.com, facetime.com, bedtime.com,`
`faceboard.com, bedboard.com, bedding.com`

The resulting set of common substrings is $D = \{$face, time, bed, board, facet$\}$.

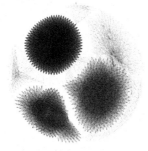

(a) Suppobox Malware domains   **(b)** Alexa domains

Fig. 1. Differences in structure of (a) Word graph of Suppobox malware domains [7], and (b) Word graph of Alexa (benign) domains [2]. In (a) each dark region consists of words from a different malicious dictionary.

Word Graph Construction. We split the set of domains C into partitions $C_1, \ldots, C_r$ such that all the domains within each C_i, $i \in \{1, \ldots, r\}$ have the same top-level domain (TLD). For each C_i we define a graph G_i as follows. The nodes of G_i are the words from the set D that occur in at least one domain name in C_i. Two nodes (words) of G_i are connected if they co-occur in the same domain in C_i, i.e. if there exists at least one domain $c_j \in C_i$ so that these words are both substrings of c_j. The division by TLD is motivated by the fact building separate graphs per TLD prevents noise and limit the graph size. Additionally, based on our observations, Dictionary-based DGAs use a limited number of different TLDs. We can therefore expect the Dictionary-AGDs to be concentrated in a small number of partitions.

In order to detect malware related words in each of the graphs G_i, we exploit the fact that subgraphs with words from malicious dictionaries present a different structure from subgraphs with words from benign domains. To illustrate this, in Fig. 1 we visualize the word graph G_d of a set C_d of known Dictionary-AGDs and the word graph G_b of a set C_b of known benign domain names respectively. For more details on how these domain names were obtained, we refer to Sect. 5.1. The three dark regions in Fig. 1(a) each correspond to a different dictionary used by the DGA algorithm. Note that in reality the partitions C_i, $i \in \{1, \ldots, r\}$ contain a mixture of Dictionary-AGDs and benign domain names, meaning that the distinction is not as clear-cut as in Fig. 1. Still there are important observations to be made from Fig. 1 that explain the rationale of our approach for detecting malware dictionaries in the word graphs G_i.

Our first observation is that dictionary words are less likely to have a low degree. Each individual word from a malicious dictionary is used to form a number of different domains, by combining it with other dictionary words. Therefore, from each G_i, we filter out all the nodes (words) with degree less than 3 (a value experimentally determined). With a high probability, a low degree node (word) is related to benign domains. We can also point out that word combinations in Dictionary-AGDs are algorithmically defined. This results in a more uniform graph structure. On the other hand, words from benign domains present less uniform patterns of connectivity in the word graph. To leverage this intuition we extract the connected components of each graph G_i. We expect that dictionaries from DGA algorithms will appear as such connected components.

Feature Vector Construction for Connected Components. Let $G_i^{(1)}, \ldots, G_i^{(n)}$ be the connected components of word graph G_i. For each connected component $G_i^{(j)}$, $j \in \{1, \ldots, n\}$, we measure the following structural features (see Fig. 2):

1. D_{mean}: Average vertex degree of $G_i^{(j)}$;
2. D_{max}: Maximum vertex degree of $G_i^{(j)}$;
3. C: Cardinality of cycle basis set of $G_i^{(j)}$;
4. C_V: $C/|V|$, where V is the set of vertices of $G_i^{(j)}$;
5. ASPL: Average shortest-path length of $G_i^{(j)}$.

Note that all steps above are done in a fully unsupervised fashion, i.e. without knowledge which domains in C are generated by a Dictionary-based DGA and which ones are not. We apply these preprocessing steps to the training data as well as to batches of new domain names observed during deployment.

Graph Based Dictionary Finding. Given a set of domains C_{Train}, we apply all the previous steps to C_{Train} and obtain all the connected components of all the graphs G_i derived from C_{Train}. We manually label every connected component in every graph G_i as DGA/non-DGA (indicated as True/False in Fig. 2). Next we train a decision tree over the training dataset of labeled feature vectors. The decision tree model is later used for classifying new vectors (connected

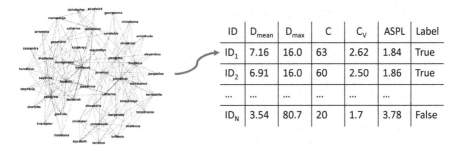

ID	D_{mean}	D_{max}	C	C_v	ASPL	Label
ID_1	7.16	16.0	63	2.62	1.84	True
ID_2	6.91	16.0	60	2.50	1.86	True
...	...	...	...	...	...	
ID_N	3.54	80.7	20	1.7	3.78	False

Fig. 2. In order to classify word graph components as DGA/non-DGA, each graph component is represented as a vector of structural features. Each description vector is part of a dataset that describes the overall word graph.

components) without human intervention, even if these connected components stem from word graphs that originate from a completely different dictionary. Each connected component that is classified as DGA by the decision tree is subsequently converted into a dictionary in a straightforward manner, i.e. by treating each node of the connected component as a word in the dictionary. An overview of the WordGraph dictionary finding phase is presented in Fig. 3.

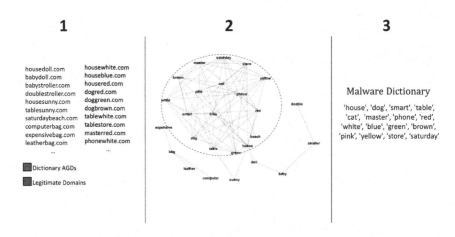

Fig. 3. An overview of the proposed WordGraph method. In **1** a dataset containing malicious and benign domains is analyzed, and frequent words are *learned* from the dataset. In **2** a word graph is built, and the structure of each graph component is analyzed to detect the malware dictionary **3**.

Classification of Domain Names. From the previous steps, we obtain a set of *detected dictionaries*, each one associated with a TLD. We flag a domain as malicious if it has at least two words from a same discovered dictionary, and it has the same TLD as the dictionary.

5   Experimental Methodology

We follow a similar approach as [10] and create an experimental setting with labeled *ground truth data* obtained from the DGArchive [15], which is a web database for DGA domains from various families, and from the Alexa top 1 million domains (a snapshot from 2016) [2]. The main goal of our experiments with labeled data is to compare our methodology with *state-of-the-art* techniques for DGA classification: classifiers based on human engineered lexical features, and classifiers based on deep neural networks. Moreover, we want to observe how robust these methods are to changes in the dictionary used for generating malicious domains. This is a question that has not been explored in the literature, to the best of our knowledge. Our method is based solely on structural features representing *how* the words from the dictionary are put together but not on the specific words themselves. Therefore, we expect our method to be robust against changes in the dictionary.

In more details, we analyze the performance of our WordGraph method and compare with classification models based on Random Forests and Deep Learning methods in three different settings:

- Training and testing datasets containing Dictionary-AGDs generated from the *same dictionary*. This experimental setting has been used in previous works [10,20,23].
- Testing datasets containing domains formed from *dictionaries that are distinct from the dictionaries used to generate the domains in the training dataset*. We want to evaluate the robustness of all models in a scenario where a botnet administrator wants to mislead a trained detection model by updating the dictionary in the malware code. This question has not been previously addressed in the literature.
- Small number of training samples. How well does each method perform when only a very small number of training samples is available?

We also evaluate the performance of the proposed WordGraph method when facing *real traffic data*. Many of the previous works are evaluated only in scenarios of synthetically created datasets. We show that the WordGraph model achieves similar performance when used for detecting Dictionary-AGDs in real DNS traffic, and moreover, it is able to detect new varieties of dictionaries and malware seeds due to its nature of pattern discovery.

5.1   Datasets

The evaluation of the proposed approach is conducted on datasets with ground truth labels and on real traffic unlabeled data.

Ground Truth Data. The ground truth data contains 80,000 benign domain names randomly selected from the Alexa top 1M domains [2]. In our experiments, we 50,000 out of the 80,000 Alexa domain names for training, while the

Table 1. Description of the datasets used in two experiments: when the train and test data are both composed of AGDs generated from the same dictionaries (Test-Familiar), and when the train and test data are composed of AGDs generated from different dictionaries (Test-Unfamiliar).

Dataset	Train				Test-Familiar				Test-Unfamiliar			
	Alexa	WL1	WL2	WL3	Alexa	WL1	WL2	WL3	Alexa	WL1	WL2	WL3
Round 1	50K	20,768	20,768	0	30K	12K	12K	0	30K	0	0	32,768
Round 2	50K	0	20,768	20,768	30K	0	12K	12K	30K	32,768	0	0
Round 3	50K	20,768	0	20,768	30K	12K	0	12K	30K	0	32,768	0

rest is reserved for testing. In addition, we use $3 \times 32,768$ AGDs obtained from the Dictionary-based DGA Suppobox [15], corresponding to three different dictionaries or wordlists, referred to as WL1, WL2, and WL3. How we split this malware data into portions for training and testing varies with the experiment.

Tables 1 provides an overview of the setup of two experiments involving the ground truth data.

- Test-Familiar: The test data consists of Dictionary-AGDs generated with the same dictionaries as the AGDs in the training data;
- Test-Unfamiliar: The test data consists of Dictionary-AGDs that were generated with a dictionary that was not known or available during training time. This experimental setting is intended to show that the model can be trained on a specific family and detect a distinct family, *unfamiliar* to the model.

Both experiments each consist of three rounds, corresponding to which wordlist is left out when training. For instance, as can be observed in Table 1, in round 1, Dictionary-AGDs generated with wordlist 3 do not appear in the training data.

Table 2. Description of imbalanced datasets used for testing and training. The imbalance present in this data is very common in real traffic, where only a very small fraction of the data corresponds to malicious activity.

Dataset	Train				Test-Imbalanced			
	Alexa	WL1	WL2	WL3	Alexa	WL1	WL2	WL3
Round 1	50,000	169	169	0	10,000	0	0	169
Round 2	50,000	0	169	169	10,000	169	0	0
Round 3	50,000	169	0	169	10,000	0	169	0

In an additional experiment, we measure the performance of all DGA domain detection methods in a scenario where very few samples of AGDs are available for training (see Table 2). The 507 AGDs involved in this experiment were selected from DGArchive; they were valid for one day only (Dec 1, 2016).

Real Traffic Data. The data used in our real traffic experiments consists of a real time stream of passive analysis of DNS traffic, as in [5]. The traffic stems from approximately 10 billion DNS queries per day collected from multiple ISPs (Internet Service Providers), schools and businesses distributed all over the world. We collected 8 days of traffic from December 2016 to perform our experiments, from Dec 8 to Dec 15 (see Table 3). From the data, we keep only A and AAAA type DNS queries (i.e. IPv4 and IPv6 address records), and exclude all domains that receive less than 5 queries in a day.

Table 3. DNS traffic data description. We collected 8 days of real traffic data to measure the performance of our proposed WordGraph model. Days 1, 2 and 3 are used for model training, and days 4 through 8 are used for model testing.

Dataset	All domains			Known AGDs (DGArchive)	
	Domains	Resolved	NX	Resolved	NX
Day 01	4,886,247	4,433,248	454,003	47	593
Day 02	4,922,618	4,532,932	390,735	67	673
Day 03	4,906,309	4,477,049	430,239	62	608
Day 04	4,350,224	3,981,514	369,673	87	662
Day 05	5,898,723	5,380,945	518,886	82	665
Day 06	5,425,651	4,963,786	463,584	73	680
Day 07	5,631,353	5,098,121	534,572	83	591
Day 08	5,254,954	4,747,867	508,319	95	635

The data stream consists of legitimate domains and malicious domains. All domains from this stream that are known to be Dictionary-based DGAs according to DGArchive [15] are marked as such. Although the number of unique Dictionary-based AGDs found in the real traffic data by cross-checking it against DGArchive is small, the total number of queries for such domains is tens of thousands per day. Furthermore, as will become clear in Sect. 6.2, the real traffic data contains more AGDs than those known in DGArchive.

5.2   Classification Models: Random Forest and Deep Learning

As stated in Sect. 1, the existing state-of-the-art approaches for classifying domain names as benign of malicious are either based on training a machine learning model with human defined lexical features that can be extracted from the domain name string, or on training a deep neural network that learns the features by itself. To show that the method that we propose in this paper outperforms the state-of-the-art, we include an experimental comparison with each kind of the existing approaches. For the approach based on human defined features, we train random forests (RFs) based on lexical features, extracted from each domain name string (see e.g. [24,25]). Within supervised learning, tree ensemble methods – such as random forests – are among the most common algorithms of choice for data scientists because of their general applicability and their state-of-the-art performance. Regarding the deep learning approach, a recent study [23] found no significant difference in predictive accuracy between recently proposed convolutional [16] and recurrent neural networks [10,20] for the task of DGA detection, while the recurrent neural networks have a substantially higher training time. In our comparative overview we therefore use a convolutional neural network (CNN) architecture as in [16].

Data Preprocessing. The strings that we give as input to all classifiers consist of a second level domain (SLD) and a top level domain (TLD), separated by a dot, as in e.g. *wikipedia.org*. As input to the CNN approach, we set the maximum length at 75 characters. The SLD label and the TLD label can in theory each be up to 63 characters long each. In practice they are typically shorter. If needed, we truncate domain names by removing characters from the end of the SLD until the desired length of 75 characters is reached. For domains whose length is less than 75, for the CNN approach, we pad with zeros on the left because the implementation of the deep neural network expects a fixed length input. For the RF and WordGraph approaches we do not do any padding. We convert each domain name string to lower case, since domain names are case insensitive.

Random Forest (RF). In each experiment, we train a random forest (RF) on the following 11 commonly used features, extracted from each domain name string: ent (normalized entropy of characters); nl2 (median of 2-gram); nl3 (median of 3-gram); naz (symbol character ratio); hex (hex character ratio); vwl (vowel character ratio); len (domain label length); gni (gini index of characters); cer (classification error of characters); tld (top level domain hash); dgt (first character digit). Each trained random forest consists of 100 trees. We refer to [22] for a detailed description of each of these features.

Deep Learning (CNN). In addition, in each experiment, following [16], we train a convolutional neural network that takes the raw domain name string as input. The neural network consists of an embedding layer, followed by a convolutional layer, two dense hidden layers, and an output layer. The role of the embedding layer is to learn to represent each character that can occur in a domain name by a 128-dimensional numerical vector, different from the original ASCII encoding. The embedding maps semantically similar characters to similar vectors, where the notion of similarity is implicitly derived (learned) based on the classification task at hand. The embedding layer is followed by a convolutional layer with 1024 filters, namely 256 filters for each of the sizes 2, 3, 4, and 5. During training of the network, each filter automatically learns which pattern it should look for. In this way, each of the filters learns to detect the soft presence of an interesting soft n-gram (with $n = 2, 3, 4, 5$). For each filter, the outcome of the detection phase is aggregated over the entire domain name string with the help of a pooling step. That means that the trained network is detecting the presence or absence of patterns in the domain names, without retaining any information on where exactly in the domain name string these patterns occur. The output of the convolutional layer is consumed by two dense hidden layers, each with 1024 nodes, before reaching a single node output layer with sigmoid activation. In all experiments, we trained the deep neural networks for 20 epochs, with batch size 100 and learning rate 0.0001.

6   Results

We report the results of all methods in terms of precision (positive predictive value, PPV), recall (true positive rate, TPR) and false positive rate (FPR). As usual, PPV = TP/(TP+FP), TPR = TP/(TP+FN) and FPR = FP/(FP+TN) where TP, FP, TN, and FN are the number of true positives, false positives, true negatives, and false negatives respectively. Blocking legitimate traffic is highly undesirable, therefore a low false positive rate is very important in deployed DGA detection systems. For parameter tuning purposes, in each experiment, we systematically split 10% of the training data off as validation data for the RF and CNN methods.

6.1   Experimental Results: Ground Truth Data

Figure 4 presents an overview of the results achieved by all models in the three different experimental settings with ground truth data described in Sect. 5.1. A first important result is that, across the board, the WordGraph method achieves a perfect TPR of 1, meaning that all Dictionary-AGDs are detected. To allow for a fair comparison, we selected classification thresholds for which the RF and CNN methods also achieve a TPR of 1. It is common for such a high TPR to be accompanied by a rise in FPR and a drop in PPV. As can be seen in Fig. 4, this is most noticeable for the RF method, and, to a somewhat lesser extent for the CNN method. The WordGraph method on the other hand is barely impacted at all: it substantially outperforms the CNN and RF methods in all experiments.

Test-Familiar Experiment. Detailed results for all methods in the "Test = Familiar" experiment are presented in Table 4. In this experiment, the train and test data contain AGDs generated from the same set of dictionaries. This experimental setup gives an advantage to classification models such as CNNs and Random Forests, since it allows the classification model to 'learn' characteristics of the words from the dictionaries.

A first observation from Table 4 is that the RF method does not do well at all. This is as expected: the lexical features extracted from the domain name strings to train the RFs have been designed to detect traditional DGAs, and Dictionary-based DGAs have been introduced with the exact purpose of evading such detection mechanisms. This is also apparent from the density plots of the features in Fig. 5: the feature value distributions for the AGDs from WL1, WL2,

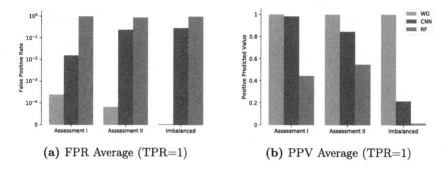

(a) FPR Average (TPR=1)   **(b)** PPV Average (TPR=1)

Fig. 4. Overview of FPR (lower is better) and PPV (higher is better) for all methods across the experimental setups on the ground truth data, for a fixed TPR=1. The WordGraph (WG) approach consistently achieves a very low FPR, of the order of magnitude of 10^{-4}, two order of magnitudes lower than the best FPR achieved by the CNN model.

and WL3 are very similar to those of the Alexa domain names, which explains the poor performance of the RF models that are based on these features.

The WordGraph method on the other hand works extremely well. It detects *all* AGDs in the test data in all rounds, while only misclassifying a very small number of benign domain names as malicious (namely 8/30,000 in round 1; 4/30,000 in round 2; and 1/30,000 in round 3). Finally, it is worth to call out that the CNN models have a very good performance as well. This is likely due to the fact that, as explained in Sect. 5.2 the CNN neural networks learn to detect the presence of interesting soft n-grams (with $n = 2, 3, 4, 5$), so, in a sense, they can memorize the dictionaries. It is interesting to point out that the CNN method performs consistently well throughout the rounds, i.e. given the fact that the dictionary was seen before by the model, there is no dictionary that is easier to 'learn'.

Table 4. Results of random forest (RF), deep learning (CNN), and our proposed WordGraph approach (WG) on balanced ground truth data, for a fixed TPR=1. The AGDs in the training and test data are generated from the same dictionaries (**"Test-Familiar"**).

Method	Round 1		Round 2		Round 3	
	FPR	PPV	FPR	PPV	FPR	PPV
WordGraph	$2.67 \cdot 10^{-4}$	0.999	$1.33 \cdot 10^{-4}$	0.999	$3.33 \cdot 10^{-5}$	0.999
CNN	0.018	0.981	0.015	0.982	0.014	0.983
RF	1.0	0.444	1.0	0.444	1.0	0.444

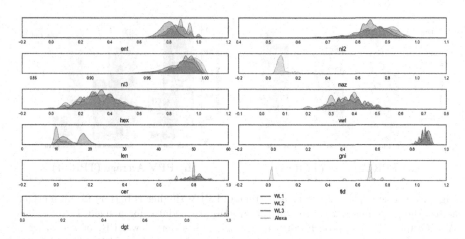

Fig. 5. Kernel density plot of the features extracted for the RF experiments where the x-axis represents the feature value and the area under the curve represents the probability of having a feature in that range of x values.

Test-Unfamiliar Experiment. In the "Test-Unfamiliar" experiment, the trained models are tested on AGDs generated from dictionaries that were not seen during training. As Table 5 shows, the WordGraph method has no problem at all detecting these new AGDs across all rounds, while, as expected, the RF method continues to struggle. Interestingly enough, unlike in the previous experimental setting, the performance of the CNN model is no longer consistently good across all rounds. In round 1, the CNN model performs significantly worse when compared to rounds 2 and 3, having a FPR higher by one order of magnitude. In round 1 the model is trained on WL1 and WL2 DGA domains, while the testing data contains WL3 AGDs. A possible explanation for the poor performance of the CNN method in round 1 is that, as observed in Fig. 5 for the 'len' feature, the AGDs in WL3 tend to be longer than those in WL1 and WL2, leading the CNN to misclassify the AGDs from WL3 as malicious because it has never seen such long malicious domain names during training.

Table 5. Results of all methods on balanced ground truth data, for a fixed TPR = 1. The AGDs in the test data are generated from dictionaries that were not available during training time (**"Test-Unfamiliar"**).

Method	Round 1		Round 2		Round 3	
	FPR	PPV	FPR	PPV	FPR	PPV
WordGraph	0.0	1.0	$6.67 \cdot 10^{-5}$	0.999	$1.33 \cdot 10^{-4}$	0.999
CNN	0.589	0.650	0.084	0.928	0.050	0.956
RF	1.0	0.522	1.0	0.522	0.723	0.602

Results on Imbalanced Ground Truth Data. The results for the models trained and tested on the imbalanced ground truth data are presented in Table 6. The trend we observed before persists: the WordGraph approach perfectly detects all Dictionary-AGDs in all rounds without misclassifying even a single benign domain name, the CNN method sometimes does well and sometimes not, and the RF method does not do well at all.

Table 6. Results of all methods on imbalanced ground truth data, for a fixed TPR=1, the three rounds of experiment are listed in Table 2 (**"Test-Imbalanced"**).

Method	Round 1		Round 2		Round 3	
	FPR	PPV	FPR	PPV	FPR	PPV
WordGraph	0.0	1.0	0.0	1.0	0.0	1.0
CNN	0.718	0.230	0.127	0.117	0.039	0.300
RF	1.0	0.017	1.0	0.017	1.0	0.017

Overall, the WordGraph method clearly outperforms the CNN and RF methods. It is able to 'find' dictionaries in data through graph analysis, even when only a small sample is available. The imbalanced experiment from Table 6 illustrates a scenario where only one infected machine is present in a network. After one day of Dictionary-AGD DNS requests, the WordGraph approach is able to extract the malicious dictionary from traffic. Out of 10,169 domains in each test dataset, only 169 domains are malicious, and the WordGraph method is able to identify 100% of the words from the malicious dictionary, with FPR=0.0 in every round of this experiment.

6.2 Experimental Results: Real DNS Traffic

To study the performance of the WordGraph method in a realistic scenario, we evaluate it on the real traffic data from Table 3. To further reduce the dataset size, we used solely NX Traffic since most of AGD queries result in Non-Existent Domain (NXDomain) responses. This approach has been consistently used in the literature [3,8].

The first three days in the real traffic dataset were used for training the graph component classifier as described in Sect. 4. The Dictionary-based AGDs in the dataset were labeled using DGA archive [15] as a source of ground truth labels. The number of Dictionary-based AGDs for each day is described in Table 3. We then evaluated the results of our method on the remaining five days of traffic.

Overall, we identified 81 dictionaries in five days of traffic. Fifteen of these discovered dictionaries are present in DGArchive. We manually verified the remaining dictionaries and confirmed they were all malicious. Since DGArchive has the complete dictionary for the 15 cases (by reverse engineering the malware) we managed to verify that our method recovered the complete dictionary in this situation. We identified several dictionaries related to malware download hosts, such as *apartonly.gq*, *oftenthere.ga* and *quitethough.cf*. We also discovered variations of the malware family Suppobox, where the generated domains in this variation present TLD ".*ru*".

Once we obtained the dictionaries, we also flagged the domains that were generated by these words in the resolved DNS traffic, giving information on active C&C (Command and Control) centers.

7   Discussion and Limitations

Computational Complexity. The most expensive part of our algorithm is the graph building with complexity $\mathcal{O}(n^2)$, where n is the number of words extracted from domains. We apply our algorithm only to NXDomains (since DGAs are mostly non-resolved) on a daily basis. The datasets have about 5 millions domains, where about 500,000 are NXdomains. The size of the graphs are about 60,000 nodes, which corresponds to the number of extracted words from traffic. The entire algorithm runs in about 30 min, considering word extraction and graph analysis phases. All experiments were run on a machine with an 2.3 GHz Intel Core i5 processor and a maximum of 16GB of allowed memory consumption.

Limitations. (1) Our WordGraph method is very successful in extracting dictionaries from AGDs. This is the case for all variations of the Suppobox family, and other unidentified families that we were able to identify in real traffic. The method leverages the fact that such families uses limited dictionaries and the reuse of dictionary words is frequent. We suggest as future work the investigation of Dictionary-based AGDs that utilizes a very large dictionary and very low word reuse rate. (2) Additionally, there are malware families, such as Matsnu, that use a DGA as a secondary resource for C&C communication, with hardcoded domains being the primary method. Such a malware family typically not only generates a very small number of DGA domains daily [18], but those domains are only queried in the case that all domains from the hardcoded list receive an NX response. Matsnu malware for instance generates only four DGA domains per day. In our real traffic dataset, we did not encounter any occurrences of Matsnu AGDs. Preliminary results on ground truth data indicate that the WordGraph method would need more than one month of observation to be able to recover the dictionary. Using one month of Matsnu AGDs from DGAarchive, we were able to extract from 590 domains a partial dictionary of 82 words, leading to the detection of 273 domains. (3) Once the dictionaries are extracted, we detect malicious domains by checking if they have two or more words from the extracted dictionaries. False positive rates were at most 10^{-4} in all the performed experiments (with real traffic and synthetic data). An adversary could, in principle, try to increase the false positive rate by using dictionaries with words commonly used in legitimate domains. However, this approach has a drawback for the adversary since several of the generated domains will already be registered and thus useless for the bot-master.

8   Conclusion

We proposed a novel WordGraph method for detection of Dictionary-based DGAs in DNS traffic. The WordGraph method consists of two main phases: (1) malicious dictionary extraction from traffic observations and (2) detection of Dictionary-AGDs present in traffic. We evaluated WordGraph on ground truth data consisting of Dictionary-AGDs from DGArchive and benign domains from Alexa. Our experiments show that WordGraph consistently outperforms random forests based on human defined lexical features as well as deep learning models that take the raw domain name string as input and learn the features themselves. In particular, unlike these existing state-of-the-art methods, WordGraph detects (nearly) all Dictionary-AGDs even when the dictionary used to generate them is changed. Furthermore, when we analyzed 5 days of real traffic from multiple ISPs with WordGraph, we were able to detect the presence of Dictionary-AGDs generated by known as well as by previously unknown malware, and we discovered domains related to C&C proxies that received thousands of requests. Due to its nature of discovering, through a graph perspective, malicious patterns of words in traffic, the WordGraph method guarantees a very low false positive rate, presenting itself as a DGA detection system with practical relevance.

References

1. Abbink, J., Doerr, C.: Popularity-based detection of domain generation algorithms. In: Proceedings of the 12th International Conference on Availability, Reliability and Security, p. 79. ACM (2017)
2. ALEXA: Top sites on the web (2017). http://alexa.com/topsites
3. Antonakakis, M., et al.: From throw-away traffic to bots: detecting the rise of DGA-based malware. In: 21st USENIX Security Symposium, pp. 24–24 (2012). http://dl.acm.org/citation.cfm?id=2362793.2362817
4. Barabosch, T., Wichmann, A., Leder, F., Gerhards-Padilla, E.: Automatic extraction of domain name generation algorithms from current malware. In: Proceedings of NATO Symposium IST-111 on Information Assurance and Cyber Defense (2012)
5. Bilge, L., Kirda, E., Kruegel, C., Balduzzi, M.: Exposure: finding malicious domains using passive DNS analysis. In: NDSS (2011)
6. Diestel, R.: Graph Theory. Graduate Texts in Mathematics, vol. 137. Springer, Heidelberg (2005)
7. Geffner, J.: End-to-end analysis of a domain generating algorithm malware family. Black Hat USA 2013 (2013)
8. Krishnan, S., Taylor, T., Monrose, F., McHugh, J.: Crossing the threshold: detecting network malfeasance via sequential hypothesis testing. In: 43rd Annual IEEE/IFIP International Conference on Dependable Systems and Networks (DSN), pp. 1–12 (2013)
9. Lind, P.G., Gonzalez, M.C., Herrmann, H.J.: Cycles and clustering in bipartite networks. Phys. Rev. E **72**(5), 056127 (2005)
10. Lison, P., Mavroeidis, V.: Automatic detection of malware-generated domains with recurrent neural models. arXiv:1709.07102 (2017)

11. Ma, J., Saul, L.K., Savage, S., Voelker, G.M.: Beyond blacklists: learning to detect malicious web sites from suspicious URLs. In: Proceedings of the 15th ACM SIGKDD International Conference on Knowledge Discovery and Data Mining, KDD 2009, pp. 1245–1254 (2009). https://doi.org/10.1145/1557019.1557153
12. Mao, G., Zhang, N.: Analysis of average shortest-path length of scale-free network. J. Appl. Math. (2013). http://dx.doi.org/10.1155/2013/865643
13. McGrath, D.K., Gupta, M.: Behind phishing: an examination of phisher modi operandi. LEET **8**, 4 (2008)
14. Mowbray, M., Hagen, J.: Finding domain-generation algorithms by looking at length distribution. In: 25th IEEE International Symposium on Software Reliability Engineering Workshops, ISSRE Workshops, pp. 395–400 (2014). https://doi.org/10.1109/ISSREW.2014.20
15. Plohmann, D., Yakdan, K., Klatt, M., Bader, J., Gerhards-Padilla, E.: A comprehensive measurement study of domain generating malware. In: 25th USENIX Security Symposium, pp. 263–278 (2016)
16. Saxe, J., Berlin, K.: eXpose: a character-level convolutional neural network with embeddings for detecting malicious URLs, file paths and registry keys. arXiv:1702.08568 (2017)
17. Schiavoni, S., Maggi, F., Cavallaro, L., Zanero, S.: Phoenix: DGA-based botnet tracking and intelligence. In: Dietrich, S. (ed.) DIMVA 2014. LNCS, vol. 8550, pp. 192–211. Springer, Cham (2014). https://doi.org/10.1007/978-3-319-08509-8_11
18. Skuratovich, S.: Matsnu technical report. Check Point Software Technologies Ltd. (2015). https://blog.checkpoint.com/wp-content/uploads/2015/07/matsnu-malwareid-technical-brief.pdf
19. Tran, D., Mac, H., Tong, V., Tran, H.A., Nguyen, L.G.: A LSTM based framework for handling multiclass imbalance in DGA botnet detection. Neurocomputing **275**, 2401–2413 (2018)
20. Woodbridge, J., Anderson, H.S., Ahuja, A., Grant, D.: Predicting domain generation algorithms with long short-term memory networks. arXiv:1611.00791 (2016)
21. Yadav, S., Reddy, A.K.K., Reddy, A.L.N., Ranjan, S.: Detecting algorithmically generated malicious domain names. In: Proceedings of the 10th ACM SIGCOMM Conference on Internet Measurement, pp. 48–61 (2010). https://doi.org/10.1145/1879141.1879148
22. Yu, B., Gray, D., Pan, J., De Cock, M., Nascimento, A.: Inline DGA detection with deep networks. In: Data Mining for Cyber Security, Proceedings of International Conference on Data Mining (ICDM 2017) Workshops, pp. 683–692 (2017)
23. Yu, B., Pan, J., Hu, J., Nascimento, A., De Cock, M.: Character level based detection of DGA domain names. In: Proceedings of IJCNN at WCCI2018 (2018 IEEE World Congress on Computational Intelligence) (2018)
24. Yu, B., Smith, L., Threefoot, M.: Semi-supervised time series modeling for real-time flux domain detection on passive DNS traffic. In: Perner, P. (ed.) MLDM 2014. LNCS (LNAI), vol. 8556, pp. 258–271. Springer, Cham (2014). https://doi.org/10.1007/978-3-319-08979-9_20
25. Yu, B., Smith, L., Threefoot, M., Olumofin, F.: Behavior analysis based DNS tunneling detection with big data technologies. In: Proceedings of the International Conference on Internet of Things and Big Data, pp. 284–290 (2016)

OTTer: A Scalable High-Resolution Encrypted Traffic Identification Engine

Eva Papadogiannaki$^{(\boxtimes)}$, Constantinos Halevidis, Periklis Akritidis,
and Lazaros Koromilas

Niometrics, Singapore, Singapore
{papadogiannaki,halevidis,akritid,koromilas}@niometrics.com

Abstract. Several security applications rely on monitoring network traffic, which is increasingly becoming encrypted. In this work, we propose a pattern language to describe packet trains for the purpose of fine-grained identification of application-level events in encrypted network traffic, and demonstrate its expressiveness with case studies for distinguishing Messaging, Voice, and Video events in Facebook, Skype, Viber, and WhatsApp network traffic. We provide an efficient implementation of this language, and evaluate its performance by integrating it into our proprietary DPI system. Finally, we demonstrate that the proposed pattern language can be mined from traffic samples automatically, minimizing the otherwise high ruleset maintenance burden.

Keywords: Traffic analysis · OTT applications · Network monitoring

1 Introduction

Over the years, the adoption of network traffic encryption has been continually growing. Mobile applications are using the SSL/TLS protocols to secure their communications, and some implement end-to-end encryption to protect the privacy of their users. Studies have shown that more than 60% of mobile application traffic is now using SSL/TLS [25].

Internet traffic analysis is commonly based on techniques like deep packet inspection (DPI). The core of traditional DPI implementations is based on pattern matching, that enables searching for specific strings or regular expressions inside the packet content. Applications of DPI include but are not limited to firewalls, intrusion detection and prevention systems, antivirus systems, L7 filtering and packet forwarding [33–35]. With the widespread adoption of network encryption, DPI tools that rely on plain text pattern matching become less effective, demanding the development of more sophisticated techniques.

In this work, we focus exclusively on analysing encrypted traffic generated by so called Over-The-Top (OTT) mobile applications—one of the most security critical (exfiltration, policy enforcement) sources of traffic. Traditional DPI

© Springer Nature Switzerland AG 2018
M. Bailey et al. (Eds.): RAID 2018, LNCS 11050, pp. 315–334, 2018.
https://doi.org/10.1007/978-3-030-00470-5_15

implementations can only extract very coarse-grained information for the majority of such traffic. Its analysis, however, is an integral operation for many network systems and needs to be improved to offer detailed traffic metrics for OTT applications. To this end, we implement a system that is able to extract essential information from encrypted traffic generated by mobile applications. Packets contain *metadata* usable even with encrypted traffic, such as packet timestamps and sizes—information that can be extracted from the packet headers or timed. In this work we focus on using patterns of packet size trains to identify OTT application events such as messaging, voice and video calls over encrypted traffic. We provide a full implementation as part of a DPI engine supporting rulesets with packet train patterns—matched using an automaton consuming packet sizes—on top of traditional substring and port number patterns, to efficiently match and report events in encrypted network traffic. Figure 1 shows a high-level overview of our approach.

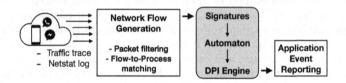

Fig. 1. High-level overview: Traffic samples are collected offline and then signatures are created either manually or using data mining. The signatures are fed to our DPI engine and compiled into an automaton for execution on live traffic keeping only usage statistics.

In this work, we make the following contributions:

- We discuss a practical methodology to collect, label, and analyse encrypted traffic generated by popular mobile OTT applications (e.g. Skype, WhatsApp, Facebook Messenger and Viber) to identify usage events such as messaging, voice and video calls
- We propose a pattern language to identify such events that is suitable for DPI systems, yet expressive enough to describe packet metadata patterns, and we confirm this experimentally
- We discuss a high-performance implementation of our pattern language, and integrate our implementation with a DPI engine to evaluate its performance against high-volume real network traffic
- We demonstrate that our pattern language is amenable to automated mining from ground truth samples.

2   Encrypted Traffic Pattern Language

During our analyses, we observed that specific sequences of packet payload sizes reliably signify discrete events inside an application. In this section we describe our proposed pattern language to express such patterns in network traffic.

2.1 Design Goals

We aim for an expressive yet simple enough language to facilitate the automated mining of rules. While offline mining techniques can be involved during the construction of the rules, we need to support very efficient and low-latency evaluation of the rules at runtime on live traffic for use in a production quality DPI system. Another consideration for a practical system is to minimize the amount of state information that a DPI engine needs to maintain per flow in order to evaluate patterns across packets of the same flow. These requirements led us to a simple regex-inspired formulation applied on trains of observed packet sizes. The advantage of our approach is that it can be implemented with an automaton without the need to retain previously observed packet sizes to support backtracking, and that it is expressive enough to capture the traffic features of interest.

2.2 Pattern Language Specification

Table 1 displays some examples of rules that we extracted during our analysis phase. The proposed pattern language uses a regex-inspired syntax, and is easy to follow, since it resembles standard regular expressions. When a network flow contains such sequences of these pre-defined payload packet sizes, expressed through a rule and in conjunction with any other traffic characteristics such as port numbers or substrings, then the application event is reported. For instance, when a captured network flow contains a series of two packets with payload sizes 3 bytes and 52 bytes respectively, then our system reports the existence of an outgoing chat message.

Table 1. Examples of application event rules.

Event	Application	Rule
Voice call	WhatsApp	3{1,3}, 56-60{1,3}, 400-800
Video call	WhatsApp	3{1,3}, 56-60{1,3}, 3{1,3}, 117 OR 3{1,3}, 56-60{1,3}, 3{1,3}, 144
Chat message	WhatsApp	3{1,3}, 52

Informally, a rule expression consists of one or more comma-separated *pieces*. Each piece is an *atom* with an optional *bound*. The atom is either a single number or a range of numbers, where *number* is a positive integer. The bound specifies an exact or relaxed (with min and max inclusive limits) number of repetitions of the atom. A formal definition can be found in Table 2.

Our proposal can be extended for additional expressiveness, for example by adding other regular expression constructs such as groups or disjunctions. In this work we kept the pattern language complexity to a minimum to avoid complicating the mining process. Disjunction, in particular, is handled by providing a disjunctive set of rules, instead of extending the language syntax with an embedded disjunctive operator. The downside is that a larger set of patterns may be required. We did not find this to be a problem in practice.

Table 2. Rule language specification; number is a positive integer.

```
expr  ::= piece | piece, expr
piece ::= atom | atom{bound}
atom  ::= number | number-number
bound ::= number | number,number
```

In order to deal with retransmitted TCP packets we could either (i) normalize traffic before applying the rule by discarding such packets or (ii) form the expression to handle the retransmitted packets, accordingly (like the rules in Table 1). The displayed expressions are able to handle retransmitted packets having a repeat range {1,3}, where 3 is the upper bound (the maximum number of retransmissions). However, handling retransmissions through the expression might be risky. Having retransmitted packets is an unpredictable network behaviour, so we might lose an application event reporting solely due to a not properly defined upper bound in the repeat range of an expression. Thus, we choose to handle retransmitted TCP packets by discarding them in a packet filtering phase.

3   Effectiveness Evaluation

In this section we demonstrate the expressiveness of the proposed pattern language by manually generating pattern signatures for a set of application events and evaluating their accuracy. We used 25% (randomly chosen) of the ground truth samples as a reference for the human analyst, and the remaining 75% for the accuracy evaluation (Sect. 3.3).

3.1   Flow Sample Collection Mechanism

We divide the mobile application network traffic into flows. A network flow is represented by the standard *5-tuple* containing (i) the source IP address, (ii) the source port number, (iii) the destination IP address, (iv) the destination port number and (v) the protocol. A network flow then, consists of the packets matching a certain *5-tuple*. To categorise the flows generated by different mobile applications, we need further information. This information should include either the domain, the process name or the process id that relates to the specific network connection. There are multiple ways to achieve this. For instance, other approaches, like [12], do domain filtering, leveraging the WHOIS protocol. We chose to employ the process id in order to obtain the required information about each network flow. In the following section we present how we implemented the network flow filtering.

Flow-to-Process Matching. `Netstat` [3] is a command-line network utility that can display among others, information about network connections. Having superuser privileges, someone can use `netstat` to determine the process id (PID) and process name of the process that owns the connection socket. In Android devices, `netstat` is available via the `BusyBox` application [2].

To collect all necessary information about each connection established during the network traffic trace collection, we continually invoke `netstat` and store the output to a file that will be later used for the flow-to-process characterisation phase (flow/process correlation), during which flows are assigned to their process and (and the corresponding PID), generating a *7-tuple*, with the following format: {*process name, process id, source IP address, source port number, destination IP address, destination port number, protocol*}.

Packet Filtering. In order for the TCP protocol to deliver data reliably, it offers many mechanisms to detect and avoid unpredictable network behaviour, like packet loss, duplication or reordering. In the proposed methodology, we choose to discard packets that do not offer substantial information to the flow (e.g. retransmitted packets). In our proposed method, we focus entirely on handling and processing packet metadata. This means that we do not take into consideration the packet payload, since we assume that it is encrypted. The information that we handle lays solely on packet metadata, such as the packet direction and payload size. Thus, packets lacking payload do not provide any valuable information to our method. To this end, we filter out ACK-flagged packets[1].

3.2   Sample Traffic Generation

To avoid extracting overly specific application event patterns, we analysed traffic traces generated during realistic usage of such applications. In addition, we used devices on both fixed and mobile networks.

Device Variations. To ensure variation, we make use of different devices, vendors, Android and kernel versions. We used four different Android mobile devices, a Sony Xperia D5503 (Android v.5.1.1, kernel v.3.4.0-gd26777b), a Xiaomi Redmi 3s (Android v.6.0.1, kernel v.3.18.20-g76f906f), a Xiaomi MI Note LTE (Android v.6.0.1, kernel v.3.4.0-gf4b741d), and finally a Xiaomi Redmi Note 3 Pro (Android v.6.0.1, kernel v.3.10.84-gda78349). In order to obtain full functionality and privileges, we used exclusively rooted Android devices, with developer options enabled. Thus, we were able to install the `BusyBox` application from Google Play store and take advantage of Unix utilities provided through a single executable [2], as well as the Android `tcpdump` tool to locally capture network traffic on the device [1]. In addition, we used Android Debug Bridge

---

[1] We discard the TCP packets with only the ACK flag set. PUSH/ACK packets are kept.

(ADB) version 1.0.39 and Wireshark 2.4.2. Due to toolset limitations, we did not include Apple devices in our study.

OTT Application Events. We chose four of the most widely used OTT Android applications to evaluate our methodology: (i) WhatsApp, (ii) Skype, (iii) Facebook Messenger and (iv) Viber[2]. Since these applications are mainly used for communication purposes, we focused on identifying (i) outgoing chat messages, (ii) voice and (iii) video calls through the encrypted network traffic. Of course, our work can be extended to support other OTT application events, such as media exchange (e.g. photo sharing), as well as iOS devices.

Overall, we collected a set of over 350 samples[3]. Each individual sample simulates either an exchange of an arbitrary number of outgoing messages (messaging), or a single voice or video call using one of the aforementioned OTT applications. Then, for each sample we collected (i) a network packet trace, (ii) a file with the information of every TCP socket that was open during the traffic capture and the process information that created it, (iii) a screen recording and (iv) a file with the device's system logs reported by the Android ADB tool, named `logcat`. Each sample contains only a single application event type (e.g. sample0: Skype/messaging).

To validate, we compare the detected application events to the device's system logs that are included in the `logcat` output and screen recordings. Using the `logcat` file and the screen recording we are able to cross-check the reported events with the actual ones. `Logcat` is a command-line tool that dumps a log of the device's system messages. We extracted information such as audio hardware on/off, camera on/off and incoming chat messages. Unfortunately, we were not able to identify a system event that matches an outgoing chat message. Thus, we had to use the screen recordings to inspect the actual time of an outgoing chat message departure, as well as the quantity of the outgoing messages.

3.3   Accuracy Evaluation

Hit Rate. Table 3 shows the resulting true positive (TP) rates. Each sample contains only a single within-application event type (e.g. sample0: Skype/messaging, sample1: WhatsApp/voice). When a signature reports a within-application event (messaging: 0 or 1, voice: 0 or 1, video: 0 or 1), then we compare it to the actual event of the application. If the event is correctly reported, then the TP counter is increased. Otherwise, we have a false positive (FP).

The TP rate of our methodology individually for each event is (i) 93% for outgoing chat message, (ii) 86% for voice and (iii) 84% for video calls. The slightly

---

[2] Through the dataset collection we make use of different application versions per application. This allows us to verify the generalisation ability and scalability of our methodology.

[3] These samples were generated using dummy accounts and non-personal mobile devices.

lower TP rate for voice and video calls, is due to a trade-off with FPs[4]. We discovered that, for all applications under investigation except Viber, video-related flows included voice-related flows as well, and, thus, a video event includes also a voice event. On the other hand, our signatures for Viber voice and video events do not follow this trend as they are not complementary to each other. Thus, we can reach the interesting conclusion, that the core implementation of the Viber application is different from all the other applications under investigation.

Table 3. TP rates of our methodology. The percentages presented are extracted through the comparison of the results of our methodology to the actual ground-truth dataset.

Application	Messaging	Voice	Video
Facebook messenger	83%	96%	96%
Skype	88%	100%	75%
Viber	100%	54%	88%
WhatsApp	100%	92%	75%

False Discovery Rate. In addition to true positives, another metric necessary for the evaluation of our methodology is the false positive rate for each application event. Reporting mobile application events using only encrypted network traffic can be considered risky since no easy cross-validation can be made. It is not only significant to correctly report the existence of events, but also to not mistakenly report absent events as existent. Table 4 shows the false discovery rates of event reporting using our signatures[5]. False discovery rates are always below 8%.

The choice of signature can significantly affect the trade-off between true positive and false discovery rates. Having a relaxed signature definition leads to almost intact TP rates, with the cost of high false positives. Similarly, a more strict signature definition gives satisfactory TP rates, keeping the false positives low. We settled on signature definitions that result in hit rates over 84% and false discovery rates below 8%.

Granularity of Messaging Event Reporting. Using our signatures for messaging reporting we achieve a total hit rate of 93%—again, compared to our ground truth data collection. This rate covers the correct identification of the existence of messaging events (i.e. outgoing text messages) within a mobile OTT application. Moving to a more fine-grained granularity, we are able not only to show that there is messaging activity within a network traffic trace, but also to

---

[4] In the following section, we discuss about how the signature formation affects the balance between TP and FP rates.

[5] False discovery rate can be calculated as $FDR = FP/(TP + FP)$.

Table 4. This table presents the false discovery rates of our methodology. The "Messaging FDR" column shows the percentages of erroneous messaging reporting in voice or video samples. Respectively, "Voice/video FDR" column shows the percentages of erroneous voice/video reporting in messaging samples.

Application	Messaging FDR	Voice/video FDR
Facebook messenger	0%	1%
Skype	5.5%	4.2%
Viber	1%	2%
WhatsApp	8%	0.6%

accurately report *when* an outgoing text message is sent, and *count* the number of text messages sent during a messaging session, something we demonstrate in Sect. 5.

4   Implementation and Performance

In this section, we discuss and evaluate an implementation of our proposed pattern language.

4.1   Efficient Automaton

We implemented a data structure to efficiently match packet trains in a streaming fashion against sets of patterns. It is inspired by string searching algorithms such as Aho-Corasick [5] but instead of characters, it operates on packet sizes represented as 16-bit integers.

The Aho-Corasick algorithm is a string searching algorithm that locates elements of a finite set of strings within an input text. It matches all strings simultaneously, so its complexity does not depend on the size of the searched set. It works by constructing an automaton executing transitions for each character of the input text. To adapt the algorithm for matching packet trains, we replaced the 8-bit characters with 16-bit packet sizes.

The algorithm constructs a finite state machine that resembles a trie with additional "failure" links between the internal nodes. These failure links are followed when there is no other matching transition and allow for fast transitions to other branches of the trie that share a common prefix, without the need for backtracking using earlier inputs. This allows for interleaving a large number of concurrent searches, such as in the case of network connections, because the state of the matcher can be preserved across input data observed at different points in time by storing a pointer to the current state of the automaton with the state maintained for each connection. Otherwise, backtracking would require us to maintain expensive per-flow state for previously-seen packet sizes.

For additional performance, a Deterministic Finite Automaton (DFA) can be built by unrolling the failure links in advance and adding appropriate transitions to map each failure directly to an appropriate node without the need to follow multiple failure links at runtime. Expanding the automaton in this way did not provide an advantage in our case where the automaton is executed for each packet size as opposed to each byte when searching for substrings, and where the length and number of patterns is much less than typical substring-based rulesets, so we opted for the more compact data structure where the failure links are followed at runtime. For a very large number of patterns, however, this optimization may be worthwhile.

We implemented packet-size repetitions with a range $m - n$ as required by our pattern language by expanding them to $n - m + 1$ separate patterns. To implement packet ranges, we attempted at first to expand them into multiple individual 16-bit characters, leading to excessively large automata in the presence of wide packet size ranges, such as 100-200{3} which would expand to 100^3 distinct sequences. To avoid this we use ranges instead of individual 16-bit characters for the arcs of the automaton. To simplify the implementation, we preprocess the expressions to collect possibly overlapping ranges used in them and extract a set of non-overlapping ranges that we use as the alphabet for the automaton constructed. For example, rule 152-156{1,5}, 150-600 contains two overlapping ranges, 152-156 and 150-600, which are expanded to an alphabet of three non-overlapping ranges: 150-151, 152-156, and 157-600. Subsequently, the repetitions in this example are expanded as shown in Fig. 2.

```
152-156,150-151
152-156,152-156
152-156,157-600
152-156,152-156,150-151
152-156,152-156,152-156
152-156,152-156,157-600
152-156,152-156,152-156,150-151
152-156,152-156,152-156,152-156
152-156,152-156,152-156,157-600
152-156,152-156,152-156,152-156,150-151
152-156,152-156,152-156,152-156,152-156
152-156,152-156,152-156,152-156,157-600
152-156,152-156,152-156,152-156,152-156,150-151
152-156,152-156,152-156,152-156,152-156,152-156
152-156,152-156,152-156,152-156,152-156,157-600
```

Fig. 2. Illustration of the complete expansion of rule 152-156{1,5}, 150-600 into a set of simple sequences of non-overlapping ranges. An alphabet of size three is used, each character corresponding to the range 150-151, 152-156, or 157-600.

4.2   DPI Engine Integration

We integrated the pattern matching data structure with our proprietary DPI engine [7] that uses an extensible signature language by implementing a plugin to add a new condition, that we called **packet_train**. The signature language uses an event-condition-action model. The DPI engine raises different events to which sets of conditions and actions can be associated with. The conditions and actions are implemented as plugins, and are free to interpret their arguments and construct the necessary state objects that are evaluated on each event. The rule engine itself handles the logic of the ruleset as a whole, and the plugins are consulted for individual conditions. Each condition plugin declares the pieces of information that it requires (such as payload or flow-tuple information) and the rule engine ensures that the respective conditions are only used in combination with events that provide the required information. One such event is the `packet` event, which contains information about packet payload and therefore packet size, that we make use of in our extension. Other events include `connection`, which is raised by the connection tracker. Information can be communicated across events by means of tags stored in the connection state, assigned by an action called `tag` and checked by a condition also called `tag`. These can be used to chain together rules triggered on distinct events, for example a rule could match a substring in a certificate to detect the application and tag the connection, while later the tag can be used in the rule that uses the `packet_train` condition to avoid evaluating flows from irrelevant applications.

Figure 3 illustrates a rule example. The conditions are evaluated as a conjunction. Disjunctions can be expressed using multiple rules, or (if the condition itself supports it, such as ours), with a list of arguments (Fig. 4). The extension API provides hooks for populating individual condition arguments into a shared object that is consulted once per event and communicates back to the rule engine any matching rules. This facilitates conditions performing simultaneous matching such as those based on Aho-Corasick or hash-tables.

```
facebook_video:
  event: packet
  conditions:
  - port: 443
  - packet_train: '399{1,2}, 51{1,2}, 1000-1260{1,2}, 38'
  actions:
    ...
```

Fig. 3. Example of rule. The underlying data representation language used is YAML.

4.3   Performance Evaluation

We evaluated the performance of the entire system experimentally using our proprietary DPI engine [7] in a live traffic test-bed. We used an HPE Proliant DL380 Gen9 server with two Intel® Xeon® E5-2699 v4 CPUs at 2.20 GHz with hyper-threading enabled, providing us with 88 logical cores (lcores), and configured with 1 TB of RAM. The system has 4 × 40 Gbps NICs, two on each CPU socket. CentOS Linux release 7.4.1708 with kernel RPM version 3.10.0-693.11.6.el7.x86_64 was used.

```
whatsapp_video:
  event: packet
  conditions:
  - packet_train:
    - '3{1,3}, 48-60{1,3}, 3{1,3}, 117'
    - '3{1,3}, 48-60{1,3}, 3{1,3}, 144'
    - '3{1,3}, 48-60{1,3}, 3{1,3}, 102'
```

Fig. 4. Example of rule with a disjunction of patterns handled internally by the packet_train extension.

The DPI engine is configured to use 8 lcores for processing the traffic from the four ports (two lcores per port). These lcores perform just sufficient packet decoding in order to load balance the traffic internally to 58 lcores configured to perform traffic inspection. These are the lcores running our implementation. The rest of the lcores in the system are dedicated to other tasks such as logging and shell access.

The traffic load consisted of real mobile user traffic that varies throughout the day between 52–153 Gbps with an average of 109 Gbps, 20–25 Gpps and between 67–230 K new connections per second with an average of 161 K/s. Throughout the experiments we confirmed that the system does not exhibit packet loss.

First we measured the baseline CPU utilization of the traffic inspection lcores using `mpstat` over 1 min intervals. For a traffic of about 130 Gbps at 1 pm local time, we measured a CPU utilization of 34.2%. After enabling our DPI engine extension, and making sure it is invoked for all packets, we measured 37.6%, an increase of about 10%. We also took a closer look using the `perf` tool, to narrow down on the specific function performing our checks, called `extension_packet_train_multiset_match`. We measured it at 3%, even without any actual patterns loaded. This number is an upper bound. If the automaton is fed only packets for pre-screened traffic that belongs only to the application (using appropriate signatures), the performance impact of our extension is expected to be less.

Subsequently, we loaded packet train signatures, increasing the number of signatures in each experiment to measure the impact of the number of signatures on the CPU utilization. We tried 1–5, 10, 15 and 20 signatures. The results were within the 2.7–3% range, with significant variance and without any observable trend. This observation shows that the bulk of the cost comes from the mere interposition of our extension into the DPI engine's pipeline and does not depend on the number of patterns, at least up to a number of 20 patterns.

5   Amenability to Data Mining

5.1   Rule Mining Methodology

In order to illustrate the robustness of our event signature approach as well as to permit fast signature extraction for numerous application - event combinations, we automated the process. The application event rules were extracted from the packet traces by using frequent pattern mining (FPM) to detect frequent packet sequences and then correlating these patterns to the ground-truth events. This approach avoids the dependence on packet statistical measures commonly employed by other studies [4,24,31]. In order to extract the rules, the following steps are taken on the training dataset:

1. *Pre-processing:* All packets with a different process id than that of the application under examination are filtered out. Similarly, as mentioned in the above, TCP retransmissions are filtered out. Finally, all local and remote IPs are considered as a single local and a single remote IP, respectively.
2. *Packet statistics:* Afterwards, the absolute frequency of all pre-processed packet (source, destination, payload length) is calculated, and packet tuples whose frequency is greater than a predetermined percentile are mapped to unique identifiers (called items in the following). All other packet tuples are grouped according to their source and destination, as previously, but with the payload length segmented in 4 equally sized buckets, and similarly mapped to identifiers. This step was taken so as to limit the effect of variable payload length on the pattern mining (e.g., a long chat message may have a greater payload length than a shorter one).
3. *Trace splitting:* The packet traces were split to bursts (or sequences) of traffic (i.e., traffic with interpacket temporal distance less than a threshold, in this case set to 1 second) [4,31]. It should be noted that as one of the type of events investigated is outgoing chat messages, a larger temporal threshold could potentially result in multiple chat messages included in one burst (chat messages sent in quick succession). Furthermore, bursts not containing any of the events under investigation are filtered out. This step is taken in order to divide the traffic to temporally correlated sequences, which, in turn, will be used as an input to the frequent pattern mining algorithm.
4. *Frequent Pattern Mining:* Frequent pattern mining techniques are used to discern the correct packet patterns corresponding to the events among potential noise. The present methodology utilises closed sequential patterns (i.e., a pattern not strictly included in another pattern of the same support) as potential application event rules in order to avoid loss of information. The patterns are mined using the ClaSP algorithm [18].
5. *Rule Generation:* Finally, the rules are generated by identifying which closed sequential patterns match well with the ground truth events (i.e., the pattern timestamp is within a margin of the ground truth event timestamp).

In order to reduce the number of possible generated rules, the supersets of the above matching patterns are used, and evaluated using the F_1 measure (i.e., placing equal emphasis to both precision and recall). Finally, the generated rule is used to detect application events on the test dataset. The training dataset consists of 25% of the samples (the same samples as those used for training in the main implementation as mentioned in Sect. 3.2).

It should be noted that the rules generated by the above mining approach differ to those of the main implementation in that they take into account the direction of packet. This can be easily included in the DFA engine by encoding outgoing packets with a preceding minus sign to the payload size.

5.2   Rule Mining Evaluation

Table 5 shows the true positive rates achieved by the automated FPM methodology as well as the difference to the main implementation results. It can be seen that the FPM methodology outperforms the main implementation in all cases except Facebook where it underperforms. Furthermore, from Table 6, it can be seen that the performance of the two approaches on the false discovery rate metric is similar.

Table 5. TP rates of the automated FPM methodology. The difference to the main implementation is given inside the parentheses.

Application	Messaging	Voice	Video
Facebook messenger	42% (−41)	54% (−42)	83% (−13)
Skype	100% (+12)	96% (−4)	100% (+25)
Viber	100% (0)	96% (+42)	100% (+12)
WhatsApp	100% (0)	100% (+8)	100% (+25)

Table 6. False discovery rates of the automated FPM methodology. The "Messaging FDR" column shows the percentages of erroneous messaging reporting in voice or video samples. Respectively, "Voice/video FDR" column shows the percentages of erroneous voice/video reporting in messaging samples. The difference to the main implementation is given inside the parentheses.

Application	Messaging FDR	Voice/video FDR
Facebook messenger	0% (0)	3% (+2)
Skype	2% (−3.5)	8.4% (+4.2)
Viber	3% (+1)	2% (0)
WhatsApp	2% (−6)	3.3% (+2.7)

The FPM methodology is able to achieve accurate detection of distinct outgoing chat messages with a true positive rate and false discovery rate (FDR) of 98.55% and 3.54%, respectively, across all applications under investigation. Figures 5 and 6 show randomly chosen packet captures from WhatsApp and Skype messaging activity. We choose not to include the equivalent graphs for the remaining applications due to space constraints. The vertical lines depict the logged timestamp of the outgoing chat messages, while *Main* and *FPM* points show the detected events using the two proposed methodologies. The slight temporal deviation of the detected events from the ground truth timestamp can be explained from the fact that the outgoing message is not truly instantaneous, but rather spans from the transmission to the delivery acknowledgement.

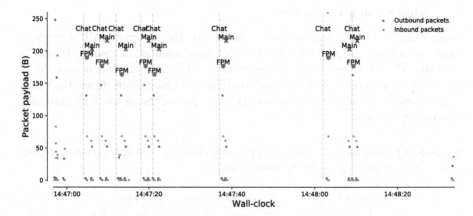

Fig. 5. Packet capture of WhatsApp messaging activity. The vertical lines depict the actual outgoing chat messages, while *Main* and *FPM* points show the detected events.

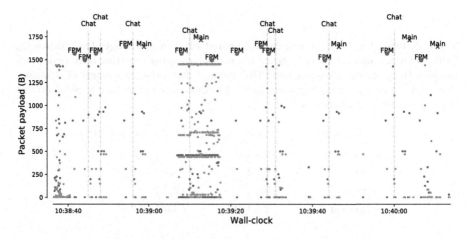

Fig. 6. Packet capture of Skype messaging activity.

Figure 5 shows a case where both our rule generation methods were able to perfectly detect the actual events, as opposed to the case shown in Fig. 6 where both false positives and false negatives are present. An interesting observation that can be derived is the increased Skype traffic during the time window 10:39:06–10:39:15. During this time, the user attempted to choose emoticons which were not pre-loaded.

6   Related Work

Traffic Analysis. Our work falls under the broad subject of traffic analysis. We briefly identify some general related work first, and subsequently expand on the most relevant areas.

Traffic analysis has been used to identify web pages transferred over encrypted tunnels established by privacy enhancing technologies such as OpenSSL, OpenVPN or TOR. For example, Herrmann et al. [19] present a classifier that correctly identifies up to 97% of web requests from packet traces.

Others used traffic analysis to extract voice information from encrypted VoIP conversations. For example, Wright et al. [39] showed that when the audio is encoded using variable bit rate codecs, the lengths of encrypted VoIP packets can be used to identify phrases spoken within a call with high accuracy.

Similarly, a cellphone's position can be located by monitoring the traffic of certain applications that provide location-based services, even over encrypted network traffic. For example, Ateniese et al. [8] show that an adversary could be able to extrapolate the position of a target user by just analysing the size and the timing of the encrypted traffic exchanged between that user and a location-based service provider.

Identification of Application Events in Encrypted Traffic. Most relevant to our work is the literature on fine-grained application event identification over encrypted traffic, surveyed in this section. The works in these section clearly motivate the feasibility of traffic analysis, often with the use of machine learning techniques. Our work builds on these feasibility results, but focuses on scalable implementation and efficient execution.

Coull et al. [14] proposed a method for traffic analysis of encrypted messaging services. Specifically, they show that an eavesdropper can learn information about user actions inside an application, the language and the size of the messages exchanged. Their results demonstrate the feasibility of gaining information about the usage of applications by observing packet lengths, but their analysis is focused on Apple's iMessage application and is an offline study. NetScope [29] is a work that performs robust inference of users' activities, for both Android and iOS devices, based on inspecting IP headers. Its main purpose is to demonstrate that a passive eavesdropper is capable of identifying fine-grained user activities within the wireless network traffic (even encrypted) generated by applications. NetScope is based on the intuition that the highly specific implementation of each app leaves a fingerprint on its traffic behaviour, such as transfer rates and packet exchanges, by learning subtle traffic behavioural differences between activities. Liu et al. [24] developed an iterative analyser for classifying encrypted mobile traffic to in-app activity. They selected an optimal set of the most discriminative features from raw features extracted from traffic packet sequences by a novel Maximising Inner activity similarity and Minimising Different activity similarity (MIMD) measurement. To develop the online analyser, they represent a traffic flow with a series of time windows, which are described by the optimal feature vector and are updated iteratively at the packet level. For their experiments, they analysed data extracted from WeChat, WhatsApp, and Facebook. Conti et al. [11,12] proposed a system to analyse encrypted network traffic to identify user actions on Android devices, such as email exchange, interactions over social network, etc. Their framework leverages information that is available in TCP/IP packets, like IP addresses and ports, among with other features, like packet size, direction and timing. They analyse diverse Android applications, such as Gmail, Facebook, Twitter, Tumblr and Dropbox. Using machine learning techniques, they conduct their experiments that show that the system can achieve accuracy and precision higher than 95% for a number of user actions. While our work is based on the same grounds (i.e., the feasibility of user activity identification over encrypted network traffic based on packet trains), we advance the state-of-the-art by (i) proposing a novel expressive pattern language specification, (ii) building a scalable and optimized implementation, which was integrated to our proprietary DPI engine and tested and evaluated on real-world traffic volumes, (iii) showing that the rule extraction is amenable to data mining techniques.

Application Identification and Classification. In this work, we focus on fine-grained event identification within the traffic of an application, and therefore rely on application identification, such as by means of server IP address ranges, or metadata available as plaintext, such as the Server Name Identification (SNI) header in TLS traffic, or plaintext information in certificates exchanged. Nevertheless, there is a large body of work on automating application identification or classification of the traffic's nature (e.g. video streaming), mostly relying on machine learning approaches, and often applicable to encrypted traffic [4,6,9,17,20,23,27,30,31,36,40,41].

Endpoint Device Tools. We used tools running on endpoint devices to collect ground truth samples. Here we survey a few related tools. Haystack [28] is a mobile application distributed via popular app stores that can correlate contextual information such as app identifiers and radio state with specific traffic flows (encrypted or not) destined to remote services, illuminating mobile application performance, privacy and security. ProfileDroid [37] is another monitoring and profiling system that can characterise the behaviour of Android applications at the static, user, OS and network layers. Finally, TaintDroid [16] performs dynamic information-flow tracking in order to identify privacy leaks.

Traffic Analysis Resistance. There have been efforts to create protocols, networks and applications that provide anonymity and privacy guarantees in the face of traffic analysis. Dissent [38] and Riposte [13] are systems that provide strong guarantees by using message broadcasting. They protect packet metadata, but may be unattractive due to scalability issues. Herd [22] is another system that tackles the case of anonymity for VoIP calls, by addressing, like the former proposals, some of the limitations of the more general-purpose Tor anonymity network [15]. Vuvuzela [32] and Atom [21] are more scalable systems (thousands of messages for millions of users) that employ differential privacy to inject noise into observable metadata. AnonRep [43] builds on top of these guarantees for the case of reputation/voting systems, TARN [42] randomises the IP addresses, while TARANET [10] employs packet mixing and splitting to achieve constant-rate transmission.

7   Ethical Considerations

Since the nature of our study may rise some ethical considerations, we dedicate this section to discuss how we avoid abusing personal and private information of "human subjects" [26]. During the offline testing of our methodology, we processed samples that were collected using non-personal mobile devices and non-private accounts for each application, explicitly for the purposes of this experiment. Thus, there should be no privacy concerns regarding the data that was processed during this phase.

During the online testing, we minimized the information collected by the system to include only the number of matches per rule, without personally identifiable information of any kind. Neither this, nor other information was retrieved from the system besides the performance measurements. All troubleshooting was conducted based on our own collected offline traces.

This study is motivated by benign uses such as customer experience/QoS assessment, data leakage detection and policy enforcement (e.g. embargo on voice), but could be abused as discussed extensively in the literature. Thus, we strongly recommend that privacy sensitive applications take precautions. We intentionally limited the scope of this work to a single direction of communication—only message sending—to avoid the possibility of correlating the user pairs that send and receive messages at the same time, and thus recovering communication graphs.

8   Conclusion

In this work, we discussed fine-grained identification of application events over encrypted network traffic with a focus on scalability and maintainability. We demonstrated that (i) a simple regex-inspired language is expressive enough to achieve a minimum hit rate of 84%, (ii) our DPI engine can scale to 130 Gbps per node, with no more than 10% of extra CPU utilization, and (iii) the rule extraction is amenable to data mining techniques. Prior work demonstrated the feasibility of such techniques. Our work focuses on a real-world implementation because we believe that just like substring pattern matching is a requirement in a state-of-the-art network monitoring system, so is packet train matching, even if techniques such as encryption and traffic analysis resistance (Sect. 6) exist to evade them.

Acknowledgements. The authors would like to thank their shepherd Roya Ensafi.

References

1. Android tcpdump. https://www.androidtcpdump.com. Accessed 09 Mar 2018-
2. Busybox (android application). https://play.google.com/store/apps/details? id=stericson.busybox&hl=en. Accessed 09 Mar 2018
3. netstat(8) - Linux man page. https://linux.die.net/man/8/netstat. Accessed 09 Mar 2018
4. Aceto, G., Ciuonzo, D., Montieri, A., Pescapé, A.: Multi-classification approaches for classifying mobile app traffic. J. Netw. Comput. Appl. **103**, 131–145 (2018)
5. Aho, A.V., Corasick, M.J.: Efficient string matching: an aid to bibliographic search. Commun. ACM **18**(6), 333–340 (1975)
6. Alan, H.F., Kaur, J.: Can android applications be identified using only TCP/IP headers of their launch time traffic? In: Proceedings of the 9th ACM Conference on Security and Privacy in Wireless and Mobile Networks, pp. 61–66. ACM (2016)
7. Anonymized for submission: DPI engine anonymized for submission
8. Ateniese, G., Hitaj, B., Mancini, L.V., Verde, N.V., Villani, A.: No place to hide that bytes won't reveal: sniffing location-based encrypted traffic to track a user's position. Network and System Security. LNCS, vol. 9408, pp. 46–59. Springer, Cham (2015). https://doi.org/10.1007/978-3-319-25645-0_4
9. Bernaille, L., Teixeira, R.: Early recognition of encrypted applications. In: Uhlig, S., Papagiannaki, K., Bonaventure, O. (eds.) PAM 2007. LNCS, vol. 4427, pp. 165–175. Springer, Heidelberg (2007). https://doi.org/10.1007/978-3-540-71617-4_17
10. Chen, C., Asoni, D.E., Perrig, A., Barrera, D., Danezis, G., Troncoso, C.: Taranet: traffic-analysis resistant anonymity at the network layer. arXiv preprint arXiv:1802.08415 (2018)
11. Conti, M., Mancini, L.V., Spolaor, R., Verde, N.V.: Can't you hear me knocking: identification of user actions on android apps via traffic analysis. In: Proceedings of the 5th ACM Conference on Data and Application Security and Privacy, pp. 297–304. ACM (2015)
12. Conti, M., Mancini, L.V., Spolaor, R., Verde, N.V.: Analyzing android encrypted network traffic to identify user actions. IEEE Trans. Inf. Forensics Secur. **11**(1), 114–125 (2016)
13. Corrigan-Gibbs, H., Boneh, D., Mazières, D.: Riposte: an anonymous messaging system handling millions of users. In: 2015 IEEE Symposium on Security and Privacy (SP), pp. 321–338. IEEE (2015)
14. Coull, S.E., Dyer, K.P.: Traffic analysis of encrypted messaging services: apple imessage and beyond. ACM SIGCOMM Comput. Commun. Rev. **44**(5), 5–11 (2014)
15. Dingledine, R., Mathewson, N., Syverson, P.: Tor: the second-generation onion router. Technical report, Naval Research Lab Washington DC (2004)
16. Enck, W., et al.: Taintdroid: an information-flow tracking system for realtime privacy monitoring on smartphones. ACM Trans. Comput. Syst. (TOCS) **32**(2), 5 (2014)
17. Fu, Y., Xiong, H., Lu, X., Yang, J., Chen, C.: Service usage classification with encrypted internet traffic in mobile messaging apps. IEEE Trans. Mobile Comput. **15**(11), 2851–2864 (2016)
18. Gomariz, A., Campos, M., Marin, R., Goethals, B.: ClaSP: an efficient algorithm for mining frequent closed sequences. In: Pei, J., Tseng, V.S., Cao, L., Motoda, H., Xu, G. (eds.) PAKDD 2013. LNCS (LNAI), vol. 7818, pp. 50–61. Springer, Heidelberg (2013). https://doi.org/10.1007/978-3-642-37453-1_5

19. Herrmann, D., Wendolsky, R., Federrath, H.: Website fingerprinting: attacking popular privacy enhancing technologies with the multinomial Naïve-Bayes classifier. In: Proceedings of the 2009 ACM Workshop on Cloud Computing Security, CCSW 2009, pp. 31–42. ACM, New York (2009)
20. Karagiannis, T., Papagiannaki, K., Faloutsos, M.: BLINC: multilevel traffic classification in the dark. ACM SIGCOMM Comput. Commun. Rev. **35**, 229–240 (2005)
21. Kwon, A., Corrigan-Gibbs, H., Devadas, S., Ford, B.: Atom: horizontally scaling strong anonymity. In: Proceedings of the 26th Symposium on Operating Systems Principles, pp. 406–422. ACM (2017)
22. Le Blond, S., Choffnes, D., Caldwell, W., Druschel, P., Merritt, N.: Herd: a scalable, traffic analysis resistant anonymity network for VoIP systems. ACM SIGCOMM Comput. Commun. Rev. **45**, 639–652 (2015)
23. Li, W., Moore, A.W.: A machine learning approach for efficient traffic classification. In: 15th International Symposium on Modeling, Analysis, and Simulation of Computer and Telecommunication Systems, MASCOTS 2007, pp. 310–317. IEEE (2007)
24. Liu, J., Fu, Y., Ming, J., Ren, Y., Sun, L., Xiong, H.: Effective and real-time in-app activity analysis in encrypted internet traffic streams. In: Proceedings of the 23rd ACM SIGKDD International Conference on Knowledge Discovery and Data Mining, pp. 335–344. ACM (2017)
25. Papadopoulos, E.P., Diamantaris, M., Papadopoulos, P., Petsas, T., Ioannidis, S., Markatos, E.P.: The long-standing privacy debate: mobile websites vs mobile apps. In: Proceedings of the 26th International Conference on World Wide Web, pp. 153–162. International World Wide Web Conferences Steering Committee (2017)
26. Partridge, C., Allman, M.: Ethical considerations in network measurement papers. Commun. ACM **59**(10), 58–64 (2016)
27. Rapoport, M., Suter, P., Wittern, E., Lhóták, O., Dolby, J.: Who you gonna call? Analyzing web requests in android applications. In: 2017 IEEE/ACM 14th International Conference on Mining Software Repositories (MSR), pp. 80–90. IEEE (2017)
28. Razaghpanah, A., et al.: Haystack: In situ mobile traffic analysis in user space. ArXiv e-prints (2015)
29. Saltaformaggio, B., et al.: Eavesdropping on fine-grained user activities within smartphone apps over encrypted network traffic. In: WOOT (2016)
30. Taylor, V.F., Spolaor, R., Conti, M., Martinovic, I.: AppScanner: automatic fingerprinting of smartphone apps from encrypted network traffic. In: 2016 IEEE European Symposium on Security and Privacy (EuroS&P), pp. 439–454. IEEE (2016)
31. Taylor, V.F., Spolaor, R., Conti, M., Martinovic, I.: Robust smartphone app identification via encrypted network traffic analysis. IEEE Trans. Inf. Forensics Secur. **13**(1), 63–78 (2018)
32. Van Den Hooff, J., Lazar, D., Zaharia, M., Zeldovich, N.: Vuvuzela: scalable private messaging resistant to traffic analysis. In: Proceedings of the 25th Symposium on Operating Systems Principles, pp. 137–152. ACM (2015)
33. Vasiliadis, G., Ioannidis, S.: GrAVity: a massively parallel antivirus engine. In: Jha, S., Sommer, R., Kreibich, C. (eds.) RAID 2010. LNCS, vol. 6307, pp. 79–96. Springer, Heidelberg (2010). https://doi.org/10.1007/978-3-642-15512-3_5
34. Vasiliadis, G., Koromilas, L., Polychronakis, M., Ioannidis, S.: GASPP: a GPU-accelerated stateful packet processing framework. In: USENIX Annual Technical Conference, pp. 321–332 (2014)

35. Vasiliadis, G., Polychronakis, M., Ioannidis, S.: MiDeA: a multi-parallel intrusion detection architecture. In: Proceedings of the 18th ACM Conference on Computer and Communications Security, pp. 297–308. ACM (2011)
36. Wang, Q., Yahyavi, A., Kemme, B., He, W.: I know what you did on your smartphone: inferring app usage over encrypted data traffic. In: 2015 IEEE Conference on Communications and Network Security (CNS), pp. 433–441. IEEE (2015)
37. Wei, X., Gomez, L., Neamtiu, I., Faloutsos, M.: ProfileDroid: multi-layer profiling of android applications. In: Proceedings of the 18th Annual International Conference on Mobile Computing and Networking, pp. 137–148. ACM (2012)
38. Wolinsky, D.I., Corrigan-Gibbs, H., Ford, B., Johnson, A.: Dissent in numbers: making strong anonymity scale. In: OSDI, pp. 179–182 (2012)
39. Wright, C.V., Ballard, L., Coull, S.E., Monrose, F., Masson, G.M.: Spot me if you can: uncovering spoken phrases in encrypted VoIP conversations. In: IEEE Symposium on Security and Privacy, SP 2008, pp. 35–49. IEEE (2008)
40. Xu, Q., et al.: Automatic generation of mobile app signatures from traffic observations. In: IEEE Conference on Computer Communications (INFOCOM), pp. 1481–1489. IEEE (2015)
41. Yao, H., Ranjan, G., Tongaonkar, A., Liao, Y., Mao, Z.M.: SAMPLES: self adaptive mining of persistent lexical snippets for classifying mobile application traffic. In: Proceedings of the 21st Annual International Conference on Mobile Computing and Networking, pp. 439–451. ACM (2015)
42. Yu, L., Wang, Q., Barrineau, G., Oakley, J., Brooks, R.R., Wang, K.C.: TARN: a SDN-based traffic analysis resistant network architecture. arXiv preprint arXiv:1709.00782 (2017)
43. Zhai, E., Wolinsky, D.I., Chen, R., Syta, E., Teng, C., Ford, B.: AnonRep: towards tracking-resistant anonymous reputation. In: NSDI, pp. 583–596 (2016)

Hardware-Assisted Security

Hardware Assisted Randomization of Data

Brian Belleville[1], Hyungon Moon[2], Jangseop Shin[2], Dongil Hwang[2],
Joseph M. Nash[1], Seonhwa Jung[2], Yeoul Na[1], Stijn Volckaert[1], Per Larsen[1],
Yunheung Paek[2(✉)], and Michael Franz[1]

[1] University of California, Irvine, Irvine, USA
{bbellevi,jmnash,yeouln,stijnv,perl,franz}@uci.edu
[2] ECE and ISRC, Seoul National University, Seoul, South Korea
{hgmoon,jsshin,dihwang,shjung}@sor.snu.ac.kr, ypaek@snu.ac.kr

Abstract. Data-oriented attacks are gaining traction thanks to advances
in code-centric mitigation techniques for memory corruption vulnerabilities. Previous work on mitigating data-oriented attacks includes Data
Space Randomization (DSR). DSR classifies program variables into a set
of equivalence classes, and encrypts variables with a key randomly chosen
for each equivalence class. This thwarts memory corruption attacks that
introduce illegitimate data flows. However, existing implementations of
DSR trade precision for better run-time performance, which leaves attackers sufficient leeway to mount attacks. In this paper, we show that high
precision and good run-time performance are not mutually exclusive. We
present HARD, a precise and efficient hardware-assisted implementation
of DSR. HARD distinguishes a larger number of equivalence classes, and
incurs lower run-time overhead than software-only DSR. Our implementation achieves run-time overheads of just 6.61% on average, while the software version with the same protection costs 40.96%.

This material is based upon work partially supported by the Defense Advanced
Research Projects Agency (DARPA) under contracts FA8750-15-C-0124 and
FA8750-15-C-0085, by the United States Office of Naval Research (ONR) under
contract N00014-17-1-2782, by the National Science Foundation under awards CNS-
1619211 and CNS-1513837, by the National Research Foundation of Korea (NRF)
grant funded by the Korea government (MSIT) (NRF-2017R1A2A1A17069478), by
the Brain Korea 21 Plus Project in 2018, and by the Institute for Information &
communications Technology Promotion (IITP) grant funded by the Korea government (MSIT) (No.2017-0-00213, Development of Cyber Self Mutation Technologies
for Proactive Cyber Defense). Any opinions, findings, and conclusions or recommendations expressed in this material are those of the authors and do not necessarily
reflect the views of the Defense Advanced Research Projects Agency (DARPA) or
its Contracting Agents, the Office of Naval Research or its Contracting Agents, the
National Science Foundation, or any other agency of the U.S. Government. The
authors also gratefully acknowledge a gift from Oracle Corporation.

B. Belleville and H. Moon—Authors contributed equally to this work.

© Springer Nature Switzerland AG 2018
M. Bailey et al. (Eds.): RAID 2018, LNCS 11050, pp. 337–358, 2018.
https://doi.org/10.1007/978-3-030-00470-5_16

1   Introduction

Memory corruption exploits remain an important attack vector in practice. Attempts to eliminate this class of vulnerabilities are being undertaken from many angles including (i) migration to type safe languages, (ii) static and dynamic program analysis, and (iii) retrofitting unsafe code with memory safety mechanisms. Automatic exploit mitigations have also been highly effective at driving up the cost of exploitation, and are transparent to developers and end-users. They also avoid the substantial overheads associated with full memory safety enforcement [26–28]. Mitigation techniques such as Address Space Layout Randomization (ASLR), Data Execution Prevention, and Control Flow Integrity (CFI) are widely deployed in modern systems. These techniques increase the difficulty of performing arbitrary code execution attacks, which has encouraged attackers to explore alternatives such as data-oriented attacks [7,13,14]. These attacks corrupt program's data flow without diverting its control flow.

Data Space Randomization (DSR) is a promising defense that mitigates data-oriented attacks [3,4]. DSR thwarts unintended data flows while leaving all legitimate data flows unaffected. To do so, DSR encrypts variables that are stored in the program's memory, and it uses different random keys to encrypt unrelated variables. Generating these keys with sufficient entropy makes the results of load and store operations that violate the program's intended data flow unpredictable, and thus hinders reliable construction of data-oriented attacks.

Prior work on DSR makes several trade-offs that favor run-time performance over security. First, existing versions of DSR do not encrypt variables that cannot be used as the base of an overflow attack. This leaves programs unprotected against temporal memory exploits such as use-after-free or uninitialized reads. Second, prior versions often use weak encryption keys to avoid the cost of handling unaligned memory accesses. Lastly, existing implementations rely on imprecise program analyses, which leads them to incorrectly classify many variables as related. As a result, these unrelated variables are encrypted with the same keys. Many unintended data flows are therefore still possible, which gives attackers some leeway to construct exploits.

This motivated our work on Hardware-Assisted Randomization of Data (HARD), a hardware-assisted implementation of more precise DSR. HARD offers greater security than prior approaches by distinguishing more unrelated variables. To do this, HARD uses a context-sensitive points-to analysis and generates encryption operations that use calling context-specific keys. HARD also encrypts *all* of the program data, and consistently uses strong 64-bit encryption keys. Thus, unlike existing schemes, HARD does not compromise its security guarantees for better run-time performance. Furthermore, HARD incurs less overhead than prior work thanks to its hardware extensions: specialized instructions to access encrypted data and efficient caches to manage encryption keys. These extensions also shield our solution against information leakage attacks because the keys are managed by the hardware and cannot be accessed from user-space.

In summary, we contribute the following:

- We propose the first context-sensitive DSR scheme, which offers greater security guarantees than prior solutions by dynamically choosing context-specific encryption keys based on the results of a context-sensitive analysis.
- We describe an ISA extension that efficiently supports our DSR scheme in hardware, and is also general enough to support all prior DSR designs.
- We implemented our DSR scheme and ISA extension in HARD and show that HARD achieves high precision with low overhead.

2   Background

Our goal is to thwart attacks that violate the intended data flow of a program. Example 1 illustrates two such violations: a *use-after-free* and an *uninitialized read*. Both types of unintended data flows are highly relevant in practice. Use-after-free is commonly exploited to attack high-profile targets such as web browsers and operating system kernels [30], and well-known Heartbleed bug was, at its core, an uninitialized read vulnerability [8].

At lines (a-1) and (a-2) in the example, the program allocates and initializes a list, X, as depicted in Fig. 1(a). At line (b-1), the program frees the second element of list X, so the Next member of the first element becomes a dangling pointer. The program then allocates a new list, Y, at line (b-2). The program now reads the contents of list Y without initialization at line (b-3). Due to the deterministic nature of common memory allocators such as *dlmalloc* [22], the two lists will likely be laid out in the memory as shown in Fig. 1(b). Thus, the data read at line (b-3) will likely include the recently free'd element of list X.

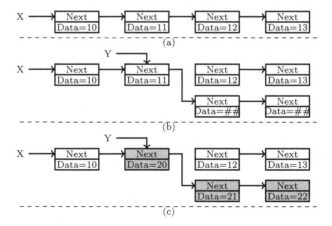

Fig. 1. The diagram shows the lists generated in Example 1. (a) shows list X after initialization at line (a-2). (b) shows the most likely layouts of lists X and Y at line (b-3). (c) shows the most likely layouts of the lists at line (c-2).

The rest of the example demonstrates the use-after-free vulnerability. The program attempts to print the contents of list X, whose second element was freed at line (b-1). A deterministic memory allocator may allocate the list X as shown in Fig. 1(c), and the dumped list includes elements of list Y.

2.1   Mitigation with DSR

DSR mitigates such unintended data flows by randomizing the representation of program data in memory. DSR relies on alias analysis to compute the points-to relations between pointers and the storage locations they can reference. Two pointers are considered aliases if they can reference the same storage location. Similarly, a pointer p may alias named object o, if p can point to o. Based on the alias analysis, DSR partitions storage locations into *equivalence classes* so that all storage locations belong to an equivalence class. Any two storage locations that may alias each other belong to the same equivalence class.

DSR encrypts storage locations belonging to different equivalence classes with distinct encryption keys. Locations belonging to the same equivalence class, however, must be encrypted with the same key. In the previous example, an ideal implementation of DSR would see that lists X and Y are disjoint, and would encrypt them with different keys. An attacker that does not know the keys cannot extract the true contents of the illegally read list element.

Unfortunately, existing implementations of DSR cannot prevent the exploits in this example [3,4]. They *do* consider lists X and Y related because of the imprecise *(context-insensitive)* alias analysis which does not consider the functions' calling contexts. In the example, both X (at line (a-2)) and Y (at line (c-1)) are passed as an argument to fillList, and the context-insensitive alias analysis will report that the formal argument L of fillList may alias both X and Y. Variables X and Y will therefore be assigned to the same equivalence class.

In this paper, we avoid this loss of precision by using a *context-sensitive* alias analysis. If we analyze our example program with a context-sensitive alias analysis, we obtain two sets of aliasing relations: one for the calling context at line (a-2) where fillList's formal argument L aliases X, and one for the calling context at line (c-1) where L aliases Y. By taking the calling context into account, we avoid having to treat X and Y as aliases and can therefore place them in different equivalence classes.

Leveraging the greater precision of context-sensitive alias analyses is challenging since the DSR instrumentation code must then take the calling context into account to determine which encryption key should be used. We discuss this challenge at length in Sect. 4, and present a novel DSR scheme that supports different contexts via dynamic key binding.

3   Threat Model

We assume the following threat model, which is realistic and consistent with related work in this area [14,33]:

- The victim program contains a memory corruption vulnerability that lets adversaries read and write arbitrary locations as long as such accesses are permitted by the MMU.
- The victim program is protected against code injection by enforcing the $W \oplus X$ policy such that no executable code is writable.
- The victim program runs in user mode and that the host system's software running in supervisor mode has not been compromised.
- We do not consider side-channel attacks, flaws in the hardware, or adversaries that have physical access to the system hosting the victim program.

Note that we do not require that ASLR is enabled, and we do not include any assumptions about it in our threat model. However HARD is fully compatible with ASLR, and additional randomness will increase security, for example by making known plaintext attacks harder (see Sect. 9).

4   DSR Design

We begin this section by providing a conceptual overview of our design, and then discuss several key components in detail. Our design can either be realized in pure software, similar to prior implementations of DSR, or supported by the hardware extensions we present in Sect. 5.

Our scheme transforms input programs at the compiler intermediate representation (IR) level. The first step is a context-sensitive alias analysis that categorizes the program's memory locations into equivalence classes based on the points-to sets computed by this analysis. We then assign two types of keys to the memory access instructions in the program, according to the equivalence classes they access. We assign a *static key* to instructions that always accesses the same equivalence class, regardless of its calling context, and a *dynamic key* to the others, which may access multiple equivalent classes depending on the calling context. The static keys are directly embedded to the data section of the program so that each instruction can fetch its key, while dynamic keys are passed to a callee through the *context frames*, which the caller should construct. Our scheme transforms (1) function call sites to construct context frames, (2) instructions that use static keys to fetch their keys from the data section, (3) instructions that use dynamic keys to fetch their keys from the context frame, (4) all store instructions to encrypt the data, and (5) all load instructions to decrypt the data.

4.1   Enabling Context Sensitivity

One of our primary goals is to support dynamic key assignment for memory instructions that may access multiple equivalence classes depending on their calling contexts. We determine the set of equivalence classes that can be accessed through dynamic keys as follows. For each function in the program, we identify the set of equivalence classes reachable from the function's pointer arguments or pointer return value. From that set, we remove any equivalence classes which contain global variables. If an instruction accesses an equivalence class that contains global variables, then that instruction always accesses that same class, regardless of which context the function is called from. Thus, such an equivalence class can safely be removed from the set. The remaining set of equivalence classes are the *dynamic classes* in that function. Other classes that are used in the function, but that are not in the set (i.e., the classes that were removed because they contain globals, and the classes that are not reachable from the pointer arguments or pointer return value), are considered *static classes*. During instrumentation, we assign dynamic keys to memory access instructions that target dynamic classes, and static keys to those that target static classes.

Managing Context Frames. We store dynamic keys in *context frames*. For each function that contains instructions with dynamic keys, we first instrument all of the function's callers to create the necessary context frame and to populate the frame with the keys for the actual callee arguments. We then instrument the callee so that instructions accessing dynamic classes read the keys from the context frame.

Handling Indirect Calls. Instrumenting indirect call sites complicates this process because if care is not taken, different target functions could require different sets of dynamic keys, even if the target functions have the same signature. To correctly instrument indirect call sites we constrain all functions that may be called from the same call site to have the same dynamic classes.

Static Equivalence Classes. Every instruction that accesses a static class will always access *that* static class, regardless of the calling context. Thus, we can safely assign static keys to instructions that access static classes.

Equivalence classes that contain global variables are always *static classes*. To understand why this is always true, consider how a flow-insensitive alias analysis constructs equivalence classes. An alias analysis evaluates all of the instructions in the program and incorporates any aliasing relationship introduced by an instruction into the points-to sets. When a flow-insensitive alias analysis such as ours evaluates a statement such as:

```
void* a = condition ? &global : &function_argument;
```

it will consider pointer a an alias for both global and function_argument, which will therefore be placed into the same equivalence class. This equivalence class will now be a static class, because, no matter which context this function is called from, any instruction that accesses this static class can now potentially access the memory storage location occupied by global.

4.2 Memory Encryption

We instrument memory access operations so that the values are xor-encrypted before they are stored to and after they are loaded from memory. The encryption/decryption instructions we add use the unique randomly-generated 8-byte key we assign to their respective target equivalence classes.

To use 8-byte keys consistently for all equivalence classes, we must carefully handle memory accesses which are not 8-byte aligned. For example, consider an equivalence class containing a structure with two fields, as shown in Fig. 2. When accessing field s.b, we should shift the key to mask the field's data with the correct part of the key (left side of the figure). Cadar et al.'s DSR implementation assigns weaker, repeating keys (right side of Fig. 2) to avoid costly shift operations [4]. We use the hardware support to efficiently handle shift operations.

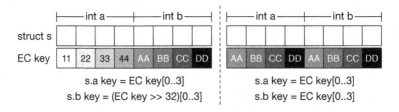

Fig. 2. Calculating keys for unaligned accesses under HARD (left side) and prior work by Cadar et al. (right side). "EC key" is the key for the equivalence class.

Our design encrypts all possible equivalence classes. To reduce the run-time overhead, prior DSR systems did not protect equivalence classes that are "safe". An equivalence class is considered safe if a static analysis can show that none of the accesses to that equivalence class can read or write outside the bounds of the target object. This weakens their protection against temporal memory errors such as use-after-free and uninitialized read. Our hardware extension enables higher level of protection with reasonable overhead.

4.3 Support for External Code and Data

We designed our scheme to allow interaction with external code. To do so, we must ensure that any encrypted data is decrypted before it is accessed by the external code, and re-encrypted afterwards. Otherwise, we cannot encrypt any equivalence classes that include the data that is passed to the external functions. To maximize the amount of memory we encrypt, we use wrapper functions around calls to known external functions, as was done in prior DSR implementations. However, we cannot encrypt accesses to external global variables because they could be accessed by external code at any point.

We must also handle function pointers that may escape to external code. An escaping function pointer could be called by the external code without the proper keys in the context frame. Therefore, calls through this pointer must not require dynamic keys. However, it is still possible to pass dynamic keys to direct calls to the same function. To handle this, we maintain two copies of the affected functions—one that accepts dynamic keys and one that does not encrypt accesses to the equivalence classes of the arguments. Note that an attacker may seek to use the version that does not expect encrypted arguments. However, in order to redirect control flow to such a function, she will need to overwrite a code pointer. This memory access will be encrypted, so the attacker will already have to bypass DSR to perform such an overwrite.

5   Hardware Design

We designed an extension of the RISC-V architecture to accelerate our DSR scheme's encryption operations and to protect the encryption keys from information leakage attacks. The primary goal of our hardware design is to achieve low overhead. To accomplish this we use a sophisticated hardware design to accelerate the encryption operations used by DSR. If both the encryption key and the data are in the cache, our hardware implementation is able to perform a load or store, key fetch, and XOR within a single instruction without any additional latency or pipeline stalls compared to a normal load or store instruction.

Overview. HARD adds or modifies several hardware components, as shown in Fig. 3. When executing a HARD'ened program, the processor uses two reserved memory regions, the *Context Stack* and the *Key Table*, to store and manage the encryption keys used by the program. The processor accesses these regions directly using their physical addresses and the regions are not mapped

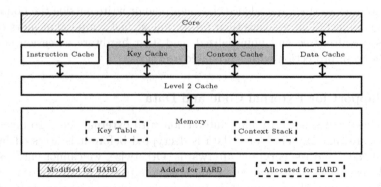

Fig. 3. Hardware overview for a HARD-enabled system.

into the virtual address space of the protected program. This design ensures that the encryption keys cannot be leaked, as the MMU forbids accesses to unmapped memory. The Key Table stores all encryption keys used in the program. To support dynamically assigned keys, programs must create context frames on the context stack and copy keys from the Key Table to the context frames.

Both the Context Stack and the Key Table have a corresponding cache: the *Context Cache* and the *Key Cache* respectively. These caches are internal to the processor and cannot be read by an attacker. Keys are always loaded through the corresponding caches, and if a key is not present in the cache, the processor will transparently fetch it from the corresponding memory region. To pair the caches with their corresponding memory regions, each cache has a base register containing the physical memory address of the associated memory region.

5.1   Hardware Initialization

The OS kernel is responsible for the initialization of the aforementioned memory regions and caches. When the OS loads a HARD'ened program, the kernel allocates the Key Table and initializes it with randomly generated encryption keys. The kernel then sets the base address register of the Key Cache and activates the cache using a control register. Finally, the kernel allocates the Context Stack and sets the base address register of the Context Cache.

5.2   New Instructions

HARD adds two sets of instructions. One set of instructions is used to load data from or store data to encrypted memory. The other set of instructions is used to manage the Context Cache and Context Stack.

Memory Access Instructions. The RISC-V instruction set architecture, which we extend, contains nine load instructions and six store instructions. For each of these, HARD adds a specialized version that decrypts data when loading or encrypts data when storing. The specialized instructions use the same mnemonic as the original instructions, but have a um suffix (for loads) or m suffix (for stores). The double-word load/store instructions, for example, look as follows:

- ldum rd, id(rb): load a double word from the virtual address stored in register rb, decrypt the data with the key at index id in the Key Table/Context Stack, and write the decrypted data to register rd.
- sdm rd, id(rb): encrypt the data in register rd with the key at index id in the Key Table/Context Stack and store the encrypted data to the virtual address in register rb as a double word.

The type of encryption key is encoded in the Most Significant Bit (MSB) of the index id. If the MSB is set to 0, the remainder of the index id is interpreted as an index into the Key Table, and the instruction therefore has a statically assigned key. We refer to these index IDs as *static IDs*. If the MSB is set to 1, the remainder of the index id is interpreted as an index into the current context frame on the Context Stack, and the instruction therefore has a dynamically assigned key. We refer to these index IDs as *dynamic IDs*.

Context Stack Management Instructions. The second group of instructions are used to manage the Context Stack. Before a new context is entered, the program should prepare a new context frame on the Context Stack and copy the keys used within the corresponding context into that frame. This newly prepared context frame must then be activated before entering the corresponding context. HARD offers four instructions to prepare, activate, and deactivate context frames.

- `mksc dest_id, src_id`: move the key at index `src_id` in the Key Table to slot `dest_id` in the context frame under preparation.
- `mkcc dest_id, src_id`: move a key from slot `src_id` of the currently activated context frame to slot `dest_id` of the context frame under preparation.
- `drpush cur_len`: deactivate the active context frame and activate the context frame under preparation. `cur_len` is the number of slots in the current frame.
- `drpop`: deactivate the active context frame and activate the previous context frame.

The `mksc`, `mkcc`, and `drpush` instructions should be used just before calling a function to provide the matching context frame. Similarly, the `drpop` instruction should be used just before a return to restore the matching frame for the caller.

6   DSR Implementation

We implemented our DSR scheme as a link-time optimization pass in LLVM/Clang 3.8 for RISC-V, and use alias analysis algorithms from the PoolAlloc module [20].

6.1   Computing Equivalence Classes

We use Bottom-up Data Structure Analysis (Bottom-up DSA) [21] to categorize memory objects into equivalence classes. Bottom-up DSA is a context- and field-sensitive points-to analysis that scales well to large programs. It is context sensitive to arbitrary length acyclic call paths, and it is speculatively field-sensitive. It is field-sensitive for type-safe code, and falls back to field-insensitive for type-unsafe code. The algorithm is unification based and is not flow sensitive. The output of Bottom-up DSA is a *points-to graph* for each function, which incorporates the aliasing effects of all callees of that function (thus "Bottom-up"). A node in the points-to graph represents a set of memory objects joined through aliasing relationships, and nodes represent disjoint sets of objects. Each node therefore identifies a distinct equivalence class within that function. For each function and its associated points-to graph, we assign equivalence classes based on Bhaktar and Sekar's mask assignment algorithm [3], with a slight modification to differentiate the static and dynamic equivalence classes.

The first step in class assignment is identifying the dynamic equivalence classes. To handle indirect calls, we constrain all possible targets of an indirect call site to have the same dynamic classes. Bottom-up DSA can create classes of functions that are all callable from the same call site. The analysis result for these functions is a single points-to graph shared by all functions in the class. Within this graph all arguments and return values for these functions will share the same set of nodes. We use this functionality to compute the set of dynamic classes for all functions in the class simultaneously. We mark all nodes that are reachable from the pointer arguments and the pointer return values of each function in the class, and then remove all nodes that contain global variables or are marked un-encryptable. The resulting nodes become the set of dynamic classes for every function in the class. We use the same procedure for functions that are only called directly, but apply the procedure individually to each function.

For each node and its associated equivalence class, we assign a dynamic ID if a node is marked as dynamic and a static ID otherwise. If a node contains a global variable, we ensure that every such class in all functions uses the same static ID. If a node is marked un-encryptable, we assign it a null static ID which indicates that memory accesses to this class should not be instrumented.

6.2 Handling External Code and Data

To minimize the number of nodes that need to be marked as un-encryptable, we implemented wrapper functions for the library functions that our benchmark programs call (cf. Subsect. 4.3). A wrapper functions decrypts the variables in equivalence classes that may be accessed by an external function, and re-encrypt them when that external function returns. The wrappers must access keys from the Context Stack and use the new instructions for memory accesses. To ensure that the correct instructions are used, the wrappers are written in C using inline assembly code. We manually implemented the wrapper functions for all 71 C library functions used in SPEC CINT 2000. Implementing new wrappers is straightforward; writing a wrapper generally takes just a few minutes after consulting documentation such as man pages. Most wrappers have a predictable structure, and generating wrappers for many common cases could be automated by adding annotations to augment the type signature of the function with additional information. For example, an annotation would distinguish between different uses of `char*` arguments, indicating if the pointer refers to a single `char` variable, an array, or a null-terminated string.

6.3 Program Transformation

Our transformation pass runs after all analysis steps have completed. It starts by creating a constructor function that runs before the `main` function. The constructor encrypts the initial values of all global variables. After we create the constructor, we annotate load and store operations with the class ID assigned to the memory location accessed by the operation. Next, we insert the instructions to manage the Context Stack. For each call site, we construct a mapping from the class IDs of the actual arguments in the caller context to the dynamic IDs of the formal arguments of the callee function. We use this mapping to insert the mksc and mkcc instructions, which initialize the callee context. We insert drpush instructions directly before call instructions to switch to the callee's context, and we insert drpop before return instructions to restore the caller's context. During code generation, we emit the annotated loads and stores as specialized instructions with the dynamic or static equivalence class ID encoded into the immediate operand.

7 Hardware Implementation

We implemented the proposed hardware architecture by extending one of the instances generated by the Rocket Chip Generator [2]. This instance is composed of a Rocket Core [24] with a 16KiB L1 instruction cache, a 16KiB L1 data cache, and a 256KiB unified L2 cache. We extended this system with the two hardware components described in Sect. 5, the Key Cache and the Context Cache. We also modified the core pipeline to interact with these caches.

7.1 Instruction Encoding

To avoid intrusive changes to the existing instruction decoder, we designed our specialized instructions to resemble the instructions they are based on. Our specialized instructions differ from their base instructions in only one respect: the specialized ones interpret their immediate fields as index IDs, rather than memory offsets. This means that, like these memory offsets, the size of the index IDs is limited to twelve bits. We use the most significant bit of the index ID to indicate whether the index should be interpreted as an index into the Key Table, or an index into the current frame on the Context Stack. This leaves us with eleven bits to encode the ID itself.

The mksc and mkcc instructions each require two index ID operands, a source ID and a destination ID. For this reason, we based these instructions on the RISC-V instruction that can encode the longest immediate field, which is 20 bits long. The semantics of the instructions defines the type of index IDs they operate on, so we do not have to encode it in the MSB. The mksc instruction has a static ID (index into the Key Table) and a dynamic ID (index into the current context frame) as its operands, and the mkcc instruction has two dynamic IDs as operands. The size of these pairs of index IDs cannot exceed the available 20 bits. We therefore limit the size of dynamic IDs to nine bits, and the size of static IDs to eleven bits. This limits the size of the Key Table to 2048 entries and the size of the context frames to 512 slots. We analyzed a large number of programs and found that 512 is a realistic limit to the number of dynamic keys in a single context frame. We discuss the security impact of the Key Table size and how to handle programs that could use a larger number of keys in Sect. 9. The other context management instructions, `drpush` and `drpop`, are pseudo-instructions using the Control and Status Registers (CSR) interface.

7.2 Processor Pipeline

We modified the core pipeline to enable interaction with the Key Cache and Context Cache, as shown in Fig. 4. The modified pipeline sends static and dynamic IDs to the Key Cache or Context Cache, which respond with the corresponding statically or dynamically assigned encryption keys respectively.

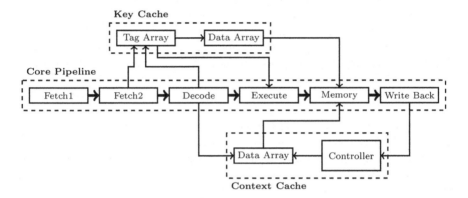

Fig. 4. Overview of the modified Rocket core, showing the interaction between the original core pipeline, the Key Cache and Context Cache added by HARD.

Key Cache. The Key Cache is a fully-associative cache that services requests for static IDs by loading the corresponding keys from its data array or from the Key Table in the memory. The Key Cache has two components: the pipeline depicted in Fig. 4 and a miss handler. The cache has a tag array, containing a set of (*valid, id, offset*) tuples. For a static ID whose key is currently present in the Key Cache's data array, this tuple gives us the offset of that static ID's corresponding encryption key in the data array. The data array has a size of 2KiB, which means that it can contain 256 keys. If the core pipeline requests a key that is not present in the data array, the miss handler loads that key directly from the Key Table. Keys are never written back to memory upon eviction from the data array because the Key Table cannot be updated at run time.

Due to the tag array access and tag matching, our Key Cache takes two cycles to respond to a request, even if the requested key is present in the data array. To avoid stalling the Execute stage, we forward the raw instruction bytes from the Fetch2 stage to the Key Cache. The Key Cache uses a minimal decoder to determine if the forwarded instruction contains a static ID. If the instruction does indeed contain a static ID, the Key Cache will look up the corresponding key immediately. This allows the Key Cache to provide the Execute stage with the appropriate key without stalling if the key was present in the cache. Otherwise, it will stall the pipeline to fetch the key from the memory.

Context Cache. The Context Cache consists of two major components, the stack controller and the data array, following the design of a hardware stack with on-chip memory presented in earlier work [32]. The cache has dedicated registers to keep track of the locations of three context frames: the previous frame, the current (activated) frame, and the next frame. The Context Cache's data array is 1KiB, which is sufficient to store the top 128 slots on the Context Stack.

When the program copies an encryption key to the Context Stack using the mkcc or mksc instructions, the key will be stored directly in the corresponding slot of the next frame in the Cache's data array. This allows the Context Stack to minimize costly memory accesses. Whenever the program executes a drpush or drpop instruction to activate a different frame, the stack controller updates the dedicated registers accordingly. After executing one of these instructions, the cache may evict the oldest entries or fetch entries from memory depending on the available space in the data array. Eviction, fetching, and changes to the context frame registers happen at the last stage of the pipeline. This creates a possible hazard for other instructions accessing the Context Cache. We therefore modified the pipeline so that whenever a drpush or drpop instruction is decoded, or an eviction or fetch is in progress, any instructions that access the context cache are stalled until the drpush/drpop has finished executing, or the eviction/fetch has completed.

8   Evaluation

We implemented and tested several configurations of HARD's analysis and instrumentation passes and compared them to prior DSR implementations:

– The **Prior DSR** configuration mimics prior DSR implementations. For this configuration, we implemented a context-insensitive points-to analysis to calculate the equivalence classes, but we did not instrument accesses to safe objects and used weak encryption keys for unaligned accesses (cf. Subsect. 4.2).
– The **Full Key Size** configuration uses the same analysis, but uses full 8-byte keys for all memory accesses (including unaligned accesses).
– The **Full Context Insensitive** configuration also uses the context-insensitive analysis, but encrypts accesses to *all* equivalence classes rather than just the unsafe ones.
– The **Context Sensitive** configuration uses HARD's context-sensitive analysis to calculate equivalence classes.

8.1   Performance

We measured the run-time overhead of all four of HARD's configurations and evaluated them with and without our architectural support. We instantiated HARD on a Xilinx Zynq ZC702 evaluation board using the *Rocket Chip Generator* [2]. The board has an FPGA running at 25 MHz and has 256 MiB of DDR3 memory. We ran the RISC-V port of the Linux kernel 4.1.17, and modified the kernel to initialize the Key Table and Context Stack on program startup. As our prototyping platform is severely resource constrained, we evaluated the run-time performance using the SPEC CINT 2000 instead of the more recent SPEC CPU 2006. For the same reason, we also ran the benchmark programs on the *train* inputs, as the board does not have enough memory to use the *ref* inputs.

Table 1 shows our evaluation results for the four configurations. For the *Prior DSR* configuration, we only have the results for software-only DSR as our hardware does not support variable-length keys. Each increasingly secure configuration incurs additional overhead, which is substantially reduced by HARD's hardware component. The overhead of the most precise configuration is 6.61% with hardware support, while the overhead of the software-only implementation is 40.96%.

Table 1. Run-time overhead of HARD and software-only DSR on SPEC CINT 2000. HARD's run-time overhead is lower than prior DSR implementations, which provide weaker security guarantee due to their less precise analyses and performance-oriented optimizations.

Benchmark	Prior DSR	Full key size		Full Ctx insensitive		Ctx sensitive	
	SW only	SW only	HW supp.	SW only	HW supp.	SW only	HARD
164.gzip	11.42%	40.17%	3.19%	70.63%	4.43%	70.94%	7.68%
175.vpr	20.14%	40.29%	8.67%	51.24%	9.64%	51.57%	9.81%
176.gcc	12.35%	22.43%	3.23%	29.00%	3.93%	34.68%	6.37%
181.mcf	7.91%	7.88%	3.70%	7.80%	3.74%	7.85%	3.69%
186.crafty	35.61%	58.81%	6.77%	68.20%	7.03%	70.83%	8.04%
197.parser	3.59%	7.21%	0.43%	17.97%	0.87%	25.17%	4.70%
252.eon	10.85%	17.51%	6.18%	18.21%	5.55%	22.59%	8.88%
253.perlbmk	1.65%	1.58%	0.46%	22.22%	1.35%	23.19%	1.11%
254.gap	14.69%	14.20%	5.75%	21.48%	6.32%	24.26%	6.64%
255.vortex	11.95%	28.32%	2.58%	28.75%	4.33%	43.68%	12.33%
256.bzip2	8.52%	76.04%	5.17%	83.92%	6.81%	83.98%	5.78%
300.twolf	16.11%	29.11%	3.51%	48.43%	4.47%	54.13%	4.70%
geomean	12.60%	26.99%	**4.11%**	36.96%	**4.85%**	40.96%	**6.61%**

8.2   Area Overhead

We used the yosys open synthesis suite to measure the hardware cost of HARD, and found that HARD adds 21% die area to an unmodified core. Since HARD makes modifications to the processor core and L1 caches only and yosys is unable to model L2 caches, the area cost is relative to the unmodified processor core + L1 cache only. This number would, in other words, be much lower if we also took L2 into consideration, or if we added HARD to a larger core such as those found in a mainstream x86 CPU.

Table 2. The number of static equivalence classes that each analysis finds. For real world programs, HARD identifies and distinguishes 88.2% more equivalence classes. The impact was notable in case of nginx (458.4%), a widely used web server.

Bench-mark	Prior DSR	Context Insensitive	Context Sensitive	Bench-mark	Prior DSR	Context Insensitive	Context Sensitive
164.gzip	77	127 (64.9%)	145 (88.3%)	nginx	250	348 (39.2%)	1396 (458.4%)
175.vpr	630	717 (13.8%)	801 (27.1%)	ProFTPD	424	646 (52.4%)	818 (92.9%)
176.gcc	1221	2115 (73.2%)	2957 (142.2%)	sshd	266	352 (32.3%)	412 (54.9%)
181.mcf	37	41 (10.8%)	41 (10.8%)	WU-FTPD	579	719 (24.2%)	745 (28.7%)
186.crafty	943	1133 (20.2%)	1161 (23.1%)	sudo	125	145 (16.0%)	178 (42.4%)
197.parser	289	343 (18.7%)	443 (53.3%)	mcrypt	177	223 (26.0%)	257 (45.2%)
252.eon	1160	1556 (34.1%)	1722 (48.5%)				
253.perlbmk	268	491 (83.2%)	528 (97.0%)				
254.gap	196	394 (101.0%)	499 (154.6%)				
255.vortex	763	911 (19.4%)	1598 (109.4%)				
256.bzip2	71	96 (35.2%)	106 (49.3%)				
300.twolf	442	692 (56.6%)	797 (80.3%)				
precision increase		(41.4%)	(68.1%)	precision increase		(31.2%)	(88.2%)

8.3   Precision

HARD can only stop data-oriented attacks if it can place the legitimate targets of attacker-controlled instructions in different equivalence classes than memory locations the attacker wishes to access. If an attacker-controlled instruction accesses a memory location in the same equivalence class as its legitimate targets, an attack will likely succeed. This property also applies to other defenses that rely on static analysis to restrict data flow, including Data-Flow Integrity [5] and WIT [1]. Thus, it is important that the analysis distinguishes memory accesses into as many distinct equivalence classes as possible.

To demonstrate the added security of our context-sensitive analysis, we compiled several programs using three of the four different configurations of HARD and we counted the number of encrypted equivalence classes under each configuration. We excluded *Full Key Size* from this comparison, as it uses the exact same equivalence classes as *Prior DSR*. Table 2 shows the number of encrypted equivalence classes for each configuration, as well as the percentage increase from the first configuration.

We observe that HARD yields an increased number of equivalence classes compared to prior work and context-insensitive DSR. The greatest increase in the number of equivalence classes was for nginx. One of the reasons for the large improvement is that nginx uses a single logging function called from many different program locations. When using a context-insensitive analysis, all arguments to this function must be placed into a single equivalence class. With the context-sensitive analysis used by HARD, the arguments to the logging function are in independent equivalence classes for different calling contexts. The loss of precision from a context-insensitive analysis increases the chances that an attacker will manage to find vulnerable code that encrypts data with the desired encryption key. It is important to note that the additional equivalence classes identified and protected by HARD include memory that is considered safe and thus left unencrypted by prior work (cf. Subsect. 4.2). This gives HARD additional resistance against temporal memory vulnerabilities such as use-after-free or uninitialized-read.

Table 3. Number of allocations per equivalence class.

Benchmark	Context Insensitive Average	Max	Context Sensitive Average	Max	Benchmark	Context Insensitive Average	Max	Context Sensitive Average	Max
164.gzip	1.21	8	1.09	8	nginx	3.56	2059	1.29	1318
175.vpr	1.21	71	1.13	48	ProFTPD	1.42	1586	0.88	1063
176.gcc	2.48	2824	1.87	2187	sshd	2.01	331	1.11	220
181.mcf	1.07	3	1.07	3	WU-FTPD	1.44	512	1.15	326
186.crafty	1.11	57	1.08	42	sudo	1.23	105	0.78	90
197.parser	1.73	379	1.41	290	mcrypt	1.01	151	0.90	140
252.eon	1.47	519	1.23	273					
253.perlbmk	4.13	1875	4.24	1872					
254.gap	4.18	1355	3.73	1270					
255.vortex	2.99	1521	3.73	1071					
256.bzip2	1.11	11	1.01	3					
300.twolf	1.05	18	0.91	9					

Another important security property is the size of the equivalence classes, since the larger an equivalence class gets, the easier it generally becomes to illegitimately access variables within that class. To quantify equivalence class sizes, we modified our analyses to track the number of allocation sites (global, stack, and heap) contained within an equivalence class. For global and stack allocations, these correspond to variable declarations, for heap allocations they are calls to heap allocator functions like malloc. We counted both the average and maximum number of allocation sites per equivalence class, as shown in Table 3. The results show that, in general, the context-sensitive analysis used by HARD gives lower number of allocation sites across the benchmarks. Note that some benchmarks actually show an increase in average number of allocation sites. This is because an allocation site can be counted multiple times in different contexts with context sensitive analysis.

8.4 Real World Exploit

We evaluated our *Context Sensitive* configuration against a recent data-oriented attack presented by Hu et al. [13]. Instead of porting the attack to the RISC-V platform, we tested the software-only variant of HARD on x86 platform. The attack exploits a format string vulnerability in the *wu-ftpd* server to perform privilege escalation. Specifically, the attack overwrites a global pointer to a struct passwd. The overwritten pointer is later read and then dereferenced by the server, and the dereferenced value is interpreted as a user ID. This user ID is subsequently used as an argument for a setuid call. By overwriting the global pointer with the address of a memory location that contains a value of 0, which is the user ID of the root user, the attacker escalates the privileges of the vulnerable application.

We built two versions of the *wu-ftpd* binary: a base and a HARD'ened version. We then tested the exploit against both versions. The exploit was successful against the base version, but did not work against the HARD'ened version. While the attacker is still able to overwrite the pointer in the HARD'ened version, the subsequent read used a different encryption key than the instruction that overwrote the pointer, making it impossible for the attacker to reliably control the outcome of the overwrite. This causes the argument to the setuid call to be an unpredictable value. HARD identifies three equivalence classes involved in this exploit: the class accessed by the vulnerable instruction during valid executions, the class of the pointer variable, and the class used for dereferences of the pointer. These classes are accessed using distinct keys, k_v, k_p, and k_d respectively. To reliably control the result of this exploit an attacker would have to guess two 64-bit secret values, $k_v \oplus k_p$ and k_d, and therefore has a low chance of succeeding.

9 Limitations

Hardware Limitations. HARD limits the size of static IDs to eleven bits, which limits the number of equivalence classes with distinct keys to 2048. To run programs with over 2048 equivalence classes, we are forced to assign some static IDs to multiple equivalence classes. Other techniques that have a space constraint imposed on the protection mechanism are also limited in the protection they can provide. For example, the entries in the color table used by WIT [1] are 1-byte long, which limits WIT to use 256 distinct colors at most. HARD's limit of 2048 IDs allows it to protect much more complex programs than WIT. The security impact of static ID reuse could be reduced by carefully choosing which equivalence classes may share IDs.

Known Plaintext Attacks. Like the other DSR schemes, HARD is vulnerable against known plaintext attacks because it uses xor operations with fixed keys to encrypt data. If an attacker discloses encrypted data and knows the plaintext data, then she can recover the key which can be used to craft a successful payload. However, to reliably disclose data, she must know the data layout of the target program. Randomizing this data layout using ASLR or more fine-grained layout randomization can therefore mitigate this attack vector [9].

Lack of Integrity. Randomizing data using xor operations does not provide any integrity checking. This gives the attacker leeway to exchange encrypted data within the same equivalence class without knowing the key. In order to craft an exploit using this technique, the attacker will still need to know the meaning of the encrypted data, although they do not need to know the exact plaintext value. This is analogous to the limitation of many CFI approaches where an adversary can swap a pointer with another pointer as long as both pointers are allowed targets for a given indirect branch. The lack of integrity checking is an example of a performance-security trade off, and like CFI, DSR makes attacks substantially harder to construct.

Attacks on Skewed Values. Another attack vector against DSR is to target variables for which the range of valid values is a small subset of the possible values for the data type. An example is Boolean variables in C programs. A memory byte representing a Boolean value can have 2^8 different values, but only one of them will be interpreted as false. If an attacker wishes to change a false value to true, the attack will have a high probability of succeeding. In practice, many C programs are written such that Boolean variables will only have a limited number of values, often just 0 or 1. Attacks targeting these values could be mitigated by using a range analysis to identify the valid ranges and inserting checks to ensure the plaintext data is always within the allowed range.

Deployment Challenges. Hardware components have a longer time-to-market than a software based solution. However, hardware vendors have shown that they are willing to develop hardware components designed to prevent memory corruption exploits. Intel now provides Memory Protection Extension for bounds checking [31], and Control-Flow Enforcement Technology for control flow integrity [16]. These commercial offerings are driven by consumer demand for effective defenses with low overhead. HARD provides protection against a wide range of exploits with low performance overhead, using moderate amounts of hardware resources, so we feel it justifies the additional deployment challenges associated with a hardware-based solution.

10   Related Work

DSR was first proposed by Bhatkar et al. [3] and Cadar et al. [4]. Compared with those works, HARD provides greater security by using context-sensitive analysis and by randomizing all data using strong keys, which can be done efficiently thanks to our hardware support.

Data-Flow Integrity (DFI) [5] and Write Integrity Testing (WIT) [1] also perform alias analysis to build a set of equivalence classes and define a data-flow policy. However, they instrument the code to enforce the data flow and do not randomize the data representation. Both DFI and WIT used a context-insensitive analysis, so HARD can stop attacks that are not detected by either

DFI or WIT due to the imprecise analysis. Thanks to its architectural support, HARD also incurs less performance overhead.

HDFI [33] introduced the notion of *Data-flow Isolation*, which allows a program to place sensitive data in isolated memory regions effectively and efficiently. The HDFI hardware is used to classify instructions and prevent those in one group from accessing the memory accessed by the instructions in the other group. However, HDFI only supports two groups because it uses one bit to distinguish each group. HARD can classify the memory regions into 2^{11} groups as it uses 11-bit IDs to identify which class an instruction should access. HDFI is not accompanied with an automated way to classify the instructions, while HARD relieves developers from this burden.

Enforcement of memory safety also mitigates data-only attacks because most attacks violate memory safety. Memory safety enforcement usually does not rely on the precision of static analysis and it provides a deterministic protection. A number of either software-only or hardware-based memory safety mechanisms have been proposed. However, some of these mechanisms cannot handle memory reallocation correctly [6,11,12,34]. Others are incompatible with unprotected external code [29,35]. More recently Softbound [27] used *fat pointers* with disjoint metadata to prevent violation of spatial memory safety and maintain compatibility with unprotected external binaries, and *low fat pointer* mechanisms [18,19] have also been proposed to reduce the performance cost. Subsequently, CETS [28] was proposed to prevent the violation of temporal safety by using identifier to track the allocation states and disjoint metadata. Later DangSan, DangNull, FreeSentry and Oscar [10,17,23,37] addressed this by nullifying, invalidating or not reusing the pointers to the freed objects.

Yang and Shin propose using a hypervisor to encrypt memory pages to provide memory secrecy from the operating system and other processes [36]. Similar to our work, this technique uses hardware (hypervisor mode) to support data encryption. However, an attempt to extend their technique to provide intra-process data isolation would change the page lifetime assumptions of their paper substantially, and incur substantial performance and memory overhead.

Works such as SeCage [25] or Intel's MPK [15] are designed to restrict memory access to protect secrets. These techniques could be used to control access to the encryption keys in HARD. However, these systems are primarily intended for infrequently used secrets, while HARD does consider any data "secret" and encrypts all program data. Our proposed hardware cache therefore provides a performant solution to protect many keys.

11   Conclusion

In this paper we present HARD, a hardware-assisted defense against memory corruption attacks. HARD provides stronger protection than prior data space randomization implementations, with lower overhead. Our protection is stronger than prior work because (i) we use a context-sensitive analysis to distinguish more illegitimate data flows, (ii) we encrypt all possible equivalence classes to protect against all types of memory errors, and (iii) we always use 8-byte encryption keys to ensure sufficient key entropy.

Our hardware extension allows us to provide strong protection with low overhead. HARD's overhead is just 6.61% on average, which is 6 times lower than a software-only implementation of the same policy. The specialized hardware also protects encryption keys from information disclosure attacks.

References

1. Akritidis, P., Cadar, C., Raiciu, C., Costa, M., Castro, M.: Preventing memory error exploits with wit. In: IEEE Symposium on Security and Privacy (S&P) (2008)
2. Asanovi, K., et al.: The rocket chip generator. Technical report, University of California, Berkeley, April 2016
3. Bhatkar, S., Sekar, R.: Data space randomization. In: Zamboni, D. (ed.) DIMVA 2008. LNCS, vol. 5137, pp. 1–22. Springer, Heidelberg (2008). https://doi.org/10.1007/978-3-540-70542-0_1
4. Cadar, C., Akritidis, P., Costa, M., Martin, J.P., Castro, M.: Data randomization. Technical report MSR-TR-2008-120, Microsoft Research (2008)
5. Castro, M., Costa, M., Harris, T.: Securing software by enforcing data-flow integrity. In: USENIX Symposium on Operating Systems Design and Implementation (OSDI) (2006)
6. Chen, S., et al.: Flexible hardware acceleration for instruction-grain program monitoring. In: Annual International Symposium on Computer Architecture (ISCA) (2008)
7. Chen, S., Xu, J., Sezer, E.C., Gauriar, P., Iyer, R.K.: Non-control-data attacks are realistic threats. In: USENIX Security Symposium (2005)
8. Mehta, N.: The Heartbleed Bug, Codenomicon (2014). http://heartbleed.com/
9. Cook, K.: Introduce struct layout randomization plugin (2017). http://www.openwall.com/lists/kernel-hardening/2017/04/06/14
10. Dang, T.H., Maniatis, P., Wagner, D.: Oscar: a practical page-permissions-based scheme for thwarting dangling pointers. In: USENIX Security Symposium (2017)
11. Dhurjati, D., Adve, V.: Backwards-compatible array bounds checking for C with very low overhead. In: International Conference on Software Engineering (ICSE) (2006)
12. Ghose, S., Gilgeous, L., Dudnik, P., Aggarwal, A., Waxman, C.: Architectural support for low overhead detection of memory violations. In: Design, Automation Test in Europe Conference Exhibition (DATE) (2009)
13. Hu, H., Chua, Z.L., Adrian, S., Saxena, P., Liang, Z.: Automatic generation of data-oriented exploits. In: USENIX Security Symposium (2015)
14. Hu, H., Shinde, S., Adrian, S., Chua, Z.L., Saxena, P., Liang, Z.: Data-oriented programming: on the expressiveness of non-control data attacks. In: IEEE Symposium on Security and Privacy (S&P) (2016)
15. Intel Inc.: Intel 64 and IA-32 Architectures Software Developer's Manual (2013)
16. Intel R. Corporation: Control-flow enforcement technology preview (2016)
17. van der Kouwe, E., Nigade, V., Giuffrida, C.: DangSan: scalable use-after-free detection. In: European Conference on Computer Systems (EuroSys) (2017)
18. Kuvaiskii, D., et al.: SGXBounds: memory safety for shielded execution. In: European Conference on Computer Systems (EuroSys) (2017)

19. Kwon, A., Dhawan, U., Smith, J.M., Knight Jr., T.F., DeHon, A.: Low-fat pointers: compact encoding and efficient gate-level implementation of fat pointers for spatial safety and capability-based security. In: ACM Conference on Computer and Communications Security (CCS) (2013)
20. Lattner, C., Adve, V.: Automatic pool allocation: improving performance by controlling data structure layout in the heap. In: ACM SIGPLAN Conference on Programming Language Design and Implementation (PLDI) (2005)
21. Lattner, C., Lenharth, A., Adve, V.: Making context-sensitive points-to analysis with heap cloning practical for the real world. In: ACM SIGPLAN Conference on Programming Language Design and Implementation (PLDI) (2007)
22. Lea, D.: A memory allocator (1996)
23. Lee, B., et al.: Preventing use-after-free with dangling pointers nullification. In: Network and Distributed System Security Symposium (NDSS) (2015)
24. Lee, Y., et al.: A 45nm 1.3GHz 16.7 double-precision GFLOPS/W RISC-V processor with vector accelerators. In: European Solid State Circuits Conference (ESSCIRC) (2014)
25. Liu, Y., Zhou, T., Chen, K., Chen, H., Xia, Y.: Thwarting memory disclosure with efficient hypervisor-enforced intra-domain isolation. In: ACM Conference on Computer and Communications Security (CCS) (2015)
26. Nagarakatte, S., Martin, M.M., Zdancewic, S.: Watchdog: hardware for safe and secure manual memory management and full memory safety. ACM SIGARCH Comput. Arch. News **40**(3), 189–200 (2012)
27. Nagarakatte, S., Zhao, J., Martin, M.M., Zdancewic, S.: SoftBound: highly compatible and complete spatial memory safety for C. In: ACM SIGPLAN Conference on Programming Language Design and Implementation (PLDI) (2009)
28. Nagarakatte, S., Zhao, J., Martin, M.M., Zdancewic, S.: CETS: compiler enforced temporal safety for C. In: International Symposium on Memory Management (ISMM) (2010)
29. Patil, H., Fischer, C.: Low-cost, concurrent checking of pointer and array accesses in C programs. Softw. Pract. Exp. **27**(1), 87–110 (1997)
30. Rains, T., Miller, M., Weston, D.: Exploitation trends: from potential risk to actual risk. In: RSA Conference (2015)
31. Ramakesavan, R., et al.: Intel memory protection extensions enabling guide (2016)
32. Schoeberl, M.: Design and implementation of an efficient stack machine. In: IEEE International Parallel and Distributed Processing Symposium (2005)
33. Song, C., et al.: HDFI: hardware-assisted data-flow isolation. In: IEEE Symposium on Security and Privacy (S&P) (2016)
34. Venkataramani, G., Roemer, B., Solihin, Y., Prvulovic, M.: MemTracker: efficient and programmable support for memory access monitoring and debugging. In: IEEE International Symposium on High Performance Computer Architecture (HPCA) (2007)
35. Xu, W., DuVarney, D.C., Sekar, R.: An efficient and backwards-compatible transformation to ensure memory safety of C programs. In: ACM SIGSOFT International Symposium on Foundations of Software Engineering (FSE) (2004)
36. Yang, J., Shin, K.G.: Using hypervisor to provide data secrecy for user applications on a per-page basis. In: Proceedings of the Fourth ACM SIGPLAN/SIGOPS International Conference on Virtual Execution Environments (2008)
37. Younan, Y.: FreeSentry: protecting against use-after-free vulnerabilities due to dangling pointers. In: Network and Distributed System Security Symposium (NDSS) (2015)

MicroStache: A Lightweight Execution Context for In-Process Safe Region Isolation

Lucian Mogosanu[1(✉)], Ashay Rane[2], and Nathan Dautenhahn[3]

[1] University POLITEHNICA of Bucharest, Bucharest, Romania
`lucian.mogosanu@cs.pub.ro`
[2] The University of Texas at Austin, Austin, USA
`ashay@cs.utexas.edu`
[3] Rice University, Houston, USA
`ndd@rice.edu`

Abstract. In this work we present, MicroStache, a specialized hardware mechanism and new process abstraction for accelerating *safe region* security solutions. In the *safe region* paradigm, an application is split into safe and unsafe parts. Unfortunately, frequent mixing of safe and unsafe operations stresses memory isolation mechanisms. MicroStache addresses this challenge by adding an orthogonal execution domain into the process abstraction, consisting of a memory segment and minimal instruction set. Unlike alternative hardware, MicroStache implements a simple microarchitectural memory segmentation scheme while integrating it with paging, and also extends the *safe region* abstraction to isolate data in the processor cache, allowing it to protect against cache side channel attacks. A prototype is presented that demonstrates how to automatically leverage MicroStache to enforce security polices, SafeStack and CPI, with 5% and 1.2% overhead beyond randomized isolation. Despite specialization, MicroStache enhances a growing and critical programming paradigm with minimal hardware complexity.

Keywords: Intra-process isolation · Safe region
Security microarchitecture

1 Introduction

Computing systems hold a significant amount of personal data. Unfortunately, applications are subject to memory safety violations that allow attackers access to application data or to take over the system. A popular and well explored solution is to provide full memory safety, which forces all data access to be safe (*e.g.,* eliminating writing outside the bounds of an object) [12,15,34,35, 40]. Despite solving the problem, full memory safety comes with too high a price, hindering its mainstream use. Instead, an emerging paradigm protects only sensitive program data, such as code pointers [30], cryptographic keys [23], or

© Springer Nature Switzerland AG 2018
M. Bailey et al. (Eds.): RAID 2018, LNCS 11050, pp. 359–379, 2018.
https://doi.org/10.1007/978-3-030-00470-5_17

programmer-defined structures [8,13]. In general, partial memory safety places *sensitive* objects into isolated memory regions, called *safe regions* [28], that can only be accessed by privileged program instructions. The result is powerful security solutions (themselves eliminating large classes of exploits) at a fraction of the cost.

Despite the demonstrable rise and power of the *safe region* paradigm, commodity protection mechanisms are inadequate. This is because safe region isolation relies heavily on the interleaving between sensitive and regular memory accesses, leaving existing mechanisms with two options: either monitor all unsafe accesses (*e.g.,* sandboxing them using SFI or MPX [8,28,39,43]) or incur costly protection domain switches (as in SGX, TrustZone, MPK, VMFUNC [28,29]). Alternatively, tag-based architectures allow policy enforcement at instruction and word granularity [9,16,41], but require significant hardware enhancements.

The core research question we investigate in this work is how to most effectively support the *safe region* paradigm, specifically seeking a hardware accelerated abstraction and mechanism. Our goal is to do so in the most general and simplest way, so that the design may be portable to alternative architectures, and to efficiently isolate regions within an address space without requiring explicit monitoring of unsafe operations or domain switching.

To this end, we propose a novel memory abstraction that is isolated by a hardware data structure. MicroStache inserts an independently addressed memory region, the *stache segment*, into the standard process environment. The stache is accessed through a small instruction set extension that operates from within program context, as an embedded but orthogonal execution domain. The stache can be used to efficiently realize *safe region* solutions by controlling when and where stache access occurs. MicroStache also includes a hardware stack that not only supports standard stack behavior but also enforces a new stack safety property, where stack access is restricted to the currently executing frame. Furthermore, we extend the MicroStache abstraction into the microarchitecture to provide static cache separation and special mechanisms that can be leveraged by programmers for cache side channel defense.

To demonstrate our system, we show that it can be used for a variety of security applications that protect sensitive program data and user secrets either manually or through automated static checking. We implement two memory safety solutions (SafeStack and Code-Pointer Integrity [30]) and find that, relative to randomization based isolation, MicroStache incurs 5% and 1.2% overhead respectively. We demonstrate our claims through a prototype MicroStache implementation for x86-64 in the Gem5 [4] simulator, along with LLVM compiler support. Overall, our contributions include:

- The design and implementation of MicroStache, a novel abstraction for sensitive data isolation by confining it to a dedicated memory segment and separating memory accesses at the ISA level (Sect. 4).
- A framework for implementing arbitrary data protection policies for user applications, either manually or automatically (using compiler support) and a demonstration of this framework on several real-world scenarios (Sect. 5).

- MicroStache Safe Stack and an attack surface analysis that illustrates the security gained through its enforcement: elimination of 60–75% of Turing-complete gadgets and mitigation of cache side channel attacks (Sect. 7).

2   Background and Motivation

The primary goal of MicroStache is to provide an abstraction for efficient and effective in-address space protection of *safe regions* [28]. Protection means preserving the integrity and confidentiality of *sensitive* data, (e.g. cryptographic keys, passwords, shadow structures and metadata used to implement partial memory safety) stored within the *safe region*. A secondary goal, is to use the abstraction as a means with which to specify and enforce data cache isolation. This section explores the degree to which existing mechanisms solve this issue. Table 1 compares software and hardware isolation mechanisms, including implementations available on commodity hardware and state of the art systems.

2.1   Safe Region Paradigm

At it's core the safe region paradigm places sensitive program data in a special memory region that is accessible only to a subset of the program's instructions. The use of this region depends on the security policy. For example, spatial memory safety approaches place object bound metadata into the safe region and verify that pointer dereferences are in bounds [12,15,34,35,40]. The approach requires that only the security runtime, which updates bounds metadata, is permitted to modify the safe region. In general, there are many security policies that employ the pattern of allocating sensitive data into the safe region and then protecting it from unprivileged access (see Koning *et al.* [28] for a thorough description of policies). Selecting which instructions are privileged is specific to the security policy and typically done by a static analysis tool, like a compiler. Additionally, these policies are best when performed "in context" because they require frequent access to the safe region.

2.2   Mechanisms

Once data and instructions are divided into privileged and unprivileged parts, a mechanism is needed to protect at runtime. Typically mechanisms use one of the following methods: (1) sandboxing, (2) separating, or (3) elevating privileges.

Sandboxing Instructions. In the sandboxing approach, the safe region is allocated into the traditional process address space, accessible to regular instructions which become privileged by definition, and unprivileged instructions are explicitly constrained from accessing the safe region. Software Fault Isolation (SFI) uses an inline reference monitor that denies unprivileged access to the safe region by checking every access [39,43]. Unfortunately, SFI incurs relatively high

Table 1. Comparison between data isolation mechanisms. **Op. Granularity**: operation granularity (smallest protected unit). **Iso Type**: type of isolation mechanism—sandboxing unprivileged instructions; separating into domains requiring context switches; or elevating privilege on a per instruction basis. **Comm.**—available in commodity systems. **HW Complexity**—complexity of the hardware support required. **Side Channel**—provides microarchitectural side channel defense. **Overhead**—run-time overhead: ranges based on the minimum and average values reported. [a]Nonderministic defense. [b]Depends on address mask. [c]Unavailable at time of writing.

Mechanism	Op. Gran.	Iso Type	Comm.	HW Complexity	Side Channel	Overhead
ASLR [30]	byte	elevate	✓	none	–	≈0%[a]
SFI [30,39]	—[b]	sandbox	✓	none	–	low-high
Segments [30,46]	byte	elevate	✓	medium	–	low
MPX [8,28]	byte	sandbox	✓	medium	–	medium
MPK [28]	page	domain	✓	medium	–	low
VMFUNC [28,31]	page	domain	✓	high	–	medium
SGX [1,3]	page	domain	✓	high	–	high
TrustZone [2,24]	page	domain	✓	high	–	high
HDFI [41]	word	elevate	–	medium	–	low-high
PUMP [38]	byte	elevate	–	high	–	low-high
IMIX [19]	page	elevate	–	low	–	low
MicroStache	byte	elevate	–	low	✓	low

overheads. Intel MPX, accelerates range checks by performing them in hardware [8,28], however, it suffers from costly bounds updating operations, must still explicitly monitor all unprivileged operations (which can be the majority), and is x86 specific.

Separating into Domains. Instead of restricting unprivileged instructions, *domain* based schemes place the safe region into an orthogonal area of memory requiring some form of context switch to access. In this way, each privileged operation must perform a domain switch, leaving regular instructions unchanged. Intel SGX, VMFUNC, and MPK, as well as ARM TrustZone provide domain switch isolation. However, all suffer from high overhead [28].

Elevating Instructions. Both prior approaches are costly, requiring either frequent checks to sandbox unprivileged access or incur expensive domain switches. Elevation based approaches leave unprivileged instructions alone and add mechanisms to increase the privilege of the sensitive instructions. Randomization mechanisms place the safe region in a random location that only the privileged instructions know [30]. Despite their efficiency, randomization techniques are probabilistic, leading to exploits [18,21,22].

Split instruction set approaches create special instructions with privileges to directly access the safe region, while normal instructions are mediated by custom hardware. In x86-32 segmentation, the safe region is placed in a separate segment, and then only special segment-based instructions can access the region. Unfortunately, segmentation has disappeared from modern architectures and its microarchitecture is complex to support in general. IMIX, adds a new safe region page permission, which is only accessible through a new instruction [19]. This scheme is comparable to MicroStache, however, details have yet to be published.

Another way of elevating specific instructions is to use a tag-based microarchitecture. In tagging schemes, each instruction can be tagged with a policy denoting its privilege. Several tagging schemes have been proposed, but more recently region based schemes, HDFI [41] and the PUMP [38], have demonstrated the ability to enforce *safe region* based polices. Despite the powerful nature of these schemes, they require complex hardware that inhibits path to adoption. Moreover, partial memory safety techniques such as CPI [30] and DCI [8] are inherently dependent on the existence of metadata and safe regions, which to our knowledge HDFI cannot easily implement.

2.3   Extending the Safe Region to Cache Level Isolation

In addition to the safe use of memory, we seek to prevent leakage of secret information through cache side channels, which have been used to break confidentiality of both cryptographic and non-cryptographic applications. Both software as well as microarchitectural solutions exist, but not without drawbacks. Software solutions sidestep microarchitectural modifications [27], thus enabling defenses on commodity processors, but they also incur substantial overheads due to their reliance on generic ISA instructions. Microarchitecture-only solutions are generally faster but lack flexibility [44], because defenses ignore contextual information about the applications. MicroStache embodies a hardware-software design that is able to leverage the best of both worlds by extending trust to portions of the microarchitecture, while also leveraging the compiler to identify the parts of the program that need protection from cache side channels. Furthermore, the abstraction boundary provided by the safe region paradigm is similar to the types of protection desired against side channels. Doing so requires specialized hardware.

2.4   MicroStache Design Goals

From our analysis, we argue that in-place solutions offer the best in terms of programmability and efficiency, and identify the following design requirements that a *safe region* abstraction should meet:

Requirement 1 (Performance Symmetry). *Regular* and *sensitive* memory accesses should impose the same performance penalty.

Requirement 2 (Programmability). Isolation mechanisms should be generally programmable, and thus allow the use of arbitrary memory safety techniques.

Requirement 3 (Cross Layer). Isolation mechanisms should provide programmers explicit access to microarchitectural state that impact data safety.

MicroStache implements all the stated requirements, being based on a simple hardware enforced isolation scheme, and exposing simple load/store memory primitives, thereby incurring minimal performance overhead on applications. Moreover, MicroStache provides a special cache for sensitive data, with an appropriate maintenance interface.

3   Threat Model and Assumptions

MicroStache prevents attacks on sensitive data integrity and confidentiality, coming from both malicious user inputs and microarchitectural side channels. We assume a program to be buggy but not malicious, and that an attacker can invoke arbitrary regular reads and writes. When combined with memory safety approaches (as described in Sect. 5), MicroStache defends against all control-flow hijack attacks. Implementing alternative safety solutions would lead to diverse threat models. We assume all hardware, operating system (OS), and compiler configuration to be correct, and read-only code and non-executable data.

We assume that the adversary can observe the victim's use of the processor cache, but that the adversary cannot observe the data values in the cache. We assume that the adversary has access to the source code of victim application, both before and after transformation using our compiler, and that the adversary cannot directly observe the victim's secret input data either due to encryption or due to isolation enforced by the OS. We do not address resource exhaustion attacks resulting from e.g. cache line locking abuse.

4   MicroStache Design

MicroStache supports the *safe region* paradigm by using the instruction elevation approach, where the safe region is placed in an external memory segment, the stache, and is only accessible through MicroStache instructions. The stache is an independently addressed segment of physical memory that uses offset-based addressing—bypassing virtual memory altogether. In this way, MicroStache integrates an isolated execution domain into the process without requiring domain switching. Figure 1 illustrates the main design elements of MicroStache. An overview of the MicroStache instruction set and their semantics are presented in Table 2. In the following we detail (i) the basic stache design, (ii) an extension that supports stack relative addressing and restricts stack access to the current frame locals (excluding return address and frame pointers), and (ii) an extension for mitigating cache side channel attacks.

4.1   Stache Segment

As depicted in Fig. 1 the stache segment is a linear region of physical memory, and its location is dynamically specified by two new privileged registers: the stache base (**xbase**) and stache end (**xend**). The operating system virtualizes the stache by storing its base and bound as a part of thread state, giving each process a unique region of physical memory, and not mapping their contents into any address space. The stache is accessed through load/store operations, **xld** and **xst**, which takes the address as (**xbase** +offset). The hardware limits all access to the (**xbase, xend**) region (avoiding arbitrary access to any physical address). A *safe region* application can use the stache by allocating data to it, and with compiler support, emit stache access instructions for its secure access.

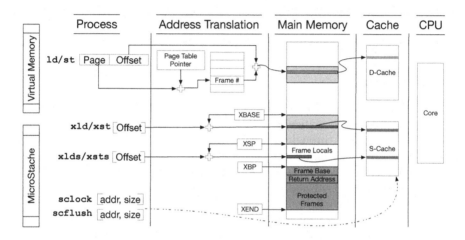

Fig. 1. MicroStache architecture.

Table 2. MicroStache interface. **reg** are general-purpose architecture registers. **addr** are memory addresses. **call** and **ret** also retain their native call/return semantics.

Abstraction	Hardware operation	Semantics
Memory	ld/st reg, addr	Access regular mapped memory
	xld/xst xbase, addr	Access stache segment, relative to **xbase**
	xlds/xsts xsp, offset	Access Safe Stack memory, relative to **xsp**
Safe Stack	call addr	Initialize new frame on Safe Stack
	xalloc size	Allocate space on the Safe Stack
	ret	Pop current frame from the Safe Stack
S-cache	scflush addr, size	Flush S-cache lines given by **addr** and **size**
	sclock addr, size	Lock S-cache lines given by **addr** and **size**

4.2   Safe Stack

In order to efficiently isolate stack data, MicroStache includes stack hardware support through the following interface: frame creation (`call`), memory allocation (`xalloc`), frame destruction (`ret`) and stack-pointer-relative stache access (`xlds/xsts`) (see semantics in Table 2). The stack is located at the end of the stache region and grows towards lower addresses, and is only accessible through `xlds/xsts` instructions. Beyond standard stack operation, MicroStache guarantees that memory addresses computed for `xlds/xsts` are always in the range of `xsp` and `xbp` (the active frame) and that even stache relative access through `xld/xst` cannot modify the stack, thus ensuring that return address and base pointer corruption (which could be used for stack pivoting) is not possible. Moreover, the Safe Stack can be used to protect a subset of program control-data and decision-making non-control data, thus reducing the attack surface for Jump-Oriented Programming (JOP) [5] and Data-Oriented Programming (DOP) [25] attacks. We quantify the value of this design in Sect. 7.

4.3   Safe Cache

A goal of MicroStache is to mitigate covert information channels without sacrificing application performance. For this purpose, MicroStache routes all sensitive memory accesses through a special cache, the safe cache (S-cache). The S-cache is a L1 cache similar to the data cache (D-cache), using the same microarchitecture-defined line update and eviction policy, but accessible only through MicroStache load and store operations. This is similar to other static cache partitioning schemes, such as Intel CAT [33].

This design point is sufficient to provide basic separation between regular and sensitive data, but it does not protect against side channel attacks on the S-cache. To make this possible, we add two new operations, `scflush` and `sclock`, that can be used by programmers to flush and lock cache lines respectively. `scflush` can be used to flush and invalidate cache lines, or the entire cache. Using `scflush`, applications and/or the operating system can implement simple policies such as flushing the S-cache on context switches. However, we expect this policy to have a significant negative impact on performance. Thus programs can prevent attackers from flushing or evicting their cache lines from the S-cache using `sclock`. However, we note that `sclock` must still be used correctly in order to ensure cache side channel protection.

5   Security Applications

In this section we describe how to use MicroStache for improving application security with minimum performance costs. In many cases, using MicroStache is a direct translation of safe region use: allocate safe-region data to the stache and issue MicroStache memory access for elevated access.

5.1   Safe Stack Protection

The safe stack approach [30] splits data on the stack into safe and unsafe based on the observation that a subset of locally-scoped data can be statically proven safe. Thus programs can make use of two separate stacks, the safe stack and the unsafe stack, to hold local variables. This technique can be automatically applied to existing programs with minimal overhead and no compatibility loss.

MicroStache protects the safe stack by modifying the existing SafeStack software infrastructure to emit MicroStache instructions instead of traditional stack instructions. More specifically, we want to (i) allocate data on the Safe Stack on function entry, using `xalloc`; and (ii) safely access local variables using `xlds`/`xsts`. This limits safe stack management to MicroStache primitives, ensuring strong Safe Stack protection against unintended memory accesses.

5.2   Code-Pointer Integrity

Code-Pointer Integrity (CPI) [30] is a technique that detects corruption of code pointers, eliminating all control-flow hijack attacks. In CPI, all pointers that may be used as a target for an indirect call or return operation are protected by placing pointer metadata and bounds information into a safe region. A compiler instruments all legitimate definitions of each pointer with a call into the CPI runtime to update pointer metadata. Then on each pointer use, CPI checks that the last update was legitimate. By using this Data-Flow Isolation (DFI) policy [9], CPI gains guaranteed control-flow hijack defense. MicroStache is used by modifying the CPI runtime to allocate metadata into the stache and replacing normal loads and stores with stache instructions.

5.3   Secret Pointer Protection

Modern systems make memory corruption attacks harder by relying on information hiding mechanisms such as ASLR [11,20]. What this effectively means is that pointers to locations of certain sections of the program, e.g. code, data, are hidden, and given to a few elevated instructions at runtime. Unfortunately, ASLR is susceptible to information leak attacks through memory corruption and cache and timing side channels [21]. We propose preventing secret pointer leaks by storing sensitive data in the stache segment. In our proof-of-concept work (Sect. 6) we show that hiding the location of the CPI safe region can be easily achieved by accessing the pointer through MicroStache, and that it requires minimal modifications to the CPI run-time.

5.4   Secret Computation Defense

We consider the general problem of information leaks through system-level attacks using cache side channels. As long as regular (non-sensitive) data doesn't depend on them, sensitive scalar values, e.g. integers, are trivially protected by MicroStache, because the computations performed, e.g. arithmetic operations, are invariant with respect to cache usage. Composite values, e.g. arrays, however may incur side channels depending on the computation that is being performed: if data dependencies involved in the computation lead to variations in cache access patterns, then these patterns can reveal parts of the data to an attacker with partial control over the cache.

We provide the possibility of efficiently performing secret computation through MicroStache by allowing programmers to lock small amounts of data into the S-cache. Listing 1.1 illustrates a simple scenario in which a global array, secret, is subject to computation that could cause leaks via cache side channels, e.g. data encryption. We make it impossible for attackers to infer bits of secret by locking it into the S-cache using the sclock primitive.

```
int secret [ARRAY_SIZE]
    __attribute__ (( secret ));
int f(int input)
{
    int result;
    sclock ( secret , sizeof ( secret ));
    /* secret computation */ \ldots
    return result;
}
```

Listing 1.1. Computation on secret data using sclock.

Note that this approach is limited to small data, i.e. not over the S-cache size. In this case, MicroStache can be combined with other hardware or software techniques, as discussed in Sect. 8.

6   Implementation

This section presents the implementation of our MicroStache prototype including: microarchitectural simulation in Gem5, LLVM compiler support, and security application details.

6.1   Gem5 Hardware Prototype

We built a proof-of-concept prototype of MicroStache for the x86 architecture. Our implementation consists of a simulated hardware prototype built using Gem5 [4]. We extended the x86 Gem5 model with MicroStache support: we added new registers, x86 micro-ops for memory operations and associated macro-ops by extending the decoder, execution and memory access Gem5 components; we extended call and ret x86 operations with Safe Stack support; finally, we extended the TimingSimpleCPU[1] generic CPU model with a new port for stache memory accesses. In a typical scenario, Gem5 MicroStache configuration involves

---

[1] http://www.gem5.org/SimpleCPU.

connecting the memory port to the S-cache, which is then connected to the system interconnect. Additionally, we added support for MicroStache in the Gem5 system call emulation mode for stache initialization.

Our current MicroStache prototype does not support S-cache flushing, S-cache locking and automatic stack frame unwinding on `ret`. We emulated S-cache programmable operations by manually loading and/or replacing data in the S-cache. Similarly, we emulated automatic stack frame unwinding through a special stack deallocation instruction.

6.2 Software Support

Integrating MicroStache with existing software requires minimal software support in the compiler toolchain, i.e. assembler (emitting MicroStache opcodes) and C compiler (MicroStache intrinsics). To demonstrate MicroStache compiler support, we added opcode emission support to both LLVM 3.8 and 3.2. We implemented high-level support for the MicroStache instruction set in two ways: partial backend support for the LLVM instruction selection passes for `alloca`, `load` and `store` instructions; and a small run-time comprising general-purpose `ustache_alloca`, `ustache_load` and `ustache_store` functions for local and global variables respectively. We used the first implementation to automatically generate instrumented code for Safe Stack use, and the second implementation to implement CPI, secret pointer, and secret computation protections.

6.3 Security Applications

We implemented Safe Stack support by: modifying the existing `SafeStack` pass in LLVM 3.8; and adding backend support for MicroStache safe stack frame management and `load`/`store` accesses to the safe stack. We modified the `SafeStack` instrumentation to leave unsafe allocations on the regular stack, and move safe allocations to the MicroStache Safe Stack, by replacing safe `alloca`s with `xalloc`s. Then for `load`/`store` instructions to `xalloc` frames, we emitted `xlds`/`xsts` instructions in the target-dependent instruction selection phase. In our work we first attempted to extend LLVM with the MicroStache memory model, which we found was extremely challenging due to the complexity of modelling Safe Stack frames in the target-independent instruction selection passes. Although this is an engineering limitation from MicroStache's perspective, it is an open area to explore how to add non-standard memory models to LLVM's backend.

In order to create a more robust toolchain we switched to LLVM 3.2 which had both SafeStack and CPI passes implemented. However, in this case we only added general stache memory access support instead of just the Safe Stack. To protect the location of the CPI safe region for randomization protection, we modified the CPI run-time to load and store the pointer to the safe region at the appropriate times. More exactly, we modified `cpi_init` to store the pointer after the initial `mmap`. Similarly, we modified `cpi_get` and `cpi_set` to load the safe region pointer from the stache segment. Due to the inability of Gem5 to load dynamically linked executables, we did not protect the GOT. Finally, we extended the LLVM 3.2 CPI run-time with full MicroStache support, using xld and xst to manage metadata on the stache.

We implemented two popular [26, 42] scenarios involving secret computation: Dijkstra's Single Source Shortest Path (SSSP) algorithm, and Top-k selection. The two algorithms operate on secret data structures: a graph and a binary heap. We used the Gem5 system call emulation (SE) mode to emulate S-cache locking by manually loading data into the S-cache before the actual computation.

7   Security and Performance Evaluation

We discuss three aspects pertaining to our MicroStache prototype: we evaluate the security of MicroStache using a safe stack as a reference scenario; we quantitatively and qualitatively analyze the security of each of the security applications presented in previous sections; and we measure the execution performance of our MicroStache prototype using standard benchmarks as well as the proof-of-concept scenarios presented in Sect. 6.

We ran all the experiments on the Gem5 TimingSimpleCPU model [4]. The TimingSimpleCPU model, in addition to instruction execution timing, simulates memory access latencies. We configured a basic Gem5 system comprising a CPU running at 1 GHz, an L1 64 KB D-cache and 32 KB I-cache, an S-cache, and a DDR3 memory controller running at 1600 MHz. We connected all the caches to the memory controller through the default Gem5 system cross-bar memory bus.

7.1   Safe Stack Security Evaluation

We evaluate the effectiveness of our safe stack protection using a security benchmark suite similar to RIPE [45]. We implemented attack scenarios for ROP, JOP and DOP, using memory corruption vectors on the stack: return addresses, function pointers, setjmp buffers and local variables used for conditional branches. We compiled the tests and ran them using our MicroStache prototype. All the benchmarks pass, with the exception of setjmp/longjmp, because setjmp buffers aren't protected in our prototype. We observe otherwise that our MicroStache prototype trivially protects sensitive local variables such as function pointers.

7.2   Security Analysis

We analyze the security of the applications designed in Sect. 5. More specifically, we: measure the effectiveness of Safe Stack at reducing ROP [6], JOP [5] and DOP [25] attack surface; discuss the effectiveness of in protecting secret pointers; and qualitatively analyze the effectiveness of our protection mechanisms against cache side channel attacks.

To measure the attack surface reduction of our Safe Stack protection, we define a new static attack surface metric that tracks the number of *protected* branches, i.e. branches that are taken correctly as a result of their dependency on data placed on the Safe Stack. Thus, in our static analysis, a given control-flow transfer instruction is considered protected if it depends exclusively on safely accessed data. The Attack Surface Reduction (ASR) metric is:

$$\text{ASR} = \frac{\text{protected branches}}{\text{protected branches} + \text{unprotected branches}}$$

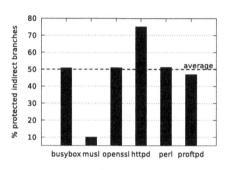

Fig. 2. ASR indirect forward flows.   **Fig. 3.** ASR conditional branches.

Safe Stack Return-Oriented Protection. The basic MicroStache Safe Stack provides full safety for function returns, even without any explicit *safe region* use. This ensures that in the event of control-flow hijack attacks, the attacker cannot obtain control of the program using ROP gadgets.

Safe Stack Forward Indirect Branch Protection. We determine the number of protected indirect forward flows at the LLVM IR level by computing the set of indirect call and indirect branch instructions. The results of this analysis are shown in Fig. 2. Overall, we observe a significant number of indirect branches protected while only protecting safe local variables, indicating a powerful element to new hybridized mitigations for JOP attacks.

Safe Stack Data-Oriented Protection. We determine conditional branch protection similarly to indirect forward flows. The results are shown in Fig. 3. On average, MicroStache protects approximately 62.7% of static branches over all the analyzed programs. Additionally, we wish to assess protection against DOP [25]. DOP attacks involve controlling conditional branches to access data-oriented gadgets. However, in order for arbitrary execution to be possible, the gadgets must be controlled using a gadget dispatcher, i.e. branch instructions must reside in a loop. Thus we determine the reduction of unsafe branches in loops, which on average is approximately 66.3%. In order to determine whether we eliminate any of the known DOP vulnerabilities, we manually analyzed the examples given by Hu et al. [25]. We found out that MicroStache protects all the branch condition variables in the ProFTPD example, which makes DOP impractical, if not impossible. We believe that a similar level of protection is provided against Control-Flow Bending (CFB) attacks [7].

Secret Pointer Protection. MicroStache can be used to protect secret pointers, i.e. pointers that point to sensitive memory locations. We illustrate this by protecting the location of the CPI safe region (Sect. 6). This ensures that the safe region is accessed through a secure interface, which removes information leaks through memory corruption. Moreover, protecting the GOT and other secret pointers can further reduce the attack surface, eliminating part of the assumptions about the layout of the address space made by Evans et al. [17].

Secret Computation Defense. MicroStache implicitly provides protection against cache side channels for scalar values when they are not part of branch conditions, since their cache location is invariant and they do not incur data dependencies measurable by the attacker. Protecting variables used in conditional branches is possible through branch normalization, either manually or by using compiler-based approaches such as Escort [37]. Composite values can be protected using sclock. In order to protect secret data for Single Source Shortest Paths (SSSP), we store and lock both the graph (our secret) and the computed distances. The reason for also storing the computed distances is that the computation of shortest paths depends on the structure of the graph, and thus cache access patterns would otherwise leak whether an edge exists between two nodes. Similarly, for Top-k selection we only store and lock the binary tree, since the only data dependencies occur between tree nodes. Thus in the worst case, the attacker can infer the size of the data being locked by inspecting S-cache access patterns.

7.3   Performance Evaluation

Our performance evaluation aims to determine: (i) the performance impact of our modifications on the Gem5 simulator; (ii) the performance impact of MicroStache enforced CPI and SafeStack relative to randomization based protection; (iii) the performance overhead of secret pointer protections; (iv) the performance overhead of cache side channel defense; and (v) the impact of S-cache size on performance, in particular of automated safe stack instrumentation.

```
// Regular stack          // MicroStache
1: sub $8, %rsp            1: xalloc $8
2: mov %rcx, (%rsp)        2: xst %rcx, $0
3: mov (%rsp), %rcx        3: xld %rcx, $0
4: loop 1b                 4: loop 1b
```

Listing 1.2. loop hot path implementation. The two versions access the regular stack and the Safe Stack using regular and MicroStache memory instructions.

Table 3. Micro-benchmark run-time overhead. The baseline is unmodified Gem5 accessing the regular stack; regular and stache represent the stack that is accessed (regular, and Safe Stack respectively); loop and recursive are two microbenchmark implementations which access the stack in a loop and recursively respectively.

Benchmark\scenario	regular	stache
loop	0.032%	−0.065%
recursive	4.168%	0.379%

Microbenchmarks. We aim to assess the impact on run-time performance of the Gem5 CPU modifications introduced in Sect. 6. MicroStache memory access instructions and their regular counterparts should have similar run-times, as we use the same logic for memory access requests; the only difference is the memory ports used, i.e. the S-cache instead of the D-cache. We wrote two micro-benchmarks that allocate space on the safe stack and read/write the allocated memory: the first, loop, uses the x86 loop instruction to do this iteratively; the second, recursive, does the same operation by calling a function recursively. We implemented two variants for each micro-benchmark, one that reads/writes to the regular stack using x86 mov instructions, and one using xlds/xsts. An example of the hot path in loop is given in Listing 1.2. We set the micro-benchmark to run the code in the loop a million times. The run-time performance of the two scenarios relative to the baseline is presented in Table 3. We observe that the performance is almost the same in each of the scenarios, with the exception of the recursive benchmark in the regular case, which has approximately 4% overhead. There are two major causes for the large overhead: the modifications to call and ret (Sect. 6), which cause it to push the return address to both the stache segment and the regular stack; and the difference in instruction size and alignment between regular and stache. The latter influences the performance of the Gem5 TimingSimpleCPU fetch unit, which prefetches 8-byte words on x86-64. This behaviour is expected to occur on real x86 processors, and thus we assume the compiler optimizes for it in real applications.

Safe Stack SPEC Benchmarks. To validate our MicroStache prototype, we compiled and ran a small subset of the SPEC CPU2006 benchmarks using our modified SafeStack LLVM pass: gobmk, hmmer, lbm and specrand. Figure 4 shows the performance of safestack using randomization based protection and stache relative to the baseline. We believe that the reasons for the high overhead is similar to that observed in the microbenchmarks, and can be further optimized at the compiler level. Many of the test did not compile due to the challenges of extending LLVM with the non-standard MicroStache memory model.

Secret Pointer Protection Test. To measure the performance impact of hiding secret pointers, we ran a small test suite for our modified version of the CPI run-time library against the original. The results show less than 1% overhead, further demonstrating of the minimal impact of MicroStache hardware.

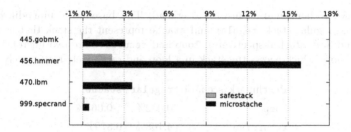

Fig. 4. SPEC CPU2006 run-time performance overhead for safe stack relative to mainline Gem5 and LLVM 3.8; `safestack` represents mainline Gem5 and LLVM 3.8 SafeStack; `microstache` represents MicroStache Gem5 and MicroStache LLVM 3.8.

Code-Pointer Integrity SPEC Benchmarks. We instrumented the SPEC benchmarks using the ASLR based implementation of SafeStack (*i.e.,* using the normal stack and regular ld/st instructions) and three variants of CPI: ASLR, SFI and MicroStache. Figure 5 illustrates the results relative to native Gem5 CPU baseline. The goal of this benchmark is to demonstrate how MicroStache performs with respect to the randomized version (no checks while using normal ld/st instructions) and the more costly SFI variant of CPI.

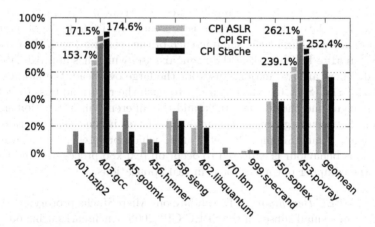

Fig. 5. CPI overhead relative to native on SPEC. On average MicroStache is 1.2% slower than randomized and 7.4% faster than SFI.

Cache Side Channel Benchmarks. Table 4 shows the performance overhead of the cache side channel protection. We compare the performance of MicroStache with Escort [37], a software solution. We observed that MicroStache is comparable with the baseline performance, and in particular in one of the two scenarios, outperforms the baseline by about 26%. The Escort prototype has a high performance overhead in the `sssp` benchmark because it relies on Intel AVX for fast

Table 4. Cache side channel protection run-time overhead. Escort and MicroStache are measured relative to the baseline (unprotected) benchmark versions. sssp is a Dijkstra single-source shortest path (SSSP) implementation; top-k is a Top-k selection implementation.

Benchmark\system	Escort	MicroStache
sssp	87.19%	−26.02%
top-k	0%	2.05%

Table 5. SPEC CPU2006 maximum run-time stache size.

Benchmark	Stache size (B)
445.gobmk	440
456.hmmer	808
470.lbm	96
999.specrand	72

memory updates, a feature which is not available in our Gem5 MicroStache prototype. The data in our MicroStache benchmark implementation is small enough that it fits in the S-cache. This would be problematic for large secret data. However, since MicroStache and Escort use orthogonal mechanisms for computation involving secrets, in principle they can be used together in the case when the secret data is too large to fit into the S-cache.

S-cache Size Impact on Performance. Adding the S-cache to the system constitutes a trade-off between processor die space and stache segment access latency. Thus we measured the maximum run-time safe stack size, results are shown in Table 5.

8   Discussion and Future Work

In this section we discuss MicroStache limitations and outline approaches to overcome them; and we compare MicroStache with closely related work, namely HDFI [41]. **Cache Side Channel Analysis:** To provide complete cache side channel protection using MicroStache, we plan to leverage automated techniques for side channel analysis [32,36,37]. Further, we aim to extend our evaluation to comprise an empirical analysis of cache side channel protection, by simulating a full-system scenario using Gem5. **Exceptional Control Flows:** While our safe stack MicroStache prototype (Sect. 6) can be used as a shadow stack, it does not provide support for exceptional control flows, such as setjmp/longjmp and try/catch. We plan to support this by integrating with related work [10,14,30]. **Comparison With HDFI:** Song et al. [41] propose fine-grained memory isolation through a hardware element called hardware-assisted data-flow isolation (HDFI). While HDFI and MicroStache have similar goals, HDFI achieves them through static 1-bit tagging, while MicroStache uses a statically-allocated memory region. Both options have benefits. HDFI tagging leaves data in place but requires a tag cache and lookup operations which impacts performance and hardware complexity, whereas MicroStache is simpler, and it can be used for a larger set of applications such as general memory safety techniques.

9   Conclusion

In this paper we explored the abstractions necessary for efficient in-address space *safe region* protection. We proposed MicroStache, a new microarchitectural isolation mechanism designed on the principle that safely accessed data can be efficiently protected by separating memory accesses at multiple abstraction levels (ISA, cache, main memory). We showed that the programmability of MicroStache allows it to be employed in a variety of use cases, with no to minimal overhead. In combination with existing compiler techniques, MicroStache can be leveraged to efficiently protect a large subset of local variables and sensitive control-flow transfers, significantly reducing the surface of jump-oriented and data-oriented attacks, as well as information leaks and memory corruption. Thus we believe MicroStache to be a significant element for fine-grained, flexible and efficient sensitive data isolation.

Acknowledgments. The authors would like to thank the anonymous reviewers, Mohit Tiwari, André DeHon, JMS, Volodymyr Kuznetsov, and George Candea, who all provided insightful feedback, improving the paper. We would like to thank our families—Filip, Andi, Bogdan, Andreea, Cornelia, Vasile, and AuNoLeZeZo—who gave us the freedom and flexibility to make this paper the best it could be. This research was funded in part by National Science Foundation grant CNS-1513687. Any opinions, findings, conclusions, or recommendations expressed in this material are those of the authors and do not necessarily reflect the views of the National Science Foundation.

References

1. Arnautov, S., et al.: SCONE: secure Linux containers with Intel SGX (2016)
2. Azab, A.M., et al.: Hypervision across worlds: real-time kernel protection from the ARM TrustZone secure world. In: Proceedings of the 2014 ACM SIGSAC Conference on Computer and Communications Security (2014)
3. Baumann, A., Peinado, M., Hunt, G.: Shielding applications from an untrusted cloud with Haven. ACM Trans. Comput. Syst. (TOCS) **33**(3), 8 (2015)
4. Binkert, N.: The gem5 simulator. ACM SIGARCH Comput. Archit. News **39**(2), 1–7 (2011)
5. Bletsch, T., Jiang, X., Freeh, V.W., Liang, Z.: Jump-oriented programming: a new class of code-reuse attack. In: Proceedings of the 6th ACM Symposium on Information, Computer and Communications Security (2011)
6. Buchanan, E., Roemer, R., Savage, S., Shacham, H.: Return-oriented programming: exploitation without code injection. Black Hat **8** (2008)
7. Carlini, N., Barresi, A., Payer, M., Wagner, D., Gross, T.R.: Control-flow bending: on the effectiveness of control-flow integrity. In: USENIX Security Symposium (2015)
8. Carr, S.A., Payer, M.: DataShield: configurable data confidentiality and integrity. In: Proceedings of the 2017 ACM on Asia Conference on Computer and Communications Security (2017). https://doi.org/10.1145/3052973.3052983
9. Castro, M., Costa, M., Harris, T.: Securing software by enforcing data-flow integrity. In: Proceedings of the 7th Symposium on Operating Systems Design and Implementation, pp. 147–160. USENIX Association (2006)

10. Christoulakis, N., Christou, G., Athanasopoulos, E., Ioannidis, S.: HCFI: hardware-enforced control-flow integrity. In: Proceedings of the Sixth ACM Conference on Data and Application Security and Privacy (2016)
11. Crane, S., et al.: Readactor: practical code randomization resilient to memory disclosure. In: IEEE Symposium on Security and Privacy (2015)
12. Criswell, J., Lenharth, A., Dhurjati, D., Adve, V.: Secure virtual architecture: a safe execution environment for commodity operating systems. In: ACM SIGOPS Operating Systems Review (2007)
13. Dautenhahn, N., Kasampalis, T., Dietz, W., Criswell, J., Adve, V.: Nested kernel: an operating system architecture for intra-kernel privilege separation. ACM SIGPLAN Not. **50**(4), 191–206 (2015)
14. Davi, L., Sadeghi, A.R., Winandy, M.: ROPdefender: a detection tool to defend against return-oriented programming attacks. In: Proceedings of the 6th ACM Symposium on Information, Computer and Communications Security, pp. 40–51. ACM (2011)
15. Devietti, J., Blundell, C., Martin, M.M., Zdancewic, S.: HardBound: architectural support for spatial safety of the C programming language. In: ACM SIGARCH Computer Architecture News (2008)
16. Dhawan, U., et al.: Architectural support for software-defined metadata processing. SIGARCH Comput. Archit. News **43**(1), 487–502 (2015). https://doi.org/10.1145/2786763.2694383
17. Evans, I., et al.: Missing the point (er): on the effectiveness of code pointer integrity. In: IEEE Symposium on Security and Privacy (2015)
18. Evtyushkin, D., Ponomarev, D., Abu-Ghazaleh, N.: Jump over ASLR: attacking branch predictors to bypass ASLR. In: 49th Annual IEEE/ACM International Symposium on Microarchitecture (2016)
19. Frassetto, T., Jauernig, P., Liebchen, C., Sadeghi, A.R.: IMIX: in-process memory isolation extension. In: 27th USENIX Security Symposium (USENIX Security 2018). USENIX Association, Baltimore (2018). https://www.usenix.org/conference/usenixsecurity18/presentation/frassetto
20. Giuffrida, C., Kuijsten, A., Tanenbaum, A.S.: Enhanced operating system security through efficient and fine-grained address space randomization. In: USENIX Security Symposium, pp. 475–490 (2012)
21. Gras, B., Razavi, K., Bosman, E., Bos, H., Guiffrida, C.: ASLR on the line: practical cache attacks on the MMU. In: Network and Distributed System Security Symposium (2017). https://doi.org/10.14722/ndss.2017.23271
22. Gruss, D., Maurice, C., Fogh, A., Lipp, M., Mangard, S.: Prefetch side-channel attacks: bypassing SMAP and kernel ASLR. In: Proceedings of the 2016 ACM SIGSAC Conference on Computer and Communications Security (2016)
23. Guan, L., Lin, J., Luo, B., Jing, J., Wang, J.: Protecting private keys against memory disclosure attacks using hardware transactional memory. In: IEEE Symposium on Security and Privacy (2015)
24. Guan, L., et al.: TrustShadow: secure execution of unmodified applications with ARM TrustZone. arXiv preprint arXiv:1704.05600 (2017)
25. Hu, H., Shinde, S., Sendroiu, A., Chua, Z.L., Saxena, P., Liang, Z.: Data-oriented programming: on the expressiveness of non-control data attacks. In: IEEE Symposium on Security and Privacy (2016)
26. Ilyas, I.F., Beskales, G., Soliman, M.A.: A survey of top-k query processing techniques in relational database systems. ACM Comput. Surv. (CSUR) **40**(4), 11 (2008)

27. Kim, T., Peinado, M., Mainar-Ruiz, G.: STEALTHMEM: system-level protection against cache-based side channel attacks in the cloud. Presented as part of the 21st USENIX Security Symposium (USENIX Security 2012), pp. 189–204. USENIX, Bellevue (2012). https://www.usenix.org/conference/usenixsecurity12/technical-sessions/presentation/kim

28. Koning, K., Chen, X., Bos, H., Giuffrida, C., Athanasopoulos, E.: No need to hide: protecting safe regions on commodity hardware. In: Proceedings of the Twelfth European Conference on Computer Systems (2017)

29. Kuvaiskii, D., et al.: SGXBOUNDS: memory safety for shielded execution. In: Proceedings of the Twelfth European Conference on Computer Systems (2017)

30. Kuznetsov, V., Szekeres, L., Payer, M., Candea, G., Sekar, R., Song, D.: Code-pointer integrity. In: 11th USENIX Symposium on Operating Systems Design and Implementation (2014)

31. Li, W., Xia, Y., Chen, H., Zang, B., Guan, H.: Reducing world switches in virtualized environment with flexible cross-world calls. In: ACM/IEEE 42nd Annual International Symposium on Computer Architecture (2015)

32. Liu, C., Harris, A., Maas, M., Hicks, M., Tiwari, M., Shi, E.: GhostRider: a hardware-software system for memory trace oblivious computation. ACM SIGARCH Comput. Archit. News 43(1), 87–101 (2015)

33. Liu, F., et al.: CATalyst: defeating last-level cache side channel attacks in cloud computing. In: IEEE International Symposium on High Performance Computer Architecture (2016)

34. Nagarakatte, S., Martin, M.M., Zdancewic, S.: WatchdogLite: hardware-accelerated compiler-based pointer checking. In: Proceedings of Annual IEEE/ACM International Symposium on Code Generation and Optimization (2014)

35. Nagarakatte, S., Zhao, J., Martin, M.M., Zdancewic, S.: SoftBound: highly compatible and complete spatial memory safety for C. ACM SIGPLAN Not. 44(6), 245–258 (2009)

36. Rane, A., Lin, C., Tiwari, M.: Raccoon: closing digital side-channels through obfuscated execution. In: USENIX Security Symposium (2015)

37. Rane, A., Lin, C., Tiwari, M.: Secure, precise, and fast floating-point operations on x86 processors. In: USENIX Security Symposium (2016)

38. Roessler, N., DeHon, A.: Protecting the stack with metadata policies and tagged hardware. In: 2018 IEEE Symposium on Security and Privacy (SP), pp. 1072–1089 (2018). https://doi.org/10.1109/SP.2018.00066

39. Sehr, D., et al.: Adapting software fault isolation to contemporary CPU architectures. In: USENIX Security Symposium (2010)

40. Simpson, M.S., Barua, R.K.: MemSafe: ensuring the spatial and temporal memory safety of C at runtime. Softw.: Pract. Exp. 43(1), 93–128 (2013)

41. Song, C., et al.: HDFI: hardware-assisted data-flow isolation. In: IEEE Symposium on Security and Privacy (2016)

42. Vishwanathan, S.V.N., Schraudolph, N.N., Kondor, R., Borgwardt, K.M.: Graph kernels. J. Mach. Learn. Res. 11, 1201–1242 (2010)

43. Wahbe, R., Lucco, S., Anderson, T.E., Graham, S.L.: Efficient software-based fault isolation. In: ACM SIGOPS Operating Systems Review (1994)

44. Wang, Z., Lee, R.B.: New cache designs for thwarting software cache-based side channel attacks. In: Proceedings of the 34th Annual International Symposium on Computer Architecture, ISCA 2007, pp. 494–505. ACM, New York (2007). https://doi.org/10.1145/1250662.1250723

45. Wilander, J., Nikiforakis, N., Younan, Y., Kamkar, M., Joosen, W.: RIPE: runtime intrusion prevention evaluator. In: Proceedings of the 27th Annual Computer Security Applications Conference (2011)
46. Yee, B., et al.: Native client: a sandbox for portable, untrusted x86 native code. In: 30th IEEE Symposium on Security and Privacy (2009)

CryptMe: Data Leakage Prevention for Unmodified Programs on ARM Devices

Chen Cao[1][✉], Le Guan[1], Ning Zhang[2], Neng Gao[3], Jingqiang Lin[3], Bo Luo[4], Peng Liu[1], Ji Xiang[3], and Wenjing Lou[2]

[1] The Pennsylvania State University, University Park, USA
{cuc96,lug14,pliu}@ist.psu.edu
[2] Virginia Polytechnic Institute and State University, Blacksburg, USA
{ningzh,wjlou}@vt.edu
[3] Institute of Information Engineering, CAS, Beijing, China
{gaoneng,linjingqiang,xiangji}@iie.ac.cn
[4] The University of Kansas, Kansas City, USA
bluo@ku.edu

Abstract. Sensitive data (e.g., passwords, health data and private videos) can be leaked due to many reasons, including (1) the misuse of legitimate operating system (OS) functions such as core dump, swap and hibernation, and (2) physical attacks to the DRAM chip such as cold-boot attacks and DMA attacks. While existing software-based memory encryption is effective in defeating physical attacks, none of them can prevent a legitimate OS function from accidentally leaking sensitive data in the memory. This paper introduces CryptMe that integrates memory encryption and ARM TrustZone-based memory access controls to protect sensitive data against both attacks. CryptMe essentially extends the Linux kernel with the ability to accommodate the execution of *unmodified* programs in an isolated execution domain (to defeat OS function misuse), and at the same time transparently encrypt sensitive data appeared in the DRAM chip (to defeat physical attacks). We have conducted extensive experiments on our prototype implementation. The evaluation results show the efficiency and added security of our design.

1 Introduction

Driven by the pressures of time-to-market and development cost, Internet-of-Things (IoT) manufacturers tend to build their systems atop existing open-source software stacks, notably the Linux kernel. Millions of IoT devices are running Linux kernel on ARM-based System-On-Chip (SoC), ranging from smart IP cameras, in-vehicle infotainment systems, to smart routers, etc. However, the swift prototyping process often comes at the cost of security and privacy. With full-blown software stacks, these devices often expose a much larger attack surface than we anticipated. Recent attacks against IoT devices have further indicated that our IoT devices are at higher and higher risk of being hacked.

© Springer Nature Switzerland AG 2018
M. Bailey et al. (Eds.): RAID 2018, LNCS 11050, pp. 380–400, 2018.
https://doi.org/10.1007/978-3-030-00470-5_18

With a full-blown software stack deployed on IoT devices, sensitive data contained in programs often spread across all layers of the memory system [7]. A vulnerability in any layer can lead to the exposure of sensitive data. Unauthorized access to sensitive data residing on a DRAM chip is particularly serious because the data contained in the DRAM frequently include unprotected sensitive information (e.g., user credentials, video frames in an IP camera, Internet traffic with health data). Its exposure can be a major security concern for IoT device users.

In this paper, we aim to address two common types of DRAM-based memory disclosure attacks. First, in a software-based attack, private data in a program could be exposed to an attacker by misusing of benign OS functions or exploiting read-only memory disclosure vulnerabilities. For example, attackers can trigger normal OS functions such as coredump [22], hibernation/swap [12,21,34], and logging [7] to export otherwise isolated private memory to external storage. The second type of DRAM-based memory disclosure attack roots in the cyber-physical characteristic of IoT devices. Specifically, IoT devices are often deployed in diverse, and sometimes ambient environments; as a result, they are usually physically unmonitored. Attackers could physically access them and extract secrets contained in the DRAM chip [11]. Cold boot attack [16], bus-monitoring attack [10] and DMA attack [5] are quite common forms of physical attack. They can break the system even if the software is free of bugs.

Memory Encryption (ME) is a promising solution to address the aforementioned memory disclosure attacks. It operates on DRAM, and encrypts a portion or all of the address space of a program at runtime [19]. However, on one hand, ME solutions relying on hardware redesign increase the cost of the chip [24], and are not feasible for incremental Commercial Off-The-Shelf (COTS) defense deployment. On the other hand, existing general software-based ME solutions [8,13,29] all leave a small working set (memory that is currently being accessed) in clear-text to ensure the correct execution of a program. As a consequence, it is still possible for the working set to be exposed.

Gap Statement. An ME solution that really works on defeating the associated threats should protect both the non-working set memory and the working set memory *at all time*. In particular, it should have the following features: (1) The non-working set memory is encrypted; (2) The working set memory is in clear-text, but does not appear in the vulnerable DRAM. (3) The working set memory cannot be accessed by other software, including the OS. Unfortunately, to the best of our knowledge, a ME solution meeting all these requirements is still missing in the literature.

Software-based ME solutions can be classified into three types, as shown in Fig. 1. Cryptkeeper [29] and RamCrypt [13] belong to Type A (see Fig. 1a). In this category, most of the program data are encrypted while a small working set is left unprotected (e.g., four pages in RamCrypt) in the DRAM. As a result, Type A ME solutions are subject to both software and physical memory disclosure attacks. Type B solutions (see Fig. 1b) eliminate all the occurrences of clear-

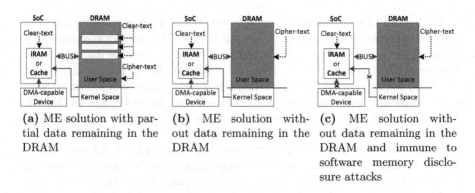

(a) ME solution with partial data remaining in the DRAM

(b) ME solution without data remaining in the DRAM

(c) ME solution without data remaining in the DRAM and immune to software memory disclosure attacks

Fig. 1. Classification of ME solutions.

text program data in the DRAM chip by further protecting the working set by constraining them in the System-on-Chip (SoC) components such as iRAM) [18] or processor cache [8]. The SoC components are commonly believed to be much more difficult to attack compared with the DRAM chip [8]. Type B ME solutions are effective in defeating cold-boot attacks to DRAM chips. Unfortunately, the clear-text working set residing in the SoC components can still be exposed by software memory disclosure or DMA-capable devices.

As shown in Fig. 1c, Type C ME solutions disable both the OS kernel and DMA-capable devices to access iRAM. To implement a Type C ME system, a straightforward solution would be to further isolate clear-text program data in iRAM/cache from the OS kernel. In the ARM platform, the TrustZone architectural extension seems to be an ideal solution. With TrustZone, an ARM processor could run in two different execution domains – secure world or normal world. The OS in the normal world cannot access iRAM monopolized by the secure world. Therefore, if we execute the program in the secure world, and integrate existing type B ME solution, the problem seems to be solved. However, this is actually very challenging based on the following observations.

- **O1**: A legacy program runs in the same world with the OS. If the iRAM is a secure resource only accessible by the secure world, the legacy program in the normal world would simply crash; on the other hand, if the iRAM is designated to be a non-secure resource, the OS can still reveal the contents of the iRAM.
- **O2**: If we instead execute the legacy program in the secure world, there is no execution environment in the secure world. In particular, system services including system calls, interruptions, and page fault, etc., are all missing in the secure world.
- **O3**: To tackle the problem mentioned in **O2**, we could duplicate a full fledged OS in the secure world. However, the code base in the secure world will be inflated, making it prone to exploits.

Our Solution. In this work, we present CRYPTME, the first type C ME solution for COTS ARM platforms. CRYPTME addresses the aforementioned challenges by offloading a program in the secure world. Instead of employing a fledged OS to respond to the system service requests, we build a thin privileged layer in the secure world. The privileged layer does not provide system services itself, but forwards the requests to the OS in the normal world. By further incorporating type B ME solution, we ensure that both the non-working set and working set memory do not appear in clear-text in the DRAM chip, and the working set memory cannot be accessed by any software in the normal world.

Specifically, we protect sensitive data (called SENDATA) by encrypting all the anonymous memory segments (i.e., memory not backed a file, such as bss, heap, stack, and anonymously mapped memory segments) and private Copy-On-Write (COW) segments (such as data segment containing global and static variables). When the encrypted data are accessed, they are transparently decrypted in the iRAM. The program code in the DRAM chip is not protected. The key insight behind this is that the code segment of a program is usually publicly available so there is no need to protect its confidentiality. To further protect data in the iRAM from software attacks, CRYPTME sets iRAM to be a secure resource. Therefore, even the OS kernel cannot access the data in it. To execute a protected process (called SENPROCESS), CRYPTME offloads it to an isolated execution domain – TrustZone secure world, and a lightweight trusted execution runtime residing in the secure world is responsible for maintaining the execution environment of the process (such as setting up page tables). In summary, CRYPTME ensures that clear-text program data *only* exists in iRAM, and we restrict accesses to iRAM from the Linux kernel by TrustZone configuration.

In summary, we made the following contributions.

- We have designed CRYPTME, an ME system that prevents the clear-text sensitive data of *unmodified* programs from leaking to the DRAM for ARM-based IoT devices.
- CRYPTME is the first ME system that is able to tackle both physical memory disclosure attacks and software attacks, including misuse of benign OS functions and real-only memory disclosure attacks.
- We have implemented CRYPTME prototype on a Freescale i.MX6q experiment board. Security validation shows that CRYPTME effectively eliminates all the occurrence of private program data in the DRAM, and thwarts software-based memory disclosure attacks.

2   Background

2.1   Memory Disclosure Attack

Though full system memory encryption has been a topic of interest, the privacy concerns for memory disclosure have not been a real threat until demonstrations of hardware-based memory disclosure attacks [5,10,16]. DMA capable devices such as Firewire were leveraged to read system memory [5]. Since DMA engine is independent of the processor, and directly talks to the DRAM chips, as long as the device is powered on, all the DRAM contents can be read out. In [16],

Halderman et al. transplanted the memory chip of a laptop onto a different one where there was no software protection on the physical memory. Using a simple dust blower to keep the memory chip cool, it was possible to extract almost all of the information from the memory. The significance of this attack is that it can bypass all the software system protections. The remanence effect of DRAM was also exploited in [6,26] to launch cold-boot attacks to smartphones, where the system is rebooted into a rouge OS to bypass the memory protection. For advanced adversaries, it might even be possible to snoop the communication between the CPU and the DRAM [10].

Memory disclosure can also occur due to misuse of legitimate OS functions or passive read-only memory disclosure attacks. For example, the memory dump function is a very useful feature in modern OSes. A core dump image provides valuable information about the execution state when a crash happens which helps developer identify the crash point. However, attackers exploited this feature to dump sensitive data of a process [22]. Taking advantage of read-only memory disclosure vulnerabilities, the authors in [17] successfully exposed the private keys of an OpenSSH server and an Apache HTTP server.

2.2   TrustZone

TrustZone is a secure extension to the ARM architecture, including modifications to the processor, memory, and peripherals [35]. Most ARM processors support this security extension. TrustZone is designed to provide a system wide isolated execution environment for sensitive workloads. The isolated execution environment is often called *secure world*, and the commodity running environment is often referred to as the *normal world* or the *rich OS*. Different system resources can be accessed depending on the world of the process. In particular, the *Security Configuration Register (SCR)* in the *CP15* co-processor is one of the registers that can only be accessed while the processor is in the secure world. *NS (non-secure)* bit in the SCR controls the security context of the processor. When the bit is set, the processor is in the normal world. When the bit is clear, the processor is in the secure world.

One of the most important components in a TrustZone-based system is *Trust-Zone Address Space Controller (TZASC)*. Registers of TZASC are mapped into the physical address of the SoC, and can be accessed via memory operations. Access policies for different physical memory regions can be programmed via these registers. With these controls, secure world code can control whether a memory region can be accessed from both secure and normal worlds, or can only be accessed from secure world. For other peripherals, such as iRAM, different SoC manufactures implement different components to configure their access policy. In a typical implementation, a *Central Security Unit (CSU)* is used by trusted secure world code to set individual security access privileges on each of the peripheral.

3 Threat Model and Security Requirements

3.1 Threat Model

CRYPTME is designed to prevent the sensitive data of a running program from being leaked into DRAM chip or other peripherals. The threats considered in this work, include (*a*) misused *benign* OS functions such as swap, hibernation, and core dump, (*b*) *passive read-only* memory disclosure attacks, and (*c*) *malicious* physical attacks targeting the DRAM chips.

We assume a benign OS kernel that runs in the normal world of a TrustZone-powered device. That is, basic OS services, such as task management, memory management and execution environment maintenance, etc. are trusted. We do not assume a compromised OS kernel. Otherwise, the process can be manipulated arbitrarily. We assume orthogonal solutions to ensure the integrity of the Linux kernel [4].

The OS is also assumed to correctly implement supplementary functions to improve efficiency (e.g., swap, hibernation), and to facilitate program analyses (e.g., core dump). However, once misused, these functions can be exploited to leak sensitive data, because they have the capability to access the whole address space of a process. There seems to be a countermeasure to deal with this issue – disabling these OS functions. However, many of them are indispensable in modern OSes. Once disabled, the whole system will be significantly affected. For example, disk swap is the key technique to support virtual memory. Without it, the system could quickly run out of memory.

The attacker could also exploit passive read-only memory disclosure attacks. When exploiting these read-only attacks, attackers often do not need to compromise the kernel to gain control flow and manipulate critical data structures. Therefore, active monitoring techniques (e.g., kernel integrity checking) cannot detect such "silent" data leakages. For example, in [17], the authors exploited two kernel vulnerabilities [27,28] to successfully extract private keys used in OpenSSH and Apache Server in several minutes. According to a statistics, this kind of "Gain Information" vulnerability contributes 16.5% of all Linux vulnerabilities as of Mar. 2018 [9].

We assume attackers are able to launch physical attacks to expose DRAM contents, bypassing the process isolation enforced by the OS. In a cold boot, the attacker is capable of dumping the entire DRAM image of a running device by rebooting it into another malicious OS from an external storage [16,26]. In DMA attacks [33], a malicious peripheral device is utilized to directly read out memory contents by issuing DMA requests. Moreover, an advanced attacker might even be able to eavesdrop data transmission between the DRAM chips and the processor by monitoring the memory bus [10].

The protected program itself must be trusted. That is, we assume a SEN-PROCESS never leaks SENDATA out of its private memory segments by itself, either intentionally or unintentionally. Since our protection is built on top of ARM TrustZone, we also assume the correctness of TrustZone implementations. The privileged codes of CRYPTME running in the TrustZone secure world are

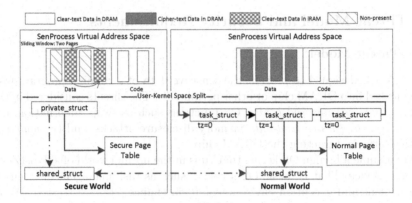

Fig. 2. CRYPTME overview with a sliding window size of two pages

assumed to be free of vulnerability, as well as the trusted boot process enabling the TrustZone-based hardware memory control. In the design and implementation of CRYPTME, we keep the privileged code base small (5.8K Lines Of Code (LOC), in the prototype system), so it is possible to formally verify its correctness. Lastly, side-channel attacks are out of the scope in this paper.

3.2 Security Requirements

Based on the threat model, we formalize the problem into the following security requirements that CRYPTME aims to meet.

R1. The DRAM chip does not contain any clear-text SENDATA.
R2. The clear-text SENDATA is constrained in the on-chip iRAM, which can only be accessed by the secure-world code.

Software-based memory disclosure attacks are thwarted by the combination of **R1** and **R2**. In addition, meeting **R1** keeps SENDATA immune to cold-boot attacks and bus-monitoring attacks, while meeting **R2** prevents DMA attacks.

4   Design

This section describes the design of CRYPTME. We start with an overview of the proposed system, then expand on several key techniques. We show how CRYPTME supports offloading CRYPTME-enabled SENPROCESSES to an isolated execution environment in the TrustZone secure world, and how page tables in this isolated environment are maintained. Finally we present the protections that CRYPTME provides for the offloaded SENPROCESSES– encryption and isolation.

4.1 Overview

In CRYPTME, a Linux OS runs in the normal world, while protected SENPRO-CESSES run in the secure world. As shown in Fig. 2, like any other processes in a Linux system, each SENPROCESS is referenced by a `task_struct` data structure in the normal OS. In fact, the `task_struct` of a SENPROCESS is no different from normal ones except for a newly added flag (`tz`) and a world-shared memory buffer (`shared_struct`). The flag identifies a process as a SENPROCESS while the shared buffer is used to exchange critical information (such as page table updates) between the two worlds.

Each SENPROCESS is still created, maintained, and scheduled by the normal OS, but executed in the secure world. The normal OS is customized so that just before a SENPROCESS is to return to user space, an `smc` instruction is issued to transfer the control to the secure world. In the secure world, there is a piece of *Secure Privileged Code* (SPC) that is responsible for maintaining the execution environment of a SENPROCESS by exchanging context information with the normal OS. Each SENPROCESS has its own `private_struct` that stores its hardware context, and `shared_struct` that is shared with the normal OS to enable data exchange.

When the SENPROCESS is executed in the secure world, its working data set is kept in clear-text in the `iRAM`, which is not accessible by the normal OS. For each SENPROCESS, SPC keeps a sliding window of `iRAM` pages for the working set. If the working set of a SENPROCESS exceeds the threshold assigned to it, SPC encrypts the oldest page in the window and copies it to the corresponding DRAM page, and then assigns the freed `iRAM` page to the virtual address that triggers the page fault.

A SENPROCESS has separate page tables in each world. Normal world page table is maintained by the normal OS with a customized page fault handler. It serves as a template for the *Secure Page Table* in the secure world. In both page table settings, the clear-text code segment is backed by the same DRAM pages, which CRYPTME takes no effort to protect. However, SENDATA, which normal world page table maps to DRAM pages, is encrypted. SENDATA contained in the sliding window in `iRAM` is decrypted to keep the SENPROCESS runnable in the secure world, as shown in Fig. 2.

CRYPTME employs the on-chip hardware-based cryptographic engine to accelerate AES computations. An AES key is generated randomly when a new SENPROCESS is about to be created. It is kept in a dedicated `iRAM` page shared by all the SENPROCESSES. The round keys and intermediate values generated during encryption/decryption are all constrained in this page, therefore, the key materials enjoy the same level of protection with that provided for SENDATA.

4.2 Executing in the Secure World

This section describes how a SENPROCESS gets offloaded to execute in the secure world. This is the prerequisite to enforce other security measures that will be discussed later. Since the secure world and the normal world are logically separated,

SPC has to maintain the essential execution environments for SENPROCESSES to run in the secure world. In this section, we introduce a naïve code offloading mechanism, in which the normal-world page table and secure-world page table share the same set of page table entries. As a result, SENPROCESS code runs in the secure world, while all the memory references are routed to DRAM pages that both worlds can access. In Sect. 4.3, we show how to improve this naïve design to encrypt SENDATA that appear in the DRAM. Then, in Sect. 4.4, we further describe how to deprive the Linux OS kernel and other peripheral devices of the privilege to access clear-text SENDATA in iRAM.

Code Offloading. CRYPTME supports memory encryption on a per-process basis. To start a SENPROCESS, the user land loader invokes a dedicated system call, similar execve, which marks the process in its task_struct.

With the capability to identify a SENPROCESS, the kernel is further instrumented to invoke an smc instruction whenever a SENPROCESS is about to be scheduled to run in user space. The smc instruction transfers control flow to the monitor mode in secure world, where the monitor mode code handles world switch, and invokes SPC to restore the hardware context of the SENPROCESS and execute it in the user space in secure world.

System Services. SENPROCESS in the secure world may incur exceptions during execution. When this happens, the SENPROCESS traps into SPC. To keep the code base of SPC small, SPC forwards all of them directly to the normal world OS kernel. In ARM platform, system calls are requested by the swi instruction, which traps the processor in the privileged SVC mode. Other exceptions such as interrupt and page fault trap the processor to the corresponding privileged CPU modes. To forward an exception to the normal world while keeping the normal OS oblivious of it, SPC needs to *reproduce* a hardware context as if the exception is triggered in the user space of the normal world. To achieve this, system registers indicating the context must be correctly set.

Re-producing Exceptions. Any SENPROCESS exception is first intercepted by the SPC. Because the monitor-mode code taking charge of world switches has ultimate privilege to access the resources of both worlds, it is possible to manually manipulate relevant registers that indicate the pre-exception context. Normally, these registers can only be set by hardware. With these registers manipulated, the system call handler in the Linux kernel can correctly parse the context information.

Page Table Synchronization. Each SENPROCESS in the secure world has its own page table. We instrument existing page fault handler in the normal Linux kernel to share the page table update information with SPC. This is based on the aforementioned exception forwarding mechanism. In particular, when a page fault exception is forwarded to the Linux kernel, it invokes its own page fault handler to populate the corresponding page in the normal world. Whenever the set_pte_at function is invoked, page table update information is duplicated in

Table 1. Cache and iRAM comparison

	Immunity to physical attacks	Capacity	Controllability	Continuous support	Intrusiveness
iRAM	✓	✗	✓	✓	✓
L2 cache	✓	✓	✗	✗	✗

the world-shared buffer `shared_struct`. The information includes the address of the page table entry, the updated value of the page table entry, the influenced virtual address, and other metadata. When the SENPROCESS is scheduled to execute in the secure world, SPC uses the shared information as a template to update the secure-world page table. In this way, SPC and the normal-world kernel maintain an identical copy of page table for each SENPROCESS.

4.3   Transparent Encryption

Barely offloading a SENPROCESS to the secure world does not gain any security benefit. This section describes how CRYPTME enforces security requirement **R1**. That is, SENDATA appears in DRAM only as cipher-text.

To execute a process, the processor should always work on clear-text program data. In our design, a SENPROCESS runs with a clear-text working set that resides on on-chip memory unit, which is more expensive for an attacker to launch a physical attack. The rest of SENDATA is kept encrypted in the DRAM. Here, two commonly used on-chip memory units are processor caches and iRAM. We show the advantages and disadvantages of each option in the next paragraphs.

Selecting On-chip Memory. On-chip caches are small static RAM that are tightly coupled with a processor. It buffers recently accessed memories with very low access latency. In the recently shipped ARM SoCs, the capacity of a Level-2 (L2) cache can achieve several megabytes. When it loses power supply, all of its contents are lost. Therefore, in literatures, many solutions seek to defeat physical attacks to the DRAM chip using L2 caches [8,36].

iRAM is another on-chip memory that is more like a traditional DRAM chip. Most manufacturers integrate a 256 KB iRAM into their products to run boot code that initializes other SoC components. After that, all of its storage is free to use. During a reboot, the immutable booting firmware explicitly erases all the iRAM content [8]. Therefore, iRAM is also immune to cold-boot attacks. Table 1 summaries pros and cons for both L2 cache and iRAM.

Both options are suitable to defeat physical attacks. However, using cache has many drawbacks. First, even though cache can be used as SoC-bound memory storage, the dynamic nature of its allocation algorithm makes it difficult to lock its mapping to the physical memory address. Second, although many ARM processors support cache locking, this feature itself only benefits programs requiring customized cache allocation to maximize cache usage. As the size of cache is growing in each generation of processors, the need for customized cache use is diminishing. As a consequence, this feature is becoming obsolete in the latest generations of ARM processors such as Cortex-A57 [3]. Furthermore, cache is designed to ease the bottleneck at the slow memory operations. Monopolizing cache for security purpose can severely degrade the overall system performances. Therefore, in CRYPTME, we choose iRAM to back the clear-text working memory.

Memory Encryption. Building atop the page table synchronization mechanism introduced in Sect. 4.2, SPC further differentiates the types of page table updates for a SENPROCESS. In particular, within the shared data structure shared_struct, a flag indicating the property of the corresponding fault page is added. The flag instructs SPC how to set up the page table – to duplicate the normal-world page table entry that points to an identical normal DRAM page (e.g., for a code page), or to allocate a new page in the iRAM (e.g., for an anonymous data page). In the latter case, SPC replaces the target normal-world DRAM page address with the newly allocated iRAM page address in the secure-world page table entry, and then maintains the mapping. Since the capacity of an iRAM chip is limited, SPC cannot meet all the page table requests of a SEN-PROCESS. We introduce a sliding window mechanism to address this problem.

Sliding Window. SPC assigns a dynamic number of iRAM pages to each SEN-PROCESS. Starting from the first available iRAM page, SPC keeps a circular index to the next available iRAM page. Page faults corresponding to SENDATA accesses continue to consume iRAM pages until the assigned pages are used up. In this case, the circular index points to the first iRAM page in the window. SPC then encrypts that iRAM page and copies it to the corresponding DRAM page. Finally, this iRAM page is assigned to be used for the newly occurred page fault request.

4.4 Disabling Access to the Sliding Window

We have ensured that no clear-text SENDATA would occur in the DRAM. However, privileged kernel can still read out any program data in the sliding window contained in iRAM. This flaw actually exists in all the existing software-based memory encryption solutions, such as Bear [18], RamCrypt [13], and Crypt-Keeper [29]. Moreover, it is possible that a local attacker issues DMA requests to iRAM. CRYPTME addresses this threat by enforcing hardware-based access control to iRAM. More specifically, during booting, CRYPTME configures the *CSU* available in TrustZone so that normal world code, including the Linux kernel, and any other peripherals, cannot access iRAM. This effectively enforces security requirement **R2**. That is, iRAM that holds clear-text SENDATA cannot be accessed by any entities other than the secure world code.

5 Implementation

We have implemented a full prototype of CRYPTME on a Freescale i.MX6q experiment board which features an ARM Cortex-A9 processor with 1 GB DDR3

DRAM and 256 KB iRAM. Our implementation includes two parts. In the secure world, the implementation of SPC comprises around 5.3K LOC of C, and 0.5K LOC of assembly. In the normal world, we instrument the Linux kernel version 3.18.24 to be CRYPTME-aware with 300 LOC of modification.

5.1   Secure World

The experiment board supports High Assurance Boot (HAB), a proprietary technology to ensure trusted boot. After power on, a proprietary boot ROM in the board executes to initialize critical system components and verify the integrity of the next stage image – in our case, the SPC. If SPC passes checking, it gets execution privilege in the secure world. Otherwise, the ROM will be reset.

To disable access to iRAM from DMA and the Linux kernel, SPC configures the CSU to set iRAM as a secure master. In our implementation, we achieve that by enabling the OCRAM_TZ_EN bit in register IOMUXC_GPR10, and setting access control policy in the low 8 bits of the CSU_CSL26 register in CSU[1]. Then SPC locks the configuration. As a result, any intentions to make modifications to the CSU configuration will trigger a system reboot, including SPC itself.

Finally, SPC hands the control to the boot loader in the normal world – uboot, which further boots the Linux OS.

5.2   Normal World

SENPROCESSES are still created and scheduled by the Linux kernel. We add a customized system call execve_enc to load a SENPROCESS. A process started with execve_enc has a tz flag set in its task_struct. We instrument the ret_to_user and ret_fast_syscall routines, so that whenever a SENPROCESS is about to return to user space, an smc instruction is issued to route the execution in the secure world. To run an unmodified program as a SENPROCESS, the user only needs to invoke a wrapper program with the path of the target program as a parameter. The wrapper program simply replaces itself with the target program by invoking the execve_enc system call.

5.3   Key Management and Encryption

When a SENPROCESS is created by execve_enc, the SPC invokes the on-board hardware-based random number generator to extract a 256-bit AES key anew. This key is used to protect all the SENDATA of this SENPROCESS. When the the process is terminated, the key can be safely discarded, because the anonymous SENDATA which it protects, do not persist across invocations.

The experiment board we use integrates Cryptographic Acceleration and Assurance Module (CAAM), which provides accelerated cryptographic computation, including AES, DES/3DES, RC4, etc. We employed CAAM to implement

---

[1] CSU_CSL is a set of registers only accessible in secure state that can set individual slave's access policy. Low 8 bits of CSU_CSL26 is marked as reserved in the manual of our experiment board, we found that it controls access to iRAM by experiments.

(a) Image dumped with a
native Linux Kernel.

(b) Image dumped when
CRYPTME is enabled.

Fig. 3. Physical memory image with and without CRYPTME enabled.

a SoC bounded cryptographic service. Specifically, during an AES computation, all the sensitive data, including the original AES key, its key schedule, and intermediate results are redirected into a single reserved iRAM page. As a result, this page, together with plain-text SENDATA, has the highest protection level in our system. In CRYPTME, we use AES-256 in CBC mode. The Initialization Vector (IV) is chosen as the virtual address of the encrypted page.

6   Evaluation

In this section, we evaluate CRYPTME in both security and performance. In terms of security, we designed and conducted experiments to validate the security requirements **R1** and **R2** in Sect. 3.2. In terms of performance, we measured the overhead introduced by CRYPTME compared with the base line in the native Linux environment. Our evaluation was performed on the same board and the same software environment as our prototype.

6.1   Security Evaluation

This section introduces several simulated attacks we designed to evaluate the security features of CRYPTME.

Meeting Security Requirement **R1**. Security requirement **R1** states that the DRAM chip contains no clear-text SENDATA. In order to obtain the contents of DRAM chip, we use the "memdump" utility to dump memory contents from the /dev/mem device file. To test the effectiveness of our system, we wrote a simple program which constantly writes a magic string ("Hack Me") into memory. Then we dump the whole DRAM image to search for this magic string.

Figure 3 depicts the results on the dumped images we obtained from the native Linux and CRYPTME. The addresses displayed in these figures are the offsets from the beginning of the dump file. The beginning of this file represents the contents of the beginning of DRAM, which has an offset from the start of physical memory map, therefore, the real physical address is calculated by deducing this DRAM offset from the displayed file offset. Figure 3a shows the result from the native Linux kernel. Clearly, we were able to locate a bunch of magic strings in the dump image. Figure 3b shows the result we obtained when CRYPTME is enabled. Throughout the searching, we did not find any occurrence of "Hack Me" string. This indicates that all the magic strings are encrypted in DRAM.

*Meeting Security Requirement **R2**.* Security requirement **R2** states that on-chip iRAM cannot be accessed by any entities other than the secure-world software. To simulate an attack targeting iRAM, we wrote a kernel module that deliberately maps iRAM to the address space of a process using the vm_iomap_memory kernel function, and attempted to read the iRAM content in the normal world. The result shows that we can only obtain zero values, regardless of what we wrote into the iRAM. On the contrary, after we disabled hardware access control enforcement on iRAM as mentioned in Sect. 4.4, we were able to read out the data that the process wrote.

Defeating Attacks Misusing Legitimate OS Functions. In a software-based attack that misuses legitimate OS functions, the whole address space of a SENPROCESS is exposed. A kind of such attacks takes advantage of the coredump function which was originally designed to assist program analyses when a crash happens. In particular, the attacker deliberately crashes the target program, and it triggers a coredump operation which allows the OS to generate an image containing target process's memory contents, CPU context etc., when the crash happens. As the image is stored in the persistent storage (i.e., flash chip in an IoT device), the attacker could easily read it out.

In order to simulate such an attack, we sent a "SIGSEGV" signal to the victim SENPROCESS to trigger a coredump after it writes a bunch of magic values (0xEF87AE12) into its anonymous memory segment. We got the coredump images of this process from the systems running with and without CRYPTME enabled. As expected, we successfully found the target value in the image dumped from the native Linux system. On the contrary, we did not find any occurrence of 0xEF87AE12 in the image dumped when CRYPTME is enabled throughout the searching process.

6.2 Performance Evaluation

To evaluate the performance overhead, we compare the benchmarks of programs in three system configurations. They are (1) **native** Linux system without modification, (2) CRYPTME using the AES algorithm to **encrypt** pages being swapped, and (3) CRYPTME using **plain** copy to swap pages. We first tested our system with the LMbench micro-benchmark [25] to measure the overhead introduced by world switches. This overhead is inevitable if we want to shield the iRAM from attacks. Next we tested our system with a self-written AES benchmark. This lightweight cryptographic primitive is frequently used in IoT devices. Finally, the performance of Nginx, a large complex web server is measured. Lots of IoT devices expose a web interface for users to access their functionality or to perform configuration changes to them. To better understand the introduced overhead, we designed experiments to measure the time consumption of different steps in the program execution.

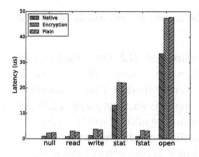

Fig. 4. System call latency.

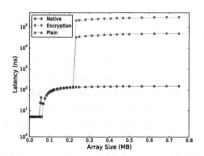

Fig. 5. Latency of memory reading with varying buffer sizes.

LMbench. SPC acts as an intermediate layer in-between the user space in secure world and kernel space in normal world. This design doubles the length of path to travel from user space to the Linux kernel and increases context-switch overhead. Therefore, we first report our results on the `lat_syscall` test, which measures the response time for various system calls.

Figure 4 depicts the results of `null`, `read`, `write`, `stat`, `fstat`, and `open` operations [25]. As shown in the figure, compared with the native Linux system, it takes CRYPTME almost 3 times longer to complete `null` and `read` operations. However, such overhead is amortized in other non-trivial operations. For example, the performance overhead for the `open()`/`close()` system call is only about 1.5 times. Moreover, CRYPTME with AES encryption and CRYPTME with plain copy exhibit very similar performance. This is expected because a system call is not likely to trigger a page swapping between DRAM and `iRAM`.

`lat_mem_rd` is a program included in the LMbemch test-suite that measures memory read latency. It reads memory buffers with varying sizes from 512 B to 768 KB. Because the maximum working set is obviously larger than the sliding window of a SENPROCESS, `lat_mem_rd` effectively exposes and even enlarges performance overhead caused by CRYPTME.

We explain the measured data as following. Since `lat_mem_rd` is a memory-intensive program, when the size of the buffer is small enough to be fit in the sliding window, very few pages need to be swapped in and out of the `iRAM`. As a result, no additional CPU cycles are needed. This is what we can see in Fig. 5 before the array size reaches 0.25 MB. At this stage, the three lines overlap with one another. When the buffer size exceeds that of the sliding window, old pages in the sliding window need to be swapped out to make room for new page requests. The introduced swapping operations indeed cause an abrupt performance degradation. Additional overhead can also be observed between CRYPTME with encryption and CRYPTME with plain copy. This is caused by the additional CPU cycles spent on the AES encryption.

Although the overhead introduced by CRYPTME appears to be significant in this experiment, we would like to argue that: (1) such extremely memory-intensive use cases are very rare in real-world applications, especially in IoT devices. And (2) with the development of hardware technologies and reduced costs, commercial IoT devices on the market are often loaded with computing powers that are significantly beyond their needs.

Table 2. AES-128 throughputs with different numbers of threads (completed AES blocks per second)

Thread #	1	2	3	4	5	6
Native	62011	63832	63862	62847	62858	62863
Encryption	63187	64213	64256	63243	63268	64316

Table 3. Nginx performance (requests per second)

	Sliding window = 16	Sliding window = 32	Sliding window = 48
Plain	109.30	247.95	574.04
Encryption	23.60	72.26	571.32

AES Benchmark. We implemented an AES benchmark based on mbed TLS [2] library. It computes AES-128 for 500,000 times using different numbers of threads. As AES is a computation-intensive program with small memory footprint, Table 2 clearly shows that CRYPTME incurs negligible overhead. Both CRYPTME and native Linux complete around 63,000 AES block calculations per second regardless of the number of computing threads.

Nginx Web Server. We also measured the overhead of CRYPTME when serving large complex programs. Many IoT devices provide their users with a web interface, through which the users are able to access the service or configure the device.

Table 4. Raw HTTP performance measurements (requests per second).

	1 KB	2 KB	4 KB	8 KB	16 KB	32 KB	64 KB	128 KB	256 KB	512 KB	1024 KB
Native	655.70	625.64	633.62	604.30	513.94	434.26	310.75	208.74	124.36	71.14	39.20
Encryption	601.97	560.68	580.87	554.98	474.72	403.92	292.52	195.08	121.51	70.18	39.05
Overhead	1.09x	1.12x	1.09x	1.09x	1.08x	1.08x	1.06x	1.07x	1.02x	1.01x	1.00x

Nginx [31] is an open-source high-performance HTTP server and reverse proxy, as well as an IMAP/POP3 proxy server. We used Nginx version 1.10.1 to run a HTTP web server, and used Apache benchmark [1] to measure the performance of the systems. The HTML file is the default 151 bytes welcome page, and the base line measured with native Linux system is 647.10 requests per second. In Table 3, we present the throughput of CRYPTME under different sliding window sizes. In Table 4, we compare the HTTP throughput of CRYPTME under 48-page sliding window size with native Linux system for different raw file sizes. When the sliding window is 48 pages, comparable performance is observed. Therefore, we would like to conclude that the overhead introduced by CRYPTME is very acceptable, because of the redundant computing power in such systems. However, as the sliding window decreases, the overhead becomes non-negligible. It is clear that frequent page swapping causes the noticeable overhead. In the following, we present a break-down measurement of additional time consumed in world switching and page swapping.

Table 5. Break-down measurement of time consumed in each period.

Operation	Time (μs)
Context switch	2.27
Encryption/decryption & copy	326.32
PTE setup	7.01

Break-down Measurement. Based on the above experiment results, CRYPTME is friendly to computation-intensive programs while exhibits ineligible overhead to memory-intensive programs. For memory-intensive programs, frequent page swapping is the key factor that influences the performance. In Table 5, we show a break-down measurement of the time spent on handling a page fault due to page swapping. Context switch is the time when completing a `getpid()` system call, which is drawn from Fig. 4. Note that this represents the minimum time for a world switch. Encryption/decryption & copy is the time spent on a encrypting/decrypting a page and copying it to normal/secure world. Note that a page swap invokes this operation twice; one for encrypting an old page into DRAM, and the other for decrypting a cipher-text page into `iRAM`. Finally, PTE setup measures the time for installing a page table entry in the secure world. It can be observed that cryptographic operation remains the dominating factor, which is the necessary price for the additional protection in memory encryption in general. However, many IoT devices are designed to be single purpose devices with limited functionality, therefore often do not require large working sets. This fixed cost for data encryption can be further reduced with more efficient hardware implementation of the cryptographic primitive.

7   Related Work

7.1   Memory Encryption

Many solutions on system memory encryption is motivated by the need to protect sensitive information stored in the memory [30]. With the rapid increase in speed and more sophisticated hardware-supported cryptographic function in modern processors, there has been recent efforts to realize practical software-based memory encryption on COTS hardware [8,13,14,18,29]. In particular, Cryptkeeper [29] and RamCrypt [13] implement ME on x86 platforms on a per-page basis with configurable security. Their implementation keeps a small set of decrypted working pages called sliding window. CRYPTME also adopts the sliding window concept, but the decrypted working set is stored in the on-chip memory, which is protected from memory attacks [16]. In [14], hypervisor is used to encrypt kernel and user space code in guest operating systems, and the decrypted working set is configured to fit the cache. Bear [18] is a comprehensive ME solution that hides working set in the on-chip memory. However, this work focuses on a "from scratch" microkernel that does not fit commodity OS. Sentry encrypts sensitive Android application when the device is locked, and employs on-chip caches to support background applications [8]. This solution is not practical for applications at normal state because substantial performance slowdown is observed. All the aforementioned approach towards full system memory encryption takes a probabilistic approach that reduces the risk of having sensitive content stored in the memory. This however leaves a door for the aforementioned software attacks that allow kernel to read the entire address space of application. Because memory coherence is maintained automatically by the processor, OS kernel could directly read out the private data in the working set, regardless they reside in DRAM, on-chip memory or caches. With CRYPTME, this decrypted working set is protected within the processor boundary in the iRAM against the cold boot attack. The iRAM is further protected by the Trust-Zone memory separation against memory disclosure attacks due to misused OS functions.

7.2   TrustZone-Based Solutions

TrustZone is a system wide security extension on ARM processors. Due to its unique ability to provide isolated execution environment even when the software of the system is compromised, TrustZone has been widely adopted in both academia research project and commercial project [4,15,20,23,32,36]. CaSE [36] is a system closely related to CRYPTME. In CaSE, sensitive workloads are encrypted and only decrypted during execution completely within the processor cache in ARM system to address the threat from physical memory disclosure. However, CaSE has limitation on the size of application binary. CRYPTME utilizes the iRAM for storing sensitive data and extends its capacity by employing a sliding-window algorithm. Therefore, it can support unmodified binaries of arbitrary size. TrustShadow [15] resembles our work in that we both offload the execution of trusted applications to the secure world. However, TrustShadow focuses on defeating malicious OSes, while CRYPTME focuses on defeating memory disclosure attacks.

8   Limitations and Future Work

Our design is not a full memory encryption solution which encrypts the whole address space of a process. Encrypted code is a compelling form of protection to thwart reverse-engineering of proprietary software. Although the current version of CRYPTME does not protect the confidentiality of program code, it is possible to extend it to encrypt code segment as well. However, we anticipate that new issues will arises. For example, how to handle shared libraries with non-SENPROCESSES is challenging. Moreover, it will inevitably introduce overhead due to increased working set.

We observed noticeable overhead for micro-benchmarks such as the memory latency test shown in Fig. 5. The overhead in the CRYPTME mainly originates from page swapping as is shown in Table 5. In the future, we plan to improve CRYPTME through the following two aspects. First, we will seek a better way to adjust the size of sliding window for individual SENPROCESSES. The provided customization allows for personalized configuration to maximum the usage of the valuable iRAM resource. Second, within a given sliding window, we plan to find a smarter page replacement algorithm to minimize the occurrence of page swapping.

9   Conclusions

In this paper, we present CRYPTME, a practical ME solution for the ARM-based IoT devices. CRYPTME supports unmodified program working on encrypted memory, mitigating the threats caused by memory leakages. Sensitive data is only decrypted in the iRAM of the SoC to protect against physical memory disclosure attacks. The trusted process is offloaded into an isolated execution domain with TrustZone. Therefore, our solution can also defeat software memory disclosure attacks from other processes or even the OS. We have implemented a CRYPTME prototype on a real ARM SoC board. Experiment results show that CRYPTME effectively defeats a wide range of memory disclosure attacks. Furthermore, CRYPTME introduces moderate overhead for computation intensive programs, and negligible overhead for programs with small memory footprints. CRYPTME enables ME for *unmodified* programs on the widely deployed ARM platforms. With small trade-off on the performance, CRYPTME provides its users with unprecedented protection for private user data.

Acknowledgement. We thank the anonymous reviewers for their valuable comments. This work was supported by NSF CNS-1422594, NSF CNS-1505664, NSF SBE-1422215, and ARO W911NF-13-1-0421 (MURI). Neng Gao and Ji Xiang were partially supported by NSFC (No. U163620068). Jingqiang Lin was partially supported by NSFC (No. 61772518).

References

1. Apache Software Foundation: Apache HTTP server benchmarking tool (2017). http://httpd.apache.org/docs/2.4/programs/ab.html
2. ARM Holdings: mbed TLS (2017). https://tls.mbed.org/
3. ARM Ltd.: Arm cortex-a57 mpcore processor technical reference manual (2013)
4. Azab, A.M., et al.: Hypervision across worlds: real-time kernel protection from the arm trustzone secure world. In: ACM CCS (2014)
5. Becher, M., Dornseif, M., Klein, C.: Firewire: all your memory are belong to us. In: 6th Annual CanSecWest Conference (2005)
6. Chan, E.M., Carlyle, J.C., David, F.M., Farivar, R., Campbell, R.H.: Bootjacker: compromising computers using forced restarts. In: 15th ACM CCS. ACM (2008)
7. Chow, J., et al.: Understanding data lifetime via whole system simulation. In: USENIX SEC (2004)
8. Colp, P., et al.: Protecting data on smartphones and tablets from memory attacks. In: ASPLOS 2015. ACM (2015)
9. CVE Details: The Ultimate Security Vulnerability Datasource (2018). https://www.cvedetails.com/vendor/33/Linux.html. Accessed 29 Mar 2018
10. FuturePlus System: DDR2 800 bus analysis probe (2006). http://www.futureplus.com/download/datasheet/fs2334_ds.pdf
11. Garcia-Morchon, O., Kumar, S., Struik, R., Keoh, S., Hummen, R.: Security considerations in the IP-based internet of things (2013)
12. Garfinkel, T., Pfaff, B., Chow, J., Rosenblum, M.: Data lifetime is a systems problem. In: 11th ACM SIGOPS European Workshop (2004)
13. Götzfried, J., Müller, T., Drescher, G., Nürnberger, S., Backes, M.: RamCrypt: kernel-based address space encryption for user-mode processes. In: 11th ACM Asia CCS. ACM (2016)
14. Götzfried, J., et al.: Hypercrypt: hypervisor-based encryption of kernel and user space. In: ARES 2016 (2016)
15. Guan, L., et al.: Trustshadow: secure execution of unmodified applications with arm trustzone. In: ACM MobiSys (2017)
16. Halderman, J.A., et al.: Lest we remember: cold boot attacks on encryption keys. In: USENIX SEC (2008)
17. Harrison, K., Xu, S.: Protecting cryptographic keys from memory disclosure attacks. In: IEEE/IFIP DSN (2007)
18. Henson, M., Taylor, S.: Beyond full disk encryption: protection on security-enhanced commodity processors. In: Jacobson, M., Locasto, M., Mohassel, P., Safavi-Naini, R. (eds.) ACNS 2013. LNCS, vol. 7954, pp. 307–321. Springer, Heidelberg (2013). https://doi.org/10.1007/978-3-642-38980-1_19
19. Henson, M., Taylor, S.: Memory encryption: a survey of existing techniques. ACM CSUR (2014)
20. Jang, J., Kong, S., Kim, M., Kim, D., Kang, B.B.: Secret: secure channel between rich execution environment and trusted execution environment. In: NDSS 2015 (2015)
21. Kleissner, P.: Hibernation file attack (2010)
22. Kolontsov, V.: Solaris (and others) ftpd core dump bug (1996). http://insecure.org/sploits/ftpd.pasv.html
23. Li, W., Li, H., Chen, H., Xia, Y.: Adattester: secure online mobile advertisement attestation using trustzone. In: ACM MobiSys (2015)

24. Lie, D.: Architectural support for copy and tamper resistant software. ACM SIG-PLAN Not. **35**, 168–177 (2000)
25. McVoy, L., Staelin, C.: Lmbench: portable tools for performance analysis. In: USENIX ATC (1996)
26. Müller, T., Spreitzenbarth, M., Freiling, F.: FROST: forensic recovery of scrambled telephones. In: 11th ACNS (2013)
27. National Vulnerability Database: CVE-2011-2707 (2011). http://www.cve.mitre.org/cgi-bin/cvename.cgi?name=2011-2707
28. National Vulnerability Database: CVE-2005-1264 (2015). https://cve.mitre.org/cgi-bin/cvename.cgi?name=CVE-2005-1264
29. Peterson, P.A.: Cryptkeeper: improving security with encrypted RAM. In: IEEE HST (2010)
30. Provos, N.: Encrypting virtual memory. In: USENIX SEC (2000)
31. Reese, W.: Nginx: the high-performance web server and reverse proxy (2008). https://nginx.org/
32. Santos, N., Raj, H., Saroiu, S., Wolman, A.: Using ARM trustzone to build a trusted language runtime for mobile applications. In: ASPLOS 2014. ACM (2014)
33. Stewin, P., Bystrov, I.: Understanding DMA malware. In: Flegel, U., Markatos, E., Robertson, W. (eds.) DIMVA 2012. LNCS, vol. 7591, pp. 21–41. Springer, Heidelberg (2013). https://doi.org/10.1007/978-3-642-37300-8_2
34. Suiche, M.: Windows hibernation file for fun 'n' profit. Black-Hat (2008)
35. Wilson, P., et al.: Implementing embedded security on dual-virtual-CPU systems. IEEE Des. Test Comput. (2007)
36. Zhang, N., Sun, K., Lou, W., Hou, Y.T.: Case: cache-assisted secure execution on arm processors. In: IEEE S&P (2016)

Software Security

PartiSan: Fast and Flexible Sanitization via Run-Time Partitioning

Julian Lettner[(✉)] [iD], Dokyung Song, Taemin Park, Per Larsen, Stijn Volckaert, and Michael Franz

University of California, Irvine, USA
{jlettner,dokyungs,tmpark,perl,stijnv,franz}@uci.edu

Abstract. Sanitizers can detect security vulnerabilities in C/C++ code that elude static analysis. Current practice is to continuously fuzz and sanitize internal pre-release builds. Sanitization-enabled builds are rarely released publicly. This is in large part due to the high memory and processing requirements of sanitizers.

We present PartiSan, a run-time partitioning technique that speeds up sanitizers and allows them to be used in a more flexible manner. Our core idea is to partition the execution into sanitized slices that incur a run-time overhead, and "unsanitized" slices running at full speed. With PartiSan, sanitization is no longer an all-or-nothing proposition. A single build can be distributed to every user regardless of their willingness to enable sanitization and the capabilities of their host system. PartiSan enables application developers to define their own sanitization policies. Such policies can automatically adjust the amount of sanitization to fit within a performance budget or disable sanitization if the host lacks sufficient resources. The flexibility afforded by run-time partitioning also means that we can alternate between different types of sanitizers dynamically; today, developers have to pick a single type of sanitizer ahead of time. Finally, we show that run-time partitioning can speed up fuzzing by running the sanitized partition only when the fuzzer discovers an input that causes a crash or uncovers new execution paths.

Keywords: Security · Privacy · Software security
Application security

1 Introduction

Although modern, safe languages could gradually replace C/C++, the sheer amount of legacy systems code forces security researchers to search for and fix memory corruption vulnerabilities in existing code in the near term. While some bugs can be found through static program analysis, many cannot. Sanitizers are dynamic analysis tools that can detect memory corruption and many other problems as well as pinpoint their occurrence during program execution [13,16, 19]. To increase coverage, sanitizer runs can be driven by a fuzzer. A fuzzer simply

© Springer Nature Switzerland AG 2018
M. Bailey et al. (Eds.): RAID 2018, LNCS 11050, pp. 403–422, 2018.
https://doi.org/10.1007/978-3-030-00470-5_19

feeds the program random inputs and records inputs that generate crashes or cause previously unexecuted code to run.

Sanitizers instrument programs—usually during compilation—to detect issues such as memory corruption and undefined behavior. This instrumentation incurs significant overheads, so sanitizers are turned off in release builds and traditionally only enabled on internal quality assurance builds that run on high-end hardware. This is less than ideal as the number of paths executed by test suites and fuzzers is outnumbered by the number of paths executed by end users.

In a recent experiment, the Tor Project released sanitizer-enabled (labeled "hardened") builds directly to its users [8]. The hardened build series was discontinued in part due to the high performance overhead and in part due to confusion among end users over which version to download. With access to PartiSan, the Tor Project developers could have released builds that automatically adapt the level of sanitization to the capabilities of the host system. Overhead can be limited by using a conservatively low, adaptive threshold by default (and possibly disabling sanitization completely on underpowered systems) while simultaneously allowing expert users to modify the default settings (thereby also eliminating the need for multiple build versions).

PartiSan clones frequently executed functions at compile time and efficiently switches among them at run time. Each function variant can be optimized and sanitized independently, and thus has different security and performance properties. In the simplest case, one variant is instrumented to sanitize memory accesses while the other one is not. PartiSan supports configurable run-time partitioning policies that determine which variant is invoked when a function is called. For example, PartiSan can execute slow variants (e.g., variants with expensive checks) with low probability on frequently executed code paths, and with high probability on rarely executed paths. This policy helps us keep the sanitization overhead below a given threshold.

This is superficially similar to the ASAP framework by Wagner et al. [22] insofar that both approaches explore the idea of reducing the amount of sanitization on the hot path. However, ASAP *statically* partitions the code into parts with or without sanitization based on previous profiling runs at compile time. PartiSan prepares programs for partitioning at compile time but does the partitioning *dynamically* at run time. This allows us to produce a single binary that adapts to each individual host system, sanitizing as many paths as possible under a given performance budget. Moreover, we can create N different function variants to support $N - 1$ types of sanitization in a single binary. Table 1 contrasts PartiSan and ASAP. Both our work and ASAP build on the assumption that security vulnerabilities in frequently executed code get discovered and patched relatively quickly, whereas vulnerabilities in rarely executed code might go unpatched for a long time.

Table 1. Conceptual comparison of ASAP and PartiSan

Statement	ASAP	PartiSan
Goal ...	Deploy sanitizers as mitigations	Find bugs efficiently
Partitioning is ...	Static (compile time)	Dynamic (run time)
Overhead reduction ...	Removal of expensive checks	Probabilistic checking
Code is ...	Deleted	Cloned
Assertions are ...	Removed	Retained
Detect bugs in cold code ...	Always	Always
Detect bugs in hot code ...	Never	Probabilistically

This paper makes the following contributions:

- We describe PartiSan[1], a framework to partition program execution into sanitized/unsanitized fragments at run time. Unlike previous approaches, the partitioning is not static but happens dynamically according to a policy-driven, run-time partitioning mechanism which selects the function variant to execute with low overhead. This lets developers release sanitizer-enabled builds to end users and thereby cover more execution paths.
- We present a fully-fledged prototype implementation of our ideas and explore three concrete run-time partitioning policies. We combined PartiSan with two sanitizers and measured the performance overhead on the SPEC CPU 2006 benchmark suite with our expected-cost partitioning policy.
- We present a thorough evaluation showing that our approach still detects the majority of vulnerabilities at greatly reduced performance overheads. For the popular ASan and UBSan sanitizers, PartiSan reduces overheads by 68% and 76% respectively.
- We demonstrate an important use case of PartiSan: improving fuzzing efficiency. We combined PartiSan with a popular fuzzer and measured consistently increased fuzzing throughput.

2   Background

LLVM [10], the premier open-source compiler, includes five different sanitizers. We demonstrate PartiSan by applying two of these sanitizers to a variety of programs. ASan, short for AddressSanitizer [16], instruments memory accesses and allocation operations to detect a range of memory errors, including spatial memory errors such as out-of-bounds accesses and temporal violations such as use-after-free bugs. UBSan, short for UndefinedBehaviorSanitizer [13], currently detects 22 types of operations whose semantics are undefined [12] by the C

---

[1] PartiSan is available upon request. Please contact the authors for a copy of the research artifacts.

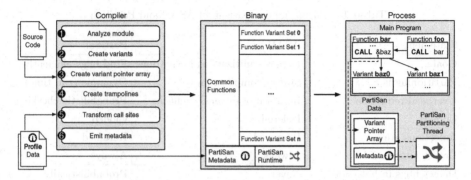

Fig. 1. System overview. The compiler (left) creates PartiSan-enabled applications (center) that have multiple variants of each function. A run-time indirection through the variant pointer array (right) ensures that the control flow calls the currently active variant. PartiSan's runtime periodically activates function variants according to the configured partitioning policy.

standard [6]. UBSan includes checks for integer overflows, uses of uninitialized or unaligned pointers, and undefined integer shifts.

We used these sanitizers with PartiSan for two reasons. First, the combination of ASan and UBSan detects many of the vulnerabilities that are security critical. Second, both sanitizers can be applied selectively.[2] Removing any of the sanitization checks from a program does not affect the correct functioning of the remaining checks. This makes these sanitizers a good fit for our framework, in which we selectively skip sanitization through run-time partitioning.

3   Design

Our goal is to reduce the run-time overhead of the sanitizers. We do this by creating multiple variants of each function, applying sanitizers to some variants, and embedding a runtime component that partitions the execution of the program into sanitized/unsanitized slices based on a policy.

Figure 1 shows an overview of the PartiSan system. To apply PartiSan to an application, the developer must compile the source code of the program with our modified compiler (left side of Fig. 1). Some partitioning policies require that the developer supply profile data.

The compiler generates an application with multiple variants for each function. To simplify the following discussion, we will focus on use cases where we generate two variants. One of the variants, which we refer to as the *unsanitized variant*, does not include any sanitizer checks. The other variant, which we call the *sanitized variant*, incorporates all sanitizer instrumentation.

---

[2] Note that ASan requires metadata to execute checks. The maintenance of this metadata constitutes residual overhead which cannot be removed.

The compiler modifies the program's control flow as follows. Rather than calling functions directly, the functions call each other through an additional level of indirection. Specifically, the compiler embeds a "variant pointer array" containing one slot for each function in the program source code. At run time, each slot holds the pointer to the currently active variant of the corresponding function. The PartiSan runtime, which is linked into the application by our compiler, selects and activates one variant of each function according to the configured partitioning policy.

The runtime currently supports three partitioning policies: random partitioning, profile-guided partitioning, and expected-cost partitioning. With the random partitioning policy, the runtime randomly selects the active variants, whereas the profile-guided and expected-cost partitioning policies select active variants with a probability that depends on the execution frequency ("hotness") and/or expected sanitization cost of that function. These policies can help us limit the cost of sanitization.

3.1   Creating Function Variants

PartiSan's compiler pass runs after the source code is parsed and converted into intermediate representation (IR) code. As its first step (Step ① in Fig. 1), our compiler pass analyzes the IR code and determines which functions to create variants for. We do not necessarily create multiple variants for each function. If the developer selects the profile-guided or expected-cost partitioning policy, and if the profile data indicates that a function is infrequently executed, then we create only the sanitized variant for that function. This design choice prevents PartiSan from unnecessarily inflating the code size of the program and is justified because checks in infrequently executed code have little impact on the program's overall performance.

Then, PartiSan creates the function variants (②). First, we clone functions that should have two variants and give them new, unique names. Then, we apply the requested instrumentations to the variants.

3.2   Creating the Indirection Layer

Once the function variants are created, our compiler pass creates the indirection layer, through which we route all of the program's function calls. This ensures that the program can only call the active variant of each function. Our indirection layer consists of three components: the variant pointer array (right side of Fig. 1), trampolines, and control-flow instructions that read their target from the pointer array.

Our compiler starts by embedding the variant pointer array into the application (③). The pointer array contains one slot for each function that has multiple variants. Each slot contains a pointer to the entry point of the currently active variant of that function.

Then, we create trampolines for externally reachable and address-taken functions (④). A trampoline jumps to the currently active variant of its associated function. We assign the original name of the associated function to the trampoline. This way, we ensure that any call that targets the original function now calls the trampoline, and consequently, the currently active variant of the original function instead.

Finally, we transform all direct call instructions that target functions with multiple variants into indirect control-flow instructions that read the pointer to the active variant of the target function from the pointer array (⑤). This optimization eliminates the need to route direct calls within the program through the function trampolines. However, the trampolines may still be called through indirect call instructions, or by external code.

3.3   Embedding Metadata

Our compiler embeds read-only metadata describing each function and its variants into the application (⑥). The metadata can consist of the function execution frequencies read from the profile data, the estimated execution costs for all function variants, and information connecting each slot in the variant pointer array to the variant entry points associated with that slot. Our partitioning mechanism bases run-time decisions on the metadata.

3.4   The PartiSan Runtime

Our runtime implements the selected partitioning policy by activating and deactivating variants. While a specific variant is active, none of the other variants of that same function can be called. To activate a variant, our runtime writes a pointer to that variant's entry point into the appropriate slot in the pointer array. PartiSan periodically activates variants on a background thread. This allows us to implement a variety of partitioning policies that do not slow down the application thread(s). Operating on a background thread also allows our runtime to run frequently, and thus make fine-grained partitioning decisions.

Random Partitioning. With this policy, our runtime component activates a randomly selected variant of each function whenever our thread wakes up. Since we only generate two variants of each function, this policy divides the execution time evenly among the sanitized/unsanitized function variants.

Profile-Guided Partitioning. With this policy, our runtime component collects the list of functions with multiple variants in the program and orders this list based on the functions' execution counts recorded during profiling. Our runtime activates the sanitized variant of a function with a probability that is inversely proportional to its order in the execution count list. The sanitized variant of the most frequently executed function is activated with 1% probability, and that of the least frequently executed function with a 100% probability. Note that this partitioning policy does not estimate the overhead impact of executing a sanitized variant instead of an unsanitized variant. It also does not consider the absolute execution count of a function. For example, the second least executed function in a program with 100 functions is sanitized 99% of the time, even if its execution count is 1000 times higher than that of the least executed function.

Expected-Cost Partitioning. This policy improves upon the profile-guided partitioning policy by calculating sanitization probabilities based on function execution counts (read from the profile data) and estimated sanitization cost. We estimate the cost of sanitization for each function by calculating the costs of all function variants using LLVM's Cost Model Analysis. We then calculate the probability of activating the sanitized variant for a function using formula:

$$P_{sanitization}(f) = \frac{sanitization\ budget(f)}{cost_{sanitization}(f) * execution\ count(f)}$$

The sanitization overhead budget is chosen by the developer and is evenly distributed among the functions in the program.

4   Implementation

Our prototype implementation of PartiSan supports applications compiled with clang/LLVM 5.0 [10] on the x86-64 architecture. Our design, however, is fully generalizable to other compilers and architectures.

4.1   Profiling

Two of our run-time partitioning policies rely on profile data to calculate the sanitization probabilities. We use LLVM's built-in profiling functionality to generate binaries that collect profile data.

4.2   Compiler Pass

Our pass instruments the program code at the LLVM IR level processing one translation unit at a time. PartiSan is fully compatible with standard build systems and program loaders. We scheduled our pass to run right before the LLVM sanitizer passes, which run late in the compiler pipeline. This allows us to define (mostly declaratively) which variants get instrumented without interfering with LLVM's earlier optimization stages.

Creating Function Variants. Of the sanitizers bundled with LLVM, our pass currently supports ASan and UBSan. We did not modify any sanitizer code and most of PartiSan's code is tool-agnostic. To create the function variants, we begin by passing the necessary `-fsanitize` command line options to the compiler. ASan's front-end pass prepares the program by marking all functions that require sanitization with a function-level attribute. With just one line of ASan-specific code, PartiSan removes this function attribute for the unsanitized variants. UBSan's front-end pass embeds many of its checks before the program is translated into IR. PartiSan contains 56 lines of code to remove these checks from the unsanitized variants.

```
foo:                      foo_0:                     bar:
  ...                       ...                        # Preserve arguments
  # Prepare arguments       # Prepare arguments        jmpq *.Lptr_array+16(%rip)
  callq bar                 callq *.Lptr_array+16(%rip)
  ...                       ...
```

(a) Original call site   (b) Transformed call site   (c) Control-flow trampoline

Fig. 2. Generated x86-64 assembly

Creating the Indirection Layer. We create the indirection layer as follows. We begin by collecting the set of functions that have multiple variants. Then, we add the variant pointer array as a global variable with internal linkage. We choose the size of the array such that it has one slot for every function in the set. Next, we create trampolines for all functions in the set. The trampoline, which takes over the name of the function it corresponds to, forwards control to the currently active variant of that function. By taking over the name of the original function, the trampoline ensures that any calls to that function will be routed to the currently active variant.

Next, we replace all call instructions that target functions in the set with indirect call instructions that read their call target from the variant pointer array. Functions outside the compilation unit will not be in the set, but might still have multiple variants. While we do not replace calls to such instructions, the call will still (correctly) invoke the currently active variant of the target function because it will be routed through that function's trampoline.

Note that the compiled program will only contain the trampolines that may actually be used at run time. If a trampoline's corresponding function is not externally visible (and thus cannot be called by external code) and it does not have its address taken (and thus cannot be called indirectly), then the trampoline will be deleted by LLVM's dead code elimination pass.

Figure 2 shows the assembly code that is generated for the trampolines and transformed call sites.

Embedding Metadata. Our runtime component needs to know which function variants are associated with each slot of the variant pointer array. Depending on the partitioning policy, it may also require function execution frequencies and estimated execution costs for all function variants. We add this information (encoded in an array of function descriptors) as read-only data to each compilation unit.

4.3   The PartiSan Runtime

The PartiSan runtime implements the three partitioning policies described in Sect. 3.4. The runtime exposes a single externally visible function used to register modules: `cf_register(const func_t* start, const func_t* end)`. Every module registers its function variants with the runtime by invoking this function from a constructor. After all modules have registered, the runtime initializes.

The runtime's initialization proceeds in four steps. First, the runtime computes the activation probabilities for each function variant, according to the configured policy. Then, we seed a secure number generator. Next, we initialize all variant pointer arrays. This is necessary because the program might call some of the variant functions before our runtime's background thread performs its first round of run-time partitioning. Finally, we spawn the background thread that is responsible for the continuous run-time partitioning.

Run-Time Partitioning. Our background thread runs an infinite loop, which invokes the partitioning procedure whenever it wakes up. This procedure iterates through the function descriptors for every registered module. For every function, we generate a random integer number X between 0 and 100, and use this to select one of the variants. If the activation probabilities for the sanitized and unsanitized variants of a function are 0.01 and 0.99, respectively, then we will activate the sanitized variant if X is less than 2, and we will activate the unsanitized variant for values greater than 1. We write the pointer to the activated variant in the variant pointer array.

We attempt to reduce cache contention by performing the write only if necessary (i.e., only if the old and new value differ). This adds a read dependency on the old pointer value which may slow down the background thread. However, the execution of the background thread is not performance critical since it runs fully asynchronously with respect to the application threads.

5   Effectiveness

We evaluate the effectiveness of PartiSan with an empirical investigation of five CVEs [15], including the infamous Heartbleed bug. Table 2 shows the CVEs we tested. Each of them was found in a popular real-world program and the types of vulnerabilities include stack-based overflows and information leaks on the heap. We used PartiSan to compile two versions of each program, applying ASan to the sanitized variants in one version and UBSan in the other version, and we configured our runtime to enforce its expected-cost partitioning policy. We detected four out of five vulnerabilities in the ASan version, and three out of five in the UBSan version. We then compiled a third version of the program with the same partitioning policy and applied both sanitizers to the sanitized variants. This third version reliably detects three out of five CVEs. The remaining two CVEs are detected in 72% and 6% of our test runs.

For each of the selected CVEs we perform the following steps:

1. Verify vulnerability exposure
2. Verify vulnerability detection
3. Collect profile data
4. Evaluate vulnerability detection with PartiSan

Each of the above steps requires a program version with different instrumentation. In step 1, we compile the vulnerable program without any instrumentation

Table 2. Evaluated CVEs

CVE #	Program (Submodule)	Vulnerability	Sanitizer	Detection
2016-6297	Php 7.0.3 (Zip extension)	Integer ovf. → Stack ovf.	UBSan, ASan	71.8%
2016-6289	Php 7.0.3 (Core engine)	Integer ovf. → Stack ovf.	UBSan, ASan	Always
2016-3191	Php 7.0.3 (Pcre extension)	Stack overflow	ASan	6.2%
2014-0160	OpenSSL 1.0.1f (Heartbeat ext.)	Heap over-read	ASan	Always
2014-7185	Python 2.7.7 (Core library)	Integer ovf. → Heap over-read	UBSan	Always

and verify that the vulnerability can be triggered. To do this, we use the proof-of-concept scripts referenced in the CVE details.

In step 2, we compile the program with ASan or UBSan enabled, but without PartiSan. We run our test script from step 1 to verify that the vulnerability is detected by the sanitizer.

Our expected-cost partitioning policy greatly benefits from profile data, so in step 3, we use LLVM's built-in profiling facilities to create an instrumented version of the program for collecting profile data. We use the tests that come with the program as the profiling workload. For vulnerabilities in submodules/extensions, we only run the tests of the submodule to increase the chance of the vulnerable code being classified as hot (since vulnerabilities in cold code are guaranteed to be detected). The test suite of the vulnerable OpenSSL version does not cover the Heartbeat extension. Therefore, if we run the test suite as-is, the function that contains the Heartbleed vulnerability is never executed. PartiSan would therefore classify this function as cold and always sanitize it, which guarantees detection. To be more conservative, we executed the vulnerable function 300 times with benign input alongside the official test suite.

Next, in step 4, we compile the program with the sanitizer enabled under PartiSan. We use PartiSan's default configuration to compile each of the programs. This means that the program contains two variants of all functions, except those that are cold and those without memory accesses. We only created sanitized variants for cold functions, and unsanitized variants for functions without memory accesses. Finally, we execute our test script from step 1 a thousand times to measure the detection rate.

Out of the five vulnerabilities, ASan and UBSan detect four and three respectively. The three vulnerabilities detected by UBSan all involve an integer overflow. The overflown value usually represents the length of some buffer, which results in out-of-bounds buffer accesses. The other two vulnerabilities are caused by a lack of bounds checking. Note that although the last CVE is classified as a heap over-read, ASan does not detect it. The reason is that the Python interpreter uses a custom memory allocator. It requests large chunks of memory from the operating system and maintains its own free lists to serve individual requests. Unfortunately, ASan treats each chunk as a single allocation and therefore is unable to detect overflows within a chunk. This shows that there is value in using multiple sanitizers that can detect different causes of vulnerabilities.

Lastly, we want to note that three out of five vulnerabilities are in code that PartiSan classifies as cold. For those cases, we manually verified that PartiSan only created the sanitized variant for the vulnerable functions. Hence, those vulnerabilities are always reported. This result supports PartiSan's underlying assumption that most bugs hide in infrequently executed code. In summary, our results show that we always detect bugs in cold code while bugs in hot code are detected probabilistically. We argue that this is a valuable property in our envisioned usage scenario: finding bugs in beta software during real usage with an acceptable performance overhead. Note that probabilistic detection is a property afforded by dynamic, but not by static partitioning.

6   Efficiency

We evaluated the performance of PartiSan-enabled programs using the SPEC CPU 2006 integer benchmark suite [20]. Since PartiSan clones code we also measured the size of the resulting binaries. Memory overheads—a small constant amount for the background thread and a few bytes of metadata for every function—are negligible (less than 1%) for all SPEC programs, so we do not report them.

We conducted all experiments on a host with an Intel Xeon E5-2660 CPU and 64 GB of RAM running 64-bit Ubuntu 14.04. We applied ASan and UBSan to all of the benchmark programs. We configure UBSan to disable error recovery, which always aborts the program instead of printing a warning message and attempting to recover for a subset of failed checks. For configurations including UBSan we also configure PartiSan to create variants of all functions, even those that do not access memory. We use the expected-cost partitioning policy with a sanitization budget of 1%, which our runtime evenly divides across all functions.

To collect profile data we use LLVM's built-in profiling facilities on the *training* workload of SPEC. Since our chosen partitioning policy greatly benefits from profile data, we make the same data available to the baseline configuration to make the comparison fair. We compile all configurations, including the baseline, with profile-guided optimization enabled, supplying the same profile data for all configurations. When measuring the runtime, we use the *reference* workload, run each benchmark three times, and report the median.

6.1   Performance

Figures 3 and 4 show the run-time overheads for ASan and UBSan with respect to the baseline for all SPEC integer benchmarks. The last column depicts the geometric mean over all benchmarks, which is additionally stated in percent by Table 3 for easier reference.

PartiSan's partitioning without any sanitization (with two identical variants) incurs a 2% overhead on average, with a maximum of 9% for `gobmk`.

For the fully-sanitized versions of ASan and UBSan (absent PartiSan) we measured an average overhead of 103% and 59% respectively. Note that the overhead introduced by ASan can be as much as 289% for `perlbench`.

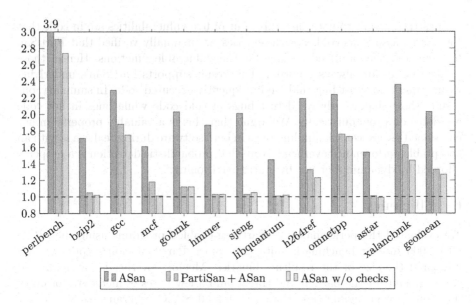

Fig. 3. SPEC run-time overheads for ASan

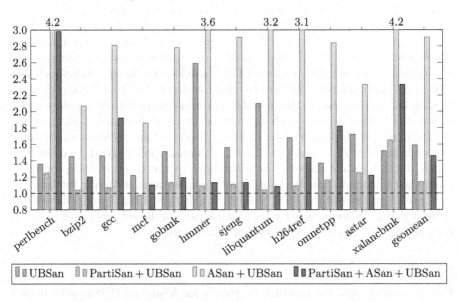

Fig. 4. SPEC run-time overheads for UBSan and ASan+ UBSan

We also created a modified version of ASan that does not execute any checks. The remaining overhead can be attributed to the maintenance of metadata and other bookkeeping tasks. This configuration represents a lower bound on the run time achievable by PartiSan since bookkeeping needs to be done in all variants. PartiSan stays close to this lower bound for many benchmarks even when using

Table 3. SPEC run-time overheads

Configuration	Overhead
PartiSan	2%
ASan	103%
ASan w/o checks	27%
PartiSan + ASan	33%
UBSan	59%
PartiSan + UBSan	14%
ASan + UBSan	191%
PartiSan + ASan + UBSan	46%

the expected-cost policy in its default configuration. For the PartiSan-enabled versions of ASan and UBSan we measured an average overhead of 33% and 14% respectively. This corresponds to a reduction of overhead levels by more than two thirds (68% and 76%) with respect to the fully-sanitized versions. We also include a configuration that enables both ASan and UBSan in Fig. 4 to show that PartiSan can handle multiple sanitizers as long as they are compatible with each other.

6.2 Binary Size

Table 4 gives an overview of the impact that PartiSan has on binary size for real-world programs. We state binary sizes of the programs used in our effectiveness evaluation for ASan and UBSan with and without PartiSan and the size increase in percent. We can navigate the size versus performance trade-off by adjusting our threshold for hot code and argue that (using our policy) the maximum size increase is limited by a factor of two (i.e., when all code is classified as hot).

Table 4. PartiSan program sizes (in kilobytes)

Program	ASan	UBSan
Php 7.0.3	20,483/21,983 (7%)	8,658/12,536 (45%)
OpenSSL 1.0.1f	19,128/25,579 (34%)	12,153/14,243 (17%)
Python 2.7.7	41,715/54,717 (31%)	22,033/28,641 (30%)

The statically-linked PartiSan runtime adds a constant overhead of 6 KB to each binary. Internally, our runtime depends on the pthread library to spawn the background partitioning thread. Usually, this does not increase program size as libpthread is a shared library.

We also measured the size of the SPEC benchmark binaries used in our performance evaluation. Since the benchmarks are small programs, the increase in relative code size is dominated by the inclusion of the ASan/UBSan runtimes. Therefore the larger programs in the suite exhibit the highest increase (9% for gcc/ASan, and 16% for xalancbmk/UBSan). The increase in binary size over all benchmarks (geometric mean) for ASan and UBSan are 2% and 5% respectively.

7   Use Case: Fuzzing

Fuzzing is an important use case for sanitization. A fuzzer repeatedly executes a program with random inputs in order to find bugs. Inputs that exercise new code paths are stored in a corpus (coverage-guided), which is used to derive further inputs (evolutionary). To aid bug detection, the program is usually compiled with sanitization. The vast majority of individual fuzzing runs do not detect bugs or increase coverage, so fuzzers rely on executing lots of runs (i.e., throughput is important). We applied PartiSan to LLVM's libFuzzer [14], an in-process, coverage-guided, evolutionary fuzzing engine, with the goal of improving fuzzing efficiency.

When we first applied PartiSan to fuzzing we noticed that it represents a specific use case that benefits from a custom partitioning policy. Specifically, the fuzzer requires the program to be executed with coverage instrumentation. The gathered coverage data is similiar (but not equivalent) to the profile data used for our partitioning policy. We adapted PartiSan to use online coverage data instead of profile data, which has two advantages. First, it simplifies the developer workflow since there is no need to collect profile data a priori. Second, it allows us to continuously refine our partitioning decisions. We integrated PartiSan with libFuzzer with minimal changes to the latter. Additionally, the main fuzzing loop provides a natural place to make partitioning decisions. We added a call into our runtime from the fuzzing loop, forgoing the background thread in favor of synchronous partitioning.

7.1   Partitioning Policy

Our policy for fuzzing is simple. For most functions we generate three variants: variant ① with coverage instrumentation, sanitized variant ②, and fast variant ③ without any instrumentation. At startup we activate variant ① for the whole program. Whenever the fuzzer discovers an input that exercises new code, we temporarily activate variant ② for all functions and re-execute the input. Finally, if a function becomes fully-explored (i.e., all its basic blocks have been executed), we activate its variant ③.

Our policy allows us to increase coverage efficiently compared to the original program whose functions contain both coverage and sanitization instrumentation. As coverage increases, functions transition from variant ① to ③, speeding up execution of the well-explored parts of the program. The downside of this approach is that it potentially reduces the chance of bug detection as well as coverage feedback to the fuzzer. Consider an input that exposes a non-crashing bug without increasing coverage. Under our policy, such inputs execute without

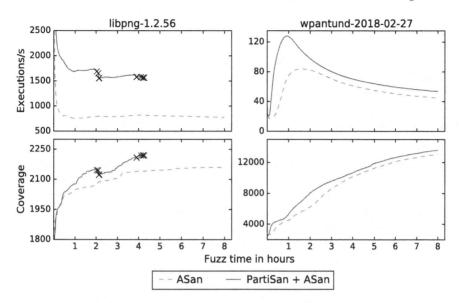

Fig. 5. Fuzzing throughput and coverage for `libpng` and `wpantund`

sanitization. Additionally, a function that we deem "fully-explored" might still provide useful coverage feedback to the fuzzer. The reason is that libFuzzer's coverage model is fine-grained (e.g., it includes execution counts) while our notion of fully-explored is binary.

7.2 Evaluation

We evaluated the PartiSan-enabled libFuzzer on a popular benchmark suite for fuzzers [4] derived from widely-used libraries. We ran all 23 included benchmarks with ASan enabled. Out of these 23 benchmarks 11 complete (find a bug) within a few minutes. For the remaining 12 benchmarks we measured fuzzing throughput and coverage and ran them for eight hours or until completion. Figure 5 shows the results for two benchmarks (geometric mean of 10 runs). The markers indicate the completion of a run (i.e., after the first marker the line represents the remaining 9 runs).

As expected, PartiSan is able to increase fuzzing throughput (executions per second) for the sanitized libraries. For 9 (of 12) benchmarks this translates to improved coverage, and 3 benchmarks complete significantly faster. For example, for the `libpng` benchmark (left side of Fig. 5) PartiSan lets us find the bug within our time budget, whereas previously we could not. However, the impact of PartiSan is not always that pronounced. For the `wpantund` benchmark (right side of Fig. 5), coverage only improves slightly. Note that fuzzing throughput generally decreases over time as the fuzzer explores longer and longer code paths.

8   Discussion

Custom Partitioning Policies. We implemented three run-time partitioning policies in PartiSan. The flexibility of our design and implementation additionally allows developers to define their own policies. To implement a custom partitioning policy, the developer can provide her own `load_policy` and `activate_variant` function when linking the final binary. Our policy for the fuzzing use case is built atop this mechanism.

Asynchronous Partitioning. We opted to offload our run-time partitioning procedure onto a background thread. The advantage of this approach is that, since partitioning happens asynchronously relative to the rest of the application, our runtime component has little impact on the application's performance. The disadvantage is that we cannot partition on a per-function call basis or depending on the calling context. That said, in the fuzzing use case we partition synchronously as part of the main fuzzing loop.

Partitioning Granularity. PartiSan partitions the program run time at function-level granularity. In particular, PartiSan might execute the sanitized variant of a hot function containing a long-running loop. Executing this sanitized variant can induce a noticeable slowdown as PartiSan does not support control-flow transfers between variants within the same function. Our design can be refined with finer-grained partitioning, though a significant engineering effort would be required to implement it. Our fundamental conclusions would not change with an improved partitioning scheme.

Selective Sanitization. Like ASAP, PartiSan does not support sanitizers that do not function correctly if they are applied selectively. Consider, for example, a multithreaded program compiled with ThreadSanitizer [17]. If two functions in the program concurrently write to the same memory location without acquiring a lock, then ThreadSanitizer will detect a data race. This would not be true in a PartiSan-enabled version of the program if we executed the sanitized variant of one function and the unsanitized variant of the other. In this case, the data race would not be detected, thus rendering ThreadSanitizer ineffective.

9   Related Work

9.1   Run-Time Partitioning

Kurmus and Zippel proposed to create a split kernel with a protected partition containing a hardened variant of each kernel function, and an unprotected partition containing non-hardened variants [9]. Whenever the kernel services a system call or an interrupt request, it transfers control flow to one of the two partitions. The protected (unprotected) partition is used to service requests from untrusted (trusted) processes and devices. Unlike PartiSan, however, it does not permit control flow transfers between the two partitions. A service request is handled in its entirety by one of the two partitions.

The ASAP framework, presented by Wagner et al., reduces sanitizer overhead by removing sanitizer checks and programmer asserts from frequently executed code, while leaving the infrequently executed code unaffected [22]. This is also a form of partitioning, as ASAP creates a sanitized and an unsanitized partition within the program. As with PartiSan, transfers between sanitized and unsanitized code are frequent with ASAP. However, contrary to PartiSan and the aforementioned work, ASAP never creates multiple variants of a function. ASAP should therefore be considered a static form of partitioning. Note that static partitioning mechanisms can neither support adaptive overhead thresholds, nor probabilistic bug detection, nor our presented fuzzing policy.

Bunshin reduces sanitizer and exploit mitigation overhead by distributing security checks over multiple program variants and running them in parallel in an N-Variant execution system [24]. The key idea is to generate program variants in such a way that any specific sanitizer check appears in only one of the variants. This distribution principle makes each variant faster than the original program and also enables the simultaneous use of incompatible tools. Bunshin achieves full sanitizer coverage by running all variants in parallel, i.e., for any given sanitizer check there will be a variant that executes it. This approach improves program latency at the cost of increased resource consumption which limits Bunshin's applicability. In a fuzzing scenario, for example, available cores can be more efficiently leveraged by running additional fuzzer instances.

9.2   Sanitizers

We applied PartiSan to two of the sanitizers that are part of the LLVM compiler framework, AddressSanitizer and UndefinedBehaviorSanitizer [13,16]. Many other sanitizers exist. MemorySanitizer detects reads of uninitialized values and, although we did not include it in our evaluation, it is fully compatible with PartiSan [21]. Sanitizers that detect bad casting [5,7,11] and variadic function misuses [1] could also benefit from PartiSan by applying checks selectively.

ThreadSanitizer instruments memory accesses and atomic operations to detect data races, deadlocks, and misuses of thread synchronization primitives (e.g., pthread mutexes) in multithreaded programs [17]. Unfortunately, it is not a good fit for PartiSan because selective sanitization renders the sanitizer ineffective (cf. Sect. 8).

FUSS, another work by Wagner, uses a separate optimization stage to increase fuzzing throughput [23, Sect. 4.3]. After a warm-up phase, FUSS collects profile data from the running fuzzer. It then re-compiles the program under test using the collected profile data to omit the most costly instrumentation code, and restarts the fuzzer with the new binary. We argue that this one-time optimization through re-compilation constitutes static partitioning (albeit integrated over time), while PartiSan optimizes dynamically and continuously.

9.3 Control-Flow Diversity

PartiSan partitions the run time of the protected program using control-flow diversity. Prior work has explored the use of control-flow diversity for security purposes. One such work, Isomeron [3], is a defensive technique that defeats just-in-time return-oriented-programming (JIT-ROP) attacks [18]. Isomeron creates diversified clones of the program's functions and switches randomly between functions on every function call and return statement. Even with precise knowledge of the gadget locations, an attacker cannot mount a reliable JIT-ROP attack, as Isomeron might transfer control flow to a non-intended location after every execution of a gadget.

Crane et al. describe how they used control-flow diversity to mitigate cache-based side-channel attacks [2]. Crane et al. create multiple variants of program functions and applies different diversifying transformations to each variant. The transformations are designed to preserve the semantics of the code, but obscure the code's memory access patterns (i.e., data access locations and execution trace). Essentially, the technique adds noise to the observable leakage in the shared cache, which raises the difficulty for the adversary.

10 Conclusion

We present PartiSan, a run-time partitioning technique that increases the performance and flexibility of sanitized programs. PartiSan allows developers to ship a single sanitizer-enabled binary *without* having to commit to either the fraction of time spent sanitizing on a given target, nor the type of sanitization employed. Specifically, PartiSan uses run-time partitioning controlled by tunable policies. We have explored three simple policies and expect future developers to define additional, application and domain-specific ones. Our experiments show that, using our expected-cost policy, PartiSan reduces performance overheads of the two popular sanitizers, ASan and UBSan, by 68% and 76% respectively. We also demonstrate how PartiSan can improve fuzzing efficiency. When integrated with libFuzzer, PartiSan consistently increases fuzzing throughput which leads to improved coverage and more bugs found.

PartiSan's dynamic partitioning mechanism enables adaptive overhead thresholds and probabilistic bug detection; neither of which are supported by static partitioning mechanisms presented in previous work. Hence, PartiSan is able to extend the usage scenarios of sanitizers to a much wider group of testers and their respective program inputs, leading to the exploration of a greater number of program paths. This will enable developers to catch more errors early, reducing the number of vulnerabilities in released software.

Acknowledgement. We would like to thank Jonas Wagner for his advice and pointing out useful previous work. We also would like to thank the anonymous reviewers for their valuable feedback.

This material is based upon work partially supported by the Defense Advanced Research Projects Agency (DARPA) under contracts FA8750-15-C-0124 and FA8750-15-C-0085, by the United States Office of Naval Research (ONR) under contract

N00014-17-1-2782, and by the National Science Foundation under awards CNS-1619211 and CNS-1513837.

Any opinions, findings, and conclusions or recommendations expressed in this material are those of the authors and do not necessarily reflect the views of the Defense Advanced Research Projects Agency (DARPA) or its Contracting Agents, the Office of Naval Research or its Contracting Agents, the National Science Foundation, or any other agency of the U.S. Government.

The authors also gratefully acknowledge a gift from Oracle Corporation.

References

1. Biswas, P., et al.: Venerable variadic vulnerabilities vanquished. In: 26th USENIX Security Symposium. SSYM 2017. USENIX Association, Vancouver (2017, to appear)
2. Crane, S., Homescu, A., Brunthaler, S., Larsen, P., Franz, M.: Thwarting cache side-channel attacks through dynamic software diversity. In: 22nd Annual Network and Distributed Systems Security Symposium. NDSS 2015. Internet Society, San Diego (2015)
3. Davi, L., Liebchen, C., Sadeghi, A.R., Snow, K.Z., Monrose, F.: Isomeron: code randomization resilient to (just-in-time) return-oriented programming. In: 22nd Annual Network and Distributed Systems Security Symposium. NDSS 2015. Internet Society, San Diego (2015)
4. Google: Fuzzer test suite (2018). https://github.com/google/fuzzer-test-suite
5. Haller, I., et al.: TypeSan: practical type confusion detection. In: 23rd ACM SIGSAC Conference on Computer and Communications Security. CCS 2016, pp. 517–528. ACM, New York (2016)
6. International Organization for Standardization: Information technology - programming languages - C. Standard, International Organization for Standardization, Geneva, CH, December 2011
7. Jeon, Y., Biswas, P., Carr, S., Lee, B., Payer, M.: HexType: efficient detection of type confusion errors for C++. In: Proceedings of the 2017 ACM SIGSAC Conference on Computer and Communications Security, pp. 2373–2387. ACM, New York (2017)
8. Koppen, G.: Discontinuing the hardened Tor browser series (2017). https://blog.torproject.org/blog/discontinuing-hardened-tor-browser-series
9. Kurmus, A., Zippel, R.: A tale of two kernels: towards ending kernel hardening wars with split kernel. In: 21st ACM SIGSAC Conference on Computer and Communications Security. CCS 2014, pp. 1366–1377. ACM, New York (2014)
10. Lattner, C., Adve, V.: LLVM: a compilation framework for lifelong program analysis & transformation. In: 2004 International Symposium on Code Generation and Optimization. CGO 2004, p. 75. IEEE Computer Society, Palo Alto (2004)
11. Lee, B., Song, C., Kim, T., Lee, W.: Type casting verification: stopping an emerging attack vector. In: 24th USENIX Security Symposium. SSYM 2015, pp. 81–96. USENIX Association, Austin (2015)
12. Lee, J., et al.: Taming undefined behavior in LLVM. In: 38th annual ACM SIGPLAN Conference on Programming Language Design and Implementation. PLDI 2017. ACM, Barcelona, June 2017
13. LLVM Developers: Undefined behavior sanitizer (2017). https://clang.llvm.org/docs/UndefinedBehaviorSanitizer.html

14. LLVM Developers: libFuzzer (2018). https://llvm.org/docs/LibFuzzer.html
15. National Institute of Standards and Technology: National vulnerability database (2017). https://nvd.nist.gov
16. Serebryany, K., Bruening, D., Potapenko, A., Vyukov, D.: AddressSanitizer: a fast address sanity checker. In: 2012 USENIX Annual Technical Conference. ATC 2012, p. 28. USENIX Association, Berkeley (2012)
17. Serebryany, K., Iskhodzhanov, T.: ThreadSanitizer: data race detection in practice. In: 2009 Workshop on Binary Instrumentation and Applications. WBIA 2009, pp. 62–71. ACM, New York (2009)
18. Snow, K.Z., Monrose, F., Davi, L., Dmitrienko, A., Liebchen, C., Sadeghi, A.R.: Just-in-time code reuse: on the effectiveness of fine-grained address space layout randomization. In: 2013 IEEE Symposium on Security and Privacy. SP 2013, pp. 574–588. IEEE, San Francisco (2013)
19. Song, D., et al.: SoK: sanitizing for security. In: 40th IEEE Symposium on Security and Privacy. SP 2019. IEEE Computer Society, San Francisco (2019)
20. Standard Performance Evaluation Corporation: SPEC CPU 2006 (2017). https://www.spec.org/cpu2006
21. Stepanov, E., Serebryany, K.: MemorySanitizer: fast detector of uninitialized memory use in C++. In: 2015 IEEE/ACM International Symposium on Code Generation and Optimization. CGO 2015, pp. 46–55. IEEE, San Francisco (2015)
22. Wagner, J., Kuznetsov, V., Candea, G., Kinder, J.: High system-code security with low overhead. In: 2015 IEEE Symposium on Security and Privacy. SP 2015, pp. 866–879. IEEE Computer Society, Washington, D.C. (2015)
23. Wagner, J.B.: Elastic program transformations: automatically optimizing the reliability/performance trade-off in systems software. Ph.D. thesis, Ecole Polytechnique Federale de Lausanne (2017)
24. Xu, M., Lu, K., Kim, T., Lee, W.: Bunshin: compositing security mechanisms through diversification. In: 2017 USENIX Annual Technical Conference. ATC 2017, pp. 271–283. USENIX Association (2017)

τCFI: Type-Assisted Control Flow Integrity for x86-64 Binaries

Paul Muntean[1](✉) , Matthias Fischer[1], Gang Tan[3] , Zhiqiang Lin[2] ,
Jens Grossklags[1] , and Claudia Eckert[1]

[1] Technical University of Munich, Munich, Germany
{paul.muntean,matthias.fischer,claudia.eckert}@sec.in.tum.de,
jens.grossklags@in.tum.de
[2] The Ohio State University, Columbus, USA
zlin@cse.ohio-state.edu
[3] The Pennsylvania State University, State College, USA
gtan@cse.psu.edu

Abstract. Programs aiming for low runtime overhead and high availability draw on several object-oriented features available in the C/C++ programming language, such as dynamic object dispatch. However, there is an alarmingly high number of object dispatch (*i.e.,* forward-edge) corruption vulnerabilities, which undercut security in significant ways and are in need of a thorough solution. In this paper, we propose τCFI, an extended control flow integrity (CFI) model that uses both the types and numbers of function parameters to enforce forward- and backward-edge control flow transfers. At a high level, it improves the precision of existing forward-edge recognition approaches by considering the type information of function parameters, which are directly extracted from the application binaries. Therefore, τCFI can be used to harden legacy applications for which source code may not be available. We have evaluated τCFI on real-world binaries including Nginx, NodeJS, Lighttpd, MySql and the SPEC CPU2006 benchmark and demonstrate that τCFI is able to effectively protect these applications from forward- and backward-edge corruptions with low runtime overhead. In direct comparison with state-of-the-art tools, τCFI achieves higher forward-edge caller-callee matching precision.

Keywords: C++ object dispatch · Indirect control flow transfer
Code-reuse attack

1 Introduction

The C++ programming language has been extensively used to build many large, complex, and efficient software systems over the last decades. A key concept of the C++ language is polymorphism. This concept is based on C++ virtual functions. Virtual functions enable late binding and allow programmers to overwrite a virtual function of the base-class with their own implementation. In

© Springer Nature Switzerland AG 2018
M. Bailey et al. (Eds.): RAID 2018, LNCS 11050, pp. 423–444, 2018.
https://doi.org/10.1007/978-3-030-00470-5_20

order to implement virtual functions, the compiler needs to generate virtual table meta-data structures for all virtual functions and provide to each instance (object) of such a class a (virtual) pointer (the value of which is computed during runtime) to the aforementioned table. Unfortunately, this approach represents a main source for exploitable program indirection (*i.e.,* forward edges) along function returns (*i.e.,* backward edges), as the C/C++ language provides no intrinsic security guarantees (*i.e.,* we consider Clang-CFI [1] and Clang's SafeStack [2] optional).

In this paper, we present a new control flow integrity (CFI) tool called τCFI used to secure C++ binaries by considering the type information from application binaries. Our work targets applications, whose source code is unavailable and that contain at least one exploitable memory corruption bug (*e.g.,* a buffer overflow bug). We assume such bugs can be used to enable the execution of sophisticated Code-Reuse Attacks (CRAs) such as the COOP attack [3] and its extensions [4–7], violating the program's intended control flow graph (CFG) through forward edges in the CFG and/or through attacks, that violate backward edges such as Control Jujutsu [8]. A potential prerequisite for violating forward-edge control flow transfers is the corruption of an object's virtual pointer. In contrast, backward edges can be corrupted by loading fake return addresses on the stack.

To address such object dispatch corruptions, and in general any type of indirect program control flow transfer violations, CFI [9,10] was originally developed to secure indirect control flow transfers, by adding runtime checks before forward-edge and backward-edge control transfers. CFI-based techniques, that rely on the construction of a precise CFG, are effective [11], if CFGs are carefully constructed and sound [12]. However, these techniques still allow CRAs that do not violate the enforced CFG. For example, the COOP family of CRAs bypasses most deployed CFI-based enforcement policies, since these attacks do not exploit indirect backward edges (*i.e.,* function returns), but rather imprecision in forward edges (*i.e.,* object dispatches, indirect control flow transfers), which in general cannot be statically (before runtime) and precisely determined as alias analysis in program binaries is undecidable [13]. Source code based tools such as: SafeDispatch [14], MCFI [15,16], ShrinkWrap [17], VTI [18], and IFC-C/VTV [19] can protect against forward-edge violations. However, they rely on source code availability limiting their applicability (*e.g.,* proprietary libraries cannot be recompiled). In contrast, binary-based forward-edge protection tools, including binCFI [20], vfGuard [21], vTint [22], VCI [23], Marx [24] and TypeArmor [25], typically protect only forward edges through a CFI-based policy, and most of the tools assume that a shadow stack [26] technique is used to protect backward edges.

Unfortunately, the currently most precise binary-based forward-edge protection tools w.r.t. calltarget reduction, VCI and Marx, suffer from forward-edge imprecision, since both are based on an approximated program class hierarchy obtained through the usage of heuristics and assumptions. TypeArmor enforces a forward-edge policy, which only takes into account the number of parameters of caller-callee pairs without imposing any constraint on the parameters' types. Thus, these forward-edge protection tools are generally too permissive. CFI-based forward-edge protection techniques without backward-edge protection are broken [27], thus these tools assume that a shadow stack protection policy is in place. Unfortunately, shadow stack based techniques (backward-edge protection) were recently bypassed [28] and add, on average, up to 10% runtime overhead [29].

In this paper, we present τCFI, which is a fine-grained forward-edge and backward-edge binary-level CFI protection mechanism, that neither relies on shadow stack based techniques to protect backward edges, nor any runtime-type information (RTTI) (*i.e.,* metadata emitted by the compiler, which is most of the time stripped in production binaries). Note that, in general, variable type reconstruction on production binaries is a difficult task, as the required program semantics are mostly removed through compilation.

At a high level, there are a number of analyses τCFI performs in order to achieve its protection objective. In particular, it (1) uses its register width (ABI dependent) as the type of the parameter for each function parameter, (2) when determining whether an indirect call can target a function, it checks whether the call and the target function use the same number of parameters and whether the types (register width) match, (3) based on the provided forward-edge caller-callee mapping it builds a mapping, back from each callee to the legitimate addresses, located next to each caller. τCFI's backward-edge policy is based on the observation that backward edges of a program can be efficiently protected, if there is a precise forward-edge mapping available between callers and callees.

We have implemented τCFI on top of DynInst [30], which is a binary rewriting framework, that allows program binary instrumentation during loading or runtime. Note that τCFI preserves the original code copy of an executable by instrumenting all code of an executable shadow copy, which is later mapped to the original binary after it was loaded and τCFI's analysis finished. τCFI works with legacy programs and can be used to protect both executables and libraries. τCFI performs per-file analysis; as such each file is protected individually. We have evaluated τCFI with several real-world open source programs (*i.e.,* NodeJS, Lighttpd, MySql, etc.), as well as the SPEC CPU2006 benchmarks and demonstrated that our forward-edge policy is more precise than state-of-the-art tools. τCFI is applicable to program binaries for which we assume source code is not available. τCFI significantly reduces the number of valid forward edges compared to previous work and thus, we are able to build a precise backward-edge policy, which represents an efficient alternative to shadow stack based techniques.

In summary, we make the following contributions:

- We present τCFI, a new CFI system that improves the state-of-the-art CFI with more precise forward-edge identification by using type information reverse-engineered from stripped x86-64 binaries.
- We have implemented τCFI with a binary instrumentation framework to enforce a fine-grained forward-edge and backward-edge protection.
- We have conducted a thorough evaluation, through which we show that τCFI is more precise and effective than other state-of-the-art techniques.

2 Background

In this section, we provide the needed technical background to set the stage for the remainder of this paper.

2.1 Exploiting Object Dispatches in C++

Figure 1 depicts a C++ code example (left) and how a COOP main-loop gadget (right) (*i.e.*, based either on ML-G (main-loop), REC-G (recursive) or UNR-G (unrolled) COOP gadgets, see [4] for more details) is used to sequentially call COOP gadgets by iterating through a loop (REC-G excluded) controlled by the attacker.

First, the object dispatch (see line 17 depicted in Fig. 1) is exploited by the attacker in order to call different functions in the whole program by iterating on an array of fake objects previously inserted in the array through, for example, a buffer overflow. Second, in order to achieve this, the attacker previously exploits an existing program memory corruption (*e.g.*, buffer overflow), which is further used to corrupt an object dispatch, ❶, by inserting fake objects into the array and by changing the number of initial loop iterations. Next she invokes gadgets, ❶ and ❸ up to ❹, through the calls, ❷ and ❹ up to ❺, contained in the loop. As it can be observed in Fig. 1, the attacker can invoke from the same callsite legitimate functions (in total ❺) residing in the virtual table (vTable) inheritance path (*i.e.*, at the time of writing this paper this type of information is particularly hard to recuperate from program binaries) for this particular callsite, indicated with green color vTable entries. However, a real COOP attack invokes illegitimate vTable entries residing in the entire initial program class hierarchy (or the extended one) with little or no relationship to the initial callsite, indicated with red-color vTable entries. Third, in this way different addresses contained in the program (1) (vTable) hierarchy (contains only virtual members), (2) class hierarchy (contains both virtual and non-virtual members) and (or) the whole program address space can be called. For example, the attacker can call any entry in the: (1) class hierarchy of the whole program, (2) class hierarchy containing only legitimate targets for this callsite, (3) virtual table hierarchy of the whole program, (4) virtual table hierarchy containing only legitimate targets for this callsite, (5) virtual table hierarchy and class hierarchy containing only legitimate targets for this callsite, and (6) virtual table hierarchy and class hierarchy of the whole program. Finally, because there are no intrinsic language semantics—such as object cast checks—in the C++ programming language for object dispatches, the loop gadget indicated in Fig. 1 can be used without constraint to call any possible entry in the whole program. Thus, making any program address the start of a potential usable gadget.

2.2 Type-Inference on Executables

Recovering variable types from executable programs is generally considered difficult for two main reasons. First, the quality of the disassembly can vary considerably from one used underlying binary analysis framework to another and

```
1  class nsMultiplexInputStream final
2  :public nsIMultiplexInputStream //A0
3  ,public nsISeekableStream //A1
4  ,public nsIIPCSerializableInputStream //A2
5  ,public nsICloneableInputStream{ //A3
6  nsTArray<nsCOMPtr<nsIInputStream>> mStreams;
7  NS_IMETHODIMP nsMultiplexInputStream::Close(){
8     MutexAutoLock lock(mLock);
9     mStatus = NS_BASE_STREAM_CLOSED;
10    //set NS_OK flag
11    nsresult rv = NS_OK;
12    //get array length
13    uint32_t len = mStreams.Length();
14    //array-based main loop gadget (ML-G)
15    for (uint32_t i = 0; i<len; ++i){
16       //(0)hijacked object dispatch
17       nsresult rv2=mStreams[i]->Close();
18       if (NS_FAILED(rv2)) {
19          rv = rv2;
20       }
21    }
22    return rv;
23 }
```

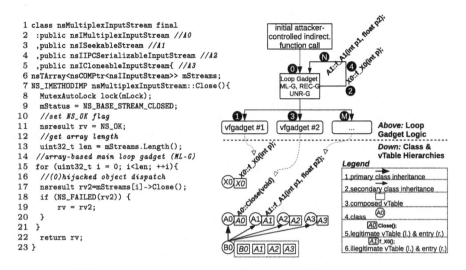

Fig. 1. COOP main loop gadget (ML-G) operation with the associated C++ code.

w.r.t. the compiler flags which were used to compile the binary. Note that production binaries can be more or less stripped (*i.e.*, RTTI or other debugging symbols may or may not be available etc.) from useful information, which can be used during a type-recovering analysis. τCFI is based on DynInst and the quality of the executable disassembly is sufficient for our needs. In contrast to other approaches, the register width based type recuperation of τCFI is based on a relatively simple analysis compared to other tools and provides similar results. For a more comprehensive review on the capabilities of DynInst and other tools, we advice the reader to review Andriesse *et al.* [31]. Second, if the type inference analysis requires alias analysis, it is well known that alias analysis in binaries is undecidable [13] in theory and intractable in practice [32]. Further, there are several highly promising tools such as: Rewards [33], BAP [34], Smart-Dec [35], and Divine [36]. These tools try more or less successfully to recover (or infer) type information from binary programs with different goals. Typical goals are: (1) full program reconstruction (*i.e.*, binary to code conversion, reversing, etc.), (2) checking for buffer overflows, and (3) checking for integer overflows and other types of memory corruptions. For a comprehensive review of type inference recovering tools in the context of binaries, we suggest consulting Caballero *et al.* [37]. Finally, it is interesting to note that the code from only a few of the tools mentioned in the previous review are actually available as open source.

2.3   Security Implications of Indirect Transfers

Indirect Forward-Edge Transfers. Illegal forward-edge indirect calls may result from a virtual pointer (vPointer) corruption. A vPointer corruption is not a vulnerability but rather a capability, which can be the result of a spatial or temporal memory corruption triggered by: (1) bad-casting [38] of C++ objects, (2) buffer overflow in a buffer adjacent to a C++ object, or (3) a use-after-free condition [3]. A vPointer corruption can be exploited in several ways. A manipulated vPointer can be exploited to make it point to any existing or added program virtual table entry or to a fake virtual table added by the attacker. For example, an attacker can use the corruption to hijack the control flow of the program and start a COOP attack [3]. vPointer corruptions are a real security threat that can be exploited in many ways as for example if there is a memory corruption (*e.g.,* buffer overflow, use-after-free condition), which is adjacent in memory to the C++ object. As a consequence, each memory corruption, which can be used to reach the memory layout of an object (*e.g.,* object type confusion), can be potentially used to change the program control flow.

Indirect Backward-Edge Transfers. Program backward edges (*i.e.,* jump, ret, etc.) can be corrupted to assemble gadget chains such as follows. (1) No CFI protection technique was applied: In this case, the binary is not protected by any CFI policy. Obviously, the attacker can then hijack backward edges to *jump* virtually anywhere in the binary in order to chain gadgets together. (2) Coarse-grained CFI protected scenarios: In this scenario, if the attacker is aware of what addresses are protected, the attacker may deviate the application flow to legitimate locations in order to link gadgets together. (3) Fine-grained CFI protection scenarios: In this case, the legitimate target set is stricter than in (2). But, assuming that the attacker knows which addresses are protected and which are not, she may be able to call legitimate targets through control flow bending. (4) Fully precise CFI protected scenarios (*i.e.,* SafeStack [26] based): In this scenario, the legitimate target set is stricter than in (3). Even though we have a one-to-one mapping between calltargets and legitimate return sites, the attacker could use this one-to-one mapping to assemble gadget chains if at the legitimate calltarget return site there is a useful gadget [27].

3   Threat Model

We follow the same basic assumptions stated in [25] w.r.t. forward edges. More precisely, we assume a resourceful attacker that has read and write access to the data sections of the attacked program binary. We assume that the protected binary does not contain self-modifying code or any kind of obfuscation. We also consider pages to be either writable or executable, but not both at the same time. Further, we assume that the attacker has the ability to exploit an existing memory corruption in order to hijack the program control flow. As such, we consider a powerful yet realistic adversary model that is consistent with previous work on CRAs and their mitigations [26]. The adversary is aware of the applied defenses and has access to the source and non-hardened binary of the target application. She can exploit (bend) any backward-edge based indirect program transfer and has the capability to make arbitrary memory writes.

4 Design and Implementation

In this section, we present a brief overview of τCFI followed by its design and implementation.

4.1 Approach Overview

Figure 2 depicts an overview of our approach. From left to right, the program binary is analyzed by τCFI and the calltargets and callsite analysis are performed for determining how many parameters are provided, how many are consumed, and their register width. After this step, labels are inserted at each previously identified callsite and at each calltarget. The enforced policy is schematically represented by the black highlighted dots (addresses, *e.g.,* *cs1*) in Fig. 2 that are allowed to call only legitimate red highlighted dots (addresses, *e.g.,* *ct1*). Next, to compute the set of addresses which a return instruction can target, the address set determined by each address located after each legitimate callsite is computed. This information is obtained by using the previously determined callsite forward-edge mapping to derive a function return backward map that uses return instructions as keys and return targets as values. This way, τCFI has a set of addresses for each function to which the function return site is allowed to transfer control. Finally, range or compare checks are inserted before each function return site. These checks are used during runtime to check if the address, where the function return wants to jump to, is contained in the legitimate set for each particular return site. This is represented in Fig. 2 by green highlighted dots (addresses *e.g.,* *ctr2*) that are allowed to call only legitimate blue highlighted dots (addresses *e.g.,* *csn1*). Finally, the result is a hardened program binary (see right-hand side in Fig. 2).

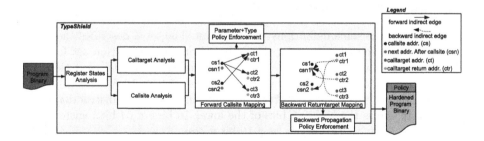

Fig. 2. Main steps performed by τCFI when hardening a program binary.

4.2 Parameter Count and Type Policy

Parameters can be passed through registers or the stack. In the Itanium C++ ABI, the first six parameters are passed through registers (*i.e.,* rdi, rsi, rdx, rcx, r8, and r9). Even when a 64-bit register is used to pass a parameter, the actual number of bits used in the register might be smaller. Therefore, we treat the used widths of parameter-storing registers as the types of the parameters. There are four types of reading and writing access on registers. Therefore, our set of possible types for parameters is $\{64, 32, 16, 8, 0\}$, where zero models the absence of a parameter. For the Itanium ABI, our analysis tracks the 6 registers used in parameter passing and classifies callsites and calltargets according to how these registers are used.

Our analysis overapproximates at callsites and underapproximates at calltargets the parameter count and types, which is due to the general difficulty of statically determining the exact number of arguments provided by a callsite and the number of parameters required by a calltarget and w.r.t. the widths of registers used in parameter passing. Specifically, at a callsite, the analysis calculates an *upper bound* for the number of arguments and for the widths of those registers that store arguments. For instance, for a function call that passes one argument with a width of 32-bit, the analysis may estimate that there are two arguments passed and the first one's width is 64-bit. Furthermore, the analysis on a calltarget (a callee function) calculates a *lower bound* for the number of needed parameters and for the widths of those registers that store parameters.

Because of the approximations in our analysis, our policy for matching callsites and calltargets allows a callsite to transfer to a calltarget if (1) the number of estimated arguments at a callsite is greater than the number of estimated parameters at a calltarget; and (2) for each argument at the callsite and its corresponding parameter in the calltarget, the estimated width of the argument is greater than the estimated width of the parameter. Part (1) is about the parameter count and is the same as the parameter-count policy in TypeArmor [25]; part (2) is about the parameter types and enables τCFI to provide a finer-grained policy than just considering the parameter count.

4.3 Instruction Read-Write Effect

We first introduce some definitions and notation. The set $\mathcal{I}$ describes the set of possible instructions; in our case, this is based on the instruction set for x86-64 processors. An instruction $i \in \mathcal{I}$ can perform two kinds of operations on registers: (1) Read n-bit from a register with $n \in \{64, 32, 16, 8\}$ and (2) Write n-bit to a register with $n \in \{64, 32, 16, 8\}$. Note that there are instructions that can directly access the higher 8 bits of the lower 16 bits of 64-bit registers. For our purpose, we treat this access as a 16-bit access.

Next, the possible effect of an instruction on one register is described as $\delta \in \Delta$ with $\Delta = \{w64, w32, w16, w8, 0\} \times \{r64, r32, r16, r8, 0\}$. Note that 0 represents the absence of either a write or read access and $(0, 0)$ represents the absence of both. Meanwhile, wn with $n \in \{64, 32, 16, 8\}$ implies all wm with $m \in \{64, 32, 16, 8\}$ and $m < n$ (*e.g.*, $w64$ implies $w32$); the same property holds for rn. The Itanium C++ ABI specifies 16 general purpose integer registers. Therefore, the read-write effect of an instruction on the set of registers can be described as $\delta_p \in \Delta^{16}$. Our analysis performs calculations based on the effect of each instruction $i \in \mathcal{I}$ via the function regEffect : $\mathcal{I} \mapsto \Delta^{16}$. Note that this function can be purely defined based on the semantics of instructions.

4.4 Calltarget Analysis

Our calltarget static analysis classifies calltargets according to the parameters they expect by taking into account the parameters' count and types. Given a set of address-taken functions[4], the static analysis performs an interprocedural analysis to determine the register states for the 6 argument registers.

Next, we present τCFI's analysis, followed by a discussion of optimizations and interprocedural analysis. The basic analysis determines, for each register and at a particular program location, that it is in one of the following states:

- rn, where $n \in \{64, 32, 16, 8\}$ represents that the lower n bits of the register are *read before written* along all control flow paths starting from the location.
- $*$ represents that, along some control flow path, the register is either written before read or there are no reads/writes on the register.

The basic analysis described above can be implemented as a classic backward-liveness analysis, except that it needs to track widths in read operations. For instance, for an instruction i, if the regEffect function shows that i reads the lower 16-bits of `rax`, then the state of `rax` immediately before the instruction is $r16$. For an instruction with multiple successors, the register states after the instruction are calculated based on the states at the beginnings of the successors. For instance, if an instruction has two successors, and the state of `rax` is $r64$ before the first successor and the state of `rax` is $r32$ before the second, then the state of `rax` after the instruction is $r32$, essentially indicating that all paths starting from the end of the instruction have a $r32$ read before write for `rax`. Recall that the calltarget analysis performs an underapproximation; so using $r32$ is safe even though one of the paths performs a $r64$ read.

The backward-liveness analysis, however, is inefficient. Our implementation actually follows TypeArmor [25] to perform a forward interprocedural analysis (with some modification to consider widths of read operations). We refer readers to the TypeArmor paper for details and give only a brief overview here.

First, note that τCFI's analysis operates at the basic block level instead of the instruction level. Second, the analysis further refines the $*$ state to be either w or c, where w (write before read) refers to a register being written to before read from along some control flow path and c (clear/untouched) represents that the register is untouched along some control flow path. The reason for such a refinement is that during forward analysis, if the states of all argument registers before a basic block b are either rn or w (e.g., when b reads or writes all argument registers), then there is no need to keep analyzing the successor basic blocks since their operations would not change the state before b; this enables an early

---

[4] Since an indirect call can target a function only if the function's address is taken, there is no need to analyze functions whose addresses are not taken; this is similar to TypeArmor.

termination of the forward analysis and is thus more efficient. On the other hand, if the state of one of the argument registers is c, then the forward analysis has to continue. This is because c indicates the register is untouched so far, but it can be read or written in a future basic block. Further, the analysis is interprocedural and maintains a stack to match direct function calls and returns during analysis. Finally, for indirect calls, however, it does not follow to the targets, but performs an underapproximation instead.

Parameter Count and Types. Once the analysis finishes, we can calculate a function's parameter count and parameter types based on the state before the entry basic block of the function. The argument count is determined using the highest argument register that is marked rn. The type of an argument register is directly given by the rn state of the register.

4.5   Callsite Analysis

Our callsite analysis classifies callsites according to the arguments they provide by considering the argument *count* and their *types*. For callsite analysis, overestimations are allowed: the callsite analysis overestimates the number of arguments and the widths of arguments. As such a callsite is allowed to target a calltarget that requires a smaller or equal number of parameters and that requires a smaller or equal width for each parameter.

For callsite analysis, we employ a customized reaching-definition analysis. The analysis determines the states of registers. At a particular program location, it determines whether or not a register is in one of the following states:

- sn, where $n \in \{8, 16, 32, 64\}$: this represents a state in which the register's lower n bit is set in a control-flow path ending at the program location.
- t (trashed): this represents a state in which the register is not set on all control flow paths ending at the program location.

τCFI's reaching-definition analysis is implemented as an interprocedural backward analysis similar to TypeArmor [25], the difference being that τCFI also tracks the widths in write operations to infer sn states. Once the analysis is finished, it uses the register state just before an indirect callsite to determine its argument count and types: If an argument register is in state sn, then it is considered an argument that uses n bits; the argument count is determined by the highest argument register whose state is sn.

4.6   Return Values

Knowing more information about return values of functions increases CFI precision. For instance, an indirect callsite that expects a return value should not call a function that does not return a value; similarly, an indirect callsite that expects a 64-bit return value should not call a function that returns only a 32-bit value.

For calltarget analysis, τCFI traverses backwards from the return instruction of a function and searches for uses of the RAX register to determine if a function has a void or a non-void return type. In case there is a write operation on the RAX register, τCFI infers that the function's return type is non-void; furthermore, it tracks the widths of write operations to infer the width of the return type. For calltarget return-value type estimation, overapproximations are allowed.

At a callsite, τCFI traverses forward from the callsite to search for reads before writes on the RAX register to determine if a callsite expects a return value or not. In case there is such a read on the RAX register, τCFI infers that the callsite expects a return value; furthermore, it tracks the widths of read operations to infer the width of the expected return value. For callsite return-value type estimation, underapproximation is allowed.

4.7 Backward-Edge Analysis

In order to protect backward edges, we have designed an analysis that can determine possible legitimate return target addresses for each callee function. Our algorithm used for computing the legitimate set of addresses for each callee works as follows. First, a map is obtained after running the callsite and calltarget analysis (see Sects. 4.4 and 4.5 for more details); it maps a callsite to the set of legal calltargets where forward-edge indirect control-flow transfer is allowed to jump. This map is then reversed to build a second map that maps from the return instruction of a function (callee) to a set of addresses where the return can transfer to.

The return target address set for a function return is determined by getting the next address after each callsite address that is allowed to make the forward-edge control flow transfer. The map is obtained by visiting a return instruction address in a function and assigning to it the addresses next to callsites that can call the function. At the end of the analysis, all callsites and all function returns have been visited and a set of backward-edge addresses for each function return address is obtained. Note that the function boundary address (*i.e.*, ret) is detected by a linear basic block search from the beginning of the function (calltarget) until the first return instruction is encountered. We are aware that other promising approaches for recovering function boundaries (*e.g.*, [39]) exist, and plan to experiment with them in future work.

4.8 Binary Instrumentation

Forward-Edge Policy Enforcement. The result of the callsite and calltarget analysis is a mapping that maps a callsite to its allowed calltargets. In order to enforce this mapping during runtime, callsites and calltargets are instrumented inside the binary program with two labels. Additionally, each callsite is instrumented with CFI checks. At a callsite, the number of provided arguments is encoded as a series of six bits. At a calltarget, the label contains six bits encoding how many parameters the calltarget expects. Additionally, at a callsite 12 bits encode the register-width types of the provided arguments (two bits for each parameter), while at the calltarget another 12 bits are used to encode the types of the parameters expected. Further, at a callsite, several bits are used to encode if the function is expecting a void return type or not, and the width of the return type if it is nonvoid (similarly for a calltarget). All this information is written in labels before callsites and calltargets. During runtime before a callsite, these labels are compared by performing an XOR operation. In case the XOR operation returns false (a zero value), the transfer is allowed; otherwise, the program execution is terminated.

Backward-Edge Policy Enforcement. Based on the previously determined reverse map, before each function return a randomly generated label value is inserted. We decided to use these kinds of values as our main requirement is to map a return to a potentially large number of return sites. The same label is inserted before each legitimate target address (the next address after a legitimate callsite). In this way, a function return is allowed to jump only to the instruction that follows next to the address of a callsite.

For callsites that target a calltarget that is also allowed by another callsite, τCFI performs a search in order to detect if the callsite already has a label attached to the address after the callsite. If so, a new label is generated and multiple labels are stored for the address following the callsite. In this way, calltarget return labels are grouped together based on the reverse map. This design allows the same number of function return sites as the forward-edge policy enforces for each callsite. Finally, in case the comparison returns true, the execution continues; otherwise, it is terminated.

4.9   Implementation

We have implemented τCFI using the DynInst [30] (v.9.2.0) instrumentation framework with a total of 5,501 lines of C++ code. We currently restricted our analysis and instrumentation to x86-64 executables in the ELF format using the Itanium C++ ABI calling convention. τCFI can deal with the level of executable obfuscation with which DynInst can deal. As such, we fully delegate this responsibility to the used instrumentation framework underneath. We focused on the Itanium C++ ABI convention as most C/C++ compilers on Linux implement this ABI. However, the implementation separated the ABI-dependent code, so we expect it to be possible to support other ABIs as well. We developed the main part of our binary analysis pass in an instruction analyzer, which relies on the DynamoRIO [40] library (v.6.6.1) to decode single instructions and provide access to its information. The analyzer is then used to implement our version of the reaching-definition and liveness analysis. Further, we implemented a Clang/LLVM (v.4.0.0, trunk 283889) backend (machine instruction) pass (416 LOC) used for collecting ground truth data in order to evaluate the effectiveness and performance of our tool. The ground truth data is then used to verify the output of our tool for several test targets. This is accomplished with the help of our Python-based evaluation and test environment implemented in 3,239 lines of Python code.

5   Evaluation

We have evaluated τCFI by instrumenting various open source applications and conducting a thorough analysis in order to show its effectiveness and usefulness. Our test applications include the following real-world programs: FTP servers *Vsftpd* (v.1.1.0, C code), Pure-ftpd (v.1.0.36, C code) and *Proftpd* (v.1.3.3, C code); Lighttpd web server (v.1.4.28, C code); two database server applications *Postgresql* (v.9.0.10, C code) and *Mysql* (v.5.1.65, C++ code); the memory cache application *Memcached* (v.1.4.20, C code); and the *Node.js* application server (v.0.12.5, C++ code). We selected these applications to allow for a fair comparison with other similar tools. In our evaluation, we addressed the following research questions (RQs): **RQ1:** How **effective** is τCFI? (Sect. 5.1); **RQ2:** What **security protection** is offered by τCFI? (Sect. 5.2); **RQ3:** Which **attacks** are mitigated by τCFI? (Sect. 5.3) **RQ4:** Are other forward-edge tools **better** than τCFI? (Sect. 5.4)? **RQ5:** Is τCFI **effective** against COOP? (Sect. 5.5) **RQ6:** How does τCFI **compare** with Clang's Shadow Stack? (Sect. 5.6) **RQ7:** What **runtime overhead** does τCFI impose? (Sect. 5.7) Our setup is based on Kubuntu 16.04 LTS (k.v.4.4.0) using 3 GB RAM and four hardware threads running on an i7-4170HQ CPU at 2.50 GHz.

5.1   Effectiveness

Table 1 depicts the average number of calltargets per callsite, the standard deviation σ, and the median. In Table 1, the abbreviation CS refers to the callsites, while CT means calltargets. Note that the restriction to address-taken functions (see column AT) is present. The label *count** denotes the best possible reduction using the parameter *count* policy based on the ground truth collected by our Clang/LLVM pass, while *count* denotes the results of our implementation of the parameter *count* policy derived from binaries. The same applies to *type∗* and *type* regarding the parameter *type* policy. A lower number of calltargets per callsite indicates better results. Note that our parameter *type* policy is superior to the parameter *count* policy, as it allows for a stronger reduction of allowed calltargets. We consider this an important result, which further improves the state-of-the-art. Finally, we provide the median and the pair of mean and standard deviation to allow for a better comparison with other state-of-the-art tools.

Table 1. Allowed callsites per calltarget for τCFI's count and type policies.

02 Target	CS total	CT total	AT total	count* limit (mean ± σ)	count* median	count limit (mean ± σ)	count median	type* limit (mean ± σ)	type* median	type limit (mean ± σ)	type median
ProFTPD	157.0	1,011.0	396.0	349.3 ± 52.8	369.0	370.1 ± 43.3	382.0	338.2 ± 64.8	361.0	354.4 ± 85.1	390.0
Pure-FTPD	8.0	127.0	13.0	8.6 ± 4.6	8.0	10.1 ± 4.8	13.0	8.1 ± 4.0	5.0	10.0 ± 4.0	10.0
Vsftpd	2.0	391.0	10.0	8.0 ± 2.0	8.0	10.0 ± 0.0	10.0	6.0 ± 2.0	6.0	7.0 ± 3.0	7.0
Lighttpd	66.0	289.0	63.0	34.3 ± 15.1	21.0	43.7 ± 14.5	51.0	34.5 ± 14.7	23.0	45.4 ± 12.1	50.0
Nginx	270.0	914.0	1,111.0	316.8 ± 146.9	266.0	447.6 ± 124.0	528.0	317.5 ± 146.4	267.0	450.9 ± 110.2	528.0
MySQL	7,893.0	9,928.0	5,896.0	338.5 ± 189.5	179.0	490.6 ± 203.3	574.0	307.9 ± 163.6	186.0	519.6 ± 147.6	540.0
PostgreSQL	687.0	6,885.0	2,304.0	423.4 ± 176.7	471.0	497.0 ± 151.8	515.0	416.2 ± 188.1	541.0	476.9 ± 162.4	562.0
Memcached	48.0	134.0	14.0	12.3 ± 2.3	14.0	13.0 ± 1.4	14.0	12.7 ± 1.0	12.0	12.8 ± 1.0	12.0
NodeJS	10,215.0	20,196.0	7,230.0	763.1 ± 329.3	806.0	1,051.2 ± 293.2	1,169.0	683.2 ± 332.9	459.0	939.8 ± 314.0	1,022.0
geomean	170.1	1,104.8	259.8	89.0 ± 31.2	79.4	110.4 ± 27.0	123.1	83.7 ± 28.1	69.3	104.7 ± 27.8	111.6

Theoretical Limits. We explored the theoretical limits regarding the effectiveness of the *count* and *type* policies by relying on the collected ground truth data; essentially assuming perfect classification. Based on the type information collected by our Clang/LLVM pass, we derived the available number of calltargets for each callsite by applying the count and type policies. From the results, (1) the theoretical limit of the *count** policy has a geomean of 89 possible calltargets, which is around 8% of the geomean of the total available calltargets (1104), and (2) the theoretical limit of the *type** policy has a geomean of 83 possible calltargets, which is 7.5% of the geomean of the total available calltargets (1104). In comparison, the theoretical limit of the *type** policy allows about 13% less available calltargets in geomean than the limit of the *count** policy (*i.e.,* 69.3 vs. 79.4).

Calltarget per Callsite Reduction. (1) The *count* policy has a geomean of 104 calltargets, which is around 9.4% of the geomean of all available calltargets (1104). This is around 24% more than the theoretical limit of available calltargets per callsite (see *count** 89 vs. 110.4). (2) The *type* policy has a geomean of 104.7 calltargets, which is 9.48% of the geomean of total available calltargets (1104). This is approximatively 25% more than the theoretical limit of available calltargets per callsite (see *type** 83.7 vs. 104.7). τCFI's *type* policy allows around 9.4% less available calltargets in the geomean than our implementation of the *count* policy (104.7 vs. 110.4), and a total reduction of more than 94% (104.7 vs. 1104) w.r.t. the total number of calltargets (CT) available once the *count* and *type* policies are applied.

5.2   Forward-Edge Policy Vs. Other Tools

Table 2 provides a comparison between τCFI, TypeArmor and IFCC w.r.t. the median count of calltargets per callsite. The values for TypeArmor [25] and IFCC [19] depicted in Table 2 have been adopted from the corresponding papers in order to ensure a fair comparison. Further, Table 2 conveys the limitations of binary-based type analysis, as the median of the possible target set size for τCFI is several times larger than the corre-

Table 2. Legitimate calltargets/callsite for 5 tools.

Target	IFCC	TypeArmor (CFI+CFC)	AT	τCFI (count)	τCFI (type)
ProFTPD	3.0	376.0	396.0	382.0	390.0
Pure-FTPD	0.0	4.0	13.0	13.0	10.0
Vsftpd	1.0	12.0	10.0	10.0	7.0
Lighttpd	6.0	47.0	63.0	51.0	50.0
Nginx	25.0	254.0	1,111.0	528.0	528.0
MySQL	150.0	3,698.0	5,896.0	574.0	540.0
PostgreSQL	12.0	2,304.0	2,504.0	515.0	562.0
Memcached	1.0	14.0	14.0	14.0	12.0
NodeJS	341.0	4,714.0	7,230.0	1,169.0	1,022.0
geomean	8.7	170.4	259.8	123.1	111.6

sponding set sizes for system using source-level analysis. Note that the smaller the geomean values are, the better the technique is. AT is a technique that allows a callsite to target any address-taken functions. IFCC is a compiler-based solution and is included here as a reference to show what is possible when the program's source code is available. TypeArmor and τCFI on the other hand are binary-based tools. τCFI reduces the number of calltargets by up to 42.9% (geomean) when compared to the AT technique, by more than seven times (7230 vs. 1022) for a single test program w.r.t. AT, and by 65.49% (170.4 vs. 111.6) in geomean when compared with TypeArmor, respectively. As such, τCFI represents a stronger improvement w.r.t. calltarget per callsite reduction in binary programs compared to other approaches.

5.3   Effectiveness Against COOP

We investigated the effectiveness of τCFI against the COOP attack by looking at the number of register arguments, which can be used to enable data flows between gadgets. In order to determine how many arguments remain unprotected after we apply the forward-edge policy of τCFI, we determined the number of parameter overestimations and compared it with the ground truth obtained during an LLVM compiler pass. Next, we used some heuristics to determine how many ML-G and REC-G callsites exist in the C++ server applications. Finally, we compared these results with the one obtained by TypeArmor.

Table 3 presents the results obtained after counting the number of perfectly estimated and overestimated protected ML-G and REC-G gadgets. As it can be observed, τCFI obtained a 96% (184 out of 192) accuracy of perfectly protected ML-G callsites for MySQL, while TypeArmor obtained a 94% accuracy for the same program. Further, τCFI obtained a 97% (131 out of 134) accuracy for Node.js, while TypeArmor obtained 95% accuracy on the same

Table 3. Parameter overestimation for the ML-G and REC-G gadgets.

Program	Overestimation						
	#cs	0	+1	+2	+3	+4	+5
MySQL (ML-G)	192	184	3	1	0	1	3
Node.js (ML-G)	134	131	1	0	1	0	1
geomean	160	155	1	1	1	1	1
MySql (REC-G)	289	273	10	2	3	0	1
Node.js (REC-G)	72	69	2	0	0	0	1
geomean	144	137	4	1	1	1	1

program. Further, for the REC-G case, τCFI obtained an 94% (273 out of 289) exact-parameter accuracy for MySQL, while TypeArmor had 86%. For Node.js, τCFI obtained an accuracy of 95% (69 out of 72), while TypeArmor had 96%. Overall τCFI's forward-edge policy obtained a perfect accuracy of 95%, while TypeArmor obtained 92%. While this is not a large difference, we want to point out that the remaining overestimated parameters represent only 5% and thus do not leave much wiggle room for the attacker.

5.4   Comparison with the Shadow-Stack

The shadow stack implementation of Abadi *et al.* [9] provides a strong security protection [11] w.r.t. backward-edge protection. However, it: (1) has a high runtime overhead ($\geq$21%), (2) is not open source, (3) uses a proprietary binary analysis framework (*i.e.,* Vulcan), (4) loses precision due to equivalent class merging. Hence, we propose an alternative backward-edge protection solution. In order to show the precision of τCFI's backward-edge protection, we provide the average number of legitimate return addresses for return instructions and compare it to the total number of available addresses without any protection.

Table 4 presents the statistics w.r.t. the backward-edge policy legitimate return targets. More specifically, in Table 4, we use the following abbreviations: total number of return addresses (Total #RA), total (median) number of

Table 4. Backward-edge policy statistics.

Program	Total #RA	Total #RATs	Total #RATs/RA	%RATs/RA prog. binary
MySQL	5,896.0	3,792.0	0.6	0.014%
Node.js	7,230.0	3,864.0	0.53	0.011%
geomean	6,529.0	3,827.0	0.58	0.012%

return address targets (Total #RATs), total (median) number of return address targets per return instruction (Total. # RATs/RA), percentage of legitimate return address targets per return addresses w.r.t. the total number of addresses in the program binary (% RATs/RA w.r.t. program binary). By applying τCFI's backward-edge policy, we obtain a reduction of 0.43 $(1 - 0.58)$ ratio (geomean) of the total number of return address targets per return address over the total number of return addresses. This means that only 43% of the total number of return addresses are actual targets for the function returns. The results indicate a percentage of 0.012% (geomean) of the total addresses in the program binaries are legitimate targets for the function returns. This means that our policy can eliminate 99.98% (100% - 0.012%) of the addresses, which an attacker can use for his attack inside the program binary. To put it differently, only 0.012% of the addresses inside the binary can be used as return addresses by the attacker. Further, we assume that the attacker cannot easily determine which addresses are still available for any given program binary, which is stripped from debug information. Note that each function return (callee) is allowed to return in geomean to around 111 legitimate addresses (MySQL 519 and NodeJS 939) in all analyzed programs. Finally, we assume that it is hard for the attacker to find out the exact set of legitimate addresses per return site once the policy was applied.

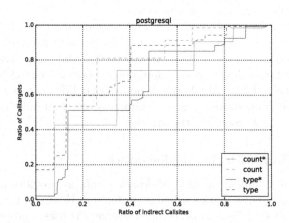

Fig. 3. CDF for the PostgreSQL program.

5.5   Security Analysis

Figure 3 depicts the cumulative distribution function (CDF) for the PostgreSQL program compiled with the Clang -O2 flag. We selected this program randomly from our test programs. The CDF depicts the relation between the ratio of indirect callsites and the ratio of calltargets, for the type and the count policies. While the CDFs for the count policies have only a few changes, the amount of changes for the CDFs of the type policies is vastly higher. The reason for this is fairly straightforward: the number of buckets (*i.e.,* the number of equivalence classes) that are used to classify the callsites and calltargets is simply higher for the type policies. Finally, note that the results depend on the internal structure of the particular program and may for this reason vary for other programs.

5.6   Mitigation of Advanced CRAs

Table 5 presents several attacks that can be successfully stopped by τCFI by deploying only the forward-edge or the backward-edge policy. For checking if the COOP attack can be prevented, we instrumented the Firefox library (libxul.so), which was used to perform the original COOP attack as presented in the original paper. We observed that due to the forward-edge policy this attack was no longer possible. For testing if backward-edge attacks are possible after applying τCFI, we used several open source ROP attacks that are explicitly violating the control flow of a C++ program through backward-edge violations. Next, we instrumented the binaries of these programs. Each attack that was using one of the protected function returns was successfully stopped.

Table 5. Stopped CRAs, forward-edge policy (FP) & backward-edge policy (BP).

Exploit	Stopped	Remark
COOP ML-G [3]		
IE 32 bit	×	Out of scope
IE 1 64-bit	✓ (FP)	Arg. count mismatch
IE 2 64-bit	✓ (FP)	Arg. count mismatch
Firefox	✓ (FP)	Arg. count mismatch
COOP ML-REC [4]		
Chrome	✓ (FP)	Void target where non-void was expected
Control Jujutsu [8]		
Apache	✓ (FP)	Target function not AT
Nginx	✓ (FP)	Void target where non-void was expected
All Backward edge violating attacks	✓ (BP)	(1)[a] or (2)[b] or (3)[c]

[a] Jump to address ∉ in the $max - min$ address range.
[b] Jump to address ≠ then a legitimate address.
[c] Jump to address label ≠ the calltarget return label.

In summary, many forward-edge and backward-edge attacks can be successfully mitigated by τCFI as long as these attacks are not aware of the policy in place and thus cannot selectively use gadgets that have their start address in the allowed set for the legitimate forward-edge and backward-edge transfers, respectively.

5.7 Runtime Overhead

Figure 4 presents the runtime overhead obtained by applying τCFI's forward-edge policy (register type; parameter count) and backward-edge policy on all C/C++ programs contained in SPEC CPU2006. Out of the evaluated programs: xala- ncbmk, namd, omnetpp, dealII, astar, soplex, and

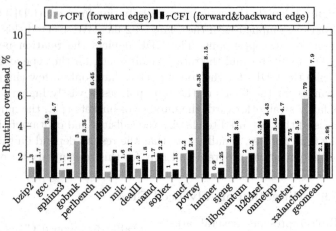

Fig. 4. Runtime overhead.

povray are C++ programs, while the rest are pure C programs. After the programs were instrumented, we measured the runtime overhead. The geomean of the instrumented programs is around 2.89% runtime overhead. One reason for the performance drop is cache misses introduced by jumping between the old and the new executable section of the binary generated by duplicating and patching. This is necessary, because when outside of the compiler, it is difficult to relocate indirect control flow. Therefore, every time an indirect control flow occurs, jumps into the old executable section and from there back to the new executable section occur. Moreover, this is also dependent on the actual structure of the target as the overhead depends on the frequency of indirect control flow operations. Another reason for the slightly higher (yet acceptable) performance overhead is our runtime policy, which is more complex than that of other state-of-the-art tools.

6 Discussion

Limitations. First, τCFI is limited by the capabilities of the DynInst instrumentation environment, where non-returning functions like exit are not detected reliably in some cases. As a result, we cannot test the Pure-FTP server, as it heavily relies on these functions. The problem is that those non-returning functions usually appear as a second branch within a function that occurs after the normal control flow, causing basic blocks from the following function to be attributed to the current function. This results in a malformed control flow graph and erroneous attribution of callsites and problematic misclassifications for both calltargets and callsites.

Second, parameter passing through floating point registers is currently not supported by τCFI, similar to other state-of-the-art tools. Tail calls are also not supported for now as they lose the one-to-one matching between callers and callees. Further, τCFI does not support self-modifying code as code pages become writable at run-time. We plan to address this limitation in future work.

Third, τCFI is not intended to be more precise than source code based tools such as IFCC/VTV [19]. However, τCFI is highly useful in situations when the source code is typically not available (*e.g.,* off-the-shelf binaries), where programs rely on third-party libraries, and where the recompilation of all shared libraries is not possible.

Finally, while a major step forward, τCFI cannot thwart all possible attacks, as even solutions with access to source code are unable to protect against all possible attacks [27]. In contrast, τCFI, our binary-based tool can stop all COOP attacks published to date and significantly raises the bar for an adversary when compared to other state-of-the-art tools. Moreover, τCFI provides a strong mitigation for other types of code-reuse attacks as well as for attacks that violate the caller-callee function calling convention.

Attacker Policy Discovery Trade-offs. In general, with usage of CFI techniques, it is relatively unchallenging for an attacker to figure out where an indirect program control flow may transfer during runtime. This is because the indirect transfer targets (backward and forward) are labeled with IDs that have to satisfy certain conditions, *e.g.,* a bitwise XOR operation between the bits of the start and target address of indirect control flow transfer should return a one or zero in case the transfer is legal or illegal, respectively.

Thus, we note that in general it is not difficult for a resourceful attacker to figure out which callees match to which calltargets or vice versa when these are labeled with IDs for example. τCFI is not exempted from this. In general, if the attacker knows where an indirect transfer is allowed to jump to, he may use this wiggle space to craft his attack with the available (reachable) gadgets. The main assumption on which CFI and τCFI are built upon is that the wiggle room is sufficiently reduced for an attacker such that the likelihood for a successful attack is greatly diminished.

7   Related Work

Mitigation of Forward-Edge Based Attacks with Binary-Based Tools. τCFI is closely related to TypeArmor w.r.t. the forward edge analysis. TypeArmor [25] ($\approx$3% runtime overhead in geomean) enforces a CFI-policy based on the parameter count policy. Compared to τCFI, TypeArmor does not use function parameter types and assumes a backward-edge protection is in place. VCI [23] and Marx [24] are both based on approximated program (quasi) class hierarchies; they (1) do not recover the root class of the hierarchy, and (2) the edges between the classes are not oriented; thus both tools enforce for each callsite the same virtual table entry (*i.e.,* index based) contained in one recovered class hierarchy represented by father-child relationships between the recovered vtables. Finally, both tools use up to six heuristics and simplifying assumptions in order to make the problem of program class hierarchy reconstruction tractable.

Compared to these tools, τCFI tries not to reconstruct a high-level metadata data structure (class hierarchy), but rather performs analysis on the usage of provided and consumed parameters at the callsites and calltargets.

Mitigation of Backward-Edge Based Attacks with Binary Based Tools. According to a comprehensive survey by Burow *et al.* [11], tools that provide backward-edge protection offer low, medium, and high levels of protection w.r.t. backward edges. Further, this survey provides runtime overhead comparisons, classifies the backward-edge protection techniques into binary-based, source code based, and other types (*e.g.,* with HW support, etc.). Due to page restriction, we review only binary tools.

The original CFI implementation of Abadi *et al.* [9], MoCFI [41], kBouncer [42], CCFIR [20], bin-CFI [43], O-CFI [44], PathArmor [45], Lock-Down [46] mostly suffer from imprecision (high number of reused labels), have low runtime efficiency, and most of them protect either forward edges or backward edges assuming a perfect shadow stack implementation is in place. In contrast, τCFI makes no assumptions on the presence of a backward-edge protection. Further, τCFI provides a technique for protecting forward edges and does not rely on a shadow stack approach for protecting backward edges.

8   Conclusion

In this paper, we have presented τCFI, a new control flow integrity (CFI) technique, which can be used to protect program control flow graph (CFG) forward edges and backward edges in executables during runtime. For the protected stripped (*i.e.,* no RTTI information) x86-64 binaries, we do not need to make any assumptions on the presence of an auxiliary technique for protecting backward edges (*i.e.,* shadow stacks, etc.) as τCFI protects these transfers, too. We have evaluated τCFI with real world open source programs and have shown that τCFI is practical and effective when protecting program binaries. Further, our evaluation reveals that τCFI can considerably reduce the forward-edge legal call-target set, provide high backward-edge precision, while maintaining low runtime overhead.

Acknowledgement. We thank the anonymous reviewers for their feedback, which helped to considerably improve the quality of this paper. Jens Grossklags' research is supported by the German Institute for Trust and Safety on the Internet (DIVSI). Gang Tan is supported by US NSF grants CCF-1723571 and CNS-1624126, the Defense Advanced Research Projects Agency (DARPA) under agreement number N6600117C4052, and Office of Naval Research (ONR) under agreement number N00014-17-1-2539. Zhiqiang Lin is partially supported by US NSF grant CNS-1812553 and CNS-1834215, AFOSR award FA9550-14-1-0119, and ONR award N00014-17-1-2995.

References

1. LLVM: Clang CFI (2017). https://goo.gl/W7aMF9

2. LLVM: Clang's SafeStack. https://clang.llvm.org/docs/SafeStack.html
3. Schuster, F., Tendyck, T., Liebchen, C., Davi, L., Sadeghi, A.R., Holz, T.: Counterfeit object-oriented programming. In: S&P (2015)
4. Crane, S., et al.: It's a TRaP: table randomization and protection against function-reuse attacks. In: CCS (2015)
5. Lettner, J., et al.: Subversive-C: abusing and protecting dynamic message dispatch. In: USENIX ATC (2016)
6. BlueLotus Team: BCTF challenge: Bypass VTable read-only checks (2015). https://goo.gl/4RYDS2
7. Lan, B., Li, Y., Sun, H., Su, C., Liu, Y., Zeng, Q.: Loop-oriented programming: a new code reuse attack to bypass modern defenses. In: IEEE Trustcom/BigDataSE/ISPA (2015)
8. Evans, I., et al.: Control Jujutsu: on the weaknesses of fine-grained control flow integrity. In: CCS (2015)
9. Abadi, M., Budiu, M., Erlingsson, Ú., Ligatti, J.: Control flow integrity. In: CCS (2005)
10. Abadi, M., Budiu, M., Erlingsson, Ú., Ligatti, J.: Control flow integrity principles, implementations, and applications. In: TISSEC (2009)
11. Burow, N.: Control-flow integrity: precision, security, and performance. CSUR **50**, 16:1–16:33 (2017)
12. Tan, G., Jaeger, T.: CFG construction soundness in control-flow integrity. In: PLAS (2017)
13. Ramalingam, G.: The undecidability of aliasing. TOPLAS **16**, 1467–1471 (1994)
14. Jang, D., Tatlock, T., Lerner, S.: SAFEDISPATCH: securing C++ virtual calls from memory corruption attacks. In: NDSS (2014)
15. Niu, B., Tan, G.: Modular control-flow integrity. In: PLDI (2014)
16. Niu, B., Tan, G.: RockJIT: securing just-in-time compilation using modular control-flow inegrity. In: CCS (2014)
17. Haller, I., Goktas, E., Athanasopoulos, E., Portokalidis, G., Bos, H.: ShrinkWrap: VTable protection without loose ends. In: ACSAC (2015)
18. Bounov, D., Gökhan K., R., Lerner, S.: Protecting C++ dynamic dispatch through VTable interleaving. In: NDSS (2016)
19. Tice, C., et al.: Enforcing forward-edge control-flow integrity in GCC and LLVM. In: USENIX Security (2014)
20. Zhang, C., et al. : Practical control flow integrity and randomization for binary executables. In: S&P (2013)
21. Prakash, A., Hu, X., Yin, H.: Strict protection for virtual function calls in COTS C++ binaries. In: NDSS (2015)
22. Zhang, C., Song, C., Zhijie, K.C., Chen, Z., Song, D.: VTint: protecting virtual function tables' integrity. In: NDSS (2015)
23. Elsabagh, M., Fleck, D., Stavrou, A.: Strict virtual call integrity checking for C ++ binaries. In: ASIACCS (2017)
24. Pawlowski, A., et al.: MARX: uncovering class hierarchies in C++ programs. In: NDSS (2017)
25. Veen, V.V.D., et al.: A tough call: mitigating advanced code-reuse attacks at the binary level. In: S&P (2016)
26. Kuznetsov, V., Szekeres, L., Payer, M., Candea, G., Sekar, R., Song, D.: Code-pointer integrity. In: OSDI (2014)
27. Carlini, N., Barresi, A., Payer, M., Wagner, D., Gross, T.: Control-flow bending: on the effectiveness of control-flow integrity. In: USENIX Security (2015)

28. Goktas, E., et al.: Bypassing Clang's SafeStack for fun and profit. In: Blackhat Europe (2016). https://goo.gl/zKMHzs
29. Dang, T., Maniatis, P., Wagner, D.: The performance cost of shadow stacks and stack canaries. In: ASIACCS (2015)
30. Bernat, A.R., Miller, B.P.: Anywhere, any-time binary instrumentation. In: PASTE (2011)
31. Andriesse, D., Chen, X., Veen, V.V.D., Slowinska, A., Bos, H.: An in-depth analysis of disassembly on full-scale x86/x64 binaries. In: USENIX Security (2016)
32. Mycroft, A.: Lecture Notes (2007). https://goo.gl/F7tUZj
33. Lin, Z., Zhang, X., Xu, D.: Automatic reverse engineering of data structures from binary execution. In: NDSS (2010)
34. Brumley, D., Jager, I., Avgerinos, T., Schwartz, E.J.: BAP: a binary analysis platform. In: Gopalakrishnan, G., Qadeer, S. (eds.) CAV 2011. LNCS, vol. 6806, pp. 463–469. Springer, Heidelberg (2011). https://doi.org/10.1007/978-3-642-22110-1_37
35. Fokin, A., Derevenets, Y., Chernov, A., Troshina, K.: SmartDec: approaching C++ decompilation. In: WCRE (2011)
36. Balakrishnan, G., Reps, T.: DIVINE: discovering variables IN executables. In: Cook, B., Podelski, A. (eds.) VMCAI 2007. LNCS, vol. 4349, pp. 1–28. Springer, Heidelberg (2007). https://doi.org/10.1007/978-3-540-69738-1_1
37. Caballero, J., Lin, Z.: Type inference on executables. CSUR **48**, 35 (2016)
38. Lee, B., Song, C., Kim, T., Lee, W.: Type casting verification: stopping an emerging attack vector. In: USENIX Security (2015)
39. Andriesse, D., Slowinska, A., Bos, H.: Compiler-agnostic function detection in binaries. In: Euro S&P (2017)
40. Bruening, D.: DynamoRIO. http://dynamorio.org/home.html
41. Davi, L., et al.: MoCFI: a framework to mitigate control-flow attacks on smartphones. In: NDSS (2012)
42. Pappas, V., Polychronakis, M., Keromytis, A.D.: Transparent ROP exploit mitigation using indirect branch tracing. In: USENIX Security (2013)
43. Zhang, M., Sekar, R.: Control flow integrity for COTS binaries. In: USENIX Security (2013)
44. Mohan, V., Larsen, P., Brunthaler, S., Hamlen, K.W., Franz, M.: Opaque control-flow integrity. In: NDSS (2015)
45. Veen, V.V.D., et al.: Practical context-sensiticve CFI. In: CCS (2015)
46. Payer, M., Barresi, A., Gross, T.R.: Fine-grained control-flow integrity through binary hardening. In: Almgren, M., Gulisano, V., Maggi, F. (eds.) DIMVA 2015. LNCS, vol. 9148, pp. 144–164. Springer, Cham (2015). https://doi.org/10.1007/978-3-319-20550-2_8

Trusted Execution Path for Protecting Java Applications Against Deserialization of Untrusted Data

Stefano Cristalli$^{(\boxtimes)}$, Edoardo Vignati , Danilo Bruschi, and Andrea Lanzi

University of Milan, Milan, Italy
{stefano.cristalli,danilo.bruschi,andrea.lanzi}@unimi.it,
edoardo.vignati@gmail.com

Abstract. Deserialization of untrusted data is an issue in many programming languages. In particular, deserialization of untrusted data in Java can lead to Remote Code Execution attacks. Conditions for this type of attack exist, but vulnerabilities are hard to detect. In this paper, we propose a novel sandboxing approach for protecting Java applications based on trusted execution path used for defining the deserialization behavior. We test our defensive mechanism on two main Java Framework JBoss and Jenkins and we show the effectiveness and efficiency of our system. We also discuss the limitations of our current system on newer attacks strategies.

Keywords: Sandbox · Anomaly detection · Java security
Software protection

1 Introduction

Deserialization of untrusted data is a cause of security problems in many programming languages [3]. For example, deserialization in Java might lead to remote code execution RCE or DoS attacks [19]. Even though it is easy to check whether preconditions for this type of attack exist in an application (that is, deserialization performed on user-controlled data), design and carry a real attack is a hard task due to the complexity of creating the attack payload. In order to exploit this type of vulnerability, an attacker should create a custom instance of a chosen serializable class which redefines the `readObject` method. The object is then serialized and send to an application which will deserialize it, causing an invocation of `readObject` and trigger the attacker's payload. Since the attacker has complete control on the deserialized data, he can choose among all the Java classes present in the target application classpath, and manually compose them by using different techniques (e.g., wrapping instances in serialized fields, using reflection), and create an execution path that forces the deserialization process towards a specific target (e.g., execution of a dangerous method with input chosen by the attacker). There are several public exploits [6] that show the impact of

© Springer Nature Switzerland AG 2018
M. Bailey et al. (Eds.): RAID 2018, LNCS 11050, pp. 445–464, 2018.
https://doi.org/10.1007/978-3-030-00470-5_21

the attack on real Java frameworks, such as JBoss and Jenkins, which are based on several common Java libraries: Oracle JRE 1.7, Apache Commons Collection 3 and 4, Apache Commons BeanUtils, Spring Beans/Core 4.x and Groovy 2.3.x.

Currently, the main defense against this issue is a whitelist/blacklist approach that allows only certain classes to be deserialized [18]. While blacklist approaches are very effective on known attacks, they cannot recognize novel exploits. Whitelists, on the other hand, suffer from one fundamental problem: the approach is based on static analysis (e.g. Look-Ahead Java Deserialization [18]) that processes the deserialization data input before the deserialization process has been executed. In such a context, static analysis fails to detect some attacks vectors when, for example, the attacker uses reflection [10] or when he is able to dynamically load classes at runtime [6]. Our method tracks dynamic of the class execution path during the deserialization events. Extracting such information from the Java execution model context is very difficult. In particular, we need to deal with several challenges due to the dynamic loading of Java classes at runtime, the JIT compilation mechanism and the native code instrumentation. Our proposed dynamic technique operates in this direction and is able to precisely reconstruct the dynamic execution path of object deserializations, and consequently mitigate the entire spectrum of the attacks based on deserialization of untrusted data.

More in detail, in this paper we propose a novel dynamic approach to protect Java applications against deserialization of untrusted data attacks. Our system is completely automatic and it is based on two phases: (1) training phase (2) detection phase. During the learning phase, the system collects important information about the behavior of benign deserialization processes and constructs the precise execution path in form of a collection of invoked Java methods (stack traces). In the second phase, the system runs a lightweight sandbox embedded inside the Java virtual machine, that acts during the deserialization process, and is able to ensure that only trusted execution paths are executed. Our tool is very flexible, and can be applied out of the box to protect any Java application. Its false positive ratio can be tuned according to the application behavior and to the desired level of protection. Our experiments, performed on two popular Java applications, JBoss and Jenkins, show the effectiveness and efficiency of our system.

To summarize, we make the following contributions:

- We design an agnostic approach to mitigate the problems of deserialization of untrusted data in the Java environment, based on the enforcement of precise execution paths. We tackle several challenges regarding the extraction of dynamic information from the Java execution model such as: JIT compilation, runtime loading of the Java classes and native code instrumentation.
- We design a lightweight sandboxing system for the Java environment that is able to limit the attacker's actions and mitigate the attacks by using information from benign stack traces. Such a sandbox is transparent to Java applications and can be tuned according to a specific desired behavior.

– We perform an experimental evaluation on two real-world Java application framework: JBoss and Jenkins, and we show that our system is able to automatically extract detailed information about object deserialization and perform a precise detection. We also analyze the limitations of our system against new types of deserialization attacks.

We present background information related to Java deserialization technologies along with our threat model in Sect. 2. In Sect. 3, we discuss the principles of our defensive mechanism. Section 4 describes the architecture and details of the system. Experimental evaluation of our tool with various Java applications is discussed in Sect. 5. Related work is presented in Sect. 6. We provide a discussion of how our current implementation can be extended to handle other sophisticated deserialization attack techniques, such as data attacks, in Sect. 7. We conclude our paper in Sect. 8.

2 Background

In this section we describe background concepts for understanding the security problems with deserialization of untrusted data in Java. In particular, we briefly describe the Java Virtual machine and the HotSpot JVM's interpreter and compiler. Then we describe the mechanisms of reflection and object deserialization in Java, and how the latter can be used to obtain malicious side effects when applied to untrusted data.

2.1 Java Virtual Machine

Java code runs on a virtual machine (the Java Virtual Machine, or JVM), which executes Java low-level instructions (bytecodes) on the host system. Several implementations for the JVM exist; in our research we focus on the HotSpot JVM, implemented by Oracle and used in both Oracle JDK and OpenJDK products. Since Java is an interpreted language, each JVM runs an interpreter, responsible for translating Java bytecodes into machine instructions for the host's architecture as programs are executed.

The *template interpreter* is the current interpreter in use in the HotSpot JVM. The HotSpot runtime generates an interpreter in memory at the virtual machine startup using the information in the TemplateTable (a structure containing *templates*, assembly code corresponding to each bytecode). The TemplateTable defines the templates and provides accessor functions to get the template for a given bytecode [14].

In order to optimize performance, the JVM can compile some of the Java bytecodes into native code. The HotSpot JVM includes two Just-In-Time (JIT) compilers, C1 and C2, responsible for code optimization at runtime. C1, the *client compiler* is optimized for compilation speed while C2, the *server compiler* is optimized for maximal performance of the generated code. The HotSpot JVM constantly analyzes the code as it runs to detect the critical parts that are executed often (called *hot spots*, from which the JVM gets its name), which are then compiled into native code [7].

2.2   Java Technologies

Java Reflection. Java allows reflection via a set of API calls. Reflective code can be used for various purposes, such as inspecting methods in classes and calling them dynamically. For example, a program could use reflection on a generic class instance i to check whether its class has a public method named doSomething, and invoke it on i in case.

Java Object Serialization. Serialization is the process of encoding objects into a stream of bytes, while deserialization is the opposite operation. In Java, serialization is used mainly for lightweight persistence, network data transfer via sockets, and Java Remote Method Invocation (Java RMI) [16]. Java deserialization is performed by the class java.io.ObjectInputStream, and in particular by its method readObject. A class is suitable for serialization/deserialization if the following requirements are satisfied [17]: (1) the class implements the interface java.io.Serializable, (2) the class has access to the no-argument constructor of its first non-serializable superclass.

A class C can specify custom behavior for deserialization by defining a private void readObject method. If present, such method is called when an object of type C is deserialized. Other methods can be defined to control deserialization:

- **writeObject** is used to specify what information is written to the output stream when an object is serialized
- **writeReplace** allows a class to nominate a replacement object to be written to the stream
- **readResolve** allows a class to designate a replacement for the object just read from the stream

As an example of custom behavior in deserialization, in Listing 1.1 we show the custom readObject method in class java.util.PriorityQueue<?>, which defines both writeObject and readObject to handle serialization/deserialization of the elements of the priority queue. We can see that queue elements are read from the ObjectInputStream one by one, by calling readObject multiple times, and then the function heapify is called at the end to organize the data in the queue internally in the heap memory.

2.3   Vulnerability Example

The code reported in Listing 1.1 does not contain evident vulnerabilities. However, there is a security problem that could potentially arise from this mechanism: function calls defined inside readObject generally operate on data read from the stream, and such data can be controlled by an attacker. In such a context, an attacker can craft nested class objects in the deserialization input stream and define a sequence of method calls that end up executing dangerous operations at the operating system level, such as filesystem activities, command

Listing 1.1. readObject in java.util.PriorityQueue

```java
private void readObject(java.io.ObjectInputStream s)
  throws java.io.IOException,
         ClassNotFoundException {
  // Read in size, and any hidden stuff
  s.defaultReadObject();

  // Read in (and discard) array length
  s.readInt();

  queue = new Object[size];

  // Read in all elements.
  for (int i = 0; i < size; i++)
    queue[i] = s.readObject();

  heapify();
}
```

execution, etc. Chains of method invocations (called "gadgets"), that lead to arbitrary command execution, have been identified in different sets of classes of various libraries [6]. In general it is hard to ensure that such gadgets do not exists in a given set of Java classes, due to the complexity in which their methods can be composed to create a valid execution.

In summary, three constraints need to be satisfied in order to obtain a successful attack on a Java application: (1) the attacker needs to define his own invocation sequence by starting from a serializable class that redefines readObject; (2) to obtain malicious behavior, the attacker has to find a path that starts from the deserialized class and reaches the invocation of one or more desired methods; (3) all the classes considered in the attack execution path must be present in the application's classpath.

To give an example of a real attack, we present some code that shows how an attacker can pilot a deserialization process and execute a dangerous native method. In Listing 1.2 we report the code for functions heapify, siftDown and siftDownUsingComparator of class java.util.PriorityQueue. In Listings 1.3 and 1.4 we show methods compare of class TransformingComparator and method transform of InvokerTransformer, from library Apache Commons Collections 4. Listing 1.5 shows an hypothetical class for wrapping a system command.

Now, let's suppose an attacker created and serialized an object as shown in Listing 1.6. When this object is deserialized, the first method invoked after reading all the data from the priority queue is heapify as defined in the source code; then siftDownUsingComparator is called (via siftDown), which uses the comparator provided by the attacker into the serialized object, in this case a TransformerComparator, for comparing the queue elements. The compare

Listing 1.2. heapify and siftDownUsingComparator in PriorityQueue

```
private void heapify() {
  for (int i = (size >>> 1) - 1; i >= 0; i--)
    siftDown(i, (E) queue[i]);
}

private void siftDown(int k, E x) {
  if (comparator != null)
    siftDownUsingComparator(k, x);
  else
    siftDownComparable(k, x);
}

private void siftDownUsingComparator(int k, E x) {
  int half = size >>> 1;
  while (k < half) {
    int child = (k << 1) + 1;
    Object c = queue[child];
    int right = child + 1;
    if (right < size && comparator.compare((E) c, (E) queue[right]) > 0)
    c = queue[child = right];
    if (comparator.compare(x, (E) c) <= 0)
    break;
    queue[k] = c;
    k = child;
  }
  queue[k] = x;
}
```

Listing 1.3. TransformingComparator.compare

```
public int compare(final I obj1, final I obj2) { final O value1 =
  this.transformer.transform(obj1); final O value2 =
  this.transformer.transform(obj2); return
  this.decorated.compare(value1, value2); }
```

Listing 1.4. InvokerTransformer.transform

```
public O transform(final Object input) {
  if (input == null) return null;
  try {
  final Class<?> cls = input.getClass();
  final Method method = cls.getMethod(iMethodName, iParamTypes);
  return (O) method.invoke(input, iArgs);
  ...
}
```

Listing 1.5. Command class

```
public class Command implements Serializable {
  private String command;

  public Command(String command) {
    this.command = command;
  }

  public void execute() throws IOException {
    Runtime.getRuntime().exec(command);
  }
}
```

Listing 1.6. Sample payload

```
final InvokerTransformer transformer =
  new InvokerTransformer("execute", new Class[0], new Object[0]);

final PriorityQueue<Object> queue =
  new PriorityQueue<Object>(2, new TransformingComparator(transformer));

queue.add(1);
queue.add(new Command("rm -f importantFile"));
```

function in `TransformerComparator` uses the field `transformer`, provided by the attacker, and calls its `transform` function on the objects being compared. `InvokerTransformer` uses reflection to call the method with name equal to its field `iMethodName` on input. The reflection in this case helps the attacker to invoke methods of generic classes; by crafting the deserialization input, the attacker is able to invoke method `execute` on an instance of the `Command` class with controlled parameters and execute arbitrary commands. In Listing 1.7 we report the stack trace collected at the execution of `Runtime.exec`, which contains all the Java methods invoked during the malicious deserialization event.

Listing 1.7. Stack trace of sample attack payload

```
Runtime.exec
Command.execute
Method.invoke
InvokerTransformer.transform
TransformingComparator.compare
PriorityQueue.siftDownUsingComparator
PriorityQueue.heapify
PriorityQueue.readObject
```

The attack vector described in this section is based on payload "Common-sCollections2" from the ysoserial repository, used in real attacks. The main difference with the original version is that no class like `Command`, which was introduced for the sake of simplicity, is generally available in the classpath. The real attack vector uses a specific gadget that leverages dynamic class loading to pass from reflective method `invoke` to an execution of `Runtime.exec` with controlled input.

2.4   Threat Model

Our threat model considers an attacker who is able to exploit (either locally or remotely) an object deserialization on untrusted and user-controlled data inside a Java application running on the machine, and execute arbitrary method calls on classes present in the Java classpath. The attacker has full control on serialized data, as well as complete knowledge on the classes defined in the application classpath and their source code. We assume that the machine is uncompromised when our defensive mechanism is loaded. Thus, we consider the protection of already infected systems to be out of the scope of this paper. We consider the Java Virtual Machine execution environment trusted and we assume that the attacker cannot compromise it by exploiting vulnerabilities such as memory errors.

3   Overview

We now briefly describe a high-level overview of our approach. For the defensive approach designed in this paper we design an application centric model based on stack trace objects. More precisely, the stack trace structure is defined as a sequence (stack) of n objects, each of them is represented by one of the Java methods invoked during the deserialization process. The first element (entry point of the stack trace), is the first class that invokes the `readObject` method, while the last (exit point) consists of a native method call. It is important to note that one stack trace is always associated with only one native method invocation, and vice versa. In our detection model, we consider only stack trace associated with native methods that interacts with the operating system (e.g., process, filesystem and network activities). By defining which stack trace a particular deserialization event can invoke, it is possible to restrict the attack surface, mitigating the attack itself. The information about which stack trace can be invoked will be part of the sandbox policy, along with other information (e.g., native call) that is used to determine the behavior of the deserialization process.

In order to define the legitimate deserialization behavior in terms of execution path, we need to dynamically collect the stack trace for a monitored application by providing the appropriate input set to stimulate the deserialization process. During this phase, called constructing phase, the system collects the entire observed benign stack trace related to deserialization events. This task is performed by dynamically monitoring a Java application at the interpreter/compiler level in the

JVM. Extracting such dynamic information and constructing the execution path is a complex task due to the nature of the Java execution model, which includes JIT compiled code, class loading at runtime (e.g., Sect. 4). Static analysis cannot be used in such a context since the complete execution sequence of the Java methods is only known at runtime. Moreover such execution model is exacerbated by the use of Java reflection, which complicates static analysis itself. For example, a single dynamic method invocation that uses reflection could in principle invoke any method in the currently loaded classes, resulting in an over-approximate call graph and consequently enlarging the attack surface [10].

Once the system has established the benign stack traces, our framework can enter in the running phase, where it performs the detection task. At the starting point, our system loads a specific set of policies for each application derived from the constructing phase. Each set of policies is characterized by three elements derived from the stack trace collection: (1) entry Java class point, (2) invocation sequence of Java methods, (3) invocation of native method. The first element is the entry point that represents the Java class that is deserialized. All the deserialization operations for a specific application must start from a Java class observed during the training phase, any other invocation of readObject from any other class is blocked. The second element is the order of the sequence of method invocations. Such a sequence has been observed during the constructing phase and it must match the actual sequence at runtime, any deviation from its order will stop the deserialization process. The third element is the native call associated with the specific stack trace. Such native call will be checked by our framework, and any invoked native method that is not defined into the permitted set will trigger an alarm, causing the deserialization process to be terminated.

Although based on fine-grained policies, our approach is very flexible. In fact, our system can be tuned based on the level of information granularity that we want to use for detecting the attack. More specifically, we can configure the length of the extracted stack traces, and restrict or enlarge the attack surface. Acting on a subset of the entire stack traces sequence has a considerable advantage: by not checking all the sequence of the Java methods, the system can lower the false positives while maintaining a good precision in detecting the attacks as showed in the evaluation Section.

4   System Design and Implementation

In this section we present the implementation details of our protection system. We describe the architectural overview and the challenges that we faced for dynamically tracing Java applications execution path.

4.1   Architectural Overview

The principles provided in the previous section show how our approach can be used for extracting stack trace related to a deserialization event. There are two main requirements that need to be satisfied for our detection system: (R1) for any stimulated event, the system needs to be able to precisely monitor the execution path of the deserialization process, so that no relevant execution is missed; (R2) the monitor component should not cause a high overhead. From an architectural point of view our system is split into two main high-level components: (1) a component, that is in charge of dynamically analyzing Java applications and extracting the precise execution path in terms of stack traces, and (2) a lightweight sandbox component that monitors applications at runtime and blocks incoming attacks, based on the rules derived by the constructing phase.

More in particular, in the constructing phase, our system intercepts all the native methods invoked by the application; for each invocation, it inspects the corresponding stack trace backwards, until it reaches the deserialization entry point (i.e., a call to readObject), and then it extracts the execution path. In case the readObject is not found on the stack we assume that the native call is invoked in a different context than deserialization one and the system discards the results. It is important to note that the presence of the invocation of readObject method on the stack cannot be tampered by an attacker since deserialization of untrusted data attack does not allow to directly write on the stack. This information is then saved into a persistent storage called sandbox policy, which will constitute the baseline for detecting malicious behavior.

Afterwards during the detection phase, when user input triggers deserialization event, the system performs only one check according to the sandbox policy: when a native method is invoked by the application, the system intercepts it and checks whether the entire stack trace executed has been already observed in the learning phase. For this check the system maintains a memory structure in the form of a hash table that contains only the execution paths that are allowed for the applications. The keys of the hash table are strings composed by the methods signatures present in each benign stack trace. Since a sequence of method signatures uniquely identifies a specific stack trace (by definition), the risk of collisions is very low, and the access to the hash table in terms of computation time is constant on average.

4.2   Building Trusted Execution Path

Both learning and protection modules, are composed by a tracing execution path component that is the core of our detection system and is in charge to efficiently and correctly intercept (requirements R1 and R2) any native method call of any Java application that is running on the system. To achieve this goal, the system needs to be able to intercept any Java method invoked after a deserialization takes place in an application. In particular, we are interested in intercepting all the execution path in form of stack trace in the following form, for every deserialized class A and every corresponding native method call X:

```
A.readObject()
method1()
method12()
...
native call X
```

In order to extract the stack traces we first need to intercept the native methods and then parse the JVM stack memory structure to collect the invoked Java methods. To this end we analyzed several approaches for our design. We first considered dynamic bytecode instrumentation, but we found it unsuitable for our purpose since native methods cannot be simply instrumented, as they do not have bytecode. In order to overcome this problem we first need to create a wrapper for each target native method, and then redirect to it all the calls inside Java code that point to that native method. Although there exists a mechanism to perform this operations [15], it would work only for classes that have not already been loaded, since the JVM does not allow insertion of extra methods to a class that is already loaded. As we would need to dynamically add methods (the wrappers) to all the classes, including ones that have already been loaded when instrumentation starts, this technique does not serve our goal.

Another idea could be to instrument every possible method in every loaded class, and check every **invoke** bytecode instruction to see whether it points to a native method. This approach fails as well, because at the time of instrumentation it is not known whether the resolved method will be native or not. Finally, trivial logging of all the method calls after **readObject** via bytecode tracing/instrumentation would be too expensive in terms of performance (R2) and the system would not scale.

After these considerations, we decided to directly modify the Java Virtual Machine to accomplish this task. Our implementation for tracing Java class methods consists of a modification to the template interpreter generator. Specifically, we modify the generation of native method entries by adding a call to our custom logging functions inside the VM runtime environment. With this approach we have two advantages:

- The system does not need to know which classes are going to be loaded, nor we have to instrument each one of them. Moreover, by running inside the JVM, our component can inspect every call to native methods, on any class (R1).
- Effectively extract only the information of our interest, focusing on native methods and their ancestor **readObject**. This gives a significant advantage in terms of performance (R2) compared to the naive solution of forward method logging starting from **readObject** calls.

We found that instrumentation of the interpreter alone was not enough to achieve the entire coverage of all the native calls. The JIT compiler constantly looks for code optimization, and our modification to the interpreter has no effect on JIT-compiled code. Since we cannot make assumptions of how much code will be compiled on the analyzed systems, and since we want to get an accurate view of all native calls, we also instrumented the generation of wrappers for native methods defined in the JIT compiler framework. By adding our custom log logic to each of these wrappers, we are able to check the stack trace every time a native call is made. In order to test the correctness of our approach, we ran Java in fully compiled mode (with option **-Xcomp**), and in fully interpreted mode (with option -Xint). We found that the interpreter component does not log any JIT compiled method, and vice versa.

4.3 Input Stimulation

In order to stimulate the deserialization process, we perform a static analysis on the Java code, searching for classes that implement the `Serializable` interface and define the `readObject` entry point. Starting from such classes we perform a manual analysis and figure out the inputs that can stimulate object deserializations. We also collect a set of inputs from the normal use of the analyzed Java frameworks, logging every object deserialization we observe. It is important to note that input stimulation is not a contribution of this paper, our system is designed to improve the whitelist mechanism in two directions: (1) providing a better detection model (precise execution path) in terms of detection so overcoming the static analysis limitations that effects actual whitelist methods, (2) and create an automatic extractor system that can operate at runtime with low overhead and it is able to reconstruct and detect a precise execution path. An automatic system for improving input stimulation is discussed in the Discussion section.

5   Experimental Evaluation

In order to evaluate our approach we analyzed two real-world Java frameworks, JBoss and Jenkins, broadly used in several companies and IT infrastructures. We also chose these frameworks since there are real attack samples available for them [6]. For each application we derive a metric that is able to show the reduction of the attack surface considering our approach. The metric, Java Class Invocation Attack Surface (JCAS), compares the number of Java classes observed during the training phase in the deserialization context with the number of potentially available classes in the monitored application's classpath. In this context, a class is *observed* in the training phase if at least one of its methods appears in at least one collected benign stack trace. Given the percentage p of the classes that were observed during monitoring, compared to all the classes in the classpath, the JCAS metric is expressed as the percentage $100\% - p$. Such a metric is able to capture the attack surface reduction since it shows how our detection model is able to restrict the set of actions of an attacker. In fact, with our detection system in place, the attacker needs to follow the execution path of the benign deserialized data and he cannot choose the gadgets (e.g. Java classes) among the entire classpath of the Java vulnerable application. Our metric exactly shows this reduction.

We also computed the overhead for each application considered in our experiments. All tests were performed using a custom build of OpenJDK 8 with our system enabled, and a clean OpenJDK 8 build as a baseline for comparison in overhead. The tests were run on a quad-core, Intel Xeon machine with 8 GB of RAM running Ubuntu 16.04 LTS.

5.1   JBoss Application Server

JBoss is an open-source Java application server, broadly used in industry. We tested JBoss 5.1.0 with our framework. We collected the benign stack traces related to native method invocations in deserializations that occur during normal operations. In particular, we stimulated the following operations: (1) server start and shutdown, (2) application deploy/undeploy, and (3) use of management consoles and deployed applications. We also trained our system on JBoss for a period of one week. During this period, several operations were stimulated by a group of users that produced hundreds of deserialization events. We collected a total of 13298 stack traces from native calls made by deserializations. We analyzed the classes necessary for computing our metric, in particular we found a total of 43250 Java classes in the JAR files present in JBoss' classpath, plus a total of 6005 present in the Java standard libraries, for a sum of roughly 49000 Java classes. The total methods called during deserialization lead to a total of 329 observed Java classes.

In Table 1 we can see the data and computed JCAS metric for JBoss, showing the reduction of the attack surface; we see that by applying our model, the attack surface is reduced by 99.2% considering the benign deserializations observed during the learning phase.

5.2   Jenkins

Jenkins is an open source automation server for tasks related to software building and continuous integration. It allows the creation of customizable and schedulable jobs for building artifacts and performing related operations. We tested Jenkins version 1.649. We collected the benign stack traces related to native method invocations in deserializations that occur during normal operations. In particular, we stimulated the following operations: (1) server start and shutdown, (2) job creation and customization, and (3) job scheduling and running. Also for Jenkins we trained our system for a period of one week, asking a group of user to access it and use it via web. As a result of our entire test, we collected a total of 6526 stack traces from native calls made by object deserializations. We analyzed the classes necessary for our metric: we found a total of 23493 classes in the JAR file present in Jenkins' classpath, plus a total of 6005 present in the Java standard libraries, for a sum of roughly 30000 classes. All the methods observed during deserialization came just from 74 classes. In Table 1 we can see the data and computed JCAS metric for JBoss, showing the reduction of the attack surface; we see that by applying our model the attack surface is reduced by 99.8% considering the benign deserializations observed during the learning phase.

5.3   Effectiveness

For each application we tested the effectiveness of our approach by running the real-world attack payloads provided in the ysoserial repository [6]. In particular,

Table 1. Attack Surface Reduction

Application	JCAS	Native method calls	Total classes in stack traces
JBoss	99.2%	13298	329
Jenkins	99.8%	6526	74

we ran payload CommonsCollections1 that uses reflection and runtime-loading Java class mechanisms against JBoss, and validated its vulnerability leading to arbitrary code execution with our system disabled; we also ran payload CommonsCollections5 against Jenkins, with the same result. Afterwards, we applied our protection by running the applications within our defensive framework. We found that our system can effectively block such attacks on both applications, after an appropriate learning phase. Both applications were then tested over a period of one week with our protection enabled, by exposing them via web to a group of users. Normal operations (including, but not limited to the ones listed above for each program) were triggered in both applications, leading to hundreds of deserialization events. No false positives were found by our system, even when enforcing the execution of all the methods in learned stack traces for an observed deserialized class.

5.4   Overhead

In this section we analyze the overhead introduced by our system. We performed a micro-benchmark and a macro-benchmark to evaluate the sandbox efficiency. The micro-benchmark focuses on local sandbox performance; we measure the time taken by our checks on the stack traces to validate native method calls. The macro-benchmark measures the overhead introduced in whole applications from the user's perspective.

Table 2. Micro-benchmark results.

Sandbox component	Mean	Standard deviation
Interpreter	2.071×10^{-5} s	6.640×10^{-5} s
Compiler	2.883×10^{-5} s	6.613×10^{-6} s

Micro-benchmark. For our micro-benchmark, we measured the time required for our checks made at each native call to analyze the stack trace, reconstruct the sequence of calls made from the `readObject` call onwards and compare it to the policy learned in the training phase; Table 2 shows the results. The test has been conducted on a number of 10000 native call traces, on which average and standard deviation were calculated. We differentiated the checks for the compiler component and the interpreter component; we can see that the time required for checking is consistent for both, and relatively small. The overhead of the system is the result of the linear composition of the time taken for the checks, triggered at each native method call.

Table 3. Macro-benchmark results for JBoss

JBoss operation	Baseline JDK	Modified JDK	Overhead
Startup time	21.0 s	29.5 s	40.5%
Console login	2.0 s	2.1 s	5.0%
Flush connections in datasource pool	1.5 s	1.9 s	26.7%
Sample WAR deployment	2.9 s	3.5 s	20.7%

Table 4. Macro-benchmark results for Jenkins

Jenkins operation	Baseline JDK	Modified JDK	Overhead
Startup time	9.0 s	10.5 s	16.7%
Homepage loading	1.8 s	2.3 s	27.8%
Login	2.0 s	2.5 s	25.0%
Job saving after creation	2.3 s	2.6 s	13.0%

Macro-benchmark. For the macro-benchmark, we computed the time for several common operations performed by end users in our test applications. Given the huge number of native calls performed during the process, and the determinism of the executed operations, this constitutes a reliable measurement for the total overhead. The values were computed both programmatically and manually (by triggering specific operations), and averaged over 10 measurements. Initially, we observed a massive overhead of over 900% for the whole startup process on JBoss. This inefficiency was due to the very high number of instrumented native calls, some of which were invoked hundreds of thousands of times in our measured runs, causing delays of several seconds with the sum of their individual analyses, as explained in the discussion on the micro-benchmark. After manually analyzing the most frequent native method calls, we established that we could exclude most of them without any security concerns, as their interaction with the OS is limited and does not constitute a threat, regardless of their input. For example, native methods `System.currentTimeMillis` and `Class.isArray` were excluded. With this tuning in place, we were able to substantially reduce the overhead introduced. Tables 3 and 4 show the result. While the overhead is still relevant in percentage, it is worth noting that our tuning of logged native calls can still be improved, and further drops of the overhead are expected; a minimum overhead would be reached if the set of analyzed native calls contained all and only the potentially dangerous invocation.

Possible Improvements and Current Impact. An additional reduction on the overhead could be made by improving the checks on native method calls. Currently, for each call we have to traverse its stack trace at least once to determine whether the call occurred during an object deserialization. Lighter checks could be designed so that the stack trace would not have to be traversed outside of deserializations, reducing the times measured in the micro-benchmark. Another idea would be to completely disable the checks on native method calls outside of the context of deserializations, bringing the overhead close to 0% for most of the executed code. In our implementation, this would require a dynamic patch to the templates produced by the JIT compiler, which would have to be done at the beginning and the end of each `readObject` call. This investigation will be part of our future research.

An important point to consider is that currently, even without these additional improvements, the net increase in the measured operations in terms of seconds is not perceived by the end user, given the relatively small absolute values of delays in the context of web applications. We can conclude that our system shows good performance from an end user's perspective, who does not perceive any substantial delay experience when they have used the protected applications.

6   Related Work

A solution to address deserialization attacks could be avoid deserialization on untrusted content, by signing serialized data and checking its signature upon deserialization. While this works perfectly in theory, in practice one cannot exclude the risk of signature counterfeiting if some bug is exploited on the signing side and an attacker gets access to the keys [9], nullifying the whole protection offered by this approach. Moreover in order to authenticate all data we need to set up a PKI infrastructure and usually such structures do not scale since they need a complex management setting. One possibility when trying to directly tackle the problem of deserialization of untrusted data is to consider a restriction of the attack surface by hardening the main deserialization entry point: the class `java.io.ObjectInputStream`. An approach to perform this type of hardening is the use of modified version of ObjectInputStream [18]. This can be done by extending the class and overriding its method, such as the `resolveClass` method, to insert security checks and perform validation before deserializing data. A Look Ahead Object Input Stream (LAOIS) [18] is an input stream relying on this logic, "looking ahead" to check whether the data presents some problem before actually deserializing it. Such method is based on static analysis that failed when applied to some classes that resolve their methods or addresses at runtime. With the reflection technique a single dynamic method could call any method in the currently loaded application, resulting in a highly inaccurate call graph for the entire application. When subclassing is not an option (for example when the code to protect is owned by a third party), it is possible to use other solutions to modify the behavior of ObjectInputStream globally, such as the use of a Java Agent for dynamic instrumentation of the classes.

The closest work to ours in terms of methodology is [5]. In this paper the authors characterize the application behavior based on the information retrieved on the stack, function name, parameters etc. However our system is different from this work in several ways: (1) first of all the attacks context is different: we operate on different programming language and data information, they mainly work on system calls invoked from C language, (2) our interception method is based on JVM internals, instead they intercept system calls at the operating system level. (3) The type of the attack is completely different: they are focusing on memory errors while we are focusing on deserialization of untrusted data attacks.

The use of sandboxes for protecting environments in which executed operations can be controlled and blocked is not new. In fact software compartmentalization has been proposed in several context and it is based on hardware and language-based techniques [2,4]. Karger proposed that fine-grained access control could mitigate malware [8]. Process-based privilege separation using Memory Management Units (MMUs) has been applied to several different applications: OpenSSH, Chromium and in Capsicum although with substantial performance overheads and program complexity. More recently, hardware primitives such as Mondriaan [22], CHERI [21], and CODOMs [20] have extended conventional MMUs to improve compartmentalization performance and programmability. Java sandboxing develops a mature and complex policy mechanism on top of language, but leaves open the possibility of misbehaving native code. Language-based capability systems, such as Joe-E [12] and Caja [13], allow safe compartmentalization in managed languages such as Java but likewise do not extend to native code. In our work we design a sandbox system that is able to intercept native methods by modifying the JVM internals. As we already showed in the paper we have tackled several design and implementation challenges in order to make our system handle the tracing of Java applications starting from the native calls.

7 Discussion

In this section we present limitations of our approach, and possible future improvements of our system.

7.1 Data Attacks

We now describe an hypothetical attack that bases its effectiveness on manipulation of the data inside the JVM's memory, as opposed to direct execution of arbitrary code. Such attacks are already present in the memory errors area [1]. Suppose that the gadget explained in Sect. 2.3 was not used to reach an endpoint for instantaneous remote command execution (or other malicious effect), but was instead targeted to invoke some method or change some fields in a class (possibly via reflection), that could later be triggered, changing the normal control flow of the application and causing the malicious effect to be activated.

Listing 1.8. Data attack entry point

```
public class Commands {
  private static lstCommandString = "ls -al";
  public static lstCommand() {
    Runtime.getRuntime().exec(lstCommandString);
  }
}
```

Listing 1.8 shows a naive example of this possibility: if the class was in the classpath and if the attacker was able to modify field lstCommandString with a gadget, class Commands would be compromised and later use could lead to remote command execution. By design, the analysis performed by our system is limited to the temporal frame of `readObject` calls; moreover it focuses on native method calls to build a recognition model for attacks. The example just presented makes it clear that with our current approach we cannot block this type of attack, due to these limitations. In order to overcome the threat posed by data attacks, our system would also have to instrument the access to data and either allow or deny it based on predefined policies; an example of policy could be to deny all write operation on sensitive data during object deserializations.

7.2   Native Call Restrictions

Another limitation of our approach is evident when considering classes that by design eventually invoke one or more potentially dangerous native calls when deserialized. Our system, as currently designed, would learn that such calls are normal benign behavior during the learning phase (provided the class is appropriately stimulated); if the execution of such calls included user controlled data (e.g. if one of the native calls used a field of the class as input), an attacker would be able to obtain malicious behavior slipping under our radar, with relatively little effort (a gadget exploiting a vulnerability of this type could be as simple as a serialized object with a particular value for a String field). One possible solution for this would be to make our model more fine-grained in the future, making it able to take into account not only native method calls and their stack trace, but also their parameters. An appropriate learning strategy would then need to be developed, to learn what constitutes benign input.

7.3   Improving Learning

The precision of our model is limited by the coverage obtained in the application during the learning phase. If learning is performed manually, even with prolonged use by experienced users that voluntarily explore the application and trigger benign deserialization behavior it is easy to argue that some possible attack entry points could never be observed, if the application is sufficiently complex. Moreover, the learning process is hard to engineer, and we cannot offer generic guidelines on how to perform it for any application. For this reason, in the future our system could benefit from a component for automated learning. This component would analyze source code (or bytecode) in applications to automatically detect where possible entry points for deserialization are located. Via static code analysis techniques, it would be possible to try and trace the execution paths that lead to such entry points, of course after facing challenges and limitations for static Java code analysis [11]. Combined with dynamic program analysis, we could measure the coverage of the deserializations found, and (1) try to generate benign variations of input to further stimulate the program automatically; we could also (2) detect if an entry point was not stimulated at all, producing a report advising users to test it.

8 Conclusion

In this paper, we propose a novel approach for protecting Java applications from deserialization of untrusted data attacks by constructing precise execution path. We have shown the principles of our design and the challenges that we tackle in order to develop our defensive framework against deserialization of untrusted data attacks. We have implemented a prototype for the Java virtual machine and by using this tool we have experimentally shown that our defensive mechanism is able to stop real-attack with affordable overhead. Finally we have provided insight into strengths and weaknesses of our tool and possible ways to defeat it.

References

1. Chen, S., Xu, J., Sezer, E.C., Gauriar, P., Iyer, R.K.: Non-control-data attacks are realistic threats. In: USENIX Security Symposium, vol. 14 (2005)
2. Cristalli, S., Pagnozzi, M., Graziano, M., Lanzi, A., Balzarotti, D.: Micro-virtualization memory tracing to detect and prevent spraying attacks. In: Proceedings of the 25th USENIX Security Symposium (USENIX Security) (2016)
3. Dahse, J., Krein, N., Holz, T.: Code reuse attacks in php: automated pop chain generation. In: Proceedings of the 2014 ACM SIGSAC Conference on Computer and Communications Security, pp. 42–53. ACM (2014)
4. Fattori, A., Lanzi, A., Balzarotti, D., Kirda, E.: Hypervisor-based malware protection with accessminer. Comput. Secur. **52**, 33–50 (2015). https://doi.org/10.1016/j.cose.2015.03.007
5. Feng, H.H., Kolesnikov, O.M., Fogla, P., Lee, W., Gong, W.: Anomaly detection using call stack information. In: Proceedings of 2003 Symposium on Security and Privacy, pp. 62–75. IEEE (2003)
6. Frohoff, C.: ysoserial repository (2015). https://github.com/frohoff/ysoserial
7. Gotz Lindenmeier, V.S.: Hotspot internals: Explore and debug the VM at the OS level. In: JavaOne Conference (2013)
8. Karger, P.A.: Limiting the damage potential of discretionary trojan horses. In: 1987 IEEE Symposium on Security and Privacy, p. 32. IEEE (1987)
9. Kim, D., Kwon, B.J., Dumitras, T.: Certified malware: measuring breaches of trust in the windows code-signing PKI. In: Proceedings of the 2017 ACM SIGSAC Conference on Computer and Communications Security, vol. 14 (2017)

10. Landman, D., Serebrenik, A., Vinju, J.J.: Challenges for static analysis of java reflection: literature review and empirical study. In: Proceedings of the 39th International Conference on Software Engineering. IEEE Press (2017)

11. Livshits, V.B., Lam, M.S.: Finding security vulnerabilities in java applications with static analysis. In: USENIX Security Symposium, vol. 14, p. 18 (2005)

12. Mettler, A., Wagner, D., Close, T.: Joe-E: a security-oriented subset of java. In: NDSS, vol. 10, pp. 357–374 (2010)

13. Miller, M.S., Samuel, M., Laurie, B., Awad, I., Stay, M.: Safe active content in sanitized javascript. Google Inc., Technical report (2008)

14. Oracle Corporation: Hotspot runtime overview (2017). http://openjdk.java.net/groups/hotspot/docs/RuntimeOverview.html

15. Oracle Corporation: Interface instrumentation (2017). https://docs.oracle.com/javase/8/docs/api/java/lang/instrument/Instrumentation.html#setNativeMethodPrefix-java.lang.instrument.ClassFileTransformer-java.lang.String-

16. Oracle Corporation: Java object serialization (2017). https://docs.oracle.com/javase/8/docs/technotes/guides/serialization/

17. Oracle Corporation: The serializable interface (2017). https://docs.oracle.com/javase/8/docs/platform/serialization/spec/serial-arch.html#a4539

18. Seacord, R.C.: Combating java deserialization vulnerabilities with look-ahead object input streams (laois) (2017)

19. Svoboda, D.: Exploiting java deserialization for fun and profit (2016)

20. Vilanova, L., Ben-Yehuda, M., Navarro, N., Etsion, Y., Valero, M.: Codoms: protecting software with code-centric memory domains. In: ACM SIGARCH Computer Architecture News, vol. 42, pp. 469–480. IEEE Press (2014)

21. Watson, R.N., et al.: Cheri: a hybrid capability-system architecture for scalable software compartmentalization. In: 2015 IEEE Symposium on Security and Privacy (SP), pp. 20–37. IEEE (2015)

22. Witchel, E., Rhee, J., Asanović, K.: Mondrix: memory isolation for linux using mondriaan memory protection. In: ACM SIGOPS Operating Systems Review, vol. 39, pp. 31–44. ACM (2005)

Malware

Error-Sensor: Mining Information from HTTP Error Traffic for Malware Intelligence

Jialong Zhang[1], Jiyong Jang[1(✉)], Guofei Gu[2], Marc Ph. Stoecklin[1],
and Xin Hu[3]

[1] IBM Research, Yorktown Heights, USA
jialong.zhang@ibm.com, {jjang,mpstoeck}@us.ibm.com
[2] Texas A&M University, College Station, USA
guofei@cse.tamu.edu
[3] Pinterest, San Francisco, USA
huxinsmail@gmail.com

Abstract. Malware often encounters network failures when it launches malicious activities, such as connecting to compromised servers that have been already taken down, connecting to malicious servers that are blocked based on access control policies in enterprise networks, or scanning/exploiting vulnerable web pages. To overcome such failures and improve the resilience in light of such failures, malware authors have employed various strategies, e.g., connecting to multiple backup servers or connecting to benign servers for initial network connectivity checks. These network failures and recovery strategies lead to distinguishing traits, which are newly discovered and thoroughly studied in this paper. We note that network failures caused by malware are quite different from the failures caused by benign users/software in terms of their failure patterns and recovery behavior patterns.

In this paper, we present the results of the first large-scale measurement study investigating the different network behaviors of both benign user/software and malware in light of HTTP errors. By inspecting over 1 million HTTP logs generated by over 16,000 clients, we identify strong indicators of malicious activities derived from *error provenance patterns*, *error generation patterns*, and *error recovery patterns*. Based on the insights, we design a new system, ERROR-SENSOR, to automatically detect traffic caused by malware from only HTTP errors and their surrounding successful requests. We evaluate ERROR-SENSOR on a large scale of real-world web traces collected in an enterprise network. ERROR-SENSOR achieves a detection rate of 99.79% at a false positive rate of 0.005% to identify HTTP errors generated by malware, and further, spots surreptitious malicious traffic (e.g., malware backup behavior) that was not caught by existing deployed intrusion detection systems.

© Springer Nature Switzerland AG 2018
M. Bailey et al. (Eds.): RAID 2018, LNCS 11050, pp. 467–489, 2018.
https://doi.org/10.1007/978-3-030-00470-5_22

1 Introduction

Malicious servers, such as command and control (C&C) servers, exploit servers and drop-zone servers, have become an essential part of recent cyber crimes. Most miscreants today rely on the malicious servers to control and monetize their malicious software (malware). However, cyber criminal structures suffer from a single-point-of-failure problem when the malicious servers are discovered and blocked by defenders. To overcome such failures, cyber criminals have developed a variety of techniques to evade possible detection and launch more stealthy malicious activities. For example, a fast-flux service [30] allows cyber criminals to quickly change the IP addresses of malicious domains to avoid IP-based access controls. A domain generation algorithm (DGA) [1,33] allows cyber criminals to dynamically generate domain names to bypass domain-based blocking. Cyber criminals also compromise a large number of legitimate web servers as "stepping stones" or "redirectors" to keep their malicious activities surreptitious.

To defend against the sophisticated cybercrime systems, most, if not all organizations have already deployed a variety of security products to detect and block the malicious servers. Blacklists and intrusion detection systems (IDSes) are widely deployed in most companies. Several modern domain reputation systems [10,14] are also designed to search for the evidence of malicious activities observed at the domain names. The competition of such sophisticated evasion techniques deployed by cyber criminals and advanced detection systems deployed by companies results in two kinds of server connectivity failures in an enterprise network: DNS failures and HTTP errors. DNS failures occur when malware tries to connect to non-existing domains, and have been widely studied by researchers for malware detection [21,41], especially for DGA-based malware [12].

In this paper, we focus on *HTTP errors* which have been less investigated in previous work. We refer HTTP errors as HTTP connection failures whose response status codes are larger than 400, as defined by the HTTP standard [2]. HTTP errors often occur when malware connects to compromised servers that have been cleared by administrators (e.g., resulting in HTTP 404 Not Found error), or to malicious servers that are blocked by an IDS or a web proxy (e.g., resulting in HTTP 403 Forbidden error) based on the policy violation.

During our investigation, we note that HTTP errors provide several new insights. First, malware often generates HTTP errors in the course of malicious activities. Most of the errors are caused by connecting to benign servers with bad parameters, connecting to compromised servers that have already been cleaned, or scanning vulnerable webpages that have been removed/protected. HTTP errors are also commonly generated because of the traffic blocks by the enterprise/ISP web proxy/gateway for policy violation or malware infection (e.g., 403 errors). Second, inspecting HTTP errors helps find out malware intelligence. When malware faces HTTP errors, it may start "recovery" behaviors to maintain the functionality of malicious infrastructures, and to ensure the reachability to the malicious infrastructure, such as connecting to some benign servers for network connectivity testing or connecting to other alternative malicious servers. Such recovery behaviors may not be easily characterized by existing IDSes, and malware bypasses security products to successfully connect to their backup malicious servers. In our experiments, we found that an IDS only detected limited parts of backup servers. Third, HTTP error-based detection is complementary to DNS failure-based detection. All the traffic related to HTTP errors have successful DNS resolution, therefore DNS failure-based detection becomes less effective. Fourth, compared to existing work [27,40] which requires the entire enterprise network traffic as an input, inspecting HTTP errors dramatically reduces the amount of traffic to be analyzed (e.g., reducing 96.8% of traffic in the real enterprise network in our experiment). Fifth, different from other existing work that relies on malicious server reputation [14] and client side behavior patterns [18], focusing on the characteristics of HTTP errors detects malware-generated traffic, including both malicious and compromised servers, without requiring multiple infections, server reputation information, or infection/URL signatures.

It is not trivial to distinguish benign traffic and malicious traffic simply based on the HTTP errors because the act of generating HTTP errors itself is not a sign of inherently malware infection. However, since cyber criminals would prepare for network failures in their malware for resilient malicious operations, there exist different error generation patterns (e.g., frequencies, sequences, and statistics) between the errors generated by malware and the errors generated by benign users/software. In addition, to conquer such possible failures, malware often employs "recovery" mechanisms when facing network failures while benign users/software may have less or no pre-arranged recovery routines. Therefore, in this paper, through examining over 1 million HTTP errors from a large enterprise network, we derive new insights to detect malicious traffic, and design a lightweight yet effective detection system, ERROR-SENSOR.

In summary, our work makes the following contributions:

- We conduct the first large-scale measurement study on 1 million HTTP errors collected in an enterprise network, and identify strong indicators of malicious activities derived from *error provenance patterns*, *error generation patterns*, and *error recovery patterns*.
- We design malware traffic detection from a new perspectives, i.e., HTTP error generating patterns and malware evasion intelligence in the face of HTTP errors, and develop ERROR-SENSOR to automatically detect malware traffic.
- ERROR-SENSOR is able to detect both compromised servers and malicious servers, even when benign servers are used by malware for Internet reachability testing, through analyzing HTTP error traffic. Furthermore, ERROR-SENSOR does not rely on any infection/URL signatures, nor require multiple infections in a network unlike existing work.
- We evaluate ERROR-SENSOR with large-scale, real-world enterprise network traces. ERROR-SENSOR achieves a detection rate of 99.79% at a false positive rate of 0.005% to identify HTTP errors generated by malware. In addition, ERROR-SENSOR finds surreptitious malware-generated traffic missed by an existing IDS, and uncovers evasion strategies employed by malware.

2   Background

2.1   HTTP Errors

A typical HTTP error is sent to the client web browser from a website when a problem is encountered while accessing a webpage. Based on the definition of HTTP response status codes in RFC 7231 [2], the 4xx class of status code is used to indicate the cases where the client caused an error.

In this paper, we focus on HTTP errors whose HTTP response status codes are in the 4xx class because we note that most errors generated by malware activities belong to this category. For example, network scanning attacks may lead to 404 Not Found errors due to scanning non-existing vulnerable target webpages, or 403 Forbidden errors due to scanning webpages in protected paths. Policy violation requests also lead to 403 Forbidden errors. The complete list of all the error codes and their corresponding reasons can be found in [2] as the part of the HTTP/1.1 standard. For the simplicity reason, the term *error* denotes the HTTP error unless stated otherwise in the remaining of the paper.

We use a combination of a client, a server, a webpage, and an error code to represent a unique HTTP error, i.e., $\langle client_i, server_j, page_k, error\ code \rangle$. For example, an HTTP request from client i to URL http://compromised.com/compromised_page.html with 404 error is denoted as $\langle client_i, compromised.com, compromised\_page.html, 404 \rangle$.

2.2   Problem Statement

In this paper, we focus on the HTTP error traffic and their nearby successful request traffic (e.g., non-error traffic of a given client at about the same time as the error traffic), and conduct a large-scale systematic analysis of HTTP errors in the wild with a special focus on the error patterns and the corresponding recovery behaviors of error generators.

We first *uncover the differences* between the errors generated by users/software and the errors generated by malware. Based on the insights obtained from the analysis, then, we design a new method to *detect malware-generated errors and extract malware evasion intelligence*. In this context, intelligence means the evasion strategies used by malware in the face of HTTP errors, such as connecting to multiple alternative malicious servers, compromised servers and other benign servers for Internet connectivity testing.

We, however, do not aim to detect all the malicious traffic in an enterprise network, and may miss malware-generated traffic that never produces errors. Rather, our approach complements existing DNS failure based detection methods which address fast-fluxing and DGA [12,21,41] because all the errors here still have successful DNS resolutions. Furthermore, our approach complements existing detection systems [26] as we identify malware evasive traffic by extracting the malware evasion intelligence without having malware samples in hand.

3   Insights into HTTP Errors

In order to gain more in-depth understanding of HTTP errors generated by both malware and users/software, we first studied one day of real-world network traffic from a large enterprise network, from which we extracted all the error traffic[1]. As a result, we collected more than 1 million HTTP error requests, and obtained 279,942 unique HTTP error requests (e.g., $\langle client_i, server_j, page_k, error\ code \rangle$), which only represents 3.2% of the entire one day of HTTP requests.

Table 1. $\mathcal{D}_{day}$ Data Sets

	# of clients	# of unique errors	# of errors
$\mathcal{B}$	16,205	71,998	925,277
$\mathcal{M}$	233	9,792	190,394
$\mathcal{M}_{IDS}$	233	965	35,239

Among the errors, 965 servers were detected as malicious servers by the deployed commercial intrusion detection system (IDS), and we labeled the errors as $\mathcal{M}_{IDS}$. Then we labeled the errors generated by the clients who sent requests to the servers in $\mathcal{M}_{IDS}$ as malicious errors $\mathcal{M}$. It is worth noting that the errors in $\mathcal{M}$ were generated by the malware infected clients; however, it *does not* mean that all of them are actually malicious errors. In this way, we collected 9,792 unique malicious errors. To collect benign errors, we first collected clients who never connected to malicious servers (servers in $\mathcal{M}$) nor generated policy violation requests. Then we labeled all the errors generated by these clients as benign errors $\mathcal{B}$, and collected 71,998 unique benign errors. Table 1 summarizes the data sets collected for the study, we label this one day of data as $\mathcal{D}_{day}$.

3.1   Key Observations

O1: Most benign errors are generated by an accident. When a client receives an error from a server, if the client makes at least one non-error connection to the same server during the observation time window[2], then we consider such an error is generated by a mistake and define it as an accidental error.

When a user faces an error, such as 404 Not Found error, the user may click other webpages on the same server either to figure out why the error is caused or to continue searching for other pages. In case of benign software, it may generate multiple different requests to the same server. Even if some of the requests are failed due to the misconfiguration, it still has some successful connections

---

[1] We excluded the cases where a client generated only a single error in the entire observation window, which might not provide sufficient insights for our study.

[2] The observation time window was set to one day for $\mathcal{D}_{day}$.

to the same server. For example, in our data set, Symantec liveupdate service always received 404 errors due to the misconfiguration of the proxy when it tried to request http://liveupdate.symantec.com/liveupdate_3.3.0.107_english_livetri. zip. However, the service also sent requests to http://liveupdate.symantec.com and other URIs on the domain liveupdate.symantec.com, which led to some successful connections. Consequently, we observed that a client encountering some errors on a server also had some successful contentions to the same server during the observation time window. However, malware may immediately try to connect to other backup servers in the face of errors. In fact, malware is typically programmed to request a certain number of pages on the same malicious servers or compromised servers. In addition, if an error is caused by an IDS or policy violation blocking, malware has no chance to establish any successful connections to the malicious servers. Therefore, we would observe fewer number of accidental errors in malware-generated errors.

While examining the errors in $\mathcal{D}_{day}$, we found that 84.95% of benign errors belonged to accidental errors while only 3.94% of malicious errors belonged to accidental errors. Further study showed that most of malicious accidental errors were generated by web browsers requesting other web resources (e.g., JavaScript and image files) on the same servers, which led to successful connections.

O2: Malware infected clients generate more errors than benign clients. We define the malware infected clients as the clients who send at least one request to malicious servers. In our study, we define all the clients in $\mathcal{M}_{IDS}$ as malware infected clients. Similarly, benign clients are the clients in $\mathcal{B}$.

Intuitively, benign clients would generate fewer number of errors than malware infected clients would do because benign HTTP requests constructed by web browsers or benign software are typically well formatted, and the remote servers would respond those requests properly. On the contrary, there exist lots of uncertainties for malware generated HTTP requests, including the request format and the response from the remote servers. For example, an IDS blocks confirmed malicious servers, and malicious requests exploiting vulnerable web pages may lead to unacceptable request formats.

During our study on $\mathcal{D}_{day}$, we found that about 94% of benign clients generated less than 10 errors per day. However, only around 38% of malware infected clients generated less than 10 errors per day. The maximum numbers of errors were 2,767 and 60 for malware infected clients and benign clients, respectively. We used the number of errors per day rather than the error ratio to evaluate clients. It was because, compared to the volume of benign traffic, the volume of malware related traffic was very small so that the error ratio could be easily influenced by different volume of benign traffic. We also filtered out the clients with less than 100 requests per day to exclude the cases where fewer errors were simply due to fewer requests by benign clients.

O3: Most benign errors are generated by benign software. *User-Agent* is the field in an HTTP header to indicate who initiates the request. Typical values of the field are different browsers, spiders, or other end user tools. To understand who generate errors, we inspect the User-Agent for each error.

We define two kinds of User-Agents: browser User-Agents and custom User-Agents. *Browser User-Agents* are the User-Agents whose values reflect the version of different browsers. [3] lists the User-Agents of commonly used web browsers. Since it is difficult to collect all the User-Agents of different browsers for different versions, in this paper, we use keywords, such as Mozilla, and Opera, to label if a User-Agent is a browser User-Agent or not. Specifically, all the User-Agents started with these keywords are labeled as browser User-Agents. In practice, unless a user changes the User-Agent of the HTTP header, browser-generated errors usually include such keywords at the beginning of their User-Agents by default. *Custom User-Agents* are defined as User-Agents other than browser User-Agents. In practice, most software uses their customized User-Agents in order to be easily recognized by the servers.

During our study on $\mathcal{D}_{day}$, we collected 15,115 and 136 User-Agents for benign errors and malicious errors, respectively. We found that only 12.52% of benign errors were generated by browsers while 93.38% of malicious errors were generated by browsers. This showed that most benign errors were generated by custom software which kept requesting no longer available resources. Since different benign software usually had different customized User-Agents, we observed a large number of diverse custom User-Agents.

O4: The errors generated by malware have different generating patterns from the errors generated by benign software. To further analyze the network patterns of errors, we first clustered the errors based on the similarity of their pages and parameters. The detailed clustering algorithm is described in Sect. 4.3. In this way, we obtained 42 clusters for malware-generated errors $(\mathcal{C}_{\mathcal{M}})$ and 716 clusters for benign errors $(\mathcal{C}_{\mathcal{B}})$.

We examined their network patterns from three perspectives: (a) error sequences, (b) error patterns, and (c) error frequencies. From the error *sequence* perspective, 72.35% of benign errors in $\mathcal{C}_{\mathcal{B}}$ were generated in a sequence. That is, the client sent requests to servers in a specific order. The sequence typically followed the order of the servers loaded in a web page, or the order of the servers listed in a configuration file, which was steady over time. Only 33.33% of malware-generated errors were observed in a sequence. From the error *pattern* perspective, all the browser-generated errors were generated in a batch when a page was loaded. Most benign software also generated errors in a batch since it immediately tried to connect to multiple alternative servers in the face of errors. In fact, most, if not all of these alternative servers, still led to errors due to the same misconfiguration, and such errors kept appearing unless a user corrected the configuration. On the contrary, malware generated errors with a delay before trying alternative servers to avoid a traffic spike and to make its activities stealthy. From the error *frequency* perspective, we found that around 70% of errors in $\mathcal{C}_{\mathcal{B}}$ had less than 10 minimum frequency while around 70% of errors in $\mathcal{C}_{\mathcal{M}}$ repeatedly sent error requests more than 10 times per day. Surprisingly, the highest frequency for benign errors was 6,398 where Microsoft-Symbol-Server kept downloading non-existing `boinc_exe.pdb` from `berkeley.edu` and microsoft.com. However, the highest frequency for malware-generated errors was only 920 where a client kept accessing file.php from three malicious servers.

O5: Malware has more recovery behaviors than benign software. Due to the possible blocks by an IDS or ill-formatted exploit requests, malware usually employs recovery mechanisms to assure their malicious activities. We explore URI path correlation and temporal correlation to characterize such recovery intelligence. For example, the recovery behavior sending the same request to multiple alternative servers to avoid a single point of failure would lead to successful requests including the same URI (path and parameters) with error requests, and testing the network connectivity when facing errors would lead to successful requests having temporal correlation with error requests.

During our study on $\mathcal{D}_{day}$, 66.67% of malware-generated errors exhibited such recovery behaviors. On the contrary, benign software typically tried a few alternative servers in the same domain or kept generating the same errors due to a lack of pre-arranged recovery methods. Only 8% of benign errors had temporal correlation with successful requests, and only 20% of them had similar pattern correlation with successful requests.

Lessons learned: Malware-infected clients usually generate more HTTP errors than benign clients, and most of the errors are related to malware activities. Based on our observation, malware-generated errors have significantly different error generating patterns and recovery behavior patterns from the errors generated by benign users/software. These different patterns exist because benign clients often lack recovery routines in the face of HTTP errors.

4   System Design

4.1   System Overview

We leverage the insights described in Sect. 3 to build a novel detection system, named ERROR-SENSOR, which aims to detect malware behaviors by examining HTTP errors. Such malware behaviors may include HTTP attacks on benign servers (e.g., scanning vulnerable pages), communication with malicious server (e.g., C&C servers and compromised servers), and other benign behaviors (e.g., testing network connectivity). Since ERROR-SENSOR relies on the network behaviors of malware in the face of errors, it detects malware traffic even when there are only a few (or just one) compromised clients in an enterprise network. In this paper, we focus on malware traffic related to HTTP errors, and malware traffic that is not correlated with errors is out of the scope of this work. We discuss the coverage of ERROR-SENSOR in Sect. 6.

Figure 1 shows the overview of ERROR-SENSOR where it takes the entire HTTP traffic as an input. The filtering component first filters out noisy error traffic, and then forwards both the remaining error traffic and the select successful request traffic surrounding the remaining errors. Then, ERROR-SENSOR groups the errors based on their HTTP URI pages and parameters, and all the errors sharing similar HTTP pages and parameter patterns are grouped together.

Fig. 1. Overview of Error-Sensor

During this process, Error-Sensor extracts various statistical features from three perspectives: error provenance, error generation and error recovery. The resulting feature vectors are then sent to the Error-Sensor classifier which is trained to distinguish malware-generated errors from benign errors.

4.2 Filtering

The goal of filtering is to reduce the amount of traffic to be processed by Error-Sensor and to filter the noisy errors. We define noisy errors as the errors generated by the clients who generate only a single error during the entire observation window[3] since it is difficult to acquire useful information from them. Since Error-Sensor relies on HTTP error patterns to identify malware-generated errors, in the filtering step, we filter out all the successful request traffic except for the successful requests within the time window T_w of error traffic. As a result, 96.8% of entire network traffic were filtered in our one day of enterprise traffic $\mathcal{D}_{day}$. As a result, 9.3% of errors were further filtered out. All the remaining HTTP requests are denoted in a form $\langle client_i, server_j, page_k, error\ code \rangle$. We acknowledge that we may miss some malware traffic by filtering out noise errors when malware probes C&C servers with a single request per day. However, it could be addressed by extending the observation time window.

4.3 Clustering

Given the filtered error traffic, the next step is to cluster them into groups. The rationale behind this step is that when facing errors, malware may start their recovery behaviors which would result in similar errors or similar successful connections. Since we rely on the recovery behaviors generated by the same client, we group the errors by each client rather than across different clients. In this way, compared to existing correlation-based detection method [18], Error-Sensor is capable of detecting malware traffic even when there is only a single infected client.

The key challenge for clustering is to determine which errors could be considered as the same. A straightforward way is to consider errors to be the same only when their URLs, including paths, pages, parameter names, are exactly matched. For example, during the vulnerable webpage scanning process, malware may send requests to multiple domains with the same target page files

---

[3] Our observation window was set to 1 day.

and the same exploit codes, or the clients may send requests to multiple compromised servers with the same compromised pages and parameters. However, certain malware campaigns may utilize obfuscated paths, such as Base64 or URL encoding for the page names. To address this problem, we set a threshold T_{len} [4] for the length of page names. If the length of the page name is shorter than T_{len}, we consider that it is unlikely an obfuscated page name, and group the errors based on **page names** and **parameters**. On the other hand, if the length of the page name is longer than T_{len}, we consider that the page is obfuscated, decode the page name with a URL decoder, and group the similar errors based on **len(page name)** and **parameters**. The clusters with a single error will be discarded because most of these errors are caused by misconfiguration where a client repeatedly sends the same requests to only one server.

4.4   Classification

In this step, ERROR-SENSOR takes the clusters of errors and their surrounding successful HTTP requests as an input, and produces a verdict on whether the clusters are malicious or not. Based on our key observations presented in Sect. 3, we develop a set of 18 features that describes the characteristics of an error cluster as summarized in Table 2.

Error Provenance Pattern (EPP): This category consists of six features for evaluating the overall reputation of an error cluster.

Client Reputation (f1) evaluates the client reputation of each cluster, which is measured by the number of errors generated by the clients in a cluster. It is worth noting that the number of errors generated by the clients includes the errors that were not initially clustered in the cluster, and the value of client reputation may be larger than the actual size of the cluster. Based on our observations discussed in Sect. 3, malware infected clients generate a lot more errors than benign clients does. In terms of reputation, the more errors a client generates, the lower reputation the client has.

Server Reputation (f2) evaluates the reputation of servers in an error cluster, which is measured by the average number of clients connecting to the servers. The more popular (i.e., more clients communicating with) a server is, the less likely the server is malicious.

A *Software Error Ratio* (f3) evaluates who generates errors, which is defined by the number of custom (non-browser) User-Agents over the total number of errors in a cluster. As noted in Sect. 3, majority of benign errors was generated by custom (non-browser) User-Agents while malware often used browser User-Agents to remain more stealthy.

An *Accidental Error Ratio* (f4) evaluates how errors are generated, which is defined by the number of accidental errors over the total number of errors in a

---

[4] T_{len} was empirically set to 25 based on [40].

Table 2. Feature selection

Category	Features	Feature domain	Novelty
Error provenance	Client reputation (f1)	Integer	New
	Server reputation (f2)	Integer	[40]
	Software error ratio (f3)	Real	New
	Accidental error ratio (f4)	Real	New
	Referer error ratio (f5)	Real	[31]
	Suspicious server ratio (f6)	Real	New
Error generation	Sequence (f7)	Boolean	New
	Periodmin (f8)	Integer	New
	Periodmedian (f9)	Integer	New
	Periodmax (f10)	Integer	New
	Frequencymin (f11)	Integer	New
	Frequencymedian (f12)	Integer	New
	Frequencymax (f13)	Integer	New
	Batchmin (f14)	Integer	New
	Batchmedian (f15)	Integer	New
	Batchmax (f16)	Integer	New
Error recovery	Temporal correlation (f17)	Boolean	[17]
	URI Path correlation (f18)	Boolean	New

cluster. As noted in Sect. 3, malware often quickly gives up failed servers and moves on to other alternative servers, resulting in a high accidental error ratio.

A *Referrer Ratio* (f5) evaluates where errors are generated. A referer provides information about the locations of the links from where a user reaches an error page. Most malware[5] and benign software typically generate errors without referers (i.e., direct requests) while users/browsers typically generate errors with referers indicating the previous page of the error page. By default, a browser automatically add a referer field to each request [5]. We define the referrer ratio as the number of unique referers in a cluster divided by the number of errors in the cluster. Malware-generated errors would have zero or very low referer ratio.

A *Suspicious Server Ratio* (f6) also measures the reputation of the servers in each error cluster. If a server generates only error traffic without any successful communication with its clients, ERROR-SENSOR flags the server as suspicious. These servers might be less popular servers which only few clients visit and generate errors, or malicious servers blocked by an IDS. The suspicious server ratio is defined as the number of suspicious servers divided by the total number

---

[5] Although it is trivial for an attacker to manipulate the Referer field, it is easy to detect by checking if the current page is embedded in the referred page.

of servers in the cluster. A higher suspicious server ratio in a cluster indicates that the cluster is more likely to be connected only by malware.

Error Generation Pattern (EGP): This category of features consists of four sub-groups of features extracted from error traffic.

A *Sequence Pattern* (f7) characterizes whether the errors in a cluster are generated in a sequence. The rationale behind the feature is that the errors generated from browsers and benign software often follow a certain sequence while malware-generate errors are often observed in an arbitrary order. For example, a client may generate a series of 404 errors to outdated Ubuntu source repositories in the same sequence over time because the source list of update servers (e.g., /etc/apt/sources.list) is fixed. However, malware may randomly select C&C servers to send requests, which leads to an arbitrary order of requests.

A *Period Pattern* (f8, f9, and f10) measures the minimum time interval for malware to generate the same errors (repeated errors). We observed that most user-generated errors did not yield repeated ones, and benign software generated errors often had short time interval of generating the same errors. However, malware typically employs some delay before reconnecting to the failed sever to avoid sudden traffic spikes. To characterize the timing pattern of repeated errors, we calculate the minimum, median, and maximum values of the minimum time interval between repeated errors.

A *Frequency Pattern* (f11, f12, and f13) measures how many recurring errors are generated for each error per day. Most benign errors are typically generated once or per usage. For example, a set of recurring 404 errors caused by using an outdated Ubuntu source list is generated only when a user issues apt-get command. However, malware may periodically try to connect to malicious C&C servers to obtain new commands or updates. Considering not all of the errors in a cluster are repeated, we assess the maximum, median, and minimum of the error frequency for each cluster to characterize the error generating frequency.

A *Batch Pattern* (f14, f15, and f16) measures the minimum time interval for malware to contact other alternative servers in a cluster. Most benign errors are often generated in a batch while malware may generate errors with some delays to avoid sudden spikes and to evade possible detection. For example, a set of 404 Not Found errors are usually generated at once when a page includes lots of missing/outdated links for scripts and resources. Typically, benign software quickly tries to reconnect to alternative servers in the face of errors. However, when malware faces errors, it may slowly complete its recovery behaviors (e.g., 1 min to send multiple requests [36]), or delay sometime before contacting to other alternative servers to remain stealthy.

Error Recovery Pattern (ERP): This feature group consists of two features to characterize the error recovery patterns of malware in the face of errors.

Temporal Correlation (f17) characterizes the recovery behaviors of malware based on temporal correlation among errors and their nearby successful traffic. The rationale behind the feature is that when malware faces errors, it would start recovery mechanisms within a certain time. For example, malware may send requests to benign servers (e.g., `google.com/xyz` and `facebook.com/xyz` as shown in Table 7) to check network connectivity after several failed connections to malicious servers. Therefore, if a server frequently appears together with error requests, it is highly likely to be a part of malware recovery routines.

To characterize temporal patterns, we define a time window T_w to set the correlation scope, and all the requests surrounding the errors within T_w time window are extracted. To quantify the temporal correlation, we utilize association rule learning [9], which is widely used to discover significant relations between variables in a large database in information retrieval. We use the association rule learning to find out associated traffic with target errors. For each error traffic e, we extract surrounding traffic of e within T_w window, defining them as an error bucket. In this way, all the traffic in the same error bucket is considered as related traffic, and a recurring error generates a set of error buckets. Then, for each error bucket, we measure support $Supp(X)$ and confidence $Conf(X)$ in association rule mining to identify highly correlated traffic. $Supp(X)$ of traffic set X is defined as the number of error buckets containing traffic set X, which reflects how frequently traffic X appears together with the target error e. $Conf(X)$ is defined as $Supp(X)$ over the frequency of traffic set X appearing in the traffic, $Conf(X) = Supp(X)/Freq(X)$, where $Freq(X)$ is the frequency of traffic X in the surrounding traffic of target error e. Therefore, if traffic set X frequently appears together with the target error e (i.e., high $Supp(X)$) and only appears together with target error e (i.e., high $Conf(X)$), traffic set X is greatly correlated with error e and is highly likely to be the traffic of recovery mechanisms for error e. As a result, temporal correlation feature returns `True` if $Supp(X)$ is higher than threshold T_{Supp}[6], and $Conf(X)$ is higher than threshold T_{Conf}[7]; otherwise, it returns `False`. For the errors with the frequency less than 2, temporal correlation feature returns `False` since it is difficult to determine if they are truly correlated or not. The correlated traffic helps to identify backup malicious servers and to understand sophisticated evasion intelligence employed by malware.

URI Path Correlation (f18) characterizes the recovery behaviors of malware based on URI pattern correlation among errors and their surrounding successful traffic. We note that malware may generate the same requests to multiple servers to avoid a single point of failure. In this case, some of malware traffic may lead to errors while others may be successful. For example, when malware connects to compromised servers, some of the compromised servers may have already been cleaned by administrators and lead to 404 errors while others may redirect clients to malicious servers. However, both error traffic and successful traffic would have similar content patterns (e.g., pages and parameters), and we measure the

---

[6] We empirically set $T_{Supp} = 2$, which means that the traffic set X appears together with target error e at least twice.

[7] We empirically set $T_{Conf} = 0.8$, which means the majority of X appear together with error e. A lower T_{Conf} leads to low false negatives with high false positives.

similarity between traffic using the method discussed in Sect. 4.3. If traffic set X is similar to target error e, path correlation feature returns True; otherwise, it returns False.

Building and Using a Classifier: Considering a set of diverse features, the classes of malicious error clusters and benign error clusters may not be linearly separable in their feature space, which makes Support Vector Machine (SVM) be less effective. In addition, tuning the parameters for diverse data is not trivial and parameter-free classifier would be desirable. Therefore, we leverage a random forest classifier (RFC) for classification, which does not require parameter tuning and is robust to handle outliers. The only two required parameters for RFC are the number of decision trees (N_t) and the number of features (N_f) per decision tree, and these parameters are independent of nuances of the data and have standard selection rules[8]. If the classifier determines that a cluster is malicious, then ERROR-SENSOR also outputs its recovery servers based on the servers extracted through temporal and URI path correlation.

5   Evaluation

We collected 5 days of real-world web proxy logs from a large enterprise network, called $\mathcal{D}_{5days}$. The logs were gathered by Symantec ProxySG [4] infrastructure deployed at multiple locations inside the enterprise network. The proxy logs consist of connection information (e.g., source/destination IP addresses, ports, and timestamps) and HTTP header fields (e.g., Hosts, URLs, User-Agents, referers, and HTTP response codes). Overall, we collected and analyzed over 170 GB of raw proxy logs including about 1.5 billion web requests and responses. The ProxySG has a built-in intrusion detection system (IDS) with blacklists which flags known threats by matching signatures.

5.1   Effectiveness of Error-Sensor

10-fold Cross Validation. The ground truth data in $\mathcal{D}_{day}$ (shown in Table 1) consisted of 716 benign error clusters and 42 malicious error clusters. Training a classifier on this unbalanced data set may bias the classification model towards the abundant class (benign errors in our case), and may be tailored for less important features, i.e., the features that may cause noises rather than contribute to the accurate classification. We addressed this problem by stratified sampling. For each client, we randomly selected a benign error cluster and keep all the malicious error clusters. As a result, our balanced training set $\mathcal{D}_{train}$ contained 136 benign error clusters and 42 malicious error clusters. We then trained a random forest model, and ran 10-fold cross validation on $\mathcal{D}_{train}$. ERROR-SENSOR achieved an average true positive rate of 98.3% at 2.2% false positive rate in terms of *error cluster* classification. The two false positive clusters included

---

[8] N_t is typically data independent and was set to 100, and the value of N_f was log(total number of features)+1.

a total of 4 errors, and the single missed false negative cluster consisted of 2 errors. Therefore, the detection rate was 99.79% at 0.005% false positive rate in terms of *individual error* classification. We also applied our trained model on the remaining ground truth data ($\mathcal{D}_{day} - \mathcal{D}_{train}$), including 580 benign error clusters, and no false positive was reported.

We further performed in-depth investigation of the misclassified cases. We checked the values in their features and compared the difference between $\langle TP, FN \rangle$ and $\langle FP, TN \rangle$ to see which features led to misclassification. For the one false negative cluster, we found that there was no suspicious server (f6 = 0), no accidental error (f4 = 0), and no recovery behaviors (f17 = False, f18 = False), which resulted in being classified as a benign cluster. For the two false positive clusters, we found that both had a high suspicious server ratio (f6 = 1), no accidental error (f4 = 0), and high period time, which looked very similar to malicious errors.

Table 3. Performance with different features

Algorithms	TP rate	FP rate	F-score	ROC Area
ERP, EGP & EPP	0.983	0.022	0.983	0.994
ERP & EGP	0.944	0.165	0.942	0.972
Only ERP	0.815	0.502	0.79	0.701

To comprehend how different feature combinations would affect the performance of the classifier, we tested different feature groups on $\mathcal{D}_{train}$. Starting with only error recovery pattern (ERP) features from Table 2, we combined other feature categories one by one (error generation pattern (EGP) features, and error provenance pattern (EPP) features), and evaluated the performance of the classifier. As shown in Table 3, we observed that using only ERP features detected the majority of malicious errors, however led to a large number of false positives. The combination of ERP features and EGP features significantly improved the detection rate, and reduced the false positive rate. By combining all feature groups, the performance of the classifier further improved.

Real-World Application. To further evaluate the effectiveness of ERROR-SENSOR, we applied it to $\mathcal{D}_{5days}$. Table 4 reports the number of the error clusters detected by ERROR-SENSOR. Since Day-4 and Day-5 were the weekend, less amount of traffic was produced and ERROR-SENSOR therefore detected fewer malicious clusters. We verified reported clusters with the ground truth. If at least one error was flagged by an IDS, we denoted it as IDS in the table. If at least one error was labeled as policy violation by the proxy, we denoted it as Policy Violation[9]. We also queried servers to VirusTotal [8] to see if the servers were blacklisted. If at least one server was labeled by VirusTotal as malicious, we

---

[9] Manual investigation confirmed all of the errors in the cluster were policy violation.

denoted the cluster as VirusTotal. We checked Whois information of the servers. If at least the registration of one server was expired, we denoted it as Expired. We believe an expired server has a higher possibility of being exploited by cyber criminals since it has a short lifetime. For the remaining errors, we conservatively labeled them as false positives as no validated malicious evidence was available.

Table 4. Malicious error clusters detected by ERROR-SENSOR

	Day-1	Day-2	Day-3	Day-4	Day-5
ERROR-SENSOR	239	216	164	45	26
IDS	32	34	17	10	6
Policy Violation	193	173	138	32	20
VirusTotal	3	0	2	0	0
Expired	1	3	0	2	0
False positives	10	6	7	1	0

For example, on Day-1, ERROR-SENSOR detected 239 malware-generated error clusters. Among them, 32 clusters were confirmed by an IDS, and 193 clusters belonged to the policy violation category. There were 3 clusters flagged by VirusTotal which were missed by the IDS and the proxy policy-based detection. There was 1 cluster containing only expired domains, indicating highly likely malicious servers. Although we had a relatively large number of false positive clusters, the sizes of the top 2 largest clusters were only 8 and 5 respectively, and all the other clusters had the size of 2 or 3. There were also several duplicate false positives recurring every day simply due to the software misconfiguration. For example, we found a client kept requesting `index.rdf` to multiple servers for RSS feeds. Some of the requests were successful while some led to 404 Not Found errors, which triggered temporal correlation and URI path correlation features.

5.2   Robustness of Error-Sensor

To evaluate the robustness of ERROR-SENSOR, we measured the gain ratio with 10-fold cross validation to quantify the most discriminant features, which has been proven to be more robust than other alternative metrics, such as the information gain or the Gini index. Table 5 presents the top-5 features in a descending order of their gain ratios. The Avg. Rank is the average rank over 10 fold cross validation, and the Avg. Merit reflects how important a feature is (the higher, the more important) averaged over the cross validation. The numbers following ± denote the standard deviations.

We also conservatively define the robustness of the features based on how difficult it is for cyber criminals to evade detection. If an attacker cannot manipulate or control a feature, we define the robustness of the feature as High. For example,

Table 5. ERROR-SENSOR gain ratios of the top 5 features

Features	Avg. Rank	Avg. Merit	Robustness
Suspicious Server Ratio (f6)	1 ± 0	0.848 ± 0.023	High
Accident Error Ratio (f4)	2 ± 0	0.566 ± 0.025	Low
Periodmedian (f9)	3.9 ± 0.94	0.475 ± 0.03	Medium
Periodmax (f10)	4 ± 0.77	0.483 ± 0.04	Medium
Client Reputation (f1)	4.8 ± 0.87	0.435 ± 0.021	High

an attacker cannot simply control how many errors are generated by a client; thus, we label the robustness of Client Reputation feature as High robustness. If an attacker is able to manipulate a feature, with some associated costs, we define the robustness of the feature as Medium robustness. For example, to influence Periodmedian feature, an attacker is required to frequently make requests with a higher risk of being flagged as suspicious due to sudden connection spikes. In other words, an attacker might be able to evade the feature while increasing the probability of being detected. For the feature that does not require a high cost for an attacker, we label them as Low robustness. For example, an attacker may simply send requests to the valid page of the target server in order to establish successful connections and avoid accidental errors. We manipulated the value of Accident Error Ratio (f4), Periodmedian (f9), and Periodmax (f10) to zero to simulate possible evasion by an attacker on these less robust features. Then, we applied our previously trained model to the prepared evasive attack, and achieved 88.09% of the detection rate.

5.3   Case Study

In this section, we demonstrate the benefits of ERROR-SENSOR with real cases detected by ERROR-SENSOR. Due to the space limit, we only include a few of malicious servers in the tables.

Table 6. Conficker botnet

	Server	Path	IDS category
IDS	149.20.56.32	/search	Malicious_Outbound_Data/Botnets
	195.22.26.231	/search	Malicious_Outbound_Data/Botnets
	96.43.141.190	/search	Malicious_Outbound_Data/Botnets
ERROR-SENSOR	205.164.24.45	/search	Placeholders
	149.20.56.33	/search	Computers/Internet
	216.172.154.35	/search	Placeholders

Case #1: ERROR-SENSOR detected *more malicious servers* missed by an existing deployed IDS. Most IDSes use blacklists or signatures to detect malicious traffic, and they may miss recent sophisticated and evasive malware traffic. Table 6 shows the Conficker botnet [28] cluster. This cluster included 6 C&C servers of the Conficker botnet, which labeled by the deployed IDS as Malicious Outbound Data/Botnets. However, there were still 3 more malicious servers missed by the IDS, but detected by ERROR-SENSOR. These severs were labeled as Placeholders and Computers/Internet categories by the IDS, and were not flagged or blocked by the IDS. On the contrary, ERROR-SENSOR captured those 3 surreptitious malicious servers through temporal correlation and path correlation, which demonstrates the capability of ERROR-SENSOR to identify stealthy attacks.

Table 7. TDSS botnet

	Server	Path	IDS category
IDS	loftgun01.ru	/wet.php	Malicious_Sources
	postbox901.ru	/wet.php	Malicious_Sources
	teranian111.ru	/wet.php	Malicious_Sources
ERROR-SENSOR	sbolt71.ru	/wet.php	Spam
	www.google.com	/efwgh/index.php	Search_Engines/Portals
	www.facebook.com	/dwrgh/index.php	Social_Networking

Case #2: ERROR-SENSOR detected the *evasive recovery mechanisms* employed by malware. Regardless of the maliciousness, the recovery mechanisms of malware provide critical information to analyze and detect sophisticated malware, which is often neglected by existing systems or IDSes. As shown in Table 7, the IDS detected 3 malicious servers used by the TDSS botnet [29]; however, the IDS mislabeled one malicious server as Spam category, and failed to block the malware traffic. ERROR-SENSOR, on the contrary, precisely detected the missed malicious server through URI path correlation, and further identified 5 benign servers used in malware evasive recovery routines (e.g., testing network connectivity by connecting to benign popular servers not to raise suspicion) through temporal correlation. Further study confirmed that those benign servers were indeed reported to be used by malware [6].

Case #3: ERROR-SENSOR detected *more decoy and malicious servers* involved in malicious activities, but missed by the IDS. Table 8 shows the Cutwail botnet [7] cluster, which is notorious for sending spam emails. Based on the malware analysis report [7], the malware embeds the list of 176 hard-coded decoy servers, and it sends dummy HTTP requests to the randomly chosen server from the decoy server list before communicating with actual C&C servers. This is to minimize the exposure of actual malicious C&C communication traffic; however, it

Table 8. Cutwail botnet

	Server	Path	IDS category
IDS	diamondcpu.com	/	Malicious_Outbound_Data/Botnets
	emailmsn.com	/	Malicious_Outbound_Data/Botnets
	erzt.com	/	Malicious_Outbound_Data/Botnets
ERROR-SENSOR	dangerous-minds.com	/	Newsgroups/Forums
	deloitte.com	/	Financial_Services
	linuxmail.org	/	Email

results in generating numerous errors to decoy servers. The IDS detected 13 of those decoy servers and one C&C server confirmed in [7]. ERROR-SENSOR detected 168 new servers missed by the IDS by leveraging URI path correlation and temporal correlation. Since all the dummy HTTP requests to the decoy servers shared the same request pattern with the requests to C&C servers, it was not trivial to distinguish C&C communication from decoy communication.

6   Discussion

Limitation: Since ERROR-SENSOR focuses on HTTP errors to detect malware traffic, it would not report malware that never generates HTTP errors. However, malware often uses HTTP [27] as either their server communication channels (e.g., C&C servers, redirectors, and payment servers) or attack channels (e.g., scanning vulnerable web pages/vulnerabilities, and attacking other web servers) because HTTP is commonly allowed to cross enterprise network perimeters [20]. This gives ERROR-SENSOR a great chance to detect malware traffic when such HTTP connections generate errors. In addition, malware may try to use HTTPS to evade detection, and this can be addressed by deploying web proxy servers that perform SSL-MITM in enterprise networks [25].

Evasion: An attacker who gains the knowledge about ERROR-SENSOR might try to mislead our system by manipulating features.

Error Provenance Pattern: This group of features characterizes the properties of error sources, and it is not trivial for an attacker to influence some features. For example, an attacker may not precisely determine when and how many malware generates connection errors, especially when malicious/compromised servers get cleaned. Malware may monitor web traffic and try to manipulate a User-Agent field; however, it requires periodic monitoring and other key features help detect malicious errors as a User-Agent alone is not the most significant feature. An attacker may also easily change a Referer field; however, forged Referers can be detected by checking if the current page is embedded in the Referer page or sending the same requests to the Referer page.

Error Generation Pattern: Malware may try to change its communication patterns to yield different error generation patterns. However, it is not trivial for an attacker to achieve the goal without raising suspicion. For example, sending requests in a batch may cause connection spikes, which could be captured by existing detection systems [36]. Furthermore, an attacker may lose their reliable control if malware sends requests too slowly or randomly [20].

Error Recovery Pattern: Malware may evade temporal correlation by adding a large delay when facing errors. This can be addressed by tuning T_w threshold to handle the requests with a larger delay at an extra processing time cost. To evade URL path correlation, malware requires to target different pages and to generate different parameters. However, depending on the vulnerabilities and malicious activities, it is complicated for malware to change its attack patterns. For example, for scanning attacks on vulnerable pages, the specially crafted URI names and parameters cannot be changed, otherwise the attack does not work.

   Although malware authors may be able to evade an individual feature, it is challenging to evade all of them. We believe ERROR-SENSOR presents a new detection perspective, and a practical complement to existing malware traffic detection approaches in the battle against malware.

7   Related Work

Malicious Traffic Detection: Malicious traffic detection has been widely studied by identifying malicious domains from different angles. Many approaches detected malicious domains from the DNS point of view. Bilge et al. [14] utilized various features to evaluate the reputation of a domain. Kopis [11] monitored DNS traffic at the upper DNS hierarchy to detect malicious domains. Another line of research focused on network traffic analysis. Some approaches [25,27] detected malicious domains by extracting signatures from malware traffic. Gu et al. [18,19] proposed anomaly-based botnet detection systems that looked for similar network behaviors across client hosts. Yen et al. [37] detected malware by aggregating traffic that shared the same external destinations or similar payload, and involved internal hosts with similar OS. Hu et al. [20] designed methods to detect regular callback patterns often generated by botnets in enterprise networks. Recently, Yen et al. [36] proposed a system to detect suspicious activities in enterprise networks by mining the features from the logs of a diverse security products. Zhang et al. [39] detected malicious servers by studying the redirection between visible servers and invisible servers. Kwon et al. [22] designed a system to detect lockstep behaviors, which captured a set of downloaders that were remotely controlled and the domains that they accessed.

Failure-based Detection: Zhu et al. [41] employed a supervised machine learning method to classify different attacks using a combination of DNS query failures and network traffic data collected for individual hosts. Yadav et al. [35] utilized the failures around successful DNS queries and the entropy of the

domains belonging to those queries to detect botnet. Jiang et al. [21] characterized DNS query failures by analyzing DNS failure graphs to identify suspicious
and malicious activities. Recently, Antonakakis et al. [12] extracted statistic features from DNS failures and built models for DGA botnets, which are then used
for online detection. Thomas et al. [32] analyzed non-existent domain queries at
several premier Top Level Domain (TLD) authoritative name servers to identify strongly connected cliques of malware related domains. Beside the DNS
failure-based study, Beverly et al. [13] used network errors (e.g., TCP timeouts,
retransmissions, reset) caused by bots for spam mitigation.

Malware Recovery Behavior Analysis: Some approaches [15,16] used the
game theory to model interactions between an attacker and a honeypot operator
to improve the information gained from honeypot. Nadji et al. [24] systematically
designed a set of rules to proactively inject false network information in order
to reveal the backup behaviors of malware. Dynamic binary analysis systems
revealed malware behaviors by forcing execution of all possible branches, as
addressed in [23,34]. Zhang et al. [38] analyzed the underlying triggering relations
of a massive amount of network events, and explored such triggering relations
to detect the stealthy malicious activities.

8   Conclusion

In this paper, we studied malware-generated web traffic from a new perspective,
i.e., HTTP errors. We conducted the first large-scale measurement study on
HTTP errors generated by both benign users/software and malware. We showed
that malware-infected clients typically generated more HTTP errors than benign
clients did, and there existed distinguishing patterns between the errors generated by malware and the errors caused by benign users/software. Leveraging our
new findings, we designed a new system, ERROR-SENSOR, to detect malware traffic. Our evaluation on real-world data sets demonstrated the effectiveness and
robustness of ERROR-SENSOR in detecting malware-generated traffic and com-
prehending the malware evasion intelligence. We believe that ERROR-SENSOR
presents a new detection method and greatly complements existing works.

Acknowledgement. This material is based upon work supported in part by the
National Science Foundation (NSF) under Grant no. 1314823. Any opinions, findings,
and conclusions or recommendations expressed in this material are those of the authors
and do not necessarily reflect the views of NSF.

References

1. Domain Generation Algorithms (DGA) in Stealthy Malware. https://www.
damballa.com/domain-generation-algorithms-dga-in-stealthy-malware
2. Hypertext Transfer Protocol (HTTP/1.1): Semantics and Content (RFC 7231).
https://tools.ietf.org/html/rfc7231
3. List of all Browsers. http://www.useragentstring.com/pages/Browserlist/

4. ProxySG (Secure Web Gateway). https://www.symantec.com/products/secure-web-gateway-proxy-sg-and-asg
5. Referer Header. http://kb.mozillazine.org/Network.http.sendRefererHeader
6. Malware TROJ_KRYPTIK.LJC (2012). https://www.trendmicro.com/vinfo/us/threat-encyclopedia/malware/troj_kryptik.ljc
7. Story of the Cutwail/Pushdo hidden C&C server (2013). https://blog.avast.com/2013/06/25/15507/
8. VirusTotal (2017). https://www.virustotal.com
9. Agrawal, R., Imielinski, T., Swami, A.: Mining association rules between sets of items in large databases. In: SIGMOD (1993)
10. Antonakakis, M., Perdisci, R., Dagon, D., Lee, W., Feamster, N.: Building a dynamic reputation system for DNS. In: USENIX Security (2010)
11. Antonakakis, M., Perdisci, R., Lee, W., Vasiloglou, N., Dagon, D.: Detecting malware domains at the upper DNS hierarchy. In: USENIX Security (2011)
12. Antonakakis, M., et al.: From throw-away traffic to bots: detecting the rise of DGA-based malware. In: USENIX Security (2012)
13. Beverly, R., Sollins, K.: Exploiting transport-level characteristics of spam. In: Proceedings of the Fifth Conference on Email and Anti-Spam (CEAS 2008) (2008)
14. Bilge, L., Kirda, E., Kruegel, C., Balduzzi, M.: Exposure: finding malicious domains using passive DNS analysis. In: NDSS (2011)
15. Carroll, T., Grosu, D.: A game theoretic investigation of deception in network security. In: ICCCN (2009)
16. Wagener, G., State, R., Dulaunoy, A., Engel, T.: Self adaptive high interaction honeypots driven by game theory. In: Proceedings of the 11th International Symposium on Stabilization, Safety, and Security of Distributed Systems (SSS 2009) (2009)
17. Gao, H., et al.: An empirical reexamination of global DNS behavior. In: ACM SIGCOMM (2013)
18. Gu, G., Perdisci, R., Zhang, J., Lee, W.: Botminer: clustering analysis of network traffic for protocol-and structure-independent botnet detection. In: USENIX Security (2008)
19. Gu, G., Zhang, J., Lee, W.: Botsniffer: detecting botnet command and control channels in network traffic. In: NDSS (2008)
20. Hu, X., et al.: BAYWATCH: robust beaconing detection to identify infected hosts in large-scale enterprise networks. In: DSN (2016)
21. Jiang, N., Cao, J., Jin, Y., Li, L., Zhang, Z.: Identifying suspicious activities through DNS failure graph analysis. In: IEEE ICNP (2010)
22. Kwon, B.J., Srinivas, V., Deshpande, A., Dumitras, T.: Catching worms, trojan horses and PUPs: unsupervised detection of silent delivery campaigns. In: NDSS (2017)
23. Moser, A., Kirda, E., Kruegel, C.: Exploring multiple execution paths for malware analysis. In: IEEE Security and Privacy (2007)
24. Nadji, Y., Antonakakis, M., Perdisci, R., Lee, W.: Understanding the prevalence and use of alternative plans in malware with network games. In: Proceedings of the Annual Computer Security Applications Conference (ACSAC 2011) (2011)
25. Nelms, T., Perdisci, R., Ahamad, M.: Execscent: mining for new c&c domains in live networks with adaptive control protocol templates. In: USENIX Security (2013)
26. Neugschwandtner, M., Comparetti, P.M., Platzer, C.: Detecting malware's failover c&c strategies with squeeze. In: ACSAC (2011)

27. Perdisci, R., Lee, W., Feamster, N.: Behavioral clustering of HTTP-based malware and signature generation using malicious network traces. In: NSDI (2010)
28. Porras, P., Saidi, H., Yegneswaran, V.: A Foray into Conficker's logic and rendezvous points. In: USENIX Workshop on Large-Scale Exploits and Emergent Threats (LEET 2009) (2009)
29. Rusakov, V., Golovanov, S.: TDSS (2010). https://securelist.com/tdss/36314/
30. Salusky, W., Danford, R.: Know your enemy: fast-flux service networks. In: The Honeynet Project (2008)
31. Stringhini, G., Kruegel, C., Vigna, G.: Shady paths: leveraging surfing crowds to detect malicious web pages. In: ACM CCS (2013)
32. Thomas, M., Mohaisen, A.: Kindred domains: detecting and clustering botnet domains using DNS traffic. In: WWW (2014)
33. Wang, T., Hu, X., Jang, J., Ji, S., Stoecklin, M., Taylor, T.: BotMeter: charting DGA-botnet landscapes in large networks. In: ICDCS (2016)
34. Wilhelm, J., Chiueh, T.: A forced sampled execution approach to kernel rootkit identification. In: Kruegel, C., Lippmann, R., Clark, A. (eds.) RAID 2007. LNCS, vol. 4637, pp. 219–235. Springer, Heidelberg (2007). https://doi.org/10.1007/978-3-540-74320-0_12
35. Yadav, S., Reddy, A.L.N.: Winning with DNS failures: strategies for faster botnet detection. In: Rajarajan, M., Piper, F., Wang, H., Kesidis, G. (eds.) SecureComm 2011. LNICST, vol. 96, pp. 446–459. Springer, Heidelberg (2012). https://doi.org/10.1007/978-3-642-31909-9_26
36. Yen, T., et al.: Beehive: large-scale log analysis for detecting suspicious activity in enterprise network. In: ACSAC (2013)
37. Yen, T.-F., Reiter, M.K.: Traffic aggregation for malware detection. In: Zamboni, D. (ed.) DIMVA 2008. LNCS, vol. 5137, pp. 207–227. Springer, Heidelberg (2008). https://doi.org/10.1007/978-3-540-70542-0_11
38. Zhang, H., Yao, D., Ramakrishnan, N.: Detection of stealthy malware activities with traffic causality and scalable triggering relation discovery. In: ASIACCS (2014)
39. Zhang, J., Hu, X., Jang, J., Wang, T., Gu, G., Stoecklin, M.: Hunting for invisibility: characterizing and detecting malicious web infrastructures through server visibility analysis. In: IEEE INFOCOM (2016)
40. Zhang, J., Saha, S., Gu, G., Lee, S., Mellia, M.: Systematic mining of associated server herds for malware campaign discovery. In: ICDCS (2015)
41. Zhu, Z., Yegneswaran, V., Chen, Y.: Using failure information analysis to detect enterprise zombies. In: Chen, Y., Dimitriou, T.D., Zhou, J. (eds.) SecureComm 2009. LNICST, vol. 19, pp. 185–206. Springer, Heidelberg (2009). https://doi.org/10.1007/978-3-642-05284-2_11

Generic Black-Box End-to-End Attack Against State of the Art API Call Based Malware Classifiers

Ishai Rosenberg[✉], Asaf Shabtai, Lior Rokach, and Yuval Elovici

Software and Information Systems Engineering Department, Ben Gurion University,
Beersheba, Israel
ishairos@post.bgu.ac.il

Abstract. In this paper, we present a black-box attack against API call based machine learning malware classifiers, focusing on generating adversarial sequences combining API calls and static features (e.g., printable strings) that will be misclassified by the classifier without affecting the malware functionality. We show that this attack is effective against many classifiers due to the transferability principle between RNN variants, feed forward DNNs, and traditional machine learning classifiers such as SVM. We also implement GADGET, a software framework to convert any malware binary to a binary undetected by malware classifiers, using the proposed attack, without access to the malware source code.

Keywords: Adversarial attacks · Malware classification
Deep neural networks · Dynamic analysis · Transferability

1 Introduction

Machine learning malware classifiers, in which the model is trained on features extracted from the analyzed file, have two main advantages over current signature based/black list classifiers: (1) Automatically training the classifier on new malware samples saves time and expense, compared to manually analyzing new malware variants. (2) Generalization to currently unseen and unsigned threats is better when the classifier is based on features and not on a fingerprint of a specific and exact file (e.g., a file's hash).

Next generation anti-malware products, such as Cylance, CrowdStrike, and Sophos, use machine and deep learning models instead of signatures and heuristics. Those models can be evaded and in this paper, we demonstrate an evasive *end-to-end attack*, generating a malware binary that can be executed while not being detected by such machine learning malware classifiers.

Application programming interface (API) calls, often used to characterize the behavior of a program, are a common input choice for a classifier and used by products such as SentinelOne. Since only the sequence of API calls gives each

© Springer Nature Switzerland AG 2018
M. Bailey et al. (Eds.): RAID 2018, LNCS 11050, pp. 490–510, 2018.
https://doi.org/10.1007/978-3-030-00470-5_23

API call its context and proper meaning, API call sequence based classifiers provide state of the art detection performance [9].

Machine learning classifiers and algorithms are vulnerable to different kinds of attacks aimed at undermining the classifier's integrity, availability, etc. One such attack is based on the generation of adversarial examples which are originally correctly classified inputs that are perturbed (modified) so they (incorrectly) get assigned a different label. In this paper, we demonstrate an attack like this on binary classifiers that are used to differentiate between malicious and benign API call sequences. In our case, the adversarial example is a malicious API call sequence, originally correctly classified, which is classified by the classifier as benign (a form of evasion attack) after the perturbation (which does not affect the malware functionality).

Generating adversarial examples for API sequences differs from generating adversarial examples for images [2], which is the main focus of the existing research, in two respects: (1) API sequences consist of discrete symbols with variable lengths, while images are represented as matrices with fixed dimensions, and the values of the matrices are continuous. (2) In adversarial API sequences one must verify that the original functionality of the malware remains intact. Attacks against RNN variants exist [7,12], but they are not practical attacks, in that they don't verify the functionality of the modified samples or handle API call arguments and non-sequence features, etc. The differences from our attack are specified in Sect. 2.

The contributions of our paper are as follows:

1. We implement a novel *end-to-end black-box method* to generate adversarial examples for many state of the art machine learning malware classifiers. This is the first attack to be evaluated against RNN variants (like LSTM), feed forward DNNs, and traditional machine learning classifiers (such as SVM). We test our implementation on a large dataset of 500,000 malware and benign samples.

2. Unlike previous papers that focus on images, we focus on the cyber security domain. We implement GADGET, an evasion framework generating a new malware binary with the perturbed features *without access to the malware source code* that allows us to *verify that the malicious functionality remains intact.*

3. Unlike previous papers, we extend our attack to *bypass multi-feature (e.g., static and dynamic features) based malware classifiers*, to fit real world scenarios.

4. We focus on *the principle* of *transferability* in RNN variants. To the best of our knowledge, this is *the first time it has been evaluated in the context of RNNs and in the cyber security domain*, proving that the proposed attack is effective against the largest number of classifiers ever reviewed in a single study: RNN, LSTM, GRU, and their bidirectional and deep variants, and feed forward DNN, 1D CNN, SVM, random forest, logistic regression, GBDT, etc.

2   Background and Related Work

Most black-box attacks rely on the concept of *adversarial example transferability* [18]: Adversarial examples crafted against one model are also likely to be effective against other models, even when the models are trained on different datasets. This means that the adversary can train a *surrogate model*, which has decision boundaries similar to the original model, and perform a white-box attack on it. Adversarial examples that successfully fool the surrogate model are likely to fool the original model as well [11]. A different approach uses the confidence score of the targeted DNN to estimate its gradients directly instead of using the surrogate model's gradients to generate adversarial examples [3]. However, attacker knowledge of confidence scores (not required by our attack) is unlikely in black-box scenarios. *Decision based attack,* which uses only the target classifier's classes, without the confidence score, result in lower attack effectiveness and higher overhead [17].

In *mimicry attacks*, an attacker is able to code a malicious exploit that mimics the system calls' trace of benign code, thus evading detection [21]. Several methods were presented: (1) *Disguise attacks* - Causing benign system calls to generate malicious behavior by modifying only the system calls' parameters. (2) *No-op Attacks* - Adding semantic *no-ops* - system calls with no effect, or those with an irrelevant effect, e.g., opening a non-existent file. (3) *Equivalence attack* - Using a different system call sequence to achieve the same (malicious) effect.

The search for adversarial examples can be formalized as a minimization problem [18]:

$$\arg_{\mathbf{r}} \min f(\mathbf{x} + \mathbf{r}) \neq f(\mathbf{x}) \ s.t. \ \mathbf{x} + \mathbf{r} \in \mathbf{D} \tag{1}$$

The input $\mathbf{x}$, correctly classified by the classifier f, is perturbed with $\mathbf{r}$ such that the resulting adversarial example $\mathbf{x} + \mathbf{r}$ remains in the input domain $\mathbf{D}$, but is assigned a different label than $\boldsymbol{x}$.

A substitute model was trained with inputs generated by augmenting the initial set of representative inputs with their FGSM [4] perturbed variants, and then the substitute model was used to craft adversarial samples [11]. This differs from our paper in that: 1) It deals *only* with convolutional neural networks, as opposed to all state of the art classifiers, including RNN variants. 2) It deals with images and doesn't fit the attack requirements of the cyber security domain, i.e., not harming the malware functionality. 3) No end-to-end framework to implement the attack in the cyber-security domain was presented.

A white-box evasion technique for an Android static analysis malware classifier was implemented using the gradients to find the element whose addition would cause the maximum change in the benign score, and add this feature to the adversarial example [5]. In contrast to our work, this paper didn't deal with RNNs or dynamic features which are more challenging to add without harming the malware functionality. This study also did not focus on a generic attack that can affect many types of classifiers, as we do. Finally, our black-box assumption is more feasible than a white-box assumption. In Sect. 5.3 we created a black-box variant of this attack.

API call uni-grams were used as static features, as well [6]. A generative adversarial network (GAN) was trained to generate adversarial samples that would be classified as benign by the discriminator which uses labels from the black-box model. This attack doesn't fit sequence based malware classifiers (LSTM, etc.). In addition, the paper does not present a end-to-end framework which preserves the code's functionality. Finally, GANs are known for their unstable training process [1], making such an attack method hard to rely on.

A white-box adversarial example attack against RNNs, demonstrated against LSTM architecture, for sentiment classification of a movie reviews dataset was shown in [12]. The adversary iterates over the movie review's words $x[i]$ in the review and modifies it as follows:

$$\mathbf{x}[i] = \arg\min_{\mathbf{z}} ||sign(\mathbf{x}[i] - \mathbf{z}) - sign(J_f(\mathbf{x})[i, f(\mathbf{x})])||\ s.t.\ \mathbf{z} \in \mathrm{D} \qquad (2)$$

where $f(\mathbf{x})$ is the original model label for $\mathbf{x}$, and $J_f(\mathbf{x})[i, j] = \frac{\partial f_j}{\partial x_i}(\mathbf{x})$. This differs from our paper in that: (1) We present a black-box attack, not a white-box attack. (2) We implement a practical cyber domain attack. For instance, we don't modify existing API calls, because while such an attack is relevant for reviews - it might damage a malware functionality which we wish to avoid. (3) We deal with multiple-feature classifiers, as in real world malware classifiers. (4) Our attack has better performance, as shown in Sect. 4.3.

Concurrently and independently from our work, a RNN GAN to generate invalid APIs and insert them into the original API sequences was proposed [7]. Gumbel-Softmax, a one-hot continuous distribution estimator, was used to deliver gradient information between the generative RNN and the substitute RNN. Null APIs were added, but while they were omitted to make the generated adversarial sequence shorter, they remained in the gradient calculation of the loss function. This decreases the attack effectiveness compared to our method (88% vs. 99.99% using our method, for an LSTM classifier). In contrast, our attack method doesn't have this difference between the substitute model and the black-box model, and our generated API sequences are shorter. This also makes our adversarial example faster. Unlike [7], which only focused on LSTM variants, we also show our attack's effectiveness against other RNN variants such as GRUs and conventional RNNs, bidirectional and deep variants, and non-RNN classifiers (including both feed forward networks and traditional machine learning classifiers such as SVM), making it truly generic. Moreover, the usage of Gumbel-Softmax approximation in [7] makes this attack limited to one-hot encoded inputs, while in our attack, any word embedding can be used, making it more generic. In addition, the stability issues associated with GAN training [1], which might not converge for specific datasets, apply to the attack method mentioned in [7] as well, making it hard to rely on. While such issues might not be visible when using a small dataset (180 samples in [7]), they become more apparent when using larger datasets like ours (500,000 samples). Finally, we developed an end-to-end framework, generating a mimicry attack (Sect. 5). While previous works inject arbitrary API call sequences that might harm the malware functionality (e.g., by inserting the *ExitProcess()* API call in the middle of the malware code), our attack modifies the code such that the original functionality of the malware is preserved (Sect. 5.1). Moreover, our approach works in real world scenarios including hybrid classifiers/multiple feature types (Sect. 5.3) and API arguments (Sect. 5.2), non of which is addressed by [7].

3   Methodology

3.1   Black-Box API Call Based Malware Classifier

Our classifier's input is a sequence of API calls made by the inspected code. In this section, it uses only the API call type and not its arguments or return value. IDSs that verify the arguments tend to be much slower (4–10 times slower, in [19]). One might claim that considering arguments would make our attack easier to detect. This could be done, e.g., by looking for irregularities in the arguments of the API calls (e.g., invalid file handles, etc.) or by considering only successful API calls and ignoring failed APIs. In order to address this issue, we don't use null arguments that would fail the function. Instead, arguments that are valid but do nothing, such as writing into a temporary file instead of an invalid file handle, are used in our framework, as described in Sect. 5. We also discuss an extension of our attack that handles API call arguments in Sect. 5.2.

Since API call sequences can be long (some samples in our dataset have millions of API calls), it is impossible to train on the entire sequence at once due to GPU memory and training time constraints. Thus, we used a sliding window approach: Each API call sequence is divided into windows with size m. Detection is performed on each window in turn, and if any window is classified as malicious, the entire sequence is malicious. This method helps detect cases like malicious payloads injected into goodware (e.g., using Metasploit), where only a small subset of the sequence is malicious. We use one-hot encoding for each API call type in order to cope with the limitations of sklearn's implementation of decision trees and random forests[1]. The output of each classifier is binary (is the inspected code malicious or not). The tested classifiers and their hyper parameters are described in Sect. 4.2.

3.2   Black-Box API Call Based Malware Classifier Attack

The proposed attack has two phases: (1) creating a surrogate model using the target classifier as a black-box model, and (2) generating adversarial examples with white-box access to the surrogate model and using them against the attacked black-box model, by the transferability property.

---

[1] For details, see: https://roamanalytics.com/2016/10/28/are-categorical-variables-getting-lost-in-your-random-forests/.

Creating a Surrogate Model. We use Jacobian-based dataset augmentation, an approach similar to [11]. The method is specified in Algorithm 1.

We query the black-box model with synthetic inputs selected by a Jacobian-based heuristic to build a surrogate model $\hat{f}$, approximating the black-box model f's decision boundaries. While the adversary is unaware of the architecture of the black-box model, we assume the basic features used (the recorded API call types) are known to the attacker. In order to learn decision boundaries similar to the black-box model while minimizing the number of black-box model queries, the synthetic training inputs are based on prioritizing directions in which the model's output varies. This is done by evaluating the sign of the Jacobian matrix dimension corresponding to the label assigned to input $\mathbf{x}$ by the black-box model, $sign(J_{\hat{f}}(\mathbf{x})[f(\mathbf{x})])$, as calculated by FGSM [4]. We use the Jacobian matrix of the surrogate model, since we don't have access to the Jacobian matrix of the black-box model. The new synthetic data point $\mathbf{x} + \epsilon sign(J_{\hat{f}}(\mathbf{x})[f(\mathbf{x})])$ is added to the training set.

Algorithm 1. Surrogate Model Training

Input: f (black-box model), T (training epochs), X_1(initial dataset), ϵ (perturbation factor)

Define architecture for the surrogate model A

for t=1..T:

  $D_t = \{(\mathbf{x}, f(\mathbf{x}))|\mathbf{x} \in X_t\}$ # Label the synthetic dataset using the black-box model

  $\hat{f}_t = train(A, D_t)$ # (Re-)Train the surrogate model

  $X_{t+1} = \left\{\mathbf{x} + \epsilon sign(J_{\hat{f}_t}(\mathbf{x})[f(\mathbf{x})])|\mathbf{x} \in X_t\right\} \cup X_t$ # Perform Jacobian-based dataset augmentation

return $\hat{f}_T$

On each iteration we add a synthetic example to each existing sample. The surrogate model dataset size is: $|X_t| = 2^{t-1}|X_1|$

The samples used in the initial dataset, X_1, were randomly selected from the test set distribution, but they were not included in the training and test sets to prevent bias. X_1 should be representative so the dataset augmentation covers all decision boundaries to increase the augmentation's effectiveness. For example, if we only include samples from a single family of ransomware in the initial dataset, we will only be focusing on a specific area of the decision boundary, and our augmentation would likely only take us in a certain direction. However, as shown in Sect. 4.3, this doesn't mean that all of the malware families in the training set must be represented to achieve good performance.

Generating Adversarial Examples. An adversarial example is a sequence of API calls classified as malicious by the classifier that is perturbed by the addition of API calls, so that the modified sequence will be misclassified as benign. In order to prevent damaging the code's functionality, we cannot remove or modify API calls; we can only add additional API calls. In order to add API calls in a way that doesn't hurt the code's functionality, we generate a *mimicry attack* (Sect. 5). Our attack is described in Algorithm 2.

Algorithm 2. Adversarial Sequence Generation

Input: f (black-box model), $\hat{f}$ (surrogate model), $\mathbf{x}$ (malicious sequence to perturb, of length l), n (size of adversarial sliding window), D (vocabulary)

for each sliding window $\mathbf{w}_j$ of n API calls in $\mathbf{x}$:

$\quad \mathbf{w}_j{}^* = \mathbf{w}_j$

$\quad$ **while** $f(\mathbf{w}_j^*) = malicious$:

$\quad\quad$ Randomly select an API's position i in $\mathbf{w}$

$\quad\quad$ # Insert a new adversarial API in position $i \in \{1..n\}$:

$\quad\quad \mathbf{w}_j^*[i] = \arg\min_{api} ||sign(\mathbf{w}_j{}^* - \mathbf{w}_j^*[1 : i - 1] \perp api \perp \mathbf{w}_j^*[i : n - 1]) - sign(J_{\hat{f}}(\mathbf{w}_j)[f(\boldsymbol{w}_j)])||$

$\quad\quad$ Replace $\mathbf{w}_j$ (in $\mathbf{x}$) with $\mathbf{w}_j{}^*$

return (perturbed) $\boldsymbol{x}$

D is the vocabulary of available features, that is, the API calls recorded by the classifier. The adversarial API call sequence length of l might be different than n, the length of the sliding window API call sequence that is used by the adversary. Therefore, like the prediction, the attack is performed sequentially on $\lceil \frac{l}{n} \rceil$ windows of n API calls. Note that the knowledge of m (the window size of the classifier, mentioned in Sect. 3.1) is not required, as shown in Sect. 4.3. $\perp$ is the concatenation operation. $\mathbf{w}_j^*[1 : i - 1] \perp api \perp \mathbf{w}_j^*[i : n - 1]$ is the insertion of the encoded API vector in position i of $\mathbf{w}_j^*$. The adversary randomly chooses i since he/she does not have any way to better select i without incurring significant statistical overhead. Note that an insertion of an API in position i means that the APIs from position $i..n$ ($\mathbf{w}_j^*[i : n]$) are "pushed back" one position to make room for the new API call, in order to maintain the original sequence and preserve the original functionality of the code. Since the sliding window has a fixed length, the last API call, $\mathbf{w}_j^*[n]$, is "pushed out" and removed from $\mathbf{w}_j^*$ (this is why the term is $\perp \mathbf{w}_j^*[i : n - 1]$, as opposed to $\perp \mathbf{w}_j^*[i : n]$). The APIs "pushed out" from $\mathbf{w}_j$ will become the beginning of $\mathbf{w}_{j+1}$, so no API is ignored.

The newly added API call is $\mathbf{w}_j^*[i] = \arg\min_{api} ||sign(\mathbf{w}_j{}^* - \mathbf{w}_j^*[0 : i] \perp api \perp \mathbf{w}_j^*[i : n - 1]) - sign(J_{\hat{f}}(\mathbf{w}_j)[f(\boldsymbol{w}_j)])||$. $sign(J_{\hat{f}}(\mathbf{w}_j)[f(\boldsymbol{w}_j)])$ gives us the direction in which we have to perturb the API call sequence in order to reduce the probability assigned to the malicious class, $f(\mathbf{x})$, and thus change the predicted label of the API call sequence. However, the set of legitimate API call embeddings is finite. Thus, we cannot set the new API to any real value. We therefore find the API call api in D whose insertion directs us closest to the direction indicated by the Jacobian as most impactful on the model's prediction. We iteratively apply this heuristic until we find an adversarial input sequence misclassified as benign. Note that in [12] the authors *replaced* a word in a movie review, so they only needed a single element from the Jacobian (for word i, which was replaced). All other words remained the same, so no gradient change took place. In contrast, since we *add* an API call, all of the API calls following it shift their position, so we consider the aggregated impact.

While the proposed attack is designed for API call based classifiers, it can be generalized to any adversarial sequence generation. This generalization is a high performance in terms of attack effectiveness and overhead (Eqs. 4 and 5). This can be seen in Sect. 4.3, where we compare the proposed attack to [12] for the IMDB sentiment classification task. In Sect. 4.3 we show why the same adversarial examples generated against the surrogate model would be effective against both the black-box model and other types of classifiers due to the principle of *transferability*.

We assume that the attacker knows what API calls are available and how each of them is encoded (one-hot encoding in this paper). This is a commonly accepted assumption about the attacker's knowledge [8].

4   Experimental Evaluation

4.1   Dataset

Our dataset contains 500,000 files (250,000 benign samples and 250,000 malware samples), including the latest variants. We have ransomware families such as Cerber, Locky, Ramnit, Matsnu, Androm, Upatre, Delf, Zbot, Expiro, Ipamor. and other malware types (worms, backdoors, droppers, spyware, PUA, and viruses), each with the same number of samples, to prevent a prediction bias towards the majority class. 80% of the malware families' (like the Virut virus family) samples were distributed between the training and test sets, to determine the classifier's ability to generalize to samples from the same family. 20% of the malware families (such as the WannaCry ransomware family) were used only on the test set to assess generalization to an unseen malware family. The temporal difference between the training set and the test set is several months (meaning all test set samples are newer than the training set samples), based on Virus-Total's 'first seen' date. We labeled our dataset using VirusTotal, an on-line scanning service which contains more than 60 different security products. Our ground truth is that a malicious sample is one with 15 or more positive (i.e., malware) classifications from the 60 products. A benign sample is one with zero positive classifications. All samples with 1–14 positives were omitted to prevent false positive contamination of the dataset.

We ran each sample in Cuckoo Sandbox, a commonly-used malware analysis system, for two minutes per sample.[2] We parsed the JSON file generated by Cuckoo Sandbox and extracted the API call sequences generated by the

---

[2] Tracing only the first seconds of a program execution might not detect certain malware types, like "logic bombs" that commence their malicious behavior only after the program has been running some time. However, this can be mitigated both by classifying the suspension mechanism as malicious, if accurate, or by tracing the code operation throughout the program execution life-time, not just when the program starts.

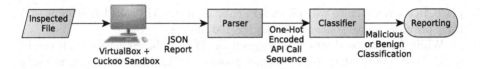

Fig. 1. Overview of the malware classification process

inspected code during its execution. The extracted API call sequences are the malware classifier's features. Although the JSON can be used as raw input for a neural network classifier (as done in [16]), we parsed it, since we wanted to focus only on API calls without adding other features, such as connected network addresses, which are also extracted by Cuckoo Sandbox.

The overview of the malware classification process is shown in Fig. 1. Figure 2a present a more detailed view of the classifier's structure.

We run the samples on a VirtualBox's snapshot with Windows 8.1 OS,[3] since most malware target the Windows OS.

Cuckoo Sandbox is a tool known to malware writers, some of whom write code to detect if the malware is running in a Cuckoo Sandbox (or on virtual machines) and if so, the malware quit immediately to prevent reversing efforts. In those cases, the file is malicious, but its behavior recorded in Cuckoo Sandbox (its API call sequence) isn't malicious, due to its anti-forensic capabilities. To mitigate such contamination of our dataset, we used two countermeasures: (1) We applied YARA rules to find samples trying to detect sandbox programs such as Cuckoo Sandbox and omitted all such samples. (2) We considered only API call sequences with more than 15 API calls (as in [13]), omitting malware that, e.g., detect a VM and quit. This filtering left us with about 400,000 valid samples, after balancing the benign samples number. The final training set size is 360,000 samples, 36,000 of which serve as the validation set. The test set size is 36,000 samples. All sets are balanced between malicious and benign samples. One might argue that the evasive malware that apply such anti-VM techniques are extremely challenging and relevant. However, in this paper we focus on the adversarial attack. This attack is generic enough to work for those evasive malware as well, assuming that other mitigation techniques (e.g., anti-anti-VM), would be applied.

4.2   Malware Classifier Performance

No open source or commercial trail versions of API calls based deep learning intrusion detection systems are available, as such products target enterprises. Dynamic models are not available in VirusTotal as well. Therefore, we created our own black-box malware classifiers. This also allows us to evaluate the attack effectiveness (Eq. 4) against many classifier types.

---

[3] While it is true that the API calls sequence would vary across different OSs or configurations, both the black-box classifier and the surrogate model generalize across those differences, as they capture the "main features" over the sequence, which are not vary between OSs.

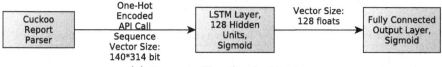

(a) Dynamic Classifier Architecture

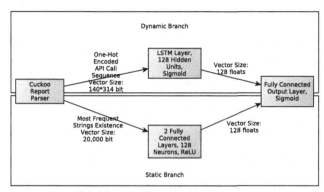

(b) Hybrid Classifier Architecture

Fig. 2. Classifier architecture overview

We limited our maximum input sequence length to $m = 140$ API calls (longer sequence lengths, e.g., $m = 1000$, had no effect on the accuracy) and padded shorter sequences with zeros. A zero stands for a null API in our one-hot encoding. Longer sequences are split into windows of m API calls, and each window is classified in turn. If any window is malicious the entire sequence is considered malicious. Thus, the input of all of the classifiers is a vector of $m = 140$ API call types in one-hot encoding, using 314 bits, since there were 314 monitored API call types in the Cuckoo reports for our dataset. The output is a binary classification: malicious or benign. An overview of the LSTM architecture is shown in Fig. 2a.

We used the Keras implementation for all neural network classifiers, with TensorFlow used for the back end. XGBoost and Scikit-Learn were used for all other classifiers.

The loss function used for training was binary cross-entropy. We used the Adam optimizer for all of the neural networks. The output layer was fully-connected with sigmoid activation for all NNs. We fine-tuned the hyper parameters for all classifiers based on the relevant state of the art papers, e.g., window size from [13], number of hidden layers from [5,9], dropout rate from [9], and number of trees in a random forest classifier and the decision tree splitting criteria from [15]. For neural networks, a rectified linear unit, $ReLU(x) = max(0, x)$, was chosen as an activation function for the input and hidden layers due to its fast convergence compared to $sigmoid()$ or $tanh()$, and dropout was used to improve the generalization potential of the network. Training was conducted

Table 1. Classifier performance

Classifier type	Accuracy (%)	Classifier type	Accuracy (%)
RNN	97.90	Bidirectional GRU	98.04
BRNN	95.58	Fully-Connected DNN	94.70
LSTM	98.26	1D CNN	96.42
Deep LSTM	97.90	Random forest	98.90
BLSTM	97.90	SVM	86.18
Deep BLSTM	98.02	Logistic regression	89.22
GRU	97.32	Gradient boosted decision tree	91.10

for a maximum of 100 epochs, but convergence was usually reached after 15–20 epochs, depending on the type of classifier. Batch size of 32 samples was used.

The classifiers also have the following classifier-specific hyper parameters: DNN - Two fully-connected hidden layers of 128 neurons, each with ReLU activation and a dropout rate of 0.2; CNN - 1D ConvNet with 128 output filters, stride length of one, 1D convolution window size of three and ReLU activation, followed by a global max pooling 1D layer and a fully connected layer of 128 neurons with ReLU activation and a dropout rate of 0.2; RNN, LSTM, GRU, BRNN, BLSTM, bidirectional GRU - a hidden layer of 128 units, with a dropout rate of 0.2 for both inputs and recurrent states; Deep LSTM and BLSTM - Two hidden layers of 128 units, with a dropout rate of 0.2 for both inputs and recurrent states in both layers; Linear SVM and logistic regression classifiers - A regularization parameter $C = 1.0$ and L2 norm penalty; Random forest classifier - Using 10 decision trees with unlimited maximum depth and the Gini criteria for choosing the best split; Gradient boosted decision tree - Up to 100 decision trees with a maximum depth of 10 each.

We measured the performance of the classifiers using the accuracy ratio, which applies equal weight to both FP and FN (unlike precision or recall), thereby providing an unbiased overall performance indicator:

$$accuracy = \frac{TP + TN}{TP + FP + TN + FN} \tag{3}$$

where: TP are true positives (malicious samples classified as malicious by the black-box classifier), TN are true negatives, FP stands for false positives (benign samples classified as malicious), and FN are false negatives. The FP rate of the classifiers varied between 0.5-1%.[4]

The performance of the classifiers is shown in Table 1. The accuracy was measured on the test set, which contains 36,000 samples.

---

[4] The FP rate was chosen to be on the high end of production systems. A lower FP rate would mean lower recall either, due-to the trade-off between them, therefore making our attack even more effective.

As can be seen in Table 1, the LSTM variants are the best malware classifiers, accuracy-wise, and, as shown in Table 2, BLSTM is also one of the classifiers most resistant to the proposed attack.

4.3 Attack Performance

In order to measure the performance of an attack, we consider two factors:

The *attack effectiveness* is the number of malware samples in the test set which were detected by the target classifier, for which the adversarial sequences generated by Algorithm 2 were misclassified by the target malware classifier.

$$attack\_effectiveness = \frac{|\{f(\mathbf{x}) = Malicious \vee f(\mathbf{x}^*) = Benign\}|}{|\{f(\mathbf{x}) = Malicious\}|} \quad (4)$$

$$s.t. \ \mathbf{x} \in TestSet(f), \hat{f}_T = Algorithm1(f, T, X_1, \epsilon),$$

$$\mathbf{x}^* = Algorithm2(f, \hat{f}_T, \mathbf{x}, n, D)$$

We also consider the overhead incurred as a result of the proposed attack. The *attack overhead* is the average percentage of the number of API calls which were added by Algorithm 2 to a malware sample successfully detected by the target classifier, in order to make the modified sample classified as benign (therefore calculated only for successful attacks) by the black-box model:

$$attack\_overhead = avg(\frac{added\_APIs}{l}) \quad (5)$$

The average length of the API call sequence is: $avg(l) \approx 100,000$. The adversary chooses the architecture for the surrogate model without any knowledge of the target model's architecture. We chose a GRU surrogate model with 64 units (different from the malware classifiers used in Sect. 4.2), which has a shorter training time compared to other RNN variants, e.g., LSTM, which provides similar attack effectiveness. Besides the classifier's type and architecture, we also used a different optimizer for the surrogate model (ADADELTA instead of Adam). In our implementation, we used the CleverHans library.

Based on Eqs. 4 and 5, the proposed attack's performance is specified in Table 2 (average of three runs).

We can see in Table 2 that the proposed attack has very high effectiveness and low attack overhead against all of the tested malware classifiers. The attack effectiveness is lower for traditional machine learning algorithms, such as SVM, due to the greater difference between the decision boundaries of the GRU surrogate model and the target classifier. Randomly modifying APIs resulted in significantly lower effectiveness for all classifiers (e.g., 50.29% for fully-connected DNN).

As mentioned in Sect. 4.1, $|TestSet(f)| = 36,000$ samples, and the test set $TestSet(f)$ is balanced, so the attack performance was measured on: $|\{f(\mathbf{x}) =$

Table 2. Attack Performance

Classifier Type	Attack Effectiveness (%)	Additional API Calls (%)	Classifier Type	Attack Effectiveness (%)	Additional API Calls (%)
RNN	100.0	0.0023	Bidirectional GRU	95.33	0.0023
BRNN	99.90	0.0017	Fully-Connected DNN	95.66	0.0049
LSTM	99.99	0.0017	1D CNN	100.0	0.0005
Deep LSTM	99.31	0.0029	Random Forest	99.44	0.0009
BLSTM	93.48	0.0029	SVM	70.90	0.0007
Deep BLSTM	96.26	0.0041	Logistic Regression	69.73	0.0007
GRU	100.0	0.0016	Gradient Boosted Tree	71.45	0.0027

$Malicious | \mathbf{x} \in TestSet(f)\}| = 18,000$ samples. For the surrogate model we used a perturbation factor of $\epsilon = 0.2$ and a learning rate of 0.1. $|X_1| = 70$ samples were randomly selected from the test set of 36,000 samples. We used $T = 6$ surrogate epochs. Thus, as shown in Sect. 3.2, the training set size for the surrogate model is: $|X_6| = 2^5 * 70 = 2240$ samples; only 70 ($= |X_1|$) of the samples were selected from the test set distribution, and all of the others were synthetically generated. Using lower values, e.g., $|X_1| = 50$ or $T = 5$, achieved worse attack performance, while larger values do not improve the attack performance and result in a longer training time. The 70 samples from the test set don't cover all of the malware families in the training set; the effectiveness of the surrogate model is due to the synthetic data.

For simplicity and training time, we used $m = n$ for Algorithm 2, i.e., the sliding window size of the adversary is the same as that used by the black-box classifier. However, even if this is not the case, the attack effectiveness isn't degraded significantly. If $n > m$, the adversary would keep trying to modify different API calls' positions in Algorithm 2, until he/she modifies the ones impacting the black-box classifier as well, thereby increasing the attack overhead without affecting the attack effectiveness. If $n < m$, the adversary can modify only a subset of the API calls affecting the black-box classification, and this subset might not be diverse enough to affect the classification as desired, thereby reducing the attack effectiveness. The closer n and m are, the better the attack performance. For $n = 100, m = 140$, there is an average decrease of attack effectiveness from 99.99% to 99.98% for a LSTM classifier.

Comparison to Previous Work. Besides [7] which was written concurrently and independently from our work, [12] is the only recently published RNN adversarial attack. The differences between that attack and the attack addressed in this paper are mentioned in Sect. 2. We compared the attacks in terms of performance. The attack effectiveness for the IMDB dataset was the same (100%), but our attack overhead was better: 11.25 added words per review (on average), instead of 51.25 words using the method mentioned in [12].

4.4 Transferability for RNN Models

While transferability was covered in the past in the context of DNNs (e.g., [18]), to the best of our knowledge, this is the first time it is *evaluated* in the context of RNNs, proving that the proposed attack is generic, not just effective against a specific RNN variant, but is also transferable between RNN variants (like LSTM, GRU, etc.), feed forward DNNs (including CNNs), and even traditional machine learning classifiers such as SVM and random forest.

Two kinds of transferability are relevant to this paper: (1) the adversary can craft adversarial examples against a surrogate model with a different architecture and hyper parameters than the target model, and the same adversarial example would work against both [11], and (2) an adversarial example crafted against one target classifier type might work against a different type of target classifier.

Both forms of transferability are evaluated as follows: (1) As mentioned in Sect. 4.3, we used a GRU surrogate model. However, as can be seen in Table 2, the attack effectiveness is high, even when the black-box classifier is not GRU. Even when the black-box classifier is GRU, the hyper parameters (such as the number of units and the optimizer) are different. (2) The attack was designed against RNN variants; however, we tested it and found the attack to be effective against both feed forward networks and traditional machine learning classifiers, as can be seen in the last six lines of Table 2. Our attack is therefore effective against all malware classifiers.

5 GADGET: End-to-End Attack Framework Description

To verify that an attacker can create an end-to-end attack using the proposed method (Sect. 3), we implemented **GADGET**: **G**enerative **A**pi a**D**versarial **G**eneric **E**xample by **T**ransferability framework. This is an end-to-end attack generation framework that gets a black-box classifier (f in Sect. 3) as an input, an initial surrogate model training set (X_1 in Algorithm 1), and a malware binary to evade f, and outputs a modified malware binary whose API call sequence is misclassified by f as benign, generating the surrogate model ($\hat{f}$ in Algorithm 1) in the process.

GADGET contains the following components: (1) Algorithms 1 and 2, implemented in Python, using Keras with TensorFlow back end, (2) A C++ Wrapper to wrap the malware binary and modify its generated API call sequence during run time, and (3) A Python script that wraps the malware binary with the

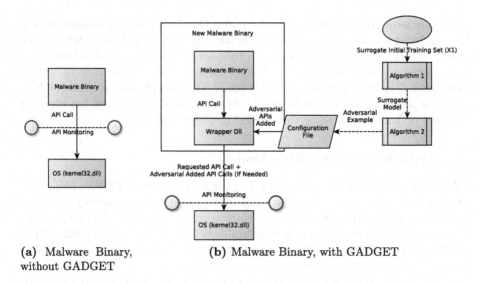

(a) Malware Binary,
without GADGET

(b) Malware Binary, with GADGET

Fig. 3. Malware binary, with and without GADGET

above mentioned wrapper, making it ready to deploy. The components appear in Fig. 3.

Adding API Calls Without Damaging Functionality. As mentioned in Sect. 3.2, we implemented Algorithm 2 using a *mimicry attack* [21]. We discarded *equivalence attacks* and *disguise attacks* (Sect. 2), since they lack the flexibility needed to modify *every API call*, and thus are not robust enough to camouflage every malware. Therefore, we implemented a *no-op attack,* adding APIs which would have no effect on the code's functionality. Since some API call monitors (such as Cuckoo Sandbox) also monitor the return value of an API call and might ignore failed API calls, we decided to implement the API addition by adding no-op API calls with valid parameters, e.g., reading 0 bytes from a valid file. This was more challenging to implement than calling APIs with invalid arguments (e.g., reading from an invalid file handle), since a different implementation should be used for each API. However, this effort can be done once and can subsequently be used for every malware, as we've done in our framework. This makes detecting those no-op APIs much harder, since the API call runs correctly, with a return value indicative of success. The functionality validation of the modified malware is discussed in Sect. 5. Further measures, such as randomized arguments, can be taken by the attacker to prevent the detection of the no-op APIs by analyzing the arguments of the API calls. Attacking a classifier with argument inputs is discussed in Sect. 5.

Implementing a Generic Framework. The requirements for the generic framework are: (1) there is no access to the malware source code (access only to the malware binary executable), and (2) the same code should work for every adversarial sample: no adversarial example-specific code should be written. The reasons for these requirements are two-fold. First, adding the code as a wrapper, without changing the malware's business logic makes the framework more robust to modification of the malware classifier model, preventing another session of malware code modification and testing. Second, with the Malware-as-a-Service trend, not everyone who uses a malware has its code. Some ransomwares are automatically generated using minimal configuration (e.g., only the CNC server is modified by the user), without source code access. Thus, the GADGET framework expands the number of users that can produce an evasive malware from malware developers to every person that purchases a malware binary, making the threat much greater.

In order to meet those requirements, we wrap the malware binary from the outside with proxy code between the malware code and the OS DLLs implementing the API calls (e.g., kernel32.dll), fulfilling requirement #1. The wrapper code gets the adversarial sequence for the malware binary, generated by Algorithm 2, as a configuration file. The logic of this wrapper code is to hook all APIs that will be monitored by the malware classifier. These API calls are known to the attacker, as mentioned in Sect. 3.2. These hooks call the original APIs (to preserve the original malware functionality), keep track of the API sequence executed so far, and call the adversarial example's additional APIs in the proper position based on the configuration file (so they will be monitored by the malware classifier), instead of hard-coding the adversarial sequence to the code (fulfilling requirement #2). This flow is presented in Fig. 3b.

We generated a new malware binary that contains the wrapper's hooks by patching the malware binary's IAT using IAT Patcher, redirecting the IAT's API calls' addresses to the matching C++ wrapper API hook implementation. That way, if another hook (e.g., Cuckoo Sandbox) monitors the API calls, the adversarial APIs are already being called and monitored like any regular API call. To affect dynamic libraries, *LdrGetProcedureAddress()\ GetProcAddress()* hook has additional functionality: it doesn't return a pointer to the requested procedure, but instead returns a pointer to a wrapper function that implements the previously described regular static hook functionality around the requested procedure (e.g., returning a pointer to a wrapper around *WriteFile()* if "Write-File" is the argument to *GetProcAddress()*). When the malware code calls the pointer, the hook functionality will be called, transparent to the user.

The code is POC and does not cover all corner cases, e.g., wrapping a packed malware, which requires special handling for the IAT patching to work, or packing the wrapper code to evade statically signing it as malicious (its functionality is implemented inline, without external API calls, so dynamic analysis of it is challenging). We avoided running Algorithm 2 inside the wrapper, and used the configuration file to store the modified APIs instead, thus preventing much greater overhead for the (wrapped) malware code.

5.1   Adversarial Example Functionality Validation

In order to *automatically* verify that we do not harm the functionality of the malware we modify, we monitored each sample in Cuckoo Monitor before and after the modification. We define the modified sample as *functionality preserving* if the API call sequence after the modification is the same as before the modification when comparing API type, return value and order of API calls, except for the added API calls, which return value should always be a success value. We found that all of the 18,000 modified samples are *functionality preserving*.

One of the families that did not exist in the training set was the WannaCry ransomware. This makes it an excellent candidate to *manually* analyze GADGET's output. First, we ran the sample via Cuckoo Sandbox and recorded its API calls. The LSTM malware classifier mentioned in Sect. 4.2 successfully detected it as malicious, although it was not part of the training set. Then we used GADGET to generate a new WannaCry variant, providing this variant the configuration file containing the adversarial sequence generated by Algorithm 2. We ran the modified WannaCry binary, wrapped with our framework and the configuration file, in Cuckoo Sandbox again, and fed the recorded API call sequence to the same LSTM malware classifier. This time, the malware classifier classification was benign, although the malicious functionality remains: files were still being encrypted by the new binary, as can be seen in the Cuckoo Sandbox snapshot and API call sequence. This means that the proposed attack was successful, end-to-end, without damaging WannaCry's functionality.

5.2   Handling API Arguments

We now modify our attack to evade classifiers that analyze arguments as well. In order to represent the API call arguments, we used MIST [20], as was done by other malware classifiers, e.g., MALHEUR [14]. MIST (Malware Instruction Set) is a representation for monitored behavior of malicious software, optimized for analysis of behavior using machine learning. Each API call translates to an instruction. Each instruction has levels of information. The first level corresponds to the category and name of a monitored API call. The following levels of the instruction contain different blocks of arguments. The main idea underlying this arrangement is to move "noisy" elements, such as the loading address of a DLL, to the end of an instruction, while discriminative patterns, such as the loaded DLL file path, are kept at the beginning of the instruction. We used MIST level 2. We converted our Cuckoo Sandbox reports to MIST using Cuckoo2Mist. We extracted a total of 220 million lines of MIST instructions from our dataset. Of those, only several hundred of lines were unique, i.e., different permutations of argument values extracted in MIST level 2. This means that most API calls differ only in arguments that are not relevant to the classification or use the same arguments. To handle MIST arguments, we modified our attack in the following way: Instead of one-hot encoding every API call type, we one-hot encoded every unique [API call type, MIST level 2 arguments] combination. Thus, *LoadLibrary* ("kernel32.dll") and *LoadLibrary* ("user32.dll") are now regarded as separate

APIs by the classifier. Our framework remains the same, where Algorithm 2 selects the most impactful combination instead of API type. However, instead of adding combinations that might harm the code's functionality (e.g., *ExitWindowsEx*()), we simply add a different API call type (the one with the minimal Jacobian value) in Algorithm 2, which would **not** cause this issue. We now assume a more informed attacker, who knows not just the exact encoding of each API type, but also the exact encoding of every argument combination. This is a reasonable assumption since arguments used by benign programs, like Windows DLLs file paths, are known to attackers [8].

Handling other API arguments (and not MIST level 2) would be similar, but require more preprocessing (word embedding, etc.) with a negligible effect on the classifier accuracy. Thus, focusing only on the most important arguments (MIST level 2) that can be used by the classifier to distinguish between malware and benign software, as done in other papers [9], proves that analyzing arguments is not an obstacle for the proposed attack.

5.3   Handling Hybrid Classifiers and Multiple Feature Types

Since our attack modifies only a specific feature type (API calls), combining several types of features might make the classifier more resistant to adversarial examples against a specific feature type. Some real-world next generation anti-malware products (such as SentinelOne) are hybrid classifiers, combining both static and dynamic features for a better detection rate.

Our attack can be extended to handle hybrid classifiers using two phases: (1) the creation of a *combined surrogate* model, including all features, using Algorithm 1, and (2) attacking *each feature type in turn* with a specialized attack, using the surrogate model. If the attack against a feature type fails, we continue and attack the next feature type until a benign classification by the target model is achieved or until all feature types have been (unsuccessfully) attacked.

We decided to use printable strings inside a PE file as our static features, as they are commonly used as the static features of state of the art hybrid malware classifiers [9], although any other modifiable feature type can be used. Strings can be used, e.g., to statically identify loaded DLLs and called functions, recognize modified file paths and registry keys, etc. Our architecture for the hybrid classifier, shown in Fig. 2b, is: (1) A dynamic branch that contains an input vector of 140 API calls, each one-hot encoded, inserted into a LSTM layer of 128 units, and sigmoid activation function, with a dropout rate of 0.2 for both inputs and recurrent states. (2) A static branch that contains an input vector of 20,000 Boolean values: for each of the 20,000 most frequent strings in the entire dataset, do they appear in the file or not? (analogous to a similar procedure used in NLP, which filters the least frequent words in a language). This vector is inserted into two fully-connected layers with 128 neurons, a ReLU activation function, and a dropout rate of 0.2 each. The 256 outputs of both branches are inserted into a fully-connected output layer with sigmoid activation function. Therefore, the input of the classifier is a vector containing 140 one-hot encoded APIs and 20,000 Boolean values, and the output is malicious or benign classification. All other hyper parameters are the same as in Sect. 4.2. The surrogate model used has a similar architecture to the attacked hybrid model described above, but it uses a different architecture and hyper parameters: GRU instead of LSTM in the dynamic branch and 64 hidden units instead of 128 in both static and dynamic surrogate branches. Due to hardware limitations, we used just a subset of the dataset: 54,000 training samples and test and validation sets of 6,000 samples each. The dataset was representative and maintained the same distribution as the dataset described in Sect. 4.1. Trained on this dataset, a classifier using only the dynamic branch (Fig. 2a) reaches 92.48% accuracy on the test set, a classifier using only the static branch attains 96.19% accuracy, and a hybrid model, using both branches (Fig. 2b) achieves 96.94% accuracy, meaning that using multiple feature types improves the accuracy.

We used two specialized attacks: an attack against API call sequences and an attack against printable strings. The API sequence attack is Algorithm 2. When performing it against the hybrid classifier, without modifying the static features of the sample, the attack effectiveness (Eq. 4) decreases to 45.95%, compared to 96.03% against a classifier trained only on the dynamic features, meaning that the attack was mitigated by the use of additional features. The strings attack is a variant of the attack described in [5], using the surrogate model instead of the attacked model used in [5] to compute the gradients in order to select the string to add, while the adversarial sample's maliciousness is still tested against the attacked model, making this method a black-box attack. In this case, the attack effectiveness is 68.66%, compared to 77.33% against a classifier trained only on the static features. Finally, the combined attack's effectiveness against the hybrid model was 82.27%. Other classifier types provide similar results which are not presented here due to space limits.

We designed GADGET with the ability to handle a hybrid model, by adding its configuration file's static features' modification entries. Each such string is appended to the original binary before being IAT patched, either to the EOF or to a new section, where those modifications don't affect the binary's functionality.

To summarize, we have shown that while the usage of hybrid models decreases the specialized attacks' effectiveness, using our suggested hybrid attack achieves high effectiveness. While not shown due to space limits, the attack overhead isn't significantly affected.

6   Conclusions and Future Work

In this paper, we demonstrated a generic black-box attack, generating adversarial sequences against API call sequence based malware classifiers. Unlike previous adversarial attacks, we have shown an attack with a verified effectiveness against all relevant common classifiers: RNN variants, feed forward networks, and traditional machine learning classifiers. Therefore, this is a true black-box attack, which requires no knowledge about the classifier besides the monitored APIs. We also created the GADGET framework, showing that the generation of the adversarial sequences can be done end-to-end, in a generic way, without access to the malware source code. Finally, we showed that the attack is effective, even when arguments are analyzed or multiple feature types are used. Our attack is *the first practical* **end-to-end** *attack* dealing with all of the subtleties of the cyber security domain, posing a concrete threat to next generation anti-malware products, which have become more and more popular. While this paper focus on API calls and printable strings as features, the proposed attack is valid for every modifiable feature type, static or dynamic.

Our future work will focus on two areas: defense mechanisms against such attacks and attack modifications to cope with such mechanisms. Due to space limits, we plan to publish an in depth analysis of various defense mechanisms in future work. The defense mechanisms against such attacks can be divided into two subgroups: (1) detection of adversarial examples, and (2) making the classifier resistant to adversarial attacks. To the best of our knowledge, there is currently no published and evaluated method to detect or mitigate RNN adversarial sequences. This will be part of our future work. We would also compare between the effectiveness of different surrogate models' architecture.

References

1. Arjovsky, M., Bottou, L.: Towards principled methods for training generative adversarial networks. In: ICLR (2017)
2. Carlini, N., Wagner, D.: Towards evaluating the robustness of neural networks. In: IEEE S&P (2017)
3. Chen, P.Y., Zhang, H., Sharma, Y., Yi, J., Hsieh, C.J.: Zoo: zeroth order optimization based black-box attacks to deep neural networks without training substitute models. In: ACM Workshop on Artificial Intelligence and Security (2017)
4. Goodfellow, I.J., Shlens, J., Szegedy, C.: Explaining and harnessing adversarial examples. In: ICLR (2015)
5. Grosse, K., Papernot, N., Manoharan, P., Backes, M., McDaniel, P.: Adversarial examples for malware detection. In: Foley, S.N., Gollmann, D., Snekkenes, E. (eds.) ESORICS 2017. LNCS, vol. 10493, pp. 62–79. Springer, Cham (2017). https://doi.org/10.1007/978-3-319-66399-9_4
6. Hu, W., Tan, Y.: Generating adversarial malware examples for black-box attacks based on GAN. ArXiv e-prints, abs/1702.05983 (2017)
7. Hu, W., Tan, Y.: Black-box attacks against RNN based malware detection algorithms. ArXiv e-prints, abs/1705.08131 (2017)
8. Huang, L., Joseph, A.D., Nelson, B., Rubinstein, B.I.P., Tygar, J.D.: Adversarial machine learning. In: ACM Workshop on Security and Artificial Intelligence (2011)
9. Huang, W., Stokes, J.W.: MtNet: a multi-task neural network for dynamic malware classification. In: Caballero, J., Zurutuza, U., Rodríguez, R.J. (eds.) DIMVA 2016. LNCS, vol. 9721, pp. 399–418. Springer, Cham (2016). https://doi.org/10.1007/978-3-319-40667-1_20
10. Papernot, N., McDaniel, P., Jha, S.H., Fredrikson, M., Celik, Z.B., Swami, A.: The limitations of deep learning in adversarial settings. In: IEEE European Symposium on Security and Privacy (2016)
11. Papernot, N., McDaniel, P., Goodfellow, I., Jha, S., Celik, Z.B., Swami, A.: Practical black-box attacks against machine learning. In: ASIA CCS (2017)

12. Papernot, N., McDaniel, P., Swami, A., Harang, R.: Crafting adversarial input sequences for recurrent neural networks. In: IEEE MILCOM (2016)
13. Pascanu, R., Stokes, J.W., Sanossian, H., Marinescu, M., Thomas, A.: Malware classification with recurrent networks. In: IEEE ICASSP (2015)
14. Rieck, K., Trinius, P., Willems, C., Holz, T.: Automatic analysis of malware behavior using machine learning. J. Comput. Secur. **19**, 639–668 (2011)
15. Rosenberg, I., Gudes, E.: Bypassing system calls-based intrusion detection systems. Concurr. Comput.: Pract. Exp. (2016)
16. Rosenberg, I., Sicard, G., David, E.O.: DeepAPT: nation-state APT attribution using end-to-end deep neural networks. In: Lintas, A., Rovetta, S., Verschure, P.F.M.J., Villa, A.E.P. (eds.) ICANN 2017. LNCS, vol. 10614, pp. 91–99. Springer, Cham (2017). https://doi.org/10.1007/978-3-319-68612-7_11
17. Rosenberg, I., Shabtai, A., Rokach, L., Elovici, Y.: Low resource black-box end-to-end attack against state of the art API call based malware classifiers, arXiv preprint arXiv:1804.08778 (2018)
18. Szegedy, C., et al.: Intriguing properties of neural networks. In: ICLR (2014)
19. Tandon, G., Chan, P.K.: On the learning of system call attributes for host-based anomaly detection. Int. J. Artif. Intell. Tools **15**, 875–892 (2006)
20. Trinius, P., Willems, C., Holz, T., Rieck, K.: A malware instruction set for behavior-based analysis. In: Sicherheit (2010)
21. Wagner, D., Soto, P.: Mimicry attacks on host-based intrusion detection systems. In: ACM CCS (2002)

Next Generation P2P Botnets: Monitoring Under Adverse Conditions

Leon Böck[1][(✉)], Emmanouil Vasilomanolakis[1], Max Mühlhäuser[1],
and Shankar Karuppayah[2]

[1] Telecooperation Lab, Technische Universität Darmstadt, Darmstadt, Germany
{boeck,vasilomano,max}@tk.tu-darmstadt.de
[2] National Advanced IPv6 Centre, Universiti Sains Malaysia (USM), Gelugor,
Malaysia
kshankar@usm.my

Abstract. The effects of botnet attacks, over the years, have been devastating. From high volume Distributed Denial of Service (DDoS) attacks to ransomware attacks, it is evident that defensive measures need to be taken. Indeed, there has been a number of successful takedowns of botnets that exhibit a centralized architecture. However, this is not the case with distributed botnets that are more resilient and armed with countermeasures against monitoring. In this paper, we argue that monitoring countermeasures, applied by botmasters, will only become more sophisticated; to such an extent that monitoring, under these adverse conditions, may become infeasible. That said, we present the most detailed analysis, to date, of parameters that influence a P2P botnet's resilience and monitoring resistance. Integral to our analysis, we introduce BotChurn (BC) a realistic and botnet-focused churn generator that can assist in the analysis of botnets. Our experimental results suggest that certain parameter combinations greatly limit intelligence gathering operations. Furthermore, our analysis highlights the need for extensive collaboration between defenders. For instance, we show that even the combined knowledge of 500 monitoring instances is insufficient to fully enumerate some of the examined botnets. In this context, we also raise the question of whether botnet monitoring will still be feasible in the near future.

1 Introduction

Botnets are networks of infected computers, that can be remotely controlled by malicious entities, commonly referred to as botmasters. Botnets have been historically used for launching a multitude of attacks, ranging from DDoS and blackmailing, to credential theft, banking fraud, etc. Recently, with the emergence of the Internet of Things (IoT), the landscape of vulnerable connected devices has increased significantly. This led to a resurgence of many new botnets infecting weakly protected IoT devices. These IoT botnets are particularly notorious for their high bandwidth DDoS attacks, bringing down even well protected websites and services.

© Springer Nature Switzerland AG 2018
M. Bailey et al. (Eds.): RAID 2018, LNCS 11050, pp. 511–531, 2018.
https://doi.org/10.1007/978-3-030-00470-5_24

An approach to remove the botnet threat, is to identify and take down the Command and Control (C2) channel used by the botmasters. For centralized botnets, this has proven to be an effective approach with many being taken down by seizing their respective C2 servers [7]. More advanced botnets overcome this Single Point of Failure (SPoF), by employing a peer-to-peer (P2P) C2 structure, where each bot acts as a server and a client. Hence, defenders have to target the majority of bots to take the botnet down. This requires knowledge about the population and inter-connectivity of the botnet, which is commonly achieved via monitoring. Monitoring mechanisms are commonly developed by reverse engineering and re-implementing the communication protocol of a botnet to gather intelligence. As botnet monitoring poses a threat for the botmasters, many botnets, e.g., GameOver Zeus [3] and Sality [6], implement monitoring countermeasures. These mechanisms increase the difficulty of monitoring operations, but do not prevent them [20]. Nevertheless, recent publications presented sophisticated countermeasures, that further limit or even prevent monitoring activities [2,14,25]. Hence, we argue that it is a matter of time until botmasters introduce such countermeasures to impede monitoring in its current form.

To deal with next-generation botnets, we need to understand the extent at which advanced countermeasures prevent monitoring operations. Investigating each of the countermeasures individually will likely end in a never ending arms race for new monitoring and anti-monitoring mechanisms. To avoid this arms race, we instead introduce a lower boundary for monitoring operations in adverse conditions, i.e., monitoring in the presence of sophisticated countermeasures.

To achieve this, we make the assumption that a botmaster can detect any behavior deviating from that of a normal bot. Therefore, the maximum intelligence that can be gathered with a single monitoring instance is limited to the information that can be obtained by any regular bot itself. As this can vary for different botnets, we analyze several botnet parameterizations to be able to evaluate how much intelligence can be gathered in different botnet designs. This allows us to evaluate the effectiveness of monitoring operations in adverse conditions, based on the parameters of the botnet protocol. To ensure that our simulations accurately replicate the behavior of real bots, we utilize churn measurements taken from live botnets [11]. Moreover, we develop and present a novel botnet churn generator that simulates churn more accurately than the state of the art. At a glance, the two major contributions of this paper are:

– An *extensive analysis* of botnet designs and parameterizations, with an emphasis to their resilience and monitoring resistance.
– A *realistic* and *botnet-focused* churn generator, namely BotChurn (BC).

The remainder of this paper is structured as follows. Sections 2 and 3, introduce the background information and the related work respectively. Section 4, presents our analysis regarding the effectiveness of monitoring in adverse conditions. Section 5, provides a detailed description of our proposed botnet churn generator. Section 6 discusses the evaluation of our churn generator and the effectiveness of monitoring in adverse conditions. Lastly, Sect. 7, concludes our work and presents outlooks with regard to our future work.

2   Background

In the following, we provide background information with regard to P2P botnets and their underlying technologies as well as introductory information regarding common monitoring mechanisms.

2.1   P2P Botnets

The decentralized nature of P2P botnets and the absence of a SPoF, makes them highly resilient against takedown attempts [20]. P2P networks can be categorized into structured and unstructured overlays. *Structured* P2P overlays such as Kademlia [16] use a concept called *Distributed Hash Table (DHT)*. As an example, Kademlia implements a ring structure on which all *peers*, i.e., participants in the P2P network, are placed based on their ID. Peers connect to a set peers, based on their distance in the ring structure. *Unstructured* P2P overlays do not have such a structure but maintain connectivity based on a Membership Management (MM) mechanism. At the core of this MM is a so called Neighborlist (NL). The NL consists of a subset of all existing peers commonly referred to as *neighbors*. To maintain connectivity within the network, peers frequently exchange NL-entries with their neighbors.

For botnets, the major difference between structured and unstructured P2P networks is related to the difficulty of monitoring. For instance, structured botnets, e.g., *Storm* [10], can be monitored efficiently [21]. More recent P2P botnets such as *Sality* [6], *GameOver Zeus* [3] and *ZeroAccess* [18] use unstructured P2P overlays. This makes them more difficult to be monitored, as the lack of a structure prevents the usage of efficient approaches applicable to structured P2P networks. Due to the greater resistance against monitoring attempts, this paper focuses on unstructured P2P botnets.

A major challenge for any P2P overlay is the handling of node churn, i.e., nodes leaving and joining the network. Churn is caused by diurnal patterns or by machines being turned off and on throughout the globe. To ensure that the network remains connected under the effects of churn, P2P overlays leverage the MM system. The MM ensures that inactive peers, in the NL of a node, are replaced with responsive peers. This is usually achieved by probing the activity of all entries in an NL at fixed intervals. Common values for such Membership Management Interval (MMIs) are between *one* second [18] and 40 min [6].

If an entry in the NL of a bot is unresponsive for several consecutive MMIs, it is removed from the NL. To replace removed peers, a node commonly asks their own neighbors for responsive candidates by sending an *NL-request*. A bot's NL can also be passively updated upon receipt of a message from a bot that is not in the bot's NL [3]. This allows the bots to maintain active connections among bots within the P2P overlay despite being affected by churn.

2.2   Botnet Monitoring Mechanisms

To obtain information about the extent of a botnet infection, one has to conduct intelligence gathering by monitoring the botnet. Monitoring a P2P botnet is achieved via the usage of crawlers, sensors or a combination of both. At a glance, crawlers are more of an active approach whereas sensors are more passive.

A *crawler* enumerates the botnet by continuously requesting NL-entries from bots. Given a list of *seed-nodes*, a crawler follows a crawling strategy such as Breadth-First Search (BFS), Depth-First Search (DFS) or Less Invasive Crawling Algorithm (LICA) [12] to discover bots within the botnet. The seed-list is updated between crawls by adding all newly discovered bots into it. This allows crawlers to quickly obtain information about participating bots and their inter-connectivity. The major drawback of crawlers is that they cannot discover bots that are behind Network Address Translation (NAT) or a firewall. Such bots usually cannot be contacted from the Internet, unless they initiate the connection first. Therefore, crawlers underestimate the population of a botnet [20]. Moreover, the aggressive sending of *NL-requests* makes crawlers easy to detect [14].

Sensors can provide more accurate enumerations of botnets by overcoming the aforesaid drawback of crawlers. A sensor imitates the behavior of a regular bot by responding to probe messages from other bots. By remaining active within the botnet for prolonged periods, sensors become popular within the botnet. That is, more bots will add the sensor to their NL and frequently contact it during their MMI. This allows a sensor to accurately keep track of the entire botnet population including those that are behind NAT-like devices. However, a major drawback for sensors is the lack of inter-connectivity information of the botnet. Therefore, sensors are commonly used as an addition to crawlers instead of a replacement. Another drawback of sensors is that they require time to become popular and therefore do not yield results as quickly as crawlers. This can again be surmounted by using a crawler to help spread information about the sensor to speed up the popularization process [27].

3   Related Work

In this section, we discuss the state of the art of: (*i*) P2P botnet monitoring techniques and (*ii*) advanced countermeasures against monitoring.

3.1   P2P Botnet Monitoring

Rossow et al. present an in-depth analysis on the resilience against intelligence gathering and disruption of P2P botnets [20]. They analyze the peer enumeration capabilities of sensors and crawlers on several P2P botnets and provide real world results. Furthermore, they analyze the resilience of these botnets against communication layer poisoning and sink-holing attacks. Their work clearly presents the drawbacks and benefits of crawlers and sensors. The authors also present an analysis of reconnaissance countermeasures implemented by botnets. Most notably, botnets such as Sality and GameOver Zeus implement rate limiting mechanisms on neighborlist replies. In addition, GameOver Zeus implements an automated blacklisting mechanism against aggressive crawlers.

Karuppayah et al. introduce a new crawling strategy called LICA [12]. Their crawling algorithm approximates the minimum vertex coverage by prioritizing nodes with high in-degree. Their approach provides a means to crawl a botnet faster and more efficiently compared to BFS or DFS. Yan et al. present a sensor popularization method called *popularity boosting* [27]. Popularity boosting leverages a mechanism that botnets commonly use to allow new bots to get into other peers NLs. For instance, in the Sality botnet, a bot can send a *server-announcement-message* upon joining the botnet. If the bot fulfills a set of conditions, such as being publicly routable, it will be added at the end of the receiving bot's NL. This mechanism allows sensors to be quickly injected into the NL of active bots in a botnet. In [13], the authors present an algorithm that efficiently extracts all entries from a bot's NL in the GameOver Zeus botnet. Contrary to a random spoofing of IDs, their strategic approach guarantees to extract all entries from a bot's NL. Lastly, botnet detection mechanisms such as [8,17] also provide monitoring information about botnets. While the main goal this research is to detect botnets within a monitored network, this information can also be used for enumeration or derivation of connectivity between individual bots.

3.2   Monitoring Countermeasures

In this section, we introduce the landscape of monitoring countermeasures. We differentiate between countermeasures that have been implemented by botmasters and novel countermeasures that have been proposed by researchers.

Existing Anti-monitoring Mechanisms: As monitoring poses a threat to botmasters, some botnets implement features specifically aimed at preventing monitoring attempts. Many botnets such as *GameOver Zeus* [3], *Sality* [6], and *ZeroAccess* [18] implement restricted Neighborlist Reply Sizes (NLRSs). This means, that when being requested, they only share a subset of their NL to the requesting bot. This significantly increases the enumeration effort for crawlers.

Furthermore, *GameOver Zeus* implements an automated blacklisting mechanism that blacklists a node if it sends more than *five* requests within a sliding window of *one* minute. The Sality botnet also implements a simple trust mechanism called *Goodcount*. For each NL-entry, such a *Goodcount* value is maintained. A bot sends periodic messages to all its neighbors and increases a nodes *Goodcount* upon receipt of a valid reply and decreases the *Goodcount* otherwise. This locally maintained reputation mechanism prevents that a bot replaces well known active NL-entries with newer entries, e.g., sensors.

Proposed Advanced Anti-monitoring Mechanisms: Andriesse et al. analyzed whether sensors and crawlers can be detected, from the botmasters' perspective, based on protocol and behavioral anomalies [2]. Their findings suggest that crawlers can indeed be detected based on anomalous behavior. The anomalies that were used for identifying the crawlers, vary from implementation-specific ones to logical and protocol level misconducts. The authors were also able to detect sensor nodes based on deviating (protocol) features.

Karuppayah et al. present another mechanism, that uses a bot's local view to identify crawlers within a P2P botnet [14]. For that, they focus on protocol violations that are common for crawlers in all P2P botnets. Upon detection, a bot can blacklist the crawler and prevent any further communication with it.

In [5,11], the authors use graph connectivity metrics to identify sensor nodes within P2P overlays. Both approaches are based on the assumption that researchers and law enforcement agencies cannot aid the botnet in any way, including the returning of valid neighbors when being asked. Böck et al. [5] use the *Local Clustering Coefficient (LCC)* mechanism to detect sensors that do not have any neighbors or groups of sensors that are fully meshed. Moreover [11], improves upon this and introduces two other mechanisms based on *PageRank* [19] and *Strongly Connected Components (SCCs)*. Their proposed mechanisms cannot be easily avoided by defenders as they require either large numbers of colluding sensors or active sharing of valid neighbors when being requested. Lastly, Vasilomanolakis et al. propose the use of computational trust for calculating trust scores for all neighbors of a bot [25]. This allows them to automatically blacklist bots that refuse to cooperate in the sharing of commands.

4   Botnet Monitoring Under Adverse Conditions

The adoption of advanced countermeasures will change the landscape of botnet monitoring. Here, we define the term adverse conditions and discuss approaches for monitoring in the presence of countermeasures. Furthermore, we introduce the idea of leveraging the Membership Management (MM) to obstruct monitoring operations. Moreover, we discuss the limitations of the MM design with regard to the trade-off between monitoring resistance and the resilience of botnets.

4.1   Identifying the Worst-Case Monitoring Scenario

We contend, that existing botnet monitoring mechanisms may no longer be feasible under adverse conditions (see Sect. 3). Therefore, new approaches to monitor botnets are urgently needed. Based on our analysis of the related work, we propose *five* approaches to conduct monitoring in adverse conditions. Namely these are: *short-term monitoring, network traffic analysis, network scanning, taking control of active bots*, and *running botnet malware in controlled environments*.

Depending on the specifics of the implemented anti-monitoring mechanisms, *short-term monitoring* may be possible for monitoring using crawlers and sensors. To avoid preemptive blacklisting of legitimate bots, anti-monitoring mechanisms may require multiple anomalous interactions before a blacklisting occurs [25]. This can allow short-time monitoring, in which the anti-monitoring mechanisms are not triggered. Furthermore, if sufficient resources are available, blacklisted IPs can be replaced to perform continuous monitoring. The major drawback of this approach is the scarcity of IP addresses which leads to higher costs and eventually IPs run out due to blacklisting.

Network traffic analysis based monitoring approaches are not affected by the anti-monitoring mechanisms described in Sect. 3. Traffic based monitoring passively analyzes the network traffic and is therefore outside the scope of advanced countermeasures. Approaches such as [8,17] can detect botnet traffic on top of Internet Service Provider (ISP) level network traces. The benefit of this approach is that it provides a centralized view on all bot infections within the network and their neighbors. Nevertheless, this approach is unlikely to provide a holistic view of the botnet unless all ISPs cooperate and share their information.

Alternatively, another approach is to scan the Internet for botnet activity on specific ports. Such a *network scanning* approach has already been done to obtain bootstrap nodes for crawling the ZeroAccess botnet [15]. This requires the botnet to use a fixed port for its communication which is the case for botnets such as the ZeroAccess family [18]. In fact, tools such as ZMAP are capable of rapidly scanning the entire IPv4 address space [1]. However, many recent botnets implement dynamic ports to avoid being scanned easily.

Another approach to obtain intelligence about a botnet can be to *take control of active bots*. This could theoretically be realized by anti-virus companies or operating system manufacturers. Once the malware is identified, the related network traffic can be analyzed to identify other infected hosts. Furthermore, if detailed knowledge about the malware is available, malicious traffic could be blocked. This would allow the controlling parties to use the infected machines themselves as monitors by analyzing the MM traffic.

In addition, it is also possible to *run and observe botnet malware in a controlled environment*, such as a bare metal machine or a controlled virtual environment. Contrary to taking control of an infected device, a clean machine is deliberately infected with the botnet malware. This allows to set up machines specifically for botnet monitoring, e.g. not storing sensitive data, rate limiting network connections, or installing software to analyze the network traffic. Even with such safeguards, legal and ethical limitations need to be considered with this approach.

Defining exactly how much information can be gathered under adverse conditions is not possible, as combinations of monitoring and sophisticated countermeasures will only lead to a never-ending arms race. However, all of the discussed monitoring approaches can gather at least as much information as a regular bot without being detected. In fact, network-based monitoring approaches on the ISP level will likely observe traffic of multiple infections at once. To avoid the aforementioned arms race, we focus on the worst-case scenario and establish a lower boundary for monitoring under adverse conditions.

Based on the findings of this section, we want to define the term Monitoring Device (MD) *as any monitoring approach, that obtains intelligence based on the view of a bot*. Similarly, we define the term *adverse conditions* as a botnet environment in which any behavior deviating form that of a normal bot can be automatically detected by botmasters. Therefore, we argue that the lower boundary for monitoring operations in adverse conditions is *limited to the knowledge/view that can be obtained by any regular bot itself.*

4.2 Limiting Monitoring Information Through the MM Design

The amount of information a single bot can obtain influences the results of monitoring in adverse conditions. Hence, it is likely that botmasters will design their botnets such that a single bot learns as less as possible about the botnet without jeopardizing the resilience of the botnet itself. This can be achieved by tweaking the MM protocol of the botnet. At its core, the MM protocol must provide three features: maintain an NL, provide a means to update the NL and frequently check the availability of neighbors. To identify how these requirements are met by existing botnets, we identified and compared the related parameters of five existing P2P botnets in Table 1.

The need of maintaining an NL is commonly addressed with two parameters, the NL-size and the Neighborlist Minimum Threshold (NLMT). The NL-size is an integer indicating the maximum size of the NL. The NLMT is another integer indicating the minimum number of bots that should always be maintained. A bot will not remove any more bots once this threshold is reached, and it will start sending *NL*-requests to obtain fresh entries. Oftentimes, botnets do not explicitly state an NLMT and instead have NL-size = NLMT. To update a bot's NL, both push or pull based NL-updates can be used. Push based updates allow a bot to insert itself into another bot's NL and are commonly only used for bots joining a botnet. Pull based updates are usually realized through *NL-request* messages, which allow a bot to ask actively for additional bots. *NL-request* messages are often affected by an Neighborlist Reply Size (NLRS) which limits the number of bots shared upon a single request, and the Neighborlist Reply Preference (NLRP) which defines how the shared bots are selected. Lastly, to check the availability of their neighbors, bots commonly probe all NL-entries during the MMI.

To illustrate how MM can be used to limit monitoring information, we consider the following scenario. The NLMT indicates the minimal number of neighbors with whom a bot communicates regularly. Thus, limiting the NLMT is an effective measure to limit the knowledge that can be obtained by a bot. However, the NLMT is not the only parameter that can limit this type of knowledge. Other parameters such as the MMI, the number of nodes returned upon an NL-request, the churn behavior of the botnet or which neighbors are returned when being requested, can influence the amount of knowledge each bot can obtain about the botnet. In Sect. 6, we examine in detail, how each parameter influences the knowledge obtainable by a single bot, i.e., the lower boundary knowledge for monitoring operations under adverse conditions.

4.3 Botnet Design Constraints

Optimizing a botnet's MM to impede monitoring operations, comes at a cost. The usage of P2P overlays for inter-bot communication was initially intended

Table 1. Analysis of common MM parameters and their values.

	GameOver Zeus [3]	Sality [6]	ZeroAccess [26]	Kelihos F. [20]	Nugache [20]
Pull based updates	Yes	Yes	Yes	Yes	Yes
Push based updates	Always	Join	Join	Join	Join
MMI	30 min	40 min	1 s	10 min	Random
NL-size	50	1000	256	3000	100
NLRS	<= 10	1	16	250 (v3), 500 (v5,v6)	100
NLMT	25	980	Unknown	Unknown	Unknown
NLRP	Custom	Random	Latest	Latest	Latest

to improve the resilience against takedown attempts. However, we expect that the resilience of a botnet's overlay is inversely proportional to the monitoring resistance of a botnet. That is, by limiting the knowledge obtainable by a bot, the robustness of the resulting overlay suffers.

This can be visualized by observing two extreme cases. On the one hand, the most resilient network architecture is a complete mesh in which each node knows all other nodes in the system. Such a network is very resilient as the failure of some nodes does not influence the connectivity of the remaining nodes. However, in a complete mesh, every bot also has complete knowledge about the botnet population. On the other hand, a minimally connected network such as a ring provides minimal knowledge to nodes at the cost of poor resilience to node failures or targeted attacks. Therefore, a botmaster has to consider both resilience and resistance against monitoring operations when designing the MM.

4.4 Connecting the Dots

Within this section, we discussed possible approaches to conduct monitoring in adverse conditions, how MM can be used to obstruct monitoring operations, and the trade-off between monitoring resistance and resilience in MM design.

We argue, that we can use this information to identify a lower boundary for the success of monitoring operations in any P2P botnet. In fact, we have discussed several approaches to monitor P2P botnets, that can at least obtain as much knowledge as any regular bot. While the information of bots can be limited through MM design, this is limited by the trade-off with resilience. Therefore, we can establish a lower bound by determining the boundaries of optimal MM designs. That is, identifying the MM parameters that provide the greatest monitoring resistance while maintaining adequate resilience. In Sect. 6, we identify and discuss, what constitutes such an optimal MM design and to what extent monitoring is possible under such adverse conditions.

5 Modeling and Simulating Botnet Churn

As one of the core contributions of this paper, we propose and verify a novel churn model and generator, focused on the simulation of botnet churn based on real world measurements. Section 5.1 discusses the shortcomings of existing churn generators with regard to simulation of real world botnet churn. Furthermore, Sect. 5.2 introduces our churn generator.

5.1   Simulation of Real World Churn Models

The availability of a bot's neighbors directly influences whether old connections are retained or if newer connections need to be established. Therefore, churn significantly impacts the overall structure of the botnet overlay. This is why we consider churn generators as a crucial feature for a P2P botnet simulator.

A recent survey by Surati et al. [24] examined the existing P2P simulators. We analyzed each of these simulators with regard to their churn generator functionalities. Out of all simulators, *Peerfactsim.kom* [22] and *OverSim* [4] provide the most advanced churn functionalities. *Peerfactsim.kom* implements a churn generator that is based on the exponential distribution, whereas *OverSim* provides the choice between random, life-time and Pareto churn models. However, according to Stutzbach et al. [23] exponential and Pareto distributions do not fit churn characteristics observed in real world P2P networks. Moreover, a random churn model is also not suitable as it only provides rudimentary presentation of churn and does not characterize the network accurately. This leaves only the option of life-time based churn models. Such a churn, which is implemented in *OverSim*, allows the usage of different probability distributions, e.g., the Weibull distribution. According to both [11,23], Weibull distributions fit well with the churn observed in regular P2P networks and P2P botnets.

However, the implementation in *OverSim* has two major drawbacks. First, the life-time and down-time of nodes is drawn from the same probability distribution. We speculate that this is done to allow for an easily adjustable active population. However, this is a critical issue, as it is highly unrealistic that life- and down-time distributions are equal, at least in the case of P2P botnets. Second, the implementation in *OverSim* requires the overall population of the simulated network to be exactly double of the desired active population. This allows to have an equal number of active and inactive nodes. In combination to nodes joining and leaving based on the same distribution the active population is approximated throughout the simulation period. Given these drawbacks of *life-time* churn, all existing churn generators present severe drawbacks with regard to a realistic simulation of churn in P2P botnets.

5.2   The BotChurn (BC) Generator

Based on the aforesaid shortcomings of existing churn simulation models, we develop BC, a novel approach to simulate P2P botnet churn based on real world measurements. To overcome the drawbacks of existing churn generators, BC focuses on addressing the following three features: (*i*) individual distributions for life- and down-times of nodes, (*ii*) support for existing P2P churn measurements, and (*iii*) independently adjustable *active* and *overall* population parameters.

Support for distinct Weibull distributions for life- and down-times:
One approach to overcome the issue of having a single distribution for life- and
down-times would be to use two different distributions as it is done for the Pareto
churn model [28]. However, obtaining accurate measurements of down-times is
often not possible as many P2P botnets do not provide unique identifiers [6,18].
Therefore, it is difficult to accurately measure when a node rejoins a system.

As an alternative, BC is based on a life-time and an inter-arrival distribution.
Theoretically, any probability distribution function can be used. However, we
currently support only the Weibull distribution for life-time and inter-arrival
measurements as it is found best suited for churn in P2P systems [11,23]. In
contrast to *life-time* churn, BC starts with all nodes being inactive. Based on
the times drawn from the inter-arrival distribution, a random inactive node is
activated. Upon activation, a *life-time* value is assigned based on the life-time
distribution. Once a bot's life-time comes to an end, it becomes inactive. This is
a continuous process, where inactive bots will eventually rejoin the system based
on the inter-arrival cycle.

Calculation of the average active population: One issue that needs to be
addressed by our approach, is that whenever a node needs to be activated, an
inactive node must be available to join the network. Therefore, the overall bot
population needs to be larger than the average active population of the simulated
botnet. This requires that we first calculate the average active number of bots
based on the two input distributions.

According to the law of large numbers, with sufficiently long simulation time
τ, with $\tau \to \infty$, the average inter-arrival time of nodes joining the system
will converge towards the mean of the inter-arrival distribution. Therefore, the
arrival-rate R_a will eventually converge towards the mean. However, the number
of nodes leaving the system is dependent on the life-time distribution and the
number of nodes active in the system. If we consider the average life-time λ and
an active number of nodes N_a, on average nodes will go off-line at a rate of $\frac{\lambda}{N_a}$.

We can therefore calculate the average active population by identifying the
active population N_a, at which the average departure-rate R_d is equal to the
average arrival-rate R_a. This is achieved by solving Eq. 1.

$$R_a = R_d = \frac{\lambda}{N_a} \Rightarrow N_a = \frac{\lambda}{R_a} \tag{1}$$

Independent active- and overall-populations: Lastly, we want to address
the need for an independently adjustable overall- and active-population. In BC,
the overall-population can be set to any desired value. However, as discussed
earlier, it should be bigger than the desired active-population.

Adjusting the active population requires additional effort. In more details, it
is necessary to modify at least one of the two distributions, as the active population is directly related to both inter-arrival and life-time distributions. While

this means that we modify the values obtained from real world measurements, this is often necessary to experiment with different sizes of botnets.

To adjust the active population, we can modify either the *inter-arrival* or the *life-time* Weibull distribution. As the reported measurements of Karuppayah [11] showed high similarity in the fitting of Weibull life-time distributions for botnets of different sizes, we maintain the input life-time distribution without any modification. Furthermore, it is not very likely that the size of a botnet has a direct influence on the life-time behavior of its individual nodes.

Therefore, we have to adjust the *inter-arrival* distribution to accommodate an adjustable active population. To adjust a Weibull distribution, one can either choose its *shape* β or *scale* α parameter. To change the real world measurements as little as possible, we want to change the parameter that is less similar across all botnets measured in [11]. The shape parameter of the reported *inter-arrival* distributions ranges from 0.61 to 1.04, whereas the scale parameter varies between 0.6801 and 160.2564. As the difference between the scale parameters is bigger across the measured botnets, we choose to modify the scale parameter α, while keeping the shape parameter β unaltered. With this modification, we can choose any desired active population value as an input to Eq. 1 and obtain the required arrival rate R_a.

6   Evaluation

Within this section, we present the evaluation of BotChurn (BC) and the influence of MM on monitoring resistance and resilience of botnets. Furthermore, an analysis on the effectiveness of monitoring in adverse conditions is also provided.

6.1   Datasets and Evaluation Metrics

In our evaluation, we utilize three datasets: (i) real world churn measurements of Sality and ZeroAccess botnets, (ii) real world graphs of the Sality botnet and (iii) a simulated dataset consisting of 1,458 combinations of different parameters.

The real-world churn measurements, that we obtained from [11], consist of *inter-arrival* and *life-time* distributions. In this paper, we focus on three particular measurements. These are the ZeroAccess 16465 (ZA65) including non-superpeers, i.e., bots behind NAT or firewalls, ZeroAccess 16471 (ZA71) and Sality version three (SalityV3). The details for these datasets are given in Table 2.

The real-world snapshots of the Sality botnet were taken from [9]. The authors, present an analysis on the graph characteristics and resilience of the Sality and ZeroAccess botnets. The metrics used in their analysis are the *number of nodes, number of edges, degree, in-degree, out-degree, density, global clustering coefficient, average path length* and the *diameter* of the botnet. We utilize their publicly available snapshot of the Sality botnet to compare it against our simulated botnet topologies. More specifically, we utilize the dataset to compare

Table 2. Churn measurements by [11]; weibull parameters as tuples (shape, scale).

	ZeroAccess 71 (ZA71)	ZeroAccess 65 including non-super peers (ZA65)	Sality v3 (SalityV3)
Inter-Arrival: $R_a(\beta, \alpha)$	(0.95, 3.0769)	(1.04, 3.8023)	(0.66, 5.814)
Life-Time: $\lambda(\beta, \alpha)$	(0.21, 76.9231)	(0.18, 12.21)	(0.28, 1139.3174)
Active Population (N_a)	165	1037	1963

the graph characteristics and resilience reported by Haas et al. [9] against those from the generated topologies.

Our last dataset is generated using our simulation framework[1]. We simulated 1,458 different parameter combinations with 20 repetitions for a duration of 75 days each. Table 3, presents all parameter types and their values. The parameters used in our simulations consist of the churn model, the MM parameters as discussed in Sect. 4, the number of MDs and the active and overall population.

It is important to note, that the maximum NL-size is not independently varied but instead dependent on the Neighborlist Minimum Threshold (NLMT). In an analysis on the influence of each individual parameter, we found that the NL-size itself only has a minor influence on the resilience or monitoring resistance. The reason for this is, that bots only search for additional neighbors if the NLMT is reached. Therefore, we set the NL-size to be twice as large as the NLMT. Furthermore, we adjusted the overall population in relation to the active population. We chose to use a factor of *three*, *four* or *five*, as our simulations of the churn model have shown, that the simulated graphs are most similar to the real world graphs at an overall population about four times larger than the active population.

Table 3. Parameter combinations used for the evaluation.

Parameter	Value
Churn Model	SalityV3, ZA65, ZA71
Membership Management Interval (MMI)	30 m, 1 h, 2 h
Max NL-size	2x NLMT
Neighborlist Minimum Threshold (NLMT)	10, 25, 50
Neighborlist Reply Size (NLRS)	1, 5, 10
Neighborlist Reply Preference (NLRP)	Latest, Random
Number of MDs	1, (10, 50, 200, 500)
Active Population (N_a)	1963, 1037, 165
Overall Population (N_t)	x3, x4, x5 Active Population

---

[1] https://git.tk.informatik.tu-darmstadt.de/SPIN/BSF.

To evaluate our work, we utilize the network *resilience* and monitoring *resistance* metrics. We measure the *resilience* of a botnet similarly to [9]. Iteratively the bot with the highest in-degree is removed from the botnet, until the ratio of nodes disconnected from the largest *weakly connected component* exceeds a threshold $t \in [0, 1]$. Therefore, the *GraphResilience(t)* denotes the fraction of bots that need to be removed, to have more than $t\%$ of the remaining bots disconnected from the botnet. Within our evaluation, we consider a threshold of $t = 0.5$, as it was least affected by outliers. The monitoring *resistance* indicates the difficulty of monitoring a botnet, i.e., the fraction of the overall population that could not be enumerated. We define monitoring resistance ρ in Eq. 2, based on the overall-population N_t, and μ the information obtained by an MD.

$$\rho = 1 - \frac{|\mu|}{|N_t|} \tag{2}$$

6.2 Simulation Setup

Within this subsection, we introduce our simulation setup. Overall we introduce three separate experiments: (i) an evaluation of BC, (ii) an analysis of the MM on monitoring resistance and network resilience, and (iii) an evaluation on how utilizing multiple MDs increases the intelligence gathered through monitoring.

For the evaluation of BC, we intend to investigate two research topics. First, the warm-up time required to reach the desired active population, and second, whether the generated topologies are more similar to the real-world characteristics reported in [9] than those created with OverSim's *life-time* churn generator.

To compare the two churn generators with the real world dataset, we run 24 simulations of the Sality botnet with each of them. To match the active population of the real world Sality graph provided by Haas et al. [9], we set the target active population to $1,422$. In addition, to compare the difference between the graph characteristics of the real world Sality botnet and the simulated topologies, we use the mean absolute error. The Mean Absolute Error (MAE) allows us to calculate the average difference between the graph characteristics of the simulated and real world dataset. To ensure, that the parameters are in comparable value ranges when calculating the error, we normalized all values through feature scaling. Furthermore, we compare the graphs with regard to their resilience.

To analyze the effects of each MM parameter with regard to monitoring resistance and botnet resilience we use our simulated dataset (see Table 3). Furthermore, to highlight the influence of each parameter, we analyze and discuss each of them individually. Every simulation is run for a period of 75 days, with the MD joining after 40 days. After the entire simulation time, we took a snapshot of the graph and then analyzed its monitoring resistance and graph resilience.

We expect, that a single MD will not yield enough intelligence to conduct successful monitoring in adverse conditions. This raises the question about how we can improve the knowledge obtained by monitoring operations. One approach is to broaden the information obtained via monitoring by increasing the number of MDs. To analyze the effects of aggregating the information of multiple MDs,

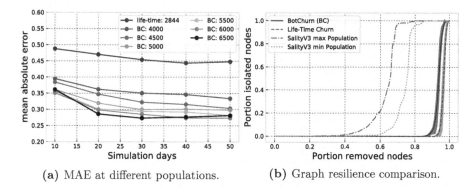

(a) MAE at different populations.   (b) Graph resilience comparison.

Fig. 1. Comparison of *life-time* churn, BC and the real world Sality botnet graph.

we repeated the simulations with the most monitoring resistant and resilient MM parameter combinations, i.e., under the most adverse conditions. To keep the number of MDs within a realistic range, we ran the simulations with 10, 50, 200 and 500 deployed MDs. Note that, 500 is close to the highest number of sensors ever reported (512) to be used to monitor a botnet [2].

6.3 Results

In this subsection, we present the results of our evaluation.

BotChurn (BC) evaluation. Before the comparison between simulated and real world graphs, we evaluated the warm-up period required by BC to reach the desired active population. The results for all three investigated churn models indicate, that the active population is reached within less than 40 days.

Figure 1a, depicts the mean absolute error between simulated graphs and a real world Sality snapshot obtained from [9]. The results clearly indicate, that the graphs generated with BC are closer to the real world botnet. Furthermore, our churn generator performs best at an overall population between 5, 500 to 6, 500. This is about twice as much as the overall population in *life-time* churn, which does not allow to adapt the overall population. While the error for BC generated botnets may still seem high, we want to point out that the error is dominated by only two out of 13 graph properties. In fact, the average path length and diameter are so similar throughout all graphs, that due to the normalization even slight changes cause large errors. For BC at a population of 6000, the average path length is 1.7045 compared to 1.5149 in Sality and the diameters are 2 and 3 respectively. If we remove these two outliers from the calculation, the error drops from 27% to only 15%.

Figure 1b, compares the average resilience of the simulated graphs against the resilience of the real world graph at its maximum and minimum population. Interestingly, the simulated networks are significantly more resilient than the real world Sality graphs. The reasoning behind this finding is that the connections

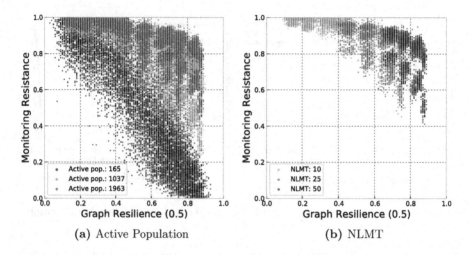

Fig. 2. Influence of individual parameters on monitoring resistance and resilience.

in all graphs are made prominently through a strongly connected core. However, the simulated graphs also have more connections among bots at the edges of the graph, which leads to the higher resilience. We speculate, that this is largely caused by the Goodcount mechanism of Sality and the botnet being active for several years. Even though, the resilience of the simulated graphs are significantly higher than the real world Sality, similar resilience has been observed for the ZeroAccess botnet [9]. In summary, the graphs generated with BC are more similar to the real-world graphs than those create with *life-time* churn.

MM Design Evaluation. We now investigate, the influence each parameter has on monitoring resistance and botnet resilience. As the first parameter, we look at the influence of the *active population*. The results depicted in Fig. 2a indicate, that the active population[2] of the botnet has a significant impact on its monitoring resistance. We argue that there is a two-fold reasoning behind this behavior. First, if more highly stable nodes are available in the botnet, they must share the in-degree of the less stable nodes and therefore, it is less likely for an MD to be within a bot's NL. Second, parameters such as the NL-size do not scale with the active population. Therefore, the information contained in a MD's NL amounts to a significantly larger fraction of the population in small botnets when compared to larger botnets.

Out of all MM parameters, the *Neighborlist Minimum Threshold (NLMT)* has the greatest influence on the resilience of a botnet. Figure 2b, highlights this influence in a scatter plot of all simulation runs with an active population of 1963. As the botnets with such a population size are most resistant to monitoring, we omit other active populations in the subsequent analysis due to clarity/space reasons. While the highest resilience obtained by botnets with an NLMT of 10

---

[2] The scatter plots depict all parameter variations, with one of them being highlighted.

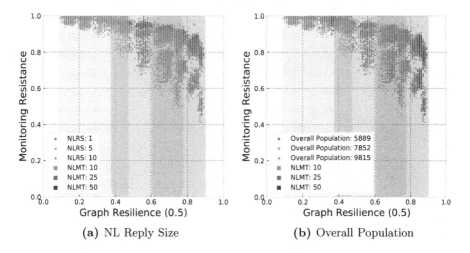

(a) NL Reply Size   (b) Overall Population

Fig. 3. Influence of individual parameters on monitoring resistance and resilience.

is approximately 40%, botnets with an NLMT of 50 approached a resilience of almost 90%. However, the increase of resilience comes at the cost of decreasing monitoring resistance (see also Sect. 4). As the resilience of the botnet is evaluated based on global knowledge of the botnet, we cannot state the best value for a botnet's NLMT. While a low NLMT hampers the gathering of information required to conduct an attack, a high NLMT is more likely to withstand an attack even if a lot of information is obtained by botnet defenders.

The effects of the *Neighborlist Reply Size (NLRS)* on the monitoring resistance of a botnet increases with higher NLMTs. Figure 3a illustrates, that with increased resilience the difference between an NLRS of 1 and 10 changes significantly. This growth of resilience is caused by the increasing NLMT, which is highlighted by the colored overlays. While the difference between an NLRS of 1, 5, or 10 does not seem to have a significant influence at an NLMT of 10, it is clear that an NLRS of 1 is superior at NLMTs of 5 and 10. We speculate, that the reason for this is, that an NL-reply is likely to contain more entries than the requesting bot needs. As an example, if a bot with 47 out of 50 neighbors receives an NL-reply with 10 entries, that is seven more bots than it required to have a full NL. Therefore, an NLRS of 1 is preferable with regard to monitoring resistance, as no unnecessary information is shared.

Similar to the active population, the *overall population* greatly influences the resilience of the botnet. Figure 3b, depicts the analysis of overall populations of 5889, 7852, and 9815 for an active population of 1963. The figure shows, that the resilience increases with a lower overall population. This pattern is repeated based on different NLMTs which are highlighted by the colored overlays. We argue, that this is caused by the increased likelihood of any node being online. As the overall population is lesser, a node will rejoin the botnet more frequently.

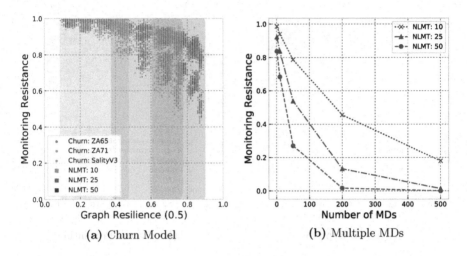

Fig. 4. Influence of parameters on monitoring resistance (and resilience).

The difference among the three observed churn models seems to be most pronounced in the resilience of the botnet. Our analysis results in Fig. 4a, indicate that the botnets differ slightly with regard to resilience and monitoring resistance. The churn models *SalityV3* followed by *ZA71* create more resilient botnets, whereas *ZA65* has the highest monitoring resistance. Nevertheless, the scaling of churn models appears to work well with only small differences between the churn models with regard to resilience and monitoring resistance.

The *NLRP*, minimally influences the monitoring resistance of a botnet. Interestingly, the preferable parameter value changes with growing NLMT. Our results indicate that a random selection is preferable for an NLMT of one, whereas returning the last seen neighbors is better for NLMTs of higher values.

The range of values we analyzed for the *MMI*, did not show any influence on monitoring resistance or resilience. Nevertheless, a lower MMI may reduce the probability of a bot getting disconnected from the botnet. At the same time, the shorter the MMI, the more communication overhead will be incurred by the botnet. We expect that with increased message overhead, it will be easier to detect the botnet. Therefore, any of the values is good with regard to monitoring resistance and resilience, but may cause the botnet to be more susceptible to detection.

In summary, we identified that among the MM parameters, NLMT and NLRS have the greatest effect on monitoring resistance and botnet resilience. Contrary, the MMI and NLRP exhibit only minor effects. We argue, based on our results, that a parameter combination of NLMT = 10, NLRS = 1, NLRP = *random* and MMI = 1*h*, exhibits the most adverse conditions for monitoring. Furthermore, our analysis of active and overall population indicates that with growing population the monitoring resistance increases significantly. Lastly, the three evaluated churn models showed similar behavior for the observed active populations.

Successful Monitoring in Adverse Conditions. For our last experiment, we analyzed how increasing the number of MDs influences the monitoring resistance of a botnet. Figure 4b, presents the results of deploying multiple MDs for the botnets with the most adverse conditions. In addition to the optimal parameter combination identified in the previous section, we varied the NLMT to cover the more resilient botnets as well. One can observe how an increase in MDs results in a decreased monitoring resistance of the botnet. However, the increase in knowledge does not increase linearly with the increase in MDs. This is the case due to two reasons: (i) knowledge gained by adding additional MDs may overlap with existing knowledge and therefore not add to the overall knowledge, and (ii) the potential increase in knowledge is limited by the total population of the botnet. Due to these factors, we can only enumerate the entire botnet for an NLMT of 50. Moreover, this is only possible with 500 deployed MDs. However, a fraction of the nodes remains unknown in the NLMT = 25 scenario, and almost 20% of the overall population remain undiscovered using 500 MDs in a botnet with an NLMT of 10.

We argue, that this clearly indicates that *short term monitoring, deploying bots in controlled environments*, or *controlling active bots* requires a large pool of diverse IP addresses to effectively monitor botnets in adverse conditions. As suggested by [2,11], this could be realized through collaboration of multiple parties. Furthermore, network based monitoring is a promising approach, as large amounts of bots can be observed at once without requiring a pool of IP addresses. However, a drawback of this approach is that it requires the collaboration of multiple ISPs which may prove to be difficult, as they are usually reluctant about sharing private data.

7   Conclusion and Future Work

In this paper, we argue that once botnets adapt more advanced countermeasures, monitoring as we know it today will no longer be feasible. We defined the term *adverse conditions* as a botnet environment in which any deviation from the behavior of a regular bot can easily be detected by the botmaster. Furthermore, we investigated the idea of designing a botnet's MM to further limit the knowledge obtainable by monitoring.

To thoroughly analyze botnets, we discussed different churn models and propose BotChurn (BC), a novel churn generator for botnets. In our experiments, we identified a lower boundary for intelligence gathering in adverse conditions. In particular, our results indicate that the MM design significantly affects both the monitoring resistance and resilience of the botnet. Finally, we conducted additional simulations in which we aggregated the intelligence obtained by multiple MDs, to observe how this increases the intelligence obtained via monitoring. The results indicate, that such a distributed approach provides a way to improve the gathered intelligence. However, this requires a significant amount of available IP addresses. To overcome this, we suggest that future research considers the concept of collaborative monitoring. If the defenders combine their resources, this would increase the quality of the gathered intelligence and also reduce the cumulative cost to conduct monitoring.

Acknowledgement. This work was supported by the German Federal Ministry of Education and Research (BMBF) and by the Hessen State Ministry for Higher Education, Research and the Arts (HMWK) within CRISP. The research leading to these results has also received funding from the European Union's Horizon 2020 Research and Innovation Program, PROTECTIVE, under Grant Agreement No 700071 and the Universiti Sains Malaysia (USM) through Short Term Research Grant, No: 304/PNAV/6313332.

References

1. Adrian, D., Durumeric, Z., Singh, G., Halderman, J.A.: Zippier zmap: internet-wide scanning at 10 gbps. In: WOOT (2014)
2. Andriesse, D., Rossow, C., Bos, H.: Reliable recon in adversarial peer-to-peer botnets. In: Internet Measurement Conference. ACM (2015)
3. Andriesse, D., Rossow, C., Stone-Gross, B., Plohmann, D., Bos, H.: Highly resilient peer-to-peer botnets are here: an analysis of gameover zeus. In: International Conference on Malicious and Unwanted Software (2013)
4. Baumgart, I., Heep, B., Krause, S.: Oversim: a scalable and flexible overlay framework for simulation and real network applications. In: Peer-to-Peer Computing, pp. 87–88. IEEE (2009)
5. Böck, L., Karuppayah, S., Grube, T., Mühlhäuser, M., Fischer, M.: Hide and seek: detecting sensors in P2P botnets. In: Communications and Network Security, pp. 731–732. IEEE (2015)
6. Falliere, N.: Sality: story of a peer-to-peer viral network. Technical report, Symantec Corporation (2011)
7. Greengard, S.: The war against botnets. Commun. ACM **55**(2), 16 (2012). https://doi.org/10.1145/2076450.2076456
8. Gu, G., Perdisci, R., Zhang, J., Lee, W., et al.: Botminer: clustering analysis of network traffic for protocol-and structure-independent botnet detection. In: USENIX Security Symposium, vol. 5, pp. 139–154 (2008)
9. Haas, S., Karuppayah, S., Manickam, S., Mühlhäuser, M., Fischer, M.: On the resilience of P2P-based botnet graphs. In: Communications and Network Security (CNS), pp. 225–233. IEEE (2016)
10. Holz, T., Steiner, M., Dahl, F., Biersack, E., Freiling, F.: Measurements and mitigation of peer-to-peer-based botnets: a case study on storm worm. In: LEET (2008)
11. Karuppayah, S.: Advanced monitoring in P2P botnets. Ph.D. thesis, Technische Universität Darmstadt (2016)
12. Karuppayah, S., Fischer, M., Rossow, C., Muhlhauser, M.: On advanced monitoring in resilient and unstructured P2P botnets. In: International Conference on Communications. IEEE (2014). https://doi.org/10.1109/ICC.2014.6883429
13. Karuppayah, S., Roos, S., Rossow, C., Mühlhäuser, M., Fischer, M.: ZeusMilker: circumventing the P2P zeus neighbor list restriction mechanism. In: International Conference on Distributed Computing Systems, pp. 619–629. IEEE (2015)

14. Karuppayah, S., Vasilomanolakis, E., Haas, S., Muhlhauser, M., Fischer, M.: BoobyTrap: on autonomously detecting and characterizing crawlers in P2P botnets. In: 2016 IEEE International Conference on Communications, ICC 2016 (2016). https://doi.org/10.1109/ICC.2016.7510885
15. Kleissner, P.: Me Puppet Master: Behind the scenes of crawling P2P botnets (2014). http://blog.kleissner.org/?p=455
16. Maymounkov, P., Mazières, D.: Kademlia: a peer-to-peer information system based on the XOR metric. In: Druschel, P., Kaashoek, F., Rowstron, A. (eds.) IPTPS 2002. LNCS, vol. 2429, pp. 53–65. Springer, Heidelberg (2002). https://doi.org/10.1007/3-540-45748-8_5
17. Narang, P., Ray, S., Hota, C., Venkatakrishnan, V.: Peershark: detecting peer-to-peer botnets by tracking conversations. In: 2014 IEEE Security and Privacy Workshops (SPW), pp. 108–115. IEEE (2014)
18. Neville, A., Gibb, R.: ZeroAccess Indepth. Technical report (2013)
19. Page, L., Brin, S., Motwani, R., Winograd, T.: The PageRank citation ranking: bringing order to the web (1999)
20. Rossow, C., et al.: P2PWNED: modeling and evaluating the resilience of peer-to-peer botnets. In: Symposium on Security & Privacy. IEEE (2013)
21. Salah, H., Strufe, T.: Capturing connectivity graphs of a large-scale P2P overlay network. In: 2013 IEEE 33rd International Conference on Distributed Computing Systems Workshops (ICDCSW) (2013)
22. Stingl, D., Gross, C., Rückert, J., Nobach, L., Kovacevic, A., Steinmetz, R.: Peerfactsim.kom: a simulation framework for peer-to-peer systems. In: High Performance Computing and Simulation (HPCS), pp. 577–584. IEEE (2011)
23. Stutzbach, D., Rejaie, R.: Understanding churn in peer-to-peer networks. In: ACM SIGCOMM Conference on Internet Measurement, pp. 189–201 (2006)
24. Surati, S., Jinwala, D.C., Garg, S.: A survey of simulators for P2P overlay networks with a case study of the P2P tree overlay using an event-driven simulator. Eng. Sci. Technol. Int. J. **20**, 705–720 (2017)
25. Vasilomanolakis, E., Wolf, J.H., Böck, L., Karuppayah, S., Mühlhäuser, M.: I trust my zombies: a trust-enabled botnet. arXiv preprint arXiv:1712.03713 (2017)
26. Wyke, J.: The zeroaccess botnet - mining and fraud for massive financial gain. Technical report, September, Sophos (2012)
27. Yan, J., et al.: Revisiting node injection of P2P botnet. In: Au, M.H., Carminati, B., Kuo, C.-C.J. (eds.) NSS 2014. LNCS, vol. 8792, pp. 124–137. Springer, Cham (2014). https://doi.org/10.1007/978-3-319-11698-3_10
28. Yao, Z., Leonard, D., Wang, X., Loguinov, D.: Modeling heterogeneous user churn and local resilience of unstructured P2P networks. In: International Conference on Network Protocols (ICNP), pp. 32–41. IEEE (2006)

IoT/CPS Security

Malicious IoT Implants: Tampering with Serial Communication over the Internet

Philipp Morgner[(✉)], Stefan Pfennig, Dennis Salzner, and Zinaida Benenson

Friedrich-Alexander-Universität Erlangen-Nürnberg, Erlangen, Germany
{philipp.morgner,stefan.pfennig,dennis.salzner,zinaida.benenson}@fau.de

Abstract. The expansion of the Internet of Things (IoT) promotes the roll-out of low-power wide-area networks (LPWANs) around the globe. These technologies supply regions and cities with Internet access over the air, similarly to mobile telephony networks, but they are specifically designed for low-power applications and tiny computing devices. Forecasts predict that major countries will be broadly covered with LPWAN connectivity in the near future. In this paper, we investigate how the expansion of the LPWAN infrastructure facilitates new attack vectors in hardware security. In particular, we investigate the threat of malicious modifications in electronic products during the physical distribution process in the supply chain. We explore to which extent such modifications allow attackers to take control over devices after deployment by tampering with the serial communication between processors, sensors, and memory. To this end, we designed and built a malicious IoT implant, a small electronic system that can be inserted in arbitrary electronic products. In our evaluation on real-world products, we show the feasibility of leveraging malicious IoT implants for hardware-level attacks on safety- and security-critical products.

Keywords: IoT · LPWAN · Implant · Serial communication
Hardware attack

1 Introduction

The Internet of Things (IoT) promises to optimize workflows, enhance energy efficiency, and to improve our everyday life. According to a recent estimation [11], 11.2 billion IoT devices will be installed by the end of 2018. These devices are connected in mostly wireless and local networks all over the world, comprising together a global IoT infrastructure. In the past, security concerns have been expressed regarding this powerful IoT infrastructure: Besides security issues in IoT devices [28,33], IoT networks [30], and IoT applications [9], the force of these billions of devices can be weaponized for targeted attacks with impactful consequences. Examples are recent denial-of-service (DoS) attacks on Internet infrastructure [3,20], in which attacker-controlled IoT nodes utilize existing IoT infrastructure to build large botnets.

© Springer Nature Switzerland AG 2018
M. Bailey et al. (Eds.): RAID 2018, LNCS 11050, pp. 535–555, 2018.
https://doi.org/10.1007/978-3-030-00470-5_25

In this paper, we explore a new threat where the connectivity of low-power wide-area networks (LPWANs) is leveraged as a communication channel to control malicious hardware. Our objective is to prove that public IoT infrastructure can be used to perform attacks at hardware level remotely, even if the target device does not feature a network interface. The underlying threat of malicious hardware arises from an untrusted supply chain, in which electronic products are manufactured and shipped in large volumes. The global supply chain of electronic products consists of a number of sequential steps from designing a new product, fabrication process, and distribution to the installation. Hereby, we focus on the physical distribution process that involves entities such as manufacturers, third-party logistics providers, distributors, retailers, and costumers. In addition, government agencies oversee the flow of goods at borders for legal and documentation purposes. Thus, an electronic product can be physically accessed and manipulated by a number of entities during distribution. These entities could be potential attackers or cooperate with an attacker, and therefore the integrity of an product should not be assumed in general. This contradicts the inherent trust of consumers that new products are not tampered with.

Inspired by the leaked NSA ANT catalog [4], we experiment with the insertion of additional hardware, referred to as hardware implants, into an existing electronic system after the fabrication process. Although the threat of hardware implants seems to be acknowledged by the academic security community, previous research on malicious hardware mainly focused on hardware trojans, i.e., diverse types of malicious hardware inserted during design phase [2,8,12,13,18,24] and fabrication phase [5,36,42] but not during the distribution phase.

We summarize our major contributions in this work as follows:

1. We comprehensively explore a new attack vector: malicious IoT implants. We show that IoT infrastructures can be abused for malicious purposes other than DoS attacks. Although the existence of hardware implants is known [4], we are the first in the scientific community that design and build a malicious IoT implant, a low-cost electronic implant to facilitate hardware-level attacks, that connects to the Internet over an IoT infrastructure.
2. We investigate new vulnerabilities on hardware level that exploit insecurities in serial communication on printed circuit boards (PCBs). We start by identifying the de-facto serial communication standards by analyzing over 11,000 microcontroller (MCU) models. Then, we show that serial communication is vulnerable to malicious IoT implants. For our implementation that focuses on the widely-adopted I^2C standard, we introduce four attack procedures in which our implant directly interferes with the communication on I^2C buses. At the end, we discuss the adoption of these attacks to other serial communication standards.

The presented threat is not considered in current threat models for hardware security [15,34] that mainly cover hardware trojans, side-channel attacks, reverse engineering, piracy of intellectual property, and counterfeiting. Also, guidelines on supply chain risks, such as NIST SP 800-161 [6], consider malicious software insertion but no malicious hardware insertion. Thus, the goal of this paper is to demonstrate and understand the feasibility of Internet-connected hardware implants and their effects on the security of arbitrary target devices to raise awareness for this novel threat.

2 Preliminaries

2.1 LPWAN Infrastructure

The global IoT infrastructure is split into millions of local networks that are interconnected via the Internet. From an application perspective, these networks can be categorized into body-area, personal-area, local-area, and wide-area networks. In this paper, we focus on LPWANs, which provide connectivity for thousands of IoT nodes across large geographical areas as their wireless range competes with the ranges of mobile telephony networks. In contrast to mobile telephony networks that support high data rates and bandwidths, LPWANs are specifically designed for low-power machine-to-machine (M2M) applications that communicate at low data rates. As of June 2018, a popular LPWAN technology with deployments in over 100 countries is LoRa [26]. LoRa operates in three frequency bands (433/868/915 MHz) at different channels and bandwidths, and uses a chirp chip spectrum modulation scheme that provides a high resistance against wireless interference. These advanced propagation properties allow transmissions of wireless data over distances of up to a few kilometers. The specifications of LoRaWAN, the LoRa network protocol, are maintained by the LoRa Alliance, a global non-profit organization consisting of more than 500 member companies [25]. From a network perspective, LoRaWAN utilizes a star-to-star architecture, in which so-called gateways relay messages either between IoT nodes or from an IoT node to the central network server and vice versa. The wireless transmissions between IoT nodes and the gateway are based on the LoRa technology, while the Internet Protocol (IP) is used for data transfers between gateways and the central network server.

The cost of deploying LPWANs is significant lower than the roll-out of mobile telephony networks such that even non-profit initiatives are able to provide network coverage for entire cities and regions. A prominent example is The Things Network (TTN), a crowd source initiative that claims to have a fast growing community with over 42,000 people in more than 80 countries. The TTN community deploys LoRaWAN gateways world-wide to achieve their objective of enabling a global network for IoT applications without subscription costs. According to TTN, 10 gateways are enough to cover a major city like Amsterdam with wireless connectivity for IoT applications. Currently, almost 4,000 TTN gateways are globally deployed. Besides non-profit initiatives, the roll-out of national-wide LPWANs driven by telecommunication companies is ongoing in many countries, e.g., India [17], Australia [32], and the USA [38]. According to a forecast [27], LPWANs will supersede mobile telephony networks in providing wireless connectivity for IoT applications by 2023.

2.2 Serial Communication

Although electronic products provide a large diversity in function, features, and appearance, their underlying hardware platform follows similar design principles. Typically, the hardware platform consists of a number of integrated circuits (ICs) that are mounted on PCBs and interconnected via on-board communication interfaces. A typical PCB comprises multiple sensors and actuators. Generally, one or more MCUs are present to process the data received from the sensors, as well as memory chips to store data persistently, and network interfaces to communicate with external entities.

For the communication between ICs exist a number of serial and parallel data transmission mechanisms. In parallel communication, multiple bits are transmitted simultaneously over multiple communication channels. This is in contrast to serial communication, where bits are sent sequentially over a single communication channel. Since the cost of ICs is also determined by the number of input and output pins, ICs on PCBs often use serial communication to interact with each other. Serial communication mechanisms can be categorized into synchronous and asynchronous systems. Synchronous systems associate a clock signal to the data signals, which is shared by all bus participants. In asynchronous systems, the data signals are transmitted without a shared clock signal. Most of the serial communication systems comprise a hierarchy of master and slave ICs. MCUs are typically masters and control the communication as well as command slaves, e.g., memory and sensors, to send data or to execute particular tasks.

To determine the most important serial communication interfaces on PCBs, we performed a parametric search on the product databases of six leading MCU suppliers: NXP, Renesas, Microchip, STMicroelectronics (STM), Infineon, and Texas Instruments (TI). In 2016, these suppliers had in sum a market share of 72% of all sold MCUs based on the revenue [16]. We analyzed more than 11,000 MCU models regarding their serial communication interfaces and found that 86.7% have a UART interface, 83.5% support I^2C and 63.8% SPI. We also analyzed the support for further serial communication interfaces, such as CAN (34.3%), USB (30.2%), and Ethernet (11.5%), which are mainly application-specific and not as widely supported as SPI, I^2C and UART. A detailed analysis can be found in Table 1. Although the support of a serial interface is no warrant that this interface is also used in a product that features this MCU, these numbers indicate the de-facto standards that are supported by leading MCU suppliers.

2.3 I^2C Communication Protocol

Although serial communication interfaces have diverse properties regarding synchronization, data rates, and complexity, there are architectural similarities from a security perspective. The most obvious property of these systems is that none of their specifications define any kind of cryptographic security measure. Therefore, the majority of the demonstrated attacks can also be adapted to other serial communication interfaces. In the implementation and evaluation of this work,

Table 1. Number of MCU models sorted by supplier and product families (as of January 2018). If a database entry of an MCU model had no parameter regarding a certain interface, we assume that this interface is not supported. *Notation: 'MS' - market share of MCU sales by revenue in 2016, 'Family' - MCU product family as advertised by the supplier (if applicable), 'Bit' - bit size of the MCU architecture, '#MCUs' - number of MCU models, 'ETH' - Ethernet.*

Supplier	MS	Family	Bit	#MCUs	#MCUs that support					
					UART	I²C	SPI	CAN	USB	ETH
NXP	19%	i.MX	32	251	243	243	243	219	243	220
		Kinetis	32	928	812	812	812	264	334	72
		LPC	32	540	534	531	482	228	276	136
		MPC	32	762	0	290	94	475	0	0
		S32	32	17	17	6	1	7	0	0
		VF	32	35	34	34	34	34	0	0
Renesas	16%	Various	8	566	550	354	3	36	1	0
		Various	16	2,358	2,304	2,226	485	340	72	0
		Various	32	2,318	2,313	2,069	1,924	1,441	1,298	585
Microchip	14%	AVR	8	49	39	43	45	0	5	0
		PIC	8	116	106	104	104	0	0	0
		PIC	16	366	366	366	366	0	58	0
		PIC	32	241	241	220	241	0	175	0
		SAM	32	255	255	255	255	0	187	0
STM	10%	STM8	8	137	30	42	33	21	0	0
		STM32	32	799	799	796	794	490	598	167
Infineon	7%	Various	8	140	140	16	135	0	0	0
		Various	16	156	156	93	145	88	0	0
		Various	32	308	205	189	206	29	14	11
TI	6%	MSP430	16	536	471	446	500	0	0	0
		DRA	32	28	28	28	28	28	18	25
		DSP	32	175	67	72	54	0	54	48
		Perform.	32	254	124	235	248	170	60	0
		Sitara	32	43	25	26	26	20	26	37
		TDA	32	12	12	12	12	12	8	12
		By bit size	8	1,008	865	559	320	57	14	0
				8.8%	85.8%	55.5%	31.7%	5.7%	1.4%	0
			16	3,416	3,297	3,131	1,496	428	130	0
				30.0%	96.5%	91.7%	43.8%	12.5%	3.8%	0
			32	6,966	5,709	5,818	5,454	3,417	3,291	1,313
				61.2%	81.9%	83.5%	78.3%	49.1%	47.3%	18.9%
		In sum		11,390	9,871	9,508	7,270	3,902	3,435	1,313
				100.0%	86.7%	83.5%	63.8%	34.3%	30.2%	11.5%

we focus on the I^2C serial bus [31] for following reasons: I^2C facilitates a sophisticated communication protocol, in contrast to UART and SPI. Furthermore, I^2C and UART are the most widely supported serial communication interfaces, and in 32-bit architectures (which make 61.1% off all evaluated MCU models), I^2C is even the most supported serial communication interface.

I^2C uses two signal lines: one clock line (denoted as SCL) and one data line (denoted as SDA). ICs are chained along these two signal lines, which are referred to as bus. In order to request and send data from one IC to another, each IC has a distinct address. Furthermore, each IC can be configured to act either as master or slave. The I^2C standard supports multiple masters, which can initiate transactions on the bus. The master that currently performs a transaction also generates the clock signal. Slaves cannot start own transactions and remain passive until they respond to the requests of masters. Typical examples of masters are MCUs and processors, while sensors, memory chips, and actuators are usually configured as slaves.

A transaction between master and slaves contains two types of frames: An *address frame* that informs all participants at the bus for which slave the message is intended, and one or more *data frames*, each consisting of an 8-bit data block. To start a new transaction, a master sends a start condition indicating its intention to occupy the bus. If more than one master aims to use the bus at the same time, the master get access that pulls the SDA line with a clock signal first. The other masters wait until the current bus master completes its transaction via a stop sequence. Upon receiving a start sequence, all slaves on the bus listen for an address frame. The master sends the 7 bit address of the corresponding slave after which only this particular slave continues listening. Then, the master sends an 8th bit to indicate whether he wants to write or read. Once these 8 bits are sent by the master, the receiving slave sends a bit to acknowledge its readiness to receive data. In case of no explicit acknowledgment bit was received, the master aborts the transaction.

After the address frame is sent, the transmission of the data frames starts. Depending on whether the master indicated its intention to read or write, either the master or the slave writes data on the SDA line and the corresponding device acknowledges the receipt. Finally, the master sends a stop condition to complete the transaction.

3   Threat Model

Serial communication on PCBs is security-critical as many high-level applications rely on correct data transmissions to function properly. For instance, spoofing of a temperature sensor with false values can have a significant impact on manufacturing processes that require a particular temperature. The injection of wrong gyroscope data into the serial communication of an unmanned aerial vehicle can lead to a crash. Eavesdropping the passcode entered into the pin pad of a safe grants an attacker access to the content without using brute force. The manipulation of loudspeakers in headphones can injure the hearing ability of the user. All these examples show that attacks on serial communication between ICs have serious impacts. To this end, we define following security goals for the serial communication between ICs on PCB boards: (a) *Confidentiality*: Only legitimate ICs have access to the data that is transmitted on the serial bus. (b) *Integrity*: The tampering with data on the serial bus during transfer is recognized by the legitimate ICs. (c) *Availability*: The legitimate ICs always have access to the transmitted data on the serial bus.

In this paper, we present a threat model that involves a so-called malicious IoT implant. Malicious IoT implants are electronic systems that are inserted into an existing system after the fabrication process, which feature a bidirectional direct wireless connection to a public IoT infrastructure. The system that hosts the implant is denoted as target system. We refer to the entity that inserts the implant into the target system as attacker. The objective of the attacker is to violate the security goals of the serial communication between ICs.

3.1   Untrusted Supply Chain

From an economic perspective, a supply chain can be described as a series of inter-related business processes ranging from the acquisition and transformation of raw materials and parts into products to the distribution and promotion of these products to the retailers or customers [29]. The supply chain process can be divided into two main business processes: *material management* and *physical distribution*. In this work, we focus on the physical distribution as malicious IoT implants are inserted into the target system after its fabrication.

We identified a number of stakeholders that are involved in the physical distribution process shown in Fig. 1: *Manufacturers* use raw materials and parts to produce goods. *Distributors* buy goods from manufacturers, store and resell them either to retailers or customers. *Retailers* sell goods to customers. *Third-party logistics providers* manage the flow of goods between point of origin and destination, which includes shipping, inventory, warehousing, and packaging. *Government agencies*, e.g., customs inspection, enforce regulations and document the flow of goods in and out of a country. *Customers* receive and consume

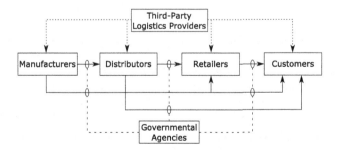

Fig. 1. Physical distribution of goods in the supply chain process. Solid lines: flow of goods. Dashed lines: flow of services (third-party logistics providers) or possibility of interception (government agencies).

goods, while having the ability to choose between different products and suppliers. Hence, the physical distribution process provides many entry points for attackers to gain physical access to a target device. Potentially any of these stakeholders can either be an attacker or cooperate with an attacker. Therefore, we assume an untrusted supply chain in our threat model.

3.2 Attacker Model

We assume that the attacker has physical access to the target device as described in Sect. 3.1, and is able to remove the device's enclosure without leaving physical traces. The attacker identifies access points on the PCB to which a malicious IoT implant can be connected within a reasonable amount of time. We further assume that the target device only requires a power supply, neither Internet nor network access are necessary. The attacker succeeds with an attack if the implant is able to interfere with the communication of the serial buses and cannot be detected without opening the enclosure of the product. Thus, we assume that the attacker targets systems that are not likely to be disassembled by the user. Furthermore, we assume that the attacker has access to a public IoT infrastructure within the wireless range of the implant. In this case, the attacker is not required to be physically present within the wireless range of the implant.

The motivations to utilize malicious IoT implants are various. Governmental organizations might have an interest to use this approach for surveillance, industrial espionage, or the manipulation of infrastructure in enemy states. Leaked documents of the National Security Agency [4] indicate the usage of similar malicious hardware for these purposes. Besides governmental entities, criminal organizations and terrorist groups can use malicious IoT implants to achieve similar goals for financial and political profit. All these groups are likely to be experienced in covert operations, and have the potential to access target devices in the supply chain.

4   Malicious IoT Implant

4.1   Design Criteria

To achieve its objectives, the attacker has certain design criteria regarding the malicious IoT implant: ① *Small Dimensions:* Size is a constraint as the implant has to be hidden inside the enclosure of the target device. In addition, small dimensions of an implant make detection harder. ② *Wireless Connectivity:* If the implant should be remotely controlled, it requires a radio transceiver. This transceiver should provide a communication interface to an LPWAN infrastructure such that physical presence of the attacker is not required. ③ *Access to Serial Communication:* The implant acts as a legitimate participant on the serial bus and is able to eavesdrop on legitimate transactions and to insert malicious transactions. ④ *Invisibility:* The implant does not influence the normal mode of operation except during an active attack. ⑤ *Low-Power:* The implant is either powered by an external power source, i.e., battery or accumulator, or supplied with power from the target device. To increase the lifetime of the implant as well as the target device, the implant should consume as less energy as possible. ⑥ *Low-Cost:* The implant should be designed in a low-cost way using mainly off-the-shelf components.

To the best of our knowledge, we are the first (in a scientific context) that design and implement an implant, which fulfills all of these design criteria.

4.2 Attack Procedures

To achieve the attacker's high-level objectives, we propose hardware-level attacks that interfere with the communication on the serial bus. To perform these procedures, the implant must be connected to the SDA and SCL signal lines of the target device.

Eavesdropping. Eavesdropping is a passive attack in which the implant observes and stores data that is transmitted on the I^2C bus. This data can then be relayed to the attacker via the wireless interface of the implant.

Denial-of-Service. A DoS disables all communication on the I^2C bus. A malicious IoT implant can perform such an active attack by permanently pulling the SDA and SCL lines to a low voltage state. As a result, no further data can be transmitted on the bus. All other bus participants have to wait until the implant releases the signal lines.

Injection of Transactions. In this active attack, the implant acts as additional master on the bus. Most implementations offer time gaps between transactions, in which the masters and slaves are in idle state. The implant has the chance to execute own transactions on the bus during this period of time. The injection of own transactions allows to perform further implicit attacks: (a) *Read out memory and configurations:* The implant can read out data from memory chips as well as the configurations of slaves. These information can then be exfiltrated to the attacker via the wireless interface. (b) *Reconfiguration:* The implant can send commands to modify the configuration of slaves consistently. For example, a pre-configured threshold can be altered or, in some cases, a slave could be completely disabled. This ultimately allows for slave impersonation attacks, in which the implant responds to messages of the legitimate master instead of the disabled slave.

On-The-Fly Bit Modification. Whenever a logical 1 is sent on the I^2C bus, the transmitting IC releases the SDA signal. A pull-up resistor connected to SDA then pulls the voltage of the signal to high level and the next clock signal carries the bit value. As an active attack, the implant can utilize this idle state to pull the SDA signal to low level, which results in the transmission of a logical 0 instead of the sent logical 1 on the bus. Due to the electronic characteristics of the I^2C bus, a modification of logical 0 to logical 1 is not possible.

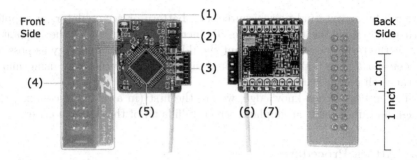

Fig. 2. Components of the malicious IoT implant: (1) indicator LED, (2) power converter, (3) I/O interface for serial bus signals (SDA, SCL) and power supply (VCC, GND), (4) removable programming and debug interface, (5) MCU, (6) wired monopole antenna, (7) LoRa radio transceiver.

4.3   Implementation

Wireless Connectivity. We use the LoRa technology (cf. Sect. 2.1) as wireless communication interface for the implant. Competing LPWAN standards to LoRa [1] exist, such as SigFox, Weightless, and LTE Narrowband IoT, but they are currently not supported by such a large community of industrial and private partners as LoRa. However, the presented attacks could also be facilitated using one of these LPWAN technologies.

TTN acts as service provider to connect the implant to the Internet using LoRa communication. Application builder can register an account at the TTN website and get access to the network infrastructure in order to connect to their deployed IoT nodes via LoRaWAN. An account can be created easily using a user name, email address and password. The purpose of the application is not checked by TTN.

Hardware Architecture. The hardware architecture of the implant consists of a PCB that is equipped with various ICs as shown in Fig. 2. The implant can be connected to a power source that provides an input voltage between 3.3 V and 16 V. Power can be supplied via the VCC and GND pads, either from the target device or using a battery.

The front side of the implant features a power converter, an I/O interface, an MCU, a number of capacitors, as well as an optional indicator LED. This LED is activated when the implant is supplied with power and blinks each time a LoRa message is sent or received. The MCU STM32F303CBT6 [39] contains an ARM Cortex-M4 core and 128 Kbytes of Flash memory. The radio transceiver RFM95W-868S2 [14] is mounted on the backside of the implant. This module supports the LoRa technology and uses the 868 MHz frequency band. We soldered a simple wired monopole antenna of length 86.4 mm (quarter of the 868 MHz wave length) to the transceiver.

For programming and debugging of the implant, a serial wire debug (SWD) interface is added to the implant. This interface can be physically removed (through breaking or cutting off) after the final version of firmware is installed on the implant.

Software Architecture. The software architecture is based on the STM32CubeMX platform [40] that includes the hardware abstraction layer and the link layer for the MCU. The real-time operating system FreeRTOS builds on top of this vendor-specific platform. A number of libraries is installed: The board support package provides drivers for the interfaces of the implant. The LMiC library [21] implements the LoRaWAN stack, and communicates with the LoRa module. The Arduino JSON library is used to decode and encode messages received within the payload of the LoRa messages. On top, so-called 'tasks' are defined. For example, the 'attack task' implements the attack procedures, while an 'LED task' defines the state of the indicator LED. The implant is registered as application belonging to the TTN account of the attacker and can be operated via the TTN web console.

5   Evaluation

Dimensions. Small dimensions are crucial in order to insert the implant into arbitrary target systems, and furthermore, to avoid visual detection. The implant has a size of 19.5×17.8 mm and a height of 4.5 mm. We measured the weight of the implant to be 3 g. Note that these dimensions are measured without the debug header, antenna, and wires connected to the target. We assert that the dimensions of the implant are small enough for many threat scenarios, in which the enclosure provides a suitable amount of space. We assume that the layout of malicious IoT implants can be further minimized if we waive the usage of off-the-shelf hardware components.

Power Consumption. The malicious IoT implant has to be powered either by the power supply of the target device, or using an external battery. We determined that the power consumption of the implant during *sleep mode* (i.e., radio is duty cycling) is $110\,\mu A$ for 3.3 V input voltage, while the implant consumes around 42 mA in *attack mode* (i.e., radio listens continuously). For comparison: a regular 3.7 V Lithium polymer battery with a capacity of 2000 mAh supplies an implant in sleep mode for more than two years, or 176 h in attack mode. Thus, attackers can wake a sleepy implant even months after the insertion into the target device.

Wireless Range. The wireless range determines from which distance an attacker is able to remotely control a malicious IoT implant. Also, it indicates in which areas the implant has coverage by an LPWAN. The implant utilizes the LoRa technology, which achieves a wireless range of 2–5 km in urban areas and up to 15 Km in sub-urban areas [1]. It is hard to make general statements about the wireless range of the implant as the propagation of radio waves depends on many variables, e.g., the enclosure of the target device, building structures and walls, nearby electrical installations, as well as other deployed wireless networks that interfere with the LoRa frequency bands.

Cost. Once we have the final schematics, we are able to build a batch of 10 implants for the hardware costs of approximately 194 Euros. The cost per unit decrease with an increasing batch size: For a batch size of 100 units, the hardware cost add up to around 1075 Euros. Thus, we can build a malicious IoT implant using mainly off-the-shelf components for less than 11 Euros per unit (assuming a batch size of 100 units). These costs comprise the customized PCB as well as all electronic components including MCU, radio transceiver, LED, power converter, and capacitors. Not included are laboratory equipment, labor costs, shipping costs, and consumable materials.

5.1   Effort of Insertion

The procedure of implanting malicious hardware into the target device consists of three steps: identifying access points on the PCB, analyzing the communication on the bus, and inserting the implant into the device.

In the first step, we open the case of the target device and look whether there is enough space to insert the implant. If so, we identify the PCBs and list the descriptors of all ICs. Then, we search for the datasheets of these ICs on the Internet. The identification of ICs on a PCB can also be automated using image recognition [19]. A datasheet usually contains a feature description as well as a pin layout, which we use to identify ICs that support I^2C. After we confirm that an IC supports I^2C, we check whether the I^2C pins are used. Optical indications are signal lines on the PCB that are connected to these pins. Then, we look for suitable solder points on the PCB where we can later attach the wires to the implant. It is not advisable to directly solder the wires onto the pins of an IC since this requires a very precise way of working and can easily lead to damages or electrical shorts with neighboring pins. Good access points are larger solder joints, for example, at surface-mounted capacitors or at through-hole connections. As second step, we use a logic analyzer to inspect the communication on the bus. Using logic diagrams, we identify the ICs that communicate with each other, the bus frequency, and the transmitted data (datasheets might help again). As a result, we configure the software of the implant accordingly. In the third step, we solder wires onto the access points after we have removed the power supply and batteries. Then, we attach the wires to the implant. If required, we fixate the implant within the target device such that the antenna does not touch other electronic parts. We supply the target device with power again, and if the insertion was successful, the indicator LED on the implant turns on. In addition, we test whether the implant can be remotely controlled. Finally, we close the casing of the target device and try to remove all traces of this modification procedure.

The danger of damaging the PCB boards during the insertion of the implant is low if we take standard precautions: The process of insertion should be performed in an electrostatic discharge protected area. In this area, all conductive materials and workers are grounded and mechanisms to prevent the build-up of electrostatic charges should be in place. Furthermore, the power supply needs to be safely removed to prevent electrical shorts. Then, the danger of damaging the target device is mainly reduced to the threat of thermal influences on the ICs from the soldering process and physical damages.

In the physical distribution process, time is crucial. Thus, the time to insert the implant into the target system should be appropriate. If we want to insert the implant into a large batch of similar target devices, the customization of the implant is only required once. From our experience, the process of customization can add up to a few hours. The insertion process needs to be performed for each target device. In our experiments, the manual inserting of the implants takes a few minutes, in some cases we were even able to insert the implant within less than a minute.

5.2   Feasibility of Attacks

We demonstrate the feasibility of the attacks outlined in Sect. 4.2 through inserting the malicious IoT implant into three exemplarily target devices: One evaluation board and two real-world products. We selected the real-world products through searching online in databases of disassembled products, e.g., iFixit, for security- and safety-relevant devices that indicate the usage of I^2C communication.

Evaluation Board. The first hardware platform is an evaluation board that was specifically designed to test the implementation of the implant. It imitates a monitoring application that observes the temperature of an industrial manufacturing process. If the temperature exceeds or undercuts a preconfigured threshold, an alarm is triggered and the light of an LED diode warns the operator. From a technical perspective, the MCU reads temperature sensor data from the registers of the sensor via I^2C, and shows the value on an LCD display. The lower and upper bounds of the temperature threshold are stored in the registers of the temperature sensor.

After attaching the implant to the SDA and SCL solder pads of the evaluation board, we are able to perform all attacks described in Sect. 4.2. During sleep mode, the implant does not interfere with the normal operation of the evaluation board. In attack mode, the implant eavesdrops the current temperature values as well as the threshold configuration, which both are requested multiple times per second by the MCU. The implant then relays these values to the attacker's operator interface. Upon receiving the DoS command from the attacker, the implant disables all communication on the bus. On the target device, the MCU cannot read data from the sensor anymore and throws an exception, which results in a bus error message on the display. Furthermore, the implant can inject own transactions to read the data stored in the registers of the sensor, and to write new values to the registers. This way, the attacker is able to reconfigure the threshold that triggers the alarm. Finally, we are able to manipulate legitimate temperature values on the bus by performing the on-the-fly bit modification attack. Exemplary, we changed one bit of a temperature value byte such that the bus transferred 0x0F instead of 0x8F. As a result, the MCU reads a temperature of 15.9 °C instead of 28.9 °C.

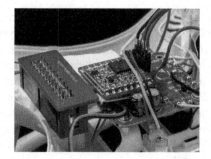

(a) Cash box   (b) Drone (implant with debug header)

Fig. 3. Malicious IoT implant (green PCB) inserted into exemplary devices.

Cash Box. As a second hardware platform, we inserted the implant into a First Alert 3040DFE cash box that allows access by entering a pin into an electronic pin pad. Each time a pin is entered into the pin pad, the MCU uses I^2C communication to read the master pin stored in an EEPROM. If the entered pin matches the master pin, the content of the cash box can be accessed. The master pin is set by pushing a red button that is located inside the cash box, and then entering the new master pin two times into the pin pad. Assuming that the attacker inserts the implant at some point during the physical distribution process, the attacker is later able to eavesdrop and set the master pin, and thus, to access the content of the box. As shown in Fig. 3a, we attached the SDA and SCL wires of the implant to solder points of a pull-up resistor and the reset button, respectively. To supply the implant with power, we attached the VCC and GND wires to solder points connected to the batteries of the cash box. The enclosure of the cash box provides plenty of space for the implant and a wired monopole antenna. Controlling the implant from the operator interface, we performed eavesdropping, DoS, and the injection of transactions. First, the attacker is able to monitor the bus to retrieve the master pin that is requested by the MCU each time a pin is entered into the pin pad. The implant then exfiltrates the master pin via the wireless interface. In addition, the implant can disable all I^2C communication upon receiving a DoS command from the attacker. Then, the MCU cannot read the master pin from the EEPROM anymore, and thus, does not unlock the cash box. Through the injection of own commands, the attacker can then read the master pin from the EEPROM and also set this pin to an arbitrary value. During sleep mode, the implant does not influence the normal operation of the cash box.

Drone. We used a Syma X5C-1 drone as third hardware platform to evaluate the malicious IoT implant. The drone features a gyroscope and accelerometer sensor that stabilizes the drone during flights. An MCU reads data from this sensor every 3 ms using I^2C communication, and subsequently adjusts the individual speed of the four rotors according to its flight position. As depicted in Fig. 3b, we attached the SDA and SCL wires of the implant to a pin of the MCU as well as a pin of the sensor. Also, we attached the GND and VCC wires to solder points that are connected to the battery power supply of the drone. The body of the drone provides enough space for the implant and its antenna. Also, the drone is capable of carrying the implant without any effects on its flight characteristics. During sleep mode, the implant does not affect the normal operation of the drone. We performed eavesdropping and DoS attacks on the drone. Using the implant, the attacker can eavesdrop on the sensor data that is requested by the MCU. This sensor data contains triple-axis angular rates as well as triple-axis accelerometer data. Parts of these aggregated information can be sent to the attacker in regular intervals. Upon receiving a DoS command from the attacker, the implant blocks the I^2C bus through pulling both lines to low. The MCU of the drone cannot read data from the gyroscope and accelerometer, and thus, the speed of the rotors is not adjusted anymore. In consequence, the flight position of drone destabilizes and the drone hits the ground.

6   Discussion

The results of our evaluation underline two major threats: As a first threat, the emergence of IoT infrastructure provide novel attack vectors besides DoS attacks on Internet infrastructure [3,20]. As we demonstrate, malicious IoT implants connected to LPWANs can be leveraged to exfiltrate secret information, manipulate the functionality of target devices, and in worst case, might even pose a threat to humans. Such attacks can be performed anonymously as one can register an account and set up the application without any identification at the website of the LoRaWAN service provider TTN. Furthermore, the attacker can control the implant from a remote location over the Internet. These attacks are not specific to LoRaWAN and can also be performed using other competing LPWAN standards. We note that the usage of traditional mobile telephony infrastructure (e.g., GSM and LTE) would not satisfy the design criteria given in Sect. 4.1 since a GSM or LTE radio transceiver consumes more energy, the attacker would have to pay for data transmissions, and in most countries a SIM card registration requires an official identification document. The effort of building such an implant is relatively low for experts since the hardware and software design is based mainly on off-the-shelf components and open-source software, respectively. Thus, the dissemination of LPWANs open up new attack vectors, which did not exist before when traditional mobile telephony infrastructure was the only wide-area connectivity provider.

As a second threat, serial communication on PCBs is vulnerable to malicious hardware inserted during physical distribution in the supply chain. While the presented malicious IoT implant is tailored to attack I^2C buses, other serial communication systems, such as UART and SPI, could be adapted with a reasonable effort. However, we might only be able to apply a subset of the presented attacks to other bus systems due to different approaches in the electronic design of these systems. In contrast to other serial buses, I^2C facilitates a communication protocol that allows multiple masters on the bus. Since the implant acts as a master, the injection of own transactions in SPI and UART communication is not easily possible. Nevertheless, we can eavesdrop the communication between ICs to exfiltrate information and perform DoS attacks through pulling all lines of the communication system to a low voltage state. In our evaluation, both attacks had a significant impact on the target devices' security and reliability.

One might ask why should attackers use malicious IoT implants when malicious software (malware) could do the same job? Although we agree that the effort of facilitating malware might be lower, malware falls short in several scenarios. First, if the target device has no Internet connection, then malware has usually no communication channel to the attacker. For this reason, neither of our three evaluation devices could be remotely attacked using malware due to missing network interfaces. Second, in case a direct interference with serial communication on hardware level is desired, e.g., to circumvent software protection mechanisms. Third, malware could be detected by other software, in contrast to implants that are "invisible" at software level. During the evaluation, the implant had no influence on the regular operation of the target device except if the attacker performs an attack. Since the attacks directly influence the communication on hardware level, an incident investigator is not able to find digital traces in the log files of the target device's software. The only indications might be exceptions triggered by the MCU and physical evidence, e.g., the presence of an implant or traces on the PCB that indicate that an implant was attached.

6.1 Limitations

The threat of LPWAN-connected malicious IoT implants comes with a number of limitations for attackers. Each implant needs to be inserted manually, which renders this attack procedure unsuitable for large-scale operations in which thousands of devices have to be modified. Furthermore, expert knowledge in electronic engineering and programming of software is necessary for the preparation and insertion of an implant. Moreover, a number of potential target devices, e.g., mobile phones and tablets, might not provide enough space within the enclosure to carry an implant that is designed using mainly off-the-shelf components. Also, the feasibility of utilizing an LPWAN-connected implant is limited through the coverage of the selected service provider's LPWAN infrastructure. Finally, the amount of exfiltrated data is restricted since LPWANs only provide low data rates to achieve their low-power objectives. Nevertheless, the bandwidth between implant and attacker is reasonable for most threat scenarios.

6.2 Countermeasures

We analyze a variety of potential approaches to encounter malicious IoT implants, which we divide into detection and safeguard mechanisms. While detection mechanisms disclose the presence of a malicious IoT implant in a system, safeguard mechanisms prohibit an implant from interfering with the serial communication.

Detection Mechanisms. A trivial approach to detect malicious IoT implants is *visual inspection* of the PCBs. The advantage is that no expensive equipment is required. On the other hand, this requires the removal of the enclosure for most products, which could be quite a cumbersome task since many products are not intended to be disassembled. Therefore, this approach becomes impractical if large batches of products should be investigated. Also, future implant layouts might become smaller and can be implemented into PCBs hidden as legitimate ICs, which makes visual detection much harder and more time-consuming. In addition, non-expert user might not be able to recognize malicious hardware elements if the implant is camouflaged as a legitimate part of the PCB.

Since malicious IoT implants have a physical appearance, another detection approach is to *compare the weight* of suspicious products with the weight of an evidently unmodified product. The advantage of this approach is low costs as only a precision scale is needed. The disadvantage is that an attacker can potentially reduce the weight of a modified device by removing small pieces of the enclosure. Also, this approach is not suitable for heavy devices since the weight of the implant might be hidden within the measurement tolerance.

In *anomaly detection*, potential side-channel effects resulting from the presence of an implant are observed. For instance, the implant consumes a certain amount of power as evaluated in Sect. 5, which might be supplied from the host system. Thus, the power consumption of manipulated products should show anomalies compared to unaltered products. Also, malicious IoT implants provide a wireless interface that emits radio waves, which can be detected with special equipment. The advantage of anomaly detection procedures is potential large-scale automation. The disadvantage is the need for hardware extensions on the products or special equipment in testing facilities.

Safeguard Mechanisms. Another way to protect against the insertion of malicious IoT implants is the adding of *tamper-evident features*. For example, the packaging of a product can be sealed in way that the attacker cannot access the product without irreversibly destroying the sealing. Also, physical security measures, such as a locked encasement or resin encapsulation, could be in place to protect the PCB against tampering. Tamper resistance does not always prevent the implementation of an implant but it increases the attacker's effort and makes the detection of malicious actions much more likely.

The usage of *cryptographic security measures* can be a countermeasure to circumvent malicious IoT implants to read and inject messages into the serial buses. Lázaro et al. [23] proposed an authenticated encryption scheme for I^2C buses. In their proposal, the I^2C data frames are encrypted and authenticated using AES-GCM, while addressing frames are not protected. The calculation of ciphertext and signature is directly implemented into the master and slave ICs. The authors assume a pre-installed key on each IC that was installed in a secure environment. The advantage of encryption is that it provides an efficient way to lock out non-authorized entities. As a disadvantage, all ICs on the bus must implement the encryption mechanism and need to be equipped with key material. Most probably, this requires a change of the I^2C specifications.

7 Related Work

Previous research investigated the insertion of malicious hardware at three stages: in the design phase, during fabrication phase, and in the post-fabrication phase. Especially hardware trojans attracted a high amount of research in the last decade. From a high level perspective, hardware trojans are malicious modifications of the hardware during the design or fabrication process. In contrast, malicious hardware implants are alien elements that are added to a system after the fabrication process.

There exist different approaches to insert malicious trojans into hardware. A first approach are modifications of the system design at hardware description language (HDL) level [8,12,13,18,24,41], which results in the adding of additional logic to the IC. Prototypes of these trojans have been mainly implemented and evaluated using FPGAs. A second approach of inserting malicious hardware is the implementation of hardware trojans at gate level during fabrication [5,22,36]. In contrast to modifications at HDL level, this approach does not add additional logic to the system but only modifies existing hardware elements. A third approach is the adding of analog circuits to the system [42].

The first ICs that relate to hardware implants were called mod chips [35], which modify functions of the target system, e.g., to circumvent copyright protection mechanisms in video playback devices or to enable restricted features in game consoles. Compared to design and fabrication phase attacks, less attention was paid by the academic community to malicious hardware attacks in post-fabrication phases. Shwartz et al. [37] demonstrated how aftermarket components, e.g., third-party touchscreens used in repairs of broken mobile devices, could be manipulated such that a malicious mobile phone app can get root access to the device. In a non-academic context, Datko and Reed [7] implemented a hardware implant inspired by the NSA Ant catalog [4]. Their proof-of-concept features a GSM interface to ex-filtrate data and connects to the target system via a VGA display adapter using I^2C communication. To relay data from the computer, a malware on the target system is assumed that sends data via I^2C to the implant. In contrast to our work, this implant does not fulfill design criteria ① and ⑥. FitzPatrick [10] presented a number of proof-of-concepts for hardware implants that connect to targeted systems via I/O pins or JTAG. Although these implants fulfill most design criteria, they lack a communication interface to an IoT or cellular infrastructure (②).

8 Conclusion

In this paper, we described the implementation and evaluation of the first malicious IoT implant showing that IoT infrastructure enables novel hardware-level attack vectors. These threats grow with the expansion of LPWANs, which will supersede mobile telephony networks in terms of providing M2M connectivity in a few years. Future threat models for hardware security have to take these threats into account.

Acknowledgement. We thank Tobias Groß for helpful comments. This work was supported by the Federal Ministry of Education and Research, Germany, as part of the BMBF DINGfest project.

References

1. Adelantado, F., Vilajosana, X., Tuset-Peiró, P., Martínez, B., Melià-Seguí, J., Watteyne, T.: Understanding the limits of LoRaWAN. IEEE Commun. Mag. 55(9) (2017). https://doi.org/10.1109/MCOM.2017.1600613
2. Agrawal, D., Baktir, S., Karakoyunlu, D., Rohatgi, P., Sunar, B.: Trojan detection using IC fingerprinting. In: IEEE Symposium on Security and Privacy. S&P 2007 (2007)
3. Antonakakis, M., et al.: Understanding the Mirai botnet. In: 26th USENIX Security Symposium. USENIX Security 2017 (2017)
4. Appelbaum, J., Horchert, J., Stöcker, C.: Shopping for spy gear: catalog advertises NSA toolbox. Spieg. Online Int. **29** (2013). http://www.spiegel.de/international/world/catalog-reveals-nsa-has-back-doors-for-numerous-devices-a-940994.html
5. Becker, G.T., Regazzoni, F., Paar, C., Burleson, W.P.: Stealthy dopant-level hardware trojans. In: Bertoni, G., Coron, J.-S. (eds.) CHES 2013. LNCS, vol. 8086, pp. 197–214. Springer, Heidelberg (2013). https://doi.org/10.1007/978-3-642-40349-1_12
6. Boyens, J., Paulsen, C., Moorthy, R., Bartol, N., Shankles, S.A.: Supply chain risk management practices for federal information systems and organizations. In: NIST SP, vol. 800, no. 161 (2015). https://nvlpubs.nist.gov/nistpubs/SpecialPublications/NIST.SP.800-161.pdf
7. Datko, J., Reed, T.: NSA Playset: DIY hardware implant over I2C. In: DEF CON 22 (2014)
8. Fern, N., San, I., Koç, Ç.K., Cheng, K.: Hardware trojans in incompletely specified on-chip bus systems. In: Design, Automation & Test in Europe Conference & Exhibition (2016)
9. Fernandes, E., Jung, J., Prakash, A.: Security analysis of emerging smart home applications. In: IEEE Symposium on Security and Privacy. S&P 2016 (2016)
10. FitzPatrick, J.: The Tao of hardware, the Te of implants. Black Hat, USA (2016)
11. Gartner: Gartner says 8.4 billion connected "things" will be in use in 2017, up 31 percent from 2016, February 2017. http://www.gartner.com/newsroom/id/3598917
12. Gomez-Bravo, F., Jiménez Naharro, R., Medina García, J., Gómez Galán, J., Raya, M.S.: Hardware attacks on mobile robots: I2C clock attacking. In: Reis, L., Moreira, A., Lima, P., Montano, L., Muñoz-Martinez, V. (eds.) Robot 2015: Second Iberian Robotics Conference. AISC, vol. 417, pp. 147–159. Springer, Cham (2016). https://doi.org/10.1007/978-3-319-27146-0_12
13. Hicks, M., Finnicum, M., King, S.T., Martin, M.M.K., Smith, J.M.: Overcoming an untrusted computing base: detecting and removing malicious hardware automatically. In: IEEE Symposium on Security and Privacy. S&P 2010 (2010)
14. HopeRF Electronic: RFM95/96/97/98(W) - low power long range transceiver module V1.0 datasheet. http://www.hoperf.com/upload/rf/RFM95_96_97_98W.pdf
15. Hunt, G., Letey, G., Nightingale, E.: The seven properties of highly secure devices. Technical report, March 2017
16. IC Insights: NXP acquires Freescale, becomes top MCU supplier in 2016, April 2017

17. Kerlink: Kerlink continues global expansion with subsidiary in India for rollout of world's largest LoRaWAN IoT network, September 2017
18. King, S.T., Tucek, J., Cozzie, A., Grier, C., Jiang, W., Zhou, Y.: Designing and implementing malicious hardware. In: USENIX Workshop on Large-Scale Exploits and Emergent Threats. LEET 2008 (2008)
19. Kleber, S., Nölscher, H.F., Kargl, F.: Automated PCB reverse engineering. In: 11th USENIX Workshop on Offensive Technologies. WOOT 2017 (2017)
20. Kolias, C., Kambourakis, G., Stavrou, A., Voas, J.M.: DDoS in the IoT: Mirai and other botnets. IEEE Comput. **50**(7), 80–84 (2017). https://doi.org/10.1109/MC. 2017.201
21. Kooijman, M.: Arduino LoraMAC-in-C (LMiC) library. https://github.com/ matthijskooijman/arduino-lmic
22. Kumar, R., Jovanovic, P., Burleson, W.P., Polian, I.: Parametric trojans for fault-injection attacks on cryptographic hardware. In: Workshop on Fault Diagnosis and Tolerance in Cryptography. FDTC 2014 (2014)
23. Lázaro, J., Astarloa, A., Zuloaga, A., Bidarte, U., Jimenez, J.: I2CSec: a secure serial chip-to-chip communication protocol. J. Syst. Arch.-Embed. Syst. Des. **57**(2), 206–213 (2011). https://doi.org/10.1016/j.sysarc.2010.12.001
24. Lin, L., Kasper, M., Güneysu, T., Paar, C., Burleson, W.: Trojan side-channels: lightweight hardware trojans through side-channel engineering. In: Clavier, C., Gaj, K. (eds.) CHES 2009. LNCS, vol. 5747, pp. 382–395. Springer, Heidelberg (2009). https://doi.org/10.1007/978-3-642-04138-9_27
25. LoRa Alliance: LoRa Alliance surpasses 500 member mark and drives strong LoRaWAN protocol deployments, June 2017
26. LoRa Alliance: LoRaWAN global networks - where are we today? October 2017
27. Machina Research: With 3 billion connections, LPWA will dominate wide area wireless connectivity for M2M by 2023, February 2015
28. Margulies, J.: Garage door openers: an internet of things case study. IEEE Secur. Priv. **13**(4), 80–83 (2015). https://doi.org/10.1109/MSP.2015.80
29. Min, H., Zhou, G.: Supply chain modeling: past, present and future. Comput. Ind. Eng. **43**(1), 231–249 (2002). https://doi.org/10.1016/S0360-8352(02)00066-9
30. Morgner, P., Mattejat, S., Benenson, Z., Müller, C., Armknecht, F.: Insecure to the touch: attacking ZigBee 3.0 via touchlink commissioning. In: Proceedings of the 10th ACM Conference on Security and Privacy in Wireless and Mobile Networks. WiSec 2017 (2017)
31. NXP: The I2C-bus specification and user manual - UM10204, April 2014
32. Reichert, C.: NNN Co and Actility announce LoRaWAN network rollout across Australia, February 2017
33. Ronen, E., O'Flynn, C., Shamir, A., Weingarten, A.: IoT goes nuclear: creating a ZigBee chain reaction. In: IEEE Symposium on Security and Privacy. S&P 2017 (2017)
34. Rostami, M., Koushanfar, F., Rajendran, J., Karri, R.: Hardware security: threat models and metrics. In: The IEEE/ACM International Conference on Computer-Aided Design (2013)
35. Safavi-Naini, R.: Digital Rights Management: Technologies, Issues, Challenges and Systems, vol. 3919. Springer, Heidelberg (2006). https://doi.org/10.1007/11787952
36. Shiyanovskii, Y., Wolff, F.G., Rajendran, A., Papachristou, C.A., Weyer, D.J., Clay, W.: Process reliability based trojans through NBTI and HCI effects. In: 2010 NASA/ESA Conference on Adaptive Hardware and Systems. AHS 2010 (2010)

37. Shwartz, O., Cohen, A., Shabtai, A., Oren, Y.: Shattered trust: when replacement smartphone components attack. In: 11th USENIX Workshop on Offensive Technologies. WOOT 2017 (2017)
38. Sigfox: SIGFOX expanding IoT network in 100 U.S. cities, February 2017
39. STMicroelectronics: STM32F303CB datasheet, May 2016
40. STMicroelectronics: STM32Cube initialization code generator datasheet, July 2017
41. Sturton, C., Hicks, M., Wagner, D.A., King, S.T.: Defeating UCI: building stealthy and malicious hardware. In: IEEE Symposium on Security and Privacy. S&P 2011 (2011)
42. Yang, K., Hicks, M., Dong, Q., Austin, T.M., Sylvester, D.: A2: analog malicious hardware. In: IEEE Symposium on Security and Privacy. S&P 2016 (2016)

Before Toasters Rise Up: A View into the Emerging IoT Threat Landscape

Pierre-Antoine Vervier[1](✉) and Yun Shen[2]

[1] Symantec Research Labs, Sophia Antipolis, France
pierre-antoine_vervier@symantec.com
[2] Symantec Research Labs, Reading, UK
yun_shen@symantec.com

Abstract. The insecurity of smart Internet-connected or so-called "IoT" devices has become more concerning than ever. The existence of botnets exploiting vulnerable, often poorly secured and configured Internet-facing devices has been known for many years. However, the outbreak of several high-profile DDoS attacks sourced by massive IoT botnets, such as Mirai, in late 2016 served as an indication of the potential devastating impact that these vulnerable devices represent. Since then, the volume and sophistication of attacks targeting IoT devices have grown steeply and new botnets now emerge every couple of months. Although a lot of research is being carried out to study new spurs of attacks and malware, we still lack a comprehensive overview of the current state of the IoT thread landscape. In this paper, we present the insights gained from operating low- and high-interaction IoT honeypots for a period of six months. Namely, we see that the diversity and sophistication of IoT botnets are both growing. While Mirai is still a dominating actor, it now has to coexist with other botnets such as Hajime and IoT Reaper. Cybercriminals also appear to be packing their botnets with more and more software vulnerability exploits targeting specific devices to increase their infection rate and win the battle against the other competing botnets. Finally, while the IoT malware ecosystem is currently not as sophisticated as the traditional one, it is rapidly catching up. We thus believe that the security community has the opportunity to learn from passed experience and act proactively upon this emerging threat.

1 Introduction

Over the last few years, security, or lack thereof, in the world of smart Internet-connected (or Internet of Things, IoT) devices has raised a lot of attention and concerns. In late 2016, several massive and high-profile DDoS attacks originated from a botnet of compromised devices, such as IP cameras and home routers, have taken part of the Internet down [7]. Although it was known for many years that there exists a lot of poorly configured Internet-facing IoT devices with default credentials or outdated firmware making them vulnerable to full device takeover, the high-profile attacks really revealed the destructive potential an army of such devices represent when used in a coordinated fashion.

© Springer Nature Switzerland AG 2018
M. Bailey et al. (Eds.): RAID 2018, LNCS 11050, pp. 556–576, 2018.
https://doi.org/10.1007/978-3-030-00470-5_26

There is a number of existing research work [7,14,18,23,30,31] that looked into these increasing threats.The most notable work is probably Antonakakis *et al.*'s forensic analysis of the Mirai botnet in 2017 [7]. Indeed, this study provides a very detailed description of the operations and evolution of the infamous botnet over a period of about one year. While this work provides an unprecedented understanding into this major IoT threat, we have seen that Mirai and its close variants only account for a limited set of IoT botnets. Additionally, Cozzi *et al.* [14] studied Linux malware but focused on their system-level behaviour. Others have proposed techniques to build honeypots to study IoT threats but these suffer from intrinsic limitations. For example, IoTCandyJar [23] requires active scanning of real IoT devices and replay parts of real attacks against these devices to build realistic models of real-device interactions. Siphon [18] relies on real devices to build high-interaction honeypots but lacks a proper instrumentation mechanism and suffer from scalability issues. Finally, IoTPot [30] by Pa *et al.* combine low-interaction honeypots with sandbox-based high-interaction honeypots but limit themselves to monitor *telnet*-based attacks. The analysis of IoT threats from these honeypot-based studies thus bears some limitations from their design. All this motivated us to carry out a global study of the IoT threat landscape. Our ultimate goal is to better answer the following questions. *What are the IoT threats we currently observe in the wild? What is the attackers' modus operandi to penetrate, infect and monetise IoT devices? How is the IoT threat landscape evolving?*

To help answer these questions, we designed an experimental environment specifically tailored for the study of the IoT threat landscape combining low- and high-interaction honeypots. We leverage embedded device firmware emulation techniques [11,13] to build high-interaction honeypots and show that it enables us to overcome major limitations in previous deployments, such as the instrumentation of the honeypots, while assuring a highly accurate real device-like interaction with attackers. We then present the results of the analysis of six months of data collected from our honeypots. We take a look at the three main stages of IoT device compromise - intrusion, infection and monetisation - and present our findings. For example, we see that while the Mirai botnet and its variants appear to be dominating the IoT threat landscape, other botnets like IoT Reaper and Hajime are fighting to grow and compromise as many devices as possible. We also see that IoT botnets are very dynamic, with rapidly changing malware hosting infrastructure and malware polymorphism. They also evolve very quickly due to, for instance, the source code release of some botnets, which means that we have to continually monitor them to detect when their behaviour changes and adapt our mitigation strategy. Finally, we observe a worrying trend of more and more IoT botnets leveraging a myriad of software vulnerabilities in specific devices to compromise them.

It is important to mention that such a work is not meant to be an one-off study but should rather be repeated over time to closely monitor the evolution of the threat landscape, that is, track existing and new botnets so as to adapt our intrusion detection and infection mitigation strategies.

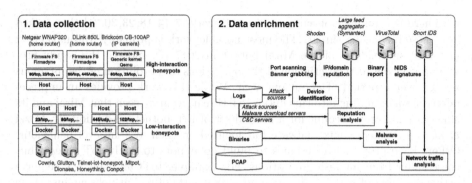

Fig. 1. Experimental environment for the study of the IoT threat landscape.

2 Data Collection Infrastructure

Studying the threat landscape in the world of smart Internet-connected (or IoT) devices is a very wide and complex task. IoT encompasses a lot of different types of devices, *e.g.*, smart televisions, surveillance systems, connected vehicles, water plant pumps, that can be deployed in a large variety of environments, *e.g.*, smart home and factories. Monitoring all these devices to detect potential compromise would be ideal but is of course infeasible. Indeed many of these devices, like industrial control systems, are deployed in very specialised environments and are also known to run on exotic and often proprietary hardware architectures and operating systems. These barriers thus makes it very hard to study the security of these devices. There is however a corpus of devices that run on commodity hardware and lightweight Linux-based operating systems. Such devices include, for instance, some home routers, IP cameras, smart televisions, DVRs and many more. These devices represent only a fraction of all the so-called "IoT" devices but, interestingly, they have been increasingly involved in cyber hazards over the last few of years due to flawed manufacturing and poor security configurations. Yet they are massively available in the consumer market.

Data Collection. Motivated by this, we thus decided to focus on the threats targeting these Linux-based IoT devices in this work. We deployed a set of honeypots mimicking various functionalities of some devices in order to observe three aspects of IoT attacks. That is, (i) the *reconnaissance* or *intrusion phase*, where attackers attempt to penetrate the defences of a device. (ii) The *infection phase*, where attackers usually take full control over the device and prepare it for whatever it is supposed to be used. (iii) Finally, the *monetisation phase* starts when the attackers use the compromised device for other nefarious purposes, such as infecting other devices, launching DDoS attacks, etc.

Figure 1 depicts the data collection and enrichment infrastructure we designed, deployed and have been operating since August 2017. The *data collection* part consists of seven different open-source low-interaction honeypots[1]. Each honeypot is running inside a docker container to isolate it from the host and easily manage how network traffic flows between the host and the honeypot-emulated services. The main advantage of these low-interaction honeypots is that they are very straightforward to deploy thus allowing to collect IoT-related threat data very quickly. These honeypots aim at tricking attackers into infecting them by offering a very basic interaction for various services/applications, such as a *telnet* remote management interface, a FTP server or an embedded web interface. Since the interaction is purposely generic, *i.e.*, independent of a specific device, and completely hard-coded into the honeypot, attackers can take advantage of this to detect them by performing some specific checks. These honeypots are also unable to observe the *monetisation* phase as their functionalities do not enable them to get compromised.

To overcome the limitations of the low-interaction honeypots, we decided to explore the design and deployment of high-interaction IoT honeypots. As described in Sect. 4, different techniques have already been proposed to build a high-interaction IoT honeypot. Having considered the different previously proposed techniques, we realised that none of them provided the required amount of flexibility, scalability and ease of deployment. To this end, we leveraged two different techniques to build our emulated high-interaction honeypots. The first technique we used is an open-source firmware emulation framework called Firmadyne [11], which enables emulation of Linux-based systems by extracting the operating system from firmware images and running it with a generic kernel inside the QEMU virtualiser. It enables us to emulate the network-facing services provided by the devices, such as a *telnet* service, a web server, etc. However, Firmadyne requires the whole operating system (except the kernel) to be embedded in the firmware images for the emulation to work. Moreover, many device operating systems appear to be tightly bound to their hardware architecture, preventing the system from being successfully emulated when, for instance, the system seeks access to specific hard-coded memory addresses. This limitation also appears to affect certain types of devices, *e.g.*, IP cameras, more than others, *e.g.*, home routers. We thus decided to leverage another technique borrowed from [13], which consists of extracting the file system from firmware images and running the specific services we are interested in, such as a web server, inside a chroot environment on a QEMU-virtualised generic operating system of the same architecture as the real device.

We built one high-interaction honeypot for the Netgear WNAP320 (home router) and the DLink 850L (home router) using Firmadyne and one for the

---

[1] Glutton: https://github.com/mushorg/glutton
Cowrie: https://github.com/micheloosterhof/cowrie
Telnet-IoT-honeypot: https://github.com/Phype/telnet-iot-honeypot
MTPot: https://github.com/Cymmetria/MTPot
Honeything: https://github.com/omererdem/honeything
Dionaea: https://github.com/DinoTools/dionaea
Conpot: https://github.com/mushorg/conpot.

Brickcom CB-100AP (IP camera) using the "chroot" technique. Since these honeypots run on emulated firmware images, we instrument them by reseting them to their original, clean state every hour.

We thus operate a total of 10 different honeypots - seven low-interaction ones and three high-interaction ones - offering a total of 15 different services on 26 ports. We also collect all incoming and outgoing traffic (the outgoing traffic from high-interaction honeypots is blocked on ports known to be used for scanning and rate-limited otherwise so that they do not involuntarily attack or scan other real devices on the Internet). Each honeypot is deployed on two different network infrastructures, namely a large cloud infrastructure that publishes its cloud-reserved IP address ranges and a tier-3 ISP cloud and hosting infrastructure. Finally, the honeypots are deployment over a set of 76 IP addresses located in six different countries and spanning two continents.

Data Enrichment. As depicted in Fig. 1 the data enrichment part of our framework essentially consists of two tasks: (i) enrich the logs generated by and the files dropped on the honeypots, and (ii) process the network traffic captured at the honeypots to extract additional attack logs and files generated by attackers. More specifically, we extract information about devices our honeypots interact with from Shodan [1] and an IP and domain reputation feed. Furthermore, we retrieve binary reports about files dropped on the honeypots from VirusTotal [2] and run the Snort IDS with the subscription rules to help us label the collected network traffic.

3   Insights into the IoT Threat Landscape

In this section we present the results obtained by analysing the data collected from our honeypot deployment over a period of six months between August 2017 and February 2018. This data consists of (i) enriched logs produced by the different honeypots, (ii) raw network traffic and (iii) files dropped by attackers.

3.1   IoT Device Reconnaissance and Intrusion

First, let us look at how attackers penetrate IoT devices in order to further compromise and monetise them. We have recorded a total of 37,360,767 connections to our honeypots from 1,586,530 unique IP addresses over the six month period. Additionally, our honeypots record peaks of up to 500K connections per day. It is noteworthy to mention that, in an effort to exclude as much as possible the basic port scanning traffic (*i.e.*, check if port is open/closed/filtered), we consider only fully-established TCP connections or at least two-packet long UDP connections. Comparably, previous IoT honeypot deployments reported about 70K *telnet* connections for IoTPot [30], 18M requests by IoTCandyJar [23] and 80K connections by the *telnet* honeypot used by Antonakakis *et al.* in their study of the Mirai botnet [7].

Looking at Attack Sources. First, we take a look at countries that originated attacks against the honeypots. Surprisingly, more than one third of the attacks originated from Brazil. Note that none of the honeypots are deployed in this country and in the South American continent. Looking into more details at this phenomenon, it turns out that no less than 25% of attacks come from one of the biggest ISP in Brazil: Telefonica. Japan's third place is also surprising and, for the big part, attributable to the largest Japanese branch of the ISP NTT. Interestingly, Antonakakis *et al.* [7] observed a similar distribution in their study of Mirai with most bots concentrated in South America and East Asia. This suggests that the issues affecting these regions have yet to be resolved. Finally, China, Russia and the United States together account for about 20% of attacks.

Now looking at the distribution of device types attacking our honeypots, we see that networking devices, such as routers, DSL/cable modems, come first supposedly due to the fact that they are widespread and typically directly reachable from the Internet. After networking devices our honeypots were heavily hit by IP cameras, digital video recorders (DVRs) and alarm systems.

Finally, we extracted the IP-based reputation of attack sources from a large feed aggregator at the time these IP addresses connected to the honeypots. This reputation feed aggregates tens of blacklists describing different malicious activity, such as bot infections, spam, C&C server hosting, web-based attacks, etc. More than two thirds of attack sources were not known to any blacklist when we observed them for the first time. Additionally, about 15% of attacking IP addresses have been flagged as compromised and already part of a botnet. This last observation is consistent with the worm-like behaviour of IoT botnets where compromised devices are trying to self-replicate themselves.

Scanned and Attacked Services. Looking at the distribution of connections per service given in Table 1, we can see that *telnet* dominates with more than 65% of connections, followed by *http* accounting for about 22% of connections. The remaining 13 decoy services represent a total of about 10% of connections. This distribution is of course skewed towards some services, such as *telnet* or *http*, which are provided by multiple of our honeypots while others, such as modbus, bacnet or mqtt, are emulated by only one honeypot. We thus provide the average number of connections per service, per day and per honeypot as a metric of the popularity (or attractiveness) of a service to attackers/scanners. With such a metric we can see that *http* ranks first, closely followed by *telnet* with an average of 5,712.97 and 4,733.02 daily connections respectively.

Since *http* and *telnet* are by far the most "attractive" and hit services at our honeypots and that these services are often provided by Internet-connected devices for remote administration, we decided to focus our investigation of IoT device intrusion mechanisms with these services.

Telnet Access. As documented in [7,30] as well as in various blog posts [21], the intrusion mechanism of a large number of IoT botnets rely heavily on the exploitation of the *telnet*-based remote management interface often provided

Table 1. Breakdown of the number of connections to and average daily hit rate of the different decoy services offered by the honeypots.

Rank	Service	No. of connections	Avg. hit rate per day ↓	Rank	Service	No. of connections	Avg. hit rate per day ↓
1	http	8,469,122	5712.97	9	s7comm	8,623	7.10
2	telnet	25,334,377	4733.02	10	snmp	4,620	4.98
3	ssh	1,061,343	1019.26	11	mqtt	698	4.78
4	upnp	208,635	761.44	12	cwmp	10,011	4.51
5	smb	1,824,945	356.37	13	pptp	512	3.51
6	https	384,863	131.57	14	bacnet	1,193	1.04
7	modbus	14,408	15.54	15	ipmi	16	0.01
8	ftp	37,401	12.38				

by IoT devices. Given the usual lack of proper security management and poor manufacturing of devices, default or hardcoded [6] *telnet* login credentials can provide an easy, dictionary-based brute-force attack vector that usually leads attackers to take full control over the devices.

We have seen a total of 11,791,128 *telnet* connections (46.5% of the total 25M) where attackers successfully logged into the box. Furthermore, attackers needed on average three attempts to guess the correct username and password associated with the different honeypots. Note that our honeypots are all configured with default or easy to guess passwords as our goal is to capture as many attacks as possible. Finally, we have seen that attackers have tried to log in with a total of 4,095 unique usernames and passwords.

Vulnerability Exploitation. Lately, anecdotal evidence suggested that IoT botnets started leveraging not only *telnet* credentials brute-forcing but also exploiting very specific software vulnerabilities in IoT device firmware [8,9]. To investigate this phenomenon, we leveraged our three high-interaction honeypots to determine how attackers have attempted to exploit them. Table 2 summarises the various vulnerabilities affecting these devices and the number of times these vulnerabilities were seen exploited by attackers[2].

We can see that both the DLink router and the Brickcom IP camera are affected by a lot of vulnerabilities, and than many of them - seven for the router and five for the camera - are being exploited in the wild. We can also see that the most exploited vulnerability for both the DLink router and the Brickcom IP camera leads to credentials disclosure, which appears to be what attackers are looking for the most. The other exploited vulnerabilities on the DLink router lead to remote command execution or full system takeover. As far as the Brickcom IP camera is concerned, apart from the XSS vulnerability, all other vulnerabilities

---

[2] We retained only vulnerabilities that can be exploited from by a remote attacker and that were related to services exposed by our honeypots.

Table 2. Software vulnerabilities affecting the high-interaction honeypot devices.

Device	Vulnerability	Discl. date	No. of exploitations
DLink 850L (home router)	Stealing login and password [17]	Sep. 2017	258
	Remote Buffer Overflow in Cookie Header [25]	Jun. 2014	49
	Full Superuser access (RCE to Root) to the device [17]	Sep. 2017	13
	Remote Command Execution via WAN and LAN [29]	Aug. 2017	6
	Buffer overflows in authentication and HNAP functionalities [26]	Nov. 2015	3
	Remote code execution (CVE-2016-5681) [5]	Jun. 2016	2
	UPnP SOAP TelnetD Command Execution [24]	Sep. 2013	1
	Updating firmware in Recovery mode [17]	Sep. 2017	0
	XSS (CVE-2017-{14413,14414,14415,14416}) [19]	Sep. 2017	0
	Retrieving admin password (CVE-2017-{14417,14418}) [19]	Sep. 2017	0
	Nonce brute-forcing for DNS configuration - CVE-2017-14423 [19]	Sep. 2017	0
	Pre-Auth RCEs as root (L2) - CVE-2017-14429 [19]	Sep. 2017	0
Netgear WNAP320 (home router)	Arbitrary command execution (CVE-2016-1555) [4]	Jan. 2016	0
Brickcom CB-100AP-3456 (IP camera)	Remote Credentials and Settings Disclosure [28]	Jul. 2017	50
	Cross-site Request Forgery [27]	Jun. 2016	11
	Hard-coded Credentials [27]	Jun. 2016	6
	Cross-site Scripting [27]	Jun. 2016	6
	Insecure Direct Object Reference/Authentication Bypass [27]	Jun. 2016	6

are related to credentials/device information disclosure and all of them are being exploited. Surprisingly, the only vulnerability affecting our Netgear router honeypot, which enables remote code execution and eventually a full device takeover, was never found to be exploited. In total 411 vulnerability exploitations have been observed across the three high-interaction honeypots over a period of four and a half month. While this number is still low compared to the number of *telnet* credentials cracking attempts, the fact that cybercriminals use so many and diverse vulnerability exploits (sometimes very recent) shows that they are putting a lot more care and sophistication into the building of their botnets. It also shows a real evolution from the first IoT botnets that were relying solely on *telnet* credentials brute-forcing. To the best of our knowledge this is the first time such a behaviour is reported with an assessment of actual vulnerability exploitations against IoT devices in the wild. It is also noteworthy that the disclosure date of the various exploited vulnerabilities vary a lot, from 2013 to the end of 2017. Moreover, the most exploited vulnerability for the DLink router and the Brickcom IP camera were both disclosed in the second half of 2017, only a few weeks before we started seeing them used against out honeypots.

To sum up, most of the time the goal of attackers is to get some privileged access to the device in order to proceed with the infection and later the monetisation. On the one hand, exploiting a software vulnerability on a specific device can facilitate the intrusion when devices are not properly patched and reduce

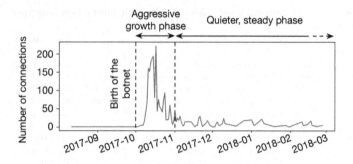

Fig. 2. Intrusion attempts from the IoT Reaper botnet.

the noise produced by the brute-forcing. However, it also requires more work and research from the botnet creator to find IoT device exploits.

A Sneak Peek at IoT Reaper. One particular botnet appears to be heavily relying on software vulnerability exploitation to spread: *IoT Reaper* [10]. The botnet emerged in late 2017. Figure 2 depicts the number of intrusion attempts attributable to the IoT Reaper botnet against our honeypots. The figure shows that the botnet exhibited an aggressive peak of intrusions at the beginning of October 2017, when the botnet was born. After one month, it initiated a quieter phase, which could be due to (i) the botmaster(s) purposely slowing down the growth of the botnet after it reached a steady size or (ii) an attempt to remain under the radar after raising a lot of attention in its first, very active month. Interestingly, the motivations behind IoT Reaper's operators is still unknown.

Browsing Attackers. Telnet credentials brute-forcing and vulnerability exploitation are not the only behaviours we observe from our honeypots. In fact, given that our high-interaction honeypots mimics almost all functionalities of the real devices they emulate, we have witnessed some attackers "browsing" through the web interfaces of the two routers and the IP camera. Table 3 shows a snippet of some URLs requested from the different devices and the action triggered or information disclosed. Furthermore, we next attempt to determine if such "browsing" behaviour is generated by individuals actually visiting the pages or if it is generated by automated scanning tools. First, we look at the time elapsed between *http* requests from each client IP address and notice that 30% of clients issue requests with an average time gap of less than one second, which means these queries are thus likely generated by automated scanning tools. On the other hand, about 10% of clients issue requests with an average time gap of several 10's of seconds, which is more compatible with a real human "browsing" behaviour. Finally, one could argue that such a behaviour, when performed in an automated way, is likely to be part of some reconnaissance or device identification phase. However, in most cases, access to specific admin pages of the remote management web interfaces requires authentication, which assumes that

Table 3. Snippet of URLs requested by "browsing" attackers.

Device	URL	Action	No. of requests
DLink 850L (home router)	GET /diagnostic.php	Display previous diagnostic reports	99
	GET /bsc_wlan.php	Wireless network settings	14
	GET /adv_wps.php	Access WiFi protection setup	14
	GET /tools.php	Access administrator settings	4
	GET /advanced.php	Access advanced setup	3
	GET /setup.php	Access internet connection setup	3
	GET /status.php	Get device information	2
	GET /st_wlan.php	Get connected wireless client list	1
	GET /st_routing.php	Get device routing table	1
	POST /routing_stat.php	Issue routing-related command	1
Netgear WNAP320 (home router)	GET /config.php?json=true	Dump router configuration	127
	GET /downloadFile.php?file=config	Download config. file containing credentials	1
Brickcom CB-100AP-3456 (IP camera)	GET /snapshot.jpg	Get snapshot from IP camera video feed	85
	POST /cgi-bin/camera.cgi	Set camera settings	9
	GET /cgi-bin/motiondetection.cgi? action=getMD& index=1	Get motion detector settings	2
	POST /cgi-bin/audiometer.cgi	Set microphone sensitivity	1

attackers have already gotten access to valid credentials and presumably already know what device they are interacting with. Moreover, we typically observe that attackers accessing more than one page of a given web interface never request inexistent pages, showing that they are either browsing through the web interface or know exactly what pages are provided by the given device.

3.2   IoT Device Infection

In the previous section, we described some of the IoT device reconnaissance and intrusion mechanisms we observed are used by cybercriminals to access and take control over IoT devices. This is usually the first step to a multi-stage attack eventually leading to compromised devices being used to perform other nefarious activities. In this section, we will discuss the second stage of an IoT device takeover where attackers prepare the device for its monetisation, usually by running some malicious code that (i) further tries to spreads itself by exploiting other devices and (ii) joins the C&C channel of an existing botnet.

In order to study the infection mechanisms against our IoT honeypots and given that, from our observations, *telnet* is by far the most prominent intrusion mechanism used by attackers, we extracted all commands issued by attackers from each *telnet* connection to our two *telnet*-enabled high-interaction honeypots, namely the Netgear router and the Brickcom IP camera, stripping away command arguments and credentials entered at the beginning of the sessions. Filtering out empty connections as well as connections where attackers didn't manage to successfully log into the box left us with a total of 169,804 out of

Table 4. Telnet session clustering results: top 10 clusters by size.

Cluster ID	Size		Malware families
	No. of connections	No. of sessions	
A	45,599 (7.46%)	5624	Linux.Downloader, Linux.Mirai, Linux.Aidra, Linux.Kaiten, Linux.Gafgyt
B	10,259 (1.68%)	5	LinuxMirai, Linux.Masuta
C	7,146 (1.17%)	8	Linux.Mirai
D	6,820 (1.12%)	6	Linux.Mirai, Linux.Gafgyt
E	4,205 (0.69%)	3	Linux.Hajime
F	3,121 (0.51%)	7	Linux.Mirai
G	2,620 (0.43%)	21	Linux.Mirai, Linux.Gafgyt
H	2,212 (0.36%)	5	Linux.Mirai, Linux.Aidra
I	1,444 (0.24%)	4	Linux.Mirai, Linux.Aidra, Linux.Gafgyt
J	1,402 (0.23%)	5	Linux.Mirai

611,429 (27.77%) connections. Next, we removed short connections where the client issued a sequence of less than two commands, which is unlikely to implement a real compromise. This step left us with 93,099 (15.23% of the total) connections. Finally, we transformed each sequence of commands into an unordered set of commands, leading to a total of 8,167 *unique telnet* sessions. We then clustered these 8K sessions with the DBSCAN clustering algorithm using the Jaccard index to compute the similarity between each pair of *telnet* sessions. We obtained a total of 70 clusters. The clustering results are summarised in Table 4. Note that only *telnet* commands were used in the clustering and the malware families were added afterwards to illustrate the clusters.

First of all we can see that the first cluster (*A*) is by far the biggest one with more than 45K `telnet` connections. It contains a lot of variety, with more than 5K unique sessions (*i.e.*, unique sets of commands). Cluster *A* can be linked to malware samples belonging to multiple families, namely Mirai, Aidra, Kaiten and Gafgyt, based on AV detections extracted from running the binaries dropped during these *telnet* sessions to VirusTotal. This observation, plus the low compactness of the cluster can be explained by the fact that the commands founds in the cluster are quite generic and common to a lot of malware families.

Cluster *B* contains about 10K *telnet* connections attributable to Mirai and Masuta. Masuta is a very recent variant of the Mirai botnet that emerged in late 2017. When digging further, we notice that the *telnet* command sequences leading to a Mirai sample and to a Masuta sample are almost identical, highlighting their common roots. In this case, the difference between the two threats resides in the dropped binaries.

Interestingly, cluster E appears to be related to the so-called "vigilante" (a.k.a. white hat) botnet *Hajime* [16]. Hajime is known to be a sophisticated, P2P-operated botnet that infects vulnerable IoT devices by brute-forcing their credentials. So far, it has not been linked to any specific type of attack, such as DDoS attacks. Interestingly, Edwards *et al.* described the Hajime infection process that would drop the malicious binary by issuing a series of `echo -ne"<hex-string>" >> <file>` commands over *telnet* in order to rebuild the binary and then execute it. This contrasts with most of IoT botnets, which drop binaries by downloading them from a remote host. However, from cluster E, it appears that Hajime has added the "download" functionality to its self-replication module. It now appears to first check whether it can download the binary and, upon failure, "echo load's" a custom dropper that downloads the main bot via HTTP.

We further looked at the number of commands issued by attackers visiting our low- and high-interaction honeypots. It is interesting to note that attackers, when getting into low-interaction honeypots are inclined to execute more unique commands during *telnet* sessions. We speculate that this phenomenon is due to the fact that low-interaction honeypots provide some default *telnet* session policies that return an empty result to the attackers. This default behaviour triggers the attackers to execute several other branches of their scripts to identify the architecture of the honeypot, alternative ways (e.g., `tftp`) to deliver binaries when `wget` failed, etc.

Looking at the *telnet* commands issued during the infection phase thus appears to provide a way to fingerprint attackers and attribute them to specific threats (or botnets). We believe that such a fine-grained profiling of attackers can greatly assist with the detection and investigation of IoT threats, for instance when writing IoCs.

Dropped Files Analysis. Over the six months of operations our honeypots have collected 3,385 files that were dropped by attackers. For the sake of comparison, previous work on the study of IoT malware analysed 43 binaries in IoTPot [30] and 434 in the Mirai botnet study [7]. Attackers use various techniques to drop files to compromise devices. (i) The most common technique consists in downloading the binary, usually via HTTP or FTP from a remote host. (ii) The other technique we have witnessed is the "echo load" where attackers rebuild the binary in the *telnet* session by "echoing" hexadecimal strings into a file. So far, we have witnessed all malware families use method (i) and only a couple of them, namely Hajime and Gafgyt use (ii) in combination to (i).

We further obtained malware families of the more than 3K binaries we collected by querying the VirusTotal binary reports and normalising AV detection labels, as presented in Table 5. Note that 2,887 out of 3,385 (85.2%) files were not known to VirusTotal before we submitted them. From the perspective of our honeypots, Mirai represents the biggest set (47.5%) of binaries we see. Hajime and Gafgyt follows, with 24.4% and 13.7% respectively. We also observed a mix of old and new botnets, *e.g.*, Masuta emerged in late 2017, Mirai, Hajime and

Table 5. Normalised AV detections of dropped binaries as given by VirusTotal.

Rank	Malware family	No. of files ↓	Rank	Malware family	No. of files ↓
1	Linux.Mirai	1,609	8	Linux.Generic	7
2	Linux.Hajime	792	9	Linux.Remaiten	9
3	Linux.Gafgyt	464	10	Linux.Amnesia	5
4	Linux.Aidra	297	11	Linux.BitcoinMiner	1
5	Linux.Kaiten	154	12	Others	4
6	Linux.Download	30	13	Undetected	3
7	Linux.Masuta	10		Total	3,385

Remaiten appeared in 2016 and the first evidence of Gafgyt dates back to 2014. Interestingly, we can see that there appears to be one instance of a cryptocurrency mining malware that infected one of our honeypots.

Finally, we looked at the observation window of individual malware sample hashes, which is plotted in Fig. 3(a). The short-lived trend here is very strong, with almost 90% of unique malware hashes seen during only one day. Additionally, four malware families - Mirai, Gafgyt, Kaiten and Hajime - have samples that are being observed for weeks and even months (with a maximum of four months and 13 days for Mirai). In case of Hajime, we witnessed only two binaries that have an observation window of several weeks. According to Edwards *et al.*'s analysis of the botnet [16], the two binaries appear to be Hajime's *stage2s* module, which corresponds to the final piece of the bot being run to fully compromise the device. Unlike the rest of Hajime's binaries we collected, these two binaries are also very likely packed, based on their Shannon entropy above 7.98 (out of 8). We speculate that malware authors decided to put more care into designing and obfuscating the *stage2s* binary, which is then observed for longer periods of time than the other first-stage binaries.

Malicious Files Download. A total 2,837 binaries were downloaded from 832 different IP addresses hosted in 146 different ASes. Figure 3(b) plots the observation window as seen from our honeypots. We can see that at least 90% of malware download servers appear to be short-lived, with a witnessed lifetime of less than five days. This is also corroborated by the fact that 60% of malware distributing IP addresses were never blacklisted throughout the six month data collection period. Such IP addresses thus appear to be used for a very short period of time to distribute IoT malware and then disposed of to move on to other IP addresses, so it is hard to rely on techniques like IP blacklisting to block them. It is also noteworthy that 40% of IP addresses are located in only five different ASes associated with large national ISPs providing hosting and cloud services. Note that 99.7% of URLs used by attackers to download files use raw IP addresses rather than domain names. Another interesting thing we observe is that attackers seem to use very limited number of IP addresses to host

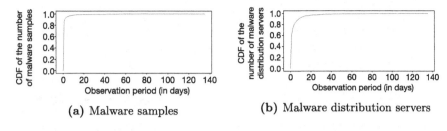

(a) Malware samples

(b) Malware distribution servers

Fig. 3. CDF of the observation window of (a) malware samples and (b) malware distribution servers.

Table 6. Top 10 ports in volume of post-infection traffic.

	Netgear router		Brickcom IP camera	
Rank	Port	No. of connections	Port	No. of connections
1	80/udp	2, 604, 683	80/udp	4, 866, 276
2	3074/udp	1, 337, 377	3074/udp	1, 461, 617
3	53/udp	1, 004, 940	53/udp	1, 384, 311
4	443/udp	764, 040	22/udp	810, 670
5	22/udp	630, 907	443/udp	805, 234
6	443/tcp	519, 864	27015/udp	618, 537
7	27015/udp	489, 547	5355/udp	164, 900
8	16837/udp	195, 545	777/tcp	98, 130
9	3074/tcp	129, 435	34/tcp	96, 703
10	8080/udp	123, 446	53/tcp	95, 490

malicious binaries. We observe, on average, 12 malicious files being hosted at a single IP address and it is worth noting that one IP address was seen hosting up to 468 malicious binaries. We also noticed that the Brickcom IP Camera (avg. 863 downloads/day) is more active than the Netgear router honeypot (avg. 163 downloads/day) in terms of malware downloads. We speculate that this is due to the widely publicised article disclosing the camera's vulnerabilities with PoCs.

3.3 IoT Device Monetisation

The final stage of an IoT device compromise usually consists, for the attacker, in leveraging its full control of the device to perform other nefarious activity, such as infecting other devices to expand its botnet, launching DDoS attacks, etc.

We define the post-infection traffic as the traffic received and generated by a honeypot excluding the intrusion and infection. The post-infection traffic thus contains all potential C&C communications as well as other attacks or malicious activity performed from the compromised honeypots. It is important to note that the following post-infection traffic analysis is different from the previous

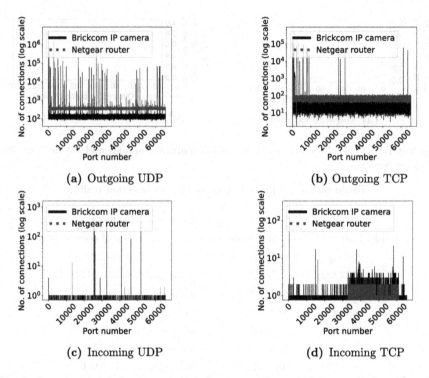

Fig. 4. Incoming and outgoing post-infection traffic per destination port (x-axis) recorded at the Netgear router and Brickcom IP camera honeypots.

research efforts due to the fact that we allow the malicious binaries in the real environment and only block or rate-limit outgoing traffic (see Sect. 2 for the detailed design information). Note in the following analysis we focus on the Netgear router and Brickcom IP camera high-interaction honeypots.

High-Level Overview. We first carry out a high-level analysis of post-infection traffic by dividing it into TCP and UDP and incoming and outgoing. The goal is to identify if the high-interaction honeypots would experience different traffic volumes due to the fact that both devices, in the real world, have different computational capabilities. Our analytical results are shown in Fig. 4. It is straightforward to notice that the router honeypot experienced more outgoing UDP and TCP traffic (see Fig. 4(a) and (b)) than the IP camera honeypot. Our interpretation of this behaviour is that the Netgear router has superior computational capabilities compared to an IP camera, hence the attackers do not need to "throttle" the performance of the payloads. It is also interesting to note that we observe outgoing traffic (on both TCP and UDP) on 65,335 different ports (see Fig. 4), which contrasts with the incoming traffic observed on only 14,560 and 5,320 ports for the Brickcom and Netgear honeypots respectively. The top 10 ports for outgoing post-infection traffic from both high-interaction honeypots

Table 7. Analysis of binaries that triggered peaked post-infection traffic.

Peak	Malware sample	Time	Top three ports per volume of traffic (port number/no. of connections)
❶ tcp (attack)	Binary 1, 2, 3 and 4	2018-02-11 16:00 − 17:00	3324/tcp (117,267), 53/udp (160), 6881/udp (75)
❷ udp (attack)	Binary 5 and 6	2018-02-20 02:00 − 03:00	80/udp (172,493), 3074/udp (167,535), 100/udp (54,772)
❸ udp (scan)	Binary 7 and 8	2018-02-25 17:00 − 18:00	21351/udp (79), 64031/udp (78), 3937/udp (77)
❹ udp (scan)	Binary 9, 10 and 11	2018-02-27 19:00 − 20:00	6881/udp (108), 35159/udp (100), 54680/udp (100)

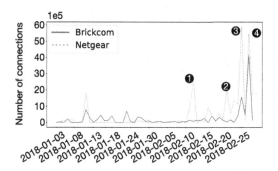

Fig. 5. Post-infection traffic analysis: traffic bursts.

are shown in Table 6. The first thing we observe is that the top 10 ports for outgoing traffic contributes to 30% of each high-interaction honeypot's total traffic. The second thing we observe is that the top three ports for outgoing traffic cover port scanning (80/udp), possible C&C communications (3074/udp) and DDoS attacks (53/udp). This traffic contributes to about 20% of each high-interaction honeypot's total traffic. We observed that even though there is a difference in the volume of traffic between the two high-interaction honeypots, however, in general, they show similar traffic patterns, *e.g.*, 80% of connections on ports 80/udp and 53/udp have less 10 packets and 80% of connections on port 3074/udp have less than 20 packets.

Spiked Traffic Analysis. After a high-level overview of the post-infection traffic, we turn our attention to the temporal analysis. As shown in Fig. 5, there are four peaks in the traffic: peak ❶ is caused by a dramatic increase in TCP traffic while peak ❷, ❸ and ❹ are triggered by elevated UDP traffic. In order to identify the root causes of these peaks, we correlate the file downloads observed during the infection phase (see Sect. 3) to these traffic peaks in order to identify the binaries that have contributed to such spikes. Note that due to the design philosophy of our high-interaction honeypots, we allow multiple binaries to run at the same in the same environment and it is hard to nail down traffic to a single binary. Taking this point into consideration, we slide an one-hour window along each day of post-infection traffic (*i.e.*, we obtain 24 traffic measurements per

Table 8. Attack, scan and mixed post-infection traffic analysis.

Honeypot	Attack (no./avg. ports/avg. binaries)		Scan (no./avg. ports/avg. binaries)		Mixed (no./avg. ports/avg. binaries)	
	udp	tcp	udp	tcp	udp	tcp
Netgear router	16/1,910/3	10/308/54	7/60,020/3	6/53,573/2	2/29,307/3	0/0/0
Brickcom IP camera	12/1,371/4	12/11/8	8/58,424/5	7/39,820/5	3/37,393/6	0/0/0

day) and rank them based upon the traffic volume. Once we have these ranked measurements in place, we identify the binaries that were downloaded during the top most active windows as the root cause of this peaked traffic. The results, shown in Table 7, are interesting. We noticed that the volume of traffic per port for the top three ports of peak ❸ and ❹ is way smaller than that of peak ❶ and ❷. For example, we observed 3,936,628 UDP connections between 19:00–20:00 in peak ❹, yet the traffic on the top three ports only cover around 0.01% of the total traffic observed during that hour. More interestingly, during the same hour, we observed outgoing traffic on 54,721 different ports. In contrast, in peak ❶, we only observed traffic on 628 different ports, yet one port covered 96% of the total traffic of that window. This observation motivates us to carry out a detail behavioural analysis.

Behavioural Analysis. In order to obtain a better understanding of the underlying communications behind the post-infection traffic, we attempted to classify it into three categories: (i) scanning traffic, (ii) attacking traffic and (iii) C&C traffic. First of all, we focus on days where we observe more than 10K connections, for TCP and UDP separately. On each day, we identify the largest hourly TCP and UDP traffic and obtain the top three ports, which are measured and ranked by the number of connections on each port. Then, if the volume of traffic on the top three ports is higher than 70% of the total hourly traffic, we classify the period as an *attack*; if the volume is lower than 20%, we classify the period as a *scan*, otherwise we consider it a *mixed* period. We can see from Table 8 that both the Netgear and Brickcom honeypots show similar volume of TCP/UDP traffic. It is interesting to observe that the UDP traffic covers a wider range of ports in the *attack* scenarios then the TCP traffic, yet in the *scan* scenario, the number of ports for TCP and UDP are comparable. This leads to our preliminary conclusion that binaries that launched TCP attacks focused on a more limited number of ports than those using UDP. However, it requires further proof from binary analysis which is out of the scope of this paper. To our best knowledge, IoTPoT [30] is the only research effort that discussed how attackers monetised the compromised devices. However, it provided limited insights into binary clusters and traffic patterns. In this paper, we were able to quantify the relationship between binaries and the traffic observed with fine granularity.

Distributed Denial of Service Attacks. IoT botnets are well known to be primarily used to launch DDoS attacks. Leveraging the classification of traffic bursts into scan traffic and attack traffic, we next attempted to estimate the total number of DDoS attacks launched from our honeypots. We observed a total of 41 high-volume traffic peaks we attributed to DDoS attacks our honeypots have taken part of. On average each attack generated 141,962 packets and lasted 143 seconds, which gives an average of 993 packets per second. From the 41 attacks, 37 were carried out over UDP and 4 over TCP. Moreover, 38 attacks were targeted towards a single IP address. We recorded five noticeably massive attacks that lasted for several minutes: four DNS (53/udp) attacks at 6K packets per second with from 25 to 54 Mb/s of traffic and one TCP SYN (25565/tcp) attack at 3K packets per second with 1Mb/s of traffic. These five attacks were targeted towards five different IP addresses, one IP address each. Interestingly, two of the IP addresses appeared to be hosting online gaming servers: one Steam and one Minecraft server. In fact, gaming servers seem to be regular targets of DDoS attacks as outlined by Krebs' article [20] and Antonakakis *et al.*'s Mirai study [7]. The three other IP addresses belong to two hosting providers and one American university network.

4   Related Work

IoT Honeypots. ScriptGen by Leita *et al.* [22] is one of the earliest efforts in building high-interaction honeypots. It analyses the sequences of message exchanged between attackers and real servers and automatically derives a state machine that represents the observed interaction. In the same spirit, IoTCandy-Jar [23] proposed a technique that captures attackers requests, then scans the internet for real IoT devices that can respond to these requests and use machine learning to build a model to be used in future interactions with the attackers. However, the ethics of this approach with respect to routing traffic to real IoT devices remains debatable. Guarnizo *et al.* [18] proposed Siphon, an architecture to build a scalable high-interaction honeypot infrastructure backed by real IoT devices. Given that Siphon relies on real devices, its scalability is thus intrinsically limited. Authors also fail to explain how they actually perform the IoT device instrumentation and reset to clean state. Pa *et al.* [30] proposed IoTPoT, a *telnet*-based IoT honeypot. Its core design philosophy is similar to ScriptGen. When an incoming command is unknown, it forwards its to a set of sandbox environments running an embedded Linux OS for different CPU architectures. The interaction between the attacker and the backend is modeled so that the system can later handle the same request without interacting with the backend. Following this design philosophy, Wang *et al.* [31] proposed ThingPot, a proof-of-concept honeypot for Philips HUE light bulbs.

Embedded Device Security and IoT Botnets. The insecurity of Internet-connected embedded devices have been studied for many years. In 2010, Cui *et al.* [15] already reported on more than 500K devices with weak or default credentials. In 2012, the Internet census powered by the IoT device-backed Carna botnet confirmed this trend [3]. In parallel, researchers have also been studying the security of embedded device firmware. Costin *et al.* performed extensive vulnerability assessment of IoT device firmware in [12,13]. Zaddach *et al.* also proposed Avatar [32] and Chen *et al.* proposed Firmadyne [11], both of which provide an emulation environment for embedded devices that further enable vulnerability assessment of firmware images. All these studies highlight the myriad of software vulnerabilities crippling IoT products.

The most notable work on the IoT threat landscape is the recent forensic study of the Mirai botnet by Antonakakis *et al.* in [7]. By combining historical and heterogeneous data sources they were able to reconstruct the whole history of the infamous botnet and track its various evolutions following the release of its source code. Pa *et al.* also leverages their IoTPot [30] infrastructure to analyse *telnet*-based intrusion mechanisms and the behaviour of the few malware samples they collected. Recently, Cozzi *et al.* [14] published a study of Linux (and Linux-based IoT) malware describing some of the trends in their behaviour and level of sophistication.

Our work serves as a follow up to these previous studies. First, we go beyond the scope of the Mirai botnet and aim at providing a global picture of the current IoT threat landscape that includes a myriad of other malware and botnets. We leverage some of the techniques used in the study of embedded device firmware security to build high-interaction IoT honeypots. Finally, unlike IoTPot and ThingPot, we do not restrict ourselves to attacks targeting a particular service or device but instead try to provide as much diversity as possible to get an accurate view into the threat landscape.

5   Conclusion

We used six months of data collected from our honeypots and enriched with various reputation feeds and binary analyses to report on the current threats targeting IoT devices. For instance, we have seen that while attackers still heavily rely on brute-forcing attacks against remote management interface of devices, a worrying and increasing number of botnets are getting equipped with a suite of exploits targeting a wide range of software vulnerabilities inside IoT device firmware, sometimes disclosed a couple of weeks before we start seeing them in the wild. Additionally, botnets powered by the Mirai malware appear to be dominating the IoT thread landscape but other new and old players, such as Hajime and IoT Reaper are aggressively claiming their share of the vulnerable IoT products. Finally, while the core business of IoT botnets is still DDoS attacks, some emerging botnets like IoT Reaper are yet to unveil their real purpose. In summary, we are now witnessing an abrupt change in the sophistication of the IoT threat ecosystem. We believe that, given the experience gained from studying the traditional malware ecosystem, we now have an opportunity to better anticipate and take proactive actions upon the evolutions of the IoT threat landscape.

References

1. Shodan. https://www.shodan.io/
2. VirusTotal. https://www.virustotal.com/
3. Internet Census (2012). http://census2012.sourceforge.net/paper.html
4. CVE-2016-1555 (2016). https://nvd.nist.gov/vuln/detail/CVE-2016-1555
5. CVE-2016-5681 (2017). https://nvd.nist.gov/vuln/detail/CVE-2016-5681
6. CVE-2017-17107 (2017). https://nvd.nist.gov/vuln/detail/CVE-2017-17107
7. Antonakakis, M., et al.: Understanding the mirai botnet. In: USENIX Security Symposium (2017)
8. Anubhav, A.: Agile QBot variant adds NbotLoader Netgear Bug in its new update, July 2017. https://blog.newskysecurity.com/agile-122bf2f4e2f3
9. Anubhav, A.: Masuta : Satori creators' second botnet weaponizes a new router exploit, January 2018. https://blog.newskysecurity.com/masuta-satori-creators-second-botnet-weaponizes-a-new-router-exploit-2ddc51cc52a7
10. Checkpoint: IoTroop Botnet: the full investigation, October 2017. https://research.checkpoint.com/iotroop-botnet-full-investigation/
11. Chen, D.D., Woo, M., Brumley, D., Egele, M.: Towards automated dynamic analysis for Linux-based embedded firmware. In: NDSS, February 2016
12. Costin, A., Zaddach, J., Francillon, A., Balzarotti, D.: A large scale analysis of the security of embedded firmwares. In: USENIX Security Symposium (2014)
13. Costin, A., Zarras, A., Francillon, A.: Automated dynamic firmware analysis at scale: a case study on embedded web interfaces. In: ASIACCS, May 2016
14. Cozzi, E., Graziano, M., Fratantonio, Y., Balzarotti, D.: Understanding Linux malware. In: IEEE Symposium on Security and Privacy, May 2018
15. Cui, A., Stolfo, S.J.: A quantitative analysis of the insecurity of embedded network devices: results of a wide-area scan. In: ACSAC, December 2010
16. Edwards, S., Profetis, I.: Hajime: analysis of a decentralized internet worm for IoT devices. Rapidity Netw. (2016)
17. Embedi: enlarge your botnet with: top D-Link routers, September 2017. https://embedi.com/blog/enlarge-your-botnet-top-d-link-routers-dir8xx-d-link-routers-cruisin-bruisin/
18. Guarnizo, J.D., et al.: Siphon: towards scalable high-interaction physical honeypots. In: CPSS, April 2017
19. Kim, P.: Pwning the Dlink 850L routers and abusing the MyDlink Cloud protocol, September 2017. https://pierrekim.github.io/blog/2017-09-08-dlink-850l-mydlink-cloud-0days-vulnerabilities.html
20. Krebs, B.: Who is Anna-Senpai, the Mirai worm author? January 2017. https://krebsonsecurity.com/2017/01/who-is-anna-senpai-the-mirai-worm-author/
21. Kumar, M.: Advanced Malware targeting Internet of the Things and Routers, March 2016. https://thehackernews.com/2016/03/internet-of-thing-malware.html
22. Leita, C., Mermoud, K., Dacier, M.: Scriptgen: an automated script generation tool for honeyd. In: ACSAC, December 2005
23. Luo, T., Xu, Z., Jin, X., Jia, Y., Ouyang, X.: IoTCandyJar: towards an intelligent-interaction honeypot for IoT devices. In: Blackhat, USA, July 2017
24. Offensive Security: D-Link Devices - UPnP SOAP TelnetD command execution (Metasploit), September 2013. https://www.exploit-db.com/exploits/28333/
25. Offensive Security: Remote buffer overflow in cookie header, June 2014. https://www.exploit-db.com/exploits/33863/

26. Offensive Security: D-Link DIR-890L/R - Multiple buffer overflow vulnerabilities, November 2015. https://www.exploit-db.com/exploits/38716/
27. Offensive Security: Brickcom corporation network cameras - multiple vulnerabilities, April 2016. https://www.exploit-db.com/exploits/39696/
28. Offensive Security: Brickcom IP Camera - credentials disclosure, July 2017. https://www.exploit-db.com/exploits/42588/
29. Offensive Security: SSD advisory - D-Link 850L multiple vulnerabilities, August 2017. https://blogs.securiteam.com/index.php/archives/3364
30. Pa, Y.M.P., Suzuki, S., Yoshioka, K., Matsumoto, T., Kasama, T., Rossow, C.: IoTPOT: analysing the rise of IoT compromises. In: WOOT, August 2015
31. Wang, M., Santillan, J., Kuipers, F.: ThingPot: an interactive IoT honeypot (2017)
32. Zaddach, J., Bruno, L., Francillon, A., Balzarotti, D.: Avatar: a framework to support dynamic security analysis of embedded systems' firmwares. In: NDSS, February 2014

Statistical Similarity of Critical Infrastructure Network Traffic Based on Nearest Neighbor Distances

Jeong-Han Yun[1]([✉]), Yoonho Hwang[2], Woomyo Lee[1], Hee-Kap Ahn[2], and Sin-Kyu Kim[1]

[1] The Affiliated Institute of ETRI, Daejeon, Republic of Korea
{dolgam,wmlee,skkim}@nsr.re.kr
[2] Department of Computer Science and Engineering, POSTECH, Pohang, Republic of Korea
{cypher,heekap}@postech.ac.kr

Abstract. Industrial control systems (ICSs) operate a variety of critical infrastructures such as waterworks and power plants using cyber physical systems (CPSs). Abnormal or malicious behavior in these critical infrastructures can pose a serious threat to society. ICS networks tend to be configured such that specific tasks are performed repeatedly. Further, for a specific task, the resulting pattern in the ICS network traffic does not vary significantly. As a result, most traffic patterns that are caused by tasks that are normally performed in a specific ICS have already occurred in the past, unless the ICS is performing a completely new task. In such environments, anomaly-based intrusion detection system (IDS) can be helpful in the detection of abnormal or malicious behaviors. An anomaly-based IDS learns a statistical model of the normal activities of an ICS. We use the nearest-neighbor search (NNS) to learn patterns caused by normal activities of an ICS and identify anomalies. Our method learns the normal behavior in the overall traffic pattern based on the number of network packets transmitted and received along pairs of devices over a certain time interval. The method uses a geometric noise model with lognormal distribution to model the randomness on ICS network traffic and learns solutions through cross-validation on random samples. We present a fast algorithm, along with its theoretical time complexity analysis, in order to apply our method in real-time on a large-scale ICS. We provide experimental results tested on various types of large-scale traffic data that are collected from real ICSs of critical infrastructures.

1 Introduction

Industrial Control System (ICS) is a general term that describes control systems and related instrumentation designed to control and monitor industrial processes using cyber physical systems. ICSs are used in a variety of national core infrastructures such as waterworks, railways, transportation, power plants,

© Springer Nature Switzerland AG 2018
M. Bailey et al. (Eds.): RAID 2018, LNCS 11050, pp. 577–599, 2018.
https://doi.org/10.1007/978-3-030-00470-5_27

and more. Abnormal or malicious behavior in these critical infrastructures can pose a serious threat to the society.

To minimize the possibility of outside intrusion, most ICSs are isolated from outside networks to a certain extent. Some old systems were built as stand-alone systems, which are disconnected completely from outside networks. However, malware can also be introduced to isolated infrastructure facilities via removable drives, and this can cause serious disasters. Many modern ICSs are connected to the Internet through a protected extension of the corporate network, and therefore they are potentially reachable from the Internet by malicious adversaries. Many studies [9] have been conducted on ICS control devices that are connected to the Internet, and there is even a search engine [1] to find them.

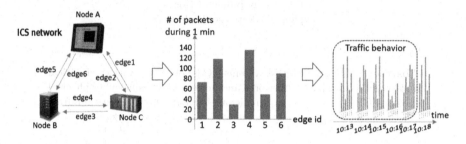

Fig. 1. ICS network traffic behavior

The anomaly-based approach (also known as behavior-based approach) is an alternative approach that overcomes the drawbacks of signature-based IDS. In this approach, a statistical model of the normal activities of an ICS is learned, and then the model is compared with the current input to detect abnormal activities in the system, caused by even unknown attacks such as zero-day and already-forgotten attacks. In order to detect anomalies, the IDS must learn to recognize normal system activities in advance, typically in the training phase of the system. There are several learning methods, and typically artificial intelligence-based techniques are employed. As ICSs become larger and more complex, it becomes increasingly difficult to ensure ICS security based on techniques that require human intervention and maintenance. Anomaly-based IDSs can be valuable in such scenarios.

Our goal is to develop a widely applicable anomaly-based IDS that only requires network traffic data of the target ICS. In this paper, we present an anomaly-based IDS with high detection rate and low false alert rate, using the nearest-neighbor search (NNS) to find normal patterns of the ICS network.

Our method learns normal behavior in the overall traffic pattern based on the number of network packets transmitted and received along pairs of devices over a certain time interval as shown in Fig. 1. The method uses a geometric noise model with lognormal distribution to model the randomness on ICS network traffic and learns solutions through cross-validation on random samples. The method then

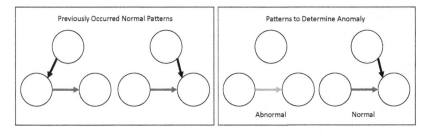

Fig. 2. An example of benefit of analyzing traffic patterns across the entire network. The red traffic that keeps the ACL is determined as abnormal. (Color figure online)

determines whether a traffic instance contains an attack or not by comparing the NNS distance of the traffic instance with the distribution. The expected benefit on this approach is that it can detect abnormalities in traffic that might appear normal from a local perspective. For example, an attack carried out by following the access control list (ACL) can appear normal when we observe only two associated nodes. However, the anomaly can be detected by analyzing the traffic patterns in the entire network, as illustrated in Fig. 2.

This approach can be widely applied to various ICS devices irrespective of the protocol used for communication or the encryption method, because it only requires the number of packets between two devices to be collected and does not require an in depth knowledge of individual devices or applications in an ICS network. In addition, practically any unknown attack introduced at the packet level can be detected, provided the attack affects traffic patterns in the network.

Our main contributions in this paper can be summarized as follows.

– We propose a new statistical model that distinguishes between normal and abnormal traffic patterns using the overall traffic flow in an ICS network.
– Based on our concrete statistical model, we provide an IDS method to detect a small amount of network traffic variation with the low false alert rates.
– We present a fast algorithm, along with its theoretical time complexity analysis, to enable our method to be used real-time in a large-scale ICS.
– We provide experimental results tested on various types of large-scale (18.5 TB) traffic data collected from real control systems of critical infrastructures.

The rest of this paper is organized as follows. Section 2 describes prior research on ICS network security. Section 3 proposes an ICS network traffic pattern learning method and an abnormal traffic detection algorithm based on the method. Section 4 presents the performance improvement of the proposed algorithm. Section 5 analyzes the experimental results of applying the proposed algorithm to the network traffic data collected from the control systems of actual infrastructures in 11 sites, and Sect. 6 concludes this paper.

2   Related Work

Numerous studies on anomaly detection techniques have been conducted. One category of techniques focuses on changes in the physical states of control systems. There have been some recent works on data set generation for ICS research [11,16,19]. Many studies have been carried out to perform anomaly detection based on the characteristics of the ICS network and control devices [10,13,20,21]. They compare the estimate with the actual current physical state to determine anomalies. However, in order for each research to be effective, it is necessary to construct a matrix containing the real-world dynamics of the physical system. In a large-scale ICS, it can be challenging to gather a byte-wise understanding of the data from the applications in the ICS, in conjunction with an understanding of the laws of physics and to implement the corresponding physical laws [7,13].

Our research focuses on the development of a practically scalable IDS by using the self-similar nature of ICS network traffic. For common IT network traffic, it has long been known that network traffic has a self-similar nature [15]. Subsequent studies have found more evidence of self-similarity with statistical characteristics, such as long-range dependency [12], the Noah effect [22], and wavelet analysis [14,18,23]. Compared to common IT networks, ICS networks operate specific tasks with fewer human interventions. Therefore, network traffic of some devices on ICS networks can be expected to possess stronger self-similar characteristics such as periodicity and auto-correlation [4,10,17] than traffic from common IT networks, but not all devices have such clear characteristics according to our experience in critical infrastructures.

Several prior studies have applied methods from IT network traffic analysis on ICS networks. However, such studies focused on analyzing ICS network traffic [2], and it is difficult to find anomalies in the ICS network based only on network traffic [3].

3   Chi-Square Distribution of NNS Distances for Normal Network Traffic

To detect a small amount of network traffic variation by analyzing ICS network traffic, we focused on the solutions provided by the NNS algorithm on network traffic data. With an analytical choice of distance metric for NNS, we prove that the distribution of NNS distances for normal network traffic follows a variant of the chi-square distribution. The traffic instance whose NNS distance is significantly different from the variant of chi-square is considered abnormal.

3.1   Representation of Normal Network Traffic

An ICS network can be abstracted as a directed graph $G(N, E)$, where N is the set of nodes, and E is the set of directed edges in G. Let m be the number of edges in G. During a fixed unit time interval U, let $\mathbf{p}$ be an m-dimensional vector, where each element of $\mathbf{p}$ represents the number of packets+1 that pass through the corresponding edge in E. The slight distortion ($+1$ for every edge) is added for subsequent analysis. By repeating this on the ICS network for n time intervals, an ordered data set for normal traffic $\mathcal{P} = \{\mathbf{p}_1, ..., \mathbf{p}_n\}$ is obtained. At a time $t > n$, the problem we intend to address can be formally defined as follows: given $\mathcal{P}$, decide whether $\mathbf{p}_t$ contains an anomaly or not.

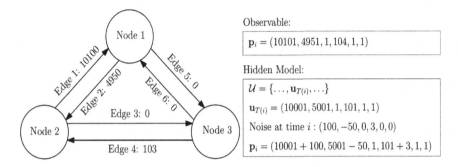

Fig. 3. An example of how our model views an actual traffic generated from the set of tasks and noise at time i.

Note that in an ICS network, specific tasks are repeated from time to time. Suppose that for a given edge in the ICS network, we can obtain the expected number of packets generated by the specific task or combinations of tasks transmitting on that edge during the time interval U. This results in a (hidden) set of m-dimensional task vectors $\mathcal{U} = \{\mathbf{u}_1, \mathbf{u}_2, ...\}$. While $\mathcal{U}$ cannot be obtained in practice, it plays an important role as a hidden model for subsequent statistical analysis. The overall network traffic $\mathbf{p}_i$ at time i comprises of $\mathbf{u}_{T(i)}$ values over all the edges, along with some noise, where $T(i)$ represents the task, or combination of tasks, in $\mathcal{U}$ that generates traffic across an edge at time i. Figure 3 illustrates this with an example on a simple ICS network.

To model the noises in the network traffic, we use a geometric noise model. Although arithmetic noise, which follows normal distribution, is more widely used, many aspects of network traffic are geometric [8]. In our case, for example, traffic changes of ± 100 are common when measuring an edge that normally transmits $10,000$ packets, but is uncommon on an edge that normally transmits 300 packets. Therefore, geometric changes help to suitably normalize the amount of noise for each edge. In the finance field, where many financial asset values tend to change geometrically with randomness, it is widely known that random geometric changes can be effectively modeled using a lognormal distribution. One famous example is BSM [6][1]. Similarly, we use a geometric model with lognormal distribution to model the randomness on ICS network traffic. Formally, for each network traffic instance $\mathbf{p}_i = \{p_{(i,1)}, ..., p_{(i,m)}\}$ and its corresponding hidden task

---

[1] The Black-Scholes option pricing model that received 1997 Nobel Memorial Prize in Economic Sciences.

$\mathbf{u}_{T(i)} = \{u_{(T(i),1)}, ..., u_{(T(i),m)}\}$, the traffic in $\mathbf{p}_i$ is generated by

$$p_{(i,j)} = u_{(T(i),j)} X_{(i,j)},\tag{1}$$

where $X_{(i,j)} \sim \ln N(0, \sigma^2)$ is an independent and identically distributed (IID) random variable following a lognormal noise at a time i on an edge j, with σ depending on the noise level of the ICS network.

3.2   Traffic Behavior Modeling Using NNS

At a time $t > n$, we decide whether $\mathbf{p}_t$ contains an anomaly or not, using the data $\mathcal{P} = \{\mathbf{p}_1, ..., \mathbf{p}_n\}$. If $\mathbf{p}_t$ was generated from normal traffic, it would be the case that a similar pattern of traffic had previously been generated by the same task.

For a traffic instance $\mathbf{p}_t$ measured at time $t > n$, we attempt to find a traffic instance in $\mathcal{P}$ that is likely to be generated by the same task as that for $\mathbf{p}_t$. One approach is to pick the traffic instance $\mathbf{p} \in \mathcal{P}$ with maximum similarity to $\mathbf{p}_t$, as the estimate for the instance that is generated by the same task. Formally, we find a $\mathbf{p}$ that satisfies,

$$\arg \min_{\forall \mathbf{p}_i \in \mathcal{P}} D(\mathbf{p}_i, \mathbf{p}_t)\tag{2}$$

where D is an m-dimensional distance metric,

$$D(\mathbf{p}_i, \mathbf{p}_t) = \sum_{j=1}^{m} (\ln(p_{(i,j)}) - \ln(p_{(t,j)}))^2\tag{3}$$

We use the squared difference of two log values as the distance metric, for two reasons. First, we deal with geometric changes of traffic and the log difference of two changes are the same if and only if their geometric changes are the same. For example, $\ln(c_1) - \ln(c_2) = \ln(c_3) - \ln(c_4)$ for some positive constants c_1, c_2, c_3, c_4 holds if and only if $\frac{c_1}{c_2} = \frac{c_3}{c_4}$. Second, D naturally works as a penalty for an extreme geometric difference, thereby preventing the traffic difference of any particular edge from dominating the results.

Note that the minimization (2) is precisely a definition of the NNS problem with distance metric (3). Let $N : \mathbb{R}^m \mapsto \mathbb{Z}$ be a traffic to time mapping function that maps $\mathbf{p}_t$ to its NNS solution $\mathbf{p}_{N(\mathbf{p}_t)} \in \mathcal{P}$. Then we estimate that $\mathbf{p}_{N(\mathbf{p}_t)}$ was generated by the same task as that for $\mathbf{p}_t$, which can be formally written as follows.

Assumption 1. $\mathbf{u}_{T(t)} = \mathbf{u}_{T(N(\mathbf{p}_t))}$

Under Assumption 1, we can offset the impact of ICS tasks on the normal network traffic by using NNS, and only the part representing the distribution of noise can be obtained as a random variable.

Lemma 1. *For a traffic instance $\mathbf{p}_t$ generated by the normal behavior of an ICS, the well normalized NNS distance $\frac{1}{2\sigma^2} D(\mathbf{p}_{N(\mathbf{p}_t)}, \mathbf{p}_t) = Z_t$ is a random variable $Z_t \sim \chi^2(m)$*

Proof. Let $s = N(\mathbf{p}_t)$. With our traffic model (1) and the Assumption 1, the distance between $\mathbf{p}_s$, the solution of the NNS, and the query $\mathbf{p}_t$, can be rewritten as follows.

$$D(\mathbf{p}_s, \mathbf{p}_t) = \sum_{j=1}^{m} (\ln(u_{(T(s),j)} X_{(s,j)}) - \ln(u_{(T(t),j)} X_{(t,j)}))^2 \tag{4}$$

$$= \sum_{j=1}^{m} (\ln X_{(s,j)} - \ln X_{(t,j)})^2. \tag{5}$$

$$= \sum_{j=1}^{m} (Y_j)^2 \tag{6}$$

where $Y_j = \ln X_{(s,j)} - \ln X_{(t,j)}$. Note that each $X_{(i,j)}$ was defined to follow $\ln \mathcal{N}(0, \sigma^2)$. By the definition of lognormal, $\ln X_{(i,j)} \sim \mathcal{N}(0, \sigma^2)$. Then, $Y_j \sim \mathcal{N}(0, 2\sigma^2)$ and $\frac{1}{\sqrt{2}\sigma} Y_j \sim \mathcal{N}(0, 1)$. Therefore, we can derive the following equations from Eq. (6).

$$\frac{1}{2\sigma^2} D(\mathbf{p}_{N(\mathbf{p}_t)}, \mathbf{p}_t) = \sum_{j=1}^{m} (\frac{1}{\sqrt{2}\sigma} Y_j)^2 \tag{7}$$

Note that the squared sum of m IID random variables that follow $\mathcal{N}(0, 1)$ follows $\chi^2(m)$.

$$Z_t \sim \chi^2(m) \tag{8}$$

Since each $\frac{1}{\sqrt{2}\sigma} Y_j$ follows $\mathcal{N}(0, \frac{2\sigma^2}{2\sigma^2})$, which is the standard normal distribution, the summation term in the right side of Eq. (7) follows $\chi^2(m)$, Chi-square distribution of degree m. Therefore, we get the following.

$$D(\mathbf{p}_{N(\mathbf{p}_t)}, \mathbf{p}_t) \overset{d}{=} 2\sigma^2 \chi^2(m) \tag{9}$$

$\square$

Lemma 1 is our core result, which has two important advantages when applied to anomaly-based IDS. First, it shows that the distances of NNS solutions for normal traffic follow a distribution associated with the well-known chi-square distribution. Thus, it is possible to set a statistically interpretable threshold that the NNS solutions of normal traffic should be present in, by observing normal traffic only. Second, in the process of deriving Lemma 1, for a normal traffic $\mathbf{p}_t$ generated by normal task in $\mathcal{U}$, the majority of the traffic generated by normal tasks is canceled out by $\mathbf{u}_{T(t)}$ and $\mathbf{u}_{N(\mathbf{p}_t)}$. In contrast, for a traffic $\mathbf{r}_t = \mathbf{p}_t + \mathbf{a}_t$ where $\mathbf{a}_t$ represents a traffic vector that is not generated from normal task in $\mathcal{U}$, the amount of traffic caused by $\mathbf{a}_t$ may not be canceled, since there is no matched task in $\mathcal{U}$. In other words, the effect of an abnormal task will be amplified in NNS distance. Moreover, we can expect that the amplification will mainly act towards increasing the NNS distance, since we define $D(,)$ as a sum of squares. Any difference between the actual traffic and its NNS solution on each edge is accumulated by the square. Therefore, we have the following observation.

Observation 1. $\mathbb{E}[D(\mathbf{p}_{N(\mathbf{r}_t)}, \mathbf{r}_t)]$ *will be larger than* $\mathbb{E}[D(\mathbf{p}_{N(\mathbf{p}_t)}, \mathbf{p}_t)]$ *during most times t.*

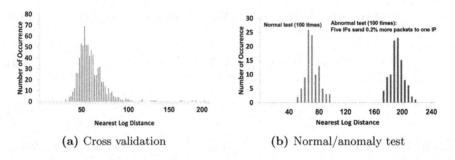

(a) Cross validation   (b) Normal/anomaly test

Fig. 4. Nearest log distance of network traffic of a site that we collected

To help understand the difference, we include brief results of the experiment in Fig. 4. Figure 4a is the cross validation of the NNS distance distribution for the number of packets transmitted per edge in one minute at site 1 of our dataset. Figure 4b shows the NNS distance distribution of the normal test and the abnormal test. The normal test shows the NNS distance of normal traffic not used for learning, and the abnormal test computes the NNS distance when five IPs send 0.2% more packets than usual to one IP. Similar results were obtained in the remaining sites of our dataset.

3.3   Learning Distribution of NNS Solution

In the previous section, we arrived at Lemma 1, which is well defined in theory. As illustrated in Fig. 4 (and we also present extensive empirical results later in Sect. 5), our theory also fits well with the empirical results. Nevertheless, real-world network traffic typically tends to contain some dirty phenomena, which makes them differ from that expressed by theory. For example, Assumption 1 may not perfectly hold for some traffic instances, which makes it hard to estimate σ for the noise $X_{(i,j)} \sim \ln\mathcal{N}(0, \sigma^2)$ used in Lemma 1. Additionally, $m = |E|$ is too large to be used for the degree of the chi-square that we derived, since the majority of edges in an ICS network never (or almost never) transmit any packets at all. Therefore, in order to use Lemma 1 for real IDS, a robust method to estimate σ and k for $2\sigma^2\chi^2(k)$ is required. We solve this problem by using n_{cv}-fold cross validation [5].

n_{cv}-fold cross validation runs our algorithm by dividing the dataset into n_{cv} equally sized pieces. Formally, let $\mathcal{P}_c \subset \mathcal{P}$ be the cth piece among n_{cv} equally divided pieces of $\mathcal{P}$. We randomly sample the n_{sp} number of traffic instances $\mathbf{p}_c \in \mathcal{P}_c$ from each $\mathcal{P}_c$, and run the NNS algorithm with each $\mathbf{p}_c$ on the dataset $\mathcal{P} \setminus \mathcal{P}_c$. After cross validation, we can achieve a set $\mathcal{D}$ ($|\mathcal{D}| = n_{cv}n_{sp}$) of NNS distances. Let $\hat{\mu}$ and $\hat{s}^2$ be the sample mean and the (unbiased) variance achieved by observing $\mathcal{D}$, respectively. By Lemma 1, we already know that each element in $\mathcal{D}$ is sampled from the distribution $2\sigma^2\chi^2(k)$ for some σ and k. Also, by the definition of $\chi^2(k)$, its mean and variance are k and $2k$, respectively. Therefore, with the large number of samples $n_{cv}n_{sp}$, we have the following equations.

$$\hat{\mu} \approx 2\sigma^2 k \tag{10}$$

$$\hat{s}^2 \approx (2\sigma^2)^2 2k \tag{11}$$

We have two unknown variables k and σ in two Eqs. (10) and (11). k and σ for $2\sigma^2\chi^2(k)$ can be easily calculated as follows.

$$k \approx \frac{2\hat{\mu}^2}{\hat{s}^2} \tag{12}$$

$$\sigma^2 \approx \frac{\hat{s}^2}{4\hat{\mu}} \tag{13}$$

By using this method, all the $n_{cv}n_{sp}$ number of NNS distances in $\mathcal{D}$ contribute to the estimation of $2\sigma^2\chi^2(k)$. Therefore, even if $\mathcal{D}$ contains several strange results, we can robustly estimate k and σ from Eqs. (12) and (13), respectively.

3.4   Detecting Anomaly of Traffic

After learning σ and k by using cross-validation, the implementation of the detection method is straightforward. Let $CCDF(k, \alpha)$ be the complementary cumulative distribution function that evaluates the probability $\mathbb{E}[A|A > \alpha]$ for a random variable $A \sim \chi(k)$. For a normal traffic instance $\mathbf{p}_t$, let $CCDF(k, \frac{1}{2\sigma^2}\mathrm{D}(\mathbf{p}_{N(\mathbf{p}_t)}, \mathbf{p}_t)) = \phi_t$. By Lemma 1, ϕ_t will be larger than $\Phi \in [0, 1]$ with probability Φ. In contrast, the NNS distance of a traffic instance containing attacks would have a smaller ϕ_t by Observation 1. Therefore, our detection algorithm sets a small Φ (i.e. 0.01) and it determines that a traffic contains an attack when $\phi_t < \Phi$.

4   An Efficient Algorithm for Anomaly Detection

The algorithm described in the section above can be used as an anomaly-based IDS with reasonable performance. Nevertheless, its performance might not be sufficient for detecting certain small amount of network traffic variation. In particular, the following three methods are common ways for hiding attacks, which also reduce their impact on network traffic. First, the attacker can minimize the short-term impact by spreading the attack over a long period. Second, the attacker can minimize the impact on the ICS network by minimizing the number of target devices to attack. Third, the attacker can mimic the normal behavior of the ICS. The full version of our IDS includes additional methods to improve the detection performance against such stealthy attacks.

We provide two extended methods to improve the detection performance: *windowed NNS* and *partitioned NNS*. A summary of the two extended methods

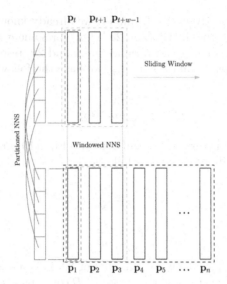

Fig. 5. Brief concepts about windowed NNS (red) and partitioned NNS (blue). (Color figure online)

is illustrated in Fig. 5. In the following subsections, we formally define windowed NNS and partitioned NNS. We also analyze how we can achieve improved detection performance with those methods, and use the findings of these analyses. Finally, we provide a fast algorithm that applies these techniques for a large-scale ICS in real-time.

4.1   Windowed NNS

We will first consider a continuous attack that lasts from time t to $t + w - 1$. In order to gather some intuition for the improvement of the detection performance of our simple version IDS, let us go back to the theoretical basis and analyze Lemma 1. Consider the normal traffic instances Z_t and Z_{t+1}. Since they come from different IID random variables (see Eq. (5)), Z_t and Z_{t+1} are also IID random variables. Let us define $Z_t^{(w)}$ as a summation of the w number of Z's as follow.

$$Z_t^{(w)} = \sum_{i=t}^{t+w-1} Z_i \tag{14}$$

Note that $Z_t^{(w)} \sim \chi^2(wm)$, since each $Z_i \sim \chi^2(m)$ is IID. Obviously, $\mathbb{E}[Z_t^{(w)}] = \sum_{i=t}^{t+w-1} \mathbb{E}[Z_t]$ by the linearity of the expectation. Let us define an inverse function $CCDF^{-1}(m, \Phi)$ that returns α, where $CCDF(m, \alpha) = \Phi$. For two constants $\alpha_1 = CCDF^{-1}(m, \Phi)$ and $\alpha_w = CCDF^{-1}(wm, \Phi)$, the linearity does not hold in general. Especially, for a small Φ, it tends to $\alpha_w < w\alpha_1$. Although the $CCDF^{-1}$

function can be expressed by a regularized gamma function, it is somewhat complex to analyze. Instead, we tested all the $CCDF^{-1}(m, 0.01)$ for m with practical ranges. Figure 6 illustrates the result of the IID chi-square random variables, for several different Φ. We empirically found that $CCDF^{-1}(m, 0.01)$ decreases *monotonically* as m increases. Therefore, we have the following Lemma.

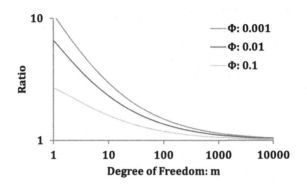

Fig. 6. The ratio $CCDF^{-1}(m, \Phi)/\mathbb{E}[\chi^2(m)]$ with respect to m (log scale)

Lemma 2. *For* Φ $=$ 0.01, *at least up to* wm $\leq$ $10,000$, $CCDF^{-1}(wm, \Phi)/\mathbb{E}[Z_t^{(w)}] < CCDF^{-1}(m, \Phi)/\mathbb{E}[Z_t]$.

Since we aim to detect unknown attacks, it is difficult to quantify the impact of the attacks. Nevertheless, we can expect that effect of the attacks on traffic will lead to an increase in the NNS distance in most cases from Observation 1. Let

$$\psi_t = D(\mathbf{p}_{N(\mathbf{r}_t)}, \mathbf{r}_t) - D(\mathbf{p}_{N(\mathbf{p}_t)}, \mathbf{p}_t) \tag{15}$$

be the increased NNS distance. For an attack that continues for a duration of w, the total increased distance is defined as follow.

$$\psi_t^{(w)} = \sum_{i=t}^{t+w-1} \psi_t. \tag{16}$$

There are two possible cases to analyze based on $\psi_t^{(w)}$.

- Case 1: Each ψ_{t+i} is similar for $i \in [t, t+w-1]$
- Case 2: One ψ_{t+i} or some ψ_{t+i}'s are very different from the others.

In Case 1, the following inequality holds for all $i \in [t, t+w-1]$ by Lemma 2.

$$CCDF(wm, \mathbb{E}[Z_t^{(w)}] + \psi_{t+i^{(w)}}) < CCDF(m, \mathbb{E}[Z_{t+i}] + \psi_{t+i}) \tag{17}$$

Therefore, the window version $CCDF(wm, Z_{t+i}^{(w)} + \psi_{t+i}^{(w)})$ has a higher probability of detecting the attack (to be smaller than Φ). In Case 2, some ψ_{t+i} is much larger than others, thereby neither window version $CCDF(m, Z_{t+i} + \psi_{t+i})$ has a higher probability of detecting the attack.

4.2 Partitioned NNS

Partition search is a method for effectively detecting an attack or anomaly where only a small fraction of the nodes have a change in the amount of packet transmission. In this method, the d-dimensional is recursively cut out randomly in half, and the log distance is obtained by looking at each partition as an independent histogram. In this case, if there is a change in the packet transmission amount within the partition, the abnormal state can be determined more effectively than the abnormal d-dimensional histogram.

Using the relationship between edges when dividing a partition in the entire histogram allows for the possibility of an attack that avoids our detection methods. To prevent this possibility, we chose to partition the edges randomly.

4.3 Anomaly Detection on All Sub-Sequences

The detection rates of both windowed and partitioned NNS can be affected by their parameters: the number of windows and the number of partitions. Instead of using a single parameter, we set the maximum number of windows and the maximum number of partitions and perform anomaly detection on all the numbers of windows and partitions smaller than this maximum value to determine the abnormal state.

A naive process of performing all calculations simply can consume a significant amount of time. However, since there is a subset relationship between multiple size windows and recursively truncated partitions, dynamic programming techniques can be used to create algorithms that work efficiently in a practical time span.

4.4 Efficient Distance Calculation

The process of finding the smallest distance value by computing (3) for every $X \in S$ can be solved by the NNS in the dw dimension. However, when a number of nodes communicate with each other on the network, if the number of nodes is N, the dimension d increases to $O(N^2)$ and the execution time increases significantly. To address this problem, we used a method to speed up the NNS in a sparse vector.

In a typical network, communication between all pairs of nodes does not always occur, and communication tends to occur only between predetermined pairs of nodes. This is even more so in a control network designed to perform a specific task. Table 1 also illustrates this fact, as there are only 614 IP $\rightarrow$ IPs (edges) between the 208 nodes based on packets transmitted in site 1, which is much smaller than the theoretical maximum of $43,056 = 208 \times (208-1)$.

Therefore, instead of storing the data in d-dimensions, we can save the time required for the nearest search by storing only the non-zero transmission edges in a sparse format as below.

[(edgeId):(logFrequency), ..., (edgeId):(logFrequency)]

In this case, the time complexity for distance calculation is $O(m_1 + m_2)$, where m_1 is the number of non-zero edges in data, m_2 is the number of non-zero edges in a query, and $m_1 + m_2 \ll N^2$.

5   Experiments

This section describes the results of applying the extended algorithm to our dataset. The results in all experiments are calculated based on the number of packets sent per an edge. Similar results are obtained when the total number of bytes is used instead of the number of packets and therefore omitted here.

Table 1. Collected traffic

Site	Volume (GB)	Period (days)	Number of IPs	Number of edges (IP → IPs)	Average number of edges per 1 min
1	366	11.7	208	614	346
2	43	7.3	40	80	37
3	188	9.8	56	117	75
4	440	8.3	47	183	59
5	66	12.0	57	210	96
6	71	5.0	91	297	117
7	1,341	29.0	375	1,341	498
8	378	7.0	174	393	133
9	300	8.7	106	249	136
10	381	3.0	126	532	270
11	15,346	21.0	780	3,743	1,893

5.1   Dataset

We collected traffic from 11 active control systems of critical infrastructure in separated networks. This section introduces the characteristics of the network traffic we collected.

The capacity and collection period of the collected traffic are shown in Table 1. The numbers of IPs and edges represent the total number of IP addresses and IP → IPs used in the collected traffic. The number of edges is not very large, considering the number of IPs.

Sites 1 through 9 are control systems of the same domain. The primary function of sites 1, 7, 8, and 9 is to periodically collect and analyze information, often requiring operator action to manage equipment and analyze data. Site 2 is a backup site for site 1, site 6 is a testbed replicating site 1, and most of the network traffic on these sites is generated by automated communication between the devices. In sites 3, 4 and 5, managers perform control operations based on the situation in the field. Sites 10 and 11 are control systems of other domains, and little human intervention is required in these sites. Most of the sites are operated based on a predetermined schedule. In sites 7, 10, and 11, network traffic was collected for all IPs in the control network, and network traffic was collected only for the main IPs in the remaining sites.[2]

In all sites, about half of all edges have the maximum number of packet transmissions of less than 10 per second, and only about 20% of edges have a maximum of 100 packet transmissions per second or more. It can be seen that the total amount of network traffic is relatively small, and a small number of edges take up most traffic. Some control devices also show various network traffic transmission patterns, but the patterns depend on the monitoring unit time. Most devices and edges do not show specific patterns.

Table 2. Precision using the extended algorithm

Site	Number of edges	Number of partitions	Precision (%)
1	614	32	99.0
2	80	8	98.6
3	117	8	99.0
4	183	16	95.2
5	210	16	99.0
6	297	16	97.4
7	1,341	128	99.8
8	393	32	99.6
9	249	16	100.0
10	532	32	98.6
11	3,743	256	99.4

5.2 Precision: Detecting Normal Traffic

The parameters for algorithm implementation were determined based on our experience. The unit time is 60 s and the number of windows is 5.

When dividing a partition, we divide the edges by half recursively, so that at least 10 edges are included in one partition. Since the total number of edges need to be considered while dividing a partition, it is not appropriate to specify the maximum number of partitions for each site equally.

Precision test results are shown as Table 2. High precision can be found at all sites, regardless of whether the site is controlled by a person or not, and whether

---

[2] For security reasons, we cannot provide more detailed information about our dataset.

the learning period is short or long. We used 80% of the collected normal network traffic as training data and then extracted 500 samples out of the remaining 20% to determine whether these samples are classified as normal. As mentioned in Sect. 3.4, if the input network traffic is included in 99% of the learning result, it is judged as normal.

5.3   Recall: Detecting Anomaly of Traffic

We tested whether the proposed algorithm detected abnormal traffic generated by modifying normal traffic not used for learning. We used the same parameters and learning data used in the precision experiments. Each experiment was performed 500 times.

Cyber attack patterns are dependent on the attacker's knowledge. It is possible to carry out an attack based on scans of the surroundings and by using a small amount of traffic causing abnormal behaviors of target devices. However, existing systems have fixed traffic transmission patterns that are intertwined with multiple systems. If an attacker modifies the operations even by a small degree, the traffic patterns will change and the impact will be evident overall. In general, cyber attacks cause additional traffic or changes in content, which do not normally occur in the ICS. Certain communications may be temporarily interrupted by cyber attacks. Sometimes cyber attacks can also change speed of traffic transmission.

We present abnormal network traffic changes as three parameters in consideration of our anomaly detection algorithm.

- **Victim windows** indicate the time when the network traffic volume changes and display the windows where the network traffic changes among the windows used in anomaly detection.
- **Victim edges** represent communication paths that change the actual network traffic throughput per victim window and are selected among IP → IPsshown in the learning process.
- **Added packets** indicates the number of added packets for each victim edge. In the proposed algorithm, the increments and decrements in the amount of network traffic produce the same effect in the calculation of the distance between network traffic instances. Therefore, in order to simplify the experiment, only the case where the number of packets increases is considered[3].

Table 3 shows the detection rate of our algorithm for anomalous network traffic activity for five minutes. It can be seen that the detection rate increases more rapidly when the number of victim edges becomes larger than the increases in the added packets. Since the log scale is used to represent the number of packets in the histogram at the current unit time, it is advantageous to select a victim edge with few or no packets when the distance based on the change in

---

[3] In our additional experiments, which are omitted in this paper, the proposed method also showed similar detection power when the total number of bytes is increased or decreased.

Table 3. Recall according to the numbers of victim edges and added packets

Site	Number of victim edges	Victim windows: 1,2,3,4,5			
		Number of added packets			
		1	5	10	20
1	1	68.4	68.4	68.4	68.4
	2	91.0	91.0	91.0	91.0
	5	100.0	100.0	100.0	100.0
	10	100.0	100.0	100.0	100.0
2	1	25.4	26.0	26.4	26.8
	2	32.8	35.0	35.0	36.0
	5	59.4	71.2	74.8	76.8
	10	67.4	90.4	94.6	96.4
3	1	10.2	10.4	11.0	14.2
	2	8.0	8.6	12.2	20.6
	5	7.6	18.0	30.6	40.8
	10	15.6	39.2	43.4	48.6
4	1	97.2	97.2	97.2	97.2
	2	99.6	99.6	99.6	99.6
	5	100.0	100.0	100.0	100.0
	10	100.0	100.0	100.0	100.0
5	1	1.2	1.2	1.2	1.2
	2	0.8	0.8	0.8	0.8
	5	2.2	2.2	2.2	2.4
	10	2.4	2.6	2.8	3.4
6	1	82.8	82.8	82.8	82.8
	2	99.6	99.6	99.6	99.6
	5	100.0	100.0	100.0	100.0
	10	100.0	100.0	100.0	100.0
7	1	58.0	58.0	58.0	58.0
	2	63.8	63.8	63.8	63.8
	5	64.0	64.0	64.0	64.2
	10	63.6	63.6	64.0	64.0
8	1	65.8	65.8	66.0	66.2
	2	93.2	93.2	93.4	93.4
	5	99.8	99.8	99.8	99.8
	10	100.0	100.0	100.0	100.0
9	1	36.4	36.4	36.4	36.8
	2	70.4	71.0	71.0	71.0
	5	93.2	93.6	93.4	93.6
	10	94.8	96.4	96.6	96.8
10	1	42.6	42.6	42.6	42.6
	2	80.2	80.2	80.6	80.8
	5	97.0	97.0	97.2	97.2
	10	97.0	97.2	97.6	97.8
11	1	82.0	82.0	82.0	82.0
	2	94.6	94.6	94.6	94.6
	5	96.8	96.8	96.8	97.0
	10	96.8	96.8	96.8	96.8

Table 4. Recall according to the number of victim windows

Site	Number of victim edges	Number of added packets: 5				
		Victim windows				
		1	1,2	1,2,3	1,2,3,4	1,2,3,4,5
1	1	1.0	13.6	43.4	58.0	68.4
	2	1.0	30.0	70.6	87.8	91.0
	5	1.2	57.8	95.6	99.6	100.0
	10	1.2	64.4	99.8	100.0	100.0
2	1	1.6	3.4	15.2	23.2	26.0
	2	2.0	3.0	14.8	19.8	35.0
	5	2.2	4.6	3.2	4.8	71.2
	10	2.2	4.6	1.8	2.6	90.4
3	1	1.0	3.2	5.0	6.8	10.4
	2	1.2	5.0	5.6	9.0	8.6
	5	1.2	7.0	4.6	12.2	18.0
	10	1.4	7.8	7.0	26.8	39.2
4	1	32.8	68.6	85.0	94.2	97.2
	2	40.2	86.4	97.4	99.8	99.6
	5	45.0	95.6	100.0	100.0	100.0
	10	45.4	95.8	100.0	100.0	100.0
5	1	1.4	0.8	0.8	1.0	1.2
	2	1.4	0.6	0.4	0.6	0.8
	5	1.6	0.4	0.4	1.0	2.2
	10	1.6	0.6	0.6	1.2	2.6
6	1	3.6	7.2	43.0	72.2	82.8
	2	3.8	9.8	76.4	95.2	99.6
	5	3.8	11.4	92.8	100.0	100.0
	10	4.0	11.6	95.4	100.0	100.0
7	1	0.2	12.2	39.4	51.2	58.0
	2	0.4	22.6	58.0	66.0	63.8
	5	0.4	28.6	62.8	63.6	64.0
	10	0.4	28.8	63.6	63.6	63.6
8	1	0.6	1.0	18.6	51.8	65.8
	2	0.6	1.6	33.2	83.2	93.2
	5	0.6	2.2	49.4	97.6	99.8
	10	0.6	2.2	52.4	98.6	100
9	1	0.0	0.4	10.8	30.6	36.4
	2	0.0	0.6	23.2	59.4	71.0
	5	0.0	1.2	46.4	81.8	93.6
	10	0.0	1.2	52.6	85.0	96.4
10	1	1.6	1.8	5.6	24.2	42.6
	2	1.6	3.6	14.0	58.6	80.2
	5	1.6	3.6	28.6	91.0	97.0
	10	1.6	4.0	34.6	97.2	97.2
11	1	1.4	13.2	40.8	73.2	82.0
	2	1.2	18.8	55.6	91.2	94.6
	5	1.2	21.8	63.2	94.8	96.8
	10	1.2	22.2	63.6	95.2	96.8

Table 5. Recall according to positions of victim windows

Site	Number of victim edges	Number of added packets: 5					
		Number of victim windows					
		2			3		
		Victim windows					
		1,2	2,4	1,5	1,2,3	1,3,5	2,3,4
1	1	13.6	18.4	13.6	43.4	41.6	49.6
	2	30.0	43.8	30.4	70.6	68.4	80.4
	5	57.8	87.0	62.4	95.6	94.4	98.2
	10	64.4	98.8	67.8	99.8	99.4	100.0
2	1	3.4	27.4	3.6	15.2	26.4	30.0
	2	3.0	55.6	3.8	14.8	52.4	27.4
	5	4.6	95.2	5.0	3.2	95.6	6.6
	10	4.6	99.8	5.4	1.8	100.0	2.0
3	1	3.2	8.0	1.0	5.0	3.6	7.4
	2	5.0	12.6	1.0	5.6	6.6	10.6
	5	7.0	19.8	1.4	4.6	9.8	10.6
	10	7.8	29.6	1.6	7.0	18.4	18.6
4	1	68.6	70.0	48.8	85.0	81.4	86.6
	2	86.4	89.6	60.6	97.4	95.8	99.0
	5	95.6	99.8	65.0	100.0	99.8	100.0
	10	95.8	100.0	65.8	100.0	100.0	100.0
5	1	0.8	1.6	1.4	0.8	2.4	1.0
	2	0.6	1.0	2.0	0.4	1.8	0.4
	5	0.4	1.2	2.0	0.4	2.4	0.4
	10	0.6	1.4	2.2	0.6	2.6	0.8
6	1	7.2	31.6	6.0	43.0	38.6	57.8
	2	9.8	50.6	8.6	76.4	72.8	85.6
	5	11.4	60.8	9.6	92.8	96.6	99.2
	10	11.6	62.6	10.0	95.4	97.2	99.8
7	1	12.2	34.0	10.0	39.4	37.6	51.2
	2	22.6	62.0	21.2	58.0	65.0	71.0
	5	28.6	83.2	27.0	62.8	82.2	71.8
	10	28.8	84.0	26.8	63.6	83.8	72.0
8	1	1.0	23.6	1.8	18.6	21.6	41.2
	2	1.6	49.0	2.0	33.2	42.0	69.0
	5	2.2	61.6	2.8	49.4	66.0	95.0
	10	2.2	63.0	2.8	52.4	69.8	96.2
9	1	0.4	21.6	0.4	10.8	10.4	27.0
	2	0.6	49.2	0.2	23.2	33.4	57.2
	5	1.2	90.4	1.6	46.4	87.2	77.4
	10	1.2	99.4	1.6	52.6	98.8	80.6
10	1	1.8	13.6	2.2	5.6	11.4	21.2
	2	3.6	27.0	3.2	14.0	32.4	48.8
	5	3.6	39.8	3.8	28.6	74.8	90.4
	10	4.0	42.8	3.8	34.6	83.2	98.0
11	1	13.2	49.2	11.8	40.8	45.4	67.6
	2	18.8	78.6	18.2	55.6	76.6	88.4
	5	21.8	91.6	21.6	63.2	90.6	95.0
	10	22.2	92.6	21.6	63.6	92.0	94.8

the number of packets is considerably different. As the number of victim edges increases, the probability of adding packets to the corresponding edge increases, which increases the detection rate significantly.

Table 4 shows the results of the experiments according to the number of victim windows. In general, the higher number of victim windows confirms the higher detection rate in Table 4. When packets are added to only one window, most sites have low detection rates. It is difficult to distinguish small amounts of traffic change with only one window due to noise. However, since the noise generated in each window is different, it is possible to find out the probability of artificially added network traffic by comparing multiple windows.

Table 5 shows that the detection rate varies with the occurrence of victim windows even if the number of victim windows is the same. The timing at which packets are added artificially determines the difference between existing traffic transmission patterns.

The actual reasons for the detection rates observed in each individual site vary.

Site 1 collects network traffic only from control devices, which perform only certain specific tasks, resulting in a high anomaly detection rate. A high detection rate is also obtained at sites 6, 8, 9, 10, and 11, where regular communication between control devices is mostly achieved. The CCDF density graph of site 11 in Fig. 7a shows that the CCDF values learned and the CCDF values in the anomaly test are well separated.

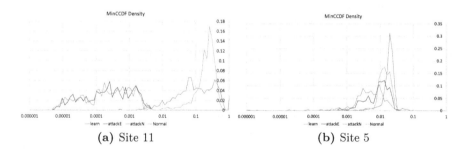

(a) Site 11   (b) Site 5

Fig. 7. CCDF density graph (blue: learning result, yellow: normal test, orange: abnormal test) (Color figure online)

Site 2 is a backup site, but the resident administrator continuously monitors the site information using the HMI. Because a network traffic throughput pattern is learned based on human operation on the small-scale site, small changes in the network traffic are difficult to detect in a short period of time. However, since human monitoring task does not require a long time to perform once, it can be seen that abnormal behavior is detected with a high probability when the traffic change time exceeds 4 min.

Sites 3 and 5 experienced a lot of administrator work during the period when the traffic data was collected. Site 5 in particular had DB server backup, failure response, and other administrator work being carried out. Because the learning traffic contains too many transmission patterns, the proposed algorithm could not detect small changes in the amount of network traffic in site 5. The CCDF density graph of site 5 in Fig. 7b shows that it is difficult to distinguish CCDF values from learning, normal test, and anomaly tests.

Site 4 only performed periodic field monitoring by control devices during the network traffic data collection, without any non-regular work. As can be seen in Table 1, site 4 has fewer IP → IPs used in one minute than in other sites. Therefore, when selecting the victim edge, the probability of choosing an edge without network traffic transmission is higher in site 4 than other sites. This has affected the high detection rate in site 4.

Site 7 has similar size and work characteristics to site 1. However, network traffic for all IPs was collected in site 7. The network traffic collected at site 7 includes non-regular and uneven patterned network traffic generated by security equipment, web server, HMI, etc. Therefore, site 7 has a lower detection rate than site 1.

Table 6. Querying time

Site	Period of learned traffic (days)	Volume of learned data (MB)	Query time (s)
1	9.36	66.4	0.902
2	5.84	4.8	0.042
3	7.84	12.0	0.118
4	6.64	7.8	0.084
5	9.60	18.4	0.292
6	4.00	9.6	0.062
7	23.20	237.6	7.030
8	5.60	15.2	0.152
9	6.96	19.2	0.228
10	2.40	13.6	0.072
11	16.80	448.0	8.736

5.4   Speed of Anomaly Detection

Our experiments were carried out on a server with Intel Xeon CPU E5-2670 2.30 GHz and 384 GB RAM, and the time to perform anomaly detection (referred to below as query) is shown in Table 6.

A more detailed analysis of the execution times for site 1 is as follows. In site 1, we collected 11.7 days of network traffic and used 80% (9.36 days) network traffic for learning data. As shown in Table 1, the capacity of converting the network traffic used for learning into the histogram every minute is 66.4 MB.

The approximate capacity of 1-minute histograms of network traffic over a year can be estimated to be 2.5 GB (365 days ÷ 9.36 days × 66.4 MB = 2.5 GB). Therefore, even if histograms for more than one year are used as learning data, it is assumed that all the data are stored in the RAM, so that the calculation time is proportional to the length of the learning data. According to Table 6, the querying time is 0.902 s when using 9.36 days network traffic as learning data. Therefore, when 1-year network traffic is used as learning data, the querying time is 35.2 s (365 days ÷ 9.36 days × 0.902 s = 35.2 s) and the query can be executed within 1 min. That is, even if 1-year network traffic is used as learning data, this algorithm can be used for real-time detection.

Sites 7 and 11 require 110.6 s and 189.8 s, respectively, for queries with one year of traffic. It is possible to shorten the detection time by performing the distance calculation of NNS in parallel by dividing the learning traffic into several parts.

6   Conclusion

In this paper, we set out to propose an anomaly-based IDS based on the NNS to learn normal traffic patterns over the entire network of an ICS. If an attack or an operation error in the equipment or communication within a system does not cause changes in the traffic patterns, it may be difficult to detect the attack or error solely through monitoring the network traffic. However, for a system that performs repetitive tasks, such as a control system, analyzing the entire network of the system can lead to the identification of unusual outliers.

We proposed a method to find anomalous signals in an ICS using the traffic transmission pattern of the control system network. We mathematically deduced whether the traffic transmission pattern can be used, and confirmed its effectiveness by applying it to the traffic collected from actual control system infrastructures.

Our experiments confirmed that small changes[4] in the amount of traffic can be detected in a small number of communication sections and that the speed of execution can be used for real-time network monitoring. We demonstrated the utility of our method to monitor the number of packets per IP→IP in this paper. Similar results are obtained when the total number of bytes is used instead of the number of packets following our experience, and our method can also be applied on a server-by-client basis.

References

1. Shodan search engine for internet-connected devices. http://www.shodan.io
2. Barbosa, R.R.R., Sadre, R., Pras, A.: A first look into SCADA network traffic. In: Network Operations and Management Symposium (NOMS), pp. 518–521. IEEE (2012)

---

[4] In the proposed algorithm, the increments and decrements in the amount of network traffic produce the same effect in detecting anomaly of traffic.

3. Barbosa, R.R.R., Sadre, R., Pras, A.: Difficulties in modeling SCADA traffic: a comparative analysis. In: Taft, N., Ricciato, F. (eds.) PAM 2012. LNCS, vol. 7192, pp. 126–135. Springer, Heidelberg (2012). https://doi.org/10.1007/978-3-642-28537-0_13

4. Berthier, R., et al.: On the practicality of detecting anomalies with encrypted traffic in AMI. In: International Conference on Smart Grid Communications (SmartGrid-Comm), pp. 890–895. IEEE (2014)

5. Bishop, C.M.: Pattern recognition. Mach. Learn. **128**, 1–58 (2006)

6. Black, F., Scholes, M.: The pricing of options and corporate liabilities. J. Polit. Econ. **81**(3), 637–654 (1973)

7. Caselli, M., Zambon, E., Kargl, F.: Sequence-aware intrusion detection in industrial control systems. In: Proceedings of the 1st Workshop on Cyber-Physical System Security, pp. 13–24. ACM (2015)

8. Downey, A.B.: Lognormal and Pareto distributions in the Internet. Comput. Commun. **28**(7), 790–801 (2005)

9. Feng, X., Li, Q., Wang, H., Sun, L.: Characterizing industrial control system devices on the internet. In: 24th International Conference on Network Protocols (ICNP), pp. 1–10. IEEE (2016)

10. Formby, D., Srinivasan, P., Leonard, A., Rogers, J., Beyah, R.: Who's in control of your control system? Device fingerprinting for cyber-physical systems. In: Network and Distributed System Security Symposium (NDSS) (2016)

11. Goh, J., Adepu, S., Junejo, K.N., Mathur, A.: A dataset to support research in the design of secure water treatment systems. In: Havarneanu, G., Setola, R., Nassopoulos, H., Wolthusen, S. (eds.) CRITIS 2016. LNCS, vol. 10242, pp. 88–99. Springer, Cham (2017). https://doi.org/10.1007/978-3-319-71368-7_8

12. Gong, W.B., Liu, Y., Misra, V., Towsley, D.: Self-similarity and long range dependence on the internet: a second look at the evidence, origins and implications. Comput. Netw. **48**(3), 377–399 (2005)

13. Krotofil, M., Larsen, J., Gollmann, D.: The process matters: ensuring data veracity in cyber-physical systems. In: Proceedings of the 10th Symposium on Information, Computer and Communications Security, pp. 133–144. ACM (2015)

14. Kwon, H., Kim, T., Yu, S.J., Kim, H.K.: Self-similarity based lightweight intrusion detection method for cloud computing. In: Nguyen, N.T., Kim, C.-G., Janiak, A. (eds.) ACIIDS 2011. LNCS (LNAI), vol. 6592, pp. 353–362. Springer, Heidelberg (2011). https://doi.org/10.1007/978-3-642-20042-7_36

15. Leland, W.E., Taqqu, M.S., Willinger, W., Wilson, D.V.: On the self-similar nature of ethernet traffic (extended version). IEEE/ACM Trans. Netw. **2**(1), 1–15 (1994)

16. Lemay, A., Fernandez, J.M.: Providing SCADA network data sets for intrusion detection research. In: Workshop on Cyber Security Experimentation and Test (CSET). USENIX Association (2016)

17. Lin, C.Y., Nadjm-Tehrani, S., Asplund, M.: Timing-based anomaly detection in SCADA networks. In: International Conference on Critical Infrastructures Security (CRITIS) (2017)

18. Rawat, S., Sastry, C.S.: Network intrusion detection using wavelet analysis. In: Das, G., Gulati, V.P. (eds.) CIT 2004. LNCS, vol. 3356, pp. 224–232. Springer, Heidelberg (2004). https://doi.org/10.1007/978-3-540-30561-3_24

19. Rodofile, N.R., Schmidt, T., Sherry, S.T., Djamaludin, C., Radke, K., Foo, E.: Process control cyber-attacks and labelled datasets on S7Comm critical infrastructure. In: Pieprzyk, J., Suriadi, S. (eds.) ACISP 2017. LNCS, vol. 10343, pp. 452–459. Springer, Cham (2017). https://doi.org/10.1007/978-3-319-59870-3_30

20. Urbina, D.I., et al.: Limiting the impact of stealthy attacks on industrial control systems. In: Proceedings of the 2016 ACM SIGSAC Conference on Computer and Communications Security, pp. 1092–1105. ACM (2016)
21. Welch, G., Bishop, G.: An introduction to the Kalman filter (1995)
22. Willinger, W., Taqqu, M.S., Sherman, R., Wilson, D.V.: Self-similarity through high-variability: statistical analysis of ethernet LAN traffic at the source level. IEEE/ACM Trans. Netw. (ToN) **5**(1), 71–86 (1997)
23. Yu, S.J., Koh, P., Kwon, H., Kim, D.S., Kim, H.K.: Hurst parameter based anomaly detection for intrusion detection system. In: International Conference on Computer and Information Technology (CIT), pp. 234–240. IEEE (2016)

Security Measurements

PostScript Undead: Pwning the Web with a 35 Years Old Language

Jens Müller[(⊠)], Vladislav Mladenov, Dennis Felsch, and Jörg Schwenk

Ruhr University Bochum, Bochum, Germany
{jens.a.mueller,vladislav.mladenov,dennis.felsch,joerg.schwenk}@rub.de

Abstract. PostScript is a Turing complete page description language dating back to 1982. It is supported by most laser printers and for a long time it had been the preferred file format for documents like academic papers. In this work, we show that popular services such as Wikipedia, Microsoft OneDrive, and Google Mail can be attacked using malicious PostScript code. Besides abusing legitimate features of the PostScript language, we systematically analyzed the security of the most popular PostScript interpreter – Ghostscript. Our attacks include information disclosure, file inclusion, and remote command execution. Furthermore, we present methods to obfuscate PostScript code and embed it within legitimate PDF files to bypass security filters. This allows us to create a hybrid exploit that can be used to attack web applications, clients systems, print servers, or printers. Our large-scale evaluation reveals that 56% of the analyzed web applications are vulnerable to at least one attack. In addition, three of the top 15 Alexa websites were found vulnerable. We provide different countermeasures and discuss their advantages and disadvantages. Finally, we extend the scope of our research considering further targets and more advanced obfuscation techniques.

Keywords: PostScript · EPS · PDF · Web application security

1 Introduction

In the early 1980s, PostScript was created as a page description language. It is a Turing complete language and allows to execute arbitrary code or to write complex functions. With respect to security, execution of arbitrary code is dangerous. Security was not among the original design goals of this language because it was primarily used for printing trusted documents or displaying graphics in local environments. Meanwhile, PostScript is a widely deployed language supported by various online services including websites offered by Google, Microsoft,

The research was supported by the German state of North Rhine-Westphalia sponsoring the research training group *Human Centered System Security*, by the German Ministry of Research and Education (BMBF) as part of the *SyncEnc* project (FKZ: 16KIS0412K), and the European Commission through the *FutureTrust* project (grant 700542-Future-Trust-H2020-DS-2015-1).

© Springer Nature Switzerland AG 2018
M. Bailey et al. (Eds.): RAID 2018, LNCS 11050, pp. 603–622, 2018.
https://doi.org/10.1007/978-3-030-00470-5_28

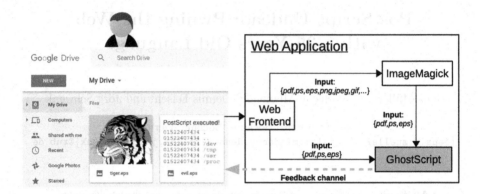

Fig. 1. Abstract overview of a web application's architecture and its components that are relevant for our attacks. The main goal of the attacker is to force the usage of Ghostscript to carry out these attacks.

or Apple. These services accept untrusted PostScript documents and present a potential danger to their providers as attackers may use many legitimate features to harm the systems processing PostScript documents. In this paper, we analyze the security implications resulting from processing PostScript documents on well-known websites. In Fig. 1, we give an abstract overview of the relevant components in scope for our attacks.

Initially, the attacker navigates her user-agent to the website where the web application is deployed. It contains a form to upload a PostScript file to the web application. The web frontend carrying out the HTTP communication receives the file and forwards it either first to an image conversion library such as ImageMagick[1] – which in turn delegates the file based on its content – or directly to the PostScript interpreter. According to our observations, in most cases this is Ghostscript[2] since it provides a rich set of output formats and features like resizing, conversion into other file types such as images, and further operations. Finally, the web application returns the resulting output of executed PostScript code as a rendered image. This gives the attacker a feedback channel to leak sensitive information and to verify if the attack had been successful.

Considering the wide deployment of PostScript and the dangers of using it, the question regarding the security of current interpreters arises.

Existing Gaps. The potential risks of processing PostScript files were first reported in 1996 by Goldberg et al. [14] and Sibert [22]. More concrete attacks were presented by Costin et al. [9,11,12] in 2010, 2011, and 2012 by attacking printers with malicious PostScript commands. In the meantime, attack vectors were not systematically analyzed; they were rather mentioned in blog posts or CVE entries.

---

[1] ImageMagick Studio LLC, *ImageMagick*, http://imagemagick.org, Mar. 2017.

[2] Artifex Software, *Ghostscript*, https://ghostscript.com/, Mar. 2017.

The first scientific paper on attacking web applications processing PostScript was published by Müller et al. [18] in 2017. They showed that Google Cloud Print could be exploited by uploading crafted files with PostScript commands. However, a thorough security analysis of web applications processing PostScript was left open for future work. Our research addresses this gap and reveals novel insights missed by previous research.

Systematization of Knowledge. To the best of our knowledge, there is no comprehensive database of existing vulnerabilities and attack vectors regarding PostScript. Therefore, the first challenge for our work was to systematically collect those. We collected all attack vectors by manually searching through vulnerability databases, individual blog posts and forums as well as by thoroughly studying the PostScript language reference. In essence, we found that attacks on PostScript interpreters can be divided into five different categories: Denial-of-Service (DoS), information disclosure, file system access, command execution, and content masking. This is consistent with attack categories that were already found by previous research on other languages such as XML [23] and PJL [18].

Evaluation. We tested two types of web applications: (Category 1) online image converters and (Category 2) the top 15 Alexa websites. Category 1 web applications were collected using search engines such as Google. We collected one hundred web applications of this type and evaluated them. The results are surprising – 56% are vulnerable against at least one attack.

To prove the impact of our attacks on prominent and more complex web applications, we decided to extend our research by evaluating Category 2 web applications. This is more challenging because the PostScript processing functionality provided by the web application has to be identified first and studied carefully with valid user accounts. We thoroughly studied the top 15 Alexa websites and finally were able to evaluate 10 out of them. Five web applications were excluded due to the duplicity (e.g. google.com and google.co.jp) or because of language barriers. Three of these web applications are vulnerable, including prominent providers such as Wikipedia and Microsoft.

Contribution

- We provide an exhaustive study regarding attacks against Ghostscript and PostScript. We systematize attack vectors and provide them in a comprehensive attack catalog.
- We evaluate the security of one hundred online image converters and ten top websites. Based on the responsible disclosure model, we reported our findings to the affected vendors and helped them to fix the issues.
- We identify various methods to include malicious PostScript code within legitimate PDF files and provide a hybrid proof-of-concept exploit.
- We discuss countermeasures mitigating or limiting the attacks. In addition, we reveal novel aspects targeting future research complementing our work.

2   Foundations

The PostScript page description language [2] was originally invented by Adobe between 1982 and 1984 for high quality printing on laser printers. However, PostScript soon became a common document exchange format, for example to share electronic versions of academic publications. It is a stack-based Turing complete programming language with a rich set of commands and data types. In this regard, Encapsulated PostScript (EPS) is also noteworthy as it is generally considered as a vector image format and supported by various applications such as LATEX processors. While EPS is limited to a subset of the PostScript language, all commands that we classify as potentially harmful are still available in EPS. An example PostScript document displaying *Hello World* is given in Listing 1.

```
1   %!PS
2   /Times-Roman findfont 75 scalefont setfont
3   100 500 moveto (Hello World) show showpage
```

Listing 1. Example PostScript document.

With respect to security, interpreting PostScript is equal to arbitrary code execution. PostScript is even capable of basic file system I/O – this was originally designed as a feature to store frequently used graphics or fonts. When running untrusted PostScript code in a sensitive environment like on a web server, such functionality can be dangerous since arbitrary files can be accessed by the attacker. In this work, the PostScript language is used to perform a variety of attacks, such as DoS and information disclosure against web applications.

Ghostscript.   The Ghostscript software suite provides interpreters for PostScript and PDF and is available on most Linux distributions. Ghostscript expects as input PDF or PostScript files. As output, multiple formats such as PNG, JPEG, and GIF are supported. Based on this rich feature set, almost all online converters use Ghostscript to convert PostScript and PDF files into other file types, for example to generate a thumbnail preview of an uploaded PDF file.

Ghostscript provides various extensions to the PostScript standard such as accessing environment variables and even shell command execution on the host system. The dangers of such powerful features have been recognized by the Ghostscript developers. For this purpose an option activating the 'more secure' execution of PostScript code was implemented. By starting Ghostscript with the -dSAFER flag, critical operations such as executing shell commands and writing to files directly on the host filesystem are disabled while reading files is limited to certain directories. Nevertheless, we will show that some attacks are still applicable even if this flag is enabled.

In the past ten years, 51 Common Vulnerabilities and Exposures (CVE) IDs have been filed for Ghostscript, with ten of them being classified as 'critical' (CVSS rating of 9 to 10). We also consider these vulnerabilities in our evaluation.

ImageMagick.   ImageMagick is an open-source software suite handling a vast variety of raster and vector image file formats. Web applications and frameworks often use ImageMagick – or forks of it such as GraphicsMagick – to convert or resize images. For working with PDF and PostScript files, ImageMagick delegates the processing to Ghostscript. Therefore, ImageMagick may be an exploit vector for malicious PostScript code.

3   Attacker Model

We assume that an attacker is able to create PostScript code and send it as input to a target web application. After that, the attacker may access the resulting image generated by the target web application from the PostScript document.

Our attacker is successful if one or more of the following five goals are achieved: (1) Processing the PostScript code forces the web application to allocate huge amounts of resources such as CPU or memory (DoS). (2) The attacker obtains non-public information useful for further attacks, such as path names or environment variables. (3) The attacker can read from or write to files on the file system of the web application. (4) The attacker can execute shell commands on the hosting machine of the web application. (5) The attacker can display different content to different users viewing the same document.

4   Attacking via PostScript

This section describes five different attacks achieving at least one of the described goals. All described attacks target the Ghostscript component, see Fig. 1.

Denial-of-Service (DoS). PostScript provides features that can be misused to allocate large amounts of resources such as CPU or RAM. Thus, if an interpreter does not impose any upper processing time or memory consumption limits, the host is prone to DoS attacks.

```
1   %!PS
2   {10000000 array} loop
```

Listing 2. Infinite memory allocation loop within a malicious PostScript document.

The example shown in Listing 2 forces the allocation of large arrays on the stack within an infinite loop. If run in the Ghostscript interpreter, all available memory is consumed within seconds. By sending this small PostScript document, an attacker could harm the availability of a machine. Furthermore, PostScript allows arbitrary strings to be printed to *stdout* and *stderr* within loops at high data rates. If error messages get logged, this allows an attacker to flood logfiles and exhaust all available disk space.

Information Disclosure. Given access to the results of executed PostScript code, an attacker can obtain reconnaissance information such as the target's system time and platform or the used PostScript interpreter version. Proprietary extensions featured by Ghostscript enable further low-level information disclosure attacks such as access to the command line arguments the program has been called with (including file names) and the full path names for configuration and font files. Older Ghostscript versions even allowed environment variables to be read even if the -dSAFER flag was set.

File System Access. The PostScript language allows reading from and writing to arbitrary files on the host file system. The Ghostscript interpreter, if called with -dSAFER, restricts access to reading certain fonts and configuration files. However, bypasses were discovered in the past such as CVE-2016-7977. Note that file inclusion may lead to further attacks such as DoS by accessing /dev/random.

Write access to Ghostscript configuration files even enables an attacker to escalate into other PostScript or Portable Document Format (PDF) files processed by the interpreter. This way, subsequent documents uploaded by users can be captured or manipulated by an attacker. Older versions of Ghostscript allowed directory listings even with activated -dSAFER mode. In current versions, an attacker can still verify if a certain file or directory exists on the file system and obtain its size and timestamp.

Command Execution. Technically, every direct access to a PostScript interpreter can already be classified as code execution. Certainly, without access to the network stack or additional operating system libraries, possibilities are limited to arbitrary mathematical calculations such as mining cryptocurrencies. However, the Ghostscript interpreter – if not called with -dSAFER – allows to invoke arbitrary shell commands to be executed using the proprietary %pipe%cmd command. Furthermore, bypasses were discovered in the past leading to command execution even in safer mode, such as CVE-2016-7976 and CVE-2017-8291.

Content Masking. The appearance of a PostScript document is dynamically generated based on its code. This enables an attacker to create a document with a different content being displayed based on conditional statements such as the current time or the host it is running on. Backes et al. [6] and Costin [12] used this feature to manipulate purchase contracts. In the context of web applications, such an approach may allow to bypass filters for illegal or offensive content: The document can be made to look different when previewed in the cloud, when opened locally, or when printed. We show that such attacks are even possible with PDF files containing PostScript overlay code. This fundamentally undermines trust in PDF documents since they are commonly assumed to display the same content, independent of their environment. Furthermore, conditional PostScript statements allow to render a different number of pages depending on whether the document is processed on a printer or a print server such as CUPS[3]. This enables an attacker to manipulate or bypass page counters used for accounting.

---

[3] Apple Inc., *Common UNIX Printing System*, https://www.cups.org/, Mar. 2017.

5   Obfuscating Malicious PostScript Files

Security related filters within the web frontend can be applied to prohibit the upload of potentially dangerous files. Usually, such filters restrict allowed files to certain types such as images. Once the file is uploaded it is just passed through to ImageMagick which – based on magic header bytes – detects the file format. There are two options for an attacker to get PostScript code deployed: Either (1) rename the PostScript file extension to a whitelisted filetype such as .png or (2) change the content type to a harmless or whitelisted header like image/png. The goal of such obfuscation is to bypass the web application's logic limiting the file upload to 'images only' by imitating other filetypes. Since ImageMagick analyzes the first bytes of the file content to determine which interpreter should be used, the attacker can still enforce the execution of malicious PostScript files.

Obfuscation with PDFs. PDF supports PostScript code defined within itself. Thus, if a web application accepts PDF files, PostScript code can be hidden and uploaded. Different tools can be used for the creation of malicious PDF files. For instance, the pdfmark [3] PostScript command in combination with tools such as ps2pdf allows to create a PDF document containing PostScript code. Another option is to use open-source tools implementing the PDF specification such as PDFBox[4]. We identified four techniques to embed PostScript within PDF.

PostScript Prepended to PDF. Many PDF interpreters such as Adobe Reader or Chrome's internal PDF viewer treat PDF files as valid if the PDF header starts within the first 1024 bytes [19]. Prepended byte streams are ignored.

```
1   %!PS
2   {malicious code up to 1023 bytes in total}
3   %PDF-1.5
4   {legitimate PDF content}
```

Listing 3. PostScript code prepended to a legitimate PDF file.

This allows an attacker to create a valid PDF file with up to 1023 bytes of PostScript code prepended. This PostScript code however is only executed if the file is processed by Ghostscript – which recognizes the PostScript header – while other PDF viewers will display the PDF content instead.

PostScript Pass-Through. Ghostscript supports a proprietary, undocumented feature which allows to hide inline PostScript code snippets within PDF byte stream containers. While other PDF viewers ignore the malicious PostScript code, Ghostscript executes it in case the PDF file is converted, e.g. to an image.

```
1   ({malicious code}) PS
```

Listing 4. Inline pass-through PostScript code within a PDF file.

---

[4] The Apache Software Foundation, *PDFBox*, https://pdfbox.apache.org/, Mar. 2017.

PostScript XObjects. The PDF standard allows to embed external objects (XObjects), e.g. images. PDF 1.1 allows XObjects containing PostScript code to be executed when printing the document. However, this feature is discouraged by the PDF 1.3 specification and is disabled in current versions of Ghostscript.

The first four lines in Listing 5 define an object within a PDF file. The type is XObject and the subtype defines that the content is PostScript code. In line 5, the beginning of a byte stream container is defined. The following lines contain the PostScript code, which ends in line 8 by closing the byte stream container.

Listing 5. PostScript code hidden in an XObject object within a PDF file.   **Listing 6.** PostScript code hidden in an Font object within a PDF file.

PostScript Fonts. The PDF standard allows fonts of various formats to be embedded. One format is of particular interest: Type 1 fonts are defined in plain PostScript itself. While these are actually limited to a subset of the PostScript language [1], Ghostscript does not consider this limitation and executes arbitrary PostScript code embedded in Type 1 fonts within a PDF file, see Listing 6.

Summary. There are various ways to obfuscate PostScript code or files in order to bypass restrictions imposed by a web application. Some of the bypasses use simple techniques such as changing the file extension or sending the wrong content type. When PDF files are processed by a web application, more sophisticated techniques can be used to hide malicious PostScript code within them. In addition, the obfuscation can be improved by deflating the PostScript code within the byte stream container. This feature is defined in the PDF specification and supported by all PDF interpreters which makes the detection of PostScript code by firewalls and Intrusion Detection Systems (IDSs) more complicated.

6   Evaluation

To evaluate PostScript based attacks as described in Sect. 4, we created a comprehensive attack catalog – implemented as a specially crafted EPS file – and uploaded it to various websites. This proof-of-concept file is available for download from http://bit.ly/ps_attacker_catalog[5]. The attack catalog serves as a

---

[5] Note that the proof-of-concept file is hosted on Dropbox. After uploading, we realized that Dropbox itself processes PostScript documents. The shown preview image therefore is the rendered result of the attack catalog executed on the Dropbox server.

blueprint to test PostScript processing applications such as websites that generate thumbnail previews of uploaded images. It can also be used to perform a security evaluation of other software like print servers or desktop applications. If processed, the attack catalog automatically checks for various features, misconfigurations, and vulnerabilities in both the PostScript language and the Ghostscript implementation. A resulting preview image after conversion by a web application running Ghostscript 9.19 is given in Fig. 4 in the appendix.

Based on the catalog, we first evaluated 100 image conversion websites to get a large-scale overview. We conducted a Google search for *online image converter* and tested the top 100 results. Second, we evaluated the Alexa top 15 sites to verify if more popular web applications are vulnerable too.

6.1   Image Conversion Websites

Given our test set of 100 image conversion sites, we could have executed malicious PostScript code on 56 of them. An overview is given in Fig. 2. Detailed results are documented in Table 2 in the appendix.

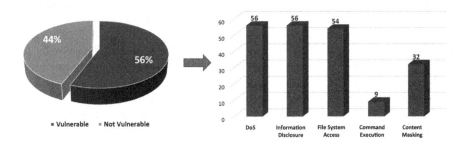

Fig. 2. Evaluation of 100 image conversion websites. 56% of them were found vulnerable to at least one attack.

Most websites do not accept PostScript or EPS files based on the file extension and content type (`application/postscript`). However, by renaming the file extension to `.png` and accordingly setting the content type (`image/png`) the attack often works. Observing this behavior of web applications, it is obvious that PostScript documents were actually not intended to be supported by the web applications but could be enforced by simple obfuscation techniques.

We did not perform any tests concerning actual DoS attacks. Instead, we measured the time it takes to calculate 10,000 MD5 hash sums, which was possible for all 56 websites and varied between 14 ms and 2,147 ms. Limited information disclosure attacks such as obtaining the system date and leaking pathnames could also be performed on all 56 PostScript processing websites. These results can be explained by the fact that even if Ghostscript is started with the -dSAFER flag, these commands are allowed. System environment variables could be dumped on

35 websites using proprietary Ghostscript commands. The reason for the lower number of affected systems is that this vulnerability is already addressed by CVE-2013-5653.

Read access to arbitrary files (LFI) could be performed on 31 websites. Such full read access is based on missing -dSAFER options or on a bypass addressed in CVE-2016-7977. By this means, older version of Ghostscript are still affected.

On 22 sites, we had only limited read access to fonts and Ghostscript configuration files. This can also be problematic since an attacker can read out the gs_init.ps file defining protection mechanisms. Disclosing this information can lead to further, more precise attack vectors bypassing the defined restrictions. On five websites we could write to arbitrary files due to missing -dSAFER options.

On 33 websites, we could get a directory listing for the whole file system. On 21 sites, we could only list the font and configuration directories, which has limited impact. This vulnerability abuses a Ghostscript configuration with less restrictive -dSAFER options, which is already documented in CVE-2013-5653.

However, we could still get status information for arbitrary files on the file system on 51 websites. Using the PostScript 'status' command, the existence of files/directories on the server including sizes and timestamps can be verified.

On nine websites we gained remote shell command execution – on five of them due to missing -dSAFER options and on four due to CVE-2016-7976. Note that we did not evaluate further known vulnerabilities and CVEs existing for the used Ghostscript versions because they are based on buffer overflows, which can harm the server and cause damage.

Because PostScript/EPS is vulnerable to content masking attacks by design, we limited such attacks to PDF files. As proof-of-concept we created a PDF file containing PostScript overlay code. In case that the converted version of the file visually differs from the unconverted PDF, the attack was successful. On 32 websites we were able to generate different views of the same document.

It is interesting to note that most websites use outdated versions of Ghostscript. Out of 56 websites interpreting PostScript, 30 use a Ghostscript version older than 9.18 (the current version for Debian/Ubuntu) which leads to multiple vulnerabilities. Furthermore, some websites with the same Ghostscript version behave differently – we assume this due to backporting.

6.2   Alexa Top 15 Sites

Image conversion websites can be considered easy targets because they are likely to be less hardened and to accept PostScript input. Therefore, we performed a test on the Alexa top 15 websites, which are frequently checked by hundreds of security researchers and bug bounty hunters around the world. Because Google's domains (google.co.in, google.co.jp) occur multiple times in this list – likely with the same technology serving them – we limited our test to the main google.com domain. Furthermore, three domains (baidu.com, qq.com, taobao.com) do not have an English interface and require a mainland China phone number to register. Thus, we could not test these.

Table 1. Evaluation of PostScript based attacks against top websites.

Rank	Domain	GS	DoS	Info Disclosure			File System Access				Cmd Exec		Masking	#
			cpu [20]	date [5]	path [5]	env [5]	read [2]	write [2]	list [2]	stat [2]	cve [10]	nosafer [5]	mask [3,4]	
1	google.com	8.54	●	●	●	✓	○	✓	○	●	✓	✓	✓	6
2	youtube.com	–	✓	✓	✓	✓	✓	✓	✓	✓	✓	✓	✓	0
3	facebook.com	–	✓	✓	✓	✓	✓	✓	✓	✓	✓	✓	✓	0
5	wikipedia.org	9.06	●	○	○	✓	○	✓	○	●	✓	✓	●	7
6	yahoo.com	–	✓	✓	✓	✓	✓	✓	✓	✓	✓	✓	✓	0
7	reddit.com	–	✓	✓	✓	✓	✓	✓	✓	✓	✓	✓	✓	0
11	amazon.com	–	✓	✓	✓	✓	✓	✓	✓	✓	✓	✓	✓	0
12	twitter.com	–	✓	✓	✓	✓	✓	✓	✓	✓	✓	✓	✓	0
13	instagram.com	–	✓	✓	✓	✓	✓	✓	✓	✓	✓	✓	✓	0
14	live.com	9.05	●	●	●	●	●	✓	●	●	✓	✓	●	8
#			3	3	3	1	3	0	3	3	0	0	2	0

Legend: ● Vulnerable ○ Vulnerability limited ✓ Not vulnerable (no PostScript)

Of the remaining ten websites, two allow the upload of EPS/PostScript files directly (google.com and live.com), while six allow PDF files to be uploaded and preview them on the server side (google.com, wikipedia.org, yahoo.com, amazon.com, and live.com). Note that Facebook uses client side JavaScript code to preview PDF files, which is out of scope for our attacks. We did not succeed in embedding and executing PostScript code within PDF files on Yahoo! and Amazon. All ten websites allow image files to be uploaded, however, we could not inject PostScript code through their image upload function. In the end, we could attack three websites discussed below. It is noteworthy to mention that all of them use outdated versions of Ghostscript. An overview of the evaluation is given in Table 1.

Google. Google Drive and Google Mail preview uploaded EPS files that contain PostScript code. However, after contacting the Google developers we learned that their conversion process is sandboxed, limiting the attacks to a virtual machine.

Wikipedia. Wikipedia, which is based on MediaWiki[6], does not allow PostScript or EPS files to be uploaded directly for security reasons. However, PDF files can be uploaded and previews are generated on the server side. Using PostScript pass-through as described in Sect. 5, we could create a specially crafted PDF file which executes PostScript code that could be used for DoS attacks. Information disclosure and accessing the file system was limited because we could only extract a limited number of bytes using this technique.

Microsoft. Microsoft OneDrive, which is hosted on live.com, allows arbitrary EPS files to be uploaded, which are processed for preview on the server side. This allowed us to dump environment variables and to read arbitrary files (LFI).

---

[6] Wikimedia Foundation, *MediaWiki*, https://www.mediawiki.org/, Mar. 2017.

6.3   Responsible Disclosure and Ethical Considerations

We responsibly disclosed all security vulnerabilities to the respective website administrators. Microsoft rewarded our findings with $5000. Ethical considerations were discussed internally during the creation of the attack catalog and before starting the tests. As a result, we defined a methodology that ensured both the verifiability of our attacks as well as minimal interference with the tested services. This includes precautions against DoS or leaking sensitive data like private keys or passwords.

7   Towards a Hybrid Exploit

Web applications are not the only systems that can be attacked with PostScript. To demonstrate the flexibility of malicious PostScript code hidden inside PDFs as described in Sect. 5 we created a hybrid proof-of-concept PostScript/PDF worm which can be used to attack various types of hosts as depicted in Fig. 3. It abuses missing –dSAFER mode, CVE-2016-7976 and CVE-2017-8291 to attack Ghostscript and CVE-2017-2741 to attack HP printers.

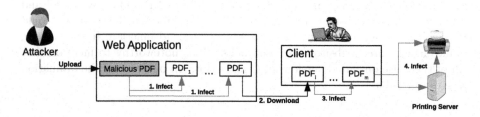

Fig. 3. A PostScript-based worm attacking and spreading on different systems.

Web Applications. When uploaded and processed by a web application vulnerable to Ghostscript-based remote code execution, the worm infects all PDF files found on the server it has write access to. Such a scenario would especially be disastrous for cloud storage providers which keep the PDFs of many users, or for scholarly research databases like *IEEE Xplore* or *ACM* which provide millions of PDF documents frequently requested by researchers around the world.

Client Systems. If any of these infected PDF files is downloaded by a victim onto a vulnerable Linux client, in turn, all PDF files on his host's file system would be infected. Infection routines could either be provided by simply replacing benign PDF files with a copy of the worm or by silently injecting malicious PostScript code into benign PDF files. The later method can be can be accomplished by restructuring the PDF content without changing the actual appearance of the document. Note that to trigger the infection it is not always necesarry to open the PDF file. It usually is sufficient to open a file manager which previews containing images and PDF files and therefore execute the malicious code. Even simple command-line tools like *less(1)*[7] are affected because on current Linux distributions, `less file.pdf` automatically converts PDFs to text to preview them in the console using Ghostscript. Note that the Windows world is not directly affected because PostScript code within PDF files is usually just ignored here. However known vulnerabilities and CVEs exist, e.g. for Adobe Reader which could be added to the malicious PDF document.

Printers and Print Servers. In April 2017, HP published CVE-2017-2741, a critical vulnerability present in various printer models without giving any details. In June 2017, Baines [7] identified specially crafted PJL commands to exploit the issue. We found another method to exploit the weakness based on PostScript code. An example exploit to gain a permanent reverse shell on printer startup is shown in Listing 7. We tested the exploit on a HP OfficeJet Pro 8210.

```
1  %!PS
2  /outfile (../var/etc/profile.d/telnetd.sh) (w+) file def
3  outfile (nc attacker.com 31337 -e /bin/sh) writestring
4  outfile closefile
```

Listing 7. Exploiting CVE-2017-2741 to gain a reverse shell on HP printers.

This exploit can be combined into the malicious PostScript/PDF file and is triggered when using direct PDF printing – which is becoming more and more popular – or from USB stick on a printer model vulnerable to CVE-2017-2741. The printer interprets and executes the PostScript code contained in PDF files leading to code execution. The worm can spread further to other vulnerable printers in the network by printing the same PostScript/PDF file (e.g. by itself sending to port 9100/tcp of all reachable network printers). In case a local print server like CUPS is in the print job deployment chain, it can also be infected because CUPS is dependent on Ghostscript for PostScript/PDF processing.

For ethical reasons, we did not evaluate the worm in the wild. But we are confident that such a hybrid exploit, viable on cloud servers as well as Linux clients and even printers is a relevant concept from an attacker's perspective.

8   Related Work

In the following, we give an introduction to significant prior research on PostScript, PDF and related security problems.

PostScript. The potential dangers of PostScript has been pointed out by Goldberg et al. [14] and Sibert [22], however we are not aware of any efforts to systematically exploit PostScript language functions. Backes et al. [6] show that PostScript documents can be crafted to force different content when opened in different viewers which allows them to manipulate sales agreements. A

---

[7] GNU Project, *GNU less*, https://www.gnu.org/software/less/, Mar. 2017.

comprehensive discussion of printer security – including a survey of malicious PostScript commands has been given by Costin [9,10,12]. Costin [12] further demonstrate how to abuse proprietary PostScript extensions to get command execution and access the memory of Xerox devices. They also demonstrate that a malicious PostScript payload can be made to execute only on a certain printer using conditional statements to check the environment the PostScript interpreter is running. [18] further demonstrate how to exploit PostScript and other languages supported by network printers and discuss the dangers of executing PostScript code in Google Cloud Print. A study conducted in parallel to our research which comes closest to our work has been conducted by [15] who use PostScript payloads to attack web applications.

PDF. In [8,20,21] the authors concentrated mainly on abusing legitimate features of PDF to create malware and to execute arbitrary code on the victim's system. The detection of potentially dangerous code within PDF files by scanning for known malicious structures is described in [5]. The authors mainly focused on detecting the execution of legitimate PDF features leading to command execution. PostScript was however not in the scope of the research. In [16] the authors use *polyglot*-based attacks by writing a code valid in multiple programming languages. The authors used PDF files as a carriage of the malicious code to invoke arbitrary URLs and bypass browser restrictions like the Same-Origin-Policy. None of the previous work considered the risks of hidden PostScript code within PDF files, which is executed in a web application context. Markwood et al. [17] show that extracted specially crafted fonts can be embedded into PDF files, which display a different text depending on whether the document is processed by a web application or a screen reader. This allows them to fool PDF indexers like search engines, plagiarism detection software and even automatic reviewer assignment systems in use by academic conferences.

9   Countermeasures

Basically, there are two approaches to mitigate the presented attacks: (1) By validating user input to globally reject PostScript code or (2) by sandboxing the PostScript interpreter. In the following, both approaches are discussed.

Input File Validation. As shown in Sect. 6 various image conversion websites support PostScript files – often without knowing it. If there is no requirement to accept PostScript, EPS or PDF files this functionality should be turned off completely. However, this is not always practical because PostScript interpreter can be deeply anchored in web applications. For example, web application frameworks simply call ImageMagick or another background library for image conversion and may not have an option to limit input files to certain types. In such cases, the web application developer has to manually whitelist uploaded files based on their 'magic' header bytes before processing them. This approach to accept only certain file types like JPEG, PNG or GIF can provide sufficient protection if implemented correctly. However, it must be noted that allowing PDF files also implies allowing arbitrary PostScript code as shown in Sect. 5.

Note that a common technique to verify if a file is actually an image and therefore protect web applications against malicious uploads is to check if the image is resizable [13]. This will not protect against malicious PostScript code: First, because EPS files are resizable and secondly because once an EPS file is resized, it is already interpreted meaning the contained malicious PostScript code has already been executed. Generally spoken, scanning for potentially dangerous PostScript code is usually based on executing the PostScript code. As a result, preventing the processing of PostScript is not possible by this countermeasure.

Interpreter Sandboxing. In case that the web application must process EPS, PostScript or PDF files the execution of PostScript code is inevitable. Differentiating between benign and malicious PostScript code can be considered hard, because the PostScript language provides dozens of obfuscation techniques. Therefore, PostScript file uploads should be treated as what they are: executing a Turing complete programming language with client input on the server side. Hence, an additional layer of security is required to mitigate the risks. Ghostscript provides a -dSAFER flag, however there have been various bypasses in the past (see Sect. 4) and even in 'safer' mode it is possible to start DoS attacks and perform information disclosure attacks like obtaining information on local files. Therefore, the conversion process should be completely isolated from the rest of the operating system. This can be provided using sandboxing techniques (Firejail, chroot, etc.) or operating-system-level virtualization (Docker, etc.). Such techniques come at the cost of implementation efforts and in some cases higher CPU usage. But they are the only safe way we know of to warp and execute PostScript code. Furthermore, the sandbox should apply resource limitation in terms of computing time, memory usage, process runtime and the number of parallel image conversion processes to be started from a single user to prevent DoS attacks. In the disclosure process we learned that sandboxing techniques are applied, for example, by Google Drive and Dropbox when thumbnails for uploaded EPS files are generated.

10   Future Work and Discussion

Based on our findings, we consider further targets and similar technologies to apply our attacks. Such targets are printers, printing services and desktop environments. In addition, we are convinced of the relevance of more advanced obfuscating techniques which should be analyzed further.

10.1   Further Targets

Besides web applications, other services and devices are capable of processing PostScript such as printers, online printing services, desktop and mobile applications, and web robots.

Direct PDF Printers. Almost all laser printers support PostScript. In 2017, Müller et al. [18] showed how dangerous the execution of PostScript on printers can be. As a reaction, many vendors restrict the dangerous features of PostScript and thus prevent or limit the impact of the attacks. However, modern printers can interpret PDF and other file formats directly. This raises the question on whether PostScript code hidden in other file formats is processed nevertheless – and whether this is done by the hardened PostScript interpreter or not.

Printing Services. Printing services such as Google Cloud Print or HP ePrint provide an interface between the user and one or multiple printers. Users do not need to install any software or printer driver. They just send the file to a server that interprets it and forwards it to the printer. Similarly, printing services like textile or digital printing offer the possibility to upload EPS files or other file types that are used to create customized products like T-Shirts, cups, calendars, or flyers. Such services may be a valuable target for attacks if malicious documents are processed.

Desktop/Mobile Clients. There is no large-scale evaluation on the security of desktop or mobile clients capable to process PostScript. Thus, the risks by opening of an unsuspicious file like PDF or PNG are barely studied. Such an evaluation should consider all popular software products like PDF readers, image viewers, and browsers on all major platforms. Commercial software products like Adobe Illustrator, PDF Studio, and even AutoCAD should be considered too.

PostScript in LaTeX. There are various services offering the compilation of LaTeXfiles and the generation of PDF files from them. Such systems like arXiv.org and ShareLaTeX.com are popular in the research community. An attacker may include malicious code within LaTeXsource files that will eventually be executed during the compilation. In addition, it may be possible that after compilation the malicious code is included in the resulting PDF file.

10.2   Obfuscation

We introduced several obfuscating techniques to bypass security measures and limitations implemented by web applications as a protection mechanism. However, further obfuscating techniques are conceivable and should be considered in future research.

Masking PDF Files as Images. The PDF format allows attackers to create polyglots – ambiguous files that allow multiple interpretations of its content. For example, an attacker may create a valid PDF document that is also a valid image such as a JPEG file when opened in an image viewer. This has been demonstrated by previous research [4,16,20].

This technique may be capable of bypassing the protection mechanisms of some web applications as discussed in Sect. 9. If one manages to create a valid image file (including 'magic' header bytes) that is identified as PDF by ImageMagick and therefore forwarded to Ghostscript, one may again inject malicious PostScript code. As a proof-of-concept, we created a polyglot file that is recognized as JPEG image by the *file(1)*[8] tool, but identified and handled as PDF by ImageMagick's *convert* tool. Thus, further research is required to develop attack and defense techniques.

Discussion. In this work, we presented a methodology to systematically analyze PostScript processing web applications for security vulnerabilities. We found 56 of 100 tested online image conversion websites to be vulnerable to at least one attack. We were further able to attack high-value targets such as Wikipedia or Microsoft OneDrive on which we could include arbitrary files. Our work was acknowledged according to the vendor's bug bounty program.

Causes. We identified three possible reasons leading to the security gaps:

1. The dangers of PostScript are poorly documented and widespread in many blogs and CVEs. Despite the fact that many of the attacks are already known, there is no document describing the *best current practices* and clarifying the risks by using PostScript interpreter. As a result, many administrators, security experts, and developers may not be aware of the existing treats. With our paper, we address the security community and reveal the need to recap our knowledge regarding the risks of PostScript.
2. The support of PostScript is hidden deep inside the frameworks used by web applications. Thus, even if a developer or administrator is aware of the risks involved in processing PostScript code, he may not be aware of it being enabled. For instance, if the Laraval PHP framework is used to resize an image, this is done by calling the `$img->resize();` function. This function calls ImageMagick, which in turn may invoke Ghostscript. As a result, the application may be vulnerable even if its developer never intended to support PostScript.
3. PostScript supports features, which can harm the host. To reduce risks, widely deployed interpreters like Ghostscript implemented restrictions with respect to security, e. g. the `-dSAFER` flag. However, even with in safer mode, attacks such as DoS are possible.

11   Conclusion

Web application and framework developers need to be aware of PostScript injection attacks and have to put more effort into addressing them. This should be done on the one side by the security community clarifying the need for preventing such attacks and on the other side by developers and administrators disabling PostScript execution by default or using it exclusively in an isolated environment with activated security restrictions.

---

[8] Christos Zoulas, *The file(1) Command*, https://github.com/file/file, Mar. 2017.

A   Comprehensive Attack Catalog

Comprehensive Ghostscript/PostScript Attack Catalog

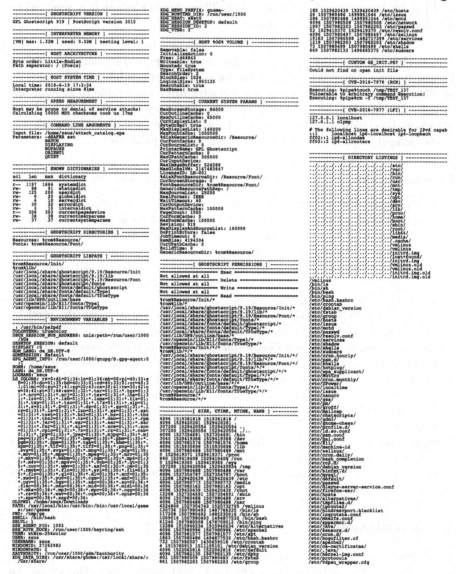

Fig. 4. Resulting preview image of a malicious proof-of-concept PostScript file, our comprehensive attack catalog, uploaded to a web application running Ghostscript 9.19.

B   Evaluation of Image Conversion Websites

Table 2. Evaluation of PostScript based attacks against web applications.

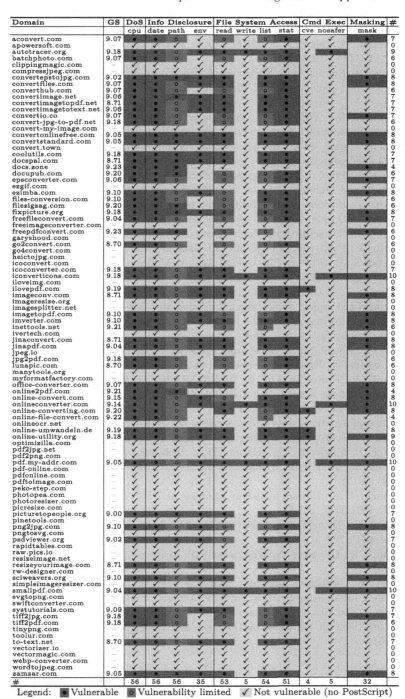

Domain	GS	DoS	Info Disclosure			File System Access				Cmd Exec		Masking	#
		cpu	date	path	env	read	write	list	stat	cve	nosafer	mask	
		56	56	56	35	53	5	54	51	4	5	32	

Legend: ■ Vulnerable ◎ Vulnerability limited ✓ Not vulnerable (no PostScript)

References

1. Adobe Systems: Adobe Type 1 Font Format (1990)
2. Adobe Systems: PostScript Language Reference Manual (1999)
3. Adobe Systems: Pdfmark Reference Manual (2005)
4. Albertini, A.: This PDF is a JPEG; or, this Proof of Concept is a Picture of Cats. PoC 11 GTFO 0x03 (2014)
5. Baccas, P.: Finding rules for heuristic detection of malicious PDFs: with analysis of embedded exploit code. In: Virus Bulletin Conference (2010)
6. Backes, M., Dürmuth, M., Unruh, D.: Vorgetäuscht/Böse Textdokumente - Postscript Gone Wild (2007). (in German)
7. Baines, J.: Rooting a Printer: From Security Bulletin to Remote Code Execution (2017). https://www.tenable.com/blog/rooting-a-printer-from-security-bulletin-to-remote-code-execution
8. Blonce, A., Filiol, E., Frayssignes, L.: Portable Document Format (PDF) Security Analysis and Malware Threats. BlackHat Europe (2008)
9. Costin, A.: Hacking printers for fun and profit. Hack.lu (2010)
10. Costin, A.: Hacking printers - 10 years down the road. Hash Days (2011)
11. Costin, A.: Postscript(um): You've Been Hacked. 28C3 (2011)
12. Costin, A.: Postscript: Danger ahead?! Hack in Paris (2012)
13. Dominique, R.: Protect File Upload Against Malicious File (2017). https://www.owasp.org/index.php/Protect_FileUpload_Against_Malicious_File
14. Goldberg, I., Wagner, D., Thomas, R., Brewer, E., et al.: A Secure Environment for untrusted helper applications: confining the wily hacker. In: Proceedings of the 6th Conference on USENIX Security Symposium, Focusing on Applications of Cryptography, vol. 6, p. 1 (1996)
15. Hong, Y., Zheng, M.: A Ghost from Postscript. Ruxcon (2017)
16. Magazinius, J., Rios, B.K., Sabelfeld, A.: Polyglots: crossing origins by crossing formats. In: Proceedings of the 2013 ACM SIGSAC Conference on Computer & Communications Security, pp. 753–764. ACM (2013)
17. Markwood, I., Shen, D., Liu, Y., Lu, Z.: PDF mirage: content masking attack against information-based online services. In: 26th USENIX Security Symposium (USENIX Security 17), (Vancouver, BC), pp. 833–847 (2017)
18. Müller, J., Mladenov, V., Somorovsky, J., Schwenk, J.: SoK: exploiting network printers. In: 2017 IEEE Symposium on Security and Privacy (SP), pp. 213–230. IEEE (2017)
19. Popescu, D.S.: Hiding malicious content in PDF documents. arXiv preprint arXiv:1201.0397 (2012)
20. Raynal, F., Delugré, G., Aumaitre, D.: Malicious origami in PDF. J. Comput. Virol. 6(4), 289–315 (2010)
21. Selvaraj, K., Gutierrez, N.: The rise of PDF malware. Symantec Security Response (2010)
22. Sibert, W.: Malicious data and computer security. In: Proceedings of the 19th National Information Systems Security Conference (1996)
23. Späth, C., Mainka, C., Mladenov, V., Schwenk, J.: Sok: xml parser vulnerabilities. In: 10th USENIX Workshop on Offensive Technologies (WOOT 2016), Austin, TX (2016)

Identifying Key Leakage of Bitcoin Users

Michael Brengel$^{(\boxtimes)}$ and Christian Rossow

CISPA, Saarland University, Saarbrücken, Germany
{michael.brengel,rossow}@cispa.saarland

Abstract. We study key leakage in the context of cryptocurrencies.
First, we consider the problem of *explicit* key leakage occurring on open-
source intelligence platforms. To do this, we monitor the Pastebin feed
from Sep 2017–Mar 2018 to find exposed secret Bitcoin keys, reveal-
ing that attackers could have stolen 22.40 BTC worth roughly $178,000
given current exchange rates. Then, we focus on *implicit* key leakage by
exploiting the wrong usage of cryptographic primitives and scan Bitcoin's
blockchain for ECDSA nonce reuse. We systematically outline how an
attacker can use duplicate r values to leak nonces and secret keys, which
goes beyond the simple case where the same nonce and the same key have
been used in conjunction more than once. Our results show that ECDSA
nonce reuse has been a recurring problem in the Bitcoin ecosystem and
has already been exploited by attackers. In fact, an attacker could have
exploited nonce reuse to steal 412.80 BTC worth roughly $3.3 million.

1 Introduction

Cryptocurrencies have become popular entities in global financial markets. A
prime example of such a currency is *Bitcoin* [17] with a current market capitalization of over $135 billion [1] or *Ethereum* [23] with a current market capital-
ization of over $44 billion [2]. As such, it comes as no surprise that malicious
actors constantly try to *steal* those currencies, i.e., change ownership of cryptocurrency assets without consent of the legitimate owners. The decentralized
and *anonymous* (or at least *pseudonymous*) nature of those currencies makes
such malicious activities more attractive, as traceback and prosecution by law
enforcement agencies is significantly harder than with traditional currencies.

In terms of stealing cryptocurrency assets, there are several possibilities. A
cryptocurrency is usually based on a *cryptographic protocol*, which uses several
cryptographic primitives such as *elliptic curves* [15] or *digital signatures* [12],
which one could try to attack. However, both the protocol and the primitives are
usually well studied and are either proven secure in theory, or have been subject
to an auditing process by experts in the field. Therefore, the best attackers can
hope for in this setting are implementation flaws, which are usually short-lived
due to the open-source nature of cryptocurrency implementations. The most
prominent incident of such an implementation flaw happened in February 2014,
when attackers found a vulnerability in the Mt. Gox Bitcoin exchange, which
allowed them to steal 850,000 BTC worth around $450 million at that time.

© The Author(s) 2018
M. Bailey et al. (Eds.): RAID 2018, LNCS 11050, pp. 623–643, 2018.
https://doi.org/10.1007/978-3-030-00470-5_29

While the attack did not affect the Bitcoin protocol itself, it exploited the inherent *transaction malleability* of Bitcoin transactions to break some assumptions of the internal accounting system of Mt. Gox [11].

While such large-scale incidents are rare, a more common and thus also severe class of attacks against cryptocurrencies aims to leak cryptographic keys. Cryptocurrency assets are cryptographically protected by a collection of *secret keys*, which is called a *wallet*. If this wallet is stored in an insecure manner, i.e., in plain on disk without any additional protection, then malware can simply scan the disk for such wallets and report them to the attacker, which in turn can use them to steal assets. Due to the popularity of cryptocurrencies, attackers have massively deployed malware that aims to leak such secret keys. A well-known case of such malware was the Pony Botnet, which operated from September 2013 to January 2014 [18]. The malware scanned the victim's machine for various confidential credentials including cryptocurrency keys, which resulted in financial damage of $220,000. Modern wallets now use more sophisticated means of key management such as additional encryption with a password, two-factor authentication or hardware-based security [13], which protects against such local attacks.

In this paper, we take a different perspective and study whether *remote* attack vectors allow leaking cryptographic keys from users. First, we study whether users (accidentally or knowingly) *explicitly* leak cryptographic keys, that is, post them publicly. To this end, we leverage the notion of *open-source intelligence* (OSINT) with respect to cryptocurrency leaks. As a case study, we consider Bitcoin as it is the most prevalent cryptocurrency currently used, but any other cryptocurrency would be suitable as well. As an OSINT platform we consider Pastebin [3], which is a popular information-sharing web application on the Internet, and has already proven to leak different types of privacy-related information [16]. However, other OSINT platforms such as Twitter, Reddit, Facebook or GitHub would also work. We envision a scenario where a victim uses Pastebin to share a piece of information including Bitcoin secrets such as a code snippet performing a transaction or the debug output of wallet software. The victim creates this *paste* to privately share the information, not knowing that it will be publicly available in the Pastebin feed. An attacker that monitors this feed can then scan each new paste for Bitcoin keys, for example using their well-known format, and use those keys to steal Bitcoins. To simulate this, we have monitored the Pastebin feed since September 2017 for Bitcoin secrets. Our results show that an attacker could have stolen 22.40 BTC during this timespan.

We then also study the possibility of *implicit* key leakage, given that cryptocurrency users (or software developers) may misapply cryptographic primitives. In particular, keeping our focus on Bitcoin, we study the incorrect use of the *Elliptic Curve Digital Signature Algorithm* (ECDSA), which, however, also applies to other cryptocurrencies that are based on this primitive. To sign a message m using ECDSA with a secret key sk, one must compute a signature, which involves a randomly chosen nonce k. It is well known that apart from the secret key, the nonce must also be kept secret, as an attacker can otherwise use the signature and k to retrieve sk. Similarly, if one signs two distinct messages

m_1 and m_2 using the same k and the same sk, then an attacker can recompute sk based on the structure of the signature and the knowledge that both the key and the nonce have been reused. While such a duplicate occurrence should not happen in practice, as the set of possible nonces is sufficiently large, i.e., almost 2^{256} in the case of Bitcoin, such duplicates can still appear for other reasons. One such reason could be the use of weak random number generators [4] or vulnerable software that is not aware of the implications of nonce reuses. Another scenario which could also be responsible for such duplicate occurrences is cloning or resetting a virtual machine, which could possibly result in reusing the same seed for the random number generator. While there is anecdotal evidence for duplicate nonces in the Bitcoin blockchain, there is no systematic study on the actual impact or the prevalence of this phenomenon, i.e., the potential financial damage that can be caused. To fill this gap, we scan the Bitcoin blockchain for duplicate nonces and simulate an attack scenario in which a malicious actor actively monitors incoming transactions to look for duplicate nonce occurrences to leak keys and steal Bitcoins. In particular, we systematically outline how an attacker can use duplicate nonces to leak secrets, which has not been shown before in such detail. This goes beyond naïve cases where the same key and nonce pair was used twice to sign two distinct messages. In fact, we show that it is also possible to leak secrets by exploiting cyclic dependencies between keys and duplicate nonces. Our results show that an attacker could have used this methodology to steal 412.80 BTC.

To summarize, our contributions are as follows: (i) We assess the threat of explicit Bitcoin key leaks using OSINT. We instantiate this idea by monitoring the public feed of Pastebin for leaked secret keys. Our results demonstrate how an attacker doing this could have stolen 22.40 BTC. (ii) We systematically demonstrate how attackers can monitor Bitcoin transactions to scan for implicit key leaks. We develop a methodology that can map signatures with duplicate nonces to linear equation systems using a bipartite graph representation. (iii) We assess the impact of implicit key leaks in the context of Bitcoin. That is, we analyze how prevalent they are and how much Bitcoins an attacker could have stolen by exploiting them. Finally, we study if such exploitation has happened in the past. Our results show that an attacker could have stolen 412.80 BTC and that attackers have exploited nonce reuse in the past to steal Bitcoins.

2   Background

In this section, we outline the preliminaries required for the scope of this paper in order to grasp our ideas using the Bitcoin technology.

Blockchain and Mining. The central component of the Bitcoin protocol is the Bitcoin *blockchain*, which is a distributed append-only log, also called a *ledger*. The idea of this ledger is to keep track of all transactions that have ever occurred in the Bitcoin network. The ledger consists of a sequence of *blocks*, each of which consists of a set of *transactions*. Adding such a block to the blockchain requires solving a computational puzzle using the Hashcash proof-of-work system [9]. The process of adding blocks to the blockchain is called *mining* and is rewarded with Bitcoins. Transactions and blocks are created and distributed by the peers of the network. Before transactions are mined, they are put in a temporary buffer called the *mempool*. *Miners*, i.e., the peers which mine blocks, will then take transactions from the mempool to build and mine a block and finally, announce a newly mined block to the network.

Transactions. A Bitcoin transaction T consists of a sequence of *inputs* $T_i = [i_1, \ldots, i_m]$ and a sequence of *outputs* $T_o = [o_1, \ldots, o_n]$ and is uniquely identified by a *transaction ID*, which is generated by computing a hash of the transaction. Inputs and outputs are therefore uniquely identified by the ID of the transaction which contains them and their index in the input list and output list, respectively. An output $o_j \in T_o$ carries a value, which is the number of *satoshis* that this output is worth. A satoshi is defined to be such that one Bitcoin (BTC) equals 10^8 satoshis. The purpose of a transaction is to spend outputs by creating new ones, which represents the money flow. To do this, every input $i_j \in T_i$ uniquely references an output of another previous transaction, i.e., the ones which will be spent, and creates new outputs that can be spent by future transactions. An output can only be referenced once, and the outputs in the blockchain which have not been referenced at any given moment in time is called the set of *unspent outputs*. Every transaction carries an implicit *transaction fee*, which is the difference between the sum of the values of the outputs and the sum of the value of the referenced outputs. Transaction fees will be paid to the miners, which thus prioritize transactions based on their fees, i.e., the higher the fee, the faster the transaction will be mined. Since a block can only be 1 MiB in size, miners will usually consider transaction fees as a function of satoshis per byte of the transaction, i.e., the larger the transaction the larger the nominal value of the fee should be. Transaction fees are an essential economical element of the Bitcoin network and change constantly depending on the number of transactions in the mempool and how much peers are willing to pay the miners. Special transactions without any inputs referencing other outputs are so-called *coinbase* transactions and are created when a block is mined to reward the miner, which is how Bitcoins are initially created. That is, before a miner mines a block, they will first create a coinbase transaction which will be put in the block and rewards them with Bitcoins. This reward is a fixed amount, which gets halved every 210,000 blocks, plus the fees of all transactions in the block.

Scripts. Transactions in the Bitcoin network are verified by using a small stack-based language, the programs of which are called *scripts*. Every input and output contains a script, which is often referred to as scriptSig and scriptPubKey, respectively. These scripts can perform arithmetic, cryptography, flow control and so on. In order for a transaction to be valid, one must concatenate the scriptSig of each input with the scriptPubKey of its referenced output, which yields a new set of scripts, i.e., one for each input. All of these scripts are then evaluated, and for the transaction to be valid, there must be only one element on the stack after evaluation and this element must be equal to *true*. The scriptPubKey can therefore be considered a means of protection, i.e., one can only redeem an output if they can provide a correct scriptSig. The scripting language contains special instructions for elliptic curve cryptography, which is used within this scripting framework to cryptographically secure transactions. In this context, every user has a *secret key* sk and a *public key* pk. The most prevalent type of transaction is called a *Pay To Pubkey Hash* (P2PKH) transaction. Outputs belonging to such transactions have a scriptPubKey that verifies that the sender of the transaction possesses the correct public key by comparing it against a hash. Additionally, the script verifies a signature, which means that a working scriptSig must provide both the public key pk as well as a valid signature that can be verified with pk, which means that the sender must know sk.

Bitcoin Addresses. A Bitcoin address is a serialized hash of pk, which is generated by hashing the public key with the SHA-256 and the RIPMED-160 hash functions and appending and prepending a version byte and checksum bytes. The hash is then serialized using base58 encoding, which is a more human-readability-friendly version of the base64 encoding and removes ambiguous-looking characters (e.g., zero ("0") and capital o ("O")). An example of such an address is 16UwLL9Risc3QfPqBUvKofHmBQ7wMtjvM. Before hashing, pk must be serialized, for which there are two options, namely the *compressed* public key and the *uncompressed* public key. We omit the technical details here as they are not required for the scope of this paper. It is only important that both serialization options yield different addresses, which means that every public key pk corresponds to *two* addresses, which can be used independently of each other. This means that if an attacker leaks a secret key, they gain control over the *balances* of two addresses. We can define the balance of a P2PKH address by using the previously mentioned scripts. For instance, we determine that the balance of a P2PKH address encoding a hash h, is the sum of the values of all unspent outputs that can be redeemed with the public key pk that h is a hash for.

3   Explicit Key Leaks: Open Source Intelligence

In this section, we will outline the methodology that we use to discover explicit Bitcoin key leaks, i.e., cases where users (knowingly or not) directly disclose sensitive Bitcoin key material to the public. To this end, we follow the general idea of *open source intelligence* (OSINT), in which an attacker harvests publicly available information to derive sensitive information. To evaluate this idea in the context of Bitcoin secrets, we chose Pastebin as an OSINT platform. Given its popularity, we expect that Bitcoin users accidentally leak secret information there. Examples of such leaks would be users publishing code snippets doing Bitcoin transactions or the debug output of some wallet software which users want to share privately, not knowing that these *pastes* are then publicly visible in the Pastebin feed. We monitored all pastes starting from September 2017 and scanned each paste for Bitcoin secrets, i.e., secret keys.

3.1   Finding Bitcoin Secrets

To scan a paste for secret Bitcoin keys, we leverage the observation that Bitcoin keys are serialized using a well-known format. A secret key is an integer sk, which we will describe further in Sect. 4.1. An agreed-upon format for serializing those keys is the *Wallet Import Format* (WIF). To convert a secret key sk into this format, the following procedure is applied. First, sk is converted to a 32-bytes-long big-endian representation, which we call b. Then, 0x80 is prepended to b and optionally 0x01 is appended if the secret key will correspond to a compressed public key. Then SHA256 is applied twice on b, and we call the last four bytes of this hash c. The WIF is defined to be the base58 encoding of $b||c$.

The last 4 bytes in this format are a checksum for the remaining bytes, which is used in practice to avoid copy and paste mistakes. However, this checksum also allows a systematic scan for instances of WIF strings in text with a very low probability of false positives. In our Bitcoin monitoring tool, we thus proceed for each new paste as follows. First, we move a sliding window over the content of the paste to discover all valid base58 encoded substrings of the paste which are 51 or 52 characters long and start with either "5", "K" or "L". Both of these constraints are a consequence of the base58 encoding and the fact that the fixed byte 0x80 is prepended. For each string which matches these criteria, we compute and verify the checksum as described above. If the checksum verifies, we have found a valid WIF string and we can compute the corresponding secret key sk. Finally, we check if the secret key is in the valid range (cf. Sect. 4.1), and if this is the case, then we consider this key for further analysis.

3.2   Results

To apply our methodology, we monitored and scanned all public pastes on Paste-bin since September 2017. We identified 21,464 secret keys, which correspond to 42,936 addresses, i.e., 2 addresses per key as described in Sect. 2. However, most of these addresses are unused, i.e., there is no transaction in the blockchain which transferred Bitcoins from or to these addresses. As of now, 391 (0.91%) of those addresses held a balance at some point in time. However, for stealing Bitcoins it is not sufficient that an address held a balance at some point in time. Instead, we also have to take into account that the address held a balance *after* we have seen the corresponding secret key in a paste. If we respect this constraint, we find that 165 (0.38%) addresses held a balance after we have seen their secret key in a paste. Those keys were scattered among a total of 34 pastes. Summing up those balances gives a total of 326.70 BTC.

It should be mentioned, though, that this is still not a guarantee that this number of Bitcoins could have been stolen. This is due to the fact that we determine the balance of an address at some point in time based on the blockchain, not the mempool. That is, we take the latest block that was mined before the paste was published and check the balance of an affected address up to this block. It could be the case that there was a transaction in the meantime which redeemed outputs from the given address, i.e., there could be a pending transaction in the mempool. In this case, an attacker could not easily create a transaction to steal the Bitcoins. Current network rules discourage the distribution of transactions that double-spend outputs unless the transaction is explicitly marked as a *replace-by-fee* (RBF) transaction. An attacker could try to mine a stealing transaction themselves or try to directly announce the stealing transaction to mining pools which do not follow these network rules. Alternatively, if the blocking transaction has a low fee, the attacker could wait until a significant number of peers do not have the transaction in their copy of the mempool anymore. This would increase the chances that the new stealing transaction will be pushed to more peers, which in turn will increase the chances that the stealing transactions will be mined. However, none of these methods guarantees success, and therefore the amount of 326.70 BTC is an upper limit.

To get a more conservative estimation of the amount of stealable Bitcoins, we have to consider pending transactions. That is, we only considered cases where there was no transaction in between which was not marked as RBF. As it turns out, this was the case for 26 addresses in 119 pastes. For the remaining cases, there was a blocking transaction in between, i.e., the paste containing the secret key was published after the blocking transaction was distributed. For example, one paste contained an address holding a balance of 40.84 BTC for which a transaction was already placed in the mempool. In total, we found that an attacker could have stolen 22.40 BTC. We excluded transaction fees in this analysis as they are highly dynamic over time and the number of stealable outputs was so small that the resulting fees would not be a significant factor.

This demonstrates that an attacker can cause significant financial loss with relatively simple means. This is amplified by the fact that an attacker could expand this methodology to other cryptocurrencies and OSINT platforms.

4   Implicit Key Leaks: Incorrectly Used Cryptography

Seeing that even explicit key leaks pose a problem to Bitcoin users, in this section, we will study how users implicitly leak secrets. To this end, we will first describe the most important cryptographic primitive in Bitcoin, namely ECDSA. We then show how the incorrect use of this primitive opens severe vulnerabilities. That is, we will systematically describe how an attacker monitoring the transactions of the Bitcoin network can use nonce reuse to steal Bitcoins, and what amount of damage could have been caused (or was caused) in the past by attackers.

4.1   Elliptic Curve Digital Signature Algorithm (ECDSA)

Bitcoin uses the *Elliptic Curve Digital Signature Algorithm* (ECDSA) to cryptographically secure transactions. The scheme is based on the computational infeasibility assumption of solving the *Elliptic Curve Discrete Logarithm Problem* (ECDLP), i.e., given two points Q and Qk on the curve, there is no polynomial-time algorithm for recovering k. Bitcoin uses the *secp256k1* curve, which is based on the equation $y^2 = x^3 + 7$ over the finite field $\mathbb{F}_p$ with the

256-bit prime number $p = 2^{256} - 2^{32} - 2^9 - 2^8 - 2^7 - 2^6 - 2^4 - 1$. Furthermore, secp256k1 uses a *generator point* G with the 256-bit *group order* $n = 2^{256} -$ 0x14551231950B75FC4402DA1732FC9BEBF, i.e., n is the smallest number such that $Gn = 0$. To create and verify signatures, we need the notion of a secret key sk and a public key pk. In the context of elliptic curve cryptography, sk is a randomly chosen integer from $\{1, \ldots, n - 1\}$ and the public key pk can be derived by multiplying the generator G with sk, i.e., $pk = Gsk$. This derivation is considered secure, as recovering sk from pk would require solving ECDLP.

To sign a message m with a secret key sk using ECDSA, the following procedure is followed: First a hash of the message $h = H(m)$ is created using a cryptographic hash function H. The hash h is then interpreted as a number and truncated so that it does not contain more bits than the group order n. In the case of Bitcoin, we have $H = \text{SHA256}^2$, i.e., applying SHA256 twice, which means that h will not be truncated as n is a 256-bit number. Then, a random nonce k is chosen from $\{1, \ldots, n - 1\}$. After that, the r *value* is computed, which is the x-coordinate of the point that is yielded by multiplying the generator point G with k, which we denote by $r = (Gk)_x \bmod n$. Finally, the value $s = k^{-1}(h + r\text{sk}) \bmod n$ is computed and the tuple (r, s) is returned as the signature. If $r = 0$ or $s = 0$, then this procedure is repeated until both r and s are non-zero. To verify that (r, s) is a valid signature for a message m using the public key pk, one proceeds as follows: First the hash $h = H(m)$ is created and truncated as before. Then, the curve point $(x, y) = (Gh + pkr)s^{-1}$ is calculated and the signature is considered valid if $x = r$. The correctness follows from the observation that $pk = Gsk$, which implies $(Gh + pkr)s^{-1} = G(h + skr)s^{-1} = Gkss^{-1} = Gk$.

In terms of key or nonce leakage, note that the equation $s = k^{-1}(h + r\text{sk}) \bmod n$ contains two unknowns and therefore cannot be used to leak the secret key or the nonce. Recovering k from $r = (Gk)_x$ would require solving ECDLP, similar to how $pk = Gsk$ cannot be used to recover sk.

4.2   Using Duplicate Nonces to Leak Keys

It is known that ECDSA fails catastrophically if *nonce reuse* occurs. Nonce reuse means that there are multiple signatures using the same nonce k, which might allow an attacker to leak secret keys under certain circumstances. For instance, if the same k (and thereby the same r value) and sk are used to create 2 signatures (r, s_1) and (r, s_2) for two distinct messages m_1 and m_2, then we have[1]:

$$s_1 = k^{-1}(h_1 + r\text{sk}) \qquad s_2 = k^{-1}(h_2 + r\text{sk}), \qquad (1)$$

This allows leaking the secret key sk with:

$$\frac{s_2 h_1 - s_1 h_2}{r(s_1 - s_2)} = \frac{h_1 h_2 + rh_1\text{sk} - h_1 h_2 - rh_2\text{sk}}{rh_1 + r\text{sk} - rh_2 - r\text{sk}} = \frac{rh_1\text{sk} - rh_2\text{sk}}{rh_1 - rh_2} = \text{sk}. \qquad (2)$$

---

[1] Note that all calculations on signatures are done modulo n, which we omit for brevity.

Similarly, k can be leaked with:

$$\frac{h_1 - h_2}{s_1 - s_2} = \frac{h_1 - h_2}{k^{-1}(h_1 - h_2 + \mathsf{sk}(r - r))} = k. \tag{3}$$

However, not every kind of nonce reuse leads to cases where an attacker can leak secrets. For instance, consider the case where a nonce k is used with two different keys sk_1 and sk_2 to sign two distinct messages, i.e.,:

$$s_1 = k^{-1}(h_1 + r\mathsf{sk}_1) \qquad\qquad s_2 = k^{-1}(h_2 + r\mathsf{sk}_2). \tag{4}$$

It turns out that it is not possible in this case to leak any secrets. To get a better understanding of this, we need to consider the fundamental underlying problem that constitutes the act of leaking secrets in this setting. If we rewrite Eq. (1) to look as follows:

$$s_1 k - r\mathsf{sk} = h_1 \qquad\qquad s_2 k - r\mathsf{sk} = h_2$$

it becomes evident that this is a system of linear equations. In particular, this system consists of 2 linearly independent equations, since $h_1 \neq h_2$, and 2 unknowns, i.e., k and sk, and is therefore uniquely solvable. On the other hand, Eq. (4) consists of 2 equations and 3 unknowns, i.e., k, sk_1 and sk_2, and is therefore not uniquely solvable as there are more unknowns than equations.

4.3 Beyond Single-Key Nonce Reuse

Interestingly, in some cases secrets leak even though the nonces are not reused with the same secret key. For example, consider the following case, where two keys $\mathsf{sk}_1, \mathsf{sk}_2$ are used with the same pair of nonces k_1, k_2, i.e.,:

$$s_{1,1} = k_1^{-1}(h_{1,1} + r_1\mathsf{sk}_1) \qquad\qquad s_{1,2} = k_1^{-1}(h_{1,2} + r_1\mathsf{sk}_2)$$
$$s_{2,1} = k_2^{-1}(h_{2,1} + r_2\mathsf{sk}_1) \qquad\qquad s_{2,2} = k_2^{-1}(h_{2,2} + r_2\mathsf{sk}_2)$$

Here, no nonce is used twice by the same key, but nonces have been reused across keys. The system thus consists of 4 linearly independent equations and 4 unknowns and is thus uniquely solvable. A solution for sk_2 that can be computed, with Gaussian elimination for example, would be:

$$\mathsf{sk}_2 = \frac{r_1 s_{1,2}(h_{2,2}s_{2,1} - h_{2,1}s_{2,2}) - r_2 s_{2,2}(h_{1,2}s_{1,1} - h_{1,1}s_{1,2})}{r_1 r_2(s_{1,2}s_{2,1} - s_{1,1}s_{2,2})}.$$

In general, we can think of this problem as follows. An attacker is given a set of signatures $\mathcal{S} = \{(h_1, r_1, s_1, \mathsf{pk}_1), \ldots, (h_n, r_n, s_n, \mathsf{pk}_n)\}$, which can be extracted from the Bitcoin blockchain, for example. Each tuple $(h_i, r_i, s_i, \mathsf{pk}_i) \in \mathcal{S}$ corresponds to a signature $(r_i = (Gk_i)_x, s_i = k_i^{-1}(h_i + r\mathsf{sk}))$ where $\mathsf{pk} = G\mathsf{sk}$. The goal of the attacker is to leak as many keys (or nonces) as possible by solving systems of linear equations. To achieve this, an attacker has to identify subsets of solvable systems. They can do so by reducing this problem to graph theory.

For instance, we build an undirected bipartite graph $G = (V_{pk} \cup V_r, E)$, where $V_{pk} = \{pk_i \mid (\cdot, \cdot, \cdot, pk_i) \in \mathcal{S}\}$, $V_r = \{r_i \mid (\cdot, r_i, \cdot, \cdot) \in \mathcal{S}\}$ and $E = \{\{r_i, pk_i\} \mid (\cdot, r_i, \cdot, pk_i) \in \mathcal{S}\}$. The graph G consists of two types of nodes, r values r_i and public keys pk_i, each of which corresponds to an unknown (a nonce k_i and a secret key sk_i). An edge $\{r, pk\}$ in this graph corresponds to a signature, which in turn corresponds to an equation in the system of linear equations that $\mathcal{S}$ constitutes. As a pre-filtering step, we first collect all the r values and public keys that appear at least twice in conjunction, i.e., we collect $F = \{r, pk \mid |\{(\cdot, r, \cdot, pk) \in \mathcal{S}\}| > 1\}$. Since this corresponds to the same nonce being used by the same key at least twice, it means that we can leak the used secrets k and sk using Eqs. (3) and (2) with the appropriate signatures. Additionally, we can leak all the secrets which correspond to the nodes that are reachable by every public key and nonce in F. To understand this, assume we have an r value $r_i \in F$, which means that we can leak the nonce k_i as described. Now assume that there is a node $pk_j \in V_{pk}$ such that $\{r_i, pk_j\} \in E$, which implies the existence of the equation $s_j = k_i^{-1}(h_j + r sk_j)$. Since we know k_i, we can leak sk_j with $sk_j = \frac{s_j k_i - h_j}{r}$. The same is analogously true if we assume a public key $pk_i \in F$ and an r value $r_j \in V_r$ such that $\{r_j, pk_i\} \in E$. By applying this argument inductively, it becomes evident that we can leak the secrets associated with all nodes that are reachable from every $r_i \in F$ and every $pk_i \in F$.

In the next step, we need to identify the nodes and edges which can be mapped to a solvable system of linearly independent equations. This can be achieved by finding non-trivial *cycles* in G, i.e., distinct nodes $r_0, pk_0, \ldots, r_n, pk_n$ for $n > 0$ such that $\{r_i, pk_i\} \in E$ and $\{pk_i, r_{i+1 \mod n}\} \in E$ for $0 \leq i \leq n$. Such a cycle contains $2(n+1)$ nodes, i.e., unknowns, and $2(n+1)$ edges, i.e., equations, and thus directly implies the existence of a solvable system of linear equations. Hence, for all such cycles we can leak the corresponding secrets, and, as before, we can also leak the secrets of the reachable nodes. The output of this whole process is two sets $V'_{pk} \subseteq V_{pk}$ and $V'_r \subseteq V_r$, which are the public keys and r values for which we have leaked the secret keys and nonces, respectively. If we remove the nodes in $V'_{pk} \cup V'_r$ and their edges from G, the resulting graph should not contain any non-trivial cycles. This means that no more secrets can be leaked and hence V'_{pk} and V'_r are optimal with respect to their size.

There is, however, a little twist to the methodology we described here. We consider two signatures (r_1, s_1) and (r_2, s_2) a case of nonce reuse if the r values coincide, i.e., if $r_1 = r_2$. This is not strictly true, as the r value is only the x-coordinate of Gk. Since elliptic curves are based on a Weierstrass equation of the form $y^2 = x^3 + bx + a$, there are always two nonces k which lead to the same r value[2]. In particular, if we have $Gk = (x, y)$, then we have $G(-k) = (x, -y)$. This means that if the r values coincide, we need to take into account that one nonce might be the additive inverse of the other rather than being equal. To respect this, we must consider for every signature (r, s) the signature $(r, -s)$ as well, which is the signature that is yielded by negating k. For each such combination we have to solve the system of linear equations and check if the

---

[2] Recall that $r \neq 0$ (cf. Sect. 4.1).

returned solutions are correct to leak the correct keys and nonces. This can be done by double-checking that each leaked secret key sk corresponds to the given public key pk, which can be done by verifying the equality $G\text{sk} = \text{pk}$.

4.4   Results

We will now outline our results regarding nonce reuse in the Bitcoin blockchain. To achieve this, we downloaded a copy of the Bitcoin blockchain up until block 506071, which was mined on 2018-01-25 16:04:14 UTC. We parsed all inputs from all P2PKH transactions to extract their ECDSA signatures.

Table 1. The 10 most frequent r values and their number of occurrences.

r value	Occurrences
0x000000000000000000000003b78ce563f89a0ed9414f5aa28ad0d96d6795f9c63	2,276,718
0x00006fcf15e8d272d1a995af6fcc9d6c0c2f4c0b6b0525142e8af866dd8dad4b	7,895
0x1206589b08a84cb090431daa4f8d18934a20c8fa52ad534c5ba0abb3232be1d9	265
0x79be667ef9dcbbac55a06295ce870b07029bfcdb2dce28d959f2815b16f81798	251
0x2ef0d2ae4c49c37703ba16a3126e27763e124ff3338fb93577ed7bd79ed0d19e	91
0x06cce13d7911baa7856dec8c6358aaa1fb119b5a77d0e4d75d5a61acae05fcfb	83
0xd47ce4c025c35ec440bc81d99834a624875161a26bf56ef7fdc0f5d52f843ad1	76
0x281d3da7518241cd8ee30cd57ae3173a1bd9ee5e3b02a46ba30f25cd5b4c6aa8	68
0x8216f63d28f4dc0b6909a330d2af09b93df9dd3b853958c4d203d530328d8ed1	64
0x5d4eb477760cf19ff00fcb4bab0856de9e1ce7764d829a71d379367684712be4	52

In total, we extracted 647,110,920 signatures and we found 1,068 distinct r values appearing at least twice and used by 4,433 keys. In total, these duplicate r values make up for 2,290,850 (0.35%) of all r values. In Table 1, we show the top 10 most frequent duplicate r values along with their number of appearances. The most frequent duplicate r value appears 2,276,671 times, which makes up 99.38% of all duplicate occurrences. This r value is special, as it is extraordinary small, given that its 90 most significant bits are all 0. Additionally, the corresponding nonce k for this r value is $k = \frac{1}{2} \mod n$. As this is unlikely to be a coincidence, it is believed that the designers of the secp256k1 curve chose the generator point G based on these values. It is also believed that this r value is used on purpose by peers to save transaction fees. Bitcoin uses the DER encoding to serialize signatures, which can compress the leading bits of this r value, which reduces the transaction size and leads to smaller transaction fees. If peers use this nonce only for the "last" transaction of an address, i.e., the final transaction which removes all funds, then this should be secure as long as the transaction is marked as non-replaceable. But since this transaction still leaks the secret key of the address, the peer needs to make sure that they will never use the address again. Our analysis revealed that this r value was primarily used in two time periods. The first block which contains this value is block 364,767 and the last one is block 477,411. In total, we identified 1,550 blocks which contain this r value. We found that the r value was used excessively in 2 time periods, which is depicted in Fig. 1. We can see that between block 365,000 and block 366,000 and between block 374,000 and block 375,000, the value is used roughly 1 million times each, which makes up almost all of its appearances.

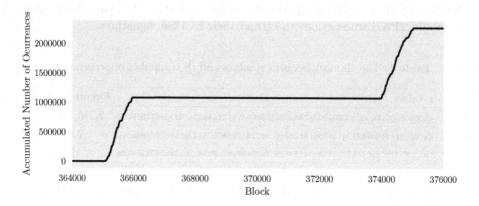

Fig. 1. Number of occurrences of the most prominent duplicate r value over time.

Inspecting the other duplicate r values a bit more closely reveals further interesting cases. The second most used r value also has 16 leading 0 bits, which is also an indication that the corresponding nonce was not chosen randomly. The fourth most used r value corresponds to the nonce $k = 1$, which is an indication of either a broken random number generator or a hand-crafted transaction where the nonce was not randomized and the creator simply took the x-coordinate of G. Another r value we found was using the nonce $k = 12345678$, which is also an indication of an ad-hoc generated transaction using a fixed nonce rather than a secure random one. Similarly, we found two other r values where the corresponding nonces where suspiciously small, i.e., in one case the nonce was $k = \texttt{0x80001fff}$ and in another case the nonce also had 74 leading 0 bits. In another case the nonce was $k = \sum_{i=0}^{32} 16^i$, i.e., $\texttt{0x0101...01}$ in hexadecimal notation, which looks like a pattern that a human would produce.

4.5   Measuring the Impact of Weak Nonces

We will now assess how much damage an attacker could have caused by using the previously described methodology for leaking keys and nonces. To do this, we put ourselves in the position of an attacker who monitors the transactions of the blockchain. That is, we use our copy of the blockchain to create an ordered sequence of signatures $[(\Delta_1, h_1, r_1, s_1, \mathsf{pk}_1), \ldots, (\Delta_n, h_n, r_n, s_n, \mathsf{pk}_n)]$ where Δ_i is a block number such that $\Delta_i \leq \Delta_j$ for $i \leq j$ and the remaining elements are the components of a signature found in a transaction of block Δ_i. We then process these entries in order as follows. We add each signature $s_i = k^{-1}(h_i + r_i)$ for a public key pk_i in block Δ_i to a database, which allows us to quickly identify duplicate r values as well as their signatures. Each identified duplicate r value r_i is then added to the graph G along with the used public key pk_i. However, before adding these 2 nodes to the graph, we make a few checks. First, we check if we have leaked both k_i and sk_i, in which case we can completely disregard both, as adding them will not lead to new leaks. Second, we check if G already contains the edge $\{r_i, \mathsf{pk}_i\}$, in which case we can leak both k_i and sk_i. Third, we check if we have already leaked either k_i or sk_i, in which case we can then leak sk_i or k_i, respectively. In the last two cases, we can also leak the secrets corresponding to all the nodes reachable from both r_i and pk_i as discussed previously. Only if none of these three conditions apply, we add the edge $\{r_i, \mathsf{pk}_i\}$ to G. After processing all signatures of a block, we look for cycles in G to identify solvable systems of linear equations in order to leak secrets as outlined previously. Whenever we find a new leak, we make sure that we remove the corresponding signatures from the database and that we remove the corresponding nodes and their edges from G, as we will otherwise redundantly reconsider the same r values and cycles.

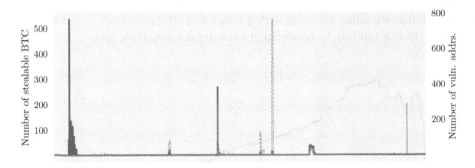

Fig. 2. Number of stealable Bitcoins + number of vulnerable Bitcoin addresses attributed to ECDSA nonce reuse over time.

Using this methodology, we managed to leak 892 out of the 1,550 possible nonces (57.55%) and 2,537 out of the 4,433 secret keys that were used in conjunction with these nonces (57.23%). In total, this gives us theoretical control over the balances of 5,074 addresses, i.e., two addresses per key. During this whole operation we identified 23 cycles in the graph and the longest cycle consisted of 12 nodes, which represents a system of 12 linear equations and 12 unknowns (6 nonces + 6 secret keys). The final shape of G did not contain any more cycles, which means that we have leaked the maximum number of secrets.

Figure 2 depicts the number of Bitcoins that an attacker could have stolen at any point in time, i.e., the block height, as well as the number of *vulnerable* addresses at each moment in time. We consider an address at a certain block vulnerable if we have leaked the key of the address and if it held a balance at that block. There are a few notable spikes for both the number of stealable Bitcoins as well as the number of vulnerable addresses. The first significant spike occurs roughly between block 221,000 and block 227,000, where the peak stealable balance is 533.82 BTC. Interestingly, there was only one vulnerable address during this spike. The next spike occurs roughly between block 296,000 and block 298,000 with a peak stealable balance of 20 BTC, which was stealable for a timespan of 3 blocks from block 297283 until block 297285. From block 297,261 up to block 297,304 there were 90 vulnerable addresses, which is also the maximum number of vulnerable addresses of the spike. The next spike is slightly shorter and happens at around block 333,300 and lasts roughly until block 333,600. During this timespan, an attacker could have stolen up to 266.73 BTC at block 333,387 and there were 290 peak vulnerable addresses at block 333,393. This is followed by two similarly long-lasting spikes between blocks 365,000 and 366,000 and blocks 374,000 and 375,000. In the former case, 11.21 BTC was stealable and there were 131 vulnerable addresses at some point, and in the latter case 15.41 BTC was stealable and there were 769 vulnerable addresses from block 374,386 to 374,386. This is also the largest number of addresses that were vulnerable at a time over the whole timespan. Finally, while the number of vulnerable addresses suddenly jumps to 289 at block 475,963, there are only 0.0064 BTC stealable at the peak. At the current state of our copy of the blockchain, there are 5 vulnerable addresses holding an accumulated balance of 4002 satoshis, i.e., 0.00004002 BTC, which is unlikely to be stolen given current transaction fees.

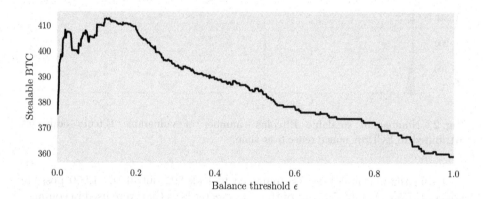

Fig. 3. Number of Bitcoins an attacker could have stolen based on a balance threshold.

To assess how much an attacker could have stolen over time, we consider two scenarios. First, we assume an attacker which steals the peak balance of each address over time. That is, we take the sum of the peak balances of each address, which gives a total of 1021.58 BTC. Here, we implicitly assume that the owner notices the fraud and therefore we ignore all future funds. However, this attack model requires an attacker to know the peak balance in advance, which is unrealistic. Therefore, we consider a second more realistic attacking scenario in which an attacker defines a balance threshold ϵ. In this setting, an attacker only steals a balance if it is equal to or larger than ϵ and we assume again that we can only steal once from an address. Figure 3 plots the number of Bitcoins that an attacker could have stolen in this scenario depending on ϵ. We let ϵ range between 0 and 1 BTC with 0.001 increments. The optimal balance threshold according to the plotted function is $\epsilon = 0.125$, which an attacker could have used to steal 412.80 BTC. Note that even though one address alone had a balance of 533.82 BTC at some point, it does not mean that an attacker in this setting can steal it completely. This is because we assume that we can steal only once from an address once its balance surpasses the balance threshold ϵ, after which we conservatively assume that the owner of the address becomes aware of the problem. While this means that choosing a large ϵ such as $\epsilon = 500$ BTC would yield a larger profit for the attacker, we believe that it is not an optimal choice. Given the current value of Bitcoin, we believe that it is unrealistic for a single individual to hold such a large balance. Additionally, if we assume that there are multiple competing attackers, then we also have to take this into consideration when choosing ϵ. We therefore let ϵ range between 0 and 1 BTC as we believe that this is a good compromise between what is currently practical and what is optimal in theory. After said optimum, the number of BTC starts to decrease steeply, and for $\epsilon = 1$, there are 359.04 stealable Bitcoins, i.e., 13.02% less than in the optimal case. Similar to our previous OSINT analysis in Sect. 3.2, we also ignored transaction fees here due to their negligible impact. Additionally, we also did not consider blocking transactions in this case, as an attacker monitoring transactions can create stealing transactions as soon as possible.

4.6   Identifying Past Attacks

Given that the phenomenon of ECDSA nonce reuse is a known problem, we now try to assess if it has been used by attackers in the past to steal Bitcoins. To do this, we tried to identify for each of the 7 spikes in Fig. 2 the moment in time when the number of stealable Bitcoins suddenly dropped. Then we tried to find transactions, which were created during that time and whose outputs referenced inputs of many vulnerable addresses. In the case of the first spike, it is hard to argue whether it was used by an attacker as only 1 address was vulnerable in this timespan. However, we identified several cases where the balance of the address suddenly dropped by over 99.99%, which one could argue is an incident where Bitcoins have been stolen. In the second, third, sixth and seventh spike we found cases where the number of stealable Bitcoins decreased suddenly and we identified in all cases a single transactions referencing all the responsible vulnerable addresses, which makes us believe that Bitcoins were stolen. In the case of the last spike, however, only 0.00064 BTC were stolen.

Regarding the fourth and fifth spike, we did not observe a similar suspicious drop regarding the number of Bitcoins, but only regarding the number of vulnerable addresses. To see the difference, consider Fig. 4, which shows and compares a zoomed in view of the second and the fifth spike. In the former, we

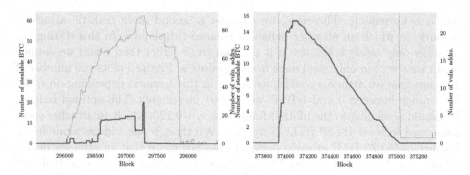

Fig. 4. Comparison of a spike where Bitcoins might have been stolen due to a sudden drop in stealable Bitcoins (left) and a case where we see a smooth decrease indicating that no coins might have been stolen (right).

can see a sudden drop in the number of stealable Bitcoins, i.e., while there are 7.49 stealable BTC at block 297,304, there are only 0.2 BTC stealable at block 297,305. We identified a single transaction which transferred all the stealable Bitcoins, indicating a theft. The fact that the number of vulnerable addresses did not decrease to 0 at the same time can be explained by various reasons. For instance, it could be possible that the attacker was not aware of the remaining vulnerable addresses. Or, it could be the case that the attacker used a balance threshold and determined that the remaining addresses are not worth stealing from based on this threshold, because as we can see, the 0.2 BTC are shared among 86 vulnerable addresses. In the second spike in Fig. 4, we observe a smooth and monotone decrease over time regarding the number of stealable Bitcoins and then a sudden decrease of the number of vulnerable addresses at the same time the stealable BTC drop. This phenomenon could be explained by the fact that all the addresses belong to the same individual and that at the end all the so-called *change addresses* are emptied by the wallet. Change addresses are addresses which are used to accumulate leftover transaction outputs. For example, if an address A wants to send 1 BTC to an address B using a single output, which is worth 5 BTC, then the resulting transaction will create two outputs, one that is worth 1 BTC and can be spent by address B and one that is worth 4 BTC and can be spent by a change address that belongs to the owner of A. The final transaction of the wallet will then use all accumulated outputs of the change addresses, which could be an explanation for the sudden drop.

5   Discussion

In this section, we will consider the ethical aspects of our work and describe how the problem of key leakage of cryptocurrencies can be tackled.

5.1 Ethical Considerations

Given that we systematically describe how attackers can steal Bitcoins abusing leaked keys, we have to address the ethical aspects that come along with such a work. On the one hand, we believe that raising awareness of these attack vectors is fundamental and important to improve the security of the cryptocurrency ecosystem. On the other hand, one could argue that the amount of detail we put into outlining these methods is not beneficial as it allows for easy reproducibility by attackers. Yet we believe that this is the right way to tackle this problem as "security by obscurity" has proven in the past to be an insufficient means in the area of security. We also note that ECDSA nonce reuse is known to be a problem and it has been reported in forum posts that this phenomenon has occurred in the Bitcoin blockchain [5–7]. However, as we have shown in Sect. 4.4, this apparently known problem still regularly occurs and is abused by attackers, with the latest case of nonce reuse appearing in a block mined on 2017-07-15. This constant recurrence leads us to believe that it will happen again, unless we emphasize this problem better, which is why we outline the attack in detail.

Another ethical aspect of dealing with attacks on cryptocurrencies is that a responsible disclosure process in terms of notifying the victims is not trivial. A fundamental downside here is that Bitcoin itself is decentralized by design and intends to ensure the anonymity (or pseudonymity) of the peers. This means that (i) we have no dedicated point of contact, which we could inform about our findings and (ii) we cannot reach out to the legitimate owners of the vulnerable addresses. We tried to handle this problem as responsibly as possible and refrain from disclosing problematic addresses and/or transactions. For example, we did not mention any vulnerable addresses or URLs to pastes containing them, as we cannot be sure that the owners of those addresses are aware of the vulnerability. While an attacker can reproduce our methodology to find any future vulnerable addresses using Pastebin, it should not be easily possible to find the addresses we have discovered, since the Pastebin feed only lists the most current 250 pastes. While Pastebin can be searched using standard search engines like Google, it should be very hard to discover the pastes we have found, since search engines only offer a keyword-based search, rather than a regex-based search which would be required to find the addresses. In our ECDSA case study, we also did not mention any vulnerable addresses. However, an attacker can fully reproduce our results here, as the Bitcoin blockchain contains all the necessary historical information. Therefore, not mentioning vulnerable addresses is not as effective as in the case of our OSINT case study. Yet we also do not see a reason to do so, as one could argue that this makes it too easy for an attacker.

5.2 Countermeasures

Explicitly leaking keys is not strictly a technical problem, as users seemingly publish private information without knowing the consequences of doing so. However, there are some technical solutions that could be applied on OSINT platforms. For example, Pastebin could include a check in their logic, which scans pastes for secrets such as Bitcoin secret keys encoded in the WIF format. In fact, they could provide immediate feedback to users about the security implications of pasting such content. We have therefore contacted Pastebin with a detailed description of our work, proposing to adopt such a methodology.

To avoid ECDSA nonce reuse, there are a few solutions that can be applied. One such solution proposed by RFC 6979 [19] is to choose the nonce k deterministically based on the message m and the key sk. As inputs differ, this scheme provides unique nonces and hardens against nonce reuse. However, since this solution is backwards-compatible with the existing ECDSA scheme, it also means that peers do not *have to* follow this proposal. In particular, one cannot verify that a signature has been created with the deterministic nonce choice as proposed by RFC 6979. Another way of dealing with this problem is to incorporate a duplicate nonce check into the Bitcoin protocol. For example, a check for duplicate r values could be incorporated into the transaction verification process. Each peer verifies each transaction of a block, which includes verifying the signature and other sanity checks. Here, the protocol could also support a check for duplicate r values, i.e., checking, for each r value of each signature, if it already occurs in the blockchain. From a performance perspective, a Bloom filter could help to scale this process. The more peers follow this, the less likely it will become that a transaction containing a duplicate r value will be added to the blockchain. However, an attacker monitoring the mempool instead of the blockchain might still be able to observe transactions containing duplicate r values. Therefore, one would need to additionally adapt the network rules such that a new rule is added, which discourages the distribution of transactions which contain duplicate nonces. If such a transaction reaches a peer which follows this new set of rules, the duplicate r value will be detected and the transaction will not be relayed further. Additionally, the peer sending the transaction should be notified with an error message about the problem to create awareness. The more peers follow this new set of rules, the less likely it becomes that transactions containing duplicate r values are distributed among the network. In total, we believe that the adoption of all proposals, i.e., deterministic ECDSA and adapting the network rules as well as the transaction verification process, are sufficient means to eliminate nonce reuse from cryptocurrencies.

6   Related Work

In this section we discuss other work in the areas of OSINT, Bitcoin key leakage and ECDSA nonce reuse, and how they relate to our work.

OSINT has been applied before to expose or harvest privacy-related information. Matic et al. [16] performed a study in which they monitored the Pastebin feed between late 2011 and early 2012 to develop a framework for detecting sensitive information in pastes. They discovered almost 200,000 compromised accounts of several websites as well as lists of compromised servers or leaked database dumps. In a slightly different vein, Sabottke et al. [20] design a Twitter-based exploit detector that can predict vulnerabilities such as code execution or

Denial-of-Service attacks solely based on tweets. Similarly, Zhu et al. [24] show how they can use academic security literature as OSINT to automatically engineer features for malware detection. While all of these works show the potential of OSINT, they are only remotely related to our work as our use case is different.

In terms of leaking Bitcoin secrets to steal money, there have been a few other papers targeting this problem. Vasek et al. [22] have outlined how one can attack passphrase-based wallets (*brain wallets*). The authors developed a tool called *Brainflayer*, which uses brute force and a dictionary to generate weak passphrases, which would have allowed an attacker to steal Bitcoins worth $100,000 at that time. This approach is similar to ours in the sense that an attacker exploits the fact that users treat sensitive information wrongly, i.e., passphrases in the case of Brainflayer and secret keys or nonces in our case. In contrast to searching for weak passphrases, we harvest OSINT and cryptographic primitives. More related are works by Castellucci et al. [10] and Valsorda [21], which both consider ECDSA nonce reuse with respect to Bitcoin. However, both only cover the basic case, where a nonce is used in conjunction with the same key twice. We generalize this concept to systems of linear equations and systematically outline how an attacker can use a graph-based approach to leak secrets.

The general problem of nonce reuse in respect to ECDSA (or the closely related DSA scheme) has been studied in other contexts. A notable incident occurred in 2010, when it was discovered that Sony reused the same nonce to sign software for the PlayStation 3 game console [8]. Furthermore, Heninger et al. [14] studied the impact of weak keys and nonce reuse in the case of TLS and SSH servers. The authors collected over 9 million signatures and found that 0.05% of these signatures contained the same r value as at least one other signature. Additionally, the authors used a subset of those signatures where a key and a nonce appear in conjunction at least twice to leak 281 secret keys. Apart from studying a different use case, i.e., Bitcoin, our work is different here in that we systematically outline how an attacker can leak keys, which goes beyond the simple case where the same key and nonce is used more than once.

7   Conclusion

We have studied the problem of implicit and explicit key leakage in the context of cryptocurrencies, which shows how an attacker can leverage OSINT or duplicate nonces to leak secret keys. Our case studies have shown the practical relevance of these issues. An attacker monitoring Pastebin or scanning transactions for nonce reuse could have stolen up to 22.40 BTC and 412.80 BTC, respectively. Our work emphasizes aspects that are important for both the users and the developers of cryptocurrencies. For instance, our Pastebin case study shows the importance of making users aware of how to deal with cryptocurrency secrets. Our results regarding ECDSA show that nonce reuse is a recurring problem and highlight the benefits of incorporating countermeasures on the protocol level. In the case that cryptocurrencies become even more popular, it will become more lucrative for miscreants to perform key leakage attacks similar to the ones we described here. This highlights the importance of our research, which apart from creating awareness of the problem, also can foster future research on the topic of explicit and implicit key leakage in the context of cryptocurrencies.

Acknowledgement. This work was supported by the European Union's Horizon 2020 research and innovation programme, RAMSES, under grant agreement No. 700326.

References

1. https://coinmarketcap.com/currencies/bitcoin/. Accessed 27 Mar 2018
2. https://coinmarketcap.com/currencies/ethereum/. Accessed 27 Mar 2018
3. https://pastebin.com. Accessed 27 Mar 2018
4. https://bitcoin.org/en/alert/2013-08-11-android. Accessed 27 Mar 2018
5. https://bitcointalk.org/index.php?topic=581411.0. Accessed 27 Mar 2018
6. https://bitcointalk.org/index.php?topic=1118704.0. Accessed 27 Mar 2018
7. https://bitcointalk.org/index.php?topic=1431060.0. Accessed 27 Mar 2018
8. https://events.ccc.de/congress/2010/Fahrplan/attachments/1780_27c3_console_hacking_2010.pdf (2010). Accessed 27 Mar 2018
9. Back, A.: Hashcash - a denial of service counter-measure (2002)
10. Castellucci, R., Valsorda, F.: Stealing Bitcoin with Math. https://news.webamooz.com/wp-content/uploads/bot/offsecmag/151.pdf. Accessed 27 Mar 2018
11. Decker, C., Wattenhofer, R.: Bitcoin transaction malleability and MtGox. In: Proceedings of the European Symposium on Research in Computer Security (ESORICS) (2014)
12. Diffie, W., Hellman, M.: New directions in cryptography. IEEE Trans. Inf. Theory **22**, 644–654 (1976)
13. Eskandari, S., Barrera, D., Stobert, E., Clark, J.: A first look at the usability of bitcoin key management. In: Proceedings of the Workshop on Usable Security (USEC) (2015)
14. Heninger, N., Durumeric, Z., Wustrow, E., Halderman, J.A.: Mining your Ps and Qs: detection of widespread weak keys in network devices. In: Proceedings of the USENIX Security Symposium (USENIX Security) (2012)
15. Koblitz, N.: Elliptic curve cryptosystems. Math. Comput. **48**, 203–209 (1987)
16. Matic, S., Fattori, A., Bruschi, D., Cavallaro, L.: Peering into the muddy waters of pastebin. ERCIM News (2012)
17. Nakamoto, S.: Bitcoin: a peer-to-peer electronic cash system (2008)
18. Naware, A.M.: Bitcoins, its advantages and security threats. Int. J. Adv. Res. Comput. Eng. Technol. (IJARCET) **5**, 1732–1735 (2016)
19. Pornin, T.: Deterministic usage of the digital signature algorithm (DSA) and elliptic curve digital signature algorithm (ECDSA) (2013). https://rfc-editor.org/rfc/rfc6979.txt
20. Sabottke, C., Suciu, O., Dumitras, T.: Vulnerability disclosure in the age of social media: exploiting Twitter for predicting real-world exploits. In: Proceedings of the USENIX Security Symposium (USENIX Security) (2015)
21. Valsorda, F.: Exploiting ECDSA failures in the bitcoin blockchain. In: Proceedings of Hack In The Box (HITB) (2014)
22. Vasek, M., Bonneau, J., Castellucci, R., Keith, C., Moore, T.: The bitcoin brain drain: examining the use and abuse of bitcoin brain wallets. In: Grossklags, J., Preneel, B. (eds.) FC 2016. LNCS, vol. 9603, pp. 609–618. Springer, Heidelberg (2017). https://doi.org/10.1007/978-3-662-54970-4_36

23. Wood, G.: Ethereum: a next-generation smart contract and decentralized application platform (2018). https://ethereum.github.io/yellowpaper/paper.pdf. Accessed 27 Mar 2018
24. Zhu, Z., Dumitras, T.: FeatureSmith: automatically engineering features for malware detection by mining the security literature. In: Proceedings of the Conference on Computer and Communications Security (CCS) (2016)

Defenses

Furnace: Self-service Tenant VMI for the Cloud

Micah Bushouse$^{(\boxtimes)}$ and Douglas Reeves

North Carolina State University, Raleigh, NC, USA
{mbushou,reeves}@ncsu.edu

Abstract. Although Virtual Machine Introspection (VMI) tools are increasingly capable, modern multi-tenant cloud providers are hesitant to expose the sensitive hypervisor APIs necessary for tenants to use them. Outside the cloud, VMI and virtualization-based security's adoption rates are rising and increasingly considered necessary to counter sophisticated threats. This paper introduces *Furnace*, an open source VMI framework that outperforms prior frameworks by satisfying both a cloud provider's expectation of security and a tenant's desire to run their own custom VMI tools underneath their cloud VMs. Furnace's flexibility and ease of use is demonstrated by porting four existing security and monitoring tools as Furnace *VMI apps*; these apps are shown to be resource efficient while executing up to 300x faster than those in previous VMI frameworks. Furnace's security properties are shown to protect against the actions of malicious tenant apps.

Keywords: Cloud security · Virtual machine introspection
Sandboxing

1 Introduction

Modern multi-tenant clouds offer their tenants accessible, affordable, and flexible computing resources. The industry is booming; some clouds are growing 40% year over year,[1] and public clouds such as Amazon Web Services (AWS), Microsoft Azure, and Google Compute Engine are relied upon to power customers' most critical systems. While clouds are increasingly essential, tenant security is a growing concern. After migrating to the cloud, tenants are unable to use Virtual Machine Introspection (VMI) for low-level security and system monitoring of their virtual machines. This lack of capability contrasts with developments outside of the cloud; since 2003, when *Livewire* [12] used a series of cleverly designed tools to infer guest activity, hypervisor-based techniques have gradually matured and are now adopted by major OS vendors,[2] antivirus companies,[3] and hypervisors [19].

---

[1] 2017 Roundup of Cloud Computing Forecasts, https://goo.gl/pJ9uj2.

[2] Microsoft Virtualization-Based Security: https://goo.gl/eixiqr.

[3] BitDefender Hypervisor Introspection: https://goo.gl/MrZFQj.

© Springer Nature Switzerland AG 2018
M. Bailey et al. (Eds.): RAID 2018, LNCS 11050, pp. 647–669, 2018.
https://doi.org/10.1007/978-3-030-00470-5_30

Hypervisor-based tools are important; as attacks have become more sophisticated, defenders increasingly rely on these tools to provide powerful methods for malware analysis and forensics [8,17], kernel integrity enforcement [28], surreptitious monitoring [5], and attack detection and response [10]. Cloud providers do not currently provide an interface for their tenants (customers) to use this growing body of hypervisor-based tools [4,15,24], and this absence of VMI in the cloud is a security gap.

The mechanism to provide tenants (or their managed security providers) with this access, a cloud VMI framework, allows the deployment of a tenant's VMI tools underneath their VMs. To be successful, a framework must satisfy two requirements. First, it must protect the cloud provider from potentially malicious tenant-supplied VMI tools. Second, it must enable these same tools to be full-featured, fast, and resource-efficient. Both requirements depend on how a framework provides access to the normally-inaccessible, privileged hypervisor APIs that VMI tools require.

There have been a variety of proposals for cloud VMI frameworks, including *CloudVMI's* [2] network-based RPC, *LiveCloudInspector's* [29] provider-curated VMI API, and *CloudPhylactor's* [27] hypervisor access control scheme. No proposal has yet met the expectations of both cloud providers and tenants. CloudVMI is slow and insufficiently secure; LiveCloudInspector provides only limited tenant VMI capabilities; and, CloudPhylactor is too costly in resources.

This paper introduces *Furnace*, an open source cloud VMI framework that leverages automated tool deployment, a software abstraction layer, and strong sandboxing to provide tenants the ability to run VMI apps directly on the cloud provider's hypervisors. A tenant writes their app using an extended version of the popular LibVMI API [19], then submits the app through Furnace's cloud API. Furnace runs the app in a sandbox on the appropriate provider hypervisor.

Furnace is underpinned by its three-partition sandbox, which uses a set of well-accepted and well-tested security mechanisms to aggressively whitelist tenant app behavior. Tenant app code runs deprivileged in the sandbox's main partition and performs work by making IPC cross-calls to Furnace-provided resource brokers in adjacent partitions. Despite the overhead of sandboxing, an app achieves similar performance to a native VMI tool through an approach called *VMI call pipelining*; this pipelining reduces IPC-related overhead by exploiting the predictability of VMI calls.

Furnace is evaluated for its ease of use, security, and performance. Furnace's flexible API is used to port four VMI-related tools, including Rekall[4] and a syscall tracer. Furnace's security claims hold against malicious tenant apps, sandbox enumeration, and fuzzing. Finally, benchmarking shows that a Furnace app approaches the speed of a native VMI tool and is up to 300x faster than Cloud-VMI.

This paper makes the following contributions:

1. The design of an open source cloud VMI framework that meets the security, performance, and feature expectations of cloud providers and their tenants.

---

[4] http://www.rekall-forensic.com/.

2. A practical, partitioned sandbox design that combines overlapping security mechanisms with a resource broker model.
3. A rich tenant API optimized for performance through VMI call pipelining.

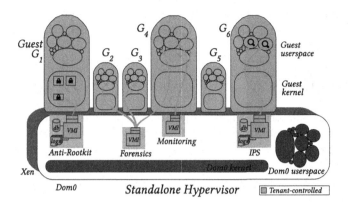

Fig. 1. Under guest G_1, an anti-rootkit VMI tool ensures kernel integrity. The forensics tool under G_2, G_3, and G_4 extracts process memory images. The monitoring tool under G_4 uses breakpoint injection to trace events occurring inside guest userspace processes. Finally, an intrusion prevention tool inspects new G_6 processes. The differing sizes of guests in the diagram indicate the variety of instance types, operating systems, and configurations found in modern clouds.

2   VMI Background

Virtual Machine Introspection (VMI) is a set of techniques to infer and influence a virtual machine's activity based on the interception, interpretation, and modification of a VM's raw bit patterns in its main memory, vCPU registers, and disk [12]. Some tools reason directly about a guest's raw memory contents, while others reconstruct a guest's high-level semantics [4,15,24]. VMI tools can also subscribe to guest events that result in VM exits, such as guest vCPU register activity, software breakpoints, and extended page table violations. In general, VMI tools offer compelling advantages over building features into a guest operating system and installing agents in a guest's userspace:

- *Privilege.* An ability to freely read and modify guest memory and vCPUs.
- *Stealthiness.* The difficulty for a guest to detect underlying VMI tools.
- *Transience.* Tools can be quickly added and removed from under a guest.
- *Visibility.* All guest layers—drivers, kernel, process, data—are observable.
- *Impunity.* A general resistance to guest attempts at interference [3,15].

Most VMI tools are designed to run on a standalone hypervisor similar to the one shown in Fig. 1, where they run as root and link directly into hypervisor

VMI APIs. This paper refers to these tools as *native VMI tools*. Specifically in the case of Xen, the hypervisor used in this work, native VMI tools typically run in Xen's privileged management domain, dom0, where VMI APIs are exposed.

While VMI's advantages often benefit security-related tools, VMI supports other use cases, including guest monitoring [1,5].

This paper introduces Furnace, a self-service framework that enables multiple cloud tenants to run VMI tools under their VMs without sacrificing either security or performance.

3   Design Goals

A cloud VMI framework's primary objective is to provide tenants with controlled access to the privileged hypervisor APIs necessary for VMI. The framework must meet two expectations. First, if a cloud provider does not feel the framework provides this access safely, the framework will not be adopted. Second, the framework's users (the tenants) must also feel it is fast, cheap, and useful enough to meet their goals.

Prior Work. The idea of a cloud VMI framework is not new, yet existing proposals have flaws that can be categorized into three types:

—*The RPC model.* One of the early frameworks was *CloudVMI (CV)* [2], which exposed an RPC server on the hypervisor. CV was flexible and easy to use because tenant VMI tools simply had to be re-compiled against CV. At runtime, these tools could then connect to a hypervisor's CloudVMI RPC server remotely across the network and have their VMI calls relayed to the hypervisor's VMI APIs. Although not implemented by CV, this method could be made reasonably secure by RPC message gateways, authentication, and encryption. However, CV's major flaw is speed. A RPC call is issued for each VMI call. Because VMI calls are analogous to individual memory accesses, this can result in hundreds of RPC network round trips per second.

—*The preset model.* *LiveCloudInspector (LCI)* [29] presents tenants with a preset list of VMI capabilities to choose from. Since the capabilities are developed and controlled by the cloud provider and activated via a simple, controlled interface, the risk that a malicious tenant could abuse them is reduced. LCI is likely faster than CV because (similar to a native VMI tool) its code runs directly on the hypervisor. However, LCI's problem is not with speed, but with choice. If a tenant's desired VMI action is not offered by the provider, they would have no reason to use the framework. This proposal also places the burden to create and maintain VMI capabilities on the cloud provider—a difficult proposition because typically VMI profiles must be maintained for every possible tenant kernel [15].

—*The VM model.* Most recently, *CloudPhylactor (CP)* [27] implemented per-VM security policies on the hypervisor that granted the ability for a tenant VM to perform VMI on a second, adjacent tenant VM. This method is fast because it uses the same APIs as native tools, and it is also flexible because a tenant is in full control of the VM performing VMI. CP's disadvantage is cost, both in terms of resources and effort. First, for each VM to be inspected, a tenant must provision (and pay for) a corresponding monitoring VM. Only a fraction of this VM's resources will end up directly supporting the VMI tool; the VM's kernel and userspace require resources as well. Second, the tenant is now responsible for managing, maintaining, and operating up to twice as many VMs along with the set of VMI tools in each.

Table 1. Desirable properties for a cloud VMI framework

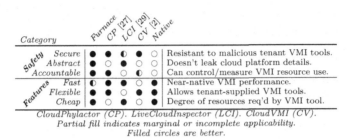

Category	Furnace	CP [27]	LCI [29]	CV [2]	Native	
Safety						
Secure	●	●	◐	●	○	Resistant to malicious tenant VMI tools.
Abstract	●	○	●	○	○	Doesn't leak cloud platform details.
Accountable	●	●	○	◐	○	Can control/measure VMI resource use.
Features						
Fast	◐	●	●	○	●	Near-native VMI performance.
Flexible	●	●	○	●	●	Allows tenant-supplied VMI tools.
Cheap	●	○	●	○	●	Degree of resources req'd by VMI tool.

CloudPhylactor (CP). LiveCloudInspector (LCI). CloudVMI (CV).
Partial fill indicates marginal or incomplete applicability.
Filled circles are better.

Requirements. Table 1 shows the desirable properties for a VMI framework[5] and compares Furnace with prior work. For illustration purposes, the table also includes the native VMI tool model where tenants use privileged accounts on the hypervisor—this model lacks any protection from malicious users. Each property is briefly discussed below.

Safety. To protect the cloud, a *secure* cloud VMI framework should contain or filter tenant VMI code to ensure it cannot execute in an unintended or uncontrolled manner. A framework should also uphold the cloud's *abstraction* model so a tenant VMI tool is prevented from inferring private cloud implementation details, i.e., a tenant should not be able to abuse the framework to determine which hypervisor is hosting their VM or what other VMs are co-resident. Finally, a framework should *account* for, measure, and control a tenant VMI tool's resource usage. This is necessary for billing and to prevent the possibility of (intentional or accidental) resource exhaustion.

Features. A tenant's VMI tool should be suitably useful and powerful. A framework should strive to run tools as *fast* as a native VMI tool. Designs that impose heavy runtime overheads are undesirable. In order to be useful, a framework should be *flexible* and expressive, allowing tenants to easily design their own custom tools. Finally, a tenant VMI tool should be *cheap*, both easy to build and inexpensive to run. This means a cloud framework should automate the deployment, execution, and management of a tenant's VMI tools, and, once running, the resources required to support the tool should be minimized.

---

[5] This list is an expansion of the five framework problems described by *CloudPhylactor*.

Assumptions and Threat Model.
Figure 2 shows a common cloud threat model [22] where the cloud management plane, hypervisor, and physical hardware are assumed to be secure. Additionally, because Furnace's security model relies on a sandbox to safely contain tenant app code, it is assumed that the underlying mechanisms used to implement this sandbox are correct and secure. Through syscall filtering, only a

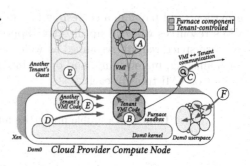

Fig. 2. Threat Model.

small set of syscalls are permitted to be used inside the sandbox; these syscalls are also assumed to be secure. Given these assumptions, Furnace is designed to be resilient against the following attack vectors:

Ⓐ *Malicious VMI Input.* A malicious tenant or third-party malicious code seizes control of the VMI tool. To do so, the tenant carefully crafts malicious input—the guest's main memory—in order to exploit a vulnerability in the tool [27]. Ⓑ *Attacks against app APIs.* A malicious tenant exploits flaws in exposed VMI APIs, allowing the leaking of private cloud implementation details or permitting a sandbox escape that yields access to the hypervisor. Ⓒ *App network snooping*: A third-party attacker tampers with messages sent between a tenant's VMI tool and external services, a concern for frameworks that provide support for this communication.

Several threats are out of scope. Furnace does not protect against a malicious Ⓓ or "curious" cloud administrator. Micro-architectural attacks Ⓔ and related side channels are considered out of scope, as are attacks targeting the cloud platform (e.g., OpenStack) itself Ⓕ. Finally, while the strong semantic gap [15] remains a concern for VMI tools, it is not in scope for Furnace.

4   Design

This section introduces Furnace as a safe, fast, and useful cloud VMI framework. Furnace is first described from the perspective of a cloud provider and later from that of a cloud tenant.

Cloud Provider Perspective. Figure 3 depicts Furnace's architecture as part of a typical cloud infrastructure. ① A tenant submits a VMI app package to the provider's public Furnace cloud service. The package contains the tenant app's source code and metadata such as the tenant's target VM and the app's allowed resource quotas. ② The Furnace cloud service parses the package contents, locates the tenant's target VM, and signals ③ the appropriate Furnace agent, which ④ provisions a Furnace sandbox under the VM and begins executing the tenant's app inside it. ⑤ The app runs as an unprivileged process inside the sandbox. ⑥ Using tenant-provided keys, Furnace provides a mechanism for

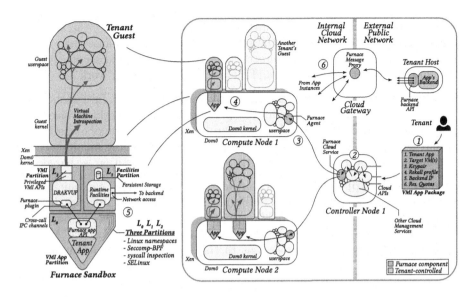

Fig. 3. The Furnace architecture from the cloud provider's perspective.

an app to securely communicate with a single tenant-controlled backend outside of the cloud. At the cloud boundary, this communication is relayed onto the public network via the Furnace message proxy.

Cloud Tenant Perspective. Figure 4 shows Furnace from the tenant's perspective. A tenant first begins by writing their VMI app. Furnace's tenant programming model means the tenant could write up to two programs: the *app* and an optional *backend*. A typical tenant use case will likely consist of many copies of the same VMI app each running under a different tenant VM and all communicating with a single backend running externally under the tenant's control. When ready to use, the app is packaged with metadata and submitted to Furnace, which starts copies of the app beneath each desired tenant VM. Once started, app

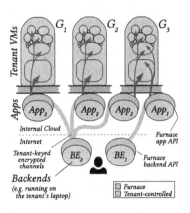

Fig. 4. Tenant model.

instances optionally establish a two-way connection with the backend, which acts as a coordination activity between app instances and the rest of the tenant's security enterprise (e.g., logging, threat feeds, databases, external blacklists, etc.). While apps are tightly constrained inside their Furnace sandbox, the tenant can run the backend anywhere. Note the Furnace-enforced abstraction in Fig. 4; as far as the tenant is concerned, both VMI and app↔backend messaging are performed by simple function calls. Furnace is responsible for handling the (sensitive) details related to function call execution. The fact the app runs in a sandbox can be ignored by the tenant. Additionally, because there is less infrastructure for the tenant to directly operate, maintain, and secure, tenants may find these abstractions safer and more scalable than prior work.

Sandbox Overview. Figure 3 also shows the Furnace sandbox. In the sandbox's L_0 partition, the tenant's app indirectly performs privileged tasks through *IPC cross-calls* to provider-controlled resource brokers in adjacent sandbox partitions L_1 and L_2. Many different apps can run under the same guest simultaneously; each app has its own L_0 and L_1 partitions while the L_2 partition is shared.

Furnace VMI App API. Tenants already familiar with VMI can quickly and easily write Furnace VMI apps. The Furnace API inside L_0 provides the core component of the LibVMI API (56 functions) and 12 Furnace-specific functions. As the tenant app executes, the VMI calls it makes to the Furnace API are translated into synchronous cross-calls to the L_2 partition where the VMI is actually performed. In the opposite direction, events produced by the guest itself are sent from L_2 to the app in L_0 either synchronously (the guest is paused until the app responds) or asynchronously (the guest continues running), with delivery occurring via a callback that the app registers at startup. The third partition, L_1, is used for communication with the app's backend and to provide persistent storage for the app.

Furnace's VMI component in L_2 is powered by *DRAKVUF* [17], a modular hypervisor-based dynamic malware analysis system, and tenant apps gain all the benefits of DRAKVUF—stealthiness, multiplexed events, and its built-in features—without having to build and configure it themselves. Furnace integrates into upstream DRAKVUF via its plugin system.

Figure 5 contains example source code that demonstrates the basic operation of a process whitelisting app. The example app first ① registers for guest CR3 register events (process context switches). For each received event, the app ② inspects the guest process that caused it. If the process is new, the app consults ③ the backend's whitelisting rules, and terminates the process if it is not allowed.

Furnace's initial implementation fully supports VMI apps written in Python. However, due to its language-agnostic cross-call interface, Furnace can potentially support tenant apps written in any language that has ZeroMQ[6] and Protocol Buffers[7] libraries.[8]

Cloud Integration. Figure 3 also shows other Furnace components elsewhere in the cloud, including the public Furnace cloud service that tenants use to create and tear down VMI apps; the per-hypervisor Furnace agent that controls app sandboxes; and the Furnace message proxy that relays app↔backend messages between the public Internet and the internal cloud network used by each sandbox's L_1 partition. The Furnace cloud service must integrate with the cloud

---

[6] https://zeromq.org/.

[7] https://developers.google.com/protocol-buffers/.

[8] Similarly, while Furnace was developed on Xen, it can also support KVM when equipped with a KVM-compatible L_2 component.

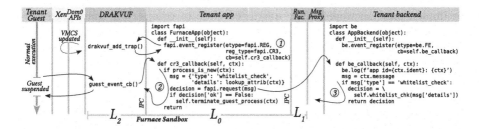

Fig. 5. Furnace tenant programming model. This example tenant app and backend work together to intercept and whitelist new guest processes.

platform to authenticate tenants, get VM state, and query for a VM's location. Furnace has the potential to be paired with many popular cloud platforms, and this integration is needed for a complete system.

Usage Model. Furnace's intended users are cloud tenants that write and deploy their own apps directly. However, Furnace can be used in other scenarios, such as tenants choosing to delegate their Furnace privileges to a third party (such as a managed security provider), or cloud providers that wish to use Furnace exclusively (such as private clouds). Furnace also would work well in use cases where there is no cloud management layer, such as distributed VMI-based malware analysis across a set of hypervisors.

4.1   Security

Because Furnace runs the tenant's app on the hypervisor, the ability for Furnace to suppress potentially malicious tenant apps is its most important requirement. Furnace's approach is to place each tenant app in a sandbox that uses existing, well-tested security mechanisms to whitelist the following allowed app activities:

1. *VMI Operations*: An app can read and write to its assigned VM's memory and vCPU registers, capture events from the VM, and pause/resume the VM.
2. *Communication*: An app can send arbitrary messages across the network to its associated tenant backend.
3. *General Computation*: An app can make limited use of hypervisor CPU and memory as a part of normal operation, including a limited ability to use the hypervisor's local disk for storage.

An app must be strictly constrained to these tasks. The Furnace sandbox must ensure that a tenant app cannot learn anything about the cloud that cannot already be discovered by a normal tenant VM. This includes preventing the app from inferring sensitive information about its hypervisor, such as its file systems, network interfaces, running processes, and co-resident VMs.

Sandbox Design. The Furnace sandbox uses a set of mutually reinforcing OS-based security mechanisms that make it unlikely that a single flaw in policy or implementation would allow untrusted code to escape. The sandbox incorporates well-tested mechanisms already successfully leveraged by the Chrome, AWS Lambda, and *Mbox* [16] sandboxes, but is notable and distinct for two reasons.

First, to a much more rigorous extent, the Furnace sandbox breaks apart the functionality of the untrusted tenant app so that a granular, tight-fitting security policy can be applied to each component. The most pronounced example of this segmentation is the sandbox's use of two resource brokers in L_1 and L_2, each with differing privileges. The Furnace sandbox also aggressively and contextually whitelists

Table 2. Sandbox comparison

	Userspace Isolation	Resource Quotas	Res. Broker Model	"Chroot"-like	Syscall Filtering	Contextual Security	Deref. Userspace	FS Size
Furnace	✓	✓	✓	✓	✓	✓	✓	≤8.9k
Chrome	✓	✗	✓	✗	✓	✗	✗	N/A
Lambda	✓	✓	✗	✓	✓	✗	✗	38.3k[a]
Mbox	✗	✗	✗	✗	✓	✓	✓	N/A

Supported: yes(✓) no(✗). FS size in # of files.
[a] https://alestic.com/2014/11/aws-lambda-environment/

the behavior of each component. A profile of whitelisted behavior is generated beforehand by the cloud provider and any deviation results in Furnace terminating the app for violating policy. Table 2 shows a feature comparison with related sandboxes:

- *Independent namespaces.* Similar to container-based sandboxes such as AWS Lambda,[9] each Furnace sandbox partition features an independent file system and employs userspace isolation.
- *Resource broker model.* Untrusted tenant code is limited to one primary external action—making cross-calls. Cross-calls are IPC messages to an external resource broker, which validates and acts upon the untrusted code's requests.
- *Syscall filtering.* Furnace employs granular syscall filtering similar to Mbox, and the full range of syscall arguments can be considered by a security policy.
- *Dynamic policy tightening.* Similar to *Pledge*,[10] Furnace can swap syscall filtering security policies based on context and does so when transitioning to a more restrictive policy immediately prior to tenant app execution.

Sandbox Implementation. Furnace's sandbox implementation achieves a base level of isolation and access control via Linux namespaces and SELinux. Seccomp-BPF is used to reduce the hypervisor kernel's exposure to an app's syscalls, and the syscalls that are allowed are inspected by a contextual syscall inspector that leverages the Linux kernel's `ptrace` interface.

Table 3. Furnace partitions

Furnace Partition	Network access	Runs As	# Init. Syscalls	# Runtime Syscalls	VMI /dev access	FS Size
App L_0	No	U	58	31	No	8.9k
Network L_1	Yes	U	42	28	No	8.9k
VMI L_2	No	R	63	24	Yes	5.7k

Unprivileged user (U). Root (R).

---

[9] Lambda represents container-based sandboxes in part because it is routinely audited.
[10] https://man.openbsd.org/pledge.2.

Finally, resource usage quotas (e.g., CPU and memory) are enforced by cgroups. Each of these sandbox security mechanisms protect against a subset of attacks and is essential to the overall security of the sandbox. When overlap between mechanisms does occur, it is because one mechanism nullifies a weakness in another.

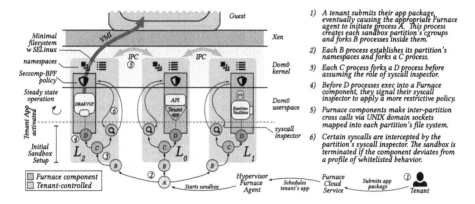

Fig. 6. From bottom to top: the sandbox is assembled when a new app is started.

Table 3 shows the details of each Furnace partition's unique security configuration, including the number of syscalls allowed at initialization and runtime (creating these security policies is discussed later in this section). Figure 6 further depicts sandbox initialization and how its components interact at runtime.

Linux Namespaces. Namespaces provide kernel-enforced userspace isolation ideal for limiting an app's ability to observe the rest of the hypervisor. Linux's support of namespaces includes user IDs, cgroups, mount points, IPCs, and network interfaces. When Furnace uses these namespaces in combination, a VMI app lacks any practical visibility outside of its assigned namespace. Mount namespaces are used to "chroot" each sandbox partition into a minimal SELinux-labeled file system tailored for its use. Process and user ID namespaces further isolate code running in each partition. The L_1 partition is the only partition given network access. To control resource quotas, Furnace places each sandbox partition in its own cgroup. Cgroups are used to limit the number of tasks allowed to exist in a partition, and how much CPU and memory these tasks can use. Minimum resource limits are statically determined based on profiling, and maximum limits are set by (and billed to) the tenant. Furnace also uses cgroups to limit apps to a single thread in order to prevent a known ptrace race condition involving multi-threaded code [25].[11]

---

[11] While this precludes multithreaded apps, Sect. 6.2 shows performance is acceptable. Heavy processing is better accomplished by the app's backend, which lacks this restriction.

#	Allowed by Seccomp-BPF	Syscall Inspector allows during runtime but checks arguments		Syscall Inspector allows only during initialization		
1	epoll_ctl	brk	madvise	access	getrandom	sched_getscheduler
2	epoll_wait	connect	mmap	arch_prctl	kill	sched_setscheduler
3	getpid	exit	mprotect	clone	lstat	set_robust_list
4	poll	exit_group	munmap	close	mkdir	set_tid_address
5	recvfrom	fcntl	open	dup	pipe2	sigreturn
6	sendto	fstat	rt_sigaction	dup2	prlimit64	socketpair
7	write	futex	sigaltstack	epoll_create	read	sysinfo
8		getpeername	socket	execve	readlink	uname
		getsockopt	stat	getcwd	rt_sigprocmask	unlink
10		ioctl		getdents	sched_getparam	vfork
11		lseek				wait4

Fig. 7. The syscall policy for the VMI app running in the sandbox's L_2 partition. The remaining $\approx$245 syscalls are denied.

SELinux. Furnace uses a SELinux policy in each sandbox partition to provide a consistent access control policy. Each partition's file system is labeled with up to four Furnace types: one for each partition's processes, and one for files.

Seccomp-BPF. Furnace uses Seccomp-BPF to filter the syscalls made by a partition. If a process attempts to make a prohibited syscall, it is terminated. Each Furnace partition has its own Seccomp-BPF policy. Of the hundreds of syscalls available in Linux, Table 2 and Fig. 7 show that Furnace whitelists $\approx$60 syscalls in a partition's most permissive state: as it is initialized. Of these, ten are related to cross-calls or basic process functionality and allowed unconditionally, while the remainder are subject to inspection by a `ptrace`-equipped security monitor called the *syscall inspector*.

Syscall Inspection. The syscall inspector provides two security functions: dereferencing userspace pointers passed as syscall arguments and dynamically tightening its current security policy based on context. One complication with Seccomp-BPF is that certain syscalls such as `open` cannot be fully filtered because Seccomp-BPF programs running in the Linux kernel cannot dereference userspace pointers [11,25]. To resolve this, Seccomp-BPF can partner with a `ptrace`-equipped userspace process that can. Furnace's three syscall inspectors monitor the Furnace component in each partition and make filtering decisions based on its syscall behavior. For example, if a tenant's app attempts to open a file not on the syscall inspector's whitelist, the app will be terminated. The syscall inspector applies its policies contextually. Based on the observation that many unique syscalls only occur while the partition and its processes are starting up, the syscall inspector initially uses a permissive security policy. Once initialized, the partition's policy is tightened.

Pertinent to Furnace's threat model, each sandbox partition has its own syscall inspector, so abnormal behavior in the L_1 and L_2 partitions will also result in app termination.

Security Policy Generation. The cloud provider supplies Furnace with three security policies: (1) a SELinux type enforcement policy; (2) a set of combined Seccomp-BPF and contextual security policies used by the three syscall inspectors; and (3) namespace-related parameters such as resource quotas. Only the

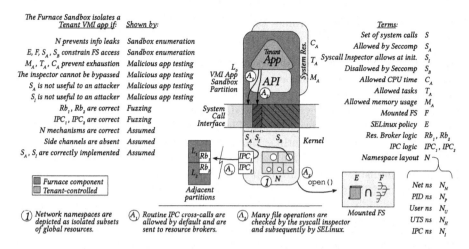

Fig. 8. This sandbox security analysis depicts the order in which security mechanisms are encountered by code running in a sandbox partition and asserts the sandbox is reasonably secure if certain criteria are met. Furnace's security evaluation will test elements of this assertion (the "shown by" column) to provide confidence that Furnace can successfully contain malicious VMI apps. *Notes: for brevity, only the L_0 partition is shown, but L_1 and L_2 are conceptually identical; the syscall inspector is not shown.*

syscall inspector policies are expected to be periodically adjusted by the cloud provider, and only on the occasion that minor adjustments need to be made. These policies are meant to apply to all Furnace sandboxes (as opposed to custom per-tenant policies).

The syscall inspector policies are created by recording all system calls (via the **strace** utility) made by each partition at runtime under a variety of benign conditions—an approach similar to *SysTrace* [20]. These system calls and their arguments are then analyzed and manually inspected. This manual inspection requires detailed familiarity with system calls and benefits from existing policy references (most notably Chromium's[12]). Only the behaviors observed during this profiling step become part of the partition's allowed syscall profile. Figure 7 shows the syscall policy applied to the tenant's VMI app running in the L_0 partition. The only syscalls a tenant app can make are either unconditionally allowed by Seccomp-BPF (column 1) or inspected by the syscall inspector (column 2).

Policies generated through profiling have been shown to be straightforward to generate and are a good starting point for refinement[13] [21]. One disadvantage of profiling is the likelihood that benign behaviors are missed and later cause unpredictable false positives at runtime. However, because the set of syscalls required by each partition is small, the profiles are quite robust, and these types of false positive were encountered rarely during testing. While a cloud provider can and

---

[12] https://chromium.googlesource.com/chromium/src.git/+/master/sandbox/linux/.
[13] https://github.com/Netflix/repokid.

should generate their own profiles (and analyze them for weaknesses [14]), Furnace comes included with a default policy set.

Interlocking Mechanisms. Some security mechanisms appear redundant. One clear example is the syscall inspector, which decides whether a file can be opened or not—something SELinux also does. The overall design could potentially be simplified if this redundancy was removed. However, each mechanism contributes to the overall security of the sandbox. The syscall inspector can choose its security policy dynamically at runtime, but lacks the more expressive and thorough approach of SELinux, which Furnace uses for broad, basic policies. These interlocking mechanisms help ensure that unknown weaknesses in security policies, implementation bugs, and profiling errors do not result in vulnerabilities. It is practical to permit some overlap in case one mechanism fails, and this point is discussed further in Furnace's security evaluation.

Attacking the Sandbox. Although restricted, an app is still allowed to perform cross-calls and make certain system calls. Furnace takes additional steps to minimize the chance these two interfaces can be successfully attacked. Figure 8 shows a security analysis that summarizes the sandbox's assumptions, security model, and how it will be evaluated.

Mitigating Exposed Kernel APIs. Flaws in existing syscalls have defeated Seccomp-BPF-based sandboxes in the past—most recently in Chrome.[14] In this case, a missing access control check in the Linux kernel's implementation of the waitid() syscall—a syscall purposely allowed by the Chrome syscall policy—led to a sandbox escape. This vulnerability demonstrates that, even in a small set of whitelisted system calls, implementation bugs can still occur and be exploited. While attacks like this remain possible, Furnace's syscall filter is more restrictive than Chrome's, reducing the number of potentially vulnerable syscalls.

Mitigating Exposed IPC Logic. Flaws in IPC logic are another source of sandbox escapes. These flaws are usually discovered through fuzzing [13,18]. Compared to the Chrome sandbox,[15] Furnace's IPC interface is simpler, so Furnace's IPC mechanism is more difficult to attack. Also, unlike Chrome, Furnace's IPC does not use shared memory, making it immune to a class of IPC-related use-after-free vulnerabilities.[16] Regardless, fuzzing remains an important part of Furnace's security evaluation.

Dom0 Complexity. Adding a new system such as Furnace to a cloud's hypervisors inherently increases the cloud's attack surface. However, not counting the Furnace sandbox's external dependencies (DRAKVUF, LibVMI, protocol buffers, and ZeroMQ), Furnace's combined 6k lines of sandbox-related code (2k Python Furnace API in L_0, 1k Python facilities daemon in L_1, and 3k C/C++ for Furnace's DRAKVUF plugin in L_2) represent a small increase in dom0's

---

[14] https://salls.github.io/Linux-Kernel-CVE-2017-5123/.

[15] http://blog.azimuthsecurity.com/2010/08/chrome-sandbox-part-2-of-3-ipc.html.

[16] https://nvd.nist.gov/vuln/detail/CVE-2017-14904.

```
1  c = list_head      # Head of guest kernel's process list      The identifier for the VMI call.
2  p = pid_offset     # Offset to pid in task_struct
3  t = tasks_offset   # Offset to tasks in task_struct            The LibVMI call function to execute.
4  n = name_offset    # Offset to comm in task_struct            An argument dictionary for the VMI call.
5  o = fapi.batch_new() # New batch object
6                                                                 The identifier for an earlier VMI call, its
7  o.add('00', fapi.PAUSE_VM)                                     results will be used as the input for this call.
8  o.add('01', fapi.READ_STR_VA,  {'vaddr': c+n-t, 'pid': 0})
9  o.add('02', fapi.READ_32_VA,   {'vaddr': c+p-t, 'pid': 0})     From it, take this field and
10 o.add('03', fapi.READ_ADDR_VA, {'vaddr': c,     'pid': 0})                          use it as input here.
11 # The results of the preceding calls are pipelined into the next set
12 for i in range(1, 120): # Batch another 119 sets
13     o.add(f'{i}1', fapi.READ_STR_VA,  {'vaddr': n-t, 'pid': 0}, f'{i-1}3', 'result', 'vaddr', fapi.ADD)
14     o.add(f'{i}2', fapi.READ_32_VA,   {'vaddr': p-t, 'pid': 0}, f'{i-1}3', 'result', 'vaddr', fapi.ADD)
15     o.add(f'{i}3', fapi.READ_ADDR_VA, {'vaddr': 0,   'pid': 0}, f'{i-1}3', 'result', 'vaddr', fapi.ADD)
16 o.add('99', fapi.RESUME_VM)
17
18 fapi.batch_send(o) # Synchronous cross-call: VMI call results stored in o
19                                                                 Add to, subtract
20 for r in o.results(): # Iterate through each call's results in order    from, or overwrite
21   if r['results'] = list_head: # The entire linked list was traversed   the existing value.
22     break
23   print(r)  # A dict of the call's results, e.g., {'name': '171', 'result': 'chrome', 'status': 0}
```

Fig. 9. A tenant app source code snippet that demonstrates the use of Furnace's VMI call pipelining API. Here, the tenant programmer creates a batch object o, populates it with several hundred VMI calls, then serializes and sends it to L_2 to be processed by calling batch_send(). By pipelining related calls together in the same cross-call message, IPC-related overhead can be greatly reduced.

attack surface, especially when compared to the 183k lines of C in common Xen dom0 libraries.[17]

There are additional security measures that cloud providers could adopt to further harden Furnace's security model, including separating Furnace sandboxes from dom0 by provisioning them in a single, per-hypervisor VMI-privileged VM.

4.2   Performance

While Furnace's inter-partition IPC channels allow the tenant app to be deprivileged, IPC overhead adds latency to every cross-call. This message-passing has implications on both guest and app performance.

Batching and Pipelining. By default, a single Furnace app VMI call is serialized into a single cross-call message that is sent between the L_0 and L_2 partitions. To minimize IPC overhead, Furnace includes a batching API that bundles multiple independent VMI calls into a single cross-call message. This amortizes IPC overhead across the entire batch, which would argue for bundling as many VMI calls as possible into a single message.

While this simple batching technique is beneficial, several commonly encountered guest kernel data structures are built in ways that force a VMI app's batch sizes to remain small. One such example is walking a linked list in guest kernel memory, where each link in the list contains a pointer to the next link. With simple batching, the entire list cannot be walked in a single cross-call because the pointers in each of the links are not known in advance.

With this problem in mind, the Furnace API further supports *VMI call pipelining.* In this model, while the L_2 partition processes a batch of VMI calls

---

[17] https://github.com/xen-project/xen/tree/master/tools.

in the same cross-call message, L_2 can be programmed to make available the results of an earlier VMI call as the input for subsequent calls. This enables a single pipelined cross-call to walk the entire length of a linked list in guest kernel memory at once.

If the length of the linked list is known, the message can include the exact number of calls needed to walk the list completely. If the size is not known, it can be estimated, and since the end of a linked list is trivial to detect, extraneous results past this mark can simply be discarded.

The tenant app programmer must choose to use pipelining. To do so, the programmer uses the Furnace API to generate a batch object, to which they then add and link VMI calls. An example of this API is shown in Fig. 9. When this batch object is ready, the Furnace API sends a single multi-part cross-call message to L_2, which extracts each VMI call from the message, resolves its dependencies, executes it, and stores the results in a multi-part reply.

Built-in Native Procedures. Furnace's API can also be used to invoke a small set of built-in native VMI procedures present in DRAKVUF. While Furnace and DRAKVUF could support an arbitrary number of built-in procedures, adding a procedure requires DRAKVUF to be recompiled and therefore would not normally be available to a tenant.

5   Case Studies

This section describes four fully-functional examples of Furnace VMI apps. All four examples are useful for memory analysis and fine-grained system monitoring—two likely use cases for Furnace. Most are written in less than 100 lines of Python code. This small size is enabled by:

- *Inherent features.* Furnace handles many low-level VMI details automatically. Through DRAKVUF, apps inherit features enhancing their stealthiness, the ability to multiplex guest events across multiple apps (such as when two apps consume events from the same guest), and built-in VMI procedures.
- *Automated deployment.* App deployment is handled by Furnace; the tenant has no concern for the process required to build, deploy, and run their app.
- *Familiar API.* Furnace's Python API function signatures are identical to Lib-VMI's Python library. Existing LibVMI tools written in Python can be placed in a Furnace app and run with minor modification.

App: Memory Analysis. *Rekall* is a popular memory analysis framework. It is typically invoked from the command line to analyze file-based memory dumps. To use Rekall, a tenant leverages Furnace's built-in Rekall app. The Rekall app must be paired with a tenant-provided backend, which issues Rekall commands to it. A 65 line backend was built for this purpose.

When a command is received, the Rekall app invokes Rekall in L_0. A Furnace-specific address space [7] was added to Rekall that converts Rekall's high-level reads and seeks into their equivalent cross-calls to L_2, allowing Rekall to run against the tenant's live virtual machine from within Furnace. Running against live memory in place avoids the requirement to snapshot and download a memory dump out of the cloud, a potentially slow and bandwidth-intensive operation unsuitable for many security use cases. In terms of raw performance, comparing Furnace's Rekall app to Rekall operating against an equivalent file-based memory dump reveals their comparable speeds (4.05 s to analyze 4 GB of memory compared to Furnace's 20.88 s).

App: Capturing and Exporting Guest Memory. While Furnace's Rekall app is useful because it quickly analyzes live guest memory, for certain use cases it is also often desirable to obtain an offline copy. To demonstrate capturing and exporting guest memory out of the cloud, a tenant app and backend were developed (87 and 67 lines, respectively).

The app idles until the tenant's backend instructs it to perform a memory capture. The app is parameterized to compress and upload some or all of guest memory, and does so asynchronously in 4 MB chunks, pausing briefly after every segment to listen for new instructions from the backend.

From a throughput performance standpoint, this app stresses each partition, the proxy, and the tenant's backend. During testing, it was found that the average end-to-end goodput was 40.47 MBps ($\approx$101 s for a VM with 4 GB RAM) for a backend running in a nearby LAN—conditions similar to if the app and backend both resided in the same cloud.

App: System Call Inspection. Furnace provides API support for tenant apps that consume syscall traces (debuggers, syscall analysis, etc.). A guest's system calls are challenging to capture due to their volume and the overhead associated with intercepting them [9]. While there is nothing preventing a tenant app from performing syscall tracing directly, managing its low-level details (injecting, single-stepping, and restoring breakpoints in guest memory) from the L_0 partition would inefficient. Instead, Furnace leverages DRAKVUF's syscall interception plugin. This plugin handles the details of tracing and sends only the results, a stream of syscall events (including the involved registers, calling process, user, and memory addresses), to the tenant app.

A 35 line tenant app was built to activate syscall tracing through the Furnace API and stream the resulting trace to its backend. During performance testing, it was found that overhead related to Furnace's cross-calls introduces a 5% in-guest performance penalty when compared to DRAKVUF tracing by itself. The small size of this syscall app indicates the ease at which a tenant can leverage Furnace to perform a complicated built-in VMI procedure. Furnace's deployment model also means it is easy for a tenant to temporarily activate an app under a guest for a specific purpose.

App: Process Event Monitoring. *Arav* [5] is a monitoring tool that uses VMI to extract events from a guest's userspace processes. Using a plugin specific to the guest program being monitored, Arav traces the program's function calls and reconstitutes its semantics. The original C source code for Arav (1219 lines) was ported to a 300 line Furnace app and a 40 line backend.

We use Arav to demonstrate Furnace's potential for integration with the tenant's security enterprise. Arav app instances were deployed under 10 Linux guests to capture and send a real-time stream of guest SSH logins/logouts and a guest kernel `commit_creds` function trace through Arav's backend into a (simulated) tenant security event manager. As a substitute for more advanced analysis, this simple manager periodically picked a username at random from the stream and used the Furnace cloud service to deploy a Rekall app under the same guest. The Rekall app ran analysis that was then returned to the event manager.

This scenario highlights the ease at which a tenant security architecture can programmatically compose and deploy multiple Furnace apps. Because an app is decoupled from its backend, the backend can be run on tenant infrastructure and directly feed information into other tenant systems.

6   Evaluation and Results

Furnace was further evaluated in two ways. First, Furnace's security properties were tested through the execution of apps containing malicious code. Second, Furnace's performance was measured and compared with that of native VMI apps and another cloud VMI framework, CloudVMI.

The evaluation environment consisted of a single Dell R920 hypervisor. The hypervisor ran Xen version 4.8.1 with a Fedora 26 dom0 and was furnished with four 2.3 GHz Intel Xeon E7-4870 processors and 256 GB RAM. Furnace sandboxes were provisioned in dom0, which also supported the Furnace cloud service, hypervisor agent, and message proxy. The evaluation's guests were fully virtualized Fedora 25 guests each with 1 vCPU, 1 GB RAM, and 5 GB storage.

6.1   Security Evaluation

The first experiments tested the security of Furnace's sandbox with a specific focus on the attack vectors described in the threat model: preventing or mitigating attacks again Furnace's VMI app APIs, sandbox construction, and resource brokers. Each test emulated an attacker's actions: first by probing the sandbox for weaknesses, then by attempting a direct escape, and finally by attempting to find and exploit vulnerabilities in the cross-call interface. These experiments are informed by previous vulnerabilities in related sandboxes [13,18].

Sandbox Enumeration. Serverless runtimes such as AWS Lambda are frequently audited by the security community.[18] An auditing app was built to perform the same steps of enumeration, such as attempting to read kernel logs, inspecting `procfs` for CPU and memory info, listing file systems and running processes, and identifying the system, kernel version, current working directory, and other environment variables.

Result: The sandbox was found to be clean, with few details available to the app. Neither the `/dev/kmsg` device, `procfs`, nor `sysfs` are mapped into L_0, so

----

[18] https://www.denialof.services/lambda/.

kernel logs, CPU and memory info, file system info, and process info are not available. Even if they were, attempts to read them (non-whitelisted behavior) would still result in the syscall inspector terminating the app. A minimum set of environment variables are artificially set in the sandbox during startup, further preventing enumeration.

Attacks by Malicious Apps. A set of malicious VMI apps that attempted to find weaknesses in the Furnace sandbox were implemented, and their execution was monitored. Recall that although Furnace components are initialized inside a permissive security policy, this policy is tightened prior to app execution.

Open Arbitrary Files. Attempts by an app to open files in directories mounted in the sandbox—/`tmp`, /`dev`, /`var`, etc.—were trapped into the syscall inspector. If the file was not on the inspector's whitelist, the inspector terminated the app. Additionally, SELinux prevented file accesses not explicitly allowed by policy. Finally, because Furnace mounts a custom filesystem as the app partition's root file system, there were no sensitive hypervisor files visible to apps.

Open a Socket. Attempts to create a TCP socket or connect to a remote socket were also intercepted by the syscall inspector. While these calls are allowed during partition startup, once the app begins execution, they are forbidden. The app's L_0 partition also lacks a network interface.

Spawn/exec a Process or Thread. Prior to app execution, the syscall inspector disallowed the `clone` and `exec` families of syscalls. Furnace also used cgroups to limit the maximum number of tasks running in a single partition.

Resource Exhaustion. An app allocated increasingly large amounts of memory and stored it to disk and also entered an infinite loop. CPU and memory abuses are prevented by Linux cgroups. Disk usage is controlled by L_1, which refuses to store additional data past the quota set in the app package manifest.

Attacks on Cross-Calls. Any crash in the sandbox's two IPC interfaces would indicate a potentially exploitable bug. A malicious app used *protofuzz*[19] to fuzz the interfaces. While this was a black-box test, the malicious app was provided the Furnace protobuf schema so it could directly create and send IPC messages. The app first broadly tested the IPC interface by generating random protobuf messages. Next, the app used a more intelligent approach [26] by mutating a set of well-formed seed messages that exercise resource broker logic, such as the code for VMI call pipelining, more thoroughly.

Result: Over 110 hours of fuzzing (150M mutated IPC messages) was unable to crash or cause unexpected behavior in the L_1 and L_2 partitions, supporting the conclusion that the interfaces are unlikely to permit escape.

6.2   Performance Evaluation

The second set of experiments compared Furnace's performance with that of a native VMI tool and the CloudVMI framework. As has been done in previous

---

[19] https://github.com/trailofbits/protofuzz.

Table 4. VMI performance comparison

		Guest Effective Performance		Time	App/Tool/CV Client				CV Service		
	Approach	calc/sec†	Δ%	ms	Calls RT	Msgs	Mem MB	CPU jiffie	Mem MB	CPU jiffie	Description
1	Native VMI	327.9	100.0	0.13±0.13	301		25.1	21.5			LibVMI example code
2	DK Native	326.2	99.7	0.84±0.02	328	1	85.0	264.4			Built-in DK procedure
3	Pipeline* app	311.4	95.0	1.71±0.01	356	1	85.6	301.2			App w/ optimized API
4	Batch app	294.1	89.7	35.54±0.21	301	100	74.9	314.2			App w/ optimized API
5	Single app	283.4	86.4	98.52±0.72	304	304	85.4	324.5			App w/ unoptimized API
6	CV Local	311.8	95.1	34.93±0.24	315	315	2.0	<0.1	34.9	22.6	RPC client on local VM
7	CV Remote	258.3	78.8	541.96±4.43	315	315	2.0	0.3	34.8	21.2	RPC client across network

Round trip (RT). CloudVMI (CV). DRAKVUF (DK). † 3 sec Sysbench CPU test. *Pipeline size: 120. All measurements are averages with 0.95 confidence interval. Measured on a guest with 100 processes.

work, the measurements focused on LibVMI's process list code example, which measures the time required to traverse the guest kernel's linked list of active processes. Several functionally identical process list programs were written to investigate differences between VMI approaches.

A variety of measurements were taken during these experiments: the time necessary for a VMI approach to perform the traversal; the slowdown caused when an approach pauses the guest to ensure guest memory consistency; the number of VMI calls issued by the approach, and, if applicable, the number of cross-call messages; and finally, the approach's resident memory and CPU time usage. Time stamps were taken immediately before and after each traversal to avoid measuring startup delays. To measure the performance penalty each VMI approach has on a guest, the sysbench CPU benchmark[20] was ran for 3 s inside a guest, during which time the process list traversal was invoked once. Comparing the average amount of work sysbench accomplished with the baseline measurement in line 1 is used to quantify each approach's performance impact on the guest. While useful for comparing approaches, this metric focuses on a single use case and is not suited to be a general measure of VMI performance.

Intuitively, CV's RPC-based method is highly sensitive to network latency. CloudVMI was measured using two topologies: line 6 ran the CV client on a VM co-resident on the same hypervisor as the target guest, as would occur in the scenario where the cloud scheduler happened to provision both on the same hypervisor—a best case scenario for CV performance; Alternatively, line 7 placed the client across a network throttled at 100 Mbps—a less ideal scenario.

Result. The results in Table 4 confirm the intuition that Furnace apps (lines 3–5) should be slower than a native VMI tool (line 1). When comparing optimized Furnace APIs (lines 3–4) to the unoptimized API (line 5), there is a clear pattern: as the number of VMI calls per cross-call message increase (line 3 shows 356:1), performance improves because fewer cross-calls are needed and less overhead occurs. Calling DRAKVUF's built-in procedures (line 2) yields Furnace's best performance, followed closely by Furnace's pipelined app. The fastest CloudVMI

---

[20] https://github.com/akopytov/sysbench.

measurement is roughly equivalent to the Furnace batching app, but its slowest is over 5x slower than the slowest Furnace app.

Furnace does require more memory and CPU time than CV. However, Furnace's results better reflect its true cost; there are no hidden costs as occur in CV or CloudPhylactor (both require a host/VM to run on, which comes with its own resource and maintenance costs). For example, with CloudPhylactor, a tenant monitoring VM with 1 GB RAM would require 12x more memory than the equivalent Furnace app ($\approx$85 MB per Table 4).

6.3 Related Work

Cloud VMI Frameworks. In addition to the previously mentioned *Cloud-VMI* [2], *CloudPhylactor* [27], and *LiveCloudInspector* [29], there have been other proposals to facilitate cloud forensics, malware analysis, and security. *CloudIDEA* [9] proposed a wide-ranging cloud analysis system consisting of several VMI-based inputs, a dedicated analysis infrastructure, and an integrated decision engine. Compared to Furnace's tenant self-service model, CloudIDEA's focus was on a centralized, provider-driven approach. *FROST* [8] proposed methods for tenants to gain access to low-level cloud VM artifacts on OpenStack clouds, including firewall logs and memory dumps. Both CloudIDEA and FROST are similar to the preset model described in Sect. 3. Self-service clouds [6] proposed allowing tenants to assign VMs special privileges to perform VMI and intercept block and network I/O. Furnace shares the tenant-empowering spirit of this proposal but not the large hypervisor architectural changes it implies. Finally, Furnace has parallels with software-defined networking (SDN) frameworks, including *FRESCO* [23], which sought to enable modular SDN app development.

Constrained Execution Environments. The namespace-based isolation used by Furnace is also leveraged by popular application containers (e.g., Docker, LXC, and rkt) and other sandbox projects such as Flatpak, Sandstorm, nsjail, and Firejail. The Furnace sandbox is distinct from these projects due to its use of `ptrace` and its resource broker model. Finally, while the use of `ptrace` has a mixed history as a sandbox mechanism [11,25], new unprivileged sandboxing mechanisms under development, including LandLock,[21] offer alternatives.

7   Conclusion

This paper proposed Furnace, a framework that enables cloud tenants to run VMI applications under their cloud VMs. Compared to prior proposals, Furnace provides better features for cloud tenants, including support for arbitrary tenant VMI apps, speed improvements and cost reductions, and less infrastructure for a tenant to maintain. Furnace also meets the expectations of cloud providers: it is safe, accountable, and protective of cloud abstractions. Furnace's sandbox withstood a multi-part security evaluation, supporting the conclusion that Furnace is a practical, adoptable cloud VMI framework.

---

[21] https://landlock.io.

Acknowledgement. We thank the anonymous reviewers, William Enck, Nathan Hicks, Luke Deshotels, and Isaac Polinsky for their comments.

References

1. Arulraj, L., Arpaci-Dusseau, A.C., Arpaci-Dusseau, R.H.: Improving virtualized storage performance with sky. In: ACM VEE (2017). https://doi.org/10.1145/3050748.3050755
2. Baek, H.W., Srivastava, A., Merwe, J.V.D.: CloudVMI: virtual machine introspection as a cloud service. In: 2014 IEEE International Conference on Cloud Engineering, pp. 153–158 (2014). https://doi.org/10.1109/IC2E.2014.82
3. Bahram, S., et al.: DKSM: subverting virtual machine introspection for fun and profit. In: 29th IEEE Symposium on Reliable Distributed Systems, October 2010
4. Bauman, E., Ayoade, G., Lin, Z.: A survey on hypervisor-based monitoring: approaches, applications, and evolutions. ACM Comput. Surv. **48**, 10 (2015)
5. Bushouse, M., Ahn, S., Reeves, D.: Arav: monitoring a cloud's virtual routers. In: Proceedings of the 12th Annual Conference on Cyber and Information Security Research (2017)
6. Butt, S., Lagar-Cavilla, H.A., Srivastava, A., Ganapathy, V.: Self-service cloud computing. In: Proceedings of the 2012 ACM Conference on Computer and Communications Security. CCS 2012, pp. 253–264. ACM, New York (2012). https://doi.org/10.1145/2382196.2382226
7. Dolan-Gavitt, B., Payne, B., Lee, W.: Leveraging forensic tools for virtual machine introspection. Technical report, Georgia Institute of Technology (2011)
8. Dykstra, J., Sherman, A.T.: Design and implementation of FROST: digital forensic tools for the openstack cloud computing platform. Digit. Invest. **10**, S87–S95 (2013)
9. Fischer, A.: CloudIDEA: a malware defense architecture for cloud data centers. In: Debruyne, C. (ed.) On the Move to Meaningful Internet Systems: OTM 2015 Conferences. OTM 2015, vol. 9415, pp. 594–611. Springer, Cham (2015). https://doi.org/10.1007/978-3-319-26148-5_40
10. Fraser, T., Evenson, M., Arbaugh, W.: VICI virtual machine introspection for cognitive immunity. In: 2008 Annual Computer Security Applications Conference. ACSAC 2008 (2008)
11. Garfinkel, T.: Traps and pitfalls: practical problems in system call interposition based security tools. In: NDSS, vol. 3, pp. 163–176 (2003)
12. Garfinkel, T., Rosenblum, M.: A virtual machine introspection based architecture for intrusion detection. In: Proceedings of the Network and Distributed Systems Security Symposium (2003)
13. Gorenc, B., Spelman, J.: Thinking Outside the Sandbox: Violating Trust Boundaries in Uncommon Ways. Black Hat, USA (2014)
14. Jaeger, T., Sailer, R., Zhang, X.: Analyzing integrity protection in the SELinux example policy. In: USENIX SEC (2003)
15. Jain, B., Baig, M.B., Zhang, D., Porter, D.E., Sion, R.: SoK: introspections on trust and the semantic gap. In: IEEE S&P (2014)
16. Kim, T., Zeldovich, N.: Practical and effective sandboxing for non-root users. In: USENIX ATC, San Jose, CA (2013)
17. Lengyel, T.K., Maresca, S., Payne, B.D., Webster, G.D., Vogl, S., Kiayias, A.: Scalability, fidelity and stealth in the DRAKVUF dynamic malware analysis system. In: Proceedings of the 30th Annual Computer Security Applications Conference. ACSAC 2014. ACM (2014)

18. Liu, Z., Lovet, G.: Breeding sandworms: how to fuzz your way out of adobe reader x's sandbox. In: Black Hat EUROPE (2012)
19. Payne, B.D., de Carbone, M., Lee, W.: Secure and flexible monitoring of virtual machines. In: Proceedings of the 23rd Annual Computer Security Applications Conference (ACSAC) (2007)
20. Provos, N.: Improving host security with system call policies. In: USENIX SEC (2003)
21. Sanders, M., Yue, C.: Automated least privileges in cloud-based web services. In: Proceedings of the Fifth ACM/IEEE Workshop on Hot Topics in Web Systems and Technologies. HotWeb 2017, pp. 3:1–3:6. ACM, New York (2017). https://doi.org/10.1145/3132465.3132470
22. Sgandurra, D., Lupu, E.: Evolution of attacks, threat models, and solutions for virtualized systems. ACM Comput. Surv. **48**(3), 46:1–46:38 (2016). https://doi.org/10.1145/2856126
23. Shin, S., Porras, P.A., Yegneswaran, V., Fong, M.W., Gu, G., Tyson, M.: FRESCO: modular composable security services for software-defined networks. In: NDSS (2013)
24. Suneja, S., Isci, C., de Lara, E., Bala, V.: Exploring VM introspection: techniques and trade-offs. In: ACM VEE (2015). https://doi.org/10.1145/2731186.2731196
25. Swiecki, R.: Promises and pitfalls of sandboxes. In: Presented at CONFidence (2017)
26. Takanen, A., Demott, J.D., Miller, C.: Fuzzing for Software Security Testing and Quality Assurance. Artech House, Norwood (2008)
27. Taubmann, B., Rakotondravony, N., Reiser, H.P.: CloudPhylactor: harnessing mandatory access control for virtual machine introspection in cloud data centers. In: 2016 IEEE Trustcom/BigDataSE/ISPA, pp. 957–964, August 2016. https://doi.org/10.1109/TrustCom.2016.0162
28. Yosifovich, P., Russinovich, M.E., Solomon, D.A., Ionescu, A.: Windows Internals, 7th edn. Microsoft Press, Redmond (2017)
29. Zach, J., Reiser, H.P.: LiveCloudInspector: towards integrated IaaS forensics in the cloud. In: Bessani, A., Bouchenak, S. (eds.) DAIS 2015. LNCS, vol. 9038, pp. 207–220. Springer, Cham (2015). https://doi.org/10.1007/978-3-319-19129-4_17

ShadowMonitor: An Effective In-VM Monitoring Framework with Hardware-Enforced Isolation

Bin Shi[1], Lei Cui[2(✉)], Bo Li[1], Xudong Liu[1], Zhiyu Hao[2], and Haiying Shen[3]

[1] State Key Laboratory of Software Development Environment, Beihang University, Beijing, China
{shibin,libo,liuxd}@act.buaa.edu.cn
[2] Institute of Information Engineering, Chinese Academy of Sciences, Beijing, China
{cuilei,haozhiyu}@iie.ac.cn
[3] Department of Computer Science, University of Virginia, Charlottesville, USA
hs6ms@virginia.edu

Abstract. Virtual machine introspection (VMI) is one compelling technique to enhance system security in clouds. It is able to provide strong isolation between untrusted guests and security tools placed in guests, thereby enabling dependability of the security tools even if the guest has been compromised. Due to this benefit, VMI has been widely used for cloud security such as intrusion detection, security monitoring, and tampering forensics. However, existing VMI solutions suffer significant performance degradation mainly due to the high overhead upon frequent memory address translations and context-switches. This drawback limits its usage in many real-world scenarios, especially when fine-grained monitoring is desired. In this paper, we present ShadowMonitor, an effective VMI framework that enables efficient in-VM monitoring without imposing significant overhead. ShadowMonitor decomposes the whole monitoring system into two compartments and then assigns each compartment with isolated address space. By placing the monitored components in the protected compartment, ShadowMonitor guarantees the safety of both monitoring tools and guests. In addition, ShadowMonitor employs hardware-enforced instructions to design the gates across two compartments, thereby providing efficient switching between compartments. We have implemented ShadowMonitor on QEMU/KVM exploiting several hardware virtualization features. The experimental results show that ShadowMonitor could prevent several types of attacks and achieves 10× speedup over the existing method in terms of both event monitoring and overall application performance.

Keywords: Virtual machine introspection · Monitor · Isolation

1 Introduction

With the prevalence of cloud computing and virtualization technology, virtual machine introspection (VMI) [7,12,15,17,28,29] has become an essential

© Springer Nature Switzerland AG 2018
M. Bailey et al. (Eds.): RAID 2018, LNCS 11050, pp. 670–690, 2018.
https://doi.org/10.1007/978-3-030-00470-5_31

technique to tackle security risks in virtualized environments. The basic idea of VMI is to place the traditional security tools into the hypervisor or a separately trusted virtual machine (VM, or guest in other literature), and then employ introspection to monitor and protect the untrusted VMs from outside, so-called out-of-VM introspection. In this way, it guarantees dependability and integrity of the security tools even if the untrusted VM has been compromised.

Existing out-of-VM introspection techniques fall into two main categories: passive technique and active technique. The passive technique usually provides several APIs to touch the state of the monitored system; it invokes the API periodically to detect whether the system is being compromised or not [15,17,34]. The main drawback is that it fails to detect the instant attack which is completed within a short while. The active technique, in contrast, adopts an event-driven way by intercepting a broad range of system events including process-switch, system calls, interruptions, etc. Therefore, it is able to detect the state change in real-time and thus detects attacks immediately [27,29]. Although the active technique is appealing in real-time detection, it introduces significant performance overhead due to frequent context-switches (VM to hypervisor) and software-based virtual address translations [34]. For example, Virtuoso takes 6 s to run the simple command *pslist* [12] which is generally completed within a few milliseconds without the interception. Drakvuf introduces 50% performance degradation of guest applications according to our experiments [21]. Although the overhead can be reduced by intercepting only a few types of events, this limits the usage of the active technique.

In addition to placing the VMI outside of the VM, some studies propose to deploy part of the monitoring components into the monitored VM, so-called in-VM introspection. The main purpose of in-VM introspection is to provide the same level of security as the out-of-VM approach without imposing significant performance loss. However, the components placed into the untrusted guests may be disabled or bypassed by the attackers who have compromised the guest. Therefore, one key concern is to ensure the security of these components placed into the guests. To achieve this, SIM [30] employs separate shadow page tables to isolate the monitor components from the guest for guaranteeing security. The same idea is adopted in other work including [8,29]. However, these works still suffer from several problems. First, they cannot prevent the address translation redirection attack [16], which is widely used to deceive the security tools with a fake address mapping [20,23,26]. For instance, SIM isolates its monitor code in an isolated address space whereas it cannot prevent the malicious kernel from employing a different address mapping. In addition, the in-VM introspection requires to insert hooks at the interception points in advance, it thus lacks the flexibility of dynamic configuration at run-time. What's worse, since they use software-level shadow page tables to provide address space isolation, they impose performance loss compared to the native mode which exploits hardware-assisted optimization (e.g., EPT [2] or RVI [1]), especially when experiencing memory-intensive operations.

Many approaches have been proposed to enhance VM security with hardware features. For example, SGX of Intel [25] places application code inside an enclave and encrypts them with specific instructions to protect the code from untrusted hardware and OS with higher privilege levels. SeCage [22] leverages hardware virtualization features to enforce strong isolation between the protected compartments and the main compartment. It ensures that only the functions inside the protected compartment can access the private data. These approaches, however, focus on isolation rather than monitoring. In addition, they require the modification of application codes, which limits their usage in practical systems.

To mitigate these problems, we propose ShadowMonitor, a general-purpose framework that provides efficient in-VM monitoring and strong isolation. The key idea of ShadowMonitor is inspired by Secage [22], which employs hardware features to enable privilege separation. ShadowMonitor decomposes the whole monitored system into two separate compartments, i.e., shadow compartment which contains the monitor tools along with the private data, and main compartment which provides the execution environments for guest OS and user applications. Then, it isolates the two compartments, so that the shadow compartment can be protected even if the guest OS (i.e., main compartment) has been compromised. To achieve this, ShadowMonitor leverages hardware virtualization features (e.g., Intel multi-EPT feature (EPTP-switching) [2]) to assign each compartment with a separate address space. Meanwhile, the address space of shadow compartment is well protected; it can only be touched through some specific gates using VMFUNC instruction [2]. In addition, exploiting these hardware features, ShadowMonitor invokes event monitoring without trapping into the hypervisor. Thus, it eliminates heavyweight operations including VM-exits and VM-enters, and consequentially accesses memory at native speed. Different from existing monitoring invoking methods [29,30], ShadowMonitor provides flexible event monitoring with a trap-stepping approach. Rather than setup hooks in advance, it configures a set of events at run-time including syscall, kernel functions, and even single instructions.

We have implemented ShadowMonitor on QEMU/KVM [4] platform. We evaluate ShadowMonitor with a set of experiments. The results show that ShadowMonitor is able to provide defenses against several types of attacks. In addition, ShadowMonitor gains a considerable speedup over existing methods when monitoring syscalls and process switches. It provides 11× memory speedup and reduces the performance loss by 58% compared to the out-of-VM introspection approach, and improves 36.1% over in-VM approach.

The main contributions of this paper are as follows:

- We propose an efficient in-VM monitoring framework which employs hardware features to separate compartments for isolating security tools from untrusted guests and discuss the challenges to realize it (Sect. 2).
- We present the solutions of providing strong isolation between compartments, efficient switching, and security event monitoring, which are key components in ShadowMonitor. (Sect. 3).

- We implement ShadowMonitor on QEMU/KVM platform (Sect. 4) and conduct a set of experiments to prove its effectiveness and efficiency (Sect. 6).
- We analyze how ShadowMonitor defends against several attacks, and show that it can detect malicious behavior and prevent itself from attacks (Sect. 5).

2   Overview

ShadowMonitor aims to achieve three main goals, (i) provide an efficient monitoring approach without introducing significant performance overhead, (ii) be robust to attacks, and (iii) support customized configuration at run-time. In this section, we will present the threat model and the basic idea of ShadowMonitor.

2.1   Threat Model

In ShadowMonitor, we follow the common assumption widely-adopted in many full virtualized environments, i.e., the hypervisor is trustworthy while the guests are not. In specific, we assume that the guest OS is trusted in the boot-up procedure, which is the same as [30]. After boot-up, the attackers are able to compromise the guest OS, yet they cannot break the underlying hypervisor and hardware nor operate the isolated address space protected by hardware. In addition, the memory region of the interrupt descriptor table (IDT) is considered to be safe, since it can be protected by setting permission flags in EPT entries and trapping operations on IDTR register [2]. Similarly, the interruptions that trigger address space switch are considered to be safe too. We also assume that the users of ShadowMonitor are trusted, so that ShadowMonitor is safely operated. It's worth noting that some attacks such as VM-escape attack, denial of service attack (DDoS), and side-channel attack may break ShadowMonitor, we will discuss them in Sect. 5.

2.2   Basic Idea

The architecture of ShadowMonitor is shown in Fig. 1. The basic idea is to decompose the monitored system into two parts, i.e., main compartment and shadow compartment, each of which is assigned with a separate hardware-enforced address space. The shadow compartment contains monitor components (e.g., code and collected data), and the main compartment provides the execution environments for guest operating systems and user applications. In this way, the Monitor Code and Monitor Data placed in the shadow compartment are invisible to the guest OS. The memory mappings of the shadow compartment are inherited from the main compartment, allowing the monitor components to access information from the guests. Entry and exit between the two compartments are enabled with specifically designated gates for safety.

ShadowMonitor can be used as an additional service for a single VM or VM clusters in clouds. Generally, the cloud provider deploys ShadowMonitor in clouds and allows the VM user to configure it. With ShadowMonitor, a user

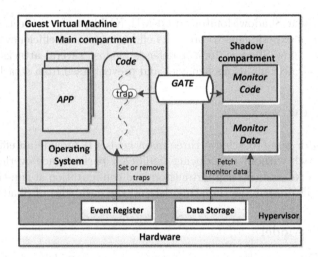

Fig. 1. Overview of ShadowMonitor

is able to monitor applications running insides the VM and manages the VM according to the monitoring data (e.g. rolling back when a potential attack is detected). The monitor points can be customized by the user with ShadowMonitor APIs. More specifically, after a safe guest boot-up, ShadowMonitor will execute the following steps. (1) The VM user requests the cloud provider to deploy the ShadowMonitor components (i.e., construct the shadow compartment and then place inside the Monitor Code). (2) Then, the user set up (or remove) traps in the guest by calling APIs of event register provided by ShadowMonitor. (3) The traps once being touched will trigger the Monitor Code in the shadow compartment so that the event, as well as its context (e.g., event address, timestamp, and arguments), can be recorded. (4) Finally, the data storage module of ShadowMonitor will collect the monitoring data periodically and report them to the VM user.

2.3 Challenges

Although the idea is simple, there are several challenges to be addressed to realize ShadowMonitor.

- *Isolation of compartments*: The guest running in the main compartment after being compromised may attempt to break the security tools deployed in the shadow compartment. Therefore, to provide strong isolation between the two is essential to ensure the security of ShadowMonitor.
- *Efficient switching between compartments*: The entry and exit to the main and shadow compartments are achieved by a designated gate. Consider that the switches between the two are frequent, how to switch with low overhead is critical to the performance of guest application and monitoring.

– *Customized event interception at run-time*: ShadowMonitor should be able to monitor a wide range of events. Meanwhile, the user should be able to register or cancel an event interception at run-time. Thus, it is important to provide dynamic and flexible event monitoring.

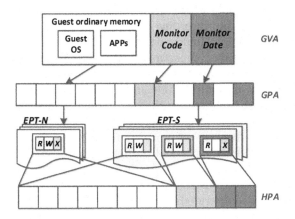

Fig. 2. Isolation between address space of two compartments.

3   System Design

In this section, we will present how to tackle the challenges above, mainly including memory isolation, low-cost compartment switching, security of monitoring execution flow, and monitoring integrity.

3.1   Isolation of Compartments

In ShadowMonitor, compartment isolation is achieved by the multi-page-mapping mechanism. Generally, in a hardware-assisted memory virtualization environment, the guest OS can only touch the first-level memory mapping which maps guest virtual address (GVA) to guest physical address (GPA), while the hypervisor manages the second-level mapping (known as extended page table (EPT)) for each guest which maps GPA to host physical address (HPA).

Unlike previous work that configures only one EPT for each guest, the recent advance in Intel CPU allows up to 512 EPTs for one guest. Exploiting this feature, ShadowMonitor provides two EPTs for each guest, one is the native EPT (EPT-N) for the guest (or the main compartment within the paper), and another one is shadow EPT (EPT-S) used for the shadow compartment. In this way, the mapping from GPA to HPA is divided into two steps, as shown in Fig. 2. The GPA belonging to the address space of the main compartment is translated to HPA by EPT-N (the left part), and the GPA from the shadow compartment is translated to HPA by EPT-S (the right part). Through address translation with different EPTs, memory access will be forwarded automatically using hardware instead of software emulation, thereby achieving native speed.

Figure 2 describes the details of memory mappings in ShadowMonitor. As can be seen, the entire GVA is divided into three regions: Monitor Code, Monitor Data, and Guest Ordinary Memory. The Guest Ordinary Memory is used for guest OS and user applications, while the Monitor Code and Monitor Data are used for monitoring and recording events of the guest. To achieve isolation between the regions, ShodowMonitor only maps the address space of Guest Ordinary Memory into the main compartment with EPT-N, and maps all the three regions into the shadow compartment. In this way, the operations of guest cannot touch the address of Monitor Code and Monitor Data. Although the Guest Ordinary Memory is shared between the two compartments, it can only be read in the shadow compartment to extract run-time information. For each memory region, the permission flags are set in associated EPT entries by the hypervisor.

By dividing the address space and configuring associated EPT entries separately, ShadowMonitor provides strong isolation between different compartments. Since the Monitor Code and Monitor Data are placed in the shadow compartment which takes a separated address space, they are invisible to the main compartment. Thus, they cannot be touched by the instructions executed in the main compartment, thereby preventing the compromised guest from breaking the monitor components. On the other hand, since the Guest Ordinary Memory region is mapped into the shadow compartment with read and write permission, with the support of hardware EPT, the Monitor Code is able to directly access the information of guest OS and user applications in native speed. This helps improve the monitoring performance a lot.

3.2   Efficient Compartment Switching

To provide efficient switching between two compartments, ShadowMonitor leverages the VM Function (VMFUNC) feature which is provided by Intel hardware virtualization extension. With VMFUNC, the guest can directly invoke virtual machine functions without triggering VM-exit, which avoids imposing heavy performance loss. Specifically, in ShadowMonitor, we load the page directory addresses of both shadow compartment and main compartment into EPTP list (EPT base pointers list). Then, by calling VMFUNC, ShadowMonitor can switch to the EPT mapping of the specified compartment. We use 2 EPTPs for the shadow compartment and the main compartment respectively (Intel supports up to 512 EPTPs), to switch between the address space of the two.

Since the Switch Gate determines the switching between the two compartments, it has to share execution permissions between the main and shadow compartments. In ShadowMonitor, we put the Switch Gate in the interrupt descriptor table (IDT) with vector id 20. To prevent the Switch Gate from being tampered by a compromised guest, we write-protect the IDT by setting permission flags of corresponding EPT-N entries. One problem is that attacks may still arise even if the IDT is write-protected. To solve this, we defend them by trapping LIDT instructions which modify the IDT pointer register (details are presented in Sect. 5). In this way, the Switch Gate can be protected in untrusted guest OS. On the other hand, the INT 20 will invoke the entry of Switch Gate in ShadowMonitor. The execution of INT 20 is triggered by two issues. The first one is the instruction 'INT 20' directly invoked by the monitor point for actively switching to a specified compartment. The other one is issued by virtualization exception (#VE, a new feature provided by Intel) which implies that the system may be operated maliciously (details are presented in Sect. 5: VMFUNC Fake Attack). By configuring the Virtual Machine Control Structure (VMCS), the EPT violations, which reflects the page table change, will lead to virtualization exceptions instead of VM-exit and finally trigger the entry of Switch Gate. This will help ShadowMonitor defend against malicious attacks issued from the guest.

To conclude, upon 'INT 20' instruction or EPT violation, the Switch Gate will be invoked by IDT vector 20. Then, the EPTP placed in the gate will be triggered and operate the switching between the two compartments.

3.3   Work-Flow of Event Monitoring

In this subsection, we will describe the execution flow of ShadowMonitor. The key concern of the design is to effectively execute the trapped instruction in single-step without introducing significant performance loss. Considering the performance issue, we will not use Monitor Trap Flag (MTF) that introduces frequent VM-exit, nor use the in-guest single-step via debug register [27] which introduces heavy overhead.

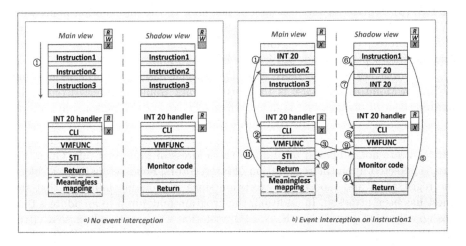

Fig. 3. Comparison between program without interceptor and program enabling interceptor

Figure 3 compares the program without event interception and that with event interception. As shown in Fig. 3a, if no event interceptor is registered, the code executes as normal in the main compartment. Meanwhile, the Switch Gate (i.e., INT 20 handler) will not be invoked and thus will not switch the compartments. On the contrary, Fig. 3b depicts the execution flow when an event has been registered. To intercept the events for monitoring applications running in the main compartment, ShadowMonitor replaces the *instruction1* with *INT 20*, which will introduce interrupt and invoke the Switch Gate (i.e., INT 20 handler). Note that the INT 20 handler firstly executes the instruction *CLI* to disable other interrupts, ensuring that the interception of the execution flow will not be diverted. Then, ShadowMonitor calls the switching instruction (i.e., *VMFUNC*) to switch to the shadow compartment. After that, the Monitor Code executing in the shadow compartment will access the state of guest and record the information into the Monitor Data. After monitoring is completed, the execution returns to the address of *instruction1*. Since the instruction after *instruction1* has been modified to *INT 20*, the INT 20 handler will be invoked again immediately after *instruction1*. In this way, ShadowMonitor switches back to the main compartment. Then, we execute *STI* instruction to enable interrupts and return to execute *instruction2* for resuming the original process. After that, one cycle of event interception and monitoring is completed.

The main advantage of the design is that it allows users to register (or cancel) an event interceptor at run-time, which is not yet supported in existing in-VM monitoring approaches (e.g., SIM). In addition, we provide several APIs to facilitate the registration (or cancellation) of the event interceptor. The user can easily configure interception as the following steps. (1) Replace the instruction which needs to be intercepted (interception point) with *INT 20* (0xcd14) in the main compartment. (2) Set the page of interception point to be executable in EPT-S. (3) Replace all the instructions neighbor to the interception point with *INT 20* in the shadow compartment. (4) Set the page of the interception point to be write-protected in EPT-N. Note that this step is essential because it ensures that the interception points will be safe in a compromised guest.

It's worth noting that there exist two special cases upon the monitoring of ShadowMonitor. One case is that *instruction2* would be overwritten if the machine code of *instruction1* is shorter than *INT 20*. For this reason, our method cannot intercept one-byte instructions, e.g. STI. Another is that *instruction1* is a jump instruction. Generally, the normal programs executing in the main compartment are not supposed to jump to the address of Monitor Code. Once this case is detected upon the registration of interceptors, ShadowMonitor will block the registration and report this exception since it probably indicates that the guest has been attacked. In addition, the program may jump to an address that has no execution permission. If so, EPT violation will occur and cause a virtualization exception. The exception will trigger the execution of INT 20, which switches back to the main compartment, as mentioned in Sect. 3.1. Finally, the program returns to the jump destination as *instruction1* is conducted. *Instruction1* may also jump to the address that is neighbor to the interception point. Similarly, since we have replaced all instructions neighbor to the interception point with *INT 20*, the Switch Gate will be invoked and execute following the procedure above.

3.4 Exploiting EPT Violation

Malicious programs may attempt to attack ShadowMonitor by modifying the interceptor points, touching the Monitor Code or Switch Gate. To prevent these, we leverage the hardware features, i.e., EPT violation, to cause either virtualization exception or VM-exit upon an unauthorized access. In specific, we set the pages of Monitor Code, Monitor Data, and Switch Gate to be write-protected in both EPT-N and EPT-S. If a malicious program tries to write these pages, EPT violation will occur and trigger the page fault handler through virtualization exception (#VE) or VM-exit. As stated before, ShadowMonitor prefers #VE since it introduces insignificant performance overhead compared to VM-exit. To achieve this, we assign 0 to the bit 63 of EPT paging-structure entries with respect to the Guest Ordinary Memory.

3.5 Functionality of Monitor Code

In ShadowMonitor, the Monitor Code is independent of untrusted regions to guarantee security. Thus, the Monitor Code should be self-contained. To achieve this, we link a copy of necessary libraries within the Monitor Code. In Monitor Code, we extract necessary information (including register content, parameter, current process information, and etc.) from the guest and then save them to Monitor Data. Generally, to verify the security state of the VM, some kernel structures should be analyzed. One feasible method is to extend existing out-of-VM approaches for parsing and identifying data structures. Moreover, if necessary, we can dump the call trace of an event in Monitor Code by extracting data from the stack. Consider that this operation is heavyweight, the user can decide to enable or disable it.

The Monitor Data will be finally saved in the persistent storage. However, saving them to the guest disk is risky because the malware may tamper the data. Therefore, we take a different method in ShadowMonitor. Specifically, the hypervisor will access the Monitor Data memory region and fetch the monitor log periodically, and then save them to the persistent storage.

Another important aspect of ShadowMonitor is that the execution of Monitor Code can be considered as an atomic operation because we execute *CLI* to disable interrupts before executing Monitor Code. Although the hypervisor can receive interrupts on behalf of guests, they will deliver them to the guest since the interrupts have been disabled. Therefore, the interrupts will not be delivered to the monitoring process.

4 Implementation

We implement ShadowMonitor on qemu-kvm-2.4.1 with Linux kernel 4.10.2 (Ubuntu 14.04 64-bit LTS). We first enable EPTP-switching and virtualization exception in KVM (they are not supported in the native KVM). Then we present how to realize the prototype of the monitor system. Although the current implementation is specific to QEMU/KVM platform, we believe that it is portable to other virtualization platforms such as Xen.

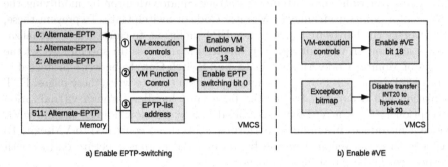

a) Enable EPTP-switching   b) Enable #VE

Fig. 4. A configuration for enabling EPTP-switching and #VE

4.1   Enabling EPTP-switching and #VE

Enableing EPTP-Switching. To enable EPTP-switching in KVM, we need to configure the processor properly following three rules. (1) The enable bit of VM function should be set 1 in Virtual Machine Control Structure (VMCS). (2) The EPTP switching bit of the VM Function Control field should be correctly set. (3) The value of pointers of the EPTP list should be stored into EPTP_LIST_ADDR. Figure 4a shows an example of the configuration. In specific, in KVM, the structure *kvm_mmu_page* is used to store the EPT, and *root_hpa* of *kvm_mmu* is used to store the EPTP which points to EPT. For EPTP-switching, we need to maintain multiple (at least two) EPTs in KVM. To this end, we modify the original structure of the page table. In detail, we use an array *ept_root_hpa_list* to save pointers of EPTs, and *kvm_mmu_page_list* to save the page directory of EPTs. By default, only the first EPT is initialized, while the other elements in these two arrays are set *NULL*. When we tend to use another EPT, we allocate a new EPT page directory in KVM and then fill the associated structures. It's worth noting that we can manage up to 512 compartments for the guest since the current Intel EPTP switching supports 512 EPTP entries.

Enabling Virtualization Exception. To enable virtualization exception, we first set the #VE bit of EPT-violation to 1 in the execution control field of VMCS, and then set bit 20 of EXCEPTION_BITMAP to 0. Figure 4b shows an example of configuration on virtualization exception. When building the EPT-S paging-structure hierarchy, bit 63 of specific EPT paging-structure entries should be 0 (which correspond to the pages that cause#VE upon EPT violation). In addition, we place a handler at vector 20 of the IDT to handle the #VE in the guest.

4.2   Deploying ShadowMonitor Framework

As described in Sect. 3, ShadowMonitor components (i.e. Monitor Code, Monitor data, and Switch Gate) are placed in the guest VM. Since the guest OS is untrusted, we should satisfy two requirements for deploying them in the guest safely and properly. First, the Monitor Code and Monitor Data are placed in a separated address space that cannot be touched by the guest to guarantee their safety, as described in Sect. 3.1; Second, the Switch Gate is write-protected by hardware features, as introduced in Sect. 3.2. To achieve this, we use a collaborative approach to cooperate guest OS and hypervisor. We first insert a kernel module after OS boot-up, which takes charge of reserving two virtual address ranges in the guest, one of which for INT 20 handler (i.e., Switch Gate) and another for Monitor Code and Monitor Data. Since we assume that the OS during the boot-up stage is safe, the module is considered to be inserted safely. Then, the kernel module will inform the hypervisor of the start address and length of the memory regions via *VMCALL* instruction. Once the hypervisor knows the information about memory regions, it creates and activates EPT-S/EPT-N, sets the permission of page table entries, and loads the Monitor Code as well as Switch Gate for event monitoring, as described in Sects. 3.1 and 3.2.

5   Security Analysis

ShadowMnitor should not only detect malicious behaviors but also prevent itself from attacks. To verify the effectiveness of ShadowMonitor, we present a comprehensive security analysis in this Section.

Rootkit Attack. Rootkit attack here tends to compromise the guest OS and thus can destroy the monitoring tools placed in the guest. ShadowMonitor can prevent such attacks because it provides strong isolation between the main and shadow compartments in which the monitoring tools are invisible to the guest. Moreover, the attacks that tend to tamper with the interceptor points and the Switch Gate will trigger page fault since the associated pages have been written-protected, thus they are easy to be detected.

Insider Attack. For each monitoring point, ShadowMonitor will execute one guest instruction in the shadow compartment. Though we have some mechanisms that check whether the instruction of guest code to be executed is benign, a sophisticated attacker may still make a tricky attack by letting malicious instruction sequences execute in shadow compartment. This attack requires the permission to register event interceptors, so it must be the insider attacker. However, **it is beyond our study** because we assume that the user who has the permission to config ShadowMonitor are trusted.

Address Translation Redirection Attack. An attack can rewrite the guest page mapping of the memory region of Switch Gate in the guest so that the Switch Gate will not be protected in the shadow compartment. Then it can tamper the content of Switch Gate and finally escape the monitoring of Shadow-Monitor. ShadowMonitor could prevent such attack by tracking the modification of page tables. It tracks only 4 page table entries for each associated page to be protected, and thus imposes insignificant performance loss.

IDT Redirection Attack. In ShadowMonitor, the Switch Gate is invoked by INT 20 instruction. If the attacker redirects the interrupt descriptor table (IDT) of the guest to a non-write-protected page, and then replace the INT 20 handler with a malware. Then, it can escape the detection of ShadowMonitor. We prevent this attack by trapping all LIDT instructions which are used to modify the IDT pointer register. The trapping can be configured in the VM-execution control field of the VMCS.

INT 20 Fake Attack. Because the Switch Gate is visible in the main compartment, the attacker may maliciously jump to the Switch Gate or invoke *INT 20* instruction, which will lead to unexpected switching of compartments. To prevent it, we adopt the same method of SIM, i.e., we check the branch that transferred execution to the entry gate using the LBR information (last branch recording) so that we can detect this attack.

VMFUNC Fake Attack. The malicious program may intentionally invoke VMFUNC instruction, thereby leading to unexpected switching of compartments. To prevent this, the executable memory code of the shadow compartment are predefined and fixedly located. This means that the memory pages containing the faked VMFUNC instructions should be not executable after completing the compartment switching. Thus, the fake operation will trigger an EPT violation and finally lead to a virtualization exception (#VE). By the design of Shadow-Monitor, the #VE will invoke the Switch Gate and then allows the operations to switch back to the main compartment. It should be pointed out that experiences attackers may carefully design the memory mapping of the guest. For example, they place the GVA of a memory page to be the prior one before the Monitor Code pages and then put the VMFUNC instruction into the last bytes of this page. In this way, if this VMFUNC is invoked, the next program counter will point to the instruction located in the Monitor Code. Once this instruction is executed, the attacker could breaks into the shadow compartment without passing the designated gate. To prevent this, we place VMFUNC instruction into the first bytes of the Monitor Code pages. Therefore, the first touch of the shadow compartment will force the malicious program to switch back to the main compartment.

We reproduce some malicious attacks that try to subvert different VMI approaches including ShadowMonitor, LibVMI, and SIM. The results in Table 1 illustrate that ShadowMonitor is able to prevent against different attacks. ShadowMonitor provides more security guarantee than SIM (in-VM monitor) and no-less than LibVMI (out-VM monitor).

Limitations. There exist some attack approaches that beyond our scope and thus cannot be directly defended by ShadowMonitor. (1) The vulnerabilities hidden in the hypervisor would enable **VM-escape attack**, which will easily destroy our system. One feasible solution for this type of attack is to deploy intrusion detection systems on the hosts. (2) In scenarios where network or hardware are untrusted, **side-channel attack** may employ wiretapping to access private

Table 1. Ability to resist different attacks

Approaches	ShadowMonitor	SIM	LibVMI
Common attack	√	√	√
ATRA attack	√	X	√
IDT redirect attack	√	X	-
INT 20 fake attack	√	-	-
VMFUNC Fake Attack	√	-	-

data. To defend such attack, we can leverage some hardware encrypting techniques such as Secage [22] and Intel SGX [25]. (3) **Bypass attack.** Since the interception points change the guest's original execution flow, the attackers may perceive their existence, identify them, and finally bypass the interception. This critical problem is common in active monitoring approaches [27,29]. One possible solution is to use code analysis or call trace analysis to detect the bypass behaviors. We will leave this as our future work.

6 Evaluation

In this section, we perform a set of experiments to demonstrate the performance loss introduced by ShadowMonitor, under both micro and macro benchmarks. The micro-benchmarks allow appreciating the raw benefit of the design while the macro-benchmarks validate the benefits for the end users. We leverage LibVMI (out-of-VM approach) and SIM (in-VM approach) as the baseline. LibVMI is an open source introspection library that provides a variety of event monitoring interfaces. It is the most representative out-of-VM approach. It's worth noting that LibVMI only supports event interception in Xen hypervisor, so the results here of LibVMI are all collected on Xen (version 4.6). SIM is a representative in-VM monitor approach, we re-implement SIM in KVM following to its design.

The hardware platform is configured with Intel Core i7-6700 3.4 GHz processors, 16 GB DDR memory, a 1000 GB WD disk with 7200 RPM and Intel I219-LM Gigabit NIC card. The operating system on the physical server is Ubuntu 14.04 with 4.10.2 64bit kernel. The virtual machines are configured with 2 vcpus, 4 GB RAM, and 100 GB Disk unless specified otherwise.

6.1 Overhead of Monitoring Invocation

The overhead introduced by ShadowMonitor is mainly from switching between compartments. We first measure the time cost of each VMFUNC instruction and then compare it with that of syscall and VM-exit. As shown in Table 2, the overhead of VMFUNC instruction is comparable to that of the syscall, i.e., 69.38 ns vs. 75.26 ns, while it is much longer for VM-exit, i.e., 653.71 ns.

To explore the monitoring overhead further, we then measure the time of invocation of monitoring, which denotes the total time to intercept an event,

Table 2. Overhead of syscall, VMFUNC, and VM-exit

Operations	Average time (ns)
Syscall	69.38
VMFUNC	75.26
VM-exit	653.71

switch to the shadow compartment and then switch back. As can be seen from Table 3, invoking the monitoring with ShadowMonitor is 11.1× faster than Lib-VMI, since it introduces less switching than LibVMI. Since the overall performance depends on the accumulation of time of single invocation, a monitor that is frequently invoked (e.g. fine-grained monitoring) would gain benefit from ShadowMonitor. It's worth noting that the overhead of ShadowMonitor is similar to SIM because both of these two methods adopt the idea of compartment switching.

Table 3. Comparison of overhead on monitoring invocation

Approaches	Average time (ns)	Standard deviation (ns)
ShadowMonitor	471	63.8
SIM	488	61.4
LibVMI	5231	139.1

Table 4. Memory acess performance comparison

Bytes	ShadowMonitor (μs)	LibVMI (μs)	SIM (μs)
4	0.357	17.3	0.187
64	0.351	17.4	0.194

6.2 Memory Access Speed

ShadowMonitor set the permission of memory pages to be protected. In this experiment, we will measure the memory access speed of guest with Shadow-Monitor. To make a fair comparison, we flush the TLB (translation lookaside buffer) and disable the cache of LibVMI. Table 4 shows the experimental results. As we can see, our ShadowMonitor method achieves hundreds of times faster than LibVMI. It should be pointed out that ShadowMonitor performs poorer than SIM, mainly because it needs the translation of the extended page table (EPT). However, in practical scenarios, we should also consider the time of handling page faults. As we will see in the next section, ShadowMonitor outperforms SIM in terms of overall system performance.

6.3   Overall System Performance

In this experiments, we intercept and monitor all the system calls and process switches in the guest, for measuring the overall performance of the guest system when VMI approach is employed. To monitor syscall, we directly set interceptor on the memory address which is pointed by MSR-LSTAR. As for process switches, we set interceptor on the kernel function *context_switch()* for ShadowMonitor and LibVMI. Note that SIM approach requires no interceptor for process switch because all the process switches will cause VM-exit in SIM. The Monitor Code will parse the arguments for syscall, and extract the process name for a process switch. We evaluate ShadowMonitor under four benchmarks: (1) **UnixBench** is a benchmark suite that measures Linux performance. With this, we can easily quantify the performance impact of many different aspects of the OS. We display four representative indicators of the Unixbench in the results, which are Whetstone (computing), Process creation (scheduling and virtual memory management), File copy (file system), and System call (kernel interface). (2) **Kernel compilation** is a memory-intensive and IO-intensive workload. It can reflect the performance impacts on VMs when they are deployed and launched in production systems. We compile the Linux 4.10.2 kernel by default configure and measure the time it spends. (3) **File Compression** is a IO-intensive and computation-intensive workload. This kind of workload is common when VMs are used as computation nodes. We use the zip algorithm to compress Linux kernel source and measure the time overhead. (4) **Apachebench** is a benchmark measuring the performance of HTTP web servers. It is IO-intensive and memory-intensive. We choose the performance index of requests per second to denote the overall performance of the Apache server in processing concurrent clients requests per second.

Table 5 demonstrates the result of our experiments. First, we can see that ShadowMonitor introduces less overhead than LibVMI for all cases. The overhead varies significantly among different benchmarks, which is mainly due to the varying frequency of the monitored events. For workloads such as kernel compilation, ShadowMonitor introduces 58% less overhead than LibVMI. Second, in some computation-intensive benchmarks (e.g. WhetStone and File Compress), ShadowMonitor introduces slightly less overhead than SIM. However, in memory-intensive benchmarks (e.g. Apachebench, kernel compilation, and process creation benchmarks), SIM introduces 36.1%, 47.5%, and 600% more overhead respectively. This is mainly because SIM uses shadow page table to manage virtual memory and associated page table updating operations, which is much slower than ShadowMonitor exploiting hardware-assisted memory virtualization features.

Table 5. Performance comparison by different benchmarks

Benchmark	No monitor	Our overhead	LibVMI overhead	SIM overhead
Kernel compile	4106.87 s	7.34%	**65.1%**	**54.8%**
Apachebench	4323 lps	5.48%	74.2%	**41.9%**
File Compress	41.69 s	1.12%	8.47%	1.55%
Whetstone	3339 Mwips	0.09%	3.83%	0.1%
Process creation	1785.8 lps	0.71%	9.1%	**613%**
File copy^a	251.1 MBps	10.1%	**93.9%**	11.3%
System call	2.7 Mlps	119%	**7134%**	123%
Average	-	20.55%	**1056%**	**120.8%**

^{a}with 256 bufsize 500 maxblocks

7   Related Works

Virtualization technology has always played important roles in system security. The very first research on gaining the security by using virtualization was proposed in [18,24]. In recent years, virtual machine introspection (VMI) technology [7] has been widely used in addressing the security problems of computer systems. It takes advantage of the hypervisor software layer to provide security support for the upper VM layer. Based on whether introspection uses the guest VM's kernel, VMI approaches can be further divided into in-VM introspection and out-of-VM introspection.

Out-of-VM introspection places the security tools into hypervisor or a separated trusted VM, and then watch and protect the untrusted guest VM from outside. Therefore, it can detect the malicious activities without facing the attacks. Existing works such as [17,28] mainly focus on bridging the semantic gap [15], namely, to reconstruct the high-level knowledge from the internal data structures of the guest operating system. And then use the reconstructed information to detect attacks. Virtuoso [12] automatically creates introspection tools by training the monitor application in a trusted VM and computing the desired introspection information from the application. The introspection tool will finally retrieve the information from outside of the target VM. VMST [13] and POG [31] bridges the semantic gap by reusing the trusted VM's kernel code to monitor the target VM's suspect behaviors. The security analysis programs run in the monitor VM and relevant data accesses are redirected to the guest's live memory. ImEE [34] points out that existing out-of-VM approaches perform badly when accessing guest memory. To reduce the significant overhead, ImEE uses an immersive execution environment with which the guest memory is accessed at native speed without any emulation. However, above-mentioned solutions only support the passive monitor. This means they all have the 'delay detection' trouble. Intruders may have issued the transient attack [26] between the inspection intervals. To detect the transient attacks, event-driven, or active, monitoring has been proposed. Lares [29] and VMDriver [6] provide the framework that enables users insert hooks inside the guest OS so that it can invoke a security application residing in another VM when a particular event occurs. Moreover, VMDriver separates semantic reconstruction module from the event interception module, so it can support different guest OS by changing different 'OS driver'. LibVMI [27] is a virtual machine introspection library based on the related XenAccess [28]. It provides APIs for accessing the VM's memory and registering interception points. LibVMI can support different OS by writing a configuration file beforehand. To our knowledge, LibVMI is the most popular opensource VMI library. Therefore, many VMI tools such as Drakvuf [21] and Volatility [32] are implemented based on LibVMI. To reduce the amount of manual intervention in the process, Tappan Zee Bridge [11] proposes a method to automatically identify locations to place useful interceptor points or hooks.

In-VM introspection is proposed to mitigate the serious performance issue of out-of-VM introspection. In general, in-VM introspection relies on the guest kernel's capabilities, so it can also save the engineering efforts when implementing the security tools. Process Implanting [14] loads monitor tools such as strace [5] and ltrace [3] into the guest VM and executes it with the camouflage of an existing process. ShadowContext [33] hijacks an existing process in the monitored VM, and then uses this process issues system calls on behalf of the introspection process. By this mean, ShadowContext can issue syscalls in the monitored VM, thereby obtaining the security states of the VM. SYRINGE [8] is similar to the ShadowContext, it runs an agent in the monitor VM and allows the introspection code to call the guest kernel functions in the agent's context. For these approaches, when the guest kernel is not trusted, the trustworthiness and effectiveness will be totally broken, because it is straightforward for a rootkit to tamper with the introspection. SIM [30] solves this problem by using hardware memory protection to create a hypervisor protected address space (SIM) where a monitor can execute. Meanwhile, hooks are placed in the guest to intercept events. When the event is intercepted, the address space switches to SIM by dedicated gates and then switches back when monitoring is done.

Some efforts also use virtualization to build high assurance execution environments which protect applications from being attacked by the untrusted OS. [19] provides application an encrypted memory view from the OS, and use hash value to detect corruption of the physical pages caused by the OS. But they do not prevent the illegal access to encrypted pages. KCoFI [9] and Virtual Ghost [10] explored to change the original architecture into a protection mode, it creates applications ghost memory that the operating system cannot read or write. SeCage [22] leverages hardware virtualization extensions to support efficient isolation of sensitive code manipulating critical secrets from the remaining code. It separates control and data plane using VMFUNC mechanism in Intel processors to transparently provide different memory views for different compartments, and allow low-cost and transparent invocation across domains without hypervisor intervention. Our idea of using hardware-enforced isolation is similar to SeCage. However, different from SeCage that focuses on the confidentiality of program data, our approach tends to provide event monitoring. In addition, with SeCage, the applications should be aware of the existence of SeCage and make modifications to cooperate with SeCage, e.g., actively switch the address space. On the contrary, our proposed approach is invisible to guest applications and thus requires no modification of them.

8 Conclusion

In this paper, we present a monitoring framework named ShadowMonitor, which enables efficient in-VM monitoring and provides hardware-enforced isolation between security tools and untrusted guests. ShadowMonitor achieves efficiency by placing monitor tools in the guest for monitoring events and achieves robustness by separating the security tools and the untrusted guest into isolated compartments exploiting Intel multi-EPT features. We described the design of ShadowMonitor and presented a comprehensive security analysis. We have implemented the prototype of ShadowMonitor on QEMU/KVM platform. The experiment results demonstrate that ShadowMonitor introduces much less overhead than existing methods. In the future, we plan to implement kernel drivers to support more types of guest kernels, such as Windows. We also plan to implement ShadowMonitor on other hypervisors, such as Xen.

Acknowledgement. We would like to acknowledge all the anonymous reviewers and Dr. Manuel Egele for their valuable comments and helps in improving this paper. This work is supported by the Chinese National Key Research and Development Program (2016YFB1000103), Chinese National Natural Science Foundation of China (grant no. 61602465), U.S. NSF grants OAC-1724845, ACI-1719397, CNS-1733596, and Microsoft Research Faculty Fellowship 8300751. This work is also supported by Beijing Brain Inspired Computing Program in BCBD innovation center. Lei Cui is the corresponding author of this paper.

References

1. AMD64 architecture programmers manual
2. Intel 64 and IA-32 architectures software developers manual
3. Ltrace. https://en.wikipedia.org/wiki/Ltrace
4. Qemu-kvm. http://www.qemu-project.org
5. Strace. https://en.wikipedia.org/wiki/Strace
6. Xiang, G., Jin, H., Zou, D., Zhang, X., Wen, S., Zhao, F.: Vmdriver: a driver-based monitoring mechanism for virtualization. In: 29th IEEE Symposium on Reliable Distributed Systems (SRDS 2010) (2010)
7. Garfinkel, T., Rosenblum, M.: A virtual machine introspection based architecture for intrusion detection. In: The Network and Distributed System Security Symposium, NDSS 2003 (2003)
8. Carbone, M., Conover, M., Montague, B., Lee, W.: Secure and robust monitoring of virtual machines through guest-assisted introspection. In: Balzarotti, D., Stolfo, S.J., Cova, M. (eds.) RAID 2012. LNCS, vol. 7462, pp. 22–41. Springer, Heidelberg (2012). https://doi.org/10.1007/978-3-642-33338-5_2
9. Criswell, J., et al.: Kcofi: complete control-flow integrity for commodity operating system kernels. In: 2014 IEEE Symposium on Security and Privacy, SP 2014 (2014)

10. Criswell, J., et al.: Virtual ghost: protecting applications from hostile operating systems. In: Proceedings of ASPLOS 2014, pp. 81–96. ACM (2014). https://doi.org/10.1145/2541940.2541986
11. Dolan, B., et al.: Tappan zee (north) bridge: mining memory accesses for introspection. In: Conference on Computer and Communications Security, CCS 2013 (2013)
12. Dolan-Gavitt, B., et al.: Virtuoso: narrowing the semantic gap in virtual machine introspection. In: 32nd IEEE Symposium on Security and Privacy, S&P 2011 (2011)
13. Fu, Y., Lin, Z.: Space traveling across VM: automatically bridging the semantic gap in virtual machine introspection via online kernel data redirection. In: IEEE Symposium on Security and Privacy, SP 2012 (2012)
14. Gu, Z., et al.: Process implanting: a new active introspection framework for virtualization. In: IEEE Symposium on Reliable Distributed Systems (SRDS 2011) (2011)
15. Jain, B., et al.: Sok: introspections on trust and the semantic gap. In: IEEE Symposium on Security and Privacy, SP 2014, Berkeley, CA, USA (2014)
16. Jang, D., et al.: Atra: address translation redirection attack against hardware-based external monitors. In: Proceedings of CCS 2014 (2014)
17. Jiang, X., Wang, X., Xu, D.: Stealthy malware detection and monitoring through VMM-based "out-of-the-box" semantic view reconstruction. ACM Trans. Inf. Syst. Secur. 13(2), 12:1–12:28 (2010). https://doi.org/10.1145/1698750.1698752
18. Kelem, N.L., Feiertag, R.J.: A separation model for virtual machine monitors. In: IEEE Symposium on Security and Privacy, pp. 78–86 (1991). https://doi.org/10.1109/RISP.1991.130776
19. Kwon, Y., et al.: Sego: pervasive trusted metadata for efficiently verified untrusted system services. In: Proceedings of ASPLOS 2016, pp. 277–290. ACM (2016). https://doi.org/10.1145/2872362.2872372
20. Lee, H., et al.: KI-Mon: a hardware-assisted event-triggered monitoring platform for mutable kernel object. In: The 22th USENIX Security Symposium (2013)
21. Lengyel, T.K., et al.: Scalability, fidelity and stealth in the DRAKVUF dynamic malware analysis system. In: Proceedings of ACSAC 2014 (2014)
22. Liu, Y., et al.: Thwarting memory disclosure with efficient hypervisor-enforced intra-domain isolation. In: Proceedings CCS 2015, 12–16 October 2015
23. Liu, Z., et al.: CPU transparent protection of OS kernel and hypervisor integrity with programmable DRAM. In: Proceedings of ISCA 2013, 23–27 June 2013
24. Madnick, S.E., Donovan, J.J.: Application and analysis of the virtual machine approach to information system security and isolation. In: Proceedings of the Workshop on Virtual Computer Systems. ACM, New York (1973). https://doi.org/10.1145/800122.803961
25. McKeen, F., et al.: Innovative instructions and software model for isolated execution. In: Proceedings of HASP 2013, p. 10. ACM (2013). https://doi.org/10.1145/2487726.2488368
26. Moon, H., et al.: Vigilare: toward snoop-based kernel integrity monitor. In: The ACM Conference on Computer and Communications Security, CCS 2012 (2012)
27. Payne, B.D.: Simplifying virtual machine introspection using LibVMI. https://doi.org/10.2172/1055635
28. Payne, B.D., Lee, W.: Secure and flexible monitoring of virtual machines. In: 23rd Annual Computer Security Applications Conference (ACSAC 2007), 10–14 December 2007, Miami Beach, Florida, USA (2007)
29. Payne, B.D., et al.: Lares: an architecture for secure active monitoring using virtualization. In: 2008 IEEE Symposium on Security and Privacy (S&P 2008) (2008)

30. Sharif, M.I., et al.: Secure in-VM monitoring using hardware virtualization. In: The Conference on Computer and Communications Security, CCS 2009 (2009)

31. Srinivasan, D., et al.: Process out-grafting: an efficient "out-of-VM" approach for fine-grained process execution monitoring. In: Proceedings of CCS 2011 (2011)

32. Walters, A.: The volatility framework: volatile memory artifact extraction utility framework (2007)

33. Wu, R., et al.: System call redirection: a practical approach to meeting real-world virtual machine introspection needs. In: 44th Annual IEEE/IFIP International Conference on Dependable Systems and Networks, DSN 2014 (2014)

34. Zhao, S., et al.: Seeing through the same lens: introspecting guest address space at native speed. In: 26th USENIX Security Symposium, USENIX Security 2017 (2017)

KASR: A Reliable and Practical Approach to Attack Surface Reduction of Commodity OS Kernels

Zhi Zhang[1,2(✉)], Yueqiang Cheng[3], Surya Nepal[1], Dongxi Liu[1], Qingni Shen[4], and Fethi Rabhi[2]

[1] Data61, CSIRO, Sydney, Australia
{zhi.zhang,surya.nepal,dongxi.liu}@data61.csiro.au
[2] University of New South Wales, Sydney, Australia
zhi.zhang@student.unsw.edu.au, f.rabhi@unsw.edu.au
[3] Baidu XLab, Sunnyvale, CA, USA
chengyueqiang@baidu.com
[4] Peking University, Beijing, China
qingnishen@ss.pku.edu.cn

Abstract. Commodity OS kernels have broad attack surfaces due to the large code base and the numerous features such as device drivers. For a real-world use case (e.g., an Apache Server), many kernel services are *unused* and only a small amount of kernel code is *used*. Within the *used* code, a certain part is invoked only at runtime while the rest are executed at startup and/or shutdown phases in the kernel's lifetime run. In this paper, we propose a *reliable* and *practical* system, named KASR, which *transparently* reduces attack surfaces of commodity OS kernels at runtime without requiring their source code. The KASR system, residing in a trusted hypervisor, achieves the attack surface reduction through a two-step approach: (1) reliably depriving *unused* code of executable permissions, and (2) transparently segmenting *used* code and selectively activating them. We implement a prototype of KASR on Xen-4.8.2 hypervisor and evaluate its security effectiveness on Linux kernel-4.4.0-87-generic. Our evaluation shows that KASR reduces the kernel attack surface by 64% and trims off 40% of CVE vulnerabilities. Besides, KASR successfully detects and blocks all 6 real-world kernel rootkits. We measure its performance overhead with three benchmark tools (i.e., SPECINT, httperf and bonnie++). The experimental results indicate that KASR imposes less than 1% performance overhead (compared to an unmodified Xen hypervisor) on all the benchmarks.

Keywords: Kernel attack surface reduction
Reliable and practical systems · Hardware-assisted virtualization

1 Introduction

In order to satisfy various requirements from individuals to industries, commodity OS kernels have to support numerous features, including various file systems

© Springer Nature Switzerland AG 2018
M. Bailey et al. (Eds.): RAID 2018, LNCS 11050, pp. 691–710, 2018.
https://doi.org/10.1007/978-3-030-00470-5_32

and numerous peripheral device drivers. These features inevitably result in a broad attack surface, and this attack surface becomes broader and broader with more services consolidated into the kernel every year. As a consequence, the current kernel attack surface gives an adversary numerous chances to compromise the OS kernel and exploit the whole system. Although we have moved into the virtualization and cloud era, the security threats are not being addressed. Instead it becomes even worse with the introduction of additional software stacks, e.g., a hypervisor layer. Recent years have witnessed many proposed approaches which realized the severity of this issue and made an effort to reduce the attack surface of the virtualized system. Specifically, schemes like NoHype [32], XOAR [7] HyperLock [35] and Min-V [24] are able to significantly reduce the attack surface of the hypervisor. In addition, several other schemes have been proposed to reduce the huge kernel attack surface, which are summarized into the following three categories.

Build from Scratch. The first category attempts to build a micro-kernel with a minimal attack surface [1,11,12,14], among which Sel4 [14] is the first OS that achieves a high degree of assurance through formal verification. Although such micro-kernel schemes retrofit security, they are incompatible with legacy applications.

Re-construction. The second category makes changes to current monolithic kernel. Nooks [31], and LXFI [21] isolate buggy device drivers to reduce the attack surface of the kernel. Considering that the reduced kernel is still large, Nested Kernel [9] places a small isolated kernel inside the monolithic kernel, further reducing the attack surface. Besides, strict access-control policies [8,28] and system call restrictions [26] also contribute a lot. A common limitation of these approaches is that they all require modifications of the kernel source code, which is usually not applicable.

Customization. The last category manages to tailor existing kernels without modifications. Tartler [33], Kernel Tailoring [18] and Lock-in-Pop [19] require the Linux source code of either the kernel or core libraries (i.e., *glibc*) to restrict user's access to the kernel. They lack the OS distribution support due to the requirement of source code re-compiling. Ktrim [17] and KRAZOR [16] rely on specific kernel features (i.e., *kprobes*) to binary-instrument kernel functions and remove unused ones. Face-Change [10] is a hypervisor-based technique to tailor the kernel code. It supports neither the Kernel Address Space Layout Randomization (KASLR) [8] nor multiple-vCPU for the target kernel. Besides, it induces a worst-case overhead of 40%, impeding its deployment in practice.

Overview. In this paper, we propose a *reliable* and *practical* virtualized system, named KASR, which is able to *transparently* reduce the attack surface of a commodity OS kernel at runtime.

Consider a specified application workload (e.g., an Apache server), whose operations do not necessarily need all kernel services. Instead, only a subset of the services are invoked to support both the target Apache process and the kernel. For example, both of them always require code blocks related to memory management (e.g., *kmalloc*, *kfree*, *get_page*) and synchronization mechanisms (e.g., *_spin_lock*). Apart from that, certain *used* kernel functions are only used during a specific period of kernel's lifetime and remain unused for the rest of the time. For instance, the initialization (e.g., *kernel_init*) and power-off actions (e.g., *kernel_power_off*) will only be taken when the kernel starts up and shuts down, respectively. In contrast to these *used* kernel code, many other kernel services are never executed. We call them *unused* kernel code in this paper. The unused kernel code resides in the main memory, contributing to a large portion of the kernel attack surface. For example, a typical kernel vulnerability, e.g., CVE-2013-2094, is exploited via a crafted system call *perf_event_open* that is unused or never invoked in the Apache workload.

Motivated by the above observation, KASR achieves the kernel attack surface reduction in two steps. The first step is to reliably deprive unused code of executable permissions. Commodity OS kernels are designed and implemented to support all kinds of use cases (e.g., the Apache server and Network File System service), and therefore there will be a large portion of kernel code (e.g., system call handlers) unused for a given use case. By doing so, this step could effectively reduce a large portion of the attack surface. The second step transparently segments used code and selectively activates it according to the specific execution demands of the given use case. This segmentation is inspired by the observation that certain kernel code blocks (e.g., *kernel_init*) only execute in a particular period, and never execute beyond that period. As a result, KASR dramatically reduces the attack surface of a running OS kernel.

We implement a KASR prototype on a private cloud platform, with Xen 4.8.2 as the hypervisor and Ubuntu Server 16.04.3 LTS as the commodity OS. The OS kernel is unmodified Linux version 4.4.0-87-generic with KASLR [8] enabled. KASR only adds about 1.2K SLoC to the hypervisor code base. We evaluate its security effectiveness under the given use cases (e.g., Linux, Apache, MySQL and PHP (LAMP)-based server). The experimental results indicate that KASR reduces more than 64% kernel attack surface at the granularity of code pages. Also, we trims off 40% of Common Vulnerabilities and Exposures (CVEs), since the CVE reduction indicates the number of CVEs that KASR could avoid. In addition, KASR successfully detects and blocks all 6 real-world kernel rootkits. We also measure the performance overhead using several popular benchmark tools as given use cases, i.e., `SPECint`, `httperf` and `bonnie++`. The overall performance overheads are 0.23%, 0.90% and 0.49% on average, respectively.

Contributions. In summary, we make the following key contributions:

- Propose a novel two-step approach to reliably and practically reduce the kernel attack surface with being agnostic to the particular OS.
- Design and implement a practical KASR system on a recent private cloud platform. KASR transparently "fingerprints" used kernel code and enables them to execute according to their execution phases.
- Evaluate the security effectiveness of the KASR system by the reductions of kernel attack surface, CVE and the mitigation of real-world rootkits.

– Measure the performance overhead of the KASR system using several popular benchmark tools. The low overhead makes KASR reasonable for real-world deployment.

Organization. The rest of the paper is structured as follows. In Sect. 2, we briefly describe our system goals and a threat model. In Sect. 3, we present the kernel attack surface, its measurement and the rationale of its reduction. We introduce in detail the system architecture of KASR in Sect. 4. Sections 5 and 6 present the primary implementation of KASR and its performance evaluation, respectively. In Sects. 7 and 8, we discuss limitations of KASR, and compare it with existing works, respectively. At last, we conclude this paper in Sect. 9.

2   Threat Model and Design Goals

Before we describe our design, we specify the threat model and the design goals.

2.1   Threat Model

In this paper, we focus on reducing the attack surfaces of commodity OS kernels in a virtualized environment. Currently, most personal computers, mobile phones and even embedded devices are armed with the virtualization techniques, such as Intel [13], AMD [2] and ARM virtualization support [3]. Thus, our system can work on such devices.

We assume a hypervisor or a Virtual Machine Monitor (VMM) working beneath the OS kernel. The hypervisor is trusted and secure as the root of trust. Although there are vulnerabilities for some existing hypervisors, we can leverage additional security services to enhance their integrity [4,6,34] and reduce their attack surfaces [7,32]. As our system relies on a training-based approach, we also assume the system is clean and trusted in the training stage, but it could be compromised at any time after that.

We consider threats coming from both remote adversaries and local adversaries. A local adversary resides in user applications, such as browsers and email clients. The kernel attack surface exposed to the local adversary includes system calls, exported virtual file system (e.g., Linux *proc* file system) for user applications. A remote adversary stays outside and communicates with the OS kernel via hardware interfaces, such as a NIC. The kernel attack surface for the remote adversary usually refers to device drivers.

2.2   Design Goals

Our goal is to design a reliable, transparent and efficient system to reduce the attack surfaces of commodity OS kernels.

G1: Reliable. The attack surface should be reliably and persistently reduced. Even if kernel rootkits can compromise the OS kernel, they cannot enlarge the reduced attack surface to facilitate subsequent attacks.

G2: Transparent. The system should transparently work for the commodity OS kernels. Particularly, it neither relies on the source code nor breaks the kernel code integrity through binary instrumentation. Source code requirement is difficult to be adopt in practice. And breaking the code integrity raises compatibility issues against security mechanisms, such as Integrity Measurement Architecture.

G3: Efficient. The system should minimize the performance overhead, e.g., the overall performance overhead on average is less than 1%.

Among these goals, G1 is for security guarantee, while the other two goals (G2 and G3) are for making the system practical. Every existing approach has one or more weaknesses: they either are unreliable (e.g., Lock-in-Pop [19] as per G1), or depend on the source code (e.g., SeL4 [14]), or break the kernel code integrity (e.g., Ktrim [17]), or incur high performance overhead (e.g., Face-Change [10]). Our KASR system is able to achieve all the above goals at the same time.

3   Design Rationale

We first present how to measure the attack surface of a commodity OS kernel, and then illustrate how to reliably and practically reduce it.

3.1   Attack Surface Measurement

To measure the kernel attack surface, we need a security metric that reflects the system security. Generally, the attack surface of a kernel is measured by counting its source line of code (SLoC). This metric is simple and widely used. However, this metric takes into account all the source code of a kernel, regardless of whether it is effectively compiled into the kernel binary. To provide a more accurate security measurement, Kurmus et al. [18] propose a fine-grained generic metric, named GENSEC, which only counts effective source code compiled into the kernel. More precisely, in the GENSEC metric, the kernel attack surface is composed of the entire running kernel, including all the Loadable Kernel Modules (LKMs).

However, the GENSEC metric only works with the kernel source code, rather than the kernel binary. Thus it is not suitable for a commodity OS with only a kernel binary that is made of a kernel image and numerous module binaries. To fix this gap, we apply a new KASR security metric. Specifically, instead of counting source lines of code, the KASR metric counts all executable instructions.

Similar to prior schemes that commonly use SLoC as the metric of the attack surface, the KASR metric uses the Number of Instructions (NoI). It naturally works well with instruction sets where all the instructions have an equal length (e.g., ARM instructions). However, with a variable-length instruction set (e.g., x86 instructions [13]), it is hard to count instructions accurately. In order to address this issue on such platforms, we use the Number of Instruction Pages (NoIP). NoIP is reasonable and accurate due to the following reasons. First, it is consistent with the paging mechanism that is widely deployed by all commodity OS kernels. Second, the kernel instructions are usually contiguous and organized in a page-aligned way. Finally, it could smoothly address the issue introduced by variable-length instructions without introducing any explicit security and performance side-effects. In this paper, the KASR metric depends on NoIP to measure the kernel attack surface.

3.2   Benefits of Hardware-Assisted Virtualization

In a hardware-assisted virtualization environment, there are two levels of page tables. The first-level page table, i.e., Guest Page Table (GPT), is managed by the kernel in the guest space, and the other one, i.e., Extended Page Table (EPT), is managed by the hypervisor in the hypervisor space. The hardware checks the access permissions at both levels for a memory access. If the hypervisor removes the executable permission for a page P_a in the EPT, then the page P_a can never be executed, regardless of its access permissions in the GPT. These mechanisms have been widely supported by hardware processors (e.g., Intel [13], AMD [2], and ARM [3]) and commodity OSes.

With the help of the EPT, we propose to reduce the attack surface by transparently removing the executable permissions of certain kernel code pages. This approach achieves all system goals listed before. First, it is reliable (achieving G1) since an adversary in the guest space does not have the capability of modifying the EPT configurations. Second, the attack surface reduction is transparent (achieving G2), as the page-table based reduction is enforced in the hypervisor space, without requiring any modifications (e.g., instruction instrumentation) of the kernel binary. Finally, it is efficient (achieving G3) as all instructions within pages that have executable permissions are able to execute at a native speed.

4   KASR Design

We firstly elaborate the design of the KASR system. As depicted in Fig. 1, the general working flow of KASR proceeds in two stages: an offline training stage followed by a runtime enforcement stage. In the offline training stage, a trusted OS kernel *Kern* is running beneath a use case (e.g., user application App_a) within a virtual machine. The KASR offline training processor residing in the hypervisor space, monitors the kernel's lifetime run, records its code usage and generates a corresponding database. The generated kernel code usage database is trusted, as the system in the offline training stage is clean. Once the generated database becomes stable and ready to use, the offline training stage is done.

In the runtime enforcement stage, the KASR module, running the same virtual machine, loads the generated database and reduces the attack surface of *Kern*. The kernel attack surface is made up of the kernel code from the kernel image as well as loaded LKMs. A large part of the kernel attack surface is reliably removed (the dotted square in Fig. 1). Still, the remaining part (the solid shaded-square in Fig. 1) is able to support the running of the use case App_a. The attack surface reduction is reliable, as the hypervisor can use the virtualization techniques to protect itself and the KASR system, indicating that no code from the virtual machine can revert the enforcement.

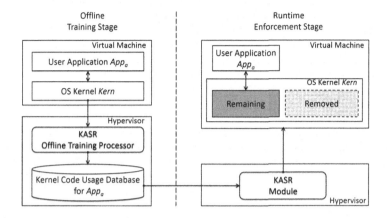

Fig. 1. The architecture of the KASR system.

4.1   Offline Training Stage

Commodity OSes are designed and implemented to support various use cases. However, for a given use case (e.g., App_a), only certain code pages within the kernel (e.g., $Kern$) are used while other code pages are unused. Thus, the KASR offline training processor can safely extract the used code pages from the whole kernel, the so-called used code extraction. On top of that, the used code pages can be segmented into three phases (e.g., startup, runtime and shutdown). The code segmentation technique is inspired by the observation that some used code pages are only used in a particular time period. For instance, the *init* functions are only invoked when the kernel starts up and thus they should be in the *startup* phase. However, for certain functions, e.g., *kmalloc* and *kfree*, they are used during the kernel's whole lifetime and owned by all three phases. The KASR offline training processor uses the *used code extraction* technique (Sect. 4.1) to extract the used code pages, and leverages the *used code segmentation* technique (Sect. 4.1) to segment used code into different phases. All the recorded code usage information will be saved into the kernel code usage database, as shown in Fig. 2.

The database will become stable quickly after the KASR offline processor repeats the above steps several times. Actually, this observation has been successfully confirmed by some other research works [17,18]. For instance, for the use case of *LAMP*, a typical *httperf* [23] training of about ten minutes is sufficient to detect all required features, although the *httperf* does not cover all possible paths. This observation is reasonable due to the following two reasons. First,

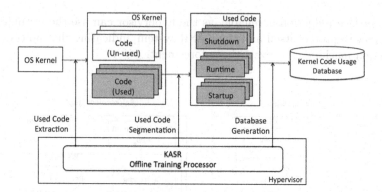

Fig. 2. Offline Training Stage. The KASR offline training processor working in the hypervisor space, extracts used code from the OS kernel, segments used code into three phases (i.e., startup, runtime and shutdown) and generates the kernel code usage database.

people do not update the OS kernel frequently, and thus it will be stable within a relatively long period. Second, although the user-level operations are complex and diverse, the invoked kernel services (e.g., system calls) are relatively stable, e.g., the kernel code that handles network packets and system files is constantly the same.

Used Code Extraction. A key requirement of this technique is to collect *all* used pages for a given workload. It means that the collection should cover the whole lifetime of an OS kernel, from the very beginning of the startup phase to the last operation of the shutdown phase. A straightforward solution is to use the trace service provided by the OS kernel. For instance, the Linux kernel provides the *ftrace* feature to trace the kernel-level function usage. However, all existing integrated tracing schemes cannot cover the whole life cycle. For example, *ftrace* always misses the code usage of the startup phase [18] before it is enabled. Extending the trace feature requires modifying the kernel source code. To avoid the modification and cover the whole life cycle of the OS kernel, we propose a hypervisor-based KASR offline training processor. The offline training processor, working in the hypervisor space, starts to run before the kernel starts up and remains operational after the kernel shuts down.

In the following, we will discuss how to trace and identify the used code pages in the kernel image and loaded LKMs.

Kernel Image Tracing. Before the kernel starts to run, the offline training processor removes the executable permissions of all code pages of the kernel image. By doing so, every code execution within the kernel image will raise an exception, driving the control flow to the offline training processor. In the hypervisor space, the offline training processor maintains the database recording the kernel code usage status. When getting an exception, the offline training processor updates the corresponding record, indicating that a kernel code page is used. To avoid this kernel code page triggering any unnecessary exceptions later, the offline training processor sets it to executable. As a result, only the newly executed kernel code pages raise exceptions and the kernel continues running, thus covering the lifetime used code pages of the kernel image. Note that the offline training processor filters out the user-space code pages by checking where the exception occurs. (i.e., the value of Instruction Pointer (IP) register).

Kernel Modules Tracing. The above tracing mechanism works smoothly with the kernel image, but not with newly loaded LKMs. All LKMs can be dynamically installed and uninstalled into/from memory at runtime, and the newly installed kernel modules may re-use the executable pages that have already been freed by other modules in order to load their code. Thus, their page contents have totally changed and they become new code pages that ought to be traced as well. If we follow the kernel tracing mechanism, such to-be-reused pages cannot be recorded into the database. Because these pages have been traced and the processor has set them to executable, they are unable to trigger any exceptions even when they are reused by other modules.

To address this issue, we dictate that only the page currently causing the exception can gain the executable permission while other pages cannot. Specifically, when a page P_a raises an exception, the offline training processor sets it to executable so that the kernel can proceed to next page P_b. Once P_b raises the exception, it is set to executable while P_a is set back to non-executable. Likewise, the offline training processor sets P_b back to non-executable when another exception occurs. By doing so, pages like P_a or P_b can trigger new exceptions if they will be re-used by newly installed modules and thus all used code pages can be traced. Obviously, this approach is also suitable for the kernel image tracing.

Page Identification. The traced information is saved in the database, and the database reserves a unique identity for each code page. It is relatively easy to identify all code pages of the kernel image when its address space layout is unique and constant every time the kernel starts up. Thus, a Page Frame Number (PFN) could be used as the identification. However, recent commodity OS kernels have already enabled the KASLR technology [8] and thus the PFN of a code page is no longer constant. Likewise, this issue also occurs with the kernel modules, whose pages are dynamically allocated at runtime, and each time the kernel may assign a different set of PFNs to the same kernel module.

A possible approach is to hash every page's content as its own identity. It works for most of the code pages but will fail for the code pages which have instructions with dynamically determined opcodes, e.g., for the *call* instruction, it needs an absolute address as its operand, and this address may be different each time, causing the failure of page identification. Another alternative is to apply the fuzzy hash algorithm (e.g., ssdeep [15]) over a page and compute a similarity (expressed as a percentage) between two pages. e.g., if two pages have a similarity of over 60%, they are identical. However, such low similarity will introduce false positives, which can be exploited by attackers to prompt malicious pages for valid ones in the runtime enforcement stage.

To address the issues, we propose a multi-hash-value approach. In this offline training stage, we trace the kernel for multiple rounds (e.g., 10 rounds) to collect all the used pages and dump the page content of each used page. Then we build a map of what bytes are constant and what bytes are dynamic in every used page. Each used page has multiple ranges and each range is made up of consecutive constant bytes. The ranges are separated by the dynamic bytes. Based on the map, we compute a hash value for every range. If and only if two pages have the same hash value for each range, they are identical. As a result, a page's identity is to hash everything within the page but the dynamic bytes. On top of that, we observe that the maximum byte-length of the consecutive dynamic bytes is 4, making it hardly possible for attackers to replace the dynamic bytes with meaningful rogue ones. Relying on the approach, the risk of abusing the false positives is minimized.

Used Code Segmentation. This technique is used to segment the used code into several appropriate phases. By default, there are three phases: *startup*, *runtime*, and *shutdown*, indicating which phases the used code have been executed in. When the kernel is executing within one particular phase out of the three, the offline training processor marks corresponding code pages with that phase. After the kernel finishes its execution, the offline training processor successfully marks all used code pages and saves their records into the database. To be aware of the phase switch, the offline training processor captures the phase switch events. For the switch between *startup* and *runtime*, we use the event when the first user application starts to run, while for the switch between *runtime* and *shutdown*, we choose the execution of the *reboot* system call as the switch event.

4.2   Runtime Enforcement Stage

When the offline training stage is done and a stable database has been generated (see details in Sect. 5.2), KASR is ready for runtime enforcement. As shown in Fig. 3, the KASR module loads the generated database for a specific workload, and reduces the kernel attack surface in two steps:

1. *Permission Deprivation.* It keeps the executable permissions of all used code pages (the solid shaded square in Fig. 3), and reliably removes the executable permissions of all unused code pages (the dotted square in Fig. 3)
2. *Lifetime Segmentation.* It aims to further reduce the kernel attack surface upon the permission deprivation. As shown in Fig. 3, it transparently allows the used kernel code pages of a particular phase to execute while setting the remaining pages to non-executable.

All instructions within the executable pages can execute at a native speed, without any interventions from the KASR module. When the execution enters the next phase, the KASR module needs to revoke the executable permissions from the pages of the current phase, and set executable permissions to the pages of the next phase. To reduce the switch cost, the KASR module performs two optimizations. First, if a page is executable within the successive phase, the KASR module skips its permission-revocation and keeps it executable. Second, the KASR module updates the page permissions in batch, rather than updating them individually.

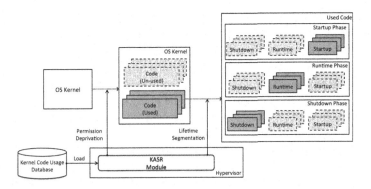

Fig. 3. Runtime Enforcement Stage. The KASR module residing in the hypervisor space reduces OS kernel attack surface in two consecutive steps. The first step (i.e., permission deprivation) reliably deprives unused code of executable permission, and the second step (i.e., lifetime segmentation) selectively activates corresponding used code according to their phases.

5   KASR Database

This section presents the implementation details of the KASR database, including database data-structure, database operations.

5.1   Data Structure

Basically, the database consists of two single-linked lists, which are used to manage the pages of kernel image and loaded modules, respectively. Both lists have their own list lock to support concurrent updates. Every node of each list representing a page is composed of a node lock, a page ID, a status flag and a node pointer pointing to its next node. The node lock is required to avoid race conditions and thus other nodes can be processed in parallel.

Page ID. The page ID is used to identify a page especially during the database updates. As kernel-level randomization is enabled within the kernel, we use the multi-hash-value approach for the identification. Specifically, we trace the kernel for 10 rounds to make sure that all the used pages are collected. Pages in different rounds are considered to be identical (i.e., a same page) if they satisfy two properties: (1) more than 3366 out of 4096 bytes (i.e., over 82%) are constant and the same among these pages; (2) the maximum byte-length of the consecutive different bytes (i.e., dynamic bytes) among these pages is no greater than 4. And then we perform a per-byte comparison of the identical pages so as to build a map of what bytes are constant and what bytes are dynamic with the pages. By doing so, each used page has multiple ranges of consecutive constant bytes and dynamic bytes are between these ranges. As a result, all the constant bytes of every range are hashed as a value and all the hash values make up the page ID.

Status Flag. The status flag indicates the phase status (i.e., *startup*, *runtime* and *shutdown*) of a used page. The flag is initialized as startup when the kernel boots up. Once the kernel switches from the startup phase to the runtime phase, or from the runtime phase to the shutdown phase, appropriate exceptions are triggered so that the offline training processor can update the flag accordingly. In our implementation, all code pages of the guest OS are deprived of executable permissions. Once the OS starts to boot, it will raise numerous EPT exceptions. In the hypervisor space, there is a handler (i.e., *ept_handle_violation*) responding to the exception, and thus the offline training processor can mark the beginning of the runtime phase by intercepting the first execution of the user-space code as well as its end by intercepting the execution of the *reboot* system call.

5.2 Database Operations

The database operations are mainly composed of three parts, i.e., populating, saving and loading.

Populate Database. To populate the database, the KASR offline training processor must trace all the used pages and thus dictates that only the page raising the exception would become executable while others are non-executable. However, we find that this will halt the kernel. The reason is that the x86 instructions have variable lengths and an instruction may cross a page boundary, which means that the first part of the instruction is at the end of a page, while the rest is in the beginning of the next page. Under such situations, the instruction-fetch will result in infinite loops (i.e., trap-and-resume loops).

To address this issue, we relax the dictation and implement a queue of 2 pages that own executable permissions. When the queue is full of two pages that have caused the first two exceptions (i.e., the first two used pages), it will then be updated by *First-in, First-out*, i.e., the newest used page will be pushed in while the oldest used page will be popped out. Besides solving the cross-page-boundary problem, we also accelerate the tracing performance. Besides, we can capture all loaded modules, as all of them have no less than 2 code pages.

To the end, it is not enough to obtain all the used pages by running the offline training stage just once. Thus, it is necessary to repeat this stage for multiple rounds until the database size becomes stable. In our experiments, 10 rounds are enough to get a stable database (see Sect. 6).

Save and Load Database. The database is generated in the hypervisor space, and stored in the hard disk for reuse. Specifically, we have developed a tiny tool in the privileged domain to explicitly save the database into the domain's disk after the offline training stage, and load the existing database into the hypervisor space during the runtime enforcement stage.

6 Evaluation

We have implemented a KASR prototype on our private cloud platform, which has a Dell Precision T5500 PC with eight CPU cores (i.e., Intel Core Xeon-E5620) running at 2.40 GHz. Besides, Intel VT-x feature is enabled and supports the page size of 4 KB. Xen version 4.8.2 is the hypervisor while Hardware-assisted Virtual Machine (HVM) is the Ubuntu Server 16.04.3 LTS, which has a KASLR-enabled Linux kernel of version 4.4.0-87-generic with four virtual CPU cores and 4 GB physical memory. KASR only adds around $1.2K$ SLoC in Xen.

In the rest of this section, we measure the reduction rates of the kernel attack surface. On top of that, we characterize the reduced kernel attack surface in the metrics of Common Vulnerabilities and Exposures (CVEs). The use cases we choose are SPECint, httperf, bonnie++, LAMP (i.e., Linux, Apache, MySQL and PHP) and NFS (i.e., Network File System). Furthermore, we test and analyze its effectiveness in defending against 6 real-world kernel rootkits. Also, we measure the performance overhead introduced by KASR through the selected use cases above. The experimental results demonstrate that we can effectively reduce kernel attack surface by 64%, CVEs by 40%, safeguard the kernel against 6 popular kernel rootkits and impose negligible (less than 1%) performance overhead on all use cases.

6.1 Kernel Attack Surface Reduction

In the runtime enforcement stage, we measure the kernel attack surface reduction through three representative benchmark tools, namely, SPECint, httperf and bonnie++ and two real-world use cases (i.e., LAMP and NFS).

SPECint [29] is an industry standard benchmark intended for measuring the performance of the CPU and memory. In our experiment, the tool has 12 sub-benchmarks in total and they are all invoked with a specified configuration file (i.e., *linux64-ia32-gcc43+.cfg*).

On top of that, we measure the network I/O of HVM using httperf [23]. HVM runs an Apache Web server and Dom0 tests its I/O performance at a rate of starting from 5 to 60 requests per second (100 connections in total).

Also, we test the disk I/O of the guest by running bonnie++ [5] with its default parameters. For instance, bonnie++ by default creates a file in a specified directory, size of which is twice the size of memory.

Besides, we run the LAMP-based web server inside the HVM. Firstly, we use the standard benchmark *ApacheBench* to continuously access a static PHP-based website for five minutes. And then a Web server scanner *Nikto* [30] starts to run so as to test the Web server for insecure files and outdated server software and also perform generic and server type specific checks. This is followed by launching *Skipfish* [22], an active web application security reconnaissance tool. It operates in an extensive brute-force mode to carry out comprehensive security checks. Running these tools in the LAMP server aims to cover as many kernel code paths as possible.

Lastly, the other comprehensive application is NFS. HVM is configured to export a shared directory via NFS. In order to stress the NFS service, we also use bonnie++ to issue read and write-access to the directory.

All results are displayed in Table 1. Note that the average results for SPECint are computed based on 12 sub-benchmark tools. We determine two interesting properties of the kernel attack surface from this table. First, the attack surface

Table 1. In every case, the kernel code pages are significantly tailored after each step. Generally, KASR can reduce the kernel attack surface by 54% after the permission deprivation, and 64% after the lifetime segmentation. (Orig.Kern = Original Kernel, Aft.Per.Dep. = After Permission Deprivation, Aft.Lif.Seg. = After Lifetime Segmentation)

Cases	Orig.Kern	Aft.Per.Dep.		Aft.Lif.Seg.	
	Page(#)	Page(#)	Reduction(%)	Page(#)	Reduction(%)
SPECint	2227	1034	54%	808	64%
httperf	2236	1026	54%	763	66%
bonnie++	2235	1034	54%	761	66%
LAMP	2238	1043	53%	817	63%
NFS	2395	1096	54%	939	61%

reduction after each step is quite significant and stable for different use cases. Generally, the attack surface is reduced by roughly 54% and 64% after the permission deprivation and lifetime segmentation, respectively, indicating that less than half of the kernel code is enough to serve all provided use cases. Second, complicated applications (i.e., LAMP and NFS) occupy more kernel code pages than the benchmarks, indicating that they have invoked more kernel functions.

CVE Reduction. Although some kernel functions (e.g., architecture-specific code) contain past CVE vulnerabilities, they are never loaded into memory during the kernel's lifetime run and do not contribute to the attack surface. As a result, we only consider the CVE-vulnerable functions that are loaded into the kernel memory. We investigate CVE bugs of recent two years that provide a link to the GIT repository commit and identify 14 CVEs that exist in the kernel memory of all five use cases.

We observe that KASR has removed 40% of CVEs in the memory. To be specific, some CVE-vulnerable kernel functions within the unused kernel code pages are deprived of executable permissions after the permission deprivation. For example, the *ecryptfs_privileged_open* function in CVE-2016-1583 before Linux kernel-4.6.3 is unused, thus being eliminated. After the lifetime segmentation, some other vulnerable functions are also removed (e.g., *icmp6_send* in CVE-2016-9919).

6.2   Rootkit Prevention

Even though the kernel attack surface is largely reduced by KASR, still there may exist vulnerabilities in the kernel, which could be exploited by rootkits. We demonstrate the effectiveness of KASR in defending against real-world kernel rootkits. Specifically, we have selected 6 popular real-world kernel rootkits coming from a previous work [25] and the Internet. These rootkits work on typical Linux kernel versions ranging from 3.x to 4.x, representing the state-of-the-art kernel rootkit techniques. All these rootkits launch attacks by inserting a loadable module and they can be divided into three steps:

1. inject malicious code into kernel allocated memory;
2. hook the code on target kernel functions (e.g., original syscalls);
3. transfer kernel execution flow to the code.

KASR is able to prevent the third step from being executed. Specifically, rootkits could succeed at Step-1 and Step-2, since they can utilize exposed vulnerabilities to modify critical kernel data structures, inject their code and perform target-function hooking so as to redirect the execution flow. However, they cannot execute the code in Step-3, because KASR decides whether a kernel page has an executable permission. Recall that KASR reliably dictates that unused kernel code (i.e., no record in the database) has no right to execute in the kernel space, including the run-time code injected by rootkits. Therefore, when the injected code starts to run in Step-3, EPT violations definitely will occur and then be caught by KASR. The experimental results from Table 2 clearly show that KASR has effectively defended against all 6 rootkits. As a result, KASR is able to defend against the kernel rootkits to a great extent.

Table 2. KASR successfully defended against all 6 kernel rootkits. (LKM = Loadable Kernel Module)

OS kernel	Rootkit	Attack vector	Attack failed?
Linux 3.x-4.x	adore-ng	LKM	✓
	xingyiquan	LKM	✓
	rkduck	LKM	✓
	Diamorphine	LKM	✓
	suterusu	LKM	✓
	nurupo	LKM	✓

6.3 Performance Evaluation

In this section, we evaluate the performance impacts of KASR on CPU computation, network I/O and disk I/O using the same settings as we measure the kernel attack surface reduction. Benchmark tools are conducted with two groups, i.e., one is called Original (HVM with an unmodified Xen), the other is KASR.

Specifically, SPECint has 12 sub-programs and the CPU overhead caused by KASR within each sub-program is quite small and stable. In particular, the maximum performance overhead is 1.47% while the average performance overhead is 0.23% for the overall system.

Httperf tests the Apache Web server inside the HVM using different request rates. Compared to the Original, the network I/O overhead introduced by KASR ranges from 0.00% to 1.94% and the average is only 0.90%.

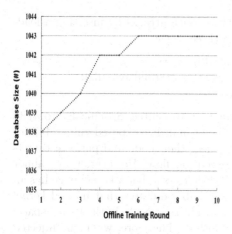
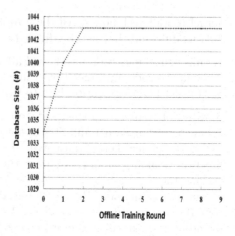

Fig. 4. In the case of LAMP, its database is built from scratch and keeps its size increasing until the round 6*th*.

Fig. 5. Incremental offline training. Compared to that of Fig. 4, only 2 more offline training rounds based on a provided database are needed to reach the same stable state, largely reducing the offline training cost.

The disk I/O results are generated by bonnie++ based on two test settings, i.e., *sequential input* and *sequential output*. For each setting, the *read*, *write* and *rewrite* operations are performed and their results indicate that KASR only incurs a loss of 0.49% on average.

6.4   Offline Training Efficiency

We take LAMP server as an example to illustrate the offline training efficiency, indicating how fast to construct a stable database for a given workload. Specifically, we repeat the offline training stage for several rounds to build the *LAMP* database from scratch. After the first round, we get 1038 code pages, 99% of the final page number. After that, 9 successive offline training rounds are completed one by one, each of which updates the database based on previous one, ensuring that the final database records all used pages. From Fig. 4, it can be seen that the database as a whole becomes steady after multiple rounds (i.e., 6 in our experiments). This observation is also confirmed in other cases.

In fact, it is still time-consuming to build a particular database from scratch. To further accelerate this process, we attempt to do the offline training stage from an existing database. In our experiments, we integrate every database generated respectively for SPECint, httperf, bonnie++ into a larger one, and try to generate the LAMP database using incremental training. Based on the integrated database, we find that only 2 rounds are enough to generate the stable database for LAMP, shown in Fig. 5, significantly improving the offline training efficiency.

7   Discussion

In this section, we will discuss limitations of our approach.

Training Completeness. Similar to Ktrim [17], KRAZOR [16] and Face-Change [10], KASR also uses a training-based approach. As the approach might miss some corner cases, it may cause KASR to mark certain pages that should be used as unused, resulting in an incomplete offline training database. Theoretically speaking, it is possible for such situations to occur. However, in practice, they have never been observed in our experiments so far. Interestingly, Kurmus al et. [18] found that a small offline training set is usually enough to cover all used kernel code for a given use case, implying that the corner cases usually do not increase the kernel code coverage. If the generated database is incomplete, EPT violations may have been triggered at runtime. For such situations, KASR has two possible responses. One is to directly stop the execution of the guest, which is suitable for the security sensitive environment where any violations may be treated as potential attacks. The other one is to generate a log message, which is friendly to the applications that have high availability requirements. The generated log contains the execution context and the corresponding memory content to facilitate a further analysis, e.g., system forensics.

Fine-Grained Segmentation. By default, we have three segmented phases (i.e., *startup*, *runtime*, and *shutdown*). Actually, the whole lifecycle could be segmented into more phases, corresponding to different working stages of a user application. Intuitively, a more fine-grained segmentation will achieve a better kernel attack surface reduction. Nonetheless, more phases will introduce more performance overhead, such as the additional phase switches. In addition, it will increase the complexity of the KASR offline training processor, and consequently increases the trusted computing base (TCB). At last, the KASR module has to deal with the potential security attacks, e.g., malicious phase switches. To prevent such attacks, a state machine graph of phases should be provided, where the predecessor, successor and the switch condition of each phase should be clearly defined. At runtime, the KASR module will load this graph and enforce the integrity: only the phase switches existing in the graph are legal, and any other switches will be rejected.

8   Related Work

In this section, we provide an overview of existing approaches to enhance the kernel security that require no changes to the kernel. Specifically, the approaches are either kernel or hypervisor-dependent.

Kernel customizations [18,33] present automatic approaches of trimming kernel configurations adapted to specific use cases so that the tailored configurations can be applied to re-compile the kernel source code, thus minimizing the kernel attack surface. Similarly, Seccomp [26] relies on the kernel source code to sandbox specified user processes by simply restricting them to a minimal set of system calls. Lock-in-Pop [19] modifies and re-compiles *glibc* to restrict an application' access to certain kernel code. In contrast, both Ktrim [17] and KRAZOR [16] utilize *kprobes* to trim off unused kernel functions and prevent them from being executed. All of the approaches above aim at providing a minimized kernel view to a target application.

In the virtualized environment, both Secvisor [27] and NICKLE [25] only protect original kernel TCB and do nothing to reduce it. Taking a step further, unikernel [20] provides a minimal kernel API surface to specified applications but developing the applications is highly dependent on the underlying unikernel. Face-Change [10] profiles the kernel code for every target application and uses the Virtual Machine Introspection (VMI) technique to detect process context switch and thus provide a minimized kernel TCB for each application. However, Face-Change has three disadvantages: (1) Its worst-case runtime overhead for `httperf` testing Apache web server is 40%, whereas our worst overhead is 1.94% (see Sect. 6.3), making it impractical in the cloud environment. (2) Its design naturally does not support KASLR, which is an important kernel security feature and has been merged into the Linux kernel mainline since kernel version 3.14. In contrast, KASR is friendly to the security feature. (3) While multiple-vCPU support is critical to system performance in the cloud environment, it only supports a single vCPU within a guest VM, whereas KASR allocates four vCPUs to the VM.

9   Conclusion

Commodity OS kernels provide a large number of features to satisfy various demands from different users, exposing a huge surface to remote and local attackers. In this paper, we have presented a *reliable* and *practical* approach, named KASR, which has *transparently* reduced attack surfaces of commodity OS kernels at runtime without relying on their kernel source code. KASR deploys two surface reduction approaches. One is spatial, i.e., the *permission deprivation* marks never-used code pages as non-executable while the other is temporal, i.e., the *lifetime segmentation* selectively activates appropriate used code pages. We implemented KASR on the Xen hypervisor and evaluated it using the Ubuntu OS with an unmodified Linux kernel. The experimental results showed that KASR has efficiently reduced 64% of kernel attack surface, 40% of CVEs in all given use cases. In addition, KASR defeated all 6 real-world rootkits and incurred low performance overhead (i.e., less than 1% on average) to the whole system.

In the near future, our primary goals are to apply KASR to the kernel attack surface reduction of a Windows OS since KASR should be generic to protect all kinds of commodity OS kernels.

References

1. Accetta, M., et al.: Mach: a new kernel foundation for UNIX development (1986)
2. AMD Inc.: Secure virtual machine architecture reference manual, December 2005

3. ARM Inc.: Armv8 (2011). https://community.arm.com/docs/DOC-10896
4. Azab, A.M., Ning, P., Wang, Z., Jiang, X., Zhang, X., Skalsky, N.C.: HyperSentry: enabling stealthy in-context measurement of hypervisor integrity. In: Proceedings of the 17th ACM Conference on Computer and Communications Security, CCS 2010, pp. 38–49 (2010)
5. Bonnie (1999). http://www.coker.com.au/bonnie++
6. Cheng, Y., Ding, X.: Guardian: hypervisor as security foothold for personal computers. In: Huth, M., Asokan, N., Čapkun, S., Flechais, I., Coles-Kemp, L. (eds.) Trust 2013. LNCS, vol. 7904, pp. 19–36. Springer, Heidelberg (2013). https://doi.org/10.1007/978-3-642-38908-5_2
7. Colp, P., et al.: Breaking up is hard to do: security and functionality in a commodity hypervisor. In: Proceedings of the Twenty-Third ACM Symposium on Operating Systems Principles, SOSP 2011, pp. 189–202. ACM (2011)
8. Cook, K.: Linux kernel ASLR (KASLR). In: Linux Security Summit (2013)
9. Dautenhahn, N., Kasampalis, T., Dietz, W., Criswell, J., Adve, V.: Nested kernel: an operating system architecture for intra-kernel privilege separation. In: Proceedings of the Twentieth International Conference on Architectural Support for Programming Languages and Operating Systems, ASPLOS 2015, pp. 191–206 (2015)
10. Gu, Z., Saltaformaggio, B., Zhang, X., Xu, D.: Face-change: application-driven dynamic kernel view switching in a virtual machine. In: 44th Annual IEEE/IFIP International Conference Dependable Systems and Networks (DSN), DSN 2014, pp. 491–502. IEEE (2014)
11. Herder, J.N., Bos, H., Gras, B., Homburg, P.: MINIX 3: a highly reliable, self-repairing operating system. ACM SIGOPS Oper. Syst. Rev. 40(3), 80–89 (2006)
12. Herder, J.N., Bos, H., Gras, B., Homburg, P., Tanenbaum, A.S.: Construction of a highly dependable operating system. In: Proceedings of the 6th European Dependable Computing Conference, EDCC 2006, pp. 3–12. IEEE (2006)
13. Intel Inc.: Intel 64 and IA-32 architectures software developer's manual combined volumes: 1, 2a, 2b, 2c, 3a, 3b and 3c, October 2011
14. Klein, G., et al.: seL4: formal verification of an operating-system kernel. Commun. ACM 53(6), 107–115 (2010)
15. Kornblum, J.: Fuzzy hashing and ssdeep (2010)
16. Kurmus, A., Dechand, S., Kapitza, R.: Quantifiable run-time kernel attack surface reduction. In: Dietrich, S. (ed.) DIMVA 2014. LNCS, vol. 8550, pp. 212–234. Springer, Cham (2014). https://doi.org/10.1007/978-3-319-08509-8_12
17. Kurmus, A., Sorniotti, A., Kapitza, R.: Attack surface reduction for commodity OS kernels: trimmed garden plants may attract less bugs. In: Proceedings of the Fourth European Workshop on System Security. ACM (2011)
18. Kurmus, A., et al.: Attack surface metrics and automated compile-time OS kernel tailoring. In: Proceedings of the 20th Annual Network and Distributed System Security Symposium, NDSS 2013 (2013)
19. Li, Y., Dolan-Gavitt, B., Weber, S., Cappos, J.: Lock-in-Pop: securing privileged operating system kernels by keeping on the beaten path. In: USENIX Annual Technical Conference, pp. 1–13. USENIX Association (2017)
20. Madhavapeddy, A., et al.: Unikernels: library operating systems for the cloud. In: ACM SIGPLAN Notices, vol. 48, pp. 461–472. ACM (2013)
21. Mao, Y., Chen, H., Zhou, D., Wang, X., Zeldovich, N., Kaashoek, M.F.: Software fault isolation with API integrity and multi-principal modules. In: Proceedings of the Twenty-Third ACM Symposium on Operating Systems Principles, pp. 115–128. ACM (2011)

22. Michal, Z., Niels, H., Sebastian, R. (2010). https://code.google.com/archive/p/skipfish
23. Mosberger, D., Jin, T.: Httperf - a tool for measuring web server performance. SIGMETRICS Perform. Eval. Rev. **26**(3), 31–37 (1998)
24. Nguyen, A., Raj, H., Rayanchu, S., Saroiu, S., Wolman, A.: Delusional boot: securing hypervisors without massive re-engineering. In: Proceedings of the 7th ACM European Conference on Computer Systems, EuroSys 2012, pp. 141–154 (2012)
25. Riley, R., Jiang, X., Xu, D.: Guest-transparent prevention of kernel rootkits with VMM-based memory shadowing. In: Lippmann, R., Kirda, E., Trachtenberg, A. (eds.) RAID 2008. LNCS, vol. 5230, pp. 1–20. Springer, Heidelberg (2008). https://doi.org/10.1007/978-3-540-87403-4_1
26. Seccomp (2005). https://lwn.net/Articles/332974
27. Seshadri, A., Luk, M., Qu, N., Perrig, A.: SecVisor: a tiny hypervisor to provide lifetime kernel code integrity for commodity OSES. In: ACM SIGOPS Operating Systems Review, vol. 41, pp. 335–350. ACM (2007)
28. Smalley, S., Vance, C., Salamon, W.: Implementing SELinux as a linux security module. NAI Labs Rep. **1**(43), 139 (2001)
29. Standard Performance Evaluation Inc.: SPECint (2006). http://www.spec.org
30. Sullo, C. (2012). https://cirt.net/nikto
31. Swift, M.M., Martin, S., Levy, H.M., Eggers, S.J.: Nooks: an architecture for reliable device drivers. In: Proceedings of the 10th Workshop on ACM SIGOPS European Workshop, pp. 102–107. ACM (2002)
32. Szefer, J., Keller, E., Lee, R.B., Rexford, J.: Eliminating the hypervisor attack surface for a more secure cloud. In: Proceedings of the 18th ACM Conference on Computer and Communications Security, CCS 2011, pp. 401–412 (2011)
33. Tartler, R., et al.: Automatic OS kernel TCB reduction by leveraging compile-time configurability. In: Proceedings of the 8th Workshop on Hot Topics in System Dependability, p. 3 (2012)
34. Wang, Z., Jiang, X.: HyperSafe: a lightweight approach to provide lifetime hypervisor control-flow integrity. In: Proceedings of the 2010 IEEE Symposium on Security and Privacy, SP 2010, pp. 380–395 (2010)
35. Wang, Z., Wu, C., Grace, M., Jiang, X.: Isolating commodity hosted hypervisors with hyperlock. In: Proceedings of the 7th ACM European Conference on Computer Systems, EuroSys 2012, pp. 127–140 (2012)

Author Index

Ahn, Hee-Kap 577
Akritidis, Periklis 315

Bai, Jiasong 161
Belleville, Brian 337
Benenson, Zinaida 535
Bertino, Elisa 114
Bi, Jun 161
Böck, Leon 511
Bos, Herbert 47
Brengel, Michael 623
Bruschi, Danilo 445
Bushart, Jonas 139
Bushouse, Micah 647
Buttery, Paula 207

Caines, Andrew 207
Cao, Chen 380
Cavallaro, Lorenzo 25
Cheng, Yueqiang 691
Coleman, Shaun 295
Coskun, Ayse K. 3
Cristalli, Stefano 445
Cui, Lei 670

Dabrowski, Adrian 184
Dautenhahn, Nathan 359
DeCock, Martine 295
Dolan-Gavitt, Brendan 273

Eckert, Claudia 423
Egele, Manuel 3
Elovici, Yuval 490

Felsch, Dennis 603
Fischer, Matthias 423
Francillon, Aurélien 92
Franz, Michael 337, 403

Gao, Neng 380
Garg, Siddharth 273
Gascon, Hugo 69
Giuffrida, Cristiano 47

Gong, Neil Zhenqiang 228
Grossklags, Jens 423
Gu, Guofei 161, 467
Guan, Le 380

Halevidis, Constantinos 315
Hao, Zhiyu 670
Hu, Xin 467
Hutchings, Alice 207
Hwang, Dongil 337
Hwang, Yoonho 577

Jang, Jiyong 467
Judmayer, Aljosha 184
Jung, Seonhwa 337

Karuppayah, Shankar 511
Kim, Sin-Kyu 577
Kinder, Johannes 25
Koromilas, Lazaros 315

Lanzi, Andrea 445
Larsen, Per 337, 403
Lee, Woomyo 577
Lettner, Julian 403
Li, Bo 670
Li, Guanyu 161
Lin, Jingqiang 380
Lin, Zhiqiang 423
Liu, Dongxi 691
Liu, Kang 273
Liu, Peng 380
Liu, Xudong 670
Lou, Wenjing 380
Luo, Bo 380

Mehnaz, Shagufta 114
Mirkovic, Jelena 250
Mladenov, Vladislav 603
Mogosanu, Lucian 359
Moon, Hyungon 337
Morgner, Philipp 535
Mudgerikar, Anand 114

Mühlhäuser, Max   511
Müller, Jens   603
Muntean, Paul   423

Na, Yeoul   337
Nascimento, Anderson   295
Nash, Joseph M.   337
Nepal, Surya   691

Paek, Yunheung   337
Papadogiannaki, Eva   315
Park, Taemin   403
Pastrana, Sergio   207
Pereira, Mayana   295
Pfennig, Stefan   535

Rabhi, Fethi   691
Rane, Ashay   359
Razavi, Kaveh   47
Reeves, Douglas   647
Rieck, Konrad   69
Rizzo, Claudio   25
Rokach, Lior   490
Rosenberg, Ishai   490
Rossow, Christian   139, 623

Sahin, Onur   3
Salzner, Dennis   535
Schwenk, Jörg   603
Shabtai, Asaf   490
Shen, Haiying   670
Shen, Qingni   691
Shen, Yun   556
Shi, Bin   670

Shin, Jangseop   337
Song, Dokyung   403
Stifter, Nicholas   184
Stoecklin, Marc Ph.   467
Stritter, Benjamin   69

Tan, Gang   423
Tatar, Andrei   47
Thomas, Sam L.   92

Ullrich, Johanna   184
Ullrich, Steffen   69

Vasilomanolakis, Emmanouil   511
Vervier, Pierre-Antoine   556
Vignati, Edoardo   445
Volckaert, Stijn   337, 403

Wang, Binghui   228
Weippl, Edgar   184
Woo, Simon S.   250

Xiang, Ji   380
Xu, Lei   161

Yu, Bin   295
Yun, Jeong-Han   577

Zhang, Jialong   467
Zhang, Le   228
Zhang, Menghao   161
Zhang, Ning   380
Zhang, Zhi   691

Printed in the United States
By Bookmasters